# VARIETIES OF VISUAL EXPERIENCE

# VARIETIES

FOURTH EDITION

# OF VISUAL

EDMUND BURKE FELDMAN
*Professor of Art, University of Georgia*

# EXPERIENCE

HARRY N. ABRAMS, INC., *Publishers*, NEW YORK

TO MERRILL

1928–1972

Project Manager: Sheila Franklin Lieber

Editor: Joanne Greenspun

Art Direction: Dirk Luykx

Designers: Gilda Hannah, with Gayle Jaeger

Photo Research: Catherine Ruello

Library of Congress Cataloging-in-Publication Data
Feldman, Edmund Burke.
    Varieties of visual experience / Edmund Burke Feldman. — 4th ed.
        p.   cm.
    Includes bibliographical references (p.  ) and index.
    ISBN 0–8109–3922–3
    1. Art—Psychology. 2. Composition (Art) 3. Visual perception.
I. Title.
N71.F42 1992b
701—dc20                                                    92–7985
                                                                CIP

Fourth Edition 1992

Published in 1992 by Harry N. Abrams, Incorporated, New York
A Times Mirror Company

Printed and bound in Japan

# CONTENTS

Preface   9

PART ONE
## THE FUNCTIONS OF ART

CHAPTER ONE   PERSONAL FUNCTIONS OF ART   12

Art and Psychological Expression   12
Love, Sex, and Marriage   15
Death and Morbidity   22
Spiritual Concern   29
Aesthetic Expression   36

CHAPTER TWO   THE SOCIAL FUNCTIONS OF ART   43

Political and Ideological Expression   45
Social Description   51
Satire   58
Graphic Communication   62

CHAPTER THREE   THE PHYSICAL FUNCTIONS OF ART   72

Architecture: The Dwelling   74
Large-Scale Design: The Community   86
The Crafts and Industrial Design   106

# PART TWO
# THE STYLES OF ART

CHAPTER FOUR  THE STYLE OF OBJECTIVE ACCURACY  123

  The Imitation of Appearances  123
  The Artist as Detached Observer  127
  The Artist as Selective Eye  129
  Variations of the Style  134
  Devices of Objective Accuracy  137

CHAPTER FIVE  THE STYLE OF FORMAL ORDER  143

  The Transient and the Permanent  144
  Kinds of Formal Order  146
  Conclusion  162

CHAPTER SIX  THE STYLE OF EMOTION  164

  Romanticism and Emotion  166
  The Role of Distortion  175
  Anxiety and Despair  175
  Joy and Celebration  181

CHAPTER SEVEN  THE STYLE OF FANTASY  186

  Myth  188
  Dreams and Hallucinations  189
  Scientific Fantasy  199
  Fantasy and Illusionism  199

# PART THREE
# THE STRUCTURE OF ART

CHAPTER EIGHT  THE VISUAL ELEMENTS: GRAMMAR  207

  Line  207
  Shape  211
  Light and Dark  217
  Color  226
  Texture  231

CHAPTER NINE  ORGANIZING THE ELEMENTS: DESIGN  234

  Unity  236
  Balance  240
  Rhythm  243
  Proportion  248
  Conclusion  249

CHAPTER TEN    PERCEIVING THE ELEMENTS: AESTHETICS    251

Aesthetic Work    251

Aesthetic Experience    252

Empathy and Psychic Distance    254

Closure and Good Gestalt    257

Funding and Fusion    260

Liking and Disliking    261

Cross-Cultural Factors    264

Conclusion    265


PART FOUR
# THE INTERACTION OF MEDIUM AND MEANING


CHAPTER ELEVEN    PAINTING    269

The Fugitive and the Permanent    270

Direct and Indirect Techniques    274

Brushwork and Emotion    278

Frottage, Grattage, and Decalcomania    291

The Picture and the Wall    294

Beyond Collage: Assemblage, Environments, Happenings    297

Minimal and Color Field Painting    314

The Shaped Canvas    317

Erotic Art    318

Conclusion    322


CHAPTER TWELVE    SCULPTURE    323

Modeling, Carving, Casting, and Constructing    323

From Monolith to Open Form    335

Constructivism    340

Sculptural Assemblage    351

Niches, Boxes, and Grottoes    360

Beyond Constructivism: Primary Structures    366

Kinetic Sculpture    368

Sculpture and the Crafts    374

Conclusion    377


CHAPTER THIRTEEN    ARCHITECTURE    380

The Classic Materials    380

Modern Materials    390

The Structural Devices    398

Constructors and Sculptors    420

CHAPTER FOURTEEN    PHOTOGRAPHY    429

Photography and Reality    430
Photography and Painting    431
The Amateur with a Camera    433
Instantaneous Seeing    437
Photojournalism    438
Principle of the Frame    441
Photography and Abstraction    442
The Photographic Slide    444
The Photographer as Artist    445
Photographic Criticism    447

CHAPTER FIFTEEN    IMAGES IN MOTION: FILM AND TELEVISION    455

The Manipulation of Space-Time    456
Film and TV Types    460
Filmed Versus Televised Imagery    461
Films and Dreams    462
The Democracy of Film    463
The Critical Appreciation of Cinema    464
Conclusion    466

PART FIVE
# THE PROBLEMS OF ART CRITICISM

CHAPTER SIXTEEN    THE THEORY OF ART CRITICISM    469

The Tools of Art Criticism    471
Types of Art Criticism    473
Kinds of Critical Judgment    476
Conclusion    486

CHAPTER SEVENTEEN    THE CRITICAL PERFORMANCE    487

Description    487
Formal Analysis    490
Interpretation    494
Judgment    503
Conclusion    510

Glossary    511
Time-Lines    516
Selected Bibliography    524
Index    528
Photo Credits    541

# PREFACE

The main purpose of this book is to show how much we can learn about the world and its people through art. To accomplish that purpose, I have tried to explain how art "works"—what it does, how it speaks, and how it asks us to respond. In doing so, I want people to feel comfortable with art and the ways it gets them to see and know and act.

Part One, "The Functions of Art," focuses on the ways in which art is used—personally, socially, and, in the case of architecture and utilitarian objects, physically. Part Two, "The Styles of Art," takes up one of the principal ways that art communicates—through style or artistic "handwriting." Here the reader learns to "read" art by recognizing and understanding style—the characteristic look and feel of the artworks produced at a certain time or place, or by a certain artist or group of artists. "The Structure of Art," Part Three, deals with the visual elements of art, the ways they are organized and how they are perceived. This section offers an alternative to the notion that visual form is what art is exclusively about; it shows that we need to know something about visual perception and social context in order to understand what art forms mean.

Part Four, "The Interaction of Medium and Meaning," deals with the relations between material and expression. Here we are brought closer to the specific character of an artwork. We learn how technique affects what artists make and what spectators see; what opportunities and constraints are created by a particular medium; how a new technology influences an artist's outlook; and how materials assist or resist an artist's intentions. Finally, Part Five examines "The Problems of Art Criticism." Here a practical guide to criticism is presented, beginning with its theory and types and ending with a method of doing criticism. In many respects, this section on art criticism, which tries to give people confidence in their own perceptions, represents the book's fulfillment: the preceding chapters supply the concepts that a critic needs; the final chapters challenge him or her to put those concepts into action.

Some of the book's pedagogical features should be mentioned. First, many of the illustrations have extended captions, which function as a second text, so to speak. With these extended captions we can amplify the main text, compare styles and themes, direct attention to technical details, demonstrate critical interpretation, and, most important, help students to develop "a good eye." Second, there are Time-Lines. Examined from top to bottom, they present a chronological listing of the major monuments of art illustrated in the book. Examined horizontally, they provide technical, social, political, economic, and religious contexts for each monument. Thus, with an art-historical option, an extensive discussion of criticism, a new chapter on aesthetics, and a book-length treatment of artistic purposes, styles, and mediums, *Varieties of Visual Experience* tries to offer a balanced and comprehensive approach to the study of art.

I hope readers will think of this book as a dialogue with the author, a dialogue whose main aim is to stimulate further discussion. While my point of view may not always be shared, I do think that the illustrations and text work together to raise provocative questions. Indeed, much of my teaching over the years has taken the form of soliciting questions from students; this book represents the answers we have formulated together. So let me pay tribute to their insight and thank them all.

## PREFACE AND ACKNOWLEDGMENTS TO THE FOURTH EDITION

Earlier editions of this book have been so well received that we have not altered its general structure. Even so, there is always room for improvement and updating. Amid great change, some principles, at least, remain valid; still, it helps to show how they apply to the most recent examples of artistic creativity.

Accordingly, the present edition has added new illustrations—some of them non-Western, many of them contemporary, and most of them in color. Also, their labels now list mediums and dimensions wherever possible. The Bibliography, too, has been updated, and the Glossary has added terms from aesthetics and art criticism. Especially important is a new chapter on Aesthetics, which tries to make an often difficult subject accessible to nonspecialists. Finally, some passages have been rewritten for the sake of greater clarity, and in all cases I have tried to make the text responsive to current ideas and issues in the art world.

Two fine publishing houses have contributed to the production of this fourth edition, and I have benefited greatly from their skill and experience. My publisher at Prentice-Hall, Norwell (Bud) Therien, Jr., has directed the development of *Varieties* for many years, giving needed advice and rarely hurting my feelings. At Abrams, Sheila Franklin Lieber, Julia Moore, and Joanne Greenspun have been consistently reliable editorial guides, while Catherine Ruello has searched the world for good photos and color transparencies—which is no easy task. I have come away from the process with a high opinion of their professionalism.

I believe an art text should, above all, be well-designed, but it should not look like a mail-order catalogue, which is all the more reason to appreciate the excellent work of Gilda Hannah and art director Dirk Luykx. They have produced a book which is both handsome and intelligent. I am grateful to all of them and to Virginia Seaquist, who prepared a difficult manuscript and never lost patience with its author.

Edmund Burke Feldman

# PART ONE

# THE FUNCTIONS OF ART

The idea that art functions, that it is useful in human affairs, may seem farfetched; we tend to believe it is the product of surplus energy and wealth. As a result, art is often considered *uniquely* useless—unnecessary for meeting the basic requirements of living. Still, the arts have existed throughout human history and they seem to be thriving today. How can we explain this? Is art tolerated because of some blunder? Can we do without it? No. We need art because it satisfies vital personal and social needs. In this book I hope to show why the visual arts—painting, sculpture, architecture, industrial design, the crafts, photography, films, and television—are essential for human survival.

Furthermore, contemporary art performs the same functions as the art of the past. It continues to satisfy (1) our personal needs for expression, (2) our social needs for communication, celebration, and display, and (3) our physical needs for useful objects and structures. But even if art gives us flashy advertising designs, soaring airport terminals, and good-looking refrigerators, we still wonder how fantastic images and constructions in paint, metal, stone, or plastics affect the quality of our lives. Merchants and manufacturers may need designers to attract buyers, but what function is performed, what need is satisfied, when paint is splashed on a canvas which is then exhibited for the amazement of honest men and women?

Why should we spend time trying to understand the work of artists who have not taken the trouble to make their meaning clear? Can't we live full lives without these visual "experiments"? Is there any connection between today's art and the masterworks of the past? Answers to these questions—or attempts to answer them—are what the following pages are about.

# CHAPTER ONE

# PERSONAL FUNCTIONS OF ART

Although we are social beings who must live in groups to survive, we have a private and separate existence, too. We can never escape the consciousness of other persons, but we also feel that thoughts occur to us uniquely. Inside each of us many events take place, and often we want others to know about them. To share these feelings and ideas we use different languages; art is one of those languages.

As a type of personal expression, art is not confined to self-revelation; it can also convey an artist's attitudes about *public* objects and events. Basic human emotions and situations like love, death, celebration, and illness constantly recur, and we see them in a fresh light because of the personal comment made by an artist. For example, adolescence has an unusual sadness in the sculpture of Wilhelm Lehmbruck; a peculiar aroma of death hovers over the pictures of Edvard Munch; and we sense an irrepressible love of living in the paintings of Frans Hals. For these artists, people, places, and events are *opportunities* to express a personal outlook, even a personal philosophy.

Almost all works of art can function as individual expressions for the artist. They may have been created to promote official ideas, but they cannot help being vehicles of the artist's private vision. Today, this subjective element is treasured above all others; the personal function of art seems to constitute its very essence.

## ART AND PSYCHOLOGICAL EXPRESSION

Visual images preceded written language as a means of communication. However, art goes beyond communicating information; it also expresses a whole dimension of human personality—our inner, or psychological, states of being.

Why distinguish between communication and expression? Because art is more than a language of standardized signs and symbols; it does not communicate in the same way as a traffic light or a newspaper headline. Art often employs standardized symbols, but fundamentally it involves the forming of lines, colors, and shapes to embody an artist's values or convictions or life experience. In this process, artistic materials and techniques become vehicles of expression; they embody an artist's intention and meaning in themselves.

Suzanne Valadon. *Reclining Nude*. 1928. Oil on canvas, 23⅝ × 31¹¹⁄₁₆". The Metropolitan Museum of Art, New York. Robert Lehman Collection, 1975

The nude and psychological expression. Notice the defensive arm, the hand nervously clutching a piece of drapery, the tightly crossed legs, and the feet that cannot relax. The model's body looks strong and healthy, but her face betrays fear, vulnerability. Compare this woman with Manet's proud, almost arrogant, Olympia (page 225).

Without art, without using certain materials in certain ways, there would be no way of discovering certain states of feeling. A poem or a song does not mean the same thing as a painting or sculpture about the same subject; different meanings are created by different materials and techniques.

*Man Pointing* by Alberto Giacometti (1901–1966) illustrates the idea. We see a uniquely visual expression of loneliness in the image of a person who is physically and spiritually distant. The same is true of Germaine Richier's (1904–1959) *La Feuille (The Leaf)*. The elongation of forms, the indistinctness of the body parts, and the proportions of the figures create an impression of human remoteness. It would be difficult to communicate with either of these men; they seem surrounded by silence. The discovery of these qualities shows that visual forms can convey exceedingly intimate emotions. They show artists commenting on a universal problem: we multiply our media of communication but fail to *reach* each other; in a sense, all of us are isolated.

While the feelings expressed by Giacometti and Richier are widely shared, the portrait of a specific person has fewer universal implications; it concentrates on individual personality. In *The Poet Max Hermann-Neisse*, George Grosz (1893–1959) presents the "map" of a singular man. The linear style, highly developed in the artist's career as a newspaper satirist, gives us a painfully truthful account of the bones of the man's skull, the veins of his temple, and the worried wrinkles in his face and forehead. The carefully drawn hands, although folded, convey a strong sense of agitation. The man's brooding quality is accentuated by his rumpled clothing: the folds seem to be in seething, turbulent motion. Grosz was a brutally honest reporter who

George Grosz. *The Poet Max Hermann-Neisse*. 1927. Oil on canvas, 23⅜ × 29⅛". Collection, The Museum of Modern Art, New York. Purchase

Alberto Giacometti. *Man Pointing*. 1947. Bronze, 70½" high, at base 12 × 13¼". Collection, The Museum of Modern Art, New York. Gift of Mrs. John D. Rockefeller 3rd

The tragedy of Giacometti's man is that he wants to communicate but "they" won't listen. So he can't break out of his spiritual isolation. Richier's man is trapped in a loser's self-image: he has defined himself as a victim, a person predestined to fail.

Germaine Richier. *La Feuille (The Leaf)*. 1948. Bronze, 54½" high. The Hirshhorn Museum and Sculpture Garden, Washington, D.C. Gift of Joseph H. Hirshhorn, 1966

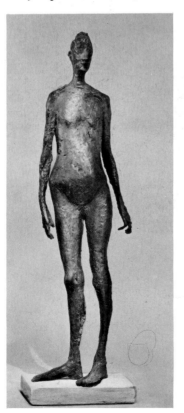

Juan Gris. *Portrait of Max Jacob*. 1919. Pencil, 14⅜ × 10½". Collection, The Museum of Modern Art, New York. Gift of James Thrall Soby

tended to stress the fact that man is, after all, a peculiar-looking creature. Obsessed with moral and social depravity, Grosz used art to express the far-from-ideal character of everything he saw. Even in a person he liked, he could not help seeing the countenance of ugliness, sickness, and perhaps cruelty.

The *Portrait of Max Jacob* by Juan Gris (1887–1927) deals with a man of about the same age in a similar pose, yet the effect is much more placid. While Grosz expresses the restless Germanic or Gothic temperament, Gris portrays the more relaxed and classic qualities of the Mediterranean world. The drawing is also excellent, but Gris does not distort what he sees: he emphasizes the sitter's gentleness. Again, we have a kind of facial map; the artist seems to be making a chart of the convolutions of his subject's face, hands,

There is a frozen quality about both groups of diners. But the immobility of Le Nain's peasants is intended to suggest their fundamental dignity and self-respect. Segal's people are immobile because they have nothing important to do.

and body. Even so, the drawing has a quality of gentle humanity; it communicates the artist's psychological insight and delicacy of feeling.

Portraits are obviously suited to the expression of personality, but landscape presents a different problem. Still, *An April Mood* by Charles Burchfield (1893–1967) reveals the psychological possibilities of Nature when human moods are projected upon her. The trees, stripped of leaves, permit Burchfield to characterize them as witches or druids. Then, by exaggerating the heaviness of the dark clouds framing the light forms in the center, the artist creates an emotionally charged stage. Nature provides theatrical occasions, but only because we see them as the working out of our private dramas of menace and threat, deliverance and jubilation. Here the upraised arms of the trees seem to join in a weird incantation, a strange imitation of primitive sun worship.

Another example of art as psychological expression is seen in George Segal's *The Dinner Table*. Segal (born 1924) creates his sculptures by placing plaster-soaked rags on the bodies of models. After the plaster sets, the rags are removed and assembled into cast-plaster figures. Therefore, the final forms are replicas of living forms, but without the exaggeration or simplification of carved or modeled figures. Then the artist installs props to create a "real" environment. Segal's creative role lies in identifying commonplace people in commonplace situations; his technique gives them a lumpy, sluggish quality. But he is not in the business of displaying sculptural virtuosity. Instead, we get grubby, ungraceful human beings—neither handsome nor ugly, not sick but not well either. The artist's theme is *the artlessness* of ordinary life; he emphasizes the vagueness and blandness of the typical human environment. Segal's people seem to have the character of overcooked vegetables.

## LOVE, SEX, AND MARRIAGE

Beyond describing the varieties of personality, art also deals with major interpersonal themes like love, sex, marriage, and procreation. The treatment of love can range from the physical embrace of Auguste Rodin's (1840–1917) *The Kiss,* to the maternal affection in Mary Cassatt's (1845–1926) *La Toilette,* to the motherly pride of Jacob Epstein's (1880–1959) *Madonna and Child.*

Usually, it is the female figure that expresses our feelings about love and sexuality. And in the work of a single sculptor, Gaston Lachaise (1882–1935), we see two variations on that theme. His *Standing Woman* of 1912–27 combines elegant hands and feet with an idealization and exaggeration of the fleshy forms associated with procreation. There is some erotic feeling, too, but it is tempered by lightness and agility in the feet and the buoyant grace of the hands. By contrast, the forms of the *Standing Woman* of 1932 are much

An early "love" object—really a fertility symbol. Here the personality of woman is wholly submerged in her biological role.

*left:* Charles Burchfield. *An April Mood.* 1946-55. Watercolor and charcoal on paper, 40 × 54". Collection of Whitney Museum of American Art, New York. Purchase, with partial funds from Mr. and Mrs. Lawrence A. Fleischman

The animation of nature. Burchfield converts the landscape into drama: the trees impersonate people against a theatrical backdrop. But Van Gogh's landscape is no stage play: he sees nature going through a real convulsion.

*below:* Vincent van Gogh. *Landscape with Olive Trees.* 1889. Oil on canvas, 28½ × 35½". Collection Mr. and Mrs. John Hay Whitney, New York

more exaggerated, with an almost athletic emphasis on childbearing. The feet are solidly planted in the earth while the muscles of the shoulders and abdomen aggressively assert the female biological role. There is less gentleness in the transitions between forms than in the earlier bronze, which results in a forceful expression of procreation; we get none of the tender meanings of love.

Auguste Rodin. *The Kiss.* 1898. Marble, over-lifesize.
Rodin Museum, Paris

Love as tender eroticism.

Jacob Epstein. *Madonna and Child.* 1927.
Bronze, over-lifesize. The Riverside
Church, New York

Love as maternal pride.

Mary Cassatt. *La Toilette.* c. 1891. Oil on canvas, 39½ × 26".
The Art Institute of Chicago. Robert A. Waller Fund

Love as protective concern.

*right:* Gaston Lachaise. *Standing Woman.* 1912–27. Bronze, 70 × 28 × 16". Collection of Whitney Museum of American Art, New York. Purchase

*far right:* Gaston Lachaise. *Standing Woman.* 1932. Bronze, 88 × 41⅛ × 19⅛". Collection, The Museum of Modern Art, New York. Mrs. Simon Guggenheim Fund

Jean Arp. *Torso Gerbe.* 1958. Collection Arthur and Molly Stern, Rochester, New York

In contrast to the fleshiness of Lachaise, Amedeo Modigliani's (1884–1920) *Reclining Nude* gives us a more elongated version of the female form. Shown in a relaxed pose, probably asleep, she is now presented in a sinuously provocative manner. Finally, we encounter a generalized idea of femaleness in *Torso Gerbe* by Jean Arp (1887–1966). Here a specific woman's character is suppressed in favor of a kind of impersonal, organic meaning. Arp carries abstraction of living form as far as he can go without abandoning what is biologically human. Yet even if the forms are impersonal and semi-abstract, the work as a whole manages to look sexy.

Our culture has produced a great deal of sarcastic humor about love in marriage. Much of it deals with losing the illusions that feed romance. Still, many of us believe in romance, which is what Marc Chagall (1887–1985) celebrates in *Birthday.* Here art is dedicated to the notion of love as perpetual courtship: exchanging gifts, pretending shyness, continuing the games of

*right:* Amedeo Modigliani. *Reclining Nude.* c. 1919. Oil on canvas, 28½ × 45⅞". Collection, The Museum of Modern Art, New York. Mrs. Simon Guggenheim Fund

Marc Chagall. *Birthday.* 1915–23.
Oil on cardboard, 31¾ × 39¼".
Private collection

Love as levitation. She skips; he
flies . . . without arms or wings.

pursuit and resistance. Chagall's fabled charm owes a lot to the hope that love
can be sustained forever if we continue the romantic rituals depicted in
*Birthday.*

Oskar Kokoschka (1886–1980) offers a sour, cynical view of love in *The
Tempest,* or *The Wind's Bride.* Here a couple is shown swirling in space under
a moonlit mountainscape. Love for them, as for Chagall's couple, has performed the miracle of levitation. But while Chagall's people are magically

Oskar Kokoschka. *The Tempest
(The Wind's Bride).* 1914. Oil on
canvas, 71¼ × 87". Offentliche
Kunstsammlung, Basel

Love as levitation. She dreams;
he can't sleep.

*above:* David Hockney. *The First Marriage (A Marriage of Styles).* 1962. Oil on canvas, 60 × 77". The Tate Gallery, London. © David Hockney 1962

Hockney's view of a May and December marriage, outdoors, next to a palm tree, under the California sun. He has one foot in the grave; she looks confidently toward the future, like an ancient Egyptian princess.

*below left:* Carl Hofer. *Early Hour.* 1935. Oil on canvas, 49¼ × 61⅜". Collection, Portland Art Museum. Oregon Art Institute, Ella M. Hirsch Fund

Love and domestic life: comfortable but still a puzzlement.

*below right:* Barbara Adrian. *Bed of Stones.* 1964. Whereabouts unknown

Love on the rocks; comfort doesn't matter.

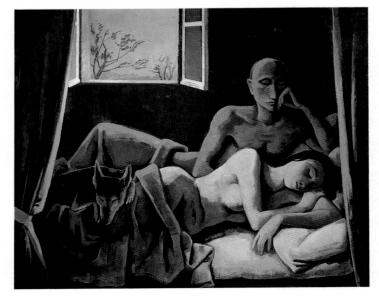

lifted up, Kokoschka's are violently *swirled*. The words in both titles—"tempest" and "wind"—suggest the *sturm und drang*, the storm and stress, of a Germanic notion of human relations. While the bride sleeps, wrapped in tender and trusting emotions, the groom stares into space—starkly awake. He may be levitated by the power of love but he seems unable to suppress strong feelings of gloom.

In *Early Hour*, Carl Hofer (1878–1955) carries the theme of *The Wind's Bride* one step further to disillusioned domesticity. The crisp morning light reveals a husband, already awake, coldly studying his wife's sleeping form. The dog at the foot of the bed completes the picture of familial routine. As for the man's head—lean and bald—it creates an impression of asceticism, of an intellectual resigned to marriage but not happy about it. It is interesting that in both works the woman is shown in contented slumber while her husband or lover is wide awake in the moonlight or skeptically contemplating his situation in the morning's clear light. In either case, the marital outlook does not look very good.

Another version of the same theme appears in *Conjugal Life* by Roger de La Fresnaye (1885–1925). Here the Cubist process of breaking up figures and converting them into geometric shapes has begun. But there is enough resemblance to visual reality to resist the depersonalizing effects of a fully developed Cubism. We recognize a casual, comradely quality about this couple, accentuated by the matter-of-factness of the woman's being nude while her clothed husband reads the newspaper and enjoys his pipe. They exhibit the mutual indifference of a comfortable intimacy based on a long-established relationship. This idea is strengthened by the way the figures lean toward each other: the main lines and masses seek the picture's center and lock the figures into a tight formal structure. Compare this composition—and the idea behind it—with the sardonic presentation by George Grosz in *Couple*. Clearly, artistic attitudes toward sex, marriage, and women serve as an interesting index of values in our culture. Contemporary art has been candid enough to address these issues.

*left:* **Roger de La Fresnaye. *Conjugal Life*. 1912. Oil on canvas, 38⁵/₁₆ × 46³/₄". The Minneapolis Institute of Arts. The John R. Van Derlip Fund**

Why isn't he undressed, too?

*right:* **George Grosz. *Couple*. 1934. Watercolor on paper, 25¼ × 17³/₄". Collection of Whitney Museum of American Art, New York. Purchase**

Why do old couples seem to look like each other?

*left:* Käthe Kollwitz. *Death and the Mother.* 1934. Lithograph, 20 × 14⁷⁄₁₆". Collection Erich Cohn, New York

*right:* Albert Pinkham Ryder. *Death on a Pale Horse (The Race Track).* c. 1910. Oil on canvas, 28¼ × 35¼". The Cleveland Museum of Art. Purchase, J. H. Wade Fund

Is this a day or a night scene? Both. Was it real or was it dreamed? Both.

# DEATH AND MORBIDITY

Death frightens and fascinates us; we cannot solve its mystery: Why do vitality and personality inhabit matter in one instant and leave it in another? From Stone Age cave images of dead animals to African sculptures of departed chiefs, art embodies our desire to understand, if not to master, the fear of death. Science may learn to control many of death's causes, but only art can express our feelings about what happens afterward. This was always the case. Sculpture originated in efforts to provide physical bodies for dead souls to inhabit. The monuments of Egyptian art were, in their principal motivation, enormous state-supported enterprises aimed at overcoming the death of a king revered as a god. Perhaps today's artistic treatment of mortality is an extension of the anxiety that everyone feels but which in ancient times was expressed mainly for the benefit of kings.

**Artistic Expressions of Mortality**     *Death and the Mother,* a lithograph by Käthe Kollwitz (1867–1945), shows us the almost insane terror that grips a mother whose child is about to die. The imagery gains much of its symbolic force from medieval personifications of the devil as the messenger of death. Notwithstanding our emergence from medieval superstition, this work disturbs us because it exploits fears we can hardly suppress. An impersonal phrase like "infant mortality" is given powerful emotional content; the viewer experiences real dread; we want to strike out against the death symbol.

A peculiar portrayal of mortality and fate occurs in *Death on a Pale Horse (The Race Track)* by the American painter Albert Pinkham Ryder (1847–1917). Here death carries his conventional attribute, a scythe, while riding a white horse around a racetrack. No one is there to witness the scene except a serpent (at bottom), and curiously there are no competitors. Like other paintings by Ryder, this one looks as if it had been dreamed. Actually, the painting was a response to a real experience: Ryder knew a man who had gambled his savings on a horse race, lost his money, and committed suicide. But the real-life origin of the painting should not interfere with our interpretation of it. (See Chapter Seventeen for a discussion of interpretation.)

Although the figure on the horse personifies death, the question remains: How does death work? Well, he cuts people down with a scythe. But why is he riding around an empty track, watched only by a snake? Here the artist's mythic imagination is at work: Ryder suggests that life is a game played by Evil and Death; the track is a magic circle that lures men with the promise of riches. But it is really a death trap; there is no possible outcome except man's destruction; the tree inside the track bears no fruit. Competing against Death and Evil (the "system"), no one can win. Ryder's dream scene gives us a *magical* explanation of Everyman's life and its inevitable end.

*The Dead Mother* by Edvard Munch (1863–1944) is even more pathetic, not so much in the image of the mother, who is beyond suffering, as in the portrayal of the child, who holds her hands to her ears as if to *stop the sound of death*. Here the psychological realism is more thoroughgoing than that of Kollwitz and Ryder, who employ conventional death symbols. Munch shows

*above:* Edvard Munch. *The Dead Mother.* 1899–1900. Oil on canvas, 39⅜ × 35⅜". Kunsthalle, Bremen

*right:* Ben Shahn. *The Passion of Sacco and Vanzetti.* 1931–32. Tempera on canvas, 84½ × 48". Collection of Whitney Museum of American Art, New York. Gift of Edith and Milton Lowenthal in memory of Juliana Force

Pablo Picasso. *Girl Before a Mirror.* 1932. Oil on canvas, 64 × 51¼". Collection,
The Museum of Modern Art, New York. Gift of Mrs. Simon Guggenheim

The image in the mirror reflects her fear of becoming a woman.

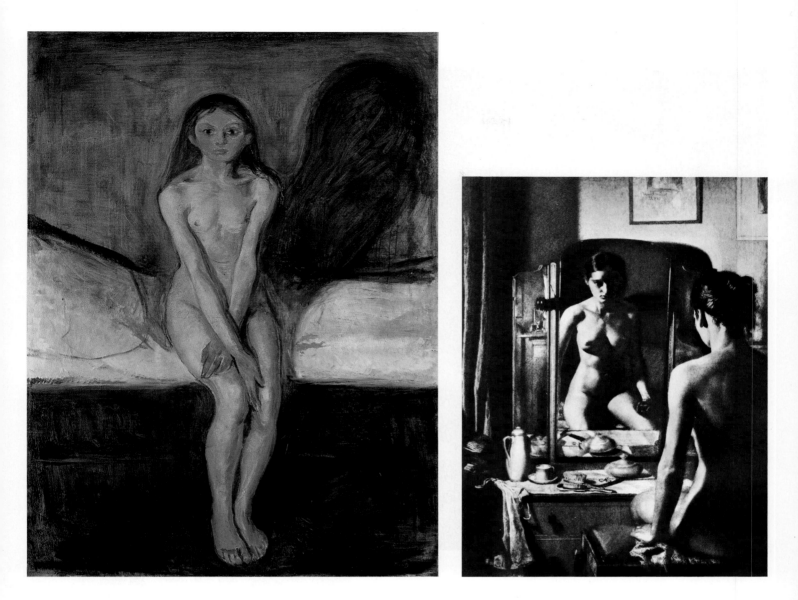

us the actual death scene and depicts its psychological impact on a child. She has no adult mechanisms for protecting herself, for softening the blow. So she acts out the meaning of death: it turns out to be a very bad sound. The date of this painting is 1899–1900, a time when art tended to sentimentalize harsh truths. But in Munch we have an artist who, like the playwright Ibsen, had the courage to examine the pain of life realistically.

*The Passion of Sacco and Vanzetti* by Ben Shahn (1898–1969) deals with the death of two men convicted of taking part in an anarchist bombing in Boston. The mourners are shown as "respectable" members of society—politicians or lawyers and an academic—who have played roles in a miscarriage of justice: they have contributed to the execution of innocent men. The background shows a courthouse and a portrait of a jurist taking his oath of office. In a scene heavy with irony, lilies, symbols of resurrection, are held over the coffins of two immigrants tried by a prejudiced judge. Sacco and Vanzetti are shown in death as foreign-looking and defenseless; their mourners look guilty and crooked. Thus Shahn expresses his bitterness and sympathy: contempt for a society that seeks vengeance, and compassion for little men (we see only pieces of their faces) caught up in a destructive chain of events. Death is the matter-of-fact, logical outcome of social and political hypocrisy.

In *Girl Before a Mirror*, Pablo Picasso (1881–1973) pictures a girl's morbid anticipations as she becomes aware of her biological womanhood. We see a kind of X-ray image of her actual figure on the left and its reflection

*left:* Edvard Munch. *Puberty.* 1895. Oil on canvas, 59⅝ × 43¼". National Gallery, Oslo

The crisis of adolescence experienced as biological dread.

*right:* Gerald Leslie Brockhurst. *Adolescence (Portrait of Kathleen Nancy Woodward).* 1932. Etching, 14½ × 10½". Courtesy of the Syracuse University Art Collection

The onset of womanhood is discovered in a magical awareness of the body's opulence.

Théodore Géricault. *Madwoman.* c. 1821. Oil on canvas, 30¼ × 25¼". The Louvre, Paris

Chaim Soutine. *The Madwoman.* 1920. Oil on canvas, 37¼ × 23¼". The National Museum of Western Art, Tokyo. Presented by Mr. Tai Hayashi, 1960

Frida Kahlo. *The Two Fridas.* 1939. Oil on canvas, 67 × 67". Collection of the Museo de Arte Moderno, Mexico City

One Frida is dressed as a bride, the other wears a Mexican costume, and both are connected (through their hearts) by a thin red artery that drips blood on the bridal gown. This is the double image of a woman trying to control a life tormented by continuous physical pain. The serenity of the faces is really a facade: it barely conceals the suffering under the skin.

in the mirror on the right. Both images deal with the shapes of female organs of reproduction and nurture. The girl's innocent face (at left) is reflected in the mirror by a dark, hollow-eyed face surrounded by black and blue moon-shaped crescents. The head on the left has a bright halo, with a yellow passage on the side where a shadow would be expected. This clear-eyed "sun-face" symbolizes the girl's unclouded youth; the "moon-face" in the mirror symbolizes reflected light, an "old" moon, a dying woman. Why does the girl's arm reach across to that fearsome image? Is she straightening the mirror? Well, the painting is vertically divided; perhaps the arm moving across the canvas is meant to unite the picture compositionally. But the gesture may also symbolize the end of the girl's innocence, an expression of sympathy for her other self—the self that ages and dies after bringing life into the world.

Picasso's painting might be compared to the treatment of the same theme by Munch in *Puberty*, and to a highly naturalistic lithograph, *Adolescence*, by the English artist Gerald Brockhurst (1890–1978). All three works show art reaching across the barriers of age, style, and gender to deal with the fears, the apprehensions, the uneasiness of the human soul.

**Artistic Expressions of Illness**   The expression of love in modern art may be sentimental or cynical (usually the latter), but when it comes to illness and disease, we see a frank, almost clinical, kind of imagery. Of course, artists are not medical pathologists, but they often use sickness as a symbol of the human condition. They may not be interested in morbidity for its own sake but they refuse to ignore a dimension of experience that helps to define our humanity.

We can see an early treatment of mental illness in Théodore Géricault's (1791–1824) *Madwoman*. Here the artist examines a woman while she seems to be confronting some real or imagined threat. She may be truly crazy, but without the title we might interpret this work as a character study, as the portrait of a somewhat suspicious, perhaps eccentric, peasant woman. Is Géricault saying that the difference between "crazy" and "eccentric" is hard to see? His picture should be compared with *The Madwoman* by Chaim Soutine (1894–1944), painted in 1920, about one hundred years later. Here the artist attempts to convey *the experience* of the sick person: every part of her trembles with fear; there is no question in our minds that she is mentally ill. Géricault maintains his objectivity whereas Soutine enters the life of his subject. Géricault is known as a Romantic painter because of his strange or emotionally demanding subject matter. Romantics tend to focus on abnormal behavior, human reactions in emergencies, or the loss of rational controls when we are under stress. We call Soutine an Expressionist because of his subject matter *and* his agitated technique. The Expressionists took the Ro-

Pablo Picasso. *The Frugal Repast*. 1904. Etching, printed in black; plate 18³/₁₆ × 14¹³/₁₆".
Collection, The Museum of Modern Art, New York. Gift of Abby Aldrich Rockefeller

mantic fascination with violence and incorporated it into the act of painting itself. Thus artistic imagery becomes a record of convulsive form and disturbed emotion. The frightened eyes and tortured hands of Soutine's woman announce her illness; nevertheless the picture rises above illness: we recognize a fellow human being who is suffering.

In Picasso's *The Frugal Repast*, an etching made when he was young and poor, we see a gaunt, emaciated couple at a meal. The man is blind; the couple seems to be starving. Their condition offers the artist an opportunity to stretch out their bodies, especially their hands, giving them a weak, feverish quality. But even if the man is handicapped and both are undernourished, the couple seem resigned to their situation; they have a little food (in France wine is a food) and each other. What we see is a highly civilized tribute to romantic love; what looks like a morbid interest in the effects of malnutrition on lovers becomes a human triumph over deprivation. Weakness is turned into tenderness; the artist discovers a peculiar beauty in the withered bodies of people who care for and love each other.

Works like *The Frugal Repast* are not meant to gloss over the reality of poverty. They demonstrate a great strength of art: its capacity to reveal the values people can create in any situation they must live with. Puccini's romantic opera *La Bohème* deals with a theme much like Picasso's: the composer creates beautiful music out of the love of a consumptive, dying girl for an impoverished poet. Picasso's etching was made in 1904 when he was twenty-two and an ardent devotee of tragic love; this was only eight years after the first performance of *La Bohème*. Both works express the romantic idea that love can reach intensity *because of* affliction and *in spite of* the world's indifference.

There is an entire aesthetic—a system of ideas about art—based on the experience of illness. In Géricault and Soutine, this interest is part of a concern with the total human condition. In Munch, death cannot be separated from living. In Shahn's *Passion*, death is part of a bitter statement about justice. In Picasso's etching the signs of deprivation have almost erotic significance. In Ivan Albright's *Self-Portrait* and Karl Zerbe's *Aging Harlequin*, a certain ugliness associated with aging (compare Domenico Ghirlandaio's [1449–1494] *An Old Man and His Grandson*) is recorded almost obsessively. Zerbe (1903–1972) enlists compassion for the harlequin, despite his ravaged countenance. Albright (1897–1983) shows himself drinking champagne and calmly contemplating the fate written in his face.

Hyman Bloom (born 1913) and Alberto Burri (born 1915) may give us the ultimate images of deterioration. In *Corpse of an Elderly Female* we witness an artist's fascination with death. Bloom employs no artistic device to soften its clinical accuracy; his interest in cadavers is probably a reaction to the slaughter of civilians during World War II. Here we are forced to confront a woman's death in all its morbid detail. The Italian artist Alberto Burri works more abstractly; his *Sacco B.* is made of burlap sacking stretched and sewn around what looks like an open wound or incision. Burri had been a military doctor, and many of his compositions are based on surgery; the dramatic focus is an opening in the flesh. Burri's works can be seen as simple arrangements of gauze, burnt wood, and burlap, but they also have an expressive purpose: the rips in the sacking seem to be the result of some mysterious, nonscientific medicine. Although the surfaces suggest disease, Burri portrays wounds and surgery as a kind of primitive handicraft: a disorderly death hovers over the whole composition. It is a far cry from the Thomas Eakins (1844–1916) painting of surgery in 1889, *The Agnew Clinic*, with its confident presentation of the doctor's technique as a triumph of science.

Examples could be multiplied. We have seen how one of the personal functions of art—now as in the past—is the confrontation of illness and death and all its associated feelings. Obviously, art cannot postpone death, but it

can help us to face the experience and understand it as part of the living process. In dealing with our most terrible fears and aversions, art may be helping us to see life clearly and whole.

## SPIRITUAL CONCERN

We should distinguish between religious art and an art of spiritual concern. Religious art usually expresses collective ideas about human existence in relation to a divine source. It may have spiritual qualities but it also functions as instruction or as history or as a kind of visual preaching. Nonreligious, or secular, art can also exhibit spiritual qualities, as in Vincent van Gogh's (1853–1890) *The Starry Night.* Ironically, religious art may exhibit very little spirituality, as in Stanley Spencer's (1891–1959) *Christ Preaching at Cookham Regatta.* Georges Rouault's (1871–1958) art, by contrast, seems to have spiritual content even when the subject matter is secular, as in his *Three Clowns.*

What accounts for this paradox? Well, religious art usually tells a sacred story, encourages morality, or tries to sustain faith in a supernatural doctrine.

Anselm Kiefer. *To the Unknown Painter (Dem unbekannten Maler).* 1983. Oil, emulsion, woodcut, shellac, latex, and straw on canvas, 9'2" square. The Carnegie Museum of Art, Pittsburgh. Richard M. Scaife Fund and A. W. Mellon Acquisition Endowment Fund

Instead of an "unknown soldier" we have an "unknown painter," who stands for all the artists and Holocaust victims lost to humanity. The ruined temple/tomb in the background is their monument; the scorched earth in the foreground symbolizes the destruction of their world and what they might have accomplished. According to Kiefer, artists and soldiers are spiritual kin: they struggle and die for impossible ideals.

*above:* Ivan Albright. *Self-Portrait.* 1935. Oil on canvas, 30⅜ × 19⅞". The Art Institute of Chicago. Mary and Earle Ludgin Collection

*left:* Domenico Ghirlandaio. *An Old Man and His Grandson.* c. 1480. Tempera and oil on panel, 24⅜ × 18⅛". The Louvre, Paris

Aging brings many indignities and a few joys. Grandchildren are one of the joys, but we need a fifteenth-century master to tell us about it.

*right:* Karl Zerbe. *Aging Harlequin.* 1946. Collection Dr. Michael Watter, Washington, D.C.

*far right:* Photograph of Melvyn Douglas as he appeared in the CBS Television Network presentation "Do Not Go Gentle into That Good Night." 1967

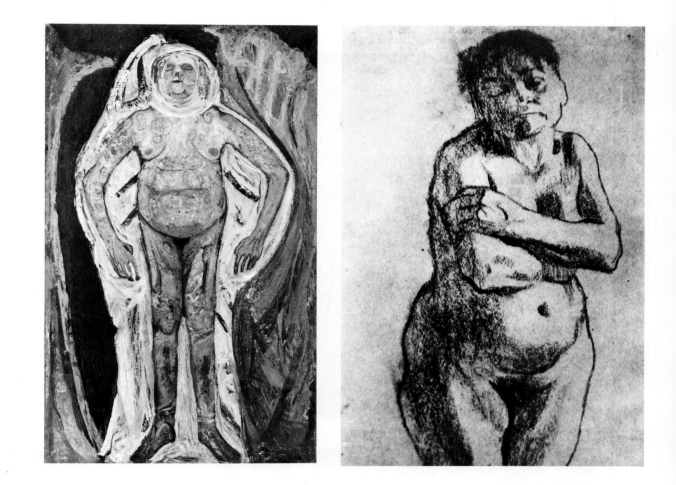

Spiritual art tries to reveal the sacred in everyday life or in human nature; often it discovers God in unexpected places. A spiritual art does not necessarily come with theological labels. Furthermore, it often expresses the *questions* artists have about our place in the universe, whereas religious art tends to deal with institutionally established *answers*. For our purposes, then, an art of spiritual concern is *any search for ultimate values through visual form.*

Today especially, the artistic enterprise is identified with search and inquiry. In the past, people had fewer doubts about life's origin and destiny, and artists could deal with commonly accepted ideas about human existence. But the modern era has witnessed profound changes in the expression of ultimate values. The scientific, industrial, and political revolutions of our times have caused almost universal questioning of inherited dogmas and philosophies, and our era has not been especially successful in providing alternatives which hold true even for a lifetime. For that reason, perhaps, today's intellectual, spiritual, and artistic activity has emphasized questioning. Artworks that deal with personal values have been characterized by uncertainty more than conviction.

Still, we cannot tolerate uncertainty forever. A deep layer of conviction may lie beneath our questions about the meaning of existence. Art makes that "layer of conviction" visible. On its surface, Van Gogh's *The Starry Night* is a picture of a village at night, with prominent cypresses in the foreground and large circles and spirals of light emanating from the stars and the moon. The scene is animated by flamelike shapes in the trees and active brushwork in the hills and sky. Everything appears to be alive and in motion; only the houses and the church are at rest. Apparently, this landscape has a kind of vitality we do not normally see; the differences between solid and void, organic and inorganic, do not exist. Van Gogh shows us the sacred where we

*left:* Hyman Bloom. *Corpse of an Elderly Female.* 1945. Oil on canvas, 70 × 42". The Chrysler Museum, Norfolk, Virginia

*right:* Käthe Kollwitz. *Nude.* 1905

The naked body of an older woman becomes a vehicle of intense personal expression. Her closed eyes, resigned mouth, and clasped arms—plus the strong, grainy modeling—add up to a gesture of complete self-acceptance.

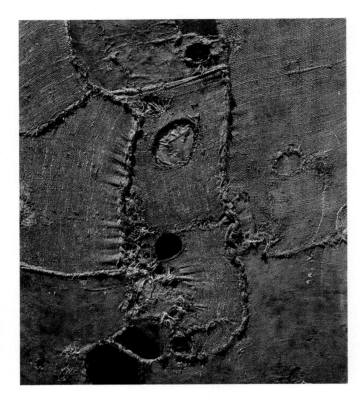

Alberto Burri. *Sacco B.* 1953. Burlap, sewn, patched, and glued over canvas, 39⅜ × 33½". Collection the artist

The ritual of surgery converted into aesthetic drama: open and closed, woven and sewn, wet and dry, alive and dead.

*below:* Thomas Eakins. *The Agnew Clinic.* 1889. Oil on canvas, 6'2½" × 10'10½". School of Medicine, The University of Pennsylvania, Philadelphia

The ritual of surgery portrayed as a triumph of mind over flesh.

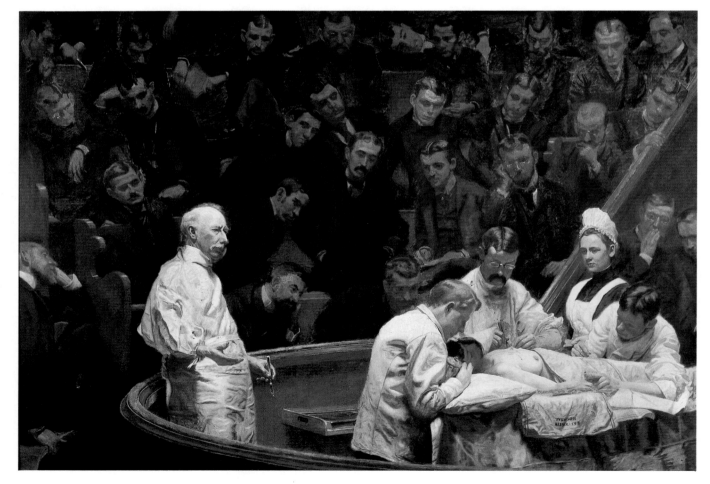

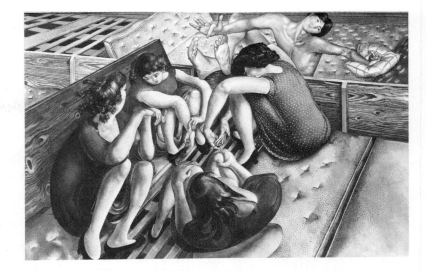

Stanley Spencer. *Christ Preaching at Cookham Regatta: Series No. VI: Four Girls Listening.* 1958. Arthur Tooth & Sons, Ltd., London

*below:* Georges Rouault. *Three Clowns.* 1917. Oil on canvas, 41½ × 29½". Collection Joseph Pulitzer, Jr., St. Louis

Vincent van Gogh. *The Starry Night.* 1889. Oil on canvas, 29 × 36¼". Collection, The Museum of Modern Art, New York. Acquired through the Lillie P. Bliss Bequest

In Van Gogh, the secular is spiritualized; this painting begins with an everyday theme and culminates in a mystical statement.

do not expect to find it. For those who do not possess his spiritual gifts, the experience of this painting offers a glimpse into a hallowed world: we share in the vision of a "God-intoxicated" man.

Rouault's art illustrates the same point in a different way. What accounts for the spiritual character of his *Three Clowns?* First, we see the similarity, with minor variations, of the three men. We view them as a group rather than as distinct personalities; collectively they symbolize all men, humanity. Second is the coarseness of their features; the artist has deliberately avoided physical beauty. Because of their rough faces and the harsh transitions from light to dark, we realize we are dealing with unbeautiful features of our species. Third is the passive, accepting expressions of the faces; the body of humanity is described as suffering but unresisting. Finally, there is the huddled arrangement of the figures; they symbolize the oppressed, fearful, and victimized condition of all who are weak.

All these factors, working together, tend to express the wretchedness of the human condition. Certain themes at the heart of Christianity—the virtue of humility and the ultimate significance of suffering—are presented in a form that gives them universal application. It appears that the artist wants to reveal our authentic nature—what humanity is really like as opposed to what man thinks he is.

While Rouault's spirituality grows out of one essential insight—the anguish of being human—the sculptor Henry Moore (1898–1986) stresses spiritual affirmation and renewal; his figures cast humanity in a monumental role. Monumental sculpture usually celebrates victories of one sort or another, but Moore celebrates survival: *the durability* of men and women, their refusal to be beaten down. Notice the massiveness and stability of his UNESCO sculpture; its powerful forms, abstracted from the thighs and the torso, look like the shapes of old hills and eroded mountains. Punctuated with deep hollows and full openings, these forms are crowned by a head which seems to symbolize the dominance of intelligence over matter. The hollows and openings are not merely "negative" shapes; they function positively, inviting the environment to participate in the sculpture.

Without obvious dramatic devices Moore's figure suggests the resurgence of a human being who has been struck down. The forms become symbols of human determination operating against adversity. The image is heroic, Promethean: man suffers but is still defiant. The reclining position of the figure may suggest defeat, as in the *Dying Gaul*, yet it is capable of physical and spiritual renewal. Compared to Rouault, Moore is less obsessed with man's helplessness and vulnerability. Instead, his sculpture expresses human tenacity, the courage of an earth creature that slowly rebuilds itself, even if it knows it will be struck down again.

A different expression of modern spirituality is found in the work of Jackson Pollock (1912–1956). *Number I, 1948* shows his typical paint surface: tangled threads of pigment dripped and spattered on the canvas; an endless maze of pattern and movement. Viewing the work as a whole, we are aware

Henry Moore. *Reclining Figure.* 1957–58. Roman Travertine marble, 16'8" long. UNESCO Headquarters, Paris

**RECUMBENT AND FALLEN FIGURES AS SYMBOLS OF DEATH AND RESURRECTION**

Epigonus. *Dying Gaul.* Pergamum. c. 225 B.C. Marble, lifesize. Roman copy of bronze original Capitoline Museum, Rome

Jackson Pollock. *Number I, 1948.* 1948. Oil on canvas, 5'8" × 8'8". Collection, The Museum of Modern Art, New York. Purchase

of an overall texture as well as repeated black calligraphic marks overlaid with paint splashes and spatters—knots and spots of color. And because the canvas is huge we feel drawn into the center of a jungle. Without representational elements, the picture directs the viewer back to the artist's act of execution. The imagery is at once dancelike and trancelike; no single movement is fathomable in terms of a deliberate departure, journey, and return. We seem to be looking at all sorts of terrain, multiple arenas of conflict, voyages begun and aborted. Yet the viewer cannot fail to be excited by the work's vitality, mainly its explosive release of painterly forces, its kinetic power. We feel entrapped, too. The experience, which intrigues us at first, can leave us visually exhausted.

The disturbing quality of Pollock's work would not have attracted such wide interest if it did not constitute a faithful reproduction of the spiritual landscape of our time. If we could see the lives of others from the inside, they might look very much like Pollock's "voyages." We might also see signs of satisfaction and hints of fulfillment. This would not invalidate Pollock's relevance to the spiritual condition of modern men and women: he remains the painter of our energetic and industrious failures.

## AESTHETIC EXPRESSION

Aesthetic needs are not the unique interest of some elite: everyone cares about what is beautiful or pleasing. Most of us are interested in harmonious forms wherever they can be found—in people, in nature, in objects of daily use. However, some artists specialize in creating images and objects that are intrinsically satisfying, apart from any use they may have. Such artworks turn out to be useful in a psychological sense: they help to satisfy our aesthetic impulses—impulses that exist at the deepest levels of personality.

In the beginning, human beings were concerned with forms, colors, shapes, and textures mainly because they were signs of danger or opportunity. Since life depended on how accurately and intelligently we could see, vision was a matter of supreme importance. We still have remarkable visual capacities for interpreting our experience. However, the conditions of modern life may not demand as much of our perceptual capacities as we are equipped to supply. In complex cultures, some forms of visual art seem to have evolved as a way of engaging unused perceptual capacity. Perhaps that is what aesthetic pleasure is—the satisfaction we feel in employing our innate capacities for perception to the fullest.

An elementary aesthetic pleasure might be called "the thrill of recognition." Obviously, recognition has always played an important role in human survival, and that may explain the popularity of art which is easily identified. When we *recognize* something in a work of art, we are in a sense rehearsing our survival technique, sharpening our capacity to distinguish between friend and foe. It is only a short step from the ability to make subtle visual discriminations to the ability to enjoy perception itself. By suspending the impulse to fight or flee, we learn to linger over visual events. And that maximizes our pleasure.

For Georges Braque (1882–1963) painting was mainly a source of visual delight. He was an early associate of Picasso in the creation of the intellectual austerities of Cubism, but he also employed Cubist principles to paint pictures of considerable sensuous appeal and decorative ingenuity. *The Round Table* displays his mastery of shape and texture and his wit in exploiting visual habits and pictorial conventions for pleasure and humor. The table can be recognized easily enough, with its top tilted up to show a set of ordinary objects: a mandolin, a knife, fruit, a magazine, a pipe, and so on. The objects in themselves are unimportant, but they have shapes, colors, and textures that Braque can rearrange. He can show the top and side view of an object at the same time; he can paint opaque objects as if they are transparent; he can reverse the expected convergence of lines in perspective; he can exaggerate ornamental shapes with white lines; he can exchange light and shadow areas arbitrarily; he can paint shadows lighter and brighter than the objects that cast them. The purpose of these surprises and "violations" is not to create a picture *of* something; the picture must *be* something, an organism that lives according

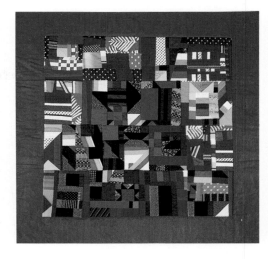

**Jean Ray Laury.** *Pieced Crazy Quilt.* **1982. Cotton, 61 × 61". Private collection, Clovis, California**

Crazy quilts originated as the nineteenth-century American answer to England's Aesthetic Movement. What was "crazy" about these quilts? Their "grotesque" designs; their seemingly random use of fabric scraps; their indifference to narrative values; their pursuit of dazzling chromatic effects. Also, women made them for *pleasurable* as well as utilitarian reasons. As we can see, the pleasurable function persists.

**Marsden Hartley.** *Indian Composition.* **1914–15. Oil on canvas, 47¼ × 47". Vassar College Art Gallery, Poughkeepsie, New York. Gift of Paul Rosenfeld**

Indian symbols, patterns, and motifs organized into a painting that functions mainly as an aesthetic object. But aesthetic potency is often rooted in magical-religious function. The forms created by the Hopi and the Crow still have the power to stir emotion.

Georges Braque. *The Round Table.* 1929. Oil on canvas, 57¼ × 44¾". © The Phillips Collection, Washington, D.C.

*opposite:* Helen Frankenthaler. *Rapunzel.* 1974. Acrylic on canvas, 9' × 6'9". Collection the artist

Whether dealing with the landscape, natural processes, or a fairy tale, Frankenthaler speaks directly in the language of sensation. Her areas of stained or brushed color communicate by size, intensity, and placement more than by shape. In other words, despite its highly personal expression of feeling, this painting is *designed.* Hanging those forms from the top edge of the canvas—and making them function simultaneously as narrative and music—is a pure feat of the aesthetic imagination. Compare this imagery to Jim Dine's *Five Feet of Colorful Tools* (page 498).

to its own cockeyed law. That "law" seems to say that any twisting, slicing, distortion, or reversal of shapes, colors, and textures is allowed if it adds to our pleasure in looking.

But how does a painter please the eye? Well, once the logic of reproducing appearances is abandoned, the possibilities are endless. The artist becomes a kind of intuitive investigator of forms that are somehow appealing, or unexpected, or both. Usually the artistic conscience will not permit the use of literary associations; our pleasure has to come from pictorial organization and painterly technique. Accordingly, Braque surrounds the table shapes with white outlines in order to flatten out the forms and destroy the illusion of deep space. He creates three-dimensional effects which are then pressed into two dimensions. The viewer is forced to read the painting as if the walls and floor were in the same plane as the table base. There is a subtle visual humor or, at least, visual trickery in Braque's painting; it doesn't make us laugh out loud, but we know that something funny is going on.

The emergence of abstract and nonobjective art has closely followed the development of an art of aesthetic purpose in our time. As painting and sculpture have departed from storytelling functions, they have increasingly concentrated on the internal problems of form creation in the hope of generating purely aesthetic emotions. José de Rivera's (1904–1985) sculpture, *Construction "Blue and Black,"* is an example. We have a work of almost absolute precision and geometric beauty that refers to nothing beyond itself. The sculpture "works" only in an aesthetic frame of reference. Perhaps some useful object will derive design inspiration from it. But we do not ask what

*above:* José de Rivera. *Construction "Blue and Black."* 1951. Painted aluminum, 47" long. Collection of Whitney Museum of American Art, New York. Purchase

*below left:* David Hare. *Juggler.* 1950–51. Steel, 80½ × 27 × 21¼". Collection of Whitney Museum of American Art, New York. Purchase

Machine-man metaphors. Hare's Juggler is having a good time; Lanceley's Personage is having a nervous breakdown.

*below right:* Colin Lanceley. *Inverted Personage.* 1965. Painted wood, 84 × 36". Albion College, Albion, Michigan

*below:* Alexander Calder. *International Mobile.* 1949. Sheet aluminum, max. dimensions 201 × 20'. The Museum of Fine Arts, Houston. Gift of Dominique and John de Menil

this work represents: its subject matter is the formal organization of the thing itself.

Alexander Calder (1898–1976) invented a sculptural type—the mobile—which pleases us almost entirely through the movement of abstract shapes. His *International Mobile* is a whimsical work in which the slightest movement of air in the surrounding space imparts a wavy, rollicking motion to the carefully balanced parts. They shift into an infinite number of constellations, arriving at temporary periods of equipoise by trembling, wriggling routes. Mobiles do not obviously resemble trees or people. Their motion can suggest anything from the sway of branches to the maneuvers of a belly dancer. But these are only one viewer's responses, stimulated by a highly original and often comic artist. Calder's work is whimsical and controlled, even in its seemingly random motion. Moreover, his sculpture "uses" the atmosphere and light of its environment. The climate of the room collaborates with the artist, who may be our greatest *ecological* artist.

The *Juggler* by David Hare (born 1917) is another work in which a playful abstraction of motion is the principal theme. Here, the juggler's muscular exertion and striving for balance become an excuse for making a strange steel "thing." It looks as if the artist was searching for a living creature that would fit into his agenda—the creation of form by using modern technologies to manipulate modern materials. The juggler represented an opportunity to make a construction out of wire and welded steel. Our aes-

*above:* Stuart Davis. *Report from Rockport.*
1940. Oil on canvas, 24 × 30". Collection Mr. and
Mrs. Milton Lowenthal, New York

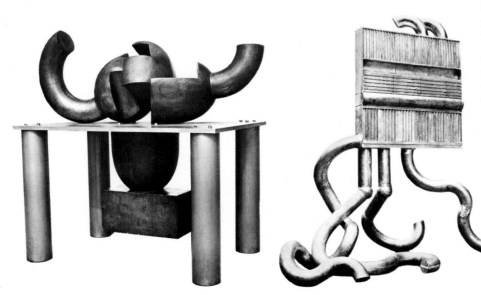

*below left:* Peter Voulkos. *Firestone.* 1965. Cast
bronze and aluminum, 80 × 48 × 72". Los
Angeles County Museum of Art. Museum
Purchase with Contemporary Art Council Funds

*below right:* Eduardo Paolozzi. *Medea.* 1964.
Aluminum, 21 × 72 × 45". Kröller-Müller
Museum, Otterlo, The Netherlands

The linear forms in Stuart Davis's 1940 street
scene fill his canvas with jazzy, comic energy.
But in the 1960s sculptures of Voulkos and
Paolozzi we see only sinister signs: amputated
arms coming out of a truncated head, and
slithery, squirmy legs attached to a terrible
machine-body-face.

Käthe Kollwitz. *Self-Portrait.* 1934. Los Angeles County Museum of Art. Los Angeles County Funds

The frontal pose, the masterly control of tones, the clear articulation of form, the regularity of the paper grain showing through the grays: all these produce a sense of aesthetic order, an order that expresses age, wisdom, and personal integrity.

thetic pleasure is based on the tension between the normal idea of a juggler and what happens to that idea as it is translated into cut, bent, hammered, and welded metal; the process has to show. Viewer expectations are crucial, too. The artist plays with the interactions between *your* idea of a juggler and *his* idea of art. So we have a game or a contest—whatever you like.

Calder's mobile and Hare's sculpture do not perform any of the world's work. But they do something for us as viewers: they yield pleasure based on our ability and willingness to follow the artist as he makes comparisons or metaphors that relate images, ideas, objects, sensations, and memories. Since these works have no practical value, we have to approach them with a fresh mental set, a different logic from the one we use in the everyday world. We are not trying to prove we know a juggler when we see one; we want to see if there is any fun or knowledge or insight in the *difference between* a juggler and a welded steel construction.

A very personal and enjoyable development of Cubism was created by the American painter Stuart Davis (1894–1964). In *Report from Rockport* he used flat, geometric, somewhat spastic shapes to describe the things he liked: street signs, billboards, gas pumps, city noise, and the architecture of Main Street. The problems that worry traffic engineers gave pleasure to Davis; he liked the confusion of signs and lights that bedevil motorists; he rejoiced in the gasoline gulches that seem to spring up along every new highway. Davis was an early and devoted follower of the jazz played in the saloons of Hoboken and Newark, and this liking is echoed in the dynamism and staccato rhythms of his painting. Building on the pictorial devices of Picasso and Braque, he developed a style which conveys the impact of our distinctively American chaos. Stuart was not a social critic: his paintings accept visual disorganization and commercial hype. But he adds to our fund of aesthetic values by teaching us to see highways and shopping districts as gloriously funny—confused, cacaphonous, and peculiarly healthy.

The range of personal statements in today's art is enormous. We have seen expressions of profound loneliness and isolation; voices crossing the boundaries of sanity; images that compare people to machines or animals or both. We have looked at strange visual puns and outrageous visual metaphors. Some works celebrate the energy and excitement of places we normally regard as ecological disasters. Beauty, defined as ideal form, is rarely encountered in our aesthetic expression. As for the human figure, it is often ugly or mutilated. In the work of Bacon, Dubuffet, and De Kooning, people tend to be angry, awkward, or hateful.

Why? The reasons are complex and beyond the scope of this chapter. It might be fair to say that, using their own peculiar methods, artists are trying to tell us something about our civilization. It is certainly true that artistic expression has never been so varied and individualized. Perhaps that is a cause for rejoicing: there has never been a wider array of aesthetic choices.

# CHAPTER TWO

# THE SOCIAL FUNCTIONS OF ART

In a sense, all works of art perform a social function since they are created for an audience. Artists may claim to work only for themselves, but this really means that they set their own standards. The artist always hopes, perhaps secretly, that there is a discriminating public which will admire his or her work. Artworks may be created because of some personal need, but they still call for a social response.

There are, however, narrower and more specific meanings for the social function of art. These meanings relate to the *character of social response* that an artwork evokes: How do groups of people act because of their art experience? Here we hope to show that art performs a social function when (a) it influences the collective behavior of human beings; (b) it is made to be seen or used in public situations; (c) it describes collective aspects of life as opposed to personal kinds of experience. In all these cases, viewers respond with the awareness that they are members of a group.

Many works are deliberately designed to influence group thinking. Artists may try to make us laugh at the same things; to accept certain religious, economic, or political ideas; to identify with a particular class or ethnic interest; or to see our social situation in new ways. The visual arts can function as languages of praise and celebration, anger and protest, satire and ridicule. In other words, art can influence collective attitudes and emotions and, ultimately, the way we act. Advertising art is a common illustration: its purpose is to influence purchasing behavior. Wartime art is another example: governments use it to stimulate patriotism, to encourage self-sacrifice, to spur enlistments, to increase production levels, to arouse hatred of the enemy. Whether the social goal is production or consumption, war or peace—art plays a role.

Some people think that art designed to influence social behavior is corrupt, impure, "mere" propaganda. And, given certain assumptions about the "appropriate" functions of art, they may be right. But we could not present a complete picture of art if we ignored its role as propaganda; the history of art offers many examples. It also shows that the excellence of an artwork is often unrelated to its official purpose. In other words, some propagandistic art may not change our opinions or behavior. But it can still be very good.

**Samuel Laroye. Bicycle mask of the Gelede Secret Society, Yoruba tribe. 1958.**

Art and social change. For the Yoruba sculptor there is nothing wrong in combining a modern man-on-a-bicycle with a traditional head mask. The mask is used in ritual, and ritual unites the past with the present. Art is the visible expression of that idea: it absorbs and assimilates everything into the *now*.

Eugène Delacroix. *Liberty Leading the People.*
1830. Oil on canvas, 8'6⅜" × 10'1". The Louvre,
Paris

Much blood, gore, and commotion: all classes
are involved in a highly "participatory" uprising,
with an allegorical figure, *la belle France,* to
inspire and guide them.

Auguste Rodin. *The Burghers of Calais.* 1886.
Bronze, 82½ × 95 × 78". The Hirshhorn Museum
and Sculpture Garden, Smithsonian Institution,
Washington, D.C. Gift of Joseph H. Hirshhorn,
1966

The public monument is a social art form. It
enables an abstraction—society—to become
humanly real; it builds our collective memory
and, we hope, our civic conscience.

ATOMKRIEG NEIN
MOUVEMENT SUISSE DE LA PAIX · SCHWEIZERISCHE BEWEGUNG FÜR DEN FRIEDEN · MOVIMENTO SVIZZERO PER LA PACE

*left:* Hans Erni. *Atomkrieg Nein (Atom War No)*. 1954. Offset lithograph, 50 × 35¼". Collection, The Museum of Modern Art, New York. Gift of the designer

*right:* David Low. *Very Well, Alone.* c. 1940. Cartoon by permission of the David Low Trustees and the *London Evening Standard*

## POLITICAL AND IDEOLOGICAL EXPRESSION

Some artists are interested in the freedom to solve special problems of style or technique. Others use style and technique to express their social and political views. They may speak of artistic responsibility: art does not exist merely to entertain; it must guide and instruct; it must improve our collective existence. As long as there are wrongs to be righted, art should enlist on the side of right: it should help shape attitudes that can improve human existence. This view is opposed by those artists who feel they serve society best when they concentrate on the honest expression of their personal experience, the creation of new form, the refinement of the styles they have inherited.

Cézanne, for example, could generate aesthetic emotions merely by painting apples or vegetables; other artists require themes with obvious social relevance. Eugène Delacroix (1798–1863) seemed to need great human spectacles to make an artistic statement; thus his *Liberty Leading the People* is one of the great monuments of revolutionary art. However, artistic liberty means different things to different artists: for some it means freedom to express private feelings without fear or censorship; for others it means the right to deal with controversial ideas any way they want to.

**Revolutionary Art: Latin America**   In this century, Mexico has produced three major artists whose work has been frankly revolutionary: José Clemente Orozco (1883–1949), Diego Rivera (1886–1957), and David Alfaro Siqueiros (1896–1974). Their paintings, often in mural form, deal with themes like the conquest of the Aztecs by Spanish invaders, the exploitation of peasants by oppressive landowners, and the poverty of the Mexican masses. These works range from obvious political propaganda to an intense concern with personal anguish. *Echo of a Scream* by Siqueiros (compare this socially oriented work with Munch's psychologically oriented *The Scream*, page 177) uses a fantastic, almost hallucinatory, pictorial device to convey the idea of poverty. The wasteland setting, the word "echo" in the title, and the repetition of the screaming child's image extend the theme of the work to the entire body of humanity; the suffering of all abandoned children is symbolized. Siqueiros employs an emotional *and a political* strategy; he forces us to confront a painful social reality and to ask "Why?"

A particularly bitter comment on society is made in Orozco's *Gods of the Modern World*, part of the fresco mural in the Baker Library at Dartmouth

Maoist poster. Library, University of Georgia, Athens

The cult of personality built around Mao Zedong did not hide powerful impulses toward Westernization, as in this patriotic poster, which borrowed heavily from the war cartoons of a Briton, David Low.

David Alfaro Siqueiros. *Echo of a Scream.* 1937. Duco on wood with applied sections, 48 × 36". Collection, The Museum of Modern Art, New York. Gift of Edward M. M. Warburg

*below:* José Clemente Orozco. *The Epic of American Civilization.* Panel 17, *Gods of the Modern World.* 1932–34. Fresco, 9'11" × 10'. Courtesy of the Trustees of Dartmouth College, Hanover, New Hampshire

With his denunciation of universities in 1932, Orozco anticipated many of today's attacks on the "relevance" of academic study.

College. We see a dissected corpse stretched on a pile of books, where it is attended by a deathly figure in academic costume. Presumably, the corpse has given birth to an infant skeleton, also in academic cap, with the death figure acting as midwife. In the background stands a collection of professors wearing their medieval regalia. The humor is especially gruesome since the mural is in the library of a distinguished American university; the academic function of preserving and transmitting knowledge is presented as a necrophilic ritual. What we see is a type of revolutionary disgust with established social institutions, a typical trait of the satirist who usually detests what he ridicules.

Diego Rivera's art has the same revolutionary commitment as Orozco's, but its formal organization is less violent; he may also be the best "designer" of the Mexican threesome. But clever designer or not, he drives his political message home with unsubtle force. *The Billionaires* and *Night of the Poor* is really a morality play: the greed of the rich, engrossed in the pursuit of profit, is contrasted with the innocent sleep of the poor, some of them studying at night to escape the blight of illiteracy. While this goes on, middle-class types in the background show their disapproval.

All of these artworks illustrate the stereotyped portrayal of social classes and racial groups according to Marxist dogma. Political ideas are presented in highly simplified form because they are intended for the uneducated. The principal objective is to persuade the masses that they belong to an exploited class. Just as early Christian art explains basic concepts of sin and expiation in simple terms, so also does revolutionary art try to explain oppressors and victims, wealth and poverty. Not surprisingly, Latin American artists, growing out of a tradition in which the religious influence on culture is very potent, employ art like the medieval Church. Ironically, the art of Rivera and his associates is violently hostile to organized religion.

Luis Cruz Azaceta. *Apocalypse: Now or Later.* 1981. Acrylic on canvas, 6 × 10'. Courtesy Allan Frumkin Gallery, New York

An ironic statement about war and the end of the world, using the biblical symbol of a horseman galloping over dead and maimed figures. In Dürer's woodcut *The Four Horsemen of the Apocalypse,* War was represented by a skeletal old man carrying a pitchfork; Azaceta's rider is a ridiculous-looking soldier blowing a silly bugle.

Diego Rivera. *The Billionaires* and *Night of the Poor.* 1923–28. Fresco. Ministry of Education, Mexico City

Mural art as an instrument for developing class consciousness.

*below:* George Tooker. *Government Bureau.* 1956. Tempera on gesso panel, 19⅝ × 29⅝". The Metropolitan Museum of Art, New York. George A. Hearn Fund, 1956

In these mechanically repeated spaces, the same sinister eyes watch the same people. According to Tooker's surreal image, we have become interchangeable units because that is what bureaucrats want us to be.

**Artistic Expressions of Humanitarian Concern**  A modern industrial state faces much different social problems from those of a feudal, agrarian society. The regulation of a complex economy, the conduct of international relations, the fair administration of justice: these functions must seem unreal to people living in a state of peonage. We have different problems—for example, the remoteness and impersonality of government, a theme expressed by George Tooker (born 1920) in *Government Bureau.* Using repetition of figure and space, like receding images in parallel mirrors, Tooker creates a quality of surreal terror in a government building: the place has the atmosphere of an orderly, methodical, thoroughly dismal nightmare. This may be the image of bureaucratic government that stands behind our fears of political overcentralization. Tooker dramatizes the vulnerability and alienation felt by ordinary citizens encountering their government in a cheerless, administrative labyrinth.

In *Employment Agency,* Isaac Soyer (1907–1981) depicts the operation of our economy in pathetically human terms. When economists speak of different kinds of unemployment—structural unemployment, transitional unemployment, the obsolescence of workers' skills, and so on—we understand only vaguely what they mean. How are real people affected? How do they cope with an economy that seems to work against them? Soyer depicts the waiting room of an employment agency as a kind of theater where several dramas are played out at once. Unemployment translates itself into the feeling of being unwanted by the world; it is one of the most painful experiences of our time. As an artist, Soyer cannot offer economic solutions, but he can make us feel what it is like, whether we have a job or not.

Can sculpture deal with industrial phenomena in social terms? Yes. In *Mine Disaster,* Berta Margoulies (born 1907) creates a kind of memorial to the wives of men who are periodically trapped and killed by mine accidents. Margoulies stresses the psychological dimensions of the event—women clinging to hope in spite of what they know. She portrays what has been the experience of mining people for generations. As in other works of social protest, the device of huddling the figures is employed, plus the portrayal of mixed emotions in faces expressing suspense, hope, and despair.

A work of human misery and hope—also a great historical document—is the famous photograph by Alfred Steiglitz (1864–1946), *The Steerage.* This

*Denver Church Opens Doors to Homeless: Eddy Wade at the Holy Ghost Roman Catholic Church.* 1982. Photograph

The social impact of "straight" photography cannot be overestimated. This jarring juxtaposition carries home a message that makes speeches, sermons, and editorials pale by comparison.

Alfred Stieglitz. *The Steerage.* 1907. Photograph. Philadelphia Museum of Art. Gift of Carl Zigrosser

picture was taken in 1907 at the height of a great migration of people from all parts of Europe to America. The steerage was the lowest, most squalid part of a ship—the cheapest way to cross the Atlantic for the desperately poor who came to the United States seeking a new life. Steiglitz has given the scene a timeless quality: his photograph reminds us of a medieval religious work in which condemned people, confined in some hellish place, emerge from the depths to greet the light.

Perhaps the greatest monument of social protest in our time is Picasso's *Guernica*. This mural-size painting was executed in 1937 to memorialize the bombing of the Basque town of Guernica by Nazi aircraft (flying for Generalissimo Franco) during the Spanish Civil War. Here Picasso invented the imagery which has influenced generations of artists in their treatment of war, chaos, and suffering. Using only black, white, and gray, Picasso endeavored to convey multiple perceptions of a single catastrophic event: the screaming of the victims, the laceration of human flesh, newspaper accounts of the bombing, and the meaning of a type of war in which civilians are the first victims. Images such as the fallen statue, the burning building, the shrieking horse, the spectator bull, and the mother and dead child describe the bombing in terms of modern *schrecklichkeit*—a new, skyborne method of terror.

While Picasso's painting relates to our time, it exists within the same frame of reference as Goya's Disasters of War series, created early in the nineteenth century. But is it equal to the challenge implied by the millions of casualties that might be sustained in a war of nuclear destruction? Probably not. Picasso could still think of war as a catastrophe which has *individual* consequences. Today, the scale of war has been enlarged to the extent that some artists feel compelled to use a more abstract, dehumanized form-language to cope with it. For an image of the really big bang, we might look at Adolph Gottlieb's *Blast II* (page 214).

## SOCIAL DESCRIPTION

Sometimes art performs a social function by describing life without implying there is a problem to be solved. By concentrating on everyday "slices of life" the artist can focus attention on the quality of our collective existence—especially as it is affected by our environment. When an artistic "frame" is con-

Pablo Picasso. *Guernica*. 1937. Oil on canvas, 11'5½" × 25'5¾". The Prado, Madrid

Francisco Goya. *"Nothing more to do."* From the series The Disasters of War. Issued 1810–63. Etching, 9⅞ × 13⅝". The Hispanic Society of America, New York

Despite the mechanization and depersonalization of war, the cruelty of individual executions has not greatly changed—from Goya's nineteenth-century etching to Segal's twentieth-century *tableau vivant*.

George Segal. *The Execution.* 1967. Mixed media (plaster, rope, wood, and metal), 8 × 11 × 8'. The Vancouver Art Gallery, British Columbia

Marisol. *The Family.* 1962. Painted wood and other materials in three sections, 6'10⅝" × 5'5½". Collection, The Museum of Modern Art, New York. Advisory Committee Fund

This imagery could have come from a snapshot taken on the front porch around 1910. Everyone squints; the kids look as if they are clones; the mother looks stout and stolid; the father is absent—or maybe she is a widow. In any case, she raises them alone. The line between social description and satire is very thin.

Ed Paschke. *Caliente.* 1985. Oil on canvas, 6'8" × 8'4". The Art Institute of Chicago. Gift of the staff of The Art Institute of Chicago

An image of human alienation. Here a man's face has been transformed by the media he watches incessantly. His features seem to be outlined in neon; his teeth glow in the dark; and his eyes look like TV tubes—bright, vibrant, and empty.

Jacob Lawrence. *Pool Parlor.* 1942. Gouache on paper, 31 × 22¾". The Metropolitan Museum of Art, New York. Arthur Hoppock Hearn Fund, 1942

*below:* George Tooker. *The Subway.* 1950. Egg tempera on composition board, 18⅛ × 36⅛". Collection of Whitney Museum of American Art, New York. Purchase, with funds from the Juliana Force Purchase Award

The subway (without graffiti) felt by urban woman and man as a descent into hell.

structed around people and places it seems easier to discern their meaning or flavor.

What about the environment of a pool hall? (Remember what Professor Harold Hill said in *The Music Man:* "You got trouble.") The *Pool Parlor* by Jacob Lawrence (born 1917) constitutes a "heavy" drama that builds on our stereotypes about inner-city life. The artist creates mock-sinister silhouettes of black men engaged in a deadly game of skill; these are "pool sharks" playing for keeps. Lawrence uses flat patterning and very angular shapes to make us believe this is a real war—a war fought under glaring lights on green felt tabletops. Actually, the picture is a parody of pool parlor folklore and the "cool" style of the black ghetto: no one will get hurt, but the scene is designed to look ominous.

The cultural patterns of ethnic groups—particularly of first- and second-generation Americans—have been the subject of many studies by sociologists. One of their findings is that the first American-born generation is anxious to forget its ethnicity. The next generation, feeling more secure, is often proud of its heritage and wants to revive the customs of its immigrant forebears. Louis Bosa (1905–1981) often deals with old-country Italian customs, perhaps because he knows how hard it is to transplant them somehow into new soil. *My Family Reunion* depicts a kind of "tribal" feast, set in Italy but seen through American eyes. Bosa emphasizes the strange seriousness of his people, especially if we view them through Anglo-Saxon lenses. These people look awkward, suspicious, and slightly conspiratorial. Their festival is clearly more than an eating occasion: individuals are being observed, information is being collected, major decisions are being made.

Images of the landscape and cityscape have social connotations whether they include people or not. There are always signs of human use—of care or neglect, of pride or abandonment. The environments people build influence their builders; at the same time they reflect human ingenuity, human choices, and human limitations of imagination. In *Landscape near Chicago*, Aaron Bohrod (born 1907) makes an ironic comment on that halfway region we can see on the outskirts of any American city, with its cinder-block architecture, piles of rusting machinery, and signs of projects begun but never finished. Bohrod's realism is ideal for painting the portrait of a house and, by implication, its inhabitants—people who occupy the undefined spaces on the outskirts of town. Much as they try, these people cannot mold their environment into a convincing imitation of a human community.

Louis Bosa. *My Family Reunion.* 1950. Oil on canvas. Whitney Museum of American Art, New York. Gift of Mr. and Mrs. Alfred Jaretski, Jr.

Louis Guglielmi. *Terror in Brooklyn.* 1941. Oil on canvas, 34 × 30 ". Whitney Museum of American Art, New York

A Surrealist version of the sense of loneliness and menace that the city's streets can evoke. Compare the terror of these Italian women with the mysteriousness of Louis Bosa's family scene in "the old country."

Jesse Tarbox Beals. Photograph of Italian children. 1900

For another building portrait we can look at Edward Hopper's (1882–1967) *House by the Railroad*, although here it is the faded glory of a Victorian mansion. Of course Bohrod's house never knew glory. But Hopper's mansion is only a relic now; perhaps it has become a rooming house. Once it stood for "class"; it represented elegance and, of course, money. The railroad changed all that. Still the house has a wilted dignity conferred by the artist's presentation of its forms as a unified, coherent, sculptural mass, isolated but wearing its dated architectural adornments with forlorn pride.

In 1936 Mark Tobey (1890–1976) tried to capture the noise and illumination of a great American thoroughfare, *Broadway*. He was fascinated by the light from a thousand signs, its capacity to express the search for fun by millions drawn like moths to an electric fire in mid-Manhattan. Later, in 1942, the Dutch abstractionist Piet Mondrian (1872–1944) surrendered to Broadway's glitter with a sparkling canvas, *Broadway Boogie Woogie*. As we can see, Tobey's painting is "written" in light, a sort of neon script that blurs into a white haze in the center of the picture. Mondrian saw the Great White Way as a musical composition, but the restrictions of the rectangle did not permit Tobey's freedom of description. Still, by employing dozens of little squares and abrupt changes of primary color, Mondrian creates a flickering, dancelike quality of light, the scurry and halt of Broadway's "mell-o-dee."

The Los Angeles Fine Arts Squad. *Isle of California.* 1971–72. Butler Avenue, West Los Angeles

An immense mural that records the effects of a real earthquake while prophesying the end of California's freeway civilization. No people, no cars, no cityscape: the sight is strangely peaceful.

Two houses facing two kinds of adversity. One house has fallen on hard times; the other never knew any good times.

Edward Hopper. *House by the Railroad.* 1925. Oil on canvas, 24 × 29". Collection, The Museum of Modern Art, New York. Given anonymously

Aaron Bohrod. *Landscape near Chicago.* 1934. Oil on composition board, 24 × 32". Collection of Whitney Museum of American Art, New York. Purchase

The neon spectacle of Broadway can be expressed as white writing, or as little squares of alternating color, or by shaping neon tubes into an abstract simulation of the whole glittering scene.

*right:* Piet Mondrian. *Broadway Boogie Woogie.* 1942–43. Oil on canvas, 50 × 50". Collection, The Museum of Modern Art, New York. Given anonymously

*below left:* Mark Tobey. *Broadway.* 1936. Tempera on Masonite board, 26 × 19¼". The Metropolitan Museum of Art, New York. Arthur Hoppock Hearn Fund, 1942

*below right:* Chryssa. *Fragments for the Gates to Times Square.* 1966. Neon and plexiglass, 81 × 34½ × 27½". Collection of Whitney Museum of American Art, New York. Purchase, with funds from Howard and Jean Lipman

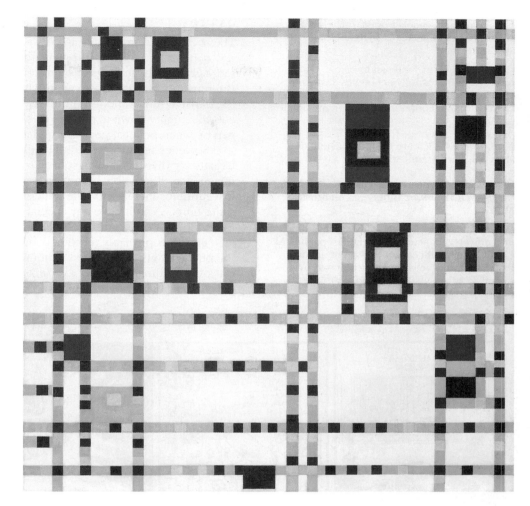

*below:* Al Capp. Panels from *Li'l Abner* Ugly Woman Contest. 1946. Copyright News Syndicate, Inc.

Capp's professional interest in comic repulsiveness was fully echoed by his readers, who generously contributed drawings of their candidates in a contest for the supreme ugliness accolade.

*bottom left:* Caricature from the ceiling of Horyu-ji, Nara, Japan. 8th century A.D.

*bottom right:* Leonardo da Vinci. *Caricature of an Ugly Old Woman.* Biblioteca Ambrosiana, Milan

When satire dwells on the ugly, it has a timeless and universal character; very little separates Al Capp's twentieth-century version of ugliness from the repulsive countenance drawn by a Japanese artist twelve hundred years ago.

# SATIRE

The social function of satire is to ridicule people and institutions *so that they will change.* Or, at least, stop what they are doing. Also, as a type of humor, satire gives us the feelings of superiority or relief we usually get from laughter. But remember: satire has an aggressive intent; it makes fun of its object—bitter, derisive fun. Although humor is involved, satire is a *serious* art form: it cuts the mighty down to size; it loves to show up hypocrisy; it dramatizes the gap between political promises and actual performance.

Societies tend to go through solemn phases when satire is considered negative or divisive or even subversive. A government may have a humorless image of itself, possibly because of self-love among high officials, or personal insecurity, or inability to take criticism. We can be sure of one thing: visual satire hurts. Does it have any special features that make it more painful than other kinds of criticism?

First, it is probably more uncomfortable to be ridiculed than scolded. If the public laughs at us, it is very humiliating; we can feel ostracized—thrown out of the human community. Second, laughter is both physiological and psychological; it involves the total organism and it fully implicates the viewer

LI'L ABNER    The Champ    By Al Capp

in an act of ridicule. We often remember the satirical image of a public figure long after we have forgotten what he or she did. Finally, artistic satire usually employs caricature, which exaggerates the physical shortcomings of its victims. Needless to say, we already know about our imperfections; to see them magnified is very painful, especially if our psychic defenses are not very strong.

Satire has roots in our fascination with the grotesque; making grotesque images of real or imagined people is a universal practice. Children are especially intrigued by fantastic or incredibly ugly faces. So are great artists: Leonardo da Vinci (1452–1519) made many caricatures; they were his investigations of deviations from the beautiful. From a psychological standpoint, such images are similar to those made by children; they seem to be explorations of the frontiers of the human. Caricatures are comparable to the rich body of spoken and written insult most of us know about. Adolescents are especially good at it, and comedians convulse audiences for hours with detailed descriptions of their ugly relatives. So the fascination with ugliness is widespread; it may be as pervasive as our interest in the beautiful. This obsession with ugliness seems vicious but its roots are only partially related to malice: we may just want to exercise our powers of aesthetic discrimination.

Perhaps the best political satirist of World War II was David Low (1891–1963). His cartoons were in many respects visual counterparts to the speeches of Winston Churchill: he could ridicule the Fascist dictators, summon the courage of Britons when they were taking a terrible beating, express defiance when England faced invasion, appeal for help from America, and grieve over the valorous dead. Low was especially good at personality formulations, notably in his characterizations of Der Führer and Il Duce. At a time when their racial and military insanity had succeeded in terrifying the civilized world, David Low made Hitler and Mussolini look like asses—dangerous, to be sure, but asses nevertheless. These cartoons encouraged a hard-pressed people to carry on. The fearsome dictators were changed into clowns, which meant they could be beaten.

Low's political satire shows well in his cartoon *Rendezvous*, which deals with one of the strange consequences of political expediency—the Russo-German nonaggression pact of 1939. By this treaty the Russians took possession of the Baltic nations, and Germany secured the neutrality of Russia during its planned attack on Poland. So, the mortal enemies, soon to be locked in a death struggle, greet each other with exaggerated gestures of courtesy while employing their customary rhetoric of insult. They meet over the body of a dead soldier; this is how Low dealt with evil: with a few brushstrokes he revealed the tragic underside of political hypocrisy.

*left:* David Low. *Rendezvous.* 1939.
"The scum of the earth, I believe?"
"The bloody assassin of the workers, I presume?"
Cartoon by permission of the David Low Trustees and the *London Evening Standard*

*above:* Jack Levine. *The Feast of Pure Reason.* 1937. Oil on canvas, 42 × 48". Extended loan from the United States WPA Art Program to The Museum of Modern Art, New York

Willem de Kooning. *Woman, I.* 1950–52. Oil on
canvas, 6'3⅞" × 4'10". Collection, The Museum
of Modern Art, New York. Purchase

Peggy Bacon. *The Patroness.* 1927. Etching,
printed in black; plate, 10 × 7¹⁵⁄₁₆". Collection,
The Museum of Modern Art, New York. Gift of
Abby Aldrich Rockefeller

H. C. Westermann. *Nouveau Rat Trap*. 1965.
Collection Mr. and Mrs. Robert Delford Brown,
New York

Art satirizing art: a semiabstract sculpture that
pokes fun at the Art Nouveau style.

We expect satire in the graphic arts, especially in news media, but it also
occurs in "serious" painting. Most of Jack Levine's (born 1915) work is satiric,
with stress on the ugly more than the humorous; *The Feast of Pure Reason* is
a typical example. There is bitter irony in the contrast between the title, which
celebrates rationality, and the realities of civic decision-making: a cop, a
politician, and a businessman meet in a dark room to "cut a deal." It is
interesting that, no matter who his target is, Levine identifies moral corruption
with physical grossness: there is nothing funny or redeeming about these
people; they are ugly, hence corrupt, hence detestable.

*Woman, I* by Willem de Kooning (born 1904) can also be seen as
satirical, although the violent execution may prevent our finding much humor
in the work. The artist depicts an older woman seated, heavyset, wearing a
flimsy shoe, holding nothing back visually or emotionally. While she may not
seem real to us, she obviously made an impression on De Kooning, who was
sufficiently provoked to portray her as a horrible spectacle. Once the forms
are established, the artist tears into them with a violent, slashing attack. What
wrath! What fury! What can she have done to him?

Another kind of satiric anger can be seen in an etching, *The Patroness*,
by Peggy Bacon (1895–1987). Here, too, the subject is a stout woman with a
low-cut dress. But her ugliness is different from that of De Kooning's woman.
Her face is twisted and pinched in contrast to her heavy hands and spreading
bulk—symbols of small-mindedness combined with too much money. Perhaps this etching expresses the artist's resentment of any patron, regardless
of his or her looks. Or perhaps it is a case of revenge—a malicious bite of the
hand that feeds the artist. The dog, lower right, probably understands the
relationship.

Satire thrives when there is freedom from political repression, and that
freedom we have usually had. But as art moves toward abstraction, we see
more satire in the titles of artworks and less in their imagery. (H. C.
Westermann's *Nouveau Rat Trap* is a rare and clever exception.) To be sure,
Pop art had considerable satiric potential, but it lacked the killer instinct for
political satire. Its target was very broad: all of modern "hard-sell" culture.
However, it was often difficult to tell whether Pop derided or celebrated the
commercialism of our environment. Still, it made us aware of optical noise,
and it developed some weapons to cope with visual garbage. For that we
have to be grateful.

# GRAPHIC COMMUNICATION

Although we tend to think of art in terms of precious objects, it is also an inexpensive public language. Cheaply reproduced visual images communicate with amazing persuasiveness, and, combined with words, their meaning is clear and unmistakable. In a culture where mass production and distribution have reached glorious heights, visual art is extensively used to sell goods, services, and ideas. Graphic design—especially of posters, packages, books, signs, and containers—is an indispensable tool of communication. Sometimes it is called advertising design, or commercial art. But labels here are not crucial; what matters is that art plays a central role in carrying information from government, business, and industry to every social group or subgroup one can imagine.

**The Problems of Communication**  What are the problems of information design that artists must solve? First is the job of arresting the public's attention: Can people be "stopped in their tracks" by artfully designed images? They certainly can. Getting attention is the main problem of all effective communication. The challenge varies from the five-second look at an outdoor poster to the eight- or ten-minute examination of a magazine page. Next is the problem of psychological strategy: What demographic group is targeted and what are its interests and motivations? Third is the problem of characterizing a product, service, or idea: How can these be presented quickly and memorably to a public which is under continuous visual assault from competing messages? Fourth is the problem of combining visual and nonvisual material: What should be seen? What should be read? What should be said? Fifth is the design of letter forms—a major graphics problem. Indeed, letter form may be more important than word choice; today's viewers are exceedingly sensitive to the look, *the image*, of a word or phrase. Finally, how should graphics specialists deal with the problems of film and television? How can visual imagery be related to unseen words or music—material that occupies aural but not optical space? What constitutes the "background"—the words, the music, or the images?

Visual logic and simplicity are important traits of modern information design. Simplicity implies a bias in favor of open space and clean, bold forms—forms that can be quickly seen, easily identified, and readily understood. By visual logic we mean *a sense of connectedness* among the elements of a design: the image of the product, the words or copy, and the layout or composition. All of these should reinforce the main message. Not surprisingly, graphic designers often draw on contemporary art to solve their problems. Following are some illustrations which show how the allegedly useless fine arts have, in fact, been used ("ripped off") by communications design.

**Graphic Solutions**  Picasso was himself a great borrower, and many have borrowed from him. Thus we can see the unmistakable influence of his harlequins and musicians in a carnival poster by the Mexican designer Segundo Freire. However, the poster artist retains only the flat patterning of Picasso's Cubism. He does not slice the figure and recompose its elements; that would have produced a somewhat confusing image. As mentioned above, simplified imagery is essential for quick recognition; hence abstract art has been a fertile source of ideas for graphic designers. Notice how the Italian designer Pino Tovaglia created his railroad poster, using, I believe, the style of Fernand Léger (1881–1955). Léger's *Three Women* may not display machinery, but it does show how organic forms can be converted into mechanical shapes. So we might think of this railroad poster as the result of an artistic triple play—from Picasso to Léger to Tovaglia.

An Alvin Lustig (1915–1955) cover design for *Fortune* magazine reveals the influence of another facet of Cubism—collage. Around 1912, Picasso and

Mel Ramos. *Chiquita Banana.* 1964. Oil on canvas, 6 × 5'. Collection Ian W. Beck, New York

Usually, advertising art borrows from fine art. Here, the relationship is reversed: Pop art borrowed everything it could from commercial art, even including the ®—Trademark Registered—over "Chiquita." Today's art belongs to the culture of reproduction, regardless of where it originates.

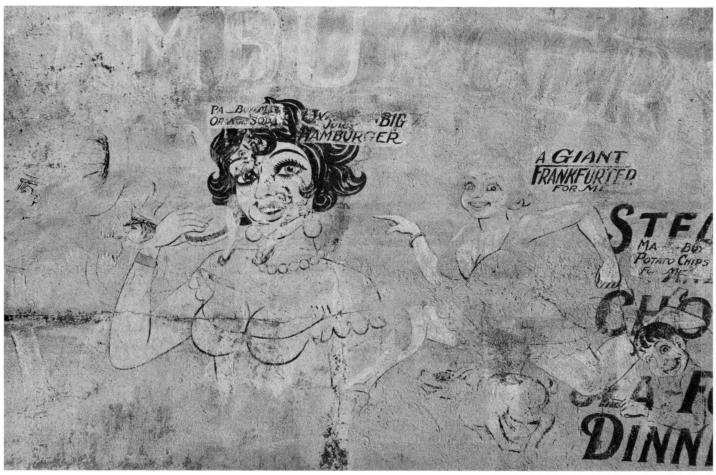

George Aptecker. Photograph of a wall at Coney Island. 1968

Communications design practiced as a folk art.

Advertisement for film *The Two of Us*. Designed by Saul Bass and Art Goodman. 1968

A word-image combination in which a maximum of characterization is achieved within very narrow formal constraints.

Bruno Munari. *Campari*. 1965. Offset lithograph, 6'5¼" × 9'1¼". Collection, The Museum of Modern Art, New York. Gift of the designer

We still do not know the full potential of computer-generated imagery for art. In this computer painting the artist builds on the bright color and low resolution of images that we see on the computer screen. Compare Nessim's effects with Lichtenstein's use of Benday screening (page 305).

Fernand Léger. *Three Women.* 1921. Oil on canvas, 6'1¼" × 8'3". Collection, The Museum of Modern Art, New York. Mrs. Simon Guggenheim Fund

Pino Tovaglia. Railway poster. 1957. Courtesy the artist and Ferrovie Nord Milano

*above:* Pablo Picasso. *La Suze.* 1912–13. Paper collage with charcoal, 25¾ × 19¾". Washington University Gallery of Art, St. Louis. University purchase, Kende Sale Fund, 1946

*right:* Alvin Lustig. Cover design for *Fortune* magazine. 1952. Courtesy Time, Inc.

Braque began to combine pasted material with drawn or painted forms, as in Picasso's *La Suze*, a picture made of construction paper, newsprint, wallpaper, and a liquor bottle label. In Lustig's design the words and type faces of the collage material reinforce a communications theme entitled "the language of advertising." Notice that the shapes are taken from billboards and television masts. Thus the designer reinforces his message two or three times and with different formal devices. The Picasso collage has no explicit message: it communicates an *aesthetic effect.* The newsprint is there to be experienced as color and texture; it is not meant to be read, except for the liquor label. Perhaps that is the essential difference between poetry and advertising.

An especially interesting example of cultural diffusion can be seen in a Japanese cosmetics poster by Tsuneji Fujiwara. His two faces are remarkably similar to those of Amedeo Modigliani, an Italian-born artist who spent most of his working life in France. Modigliani began as a sculptor and was especially influenced by African wood carving, as in the example illustrated. We can see how Modigliani translated its basically African forms into the small mouth, ovoid face, and stylized arches over the eyes of the woman in his painting. And that is what Fujiwara must have seen as an ideal of female elegance. Connecting that ideal with soap or cologne or face powder represents a triumph of the design imagination.

We can easily trace the forms in the Saul Bass (born 1921) poster to Joan Miró (1893–1983). What interests us is the adaptation of Surrealist imagery to advertise house paint. And the design strategy makes marketing sense: a manufacturer wants to persuade women that they can do house painting—do it and enjoy it. Now Miró's work is a kind of "research" into childlike imagery: it emphasizes fun and games and an occasional ghost or goblin. That imagery says in effect that we can face our fears and laugh at them. The woman with the paintbrush in the Bass poster is having a good time: house painting is a romp, easy enough for a child to do. The poster also tells us something about the advertiser's perception of women and their purchasing behavior. The image is exceptionally simple, but it makes sophisticated use of unconscious suggestion to attain its objective.

With these examples the dependence of information design on "fine art" should be clear. Yet, there is considerable originality and quality in graphics,

*above left:* Mask, from Ivory Coast. Collection Peter Moeschlin, Basel

*above:* Amedeo Modigliani. Detail of *Anna Zborowska.* 1917. Collection, The Museum of Modern Art, New York. Lillie P. Bliss Collection

*left:* Tsuneji Fujiwara. Cosmetics poster. 1957

Here is the best possible demonstration of the internationalism of today's art and the interchangeability of its forms.

TEXTOS: IGNÁCIO DE LOYOLA BRANDÃO, GIOVANNI DE BOURBON - SICILES, HÉLIO PELLEGRINO, PEDRO BLOCH, VIVI NABUCO, NORMA COURI E RUDI CRESPI. CRIAÇÃO: ZARAGOZA.

*above:* José Zaragoza. Cover for Brazilian edition of *Vogue* magazine, on the subject of plastic surgery. 1984

An elegant use of the Cubist devices of overlapping, displacement, and repetition of shapes in graphic communication. The subject—plastic surgery—might suggest blood and pain, but here it appears as the epitome of high fashion.

B. Martin Pedersen. Dustjacket for *Typography 5,* the Annual of the Type Directors Club of the United States. 1985

This graphic image operates simultaneously at several levels: as a discreet announcement of *Typography* plus the number *5*; as a demonstration of the Gestalt principle of figure-ground ambiguity; and as a painting in which bold, abstract shapes bend, squeeze, and float in a golden space.

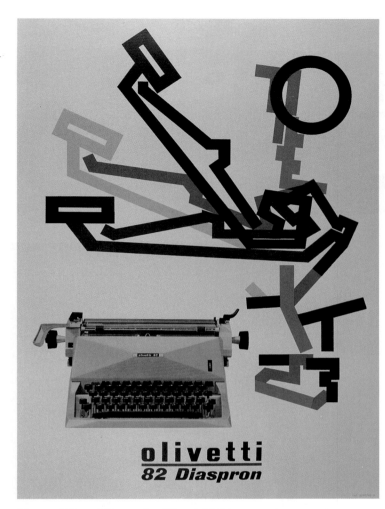

Giovanni Pintori. Poster for Olivetti 82 Diaspron. Courtesy the artist

Purely visual communication. This work represents a brilliant wedding of the qualities of the machine—accuracy of engineering, measured shape, controlled motion—and the traits of its product: the scrutable mark, the precise word, the significant symbol.

Paul Rand. Poster for Advertising Typographers' Association of America. Courtesy the artist

The picture of an idea that was first expressed by the philosopher Alfred North Whitehead. It succeeds through a clever graphic creation: the arrow penetrates the apple, and that makes its red "blood" flow down into the letter A.

Walter Allner. Cover design for *Fortune* magazine, February, 1965. Courtesy Time, Inc.

Here a graphic designer functions almost like a sculptor. Working for an audience of industrial executives, Allner created a dazzling composition of old and new metallic objects. The design has a powerful tactile appeal, yet it operates within a graphic format. Why? Because the miracle of photography makes us believe this imagery is real; we can touch it with our eyes.

Joan Miró. *Nursery Painting*. 1938. Oil on canvas, 2'7⅝" × 10'4". Collection Mr. and Mrs. Richard K. Weil, St. Louis

Saul Bass. Poster for Pabco Paint Company. 1957. Courtesy Napko Corporation, Houston

which proves that the relationships among patrons, artists, clients, and designers are very complex in our culture. Unfortunately, fine artists usually live in the time-honored tradition of economic malnutrition, whereas designers do quite well, thank you. But perhaps we can look forward to a new Renaissance in which there is no line between gallery artists, illustrators, and designers because, with few exceptions, they are the same persons.

Victor Vasarely. *Vega*. 1957. Oil on canvas,
76¾ × 51⅛". Collection the artist

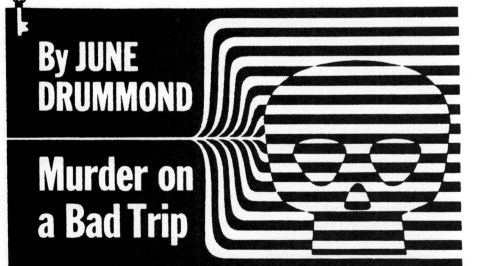

Advertisement for *Murder on a Bad Trip*
by June Drummond. Holt Rinehart and
Winston, Inc., 1968. Courtesy Denhard &
Stewart, Inc., New York

Since many viewers are disoriented by Op
art, it seems logical to exploit Op-art
effects in the jacket design for a murder
mystery dealing with hallucinatory drugs.

71

# CHAPTER THREE

# THE PHYSICAL FUNCTIONS OF ART

Paintings and buildings can be symbols, but only buildings perform a physical function. By "physical function" we mean art objects that work as tools or containers. By "containers" we mean objects that range from a carton of milk to an office building. Both have to be built and shaped according to the requirements of their contents (if people can be thought of as "contents"). As for a "tool," it can be a tablespoon or a locomotive: simple and small, or large and complex. Both have to be designed to operate efficiently, but an important aspect of their operation is appearance: they are seen as well as used. In other words, a tool or machine *looks like* something; it has to look like what it does, and it has to look good.

The difference between a painting and a building is that we use a painting only by looking at it; a building or tool is used by doing something *in* it or *with* it. Once we thought artists created skins or garments to conceal the working parts of useful objects. This notion survives in a debased conception of industrial design called styling: engineers solve functional problems while artists take care of surface beauty. But now we realize that appearance and function are closely linked. Some useful objects are *totally* created by artist-designers. Their profession—industrial design—constitutes a fruitful synthesis of art and engineering—and marketing too.

During the Renaissance, artists could be architects and engineers simultaneously. The separation of art from the functional aspects of making and building took place during the eighteenth-century Industrial Revolution. That was when civil and mechanical engineering developed as professions separate from art and architecture. As a result, society experienced an upsurge of ugliness in the large- and small-scale environment. Of course, engineers can be good designers, but in the early stages of mass production, their technical specialization produced a great deal of machine-made trash.

Between the eighteenth and twentieth centuries the handicrafts survived mainly as obsolescent vestiges of preindustrial modes of making, as status symbols for those who could resist engineer design, or as focal points of idealism for craftsmen like William Morris. Morris hoped to reverse the march of industrialization and capitalism by reviving medieval artisanship under socialist auspices. But while his motives were pure, his solution was unworkable.

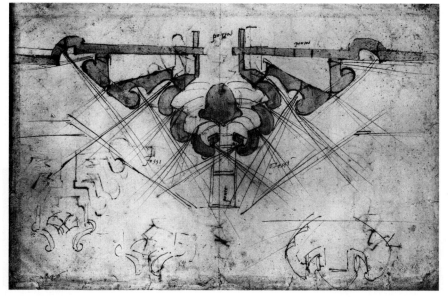

Leonardo da Vinci. *Drawing for an automated spool-winding machine.* c. 1490. In Codex Atlanticus, folio 393 v. Biblioteca Ambrosiana, Milan

Both Leonardo and Michelangelo were "designers"; they could tackle anything—from fortifications to industrial machinery. For the Renaissance artist, drawing was a process of discovery, invention, and visualization—from inside to outside or from surface to depth. The radical separation of art and engineering had not yet taken place.

Michelangelo. *Drawing for the Fortification of Florence.* c. 1529. Pen and wash, 11½ × 16¼". Casa Buonarroti, Florence

Today we have product designers who can create anything—handsome automobiles, glamorous refrigerators, and noble pencil sharpeners. Art shares responsibility for the entire built environment: how it looks and how it works. And here "art" means more than embellishing or beautifying surfaces. A successful environmental design is the end product of a sensitive relationship between art, law, sociology, politics, and engineering. Most important, environmental design has to be done in the light of a total philosophy of human behavior, social interaction, and aesthetic response.

The physical functions of art, therefore, affect us in our private lives and in our public existence—as people who use and are used by an artificial organism called the community. The most familiar unit of that organism is the house, or dwelling.

# ARCHITECTURE: THE DWELLING

Of all building types, the dwelling is the earliest, the closest to our daily lives, and perhaps the best illustration of the combined effects of art, technology, and design. Architecture is a social art, and in the dwelling we see how it influences a prime social institution: the family. Here we might examine some of the interactions between family life and domestic architecture.

Today's home is intended almost exclusively for a couple, or for a small child-rearing family. Usually it has no room for aunts, uncles, grandparents, or other relatives. It rarely has a library, parlor, pantry, or front porch. Instead, there may be new rooms or spaces—a game room, family room, recreation room, sauna, sundeck, and carport. Compared to earlier homes there is more open planning, less privacy, and fewer single-purpose spaces. Partitions are often eliminated or do not go from floor to ceiling; they rarely insulate sounds. In addition, houses are usually built on one level or on split levels; seldom do they have three or four distinct layers. One-level living has its advantages: the ranch-type dwelling promotes mobility while it sacrifices privacy. But privacy may be obsolete.

Multipurpose rooms reduce the overall size of a house and intensify the use of space and the wear of equipment. Labor-saving devices and gadgets absorb more of the home's cost, and for many people they are a principal index of its value—economic and aesthetic. That is, we probably love our dishwashers, air conditioners, microwave ovens, jacuzzis, and stereo sets more than the qualities of light, space, and circulation that good design can bring to the home.

Perhaps Le Corbusier's dictum—"The house is a machine to be lived in"—has been accepted in practice if not in theory. What has made it possible for the modern dwelling to operate like a machine without losing the warmth of the idea of home? Technology: heating and cooling, laundering and house cleaning, decoration and maintenance, food preparation and storage. Modern building materials have greatly increased the designer's options: light, strong structural elements, some of them metal and plastic instead of wood; new insulation materials, adhesives, and fasteners; new surface materials, especially plastics and man-made fibers; and prefabricated units, notably in kitchens and bathrooms. More important than materials is the almost universal availability of low-cost electricity.

Beverly Buchanan. *Shack South: Inside and Out.* 1990. Cedar, pine, tin, and cardboard, 78" high. Courtesy Bernice Steinbaum Gallery, New York

The rural African-American shack. Once it was an actual dwelling; now it has been re-created for a museum. Transformed into sculpture, the shack symbolizes the existence of aesthetic impulses even under the most desperate living conditions.

Bruce Davidson. Photograph of people on East 100th Street, New York. 1967

Architecture is a social art—design for human beings living together. The trouble is that poor people cannot afford to live in spaces designed around their needs. So, like most of us, they make do.

**Kenneth Isaacs. Ultimate Living Structure. 1968**

All of an individual's physical needs for domestic living have been packaged in a single double-decker unit. It looks like a triumph of rationality—a real "machine for living." But without social interaction, design is easy.

Plate glass may be the most influential material affecting home design. Ideal for warm climates, it is widely used in temperate and cold climates because it brings the outdoors in, optically. We have enthusiastically accepted one of the main principles of modern domestic architecture: indoor and outdoor space should interpenetrate. The contemporary house is designed so that its outer shell is a screen more than a barrier. The one-level dwelling keeps us in close touch with the environment. Visually, there is the well-known lamp-and-picture-window combination facing what we hope is more inspiring than someone's backyard. That picture window is so essential that even apartment dwellers have them, with a balcony substituting for a patio (although the balcony is rarely used). The main point is that plate glass makes it possible for nature (or city traffic) to be part of our interior decoration.

There are good technical and structural reasons for the widespread use of glass: (1) the walls of modern buildings can be penetrated at almost any point because they do not bear weight; (2) the loss of heat through glass can be reduced by double paning if the glass framing is tight and well-insulated; (3) plate glass is strong and durable, even over fairly large areas; (4) intelligent orientation of a house on its site and proper location of windows admit sun when it is wanted. Architects can cooperate with nature by designing eaves, overhangs, or sunbreaks so that summer sun is blocked out while winter sun is invited in.

Air-conditioning has become a symbol of philosophic disagreement in modern architecture. We have the technology (expensive, of course) to air-condition all interior living space. (Someday, we may be able to air-condition the out-of-doors, too.) Already, shopping centers, department stores, and sports arenas are air-conditioned. Yet our domestic architecture, especially under the influence of Frank Lloyd Wright, seeks *continuity* with nature; we want technology to make structures look as if *they belong to and grew out of* their surroundings.

The philosophy of the International Style architects, exemplified by Walter Gropius, Ludwig Mies van der Rohe, and Marcel Breuer, conceived of the dwelling—or any building—as *wholly separate* from nature. They have designed buildings without windows, without modifying exterior form in response to climate or view or topography. Masterful engineering enables us to ignore the environment, so the architect can concentrate on designing beautiful interior spaces. And where the focus of activity is almost wholly internal—as in a museum, a laboratory, a department store, a gymnasium, a factory—such buildings can be successful.

But again, technology affects aesthetics. The high-speed elevator, the steel-frame skeleton, and light curtain-wall construction enable us to build almost as high as we wish. With computerized controls we can create a uniform atmosphere throughout a structure. Sometimes. There may be some disturbing rumbles, too: the costs of climate control are getting too high; and when the technology is not working well, uncomfortable temperature variations develop. When there are no windows, the inhabitants want to look out. When the air-conditioning does work, people wish they could smell spring. Or they hanker for the odor of gasoline fumes and damp city streets, the sound of automobile horns, and the scuttle of pedestrians racing for cover. Office workers may need certain noises and aromas to remind them that they have sense organs. Just like dwellers in the suburbs, for whom the sound of a neighbor's lawn mower and the fragrance of burned barbecue are worth the interest on the mortgage.

**Frank Lloyd Wright**   Frank Lloyd Wright (1869–1959) was perhaps our greatest artist-poet of the dwelling. In a long and controversial career he brought a pioneering and distinctively American genius to the art of creating human shelter. He was independently ahead of European architects in many ways: in understanding how to use modern technology; in his revolt against the architectural baggage of the past; and in his aesthetic originality—that is, his ability to deal with the dwelling as an art object, as something beautiful to look at and live in. Wright's adventures in social philosophy and community planning have not been universally praised, but his houses—especially his Prairie Houses—are great monuments. Indeed, when we look at a building as fresh and vital as the Robie House, it is hard to realize that it was built in 1909.

The most widely reproduced house by Wright is probably Fallingwater, built in 1936 at Bear Run, Pennsylvania. It is at once a triumph of architectural romanticism and an example of the brilliant exploitation of technology. Only steel-and-concrete cantilever construction would allow those massive overhanging slabs, complementing the rugged natural setting with their rectangular precision. There is an echo of the International Style in these crisp, cubical masses, but the overall conception is romantic. Heavily textured masonry in the vertical forms connects the house to the materials on the site, an important association in Wright's philosophy of building.

Some Wrightian ideas about the internal organization of a house provoke controversy, although many have been accepted. He believed that a huge hearth should be the physical and psychological center of the home. And he had strong dislikes: basements and attics; materials like paint, plaster, and varnish; and wood trim. Ornament should not be *applied*; it should result from the natural textures of materials; it should grow logically out of the processes of forming and fabrication. Cooking and dining facilities should be next to the living room, which should be located in the center of the house, away from exterior walls. He called the kitchen a "work area"—a tall space behind the fireplace. Wright believed that cooking odors should flow up and out rather than into the house. And there we may differ.

Rooms should radiate from the fireplace core; hence Wright's houses

Frank Lloyd Wright. Interior, Taliesin East, Spring Green, Wisconsin. 1925

usually have a cross-shaped plan. The arms of the cross are thus open to the outdoors on three sides, with horizontal bands of windows around them and wide eaves creating porchlike spaces underneath. Of course, this increases exterior wall area, adding to heating costs, but Wright was a genius, and genius doesn't worry about money.

The interior of Mr. Wright's house, Taliesin East, in Spring Green, Wisconsin, shows the inviting warmth and variety of surface, space, and light that he built into his Prairie Houses. Oriental rugs are used to break up the floor space and to define functional areas, with Chinese and Japanese art objects located on ledges set at different heights so that the eye will be encouraged to linger and refresh itself. Wright's interiors were sometimes criticized for being too dark, but he calculated the *modulation* of light more than designers who simply flood a room with light: Wright did not force people to install acres of drapery to gain privacy and control over outside illumination. His corners are delightful little zones of peace or sociability. To be sure, a Wrightian living room suggests a cave more than a tent or a metal cage. Why not? Wright understood our atavistic desires—the deep feelings of safety we inherit from our Stone Age ancestors; he remembered what we remember.

**Ludwig Mies van der Rohe**   The austere style of Mies van der Rohe (1886–1969) can best be understood against the background of Art Nouveau, a somewhat frivolous style of design and decoration that affected the arts early in the twentieth century. The subway, or Métro, station, designed for the city of Paris by Hector Guimard (1867–1942) shows a number of Art Nouveau features: ornamental and structural elements of cast iron, the concealment of right angles, heavy reliance on a serpentine or "whiplash" line, and curves at every joint or change of direction. This style had an international revival after World War II and reached a peak in the early 1960s.

Perhaps wealth encourages playful impulses in design and fashion. The somber doctrine of Mies that "less is more" seemed life-denying to people who wanted elegance or playfulness or both. But Art Nouveau was not elegant in the classical manner; instead it tried to unite art and nature almost literally. Nature was conceived as a forest grove or a garden filled with plants, vines, and creepers.

International Style architects loved the severe right angle as much as the Art Nouveau designers loved the S-curve. Accordingly, from the 1920s until about 1942—with the exception of Wright and his followers—avant-garde houses were plain white cubes, empty of ornament, faced with glass, and covered by no-nonsense flat roofs without eaves. Small wonder that the popular reaction to these buildings was chilly and that the style was known to some as "gas-station moderne."

In the hands of a master like Mies, the International Style was restrained but rich, as can be seen in his Tugendhat House in Czechoslovakia, designed in 1930. Floor-to-ceiling glass, black marble partitions, polished metal columns, silk curtains, and Oriental rugs: these created an atmosphere of refinement and sensuous appeal within a controlling intellectual framework. Despite his austerity, Mies had the instincts of a craftsman; he never abandoned the ideal of beauty achieved through well-made, well-proportioned parts. Unfortunately, his less imaginative followers became addicted to design as the simple multiplication of standardized units.

In the Farnsworth House of 1950 built in Plano, Illinois, Mies employed a vocabulary similar to the one he used again in his School of Architecture for the Illinois Institute of Technology in 1952. Both buildings are approached from a raised platform, and both use a series of slablike steps to make the transition from ground level to the plane of the floor. In the Farnsworth House, large expanses of glass produce reflected images that help establish continuity with nature. We see an extreme simplification of form and function in the white posts that support the roof, acting like stilts that raise the house off the ground. In the Illinois Tech building, Mies hung the ceiling from imposing steel girders stretching across the roof and connecting to black exterior steel columns which work as vertical accents. The building is not lifted off the ground like the Farnsworth House, but its platform and gently rising steps create that impression. Finally, the repeated horizontals of the steps help balance the vertical rhythm of the columns, giving the structure a sense of classic dignity and repose.

A Miesian house is essentially *one large cube*, with functional space divisions achieved by nonstructural partitions. For Mies, the real work of architecture was the creation of open interior space which occupants could subdivide as they wished. Philip Johnson's (born 1906) glass house of 1949

Hector Guimard. **Métropolitain station, Place de L'Etoile, Paris. 1900. (Demolished)**

Ludwig Mies van der Rohe. Living Room,
Tugendhat House, Brno, Czechoslovakia. 1930

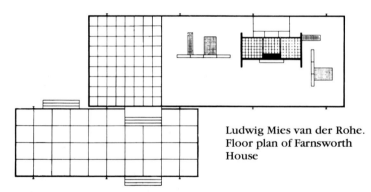

Ludwig Mies van der Rohe.
Floor plan of Farnsworth
House

Ludwig Mies van der Rohe. Crown Hall, Illinois
Institute of Technology, Chicago. 1952

Ludwig Mies van der Rohe. Farnsworth House, Plano, Illinois. 1950

in New Canaan, Connecticut, expresses the same point of view, although it probably would not work for a family. But Mies and Johnson were not much concerned about *who* lives in a building, or how interior areas will be used. They concentrate instead on designing one of the rarest, most precious commodities in the modern world—pure, unobstructed space.

**Le Corbusier**   Le Corbusier (Charles-Édouard Jeanneret-Gris, 1887–1965) began with assumptions similar to those of Mies but grew in a more sculptural direction. He preferred poured-concrete forms, leaving the steel, glass, and brick vocabulary to others. Le Corbusier's Villa Savoye, built in 1929, shows how much he was influenced by Cubist painting (Le Corbusier was himself an active abstract painter). The house also shows his use of stilts, a structural

*left and below:* Philip Johnson. Glass House, New Canaan, Connecticut. 1949

Le Corbusier. Villa Savoye,
Poissy-sur-Seine, France. 1929–30

Frank Lloyd Wright. Interior,
Johnson Wax Administration
Building, Racine, Wisconsin.
1936–39

device which has been widely adopted. These reinforced concrete columns
exploit the fact that steel-and-concrete technology can lift whole structures
into the air, freeing the space at ground level. The result is a strong shadow
pattern at the building's base, which defines the forms above it in almost
sculptural terms.

Wright had developed "mushroom" pillars (something like stilts) in the
interior of his Johnson Wax Building; they were a structural and decorative
device. Since his houses generally rose from a concrete pad, he used cantilevers to open up ground space and to create a strong light-and-dark pattern.
But Wright was a horizontal architect—temperamentally attached to the earth,
whereas Le Corbusier and the Bauhaus designers would have suspended
buildings from a sky hook if they could. Indeed, they designed several classic
chairs based on suspension and tension principles.

In the Villa Shodan, built for an Indian businessman in 1952, Le Corbusier
shows his development along the directions of his Villa Savoye. His mastery
of poured concrete was now well established, with textures imprinted by
rough wooden formwork; this was meant to overcome any mechanical slick-
ness of surface. He also developed the *brise-soleil*, or sunbreak, a device
which is especially useful in tropical climates. The occupants can see out, yet

the exterior rooms are shaded against the steady sun. From the outside, a delightful articulation of surface is produced.

The complicated wooden formwork needed to build virtually sculptured structures is feasible only in countries with cheap sources of hand labor. Thus Le Corbusier could use his poured-concrete vocabulary to build an entire city at Chandigarh, India. But in industrially advanced countries, construction time is precious; variations in shape and space are very expensive and must be held to a minimum. So a building vocabulary of steel frame, glass wall, and metal panels is more often used. A notable exception to this practice can be seen in the Yale art school designed by Paul Rudolph (born 1918). Here there is a lavish use of poured concrete combined with a special aggregate to give the building's surface a rich, coarse texture. After the concrete set, its surface was hand-hammered by workmen, adding to its cost but enhancing its sturdy, grainy qualities, which may be just right for artists and architects.

**Le Corbusier. Interior, Villa Shodan, Ahmedabad, India. 1952**

In the interior of the villa, Le Corbusier virtually paints with light through the design of the window perforations, much as in his chapel at Ronchamp (page 213)

Le Corbusier. High Court Building, Chandigarh, India. 1955–56

Paul Rudolph. Art and Architecture Building,
Yale University, New Haven, Connecticut. 1963

Le Corbusier. Unité d'Habitation, Marseille.
1947–52

**The Apartment House**   If Wright was poet of the house, Le Corbusier was poet of the apartment and the multiple dwelling. His Unités d'Habitation (apartment houses) have been widely imitated, especially the one at Marseille. Le Corbusier conceived of the building as a huge chest of drawers; each apartment is a self-contained, two-level unit that "slides" into a standardized cavity in the building's skeleton. If mass-production methods were fully extended to housing, such "drawers" could be fabricated in factories, hoisted into place in the building skeleton, and plugged in. At Marseille, the apartments are sound-insulated by lead sheets between the common walls, something our apartment dwellers would appreciate: acoustical privacy is rare today. The kitchens are air-conditioned; living rooms are two stories high and face a balcony with a sunbreak and a view. On every third floor there is a corridor called an "interior road," which runs the length of the building. On floors seven and eight, these interior roads have an indoor shopping center.

While it had many of the features of a resort hotel, Le Corbusier's Unité was intended for permanent residents. It could accommodate couples, large families, or singles. The seventeenth floor had a kindergarten and nursery; on the roof there was a garden, plus a swimming pool, gymnasium, running track, solarium, and snack bar. The roof structures for elevators, ventilation, and storage were also designed as playful sculptures, while the machinery for generators, air-conditioning, and so on was tucked under the first floor, above the stilts.

Le Corbusier wanted urban living to be a supremely satisfying experience, not merely a compromise for people who would rather be elsewhere. His ideas seem relevant to American needs; our population has become increasingly urbanized and, it seems, increasingly unhappy with the quality of urban life. We have built immense multiple dwellings for persons of all economic levels, but however "modern" these structures look from the outside, they don't seem to promote satisfying patterns of life within. At least, many of those who can escape do so. What is the reason for these costly failures? Do we design and build badly? Is it that Le Corbusier's pattern does not work? Are Americans psychologically incapable of living close to each other? That may be the problem. But the realities of urban space prevent horizontal spread. So those who can, head for the suburbs, where they hope to enjoy low-density life; at least they don't have to live on top of each other. However, they pay a price beyond money.

**The Modern Dwelling**   Wright, Mies, and Le Corbusier were the great innovators of modern architecture. Their contributions to design have been enormously influential, extending even to non-Western societies. The genius of these "form-givers" lay in their ability to create new conceptions of *lebensraum* (dwelling space) based on strong convictions about the nature of living and working together; about the requirements of urban living in an industrial age; and about the visual options created by modern technology.

What lessons or guiding ideas about the domestic dwelling do we get from these masters of modern architecture?

1. A house does not exist in a physical or social vacuum; it is not primarily a form of self-expression. A house should be oriented to its site so that it seems to belong there. From that orientation it can derive aesthetic as well as practical advantages. Finally, a house must not shut out the environment; it should include parts of the environment within itself.

2. The real substance of a dwelling is the shape of its space, not its fixtures and gadgets. These can be replaced, but the spaces we live in remain fairly constant; space and light are the chief causes of pleasure in a dwelling. A house plan should be shaped around patterns of living rather than the requirements of fashion. This calls for self-knowledge and a realistic assessment of our needs, habits, and resources.

Pierre Paulin. *Undulating furniture.* 1970.
**Designed for Artifort Holland. Distributed by**
**Turner Ltd., New York**
Furniture is part of architecture—often the
expressive part. Here it tries to revive prenatal
memories. The repetition of undulating forms in
a soft, billowy material reminds us of the
security of the womb.

3. The outside of a dwelling is a membrane that reflects the shape of its interior space and selectively transmits light and heat. Traditional features of building—cornices, gables, cupolas—are often costly survivals of obsolete building technologies. On the other hand, the old-fashioned porch probably deserves a revival: it gave much pleasure without being very expensive. As for exterior surfaces, beware of too many changes of material—combinations of wood, brick, stone, stucco, glass, marble, metal, and plastic; they may be over-compensations for design failures. Simplicity of material is a virtue in building.

4. Interior decoration (Wright called it "inferior desecration") means more than selection of furniture, application of ornament, or the display of objects. But since interiors are experienced visually as well as used physically, they have to be considered from an aesthetic as well as a practical standpoint. In apartments, where architectural options are generally limited, choices of furniture, color scheme, and lighting are crucial. Ultimately, the problems of unity, focus, and expressiveness have to be solved by reconciling a given space to the needs of particular individuals. This is not easy, but it has to be done, no matter how rich or poor they may be. We can learn to do it, and do it well.

**Conclusion**   Since the time when people lived in caves and tents, domestic dwellings have gone through immense changes; our needs and ambitions have also changed. Today, space exploration and scientific fantasy promise residence on distant planets in strange or nonexistent atmospheres; outer-space technologies may transform our approach to living on earth. The astronaut's microclimate can be controlled through his or her clothing; so, in time, our only shelter might be our clothing—and that for privacy, not protection. Our dwellings may become no more than storage places for personal possessions, while our lives are lived in special structures designed for certain purposes. There may be special structures for enjoying privacy, just as there are buildings where we go for collective dreams—motion picture theaters. The difference between home and community may disappear. Perhaps people will live in disposable dwellings like the nests that birds build and discard each year. Designers can accomplish such wonderful (or dreadful) things now, if we wish. But do we wish? Before deciding, we have to consider what it is that gives our communities their architectural shape.

## LARGE-SCALE DESIGN: THE COMMUNITY

Everyone knows about our problems of crowding, air pollution, traffic snarls, and visual chaos. We know, too, that communities need not be troubled places. Cities and towns are built by people, so people are responsible for the predicament we are in: only people can get us out. What remedies have been proposed to make cities and towns truly livable? If a community is a work of art—badly or well executed—what are the elements of that art?

We know how to design and construct good buildings and roads, but we seem unable to put them together so that the results are anything short of lethal. If the automobile is a deadly weapon, can we minimize its destructiveness? Can we build cities and towns which are not completely at the mercy of poisonous exhausts and murderous fenders? Is peaceful coexistence possible? Since we are social beings, can we create physical arrangements that will allow us to enjoy social life?

Philosophers and architects, engineers and planners, have considered these problems and made proposals ranging from extreme utopianism to cautious reform. Here we shall examine a few of their ideas.

**Ebenezer Howard: The Garden City**   In the nineteenth century, as today, people left farms in droves, adding to the congestion of cities. The

countryside was depopulated and the cities teemed. In 1898 Ebenezer Howard, an Englishman without architectural training, realized that it was not enough to reverse the flow of migration: it was necessary to create communities that would combine the advantages of urban and rural living. His solution: "Town and country *must be married*, and out of this union will spring a new hope, a new life, a new civilization." He wrote a book advancing the concept of the "garden city," a community of concentric belts of land alternately used for commerce or manufacturing and "greenbelts" or park land. These greenbelt communities would separate functional areas from each other while providing recreation space and a good balance of rural and urban amenities—the balance needed for a healthy and satisfying existence. Administrative and recreational buildings would be located at the core of these communities, functioning like the squares and village greens which gave emotional and visual focus to early American towns and cities.

Land would not be individually owned but would be held and developed by a common body which would limit growth to about thirty thousand; this would prevent high density, land speculation, and impossible costs. Beyond this population it would be necessary to start a new garden city. The outermost belt of each community might be used to grow food for local consumption, or it would be left uncultivated so it could be used for recreation.

Howard hoped his plan would lead to the decentralization of London—something that never happened. But it *was* translated into reality in several English and American suburbs. The word "greenbelt" has been widely adopted, although Howard's principles have rarely been applied in a single community: controlled growth; ownership of land by a common authority; and the separation of residential, industrial, recreational, and administrative functions.

It should be stressed that Howard's garden city was to be a *balanced* community—a place where people would live *and* work. Today's suburbs or satellite towns are often one-function communities; they have been called "dormitory suburbs." Without an industrial base, it is difficult for them to pay for good schools, libraries, and other essential services. And, as industries are lured into these communities, as highways to the central city grow crowded, and as industrial facilities sprawl beyond their corporate limits, the suburbs lose the advantages of decentralization. But that was the purpose of leaving the city! Aside from the morality of suburban parasitism—using urban services without contributing to their support—there are practical disadvantages in arrangements which grow increasingly insupportable from an economic standpoint. We have learned, alas, that no community is an island.

**Daly City, California**

Land on the California coast is precious, and the Daly City developers have eaten up every buildable piece of it. Can everyone have "a place in the country"? Does everyone *want* a place in the country? Is this "country"? Is this sprawl necessary?

**Conklin and Wittlesey. Town center, Reston, Virginia. 1961**

Ebenezer Howard's Garden City concept is given contemporary expression in the American town of Reston.

Photograph of a slum scene in Harlem

Frank Lloyd Wright. Broadacre City plan. 1933–40. Reprinted from *The Living City* by Frank Lloyd Wright, copyright 1958. By permission of the publisher, Horizon Press, New York

**Frank Lloyd Wright: Broadacre City**   Of course, one way to deal with the problems of urbanism is to abandon cities, to start all over again by reorganizing society into small, self-sufficient communities. If the problems of cities are too deep-seated to be solved, we can reform *part* of society by creating ideal communities outside the megalopolitan monsters. This might be called the Noah's Ark approach to urban redesign: save at least some of the people. Spreading out some of the population might overcome the spatial and social problems of urbanism.

Decentralization would enable people to establish a better relationship to the land and to nature. That is what Frank Lloyd Wright proposed with his Broadacre City plan of the 1930s. His solution: an acre of land for each person. Farmers would have ten acres, but all would raise some of their own food, supplementing what full-time farmers grow. This procedure would not be very efficient from the standpoint of yield per acre, but Wright believed, like Thomas Jefferson, that moral benefits accrue to people who till the soil at least part of the time. That is why some people live in agricultural communes today; they are as much concerned with the moral advantages of group living as with escaping the evils of urbanism.

In a land area of four square miles, fourteen hundred families or six thousand people could live, produce some food, provide each other with personal services, and engage in some light manufacturing. Wright believed that the automobile and helicopter liberate us residentially and industrially: we need not live next to where we work. The telephone lets us communicate easily with cities, if we need to; radio and television broadcast news and entertainment; we can shop by mail; we can see movies at home. We do not have to live in cities to use the goods and services they create.

But can communities of six thousand create the necessities of modern civilization? How many people are needed to support a good high school? Or a hospital? Thirty-five thousand? Fifty thousand? How many are needed to support a museum, a theater, a symphony orchestra? These are rarely found in small towns.

However, Wright did not plan to eliminate cities at once; he expected them to wither away. The existence of the city was assumed, since some residents of Broadacre would commute there to work. (Today, commuters may wonder whether two or three hours of daily travel are sufficiently rewarded by character-building activities in the suburbs like raising tomatoes and mowing the lawn.) But contemporary suburban life is a caricature of Wright's idea: he really wanted people to raise their own food, to improve the land, to be independent of bosses and wages. Their houses would be beautiful—designed by architects like himself, who knew how to relate dwellings to the shape of the terrain. People would not own land but they could hold it as long as they made productive use of it. Land would not be a commodity traded for profit; it would be a source of sustenance and delight.

As we know, Wright had strong opinions and strong dislikes. We can tell what they were from his list of principles governing the organization of Broadacre City:

> No private ownership.
> No landlord and tenant.
> No "housing." No subsistence homesteads.
> No traffic problems. No back-and-forth haul.
> No railroads. No streetcars.
> No grade crossings.
> No poles. No wires in sight.
> No ditches alongside the roads.
> No headlights. No light fixtures.
> No glaring cement roads or walks.
> No tall buildings except as isolated in parks.
> No slum. No scum.
> No public ownership of private needs.

A truly agrarian utopia, the very opposite of Le Corbusier's ideal.

**Le Corbusier: La Ville Radieuse**   The garden city is a suburb and the suburb is a tentacle of the city. According to Le Corbusier it creates more problems than it solves: commuting, too many vehicles, expensive utilities, costly maintenance. And eventually the garden city is absorbed by the spreading central city. In its place Le Corbusier proposed his Ville Radieuse, a plan for as many as three million people. Unlike Wright, who detested skyscrapers, Le Corbusier found them absolutely essential: in effect he would create *vertical* garden cities.

The Ville Radieuse would have a higher population density than present cities and yet *more* open space. The explanation lies in its huge but widely separated office buildings and apartment houses. Instead of being lined up next to each other to form canyons, as in Manhattan, they would be far apart, exposed to light and air, surrounded by parks, and approached by unimpeded highways on multiple levels. Highways and subways would radiate outward from the center of the city, like the streets of Washington, D.C. At the outer rings of the city would be large apartment houses of the type at Marseille, fifteen or twenty stories high, with some individual dwellings scattered among them. Industry would be located even farther out from the city, but not too far from the apartments where their workers lived.

The space opened up in the city by high-density skyscrapers could be safely used by pedestrians since each kind of transportation would have its own levels—an ideal we still cannot seem to reach. Modern urban redevelopment schemes continue to locate parking garages in the city's core, drawing vehicles and pedestrians together and forcing them to compete for the same space.

Le Corbusier was reconciled to the existence of cities and their unique culture; he did not seek to escape the city but to change it. And society seems

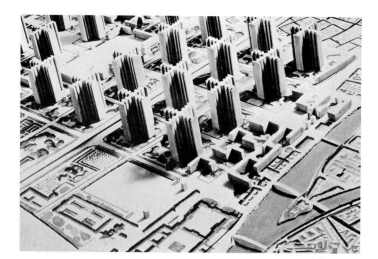

Le Corbusier. Ville Radieuse: Voisin Plan for Paris. 1925

to have accepted his commitment to high-rise structures. But, until recently, we have been unwilling to carry out the radical surgery necessary to rationalize the city's transport systems and to admit light, sun, and air to downtown areas by opening up the space around our skyscrapers.

Le Corbusier admired Manhattan's skyline—from a distance. He deplored the living and working arrangements which it implied: "Our American friends have erected skyscrapers and made them work. They are constructions of an astonishing technique, tangible proofs of present possibilities. But, from the planning point of view, their skyscrapers are tiresome and their towns wretched to live in (though vibrant and meriting the closest attention)." As for detached single dwellings, he said: "Instead of multiplying innumerable suburban houses let us equip ourselves with impeccable dwelling-units [that is, apartment houses] of an appropriate stature."

Since cities are an inescapable fact of life, Le Corbusier insisted that the rational ordering of space would make urban life satisfying, even exciting. Great architecture is possible without returning to the building techniques of the past. Reinforced-concrete construction ("reconstituted stone," as he called it) can be spiritually satisfying, functionally adequate, and reasonable in cost. Artistic sensitivity wedded to modern technology and a realistic assessment of social, industrial, and human needs would produce good urban design.

Following are some of the main principles of town planning advocated by Le Corbusier:

Town planning means designing for four major functions: Living, Working, Recreation, and Circulation.

The *materials* of town planning are sunlight, space, greenery, and steel-reinforced concrete.

Enough dwellings should be concentrated in one building to liberate the space around it.

Pedestrian routes and mechanized-transportation routes should be separated.

The distance between home and work should be minimized.

Living quarters should get the best urban sites.

Pedestrian paths should not be obstructed by buildings, which should be elevated on stilts.

Autos, buses, and other vehicles should travel on elevated roadways, beneath which utilities should be housed; the result is easier installation, maintenance, and repair.

Industrial and residential areas should be separated by greenery.

Architectural monuments should be safeguarded.

**Elements of Planning: Residential Grouping**  Almost all community plans call for special areas set aside for residential purposes. Mainly, they are

**New town in Cumbernauld, Scotland. 1965**

A plan that avoids the monotony of the grid. We see honeycomb patterning and tilted siting—both attempts to gain visual variety and sunny exposures in low-cost housing with "add-on" possibilities.

occupied by detached, single-family dwellings. These dwellings vary greatly in cost, quality of design, and orientation on their sites. Most are built speculatively in huge developments; others are built on an individual, custom-made basis. But cost of construction rarely governs the patterning of roads, open spaces, and home sites. Hence the builder of a large development may have the best opportunity to plan for good, overall design.

What objectives are sought in the grouping of houses, the design of roads, and the shaping of open space? The goal of most people who buy separate dwellings is to capture the charm of village life while enjoying urban conveniences. They hope their houses will blend gracefully into the landscape, afford easy access to neighbors, and provide nearby roads to shops, schools, and churches. Most of all they want visual harmony—residence in a community where individualism has not run amok: aesthetically speaking, they want unity in variety.

To provide visual interest and variety, curving roads are preferred; also, they slow down motorists. Main thoroughfares should not pass through residential areas. Where straight roads are necessary, houses need not be set parallel to the road; they can be given a slight, consistent tilt to create varied space intervals and for good orientation to sun and view. But if every house in a group is independently tilted, the result will be chaotic. This can be prevented by zoning ordinances for uniform setbacks and minimum distances between houses. As for intersections, the four-corner intersection should be avoided; the simple T-intersection is better. When connecting to large arteries, a variety of road types can be employed: the dead end, the cul-de-sac, the loop street, and the collector road. Natural contours should be respected; that is, good trees and interesting stone outcroppings ought to be preserved. And the bulldozer should be used sparingly.

Flat terrain lends itself to many patterns, but designers should try to avoid the obvious, especially the rectangular grid. Design should aim at variety where nature has not been generous with trees or rolling landscape. In highways it has been found that a good view is improved if it is approached by a curved route. Accordingly, even an ordinary row of houses will look better if we do not see them all at once—lined up like boxes on a shelf. In addition to horizontal curves, the vertical curve—the rise and dip of the road—can add interest to a group of dwellings. Also, we like to see dominant roof lines following the slope of the land; houses tend to harmonize if there is some continuity between their roof lines. In general, we like to see houses flow together, and good landscaping can promote that effect.

Whether it is efficient or not, the detached dwelling seems to be something everyone wants, although not everyone can afford it. For most Americans it constitutes a better solution to the problems of shelter than living in a small box, inside a large box, within a large block, in an anonymous grid. That solution is increasingly reserved for the very rich or the very poor. But unfortunately, the poetic promise of the dwelling, inherited from Frank Lloyd Wright, has not been realized in housing for the millions. Can it ever be realized? Perhaps this is a case where architecture and planning are ahead of politics and economics. The professionals know how to design better communities than they are allowed to build. The solution? Better clients for our designers.

**Elements of Planning: The Highway**   Trains and buses are more efficient than automobiles. Nevertheless, if we have a choice we prefer to drive. Why? Because automobiles give us a greater sense of freedom and personal control. Modern life may be increasingly mechanized and automated, but driving provides the opportunity to exercise judgment and skill. The automobile is felt as an extension of our bodies; we want to test it against the rigors of distance, the demands of the road, the challenge of the unexpected, the cars of other drivers. Along with the shopping trip, the auto voyage is one of the great experiences of twentieth-century mankind. Despite transportation alternatives and casualty statistics, we are drawn toward concrete and asphalt like lemmings drawn to the sea.

What appeals to us in addition to going somewhere is the opportunity to feel the land moving under our vehicles, seeing the changing sky and countryside at 75 mph, sensing the car's response to the shifting shape of the road. For these reasons it is not too much to say that highways, bridges, parkways, and viaducts constitute public art forms—sources of aesthetic experience for the millions.

Safety is the main goal of highway designers, but aesthetic considerations are intimately related to safety. Designers know how far drivers can see at given speeds, their degree of peripheral vision, their ability to discriminate objects. They know how comfort and pleasure are affected by the banking and grading of a road, and the transition into and out of a curve. The well-

**Sven Markelius. Vällingby, Sweden. Begun 1953**

Le Corbusier's urban planning ideas applied in Sweden. But those connected units, lower left, look like freight cars. Maybe the S-curve helps.

*left:* Alfred Neumann and Zvi Hecker. Apartment house, Ramat Gan, Israel. 1960-63

The sculptural excitement in the apartment building (left) proves that modern technology can generate the same feeling of community that we sense in the adobe pueblo, America's oldest high-rise dwelling (right).

*right:* Indian village, Taos Pueblo, New Mexico. c. 1935. Courtesy Museum of New Mexico, Santa Fe

*opposite above:* Expressway through Lefrak City in Queens, New York

An automotive conveyor belt surrounded by an anonymous collection of boxes for middle-income apartment dwellers. The result of this architectural relationship is human indifference.

*opposite below:* Complex freeway interchange in Los Angeles

An engineering marvel that looks good from the air. In a car, it's best to close the windows, turn on the stereo, and stay in the same lane.

designed highway *leads* the driver's eye; it prepares us for certain operations while offering enough stimulation to avoid monotony. Unity and predictability versus variation and surprise: these are aesthetic considerations. It is well known that monotonous highway design can be dangerously hypnotic; in other words, bad design is harmful to your health.

The construction of bridges, viaducts, interchanges, side slopes, retaining walls, safety rails, and embankments presents artistic as well as engineering problems. These problems arise whenever we try to bring a highway through a city. Can it be done harmoniously? Can major arteries be visually integrated with the natural and man-made structures that surround them? How should we treat the areas created by the crossing, paralleling, rising, or descending of exit ramps as they meet local traffic patterns?

And there are other questions: What should be done with road signs? Can we get the visual information we need more concisely, and *before we need to use it?* What about the billboards that invade our privacy, exploiting our attention without our permission? Vision is essential to driving, and billboards cannot be "turned off." Thus, the best efforts of planners and designers are frustrated because the visual relationships they create are not protected. Perhaps the modern highway illustrates our resemblance to the ancient Romans—solid builders and administrators but not especially sensitive to human relationships.

Since 1946, Germany and Switzerland have demonstrated great sensitivity to the highway as an art form. But the world's greatest democracy will not spend public funds to enliven its expressways. Edward Hopper's painting, *Gas*, tells the story well. Or perhaps Stuart Davis was right (see page 41): our sculptures are gas pumps! We have yet to learn that with our frontiers gone and natural resources limited, visual pollution of the landscape must stop. Highways represent an ecological and aesthetic opportunity: they might be our last chance to enjoy the countryside and preserve it unravaged.

**Elements of Planning: Plazas, Malls, and Civic Centers** Television has made our public life a living-room experience. Today we witness momentous events from the same sofa that was formerly used for conversation and courtship. We experience the death of a president on television with the same sense of distress as do the members of his family. For some time it has been clear that we cannot gather in a single square to watch our leaders debate the

Terracing along Highway 70 outside Denver, Colorado

Good highway engineering here creates an impressive geologic display as well as an aesthetic effect appropriate to the grandeur of the Rocky Mountain setting.

issues; our sense of community comes mainly from the media of news and information. But although the media create a community of ideas, opinion, and entertainment, they do not bring us together physically. In fact, they separate us physically. So we still need places—open spaces—where we can come together out of the darkness of our TV dens. There is no substitute for the exhilaration of *being with* people, as opposed to *looking at* or *reading about* them.

What are the places that bring large numbers of people together? Amusement parks, shopping malls, civic squares, sports arenas, bus terminals, airports, museum gardens, public parks. These are the places where we can stroll, window-shop, sit on benches and watch the passing parade. Given the chance, we would like to browse in an outdoor book stall, shop in an open market, explore a crooked little street, discover a square with a little church, some statuary, a fountain, and some children playing: that sounds like a civilized way to spend time. Must we go to Europe to do it?

Jacques Moeschal. Sculpture for Mexico City's Route of Friendship. 1968. Gray-green painted concrete, 68' high

*above:* Edward Hopper. *Gas.* 1940. Oil on canvas, 26¼ × 40¼". Collection, The Museum of Modern Art, New York. Mrs. Simon Guggenheim Fund

*right:* Red Grooms and Mimi Gross. Detail of vinyl tower featuring Blissberg's Old Folks Home from *Ruckus Manhattan.* 1975. Courtesy Marlborough Gallery, New York

The imageries of Dubuffet and Grooms have common origins in children's drawings, street graffiti, and the art of the insane. Both artists are amazed by the idea of people housed like insects in multicelled containers; both think of cities as crazy, rollicking machine-organisms. Both are fascinated by fun, terror, and lunacy.

*below:* Jean Dubuffet. *Dévidoir enregistreur.* 1978. Acrylic and paper collage on canvas, 6'7" × 9'6". Albright-Knox Art Gallery, Buffalo, New York. George B. and Jenny R. Mathews Fund, 1979

Donald Ray Carter. Photograph of Galleria
Vittoria Emanuele, Milan

Street life raised to the level of an art form. This
is what we are trying to accomplish with our
shopping-mall architecture. Too bad we can't do
it downtown.

Stamford Town Center Mall, Connecticut

Well, the shopping mall is America's answer to the European square—our version of an exciting public space. Of course, it tempts us to buy things: the visual and spatial amenities have to be paid for. But it is also possible to stroll through for free. Usually, a shopping mall is an enclosed structure, with natural light admitted at the top; often it has generous and exotic plantings, and air-conditioning throughout. (Americans can always improve on nature.) Some malls are created by closing off downtown streets—converting a few downtown canyons to pedestrian use and reclaiming the city for people. We are also learning that good buildings need not be torn down: auto traffic can be rerouted and people can rediscover their feet. But what about the slums and obsolete structures that surround downtown areas? Mostly, they are destroyed, or expensively redesigned and their inhabitants relocated. A better solution is to attract artists: they tend to inhabit marginal areas, and they will fix most things with their own labor. Moreover, the results will be better looking and less plastic.

So far as massive redesign is concerned, Rockefeller Center in New York City is our great model. Begun in 1931, it provided the impetus for the construction of public buildings and plazas in the high-density core of a modern metropolis. Consisting of sixteen buildings occupying fourteen acres of choice Manhattan real estate, the Center formed a complex surrounding a pedestrian mall and a sunken plaza, which is an ice-skating rink in the winter and an outdoor restaurant in the summer. Its massive, slablike buildings represented the first significant departure from the idea of the skyscraper as a sort of oversized church steeple. They also embodied a frank, if unspectacular, solution to the problem of getting natural light and fresh air into the interior of very large structures. An early example of ecological design.

The unbroken curtain-wall surfaces of the Rockefeller Center buildings provide an important psychological dividend—a sense of enclosure and protection for the plaza and mall on the ground. That means *the people* on the ground: we have tall buildings that do not intimidate. In addition, Rockefeller Center gives pedestrians the feeling of being at the focal point of an exciting city. Excitement and a sense of protection: that is the combination we want in public spaces. Great cities can be depressing as well as exciting;

*right:* Piazza San Marco, Venice. Begun 1063

Two public squares almost a thousand years apart, and yet they perform essentially the same function. They bring people together in an enclosed space to create one of the great spectacles of civilized life: human beings moving freely against a background of monumental architectural forms.

*below right:* Lincoln Center for the Performing Arts, New York. 1962–69

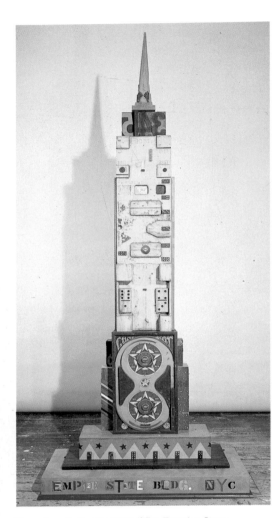

Tony Lordi. *Lucky Star/The Empire State Building.* 1989. Wood, games, found objects, and metal parts, 8'8" high. Courtesy Broadway Windows, New York University

New York's Empire State Building dressed up with old toys and furniture parts. What does this funky, human-size sculpture seem to say about the city and its most celebrated architectural icon? That we relate to buildings as if they were persons, that we want the city to be fun again.

*opposite:* Charles Moore and William Hersey. Piazza d'Italia, New Orleans. 1974–78

Urban fun architecture—part stage set, part sculpture, and part Pop painting. Intended to honor the Italian immigrants of New Orleans, the Piazza is not so much a space as it is a potpourri of classical architectural fragments, modern glitzy materials, and hotel-lobby glitter.

individuals lost in depersonalized routines need to be reminded of their humanity, their capacity to experience emotions that enlarge the self. That may be the real reason we feel a sudden urge to visit Paris, Rome, or Venice. The time has come to go to San Francisco, Seattle, and Toronto. And Savannah.

**Elements of Planning: Industrial and Commercial Structures**   Not long ago, a factory was an ugly place—grimy, surrounded by clutter, refuse, and foul smells. Crossing the New Jersey meadows and looking at the industrial sprawl from the train window, one wondered how people could tolerate the sights and sounds once they had overcome the stench. The same was true of the pulpwood mills in the South, the steelmill towns along the Ohio River, the slaughterhouses of Chicago or Kansas City, and the scarred mining towns of Pennsylvania and West Virginia. Their active and obsolete remains still mark the places where we live and work.

But most of these sights and sounds are disappearing, mainly because their operation has become uneconomic: those mills and factories and slaughterhouses were in the wrong location; they were too costly to maintain; they could not be automated; or their managements became environmentally aware. The Victorian notion that industry is inherently ugly has given way to the idea that order, precision, and harmony are essential features of a success-

Frank Lloyd Wright. Johnson Wax Administration
Building and Research Tower, Racine, Wisconsin.
1936–39, 1947–50. Views by day and by night

ful enterprise. These qualities have to be visible wherever products are
planned, manufactured, and distributed. Consumers have become choosy or
aesthetically sensitive: they associate products with the places where they are
made and sold.

Again, a pioneering industrial statement was made by Frank Lloyd Wright
in his administration building and research tower for the Johnson Wax Company in Racine, Wisconsin. To be sure, the structural vocabulary (with the
exception of the tower) seems more related to a domestic dwelling than a
corporate headquarters. But is that bad? What should a factory or research
center look like? A museum? A college campus? Why not? If morale is improved, management can attract and hold the people it needs to survive in a
modern, competitive economy.

The Johnson buildings are located in the center of a city that values
architectural excellence. Hence the structural forms have a bold, sculptural
quality. This is especially apparent in the research tower rising dramatically
from a hovering platform. Its horizontal bands repeat the lines of the administration buildings, and its circular roof turrets offer a good solution to that
eternal problem of the high-rise—how to top it off. The cantilevered floors of
the structure are clearly revealed at night, which gives us the Wrightian
concept of a tall building as opposed to the New York idea of a skyscraper.
Today, such structures resting on platforms are used increasingly and with
conspicuous success, as in New York's Lever House. The tower is efficient
and symbolically potent; the platform unites it with the site while creating a
useful protected space underneath. Does that idea belong to Wright or to Le
Corbusier? Well, good ideas don't care who invented them.

Dramatic industrial and commercial structures can also be seen in Ely
Kahn's (1884–1972) Municipal Asphalt Plant in New York City, in the St. Louis
airport terminal by Minoru Yamasaki (1912–1986), and in the North Carolina
State Fair Arena by Matthew Nowicki (1910–1949) and W. H. Deitrick (born

Skidmore, Owings and Merrill. Lever House, New York. 1952

*below:* Epstein & Sons. Kitchens of Sara Lee Administration Building, Deerfield, Illinois. 1964

Compare this building with Mies van der Rohe's Crown Hall at Illinois Institute of Technology (page 80)

Kahn & Jacobs. Municipal Asphalt Plant (now occupied by the George and Annette Murphy Center), New York. 1944

From industrial plant to temple for arts and sports. A good building is worth keeping, regardless of its original function.

*above:* Minoru Yamasaki. St. Louis Airport Terminal. 1954

*above right:* Matthew Nowicki and William H. Deitrick. J. S. Dorton State Fair Arena, Raleigh, North Carolina. 1953

Eero Saarinen. TWA Terminal, Kennedy International Airport, New York. 1962

1905). Eero Saarinen (1910–1961) displayed almost theatrical gifts in his TWA Terminal for Kennedy International Airport. All these examples show that the gap between art and science, or between architecture and engineering, is steadily closing. Great and enduring monuments are created when the artistic imagination is not restricted by a false professional separation.

Ours is a time of frantic urban and regional transformation. The convergence of several forces has brought this about: (1) we realize that many social problems, now at the stage of crisis, originate in the physical design of the community; (2) we realize that problems of transportation, work, health, and recreation transcend traditional political units; (3) modern technology has made it practical to think in terms of large-scale, comprehensive design; (4) specialists like architects, engineers, ecologists, lawyers, and land-use experts have developed patterns of unified action in community design; (5) architectural education now embraces the design of regional environments as well as individual structures.

*top:* **John Andrews. Scarborough College, University of Toronto. 1966**

The "megastructure" approach to the architecture of great institutions and even of whole cities. Such continuous structures are open to social and technological change because they are designed to receive "add-on" or "clip-on" units, which are mass produced by industrial methods instead of being custom-made on the site.

*above:* **Safdie, David, Barott, and Boulva. Habitat, EXPO 67, Montreal. 1967**

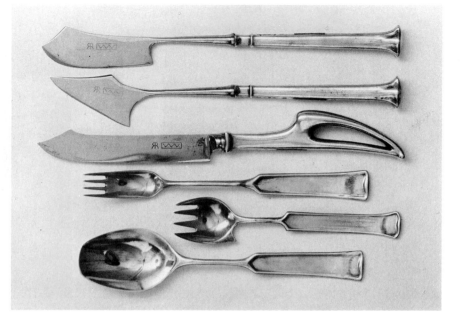

## THE CRAFTS AND INDUSTRIAL DESIGN

We have seen how art performs physical functions through the design of
large-scale containers—from single buildings to whole communities. The
important point is that art is not only decorative or symbolic; it is also
utilitarian. While there are significant differences between handmade and
machine-made objects, we should remember that shaping them to satisfy
human needs is an artistic problem.

At different times the person responsible for making pots and pans has
been called an artisan, a craftsman, an engineer, or a designer. In the past,
families produced most of their own tools and utensils. The hardworking
colonial housewife was not called a craftsman or designer, but she spun and
wove her own cloth, cut and sewed garments, made blankets and rugs, and
painted and embroidered textiles. She did the job but she didn't have the title.
However, we are not interested in labels at this point; we are concerned with
the forms of useful objects, how the forms are affected by machine tools,
where the human contribution appears, and whether the results have aesthetic quality.

The water jug made by a potter and the aluminum pitcher stamped out
by a machine may be similar in form and function. But a potter's fingers made
the clay jug; making the aluminum pitcher was different: the pitcher grew out
of a man-machine *collaboration*. Did it cease to be art when the machine
entered the scene? Or do we have something new called "machine art"? If so,
do people respond to it differently? Should they? Here we can examine some
of the historical, technical, and psychological factors involved in the transition
from clay pot to metal container. In effect, we ask these questions: "Have
machines learned to create art? If so, is it any good? Or was it all a mistake?"

**Qualities of Handcraft**     Usually, a craft object is planned and made by the
same person. In the village and cottage crafts of preindustrial economies there
was some division of labor between members of a family, between men and
women, between children and adults, between skilled and unskilled workers.
Even so, there was a certain unity of control in the making of a craft object.
The "professional" craftsman is different: he or she does all the work, adjusting a design according to the requirements of a customer. A good illustration
would be the tailor who makes a garment "to order," that is, according to an
individual's personal measurements. Hence, the characteristics of handcraft
usually include (1) unified execution of the object; (2) unified responsibility
for the object; and (3) adjustment of design to individual needs.

The result of the craft process inevitably exhibits variation. That is why we can speak of a craft object as "one of a kind," even if it is similar to other objects of its type. The uniqueness of the object may be due to the craftsman's idiosyncrasies or the special desires of a patron. In either case, that uniqueness is often considered the essence of art. It pleases us to know that we own, or are looking at, an object which is absolutely singular. Nobody has one exactly like it.

Another feature of handcraft is, paradoxically, its relative sameness. Variations in detail occur because absolute duplication is impossible in hand-made articles. Also, the "true" craftsman does not look kindly on change for its own sake. Peasants, folk artisans, and craftsmen change their modes of thinking and making slowly; they prefer to use patterns and formulas inherited for generations. These patterns and traditions promote a high degree of technical skill; folk craftsmen, especially, concentrate on mastery of skill more than originality of expression. For them, the problems of design and meaning have been largely solved. The result is a timeless quality in craft objects, a quality that charms tourists—visitors from cultures that change their tastes every month or so.

While the old craft traditions care little for novelty, they do stress the right use of tools and materials and the importance of durability. "Right" means using tools correctly, that is, according to inherited techniques and with due respect for the working properties of materials. Since the patron-craftsman relationship is close, the craftsman cannot escape responsibility for what he or she has made. This gives us a special insight into the meaning of crafts-manship: the value of an object is based on a relationship of trust between user and maker. You can go back to a tailor or dressmaker to adjust your garment because you have gained weight; try that at your local department store.

Another handcraft trait may account for the survival of craftsmen today, notwithstanding their struggle with the economic facts of life: it is difficult to produce a great many ugly products by hand. To be sure, there are bad craftsmen, but they are usually weeded out. Furthermore, it is difficult for a human being to make something badly again and again; inevitably, we improve a little bit. But machines can produce trash at a fantastic rate; the results improve only if the designer improves. In the meantime, a vast amount of rubbish is manufactured. Furthermore, excellence in an industrial civilization is often defined in terms of mass acceptance, an acceptance that can be engineered by advertising.

*above:* Roy Lichtenstein. *Ceramic Sculpture I.* 1965. Glazed ceramic, 9" high. Private collection

These works rely for their Surrealist impact on the deliberate violation of the craftsman's aesthetic: appropriateness of material and form to the function of the object.

*left:* Meret Oppenheim. *Object.* 1936. Fur-covered cup, saucer, and spoon; cup, 4⅜" diameter; saucer, 9⅜" diameter; spoon, 8" long; overall height 2⅞". Collection, The Museum of Modern Art, New York. Purchase

For most of human history, objects of daily use have been made with the aid of small hand tools functioning as extensions of our senses and fingers. Thus we have been thoroughly habituated to the visual and tactile characteristics of handcraft, and it is doubtful that we shall ever escape our emotional attachment to materials worked by hand. But civilization as we know it depends on mechanical and automated forms of making. Since the Industrial Revolution we have been going through a conflict between our emotional attachment to the crafts and the mechanical basis of our economy. Today, that conflict is almost over.

Machine-made products have been accepted by almost all societies. Computer-aided design (CAD) and computer-aided manufacture (CAM) are spreading rapidly. Those newly emerging nations which still depend on handcraft are trying desperately to become industrialized. For them, mechanical-industrial production is a symbol of national prestige, and handcraft is regarded as a survival of colonial dependence. For us, ironically, the practice of the crafts and the ownership of craft objects is often a symbol of taste and cultivation; or perhaps it is hankering for the past. In any case, something in our bones and organs—especially our eyes—craves the sight and touch of hand-made objects. How, then, did we get "hooked" on the mass-production habit?

**The Origin and Principles of Mass Production**   Clearly, we have to understand the basic processes of mechanization and mass production. Only then can we look at industrial design and the aesthetic implications of machine art.

The main principles of mass production are *duplication, accuracy, interchangeability*, and *specialization*. Casting, the oldest method of duplication, goes back to the Neolithic era—about 8000 B.C. From this *art* (it was art, magic, and technology rolled into one) the metal foundries of the present evolved. Today, there are few manufactured products which do not contain cast metal or plastic parts. A second Neolithic invention, the potter's wheel, led to the wood lathe and the metal lathe, which is the basic machine tool of metalworking. Die stamping, another method of duplication, was used by the Persian king Darius to manufacture coins in the fifth century B.C. Gutenberg's invention of movable type (c. 1440) was another duplication method which had effects extending far beyond printing. Movable type involved a kind of *interchangeability* since the same letters could be used again and again in different combinations. However, *accuracy* was not very great, and the interchangeable principle was used only on a two-dimensional surface without moving parts. By the eighteenth century, a fair degree of three-dimensional accuracy was developed in steam engines and watches, leading to *interchangeability of parts*: manufacturing could be done in one place and assembling in another. These developments depended on *accuracy*, uniform standards of measure, agreement about the meaning of dimensions—something handcraftsmen did not have because each craftsman was a law unto himself.

*Specialization* in mass production refers not only to workers but also to machine tools. The ideal machine was designed to carry out a single operation or set of operations on a particular product. Today, there is talk of versatile robots, that is, multipurpose robots, but this may be a matter of semantic play; efficiency in mass production depends on specialized, reliable machines. The ideal factory consists of a series of such machines connected to each other and electronically guided by instructions from a computer. Well, who guides the computer? Here we approach the role of the designer.

An assembly line is a manufacturing system that fully employs duplication, accuracy, interchangeability, and specialization in machines and, to some extent, workers. We associate it with Henry Ford, although Eli Whitney set up an assembly-line system to manufacture guns in the eighteenth century.

**Ford Motor Company assembly line. Early 1900s**

The technology of the Ford assembly line might be compared to Tinguely's sculpture *Méta-Mécanique* (page 373)

Early in the twentieth century, Ford realized he could not tolerate hand-fitting because it wasted time. Ironically, higher quality production could be achieved by eliminating the possibility of human error. And error could be reduced by taking the human hand out of the process of making!

So the basic idea of mass production might be summarized as follows: the quality of a product can be raised, its price lowered, and greater numbers produced, if component parts are made accurately with specialized tools operated by workers who do not possess the skills to make the whole product. The skill resides in the system, not the person who tends a machine or assembles parts.

Modern manufacturing operations (computerized or not) fall into three distinct phases: plant layout and tooling, duplication of parts, and assembly of duplicated units. These phases follow decisions to manufacture a new product or model—decisions that are guided by research, capitalization, design, engineering, and marketing. Obviously, the design function interacts with all the other factors, suggesting that an *artistic element* influences every aspect of production. In addition, there is *re*design, which entails costly retooling in the light of new needs. Beyond redesign, there is *styling*—a type of designing which mainly changes the appearance of a product, usually in response to marketing pressures. In the following section we examine some of the ethical and aesthetic questions it raises.

**The Emergence of Industrial Design**  As we have seen, the Industrial Revolution and mass production caused a steady replacement of the human hand. Until the eighteenth century, no basic changes in making had taken place since the Bronze Age; tools were more refined but principles of operation remained the same. Then, suddenly, handcraft methods of manufacture became obsolete.

Preindustrial manufacture assumed that craftsmen added skill and imagination to raw materials which, when formed into finished products, had added value. After the Industrial Revolution, craftsmen became *workers* who ceased to contribute skill and imagination: they offered only labor, which became a commodity like wool or leather or wood. Machines tended by men (or women and children) produced the changes from raw material to finished product with results that were uniform and predictable. Craftsmen ceased to be important variables in production: they became an anonymous, invariable factor.

From a human standpoint the consequences of the Industrial Revolution were disastrous. As craft skills lost their unique value, work was turned into labor and, often, drudgery. Women and children competed to sell their labor with steadily diminishing bargaining power; workers' wages and living conditions were wretched. Ironically, the machines that created wealth and jobs brought poverty and lowered standards of living for those who tended them.

The sordidness of cities, the misery of the working classes, and the monotony of machine jobs led to a romantic escapism in the arts. Sensitive people could not conceive of art in a context which was so ruinous of human resources. And the early products of mechanization gave little contrary evidence: machine tools tried to imitate handmade ornament, with results totally unsuited to the materials and processes used. Craft revivals were attempted, notably by John Ruskin and William Morris; but they could not change the economic facts of life or art. The artistic problems raised by mass production were not effectively faced until Walter Gropius (1883–1969) established a new kind of educational and industrial institution—the Bauhaus—in the twentieth century.

Gropius realized that the essential difference between craft and machine production lay in *the control* of the process of making: one person in the crafts; a division of labor in industry. He had written a paper, "Industrial Prefabrication of Homes on a Unified Artistic Basis," which urged mass-pro-

**Mimi Vandermolen. Dashboard of the 1985 Ford Taurus. The New York Times Pictures**

Abstract sculptural quality in a mass-produced product. The soft shapes and rounded corners of the dash have practical as well as aesthetic values: safety, simplicity, logical organization, and easy legibility—which add up to a "user-friendly" instrument panel. Who could have imagined it when Ford set up his assembly line in 1909?

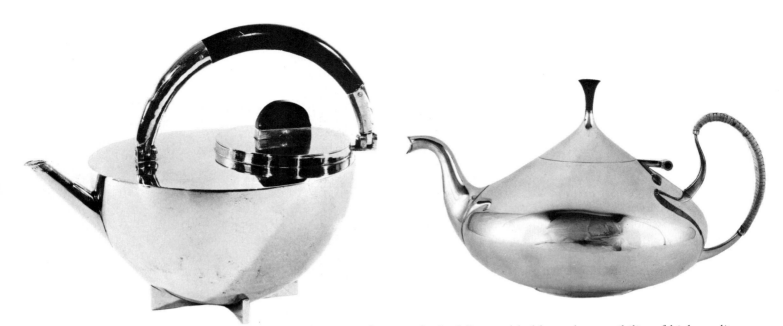

*above:* Marianne Brandt. Teapot. 1924. Nickel silver and ebony, 7" high. Collection, The Museum of Modern Art, New York. Phyllis B. Lambert Fund

The Bauhaus-type teapot of 1924, with its perfect geometry and no-nonsense surfaces, was the product of a love affair with mechanization. An ideological love affair. By 1953, craftsmen felt free to express their organic feelings: machine-form is still honored, but now the shapes are sexier. The idea of biological growth has slipped in.

*above right:* John Prip. Silver teapot. 1953. Museum of Contemporary Crafts, New York. Permanent Collection

German Rose Engine. c. 1750. Brass, 20½" high; weight about 50 lbs. British Crown Copyright, Science Museum, London

How could the machine tool be humanized? By converting it into "art"—by covering all its surfaces with irrelevant ornament.

duction techniques for building and held out the possibility of high-quality production through industrial methods. The net result of these ideas was the opening of the Bauhaus at Weimar, Germany, in 1919, with Gropius as its director: it was formed by combining a trade school with a school of fine arts.

At first, each Bauhaus student had two teachers, one an artist and the other a master craftsman, because there were no instructors who possessed the qualities of both. It was necessary to give art students experience with machine production so they could provide industry with the *integrated control* it lacked. Beyond machine forming and craftsmanship, the Bauhaus taught science and economics as well as the typical fine-arts curriculum of drawing, painting, sculpture, composition, and art history. In this way, industrial designers as we know them were first trained.

In 1925 the Bauhaus left Weimar and reestablished itself at Dessau, where a new faculty, now composed of Bauhaus graduates, combined the technician and artist in the same instructor. The school became an experimental workshop where models for mass production were continually developed by students and faculty. A mechanical idiom, or "machine style," was created, one that was distinctly different from handcraft styles. Of particular importance, hierarchies and status distinctions between "fine" artists, architects, and craftsmen were largely eliminated.

In 1933, when the Nazis came to power, the Bauhaus was driven out of Germany. Subsequently, one of its younger instructors, Lázló Moholy-Nagy (1895–1946), established an American branch in Chicago, where it was eventually absorbed into the Illinois Institute of Technology. By World War II, it was plain that the Bauhaus had created a new profession, industrial design; at the same time the education of artists throughout the world was fundamentally transformed.

**Form and Function**   Louis Sullivan (1856–1924), Frank Lloyd Wright's beloved teacher, originated the phrase, "Form follows function." Applied to architecture or manufactured objects, the phrase became an axiom for all modern design. It means that the outer shape or appearance of an object results from its inner operation; an object should look like what it is and does. There should be no deceptive appearances: metal should not imitate wood, plastic should not imitate marble. Usually, the design of buildings and objects began with an outer shell or facade, and then proceeded to divide and arrange interior space. As for function or working processes, ornament was "applied" to cover their nakedness, so to speak. Thus architecture and product design grew increasingly decorative; instead of following function, the form of a product followed prevailing tastes in period styles and ornamentation.

**Automobile grilles. Courtesy *Design Quarterly* magazine**

During the 1950s, American automobile designers embarked on a monumental "front-end" binge, which they followed with a tailfin orgy. A true example of American Baroque, the phenomenon had an industrial father and a psychological mother: the manufacturer's need for salable packages mated with the stylist's need to express his sculptural impulses.

Industrial design originated as an effort to bring unity and logic to the planning and production of machine-made objects. As it evolved, however, artistically irrelevant factors entered the scene. "Appearance design" emerged when manufacturers discovered that consumers could not tell the difference between functional redesign and a new look. Merchants discovered that any "redesign" had sales appeal. The new "machine style" could be used to make a product look as if it had been basically transformed. We got "streamlining" —slick surfaces for everything from automobiles to wristwatches.

We come, then, to a false kind of industrial design—styling. The periodic redesign or styling of products stimulates sales *whether or not* changes in physical function have taken place. And as we know, a newly styled product has the effect of making older designs look bad. The cycle of design, redesign, and new styling, leading to an apparent loss of value in older product models, is called *planned obsolescence*; it creates a peculiarly modern dilemma.

The planned obsolescence of useful objects has major economic implications. Industries need to use most of their productive capacity to keep their workers employed because unemployed workers cannot buy automobiles and refrigerators. So, persuading the public to use and discard goods rapidly is vital to maintain a healthy economy. Surely, planned obsolescence has helped create the American standard of living by making greater use of the productive capacity of industry. However, our standard of living may be defined too exclusively in terms of *how many* things we own and *how often* we replace them. Today, planned obsolescence and disposable design haunt

**Wilhelm von Debschitz. Inkstand. 1906. Bronze, 2⅜ × 6¾ × 8⅝". Württenbergisches Landesmuseum, Stuttgart**

An impressive but pretentious solution to the design of a useful object: Von Debschitz tried to transcend utility by disguising the function of the object beneath sculptural gestures.

us in the form of wasted energy, pollution, and uglification of the environment.

Now, industrial designers belong to the worlds of economics and marketing as well as art. They are trained to analyze a product and find the best combination of materials, processes, and forms to suit its function; their knowledge of production methods equips them to keep manufacturing costs to a minimum consistent with quality; they can design for every phase of production, including packaging, information, and display. But often they merely fabricate a new "skin" for a product—arriving at a result which is spuriously different. Can this be changed? Perhaps the competitive forces which made design crucial for commercial success will raise the designer's ethical level. Generally, we can rely on the integrity of the engineer who designs a bridge, or the dentist who extracts a tooth. We should also be able to rely on the integrity of designers—those who are responsible for what we see—from refrigerators to saucepans, from locomotives to chairs.

**Industrial Design: The Chair**   Until we sit on it, a chair is an abstract sculpture; it is also a complex engineering problem. The habit of sitting in chairs is carried on in many positions, for varied purposes, and with different physical equipment. We expect comfort, support, and stability from our seating, and we would like to get into and out of a chair with a certain amount of dignity. Some chairs have to be portable and light, others must be sturdy to resist abuse. Generally, chairs should not be bulky; today's dwellings cannot afford to invest in chairs that occupy space like piles of mattresses.

As sculpture, chairs possess symbolic value: they can look like thrones, beds, swings, saddles, or wire cages, reminding us of kings, queens, bishops, cowboys, or canaries. Chairs are masculine or feminine, juvenile or adult, shy or assertive. To a kitten or a crawling child, chairs are a forest of legs. To a mother of small children, chairs may represent nonwashable surfaces covered with peanut butter. Thus the symbolic, the practical, and the aesthetic combine in a chair to make it a formidable design problem.

A chair can reveal a complete philosophy. Designers often use it to express their convictions about structure, truth, strength, comfort, and decoration. For example, the famous Barcelona lounge chair by Mies van der Rohe eloquently demonstrates his architectural philosophy: God is in the details; use a minimum of materials; keep it simple; and "less is more." Technological innovation is also prominent: the cantilever principle is used in conjunction with the elasticity of metal; the same continuous metal bar serves as curved leg and back support. Aesthetically, the tufted leather cushions provide bulk, warmth, and color in contrast to the thin metal members. A masterpiece of

*left:* Constantin Brancusi. *The Beginning of the World: Sculpture for the Blind.* 1916. Marble, 12 × 6"; base (plaster), 10" high. Philadelphia Museum of Art. The Louise and Walter Arensberg Collection

The biomorphic perfection of the egg can be exploited at several design levels: it can yield practical dividends (the Aarnie chair); or it can be enlisted in the service of tactility (the Brancusi sculpture).

*right:* Eero Aarnie. Gyro Chair. c. 1965–66. Polyester reinforced fiberglass, 21 × 36¾ × 36¾". Distributed by Stendig, Inc., New York

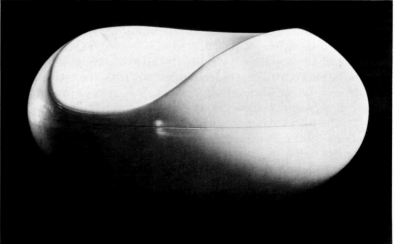

Ida Kohlmeyer. *Mythic Chair.* 1984. Mixed media on wood, 40 × 25 × 24". Courtesy Arthur Roger Gallery, New Orleans

A painter's approach to a chair. The basic bentwood shapes already suggest the armature of a growing thing; Kohlmeyer has taken the hints offered by the wooden framework and added organs in hot color. Now the tubular forms really live.

design, the Barcelona chair will probably endure as a modern classic for years to come—remarkable when we consider its date, 1929.

Where cheap, easily stacked and transported seating is needed—especially for public purposes—designers often use molded plastic forms with tubular metal legs and supporting elements. Since cost is a factor, molded plastics can replace expensive and destructible leather or fabric coverings. Because the philosophy of modern design was built on the requirements of a mass market and low unit cost, expensive chair ideas have been regularly "adapted" and sold to a large public at low prices. This was the economic as well as aesthetic achievement of our "pioneers" of design: Charles Eames, George Nelson, Henry Dreyfuss, Russel Wright, and Raymond Loewy; they brought good design to the American masses, creating markets, jobs, and "taste"—a hunger for excellence at low cost.

Today a huge world market for good design has emerged. Production facilities are widely dispersed, international transportation is cheap, and people in remote places have acquired appetites for quality at reasonable prices. We are entering an era in which the tools of production will be radically transformed—miniaturized, computerized, and electronically linked. There will be many new centers of production and distribution. In this new era, industrial design will be a crucial factor in capturing and holding markets, conserving energy and raw materials, and satisfying human needs yet to be discovered. Or created. The connections between aesthetics and ethical design will become ever more important. We shall have to answer such urgent questions as the following: Is it useful? Do we need it? Is it durable? How will it affect the environment? Does it deserve to last?

**Wendell Castle. Oak-and-leather chair. 1963**

Castle is a contemporary craftsman who chose to develop the sculptural possibilities of the Thonet furniture of the 1860s, the Art Nouveau swirls of the early 1900s, and the tubular-metal construction of the 1920s.

Gebrüder Thonet. Rocking chair. 1860. Bent beechwood; cane, 37½" high. Collection, The Museum of Modern Art, New York. Gift of Café Nicholson

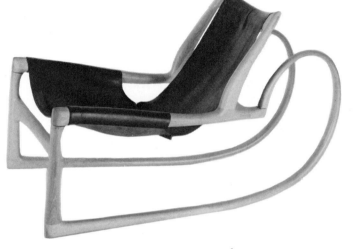

Charles Eames. Lounge chair. 1958. Polished die cast aluminum, black painted tube, charcoal Naugahyde padded with vinyl foam, nylon glides, 35 × 22 × 27". Collection, The Museum of Modern Art, New York. Gift of the manufacturer: Herman Miller, Inc.

Ludwig Mies van der Rohe. "Barcelona" chair. 1929. Chrome-plated flat steel bars with pigskin cushions, 29⅞ × 29½ × 29⅝". Collection, The Museum of Modern Art, New York. Gift of Knoll International

**Gunnar Aagaard Andersen. Armchair. 1964. Polyurethane, 29½ × 44¼ × 35¼". Collection, The Museum of Modern Art, New York. Gift of the designer**

Ostensibly, this chair of poured urethane plastic represents the creative marriage of art and technology. But the object makes no real contribution to chair design: it functions mainly as a demonstration of liquid tactility.

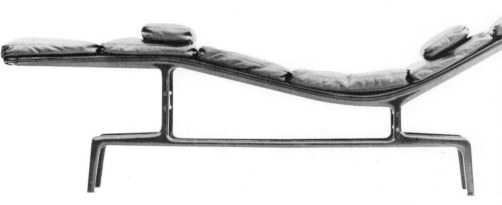

Le Corbusier, Pierre Jeanneret, and Charlotte Perriand. Chaise longue. 1927. Chrome-plated tubular steel, painted steel, fabric, and leather, 24 × 19⁹⁄₁₆ × 62⁵⁄₁₆". Collection, The Museum of Modern Art, New York. Gift of Thonet Brothers, Inc.

**Charles Eames. Chaise longue. 1968. Nylon coated aluminum frame, 28¾ × 75 × 17½". Designed for Herman Miller, Inc., New York**

The 1968 chaise by Charles Eames builds on Le Corbusier's architectural solution to the reclining chair (1927). But Eames has new materials to work with: foam-rubber cushions, zippered pillows, and a cast-aluminum frame covered with dark nylon.

**Olivier Mourgue. Chairs. 1965**

The influence of painters Arp and Miró on a modern French furniture design.

**Wooden door with carving in relief, from Baule, Ivory Coast. 51⅛ × 24⅜". Rietberg Museum, Zurich. Von der Heydt Collection**

There is no difference between "fine" and "applied" in African art: utilitarian purpose and expressive form coexist harmoniously.

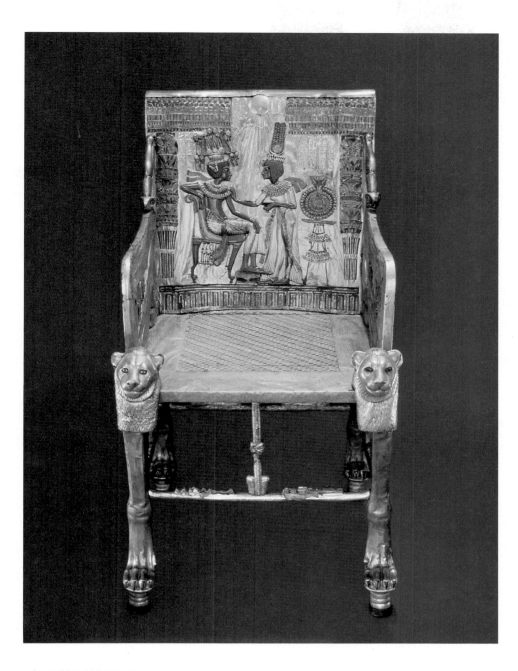

*above:* Tutankhamen's throne. c. 1350 B.C. Gold-sheathed wood, carved and inlaid with precious stones, 40⅜ × 23⅜". Egyptian Museum, Cairo

The royal seat is protected by lions, but they don't look very ferocious. Emphasis is on the symbolism and prerogatives of power: gold-covered carving, inlays of gems, the image of an attentive queen, and the sun god shining down on the king, his lineal descendant.

*right:* Benvenuto Cellini. *Saltcellar of Francis I.* c. 1540. Gold and enamel, 10¼ × 13⅛". Kunsthistorisches Museum, Vienna

Fine art or craft? Obviously, there is more here than a salt-and-pepper container. An extravagant allegory (he represents salt, she represents pepper) was needed to satisfy the taste of a Renaissance monarch.

Polynesian game board (*konane*) from the
Hawaiian Islands. 8" high. National Park Service,
Hawaii Volcanoes National Park. Gift of Mrs.
Harry Edmondson, 1956

Only eight inches high, this little table could
pass for a monumental sculpture. Why? Because
the Polynesian carver concentrated on the
essential forms needed to dramatize the
supporting function of those fierce little men (or
animals). Thus the structural elements have
tremendous energy. What a powerful game of
checkers could be played on that board!

Ice bucket with lid. Magnus Stephensen design
executed by G. Pedersen for Georg Jensen Ltd.,
Copenhagen, Denmark. 1951. Sterling silver and
raffia, 42½ × 6¾". Collection, The Museum of
Modern Art, New York. Gift of Philip Johnson

This silver container is surely a craft object—
handwrought in a precious metal. But notice
how its form reflects the influence of machine
manufacture. No allegory, no symbolism; all we
have is an elegant way to carry ice cubes from
the refrigerator to the place where an empty
glass is waiting.

118

**Micronesian stool for grating coconuts, from the Mariana Islands**

Ancient folk-craft objects created by anonymous artisans. The jug is one of thousands like it; the stool is a variant of a standard type. Both have almost mechanical qualities of clarity and precision; both exhibit exquisite formal relationships. These objects show that good design is universal and ageless; they would be elegant and graceful even if they were mass-produced in Detroit or Grand Rapids.

Jug, from Kültepe, northern Anatolia. 18th century B.C. Clay with red-brown slip, 13¾" high. Museum of Archaeology, Ankara

*above:* Umberto Boccioni. *Development of a Bottle in Space.* 1912. Silvered bronze (cast 1931), $15 \times 12\frac{7}{8} \times 23\frac{3}{4}$". Collection, The Museum of Modern Art, New York. Aristide Maillol Fund

*left:* Lawrence Vail. *Bottle with Stopper.* 1945. Collection Mr. and Mrs. Bernard Reis, New York

*right:* Claes Oldenburg. *Lipstick Ascending on Caterpillar Tracks.* 1969 (reworked 1974). Painted fiberglass tip, aluminum tube, and steel body, 10" high. Yale University Art Gallery, New Haven, Connecticut. Gift of the Colossal Keepsake Corporation

Three objects that tell the story of craft and industrial design. Vail's bottle is a fetish object; it could be the container for a sorcerer's magic potion. Boccioni's bottle is so intellectual it can't hold anything: it represents a search for the object's inner geometry. Oldenburg's *Lipstick* is a gigantic "put-on"—a burlesque of sex, advertising, mass production, and the Pentagon.

# PART TWO

# THE STYLES OF ART

The concept of style is indispensable for the study of art, and yet it can confuse us because the word has so many meanings. Usually, it means the art of a particular historical period, but it may also refer to the art of a nation (the Italian Renaissance), or a region (the Barbizon style) or a group of artists (the Pre-Raphaelites). It can designate an individual artist's manner (Titianesque, Rubensian, Cézannesque), or it can refer to a technical or artistic approach (Color Divisionism, Pointillism, Photorealism). Style can also be used as a term of approval: "He (or she) has *style*." Or, it may refer to a new look in cars, clothes, and kitchen appliances; here "style" is equivalent to the latest fad or fashion. All the uses of the concept have one purpose—the arrangement of a variety of objects into categories that make them easier to recognize, understand, and talk about. At the most general level, therefore, a style is a grouping or classification of artworks (by time, region, appearance, technique, etc.) that makes further study and analysis possible.

As with scientific classification, the sorting of phenomena into categories is based on the observation of common traits or qualities. Styles of art, therefore, can be thought of as families. Just as members of a family have features which give them a "family resemblance," works of art may also look like each other. They may have differences, too, but they have *some* common traits which we can see or sense, and that makes classification possible. That recognizable element may consist of a certain use of line, color, or shape; or it may be felt in a qualitative sense. In other words, style may be visible on the surface of an artwork or in its overall feeling. This overall, or *pervasive* quality of a work is often the basis for its classification; stylistic terms like "classical" and "romantic" seem to rely on the viewer's feelings about an artwork as much as on the artist's technique.

With an understanding of styles, we can read the so-called hidden language of art. Style helps us find meanings beneath the subject matter and apparent purpose of an artwork. Just as handwriting reveals meanings that are not in words alone, style can tell us much about an artist's environment, values, and heritage. Indeed, archaeologists and anthropologists use style to reconstruct whole cultures: they put pieces of stylistic evidence together like a mosaic, trying to form a complete picture or idea of a culture. Similarly, we can study an art style to build an idea of the inner condition of an artist, a people, or perhaps, the evolution of human consciousness as a whole.

# STYLISTIC CHANGE

Although several styles may coexist—especially in modern cultures—there have been periods when a single style was dominant. However, every style is succeeded by another, and in recent years styles have succeeded each other very rapidly. Of all the styles described by art history, only folk or peasant styles seem to persist regardless of social change—a phenomenon which is probably due to the isolation of folk cultures. Today, however, few groups are completely isolated from world culture; consequently, folk and peasant art is disappearing. This disappearance calls attention to the dynamic character of styles in the mainstream cultures.

In the mainstream cultures, then, what accounts for stylistic change? New scientific knowledge? New forms of technology? Fresh artistic responses to the social and spiritual environment? Can we say that artists invent styles out of whole cloth, so to speak? Do styles catch fire, grow into conflagrations, and then burn themselves out?

Scholarly answers to these questions differ according to the discipline of the observer. Art historians may attribute stylistic change to artists working out the possibilities of the styles they have inherited. Critics may see artists generating whole new ways of seeing—ways that become part of our common visual and emotional equipment. Social scientists may attribute stylistic change to shifts in the political and economic climate; thus artists react more than they innovate. I am inclined to believe they do all these things: they react and they invent; they inherit and they transform.

Why do we try to explain stylistic change? Because we suspect that changes in style may anticipate changes in life as a whole. Perhaps a style that many artists adopt represents a form of adaptation to change in the total culture. In that case, artists act as social antennae—as scouts, heralds, and prophesiers. Also, there is the possibility that artists *cause* changes in the way people see the world and cope with their experience. In other words, artists may be the ship's rudder rather than its radar.

Regardless of our views about stylistic change, we think we can recognize the emergence of new styles and the decline of old ones. They seem to have the traits of living organisms; we speak of their life cycles as if they were flowers that bud, bloom, and wilt; like people they have a childhood, maturity, and old age. These analogies may be inexact but they call attention to something we are all aware of: style seems to have a secret connection to large trends in human affairs.

The reasons for studying the styles, then, are as follows: (1) to acquire useful categories for thinking about the common traits of artworks produced at various times and places; (2) to understand the artists, periods, countries, and regions in whose art a style frequently reappears; (3) to compare or judge works of art that seem related by look or feeling or subject matter; (4) to understand the connections between an artist's creative strategy and our reactions to his or her work; (5) to get special information—"inside dope"—about impending social changes.

# THE STYLE OF OBJECTIVE ACCURACY

The style of objective accuracy is familiar to most people whether they have studied art or not. They feel confident about judging works in this style since they can compare a painting or sculpture with its real-life original. (Of course, the real-life original has to be remembered—which is not always easy.) Still, optical accuracy, or convincing resemblance to life, is for many persons the principal way of evaluating artistic excellence.

Most of us have good eyesight, so we believe we are good judges of an artist's skill in creating illusions of reality. To create such illusions, some artists reproduce every visual detail of a model, assuming that a convincingly real work is the sum of carefully observed and rendered parts. Sometimes this kind of artistic approach is called "realistic," although the invention of photography has made it almost obsolete. Yet recently it has made a phenomenal comeback: realism has enormous staying power.

The masters of the past knew how to create realistic illusions without reproducing everything the eye sees: the idea was to seize the essentials. Today, many artists see little reason to compete with the camera; for them the main problem of art is to create credible images through a selective use of the visual facts. Well, what are the right facts? And are they the same for every artist? Objective accuracy seems to require more than good eyesight to be successful.

In this chapter we discuss the varieties of expression possible within an objectively accurate style. We examine the different ways artists represent reality without reproducing all of its details. Also, we ask why some artists prefer accuracy of representation to abstraction or distortion. The style of objective accuracy rises and falls in popularity, but it appears to be a permanent way of expressing feelings and ideas. To discover those feelings and ideas we need to distinguish between the thoughtless rendering of optical facts and the use of objective representation to convey meanings beyond the immediately visible.

## THE IMITATION OF APPEARANCES

What accounts for our fascination with a painting or sculpture that looks exactly like its real-life model? Why do artists try to imitate precisely what the eye sees or the camera records? These are fundamental questions since so

Duane Hanson. *The Shoppers.* 1976. Cast vinyl, polychromed; lifesize. The Nerman Family Collection

Perhaps this is the ultimate in objective accuracy, that is, realism without the artist's "personal" interference. But in his choice of people, clothes, and accessories, Hanson expresses a definite point of view. What is it?

many people believe accurate representation is the basis of art. Also, there is the evidence of our earliest known art—Paleolithic cave painting: it is highly representational, beautifully accurate. Children, too, want to represent objects realistically, although they do not succeed at first. That is because they don't understand adult notions of visual logic; but as they grow older, they try to imitate appearances truly. Accurate imitation, it seems, is part of coming to terms with the world.

Psychologically, the imitation of reality represents an effort to *control* reality. At deep levels of awareness, our desire to paint a head so that it seems alive is part of an effort to develop mastery over life itself. Drawing an object over and over again creates confidence in our ability to know it, to dominate it, to make it our own. We think we are less likely to be victims of chance in a world we cannot understand if we make images that are good enough to replace pieces of reality—pieces of the world we must deal with.

For viewers, realistic works may be fascinating because we admire the artist's skill. At another level, viewers are attracted by convincing imitations because they know they are looking at *artistic* effects—not real flesh, leaves, cloth, and so on. For that reason many of us enjoy fool-the-eye paintings; we get a peculiar pleasure in being deceived. There are stories going back to the ancient Greeks about artists who could paint grapes so faithfully that even the birds pecked at them. Perceptually, the appeal of a lifelike work relies on a peculiar tension between appearance and reality: we engage in a continuous comparing or matching operation between what we see and what we know.

Another kind of accuracy grows out of the interest in narration—telling the viewer as honestly as possible what really happened. From its beginning, art has played a role in transmitting information. Today, artists have been largely replaced by photojournalists as recorders of events; nevertheless, artists continue to work in a storytelling mode. Thus Andrew Wyeth (born

Grant Wood. *American Gothic.* 1930. Oil on board, 29⅞ × 24⅞". The Art Institute of Chicago. Friends of American Art Collection

Otto Dix. *My Parents.* 1921. Oil on canvas, 39¾ × 45¼". Kunstmuseum, Basel

1917) employs a straightforward descriptive style to tell his stories about the lives of plain people and places. In *Christina's World*, for example, he pictures the lonely struggle of a physically handicapped woman. Through close attention to detail Wyeth establishes a mood of grim reality—plus hope. The tempera medium gives this picture a dry, matter-of-fact quality that heightens our awareness of Christina's hard existence. The selection and placement of details are crucially important; notice the high horizon and the low position of Christina's figure. We see more of the earth than of the sky, and this connects her body closely to the ground; distances must be tremendous in her groping world. Wyeth also generates emotion through the use of perspective—in the small, distant building, and in the vast expanse of field between Christina and the house. It is not easy to paint a large area of unimportant material—grass—and keep it interesting to the viewer. Yet Wyeth manages to give the field a powerful psychological charge—mainly because of the tension between the woman and the house: we view the grass as space that has to be painfully crossed.

Americans usually favor accurate, matter-of-fact descriptions of everyday life. This may have grown out of frontier suspicions of old-world wealth; traditional civilizations were associated with corruption caused by the pursuit of luxury, whereas we were too young or poor to be decadent. *American Gothic* by Grant Wood (1892–1942) hints at this idea in its celebration of the plain, hard-working virtues of rural life. The picture and its title constitute an ironic comparison with the soaring complexity of real Gothic architecture. In the background we see a wood-frame dwelling in the so-called Carpenter Gothic style—our version of the illustrious European style ornately carved in stone. But the sardonic force of this work is based mainly on the faces of the farm couple: they are as plain as Gothic is fancy. Their simplicity is severe and slightly pathetic; but authentic, too.

Wood's homely couple might be compared with the double portrait, *My Parents*, by the German artist Otto Dix (1891–1969). We seem to see similar human types although Dix is less photographic in creating his overwhelmingly realistic impression. He uses enlarged hands and deep wrinkles—wrinkles echoed in the clothing—to convey a feeling of struggle and awkwardness, a feeling that Europeans associate with the peasantry. Wood distorts his heads only slightly, to stress their oval shape (repeated in the shape of the pitchfork) whereas Dix employs much more distortion and exaggeration—traits we usually call Expressionist. Then, can this be a work of objective accuracy? Yes, because the narrative element, the reportorial

Andrew Wyeth. *Christina's World.* 1948. Tempera on gesso panel, 32¼ × 47¾". Collection, The Museum of Modern Art, New York. Purchase

details, and those highly believable faces dominate the painting. We are convinced that we are looking at the facts, the *real* facts.

## THE ARTIST AS DETACHED OBSERVER

Another characteristic of objective accuracy is concealment of technique. It looks as if the artist wants to deny that a picture is made of paint, or that a sculpture is made of clay: the final product must not show the marks of the artist's tools. This is because the artist wants to focus attention on the subject, not on the way the picture was made. There is a certain modesty implied by this approach—artistic self-effacement for the sake of heightening the illusions in the image. At one extreme, Soutine (page 26) deliberately reveals his brushstrokes; at the other, Charles Sheeler conceals them. Soutine expresses his subject's anxiety; Sheeler uses a smooth, impersonal technique to create a purely "factual" image.

Normally, a realistic style does not tell us much about the artist's personality. If we learn anything about the artist as an individual, it is through choice of theme or overall organization of forms. There is a scientific flavor in this approach: scientists, as we know, try to separate their observations from their private feelings. They hope other investigators will come to the same conclusions if they perform the same experiment and examine the same data. The artist-as-realist has a similar goal: his or her work must look true regardless of the observer's bias or personality. The artwork should appear to be almost anonymous, with only the signature revealing the author.

Perhaps the suppression of personality is due to the artist's wish to make vision—the act of seeing—the real point of experiencing his work. In a sense, the Impressionists fit this description: using scientific theories of color and optics, they concentrated on appearances more than their feelings; their images look as if they were suddenly captured by an impersonal eye. The Rouen Cathedral series of Claude Monet (1840–1926) constitutes a determined effort to represent the same building under different light conditions according to a theory of color that was considered very "realistic"—that is,

Charles Sheeler. *City Interior.* 1936. Aqueous adhesive and oil on composition board, 22⅛ × 28". Worcester Art Museum, Worcester, Massachusetts. Purchased in memory of Jonathan and Elizabeth M. Sawyer

based on a solid foundation in color physics. So we can think of Impressionism as a style of objective accuracy; it was a disciplined endeavor to use the science of color to depict objects in their actual atmospheric settings. The Impressionists realized that it is essential for artists to consider the illumination and atmosphere that enable them to see. That realization may not account for the beauty of their canvases, but it does indicate how scientific seeing—objective accuracy—can have important aesthetic consequences.

In the work of Edgar Degas (1834–1917), we see a style of rich, Impressionist color combined with extreme faithfulness to the reality of objects. In *The Glass of Absinthe*, Degas seems to play the role of reporter, of detached observer of humanity: he lets us read the character of the figures for ourselves. They are caught casually, toward the side of the picture, as if the artist were using a candid camera. As a matter of fact, Degas was influenced by the seemingly accidental compositions of photography; his pictures are designed to look as if their subjects had been suddenly discovered. As a result, Degas's ballet dancers, jockeys, and bathers look exceptionally truthful; we sense they are not theatrically staged. Henri de Toulouse-Lautrec (1864–1901) also employed a photographic sort of composition combined with psychological honesty. His portrait *M. Boileau at the Café* uses a similar diagonal device, except that the main figure is more centrally located. To be sure, M. Boileau is not portrayed as drunk, depressed, or hard-up; on the contrary, he is alert, well-fed, and well-heeled—the solid embodiment of bourgeois self-satisfaction. Whether the subject is prosperous or down-and-out, the style of objective accuracy is neutral.

*below:* Claude Monet. *Cathedral in Sunshine.* 1894. Oil on canvas, 42⅛ × 28⅞". Musée d'Orsay, Paris. Bequest of Isaac de Camondo, 1911

*right:* Claude Monet. *Cathedral in Fog.* 1894. Oil on canvas, 39⅜ × 25⅝". Musée d'Orsay, Paris. Bequest of Isaac de Camondo, 1911

Degas and Lautrec used Impressionist color, a photographic way of seeing details, and a compositional method borrowed from the Japanese. Their basic psychological stance was also similar; as detached observers of human behavior they did not insinuate their own moral judgments. We might call them the radical empiricists of painting: artistic forms should be based on observation of the real world, regardless of how we feel, and regardless of what we think we know.

For the detached observer, omission of the observed facts is a vice, a type of visual deceit, a form of artistic immorality. The Philadelphia painter Thomas Eakins (1884–1916) fits that ideal of honesty; he spent much of his career in an almost fanatical pursuit of visual truth—the sort of truth that results from scientific knowledge of what is seen. Eakins's students were taught human anatomy by dissecting cadavers; and in his own work he was determined to tell "the whole truth and nothing but . . ." This is clear in his portrayal of the unvarnished facts of surgical technique in *The Agnew Clinic* of 1889. The picture did not especially please Dr. Agnew; it was not pleasant for him to be shown lecturing with blood on his hands. But Eakins was too stubborn to compromise the facts; he had been just as honest in portraying a blood-spattered surgeon and assistants in *The Gross Clinic* of 1875. Eakins insisted on telling everything, whereas those surgeons probably wanted a painting like Rembrandt's (1606–1669) *Anatomy Lesson of Dr. Tulp*. There we see a respectful tribute to the medical pursuit of learning. To be sure, Rembrandt shows a cadaver—not a pretty subject—but he manages to focus our attention on the searching mind more than the dead man's flesh.

## THE ARTIST AS SELECTIVE EYE

The artistic concern with accuracy need not result in photographic realism. Often illusions of reality can be created by simplification—eliminating details the eye might see. Or there can be a piling up of detail—more than would be visible at one time. This can happen when the artist becomes obsessed with

*left:* Edgar Degas. *The Glass of Absinthe.* 1876. Oil on canvas, 36½ × 26¾" Musée d'Orsay, Paris. Bequest of Isaac de Camondo, 1911

*above:* Henri de Toulouse-Lautrec. *M. Boileau at the Café.* 1893. Gouache on cardboard, 31½ × 25". The Cleveland Museum of Art. Hinman B. Hurlbut Collection

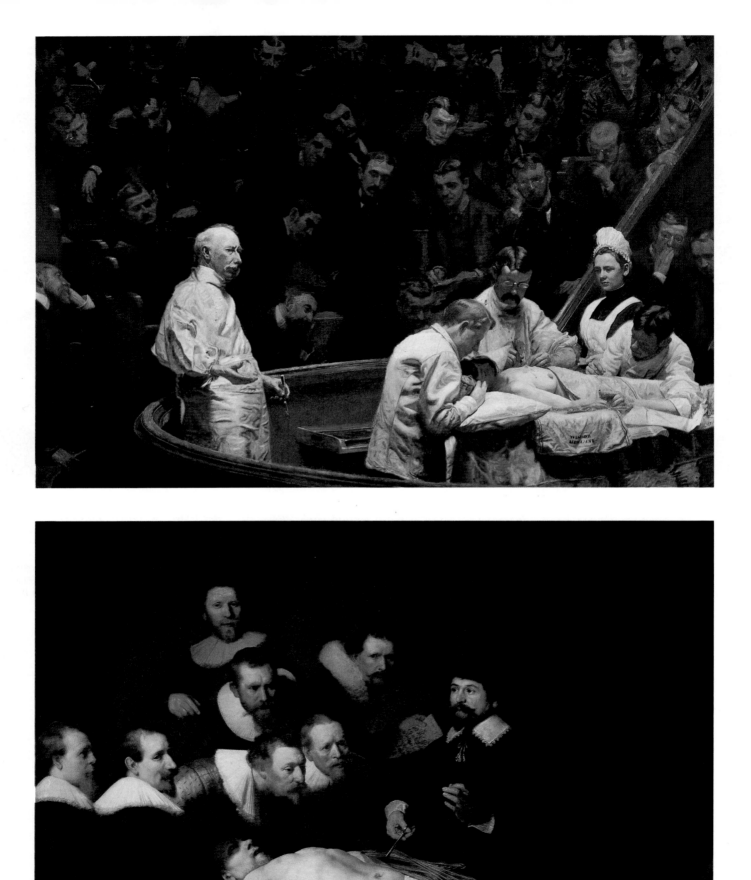

*opposite above:* Thomas Eakins. *The Agnew Clinic.* 1889. Oil on canvas, 6'2½" × 10'10½". School of Medicine, The University of Pennsylvania, Philadelphia

*opposite below:* Rembrandt van Rijn. *The Anatomy Lesson of Dr. Tulp.* 1632. Oil on canvas, 66¼ × 85¼". Royal Cabinet of Paintings, Mauritshuis, The Hague, The Netherlands

*left:* Thomas Eakins. *The Gross Clinic.* 1875. Oil on canvas, 96 × 78". The Jefferson Medical College of Philadelphia

*below:* Ivan Albright. Detail of *The Picture of Dorian Gray.* 1943–44. The Art Institute of Chicago. Gift of the artist

a subject and has trouble leaving it; some artists embellish and enrich a surface for years, selecting more and more, eliminating less and less: the image becomes a kind of visual storehouse. Ivan Albright's paintings result from that long, patient accumulation of detail. Appropriately enough, he was chosen to paint the portrait for a film based on Oscar Wilde's *The Picture of Dorian Gray.* As in Wilde's story, Albright's painting grew old and ugly along with its subject. Viewers approach such detailed works with great seriousness; the evidence of long and sustained effort creates a special type of empathy. And the artist benefits from that empathy; we respect work, and our respect is converted into belief: Albright *has* to be telling the truth.

Edward Hopper is different; he simplifies while maintaining the strong sense of a real place. *Nighthawks*, for example, is built out of quiet, uncomplicated areas of color and tone. The brushwork is hardly evident; instead we sense the physical materials of the scene. A mood of silence—of a great city asleep—is created by small inactive figures, crisp shadows thrown by artificial light, and the dominance of vertical and horizontal lines. Hopper is not a tricky or dextrous painter; he shows us just enough of a person or building to permit identification; each area of the canvas is pruned of nonessentials. Like Wyeth, Hopper relies on placement and size relationships for psychological effect. As for his unexciting execution, it builds its own kind of quiet drama. Notice, too, that the mood of this painting depends on an abstract design: the intersection of two horizontal rectangles. Within those rectangles Hopper skillfully manipulates paint thicknesses to produce variations of light and dark: it is *paint* that gives us the solidity of the place and the heaviness of the hour.

In Albright's *Into the World There Came a Soul Called Ida*, accumulated

Edward Hopper. *Nighthawks*. 1942. Oil on canvas, 30 × 60". The Art Institute of Chicago. Friends of American Art Collection

detail is used to describe the wear and tear of the aging process. We also see that physical and psychological deterioration fascinate the artist. But we may also sense the artist's compassion; Ida's face is shown in a tragic light, as she realizes that clothes and cosmetics cannot restore her youth. Not even hope. The buildup of homely detail seems to create a new organism, Ida, who is both painted surface and human document—a person trapped by time, flesh, and sad experience.

The portrait of Elsa Maxwell by René Bouché (1896–1963) employs a different kind of accuracy to express the drama of aging. Bouché views his subject from below her eye level—which is not very flattering to a stout, elderly person. Also, the lighting is harsh and Elsa's figure overfills the canvas. Finally, there is a nervous, comic quality about her expression. Yet oddly, a peculiar kind of respect is earned by someone who is presented honestly, without heroics or prettification. The image of this woman reaches a level of human dignity despite—or because of—the fact that the artist presents her in a hard light, at a bad angle, in an uncomfortable position.

In sculpture, the Italian artist Giacomo Manzù (1908–1991) offers us a refined sort of realism. It has roots in Renaissance classicism and yet it appeals to modern tastes nourished on abstraction. *Girl in Chair* combines careful observation with an elimination of detail so subtle that it is hard to say where the figure has been simplified. Actually, the basic forms have been stripped of all but their most essential qualities of size and shape. Yet the figure has extraordinary psychological presence. Even the chair has a curious perfection: its spare, open form provides just the right contrast to the roundness of the girl's figure. In choosing a subject who is neither child nor woman, Manzù faced a difficult challenge: he had to suggest the changing body and personality of a nice-looking girl without making her look like a dressmaker's dummy. His solution was to combine accuracy in the overall dimensions with slightly softened modeling in the subordinate forms. The result is a strong awareness of the figure's geometry and weight distribution; Manzù approaches abstraction while staying in touch with observed reality.

Ivan Albright. *Into the World There Came a Soul Called Ida.* 1929-30.
Oil on canvas, 55 × 46". The Art Institute of Chicago. Gift of the artist

René Bouché. *Elsa Maxwell.* 1958-59.
Collection Mrs. René Bouché, New York

Wilhelm Lehmbruck. *Seated Youth (the Friend).* 1917. Composite tinted
and plaster, 40⅝ × 30 × 45". National Gallery of Art, Washington, D.C.
Andrew W. Mellon Purchase Fund

Giacomo Manzù. *Girl in Chair.* 1955.
Bronze, 44¾" high. The Hirshhorn
Museum and Sculpture Garden,
Smithsonian Institution, Washington,
D.C. Gift of Joseph H. Hirshhorn, 1966

Manzù's pubescent girl might be compared to *Seated Youth* by Wilhelm Lehmbruck (1881–1919). Here, too, we see careful observation of the youthful body together with simplification of surfaces. But Lehmbruck's figure expresses fatigue or despair in contrast to the girl's more confident attitude. Also, Lehmbruck departs from objective accuracy in his elongation of forms. This stretching of the figure's normal dimensions conveys the idea of rapid growth—the physical unease and psychological tension that adolescents often feel. When working in a realistic style, the artist can heighten the possibilities of emotional expression by departing—even slightly—from complete physical accuracy.

Suppression of detail does not succeed, however, unless the artist has observed a subject carefully. He must *know* that subject as well as see its surface characteristics. Otherwise, essential traits will be lost: the result will be simple and empty rather than simple and significant. An artwork is the end result of a long process of observation and simplification—in Albright's richly elaborated canvases, or in the simplified surfaces of Manzù and Lehmbruck. But notice that in departing from the facts, Lehmbruck *created new facts*; his use of distortion represented a decision to sacrifice accuracy in favor of heightened emotional appeal. Apparently, art involves trade-offs; it is a game played according to rules the artist recognizes. One of our tasks is to find out what those rules are; then we can decide how well the game has been played.

## VARIATIONS OF THE STYLE

Merely by reporting what they see, artists reveal their individual viewpoints. For example, in his painting *Handball*, Ben Shahn uses a set of strangely separated figures to express his feelings about inner-city life. Those clumsy-looking boys belong to a totally different world from Christina's. Yet both

pictures employ isolated figures, and both show large areas of relatively uncluttered space. Shahn paints some urban detail around the edges of the canvas to establish the setting, just as Wyeth shows some farm buildings at the top of his canvas, silhouetted against the horizon. Like Wyeth, Shahn also freezes the action of his characters. But Shahn's figures look rumpled and lumpy; their bodies lack Christina's peculiar grace. Awkward or not, they are trying to find excitement in a very dreary place. If Shahn's figures look pathetic, it is a general, collective pathos: they are infected by the sadness of their environment. Christina's tragedy is more personal because Wyeth has painted her as the victim of a misfortune which is hers alone. Shahn's realism is devoted to the problems of people in the aggregate; Wyeth concentrates on the drama of the individual.

What about the realistic examination of the self? John Kane's (1860–1934) *Self-Portrait* shows how an untrained artist looks at himself honestly and tries to tell the truth about what he sees. Stripped to the waist, and looking straight ahead, he paints his aging body as accurately as he can. The resulting image reveals a combination of pugnacity, pride in strength, and exceptional candor about the kind of man he is. Notice that the edges of the forms are hard and sharp: the modeling of flesh has been achieved with difficulty. Naive artists tend to use rigid outlines to describe the world. They can rarely use masses of color and tone skillfully; that normally calls for art-school training. But if Kane wanted to gloss over the facts, he wouldn't know how; it was a matter of pride to tell the truth straight and plain. This explains why we admire primitive portraits: the artist doesn't know any tricks, so he shows us people as they really are.

The art of Charles Sheeler (1883–1965) seems closely related to photography; he was, in fact, a distinguished photographer. However, in paintings like *Upper Deck* there is an emphasis on geometric purity of form rather than the real surfaces and edges of things. The machinery in this picture is immaculately white, perfectly regular in shape, without blemish or wear. Sheeler

*left:* John Kane. *Self-Portrait.* 1929. Oil on canvas over composition board, 36⅛ × 27⅛". Collection, The Museum of Modern Art, New York. Abby Aldrich Rockefeller Fund

*above:* Stanley Spencer. *Self-Portrait.* 1936. Oil on canvas, 24½ × 18⅛". Stedelijk Museum, Amsterdam

Although his painterly technique is more accomplished, Spencer exhibits the same attitude toward the self—the same asceticism and absence of posturing—that we see in Kane's self-portrait.

*opposite above:* Diego Velázquez. *Sebastian de Morra.* 1643–44. Oil on canvas, 41¾ × 31⅞". The Prado, Madrid

Here the style of objective accuracy reveals its capacity for moral sensitivity. Velázquez presents us with a dignified and compassionate portrayal of a dwarf kept as a living toy by the Spanish court.

*opposite below:* Ben Shahn. *Handball.* 1939. Tempera on paper over composition board, 22¾ × 31¼". Collection, The Museum of Modern Art, New York. Abby Aldrich Rockefeller Fund

Charles Sheeler. *Upper Deck.* 1929. Oil on canvas, 29⅛ × 22⅛". Fogg Art Museum, Harvard University, Cambridge, Massachusetts. Louise E. Bettens Fund

The pristine whiteness of these motors and ducts expresses a kind of reverence for machinery.

William M. Harnett. *Old Models.* 1892. Oil on canvas, 54 × 28". Courtesy, Museum of Fine Arts, Boston. The Hayden Collection

seems to be a realist but he actually portrays a world in which age, noise, dirt, and confusion have been eliminated. Accurate representation combined with an almost photographic technique create a highly convincing result. However, it is an idealized result because accidents and natural variation—the effects of time and chance—have been eliminated.

Another type of realism—"magic realism"—falls within the style of objective accuracy. A good nineteenth-century example is *Old Models* by William M. Harnett (1848–1892). Such pictures re-create the retinal image of arranged objects—much like a photograph, but without the texture of paint on canvas. In addition, the arrangement of old or much-loved objects provides a comfortable set of associations: the viewer is invited to enjoy little moments of philosophic contemplation in recognizing the relatedness of things and the beauty of common substances, plus the failure of art to capture reality absolutely. And there are the visual thrills of seeing painted nails driven into painted wood, painted letters on painted paper, and so on. The "magic" of this realism lies in the fact that our eyes can be deceived. A painter—a visual artist—forces us to question the reliability of vision itself.

Harnett and the "little masters" of seventeenth-century Holland (who were magic realists, too) may have anticipated Surrealism, which also relies on magical illusions. However, the Surrealists preferred weird or uncanny juxtapositions of objects, using them to generate psychological shock and a retreat into the unconscious. Harnett, at most, wanted to challenge our faith in sense experience as the only guide to truth. But it is a comfortable sort of challenge; we come away from his paintings feeling fairly good about our optical equipment.

## DEVICES OF OBJECTIVE ACCURACY

We have seen several examples of the ways artists create convincing representations of reality. Obviously, accuracy of size and shape relationships—"correct" drawing and modeling—are important. This mastery of representation can be learned, but not easily. However, reasonably good accuracy can be achieved with the assistance of photographs, tracings, pantographs, and other reproduction devices. Commercial artists and illustrators often use such mechanical aids because they work against deadlines. But even a hand-copied photograph will show departures or omissions from the original; and those departures or omissions can be more interesting than an exact reproduction. It is the drawing "error" due to an artist's personality, attitude, or characteristic touch that generates *aesthetic* interest.

In addition to accurate size and shape relationships, the control of illumination helps create realistic images. The source of light, the amount of light received and reflected, the transitions from light to dark, the shapes and edges of shadows: artists learn to observe and control these things by skillful manipulation of their media. Through the representation of light alone, objects and spaces can be modeled illusionistically. This applies to sculpture as well as drawing and painting: from Michelangelo to Rodin, sculptors have studied the action of light in attempting to control the way it falls over forms.

Another artistic device is focus: sharpness or softness and sameness or contrast in contour and form. An elementary fact about optics—that objects lose distinctness at the periphery of our field of vision—becomes a tool for governing the spectator's attention. Other things being equal, our eyes are drawn to the center of distinctly represented forms. If the edges of a painted form are softened or blurred, we tend to see them as further away. In contour drawing, forms in the same plane can be made to advance or recede, depending on the "hard-and-soft," "lose-and-find" characteristics of the drawing line. Masters of drawing from Michelangelo (see page 274) to Picasso (see page 208) have used these focal properties of line to make forms seem to move back and forth in the visual field.

Auguste Rodin. Head of Eustache de St. Pierre (detail of *The Burghers of Calais*). 1886. Rodin Museum, Paris

Jacob Epstein. *Head of Joseph Conrad.* 1924–25. Bronze, 16½ × 11¾ × 10". The Hirshhorn Museum and Sculpture Garden, Smithsonian Institution, Washington, D.C. Gift of Joseph H. Hirshhorn, 1966

In sculpture, forms may be sharply raised or softly blended, thus controlling visual and psychological attention. The degree to which a form emerges into "full round" becomes a tool of artistic expressiveness. We saw a certain amount of soft focus in Manzù's *Girl in Chair* (page 133) and it appears again in Rodin's head of Eustache de St. Pierre. By contrast, Jacob Epstein's portraits are highly focused to heighten the sense of the subject's aliveness. The modeling is exaggerated—that is, the hollows of the eyes, cheeks, and mouth are deeper than in real life. Using rough projections of clay, Epstein catches the light and brings out the forms very sharply. That sharpness creates a kind of agitation, a sense of emotional activity, even in a head at rest. Compare this with the melting forms of the Rodin head. Here we are aware of resignation— a slightly unfocused quality that can be seen in the eyes, too. Even so, both heads are convincingly realistic.

Color, of course, is a powerful instrument of representation. Modern painters often create form by color alone; if line or light appears in their work, it is through the edges of color areas or the sharp contrast between light and dark colors. Traditional painters tended to use color descriptively: color was modulated according to the light source and location in space. From Leonardo onward, they realized that focus grows less distinct as objects recede, that color loses intensity as objects recede. Conversely, brightly colored forms seem to advance. So, if brilliance of color is combined with sharpness of focus we have a powerful device for attracting attention— defining forms so that they seem to be vividly and psychologically present.

Here is an interesting variation: some artists use arbitrary color for its emotional impact and combine it with precise, representational drawing. Even "realistic" artists may exaggerate color while remaining faithful to the observed contours of things. It seems that where color is concerned artists have a kind of poetic license: chromatic inventiveness is permitted but there can be few if any deviations from optical truth in drawing. Again, we have to know what "rules" the artist wants to obey.

Perspective may be the pictorial device most of us know about. It is a science that enables artists to create illusions of deep space on a flat surface

*below:* Andrea Mantegna. *The Lamentation.* c. 1490–1500. Tempera on canvas, 26¾ × 31⅞". Pinacoteca di Brera, Milan

Extreme foreshortening in the Christ figure adds to the pathos of the scene. Notice that the crying women are shown in normal perspective, increasing the contrast between life and death.

*right:* Édouard Manet. *The Dead Christ with Angels.* 1864. Oil on canvas, 70⅝ × 59". The Metropolitan Museum of Art, New York. The H. O. Havemeyer Collection. Bequest of Mrs. H. O. Havemeyer, 1929

Compared with the Mantegna, the foreshortening is less extreme: our eye-level is at the knees, not at the soles of the feet. Manet gets a ghastly, death-white quality from the flat lighting that seems to come from below.

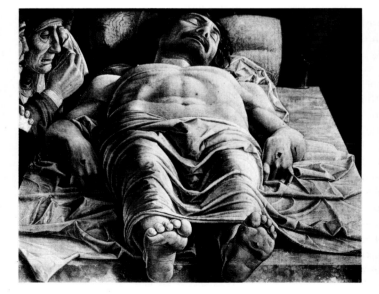

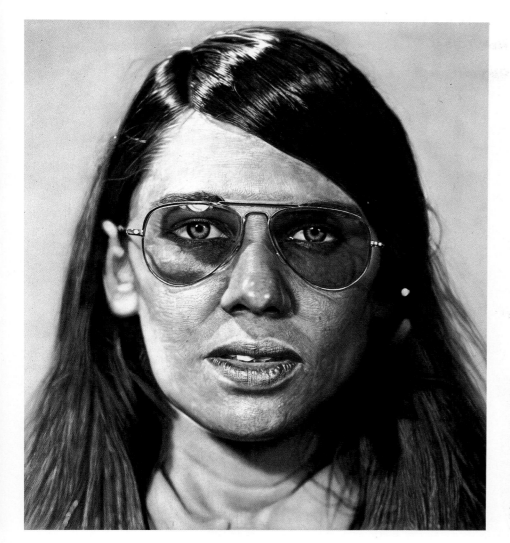

**Chuck Close. *Susan*. 1971. Acrylic on canvas, 8'4" × 7'6". Morton G. Newmann Family Collection, Chicago**

The pursuit of realism by imitating the camera's one-eyed optic. Notice how Susan's ear and neck are ever so slightly out of focus, but we can see each crack in her lips and each pore in her skin. This is not really a picture of Susan: it's a picture of Chuck Close pretending to copy a *photograph* of Susan. There are other ways to reproduce that photograph, yet Close uses an old-fashioned technology: paint on canvas. Why?

through diminishing size relationships. The technical features of linear and aerial perspective—the perspective of shadows and reflections, of receding measured forms, of advancing or foreshortened forms, of single- and multiple-point systems—are quite complex. But even a simple understanding of perspective makes it possible to simulate optical experience credibly. Modern painting, however, has questioned and abandoned the simulation of depth. The Surrealists used it dramatically to create illusions of infinitely receding space—often as a symbol of timelessness. But in the Cubism of Picasso, Braque, and Gris, traditional perspective devices were combined with anti-illusionistic devices. They probably wanted us to unlearn what we had learned from the Renaissance: reading pictures like vistas seen through an open window. The Cubists employed a totally different pictorial logic, and objective accuracy had nothing to do with it.

Even so, artists continue to use illusionistic devices. Certainly, many modern masters possess the skills for reporting their experience optically; and these skills have served them even in highly abstract creations. But realistic technique is not learned merely to gain confidence, to discard it later, or to suffer. Drawing accurately teaches artists to see, that is, to *understand* what they are looking at. Only then can they distinguish between surface copying and knowledgeable representation. As for viewers, we benefit from the artist's struggle to see clearly and represent truly. We also learn to compare the artist's rendering of reality with the world as we know it. The difference between the two holds many of the secrets of art.

# MODERN FIGURATIVE MODES

*above:* Morris Broderson. *The Earth Says Hello.* 1969. Pastel, 36 × 24". Collection Joan F. Apt

Using a soft, rubbed-pastel technique, Broderson combines accurate modeling with lush, exaggerated color. Notice the blues and violets in the shadows of the breasts and the flowing reds, oranges, and yellows in the flesh tones. The result is an eerie sort of sensuality—a strange mixture of voluptuousness and innocence.

*opposite above:* Willem de Kooning. *Two Women.* c. 1952–53. Pastel on paper, 18⅞ × 24".
The Art Institute of Chicago. The Joseph H. Wrenn Memorial Collection

Pastel again, but the intense color is more aggressively applied. The signs of artistic outrage are everywhere, especially in the treatment of the heads, hands, and feet.

*opposite below left:* Philip Pearlstein. *Two Seated Models.* 1968. Oil on canvas, 60 × 48".
Collection Mr. and Mrs. Gilbert Carpenter, Greensboro, North Carolina

Accurate drawing and modeling combined with understated monochromatic color. Compare these two women with De Kooning's. In both pictures, faces and feet have been arbitrarily cut off. But Pearlstein's almost photographic rendering produces a sense of anonymous, soulless flesh. De Kooning's multicolored torsos look richer and juicier even though their owner's personalities have been destroyed.

*opposite below right:* Chaim Soutine. *The Madwoman.* 1920. Oil on canvas, 37¼ × 23¼".
The National Museum of Western Art, Tokyo. Presented by Mr. Tai Hayashi, 1960

Loaded-brush technique can be used to express agitated pathological states—in the subject or in the artist. Here twisted contours and convulsive brushwork enlist our sympathy for the subject.

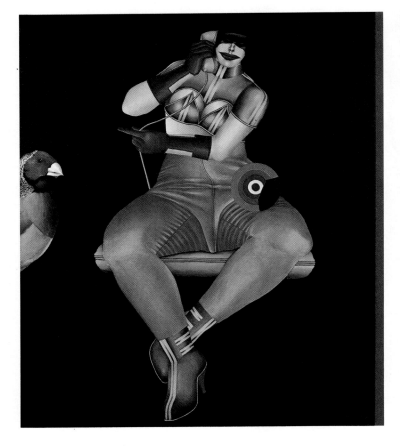

Richard Lindner. *Hello*. 1966. Oil on canvas, 70 × 60". The Harry N. Abrams Family Collection, New York

The pose, the clothing, the low angle of vision, the space-age rendering—all combine to create a fearsome Amazonian creature.

Max Beckmann. *Columbine*. 1950. Oil on canvas, 53½ × 39¾". Collection Morton D. May, St. Louis

Another antifeminine version of a woman, this time in circus costume. Both Beckmann and Lindner revert to a Stone Age fertility image—the so-called displayed or shameless woman motif. But why has this image been revived?

# CHAPTER FIVE

# THE STYLE OF FORMAL ORDER

The style of formal order is the expression of a preference for stability in art and, by implication, in the world. To the extent that Western civilization carries the imprint of ancient Greek thought, formal order has been its constant ideal. The Greeks pursued it through measured form and proportion—through the expression of ideal mathematical relationships. For us, formal order means balance, harmony, and stability in art. It is another term for classicism—a classicism found in the art of many peoples.

The immediate source of proportions for order and hence of beauty was, for the Greeks, the nude human figure. They realized that what we call "beautiful" is the result of a harmonious set of relationships—or proportions—among the parts of any whole. The proportions of the human body are beautiful, they believed, because they reflect the fundamental order in the universe. The problem of the artist was to apply that universal order to the design of buildings, the writing of music, and the making of images. Major works of figurative art were rarely drawn from specific personalities; they were "idealized"—that is, they were based on mathematical averages of the best models the Greeks knew. Artistic creation becomes a search for perfection: right shape, correct proportion, and complete finish.

To be sure, we in the West have not always followed the classical ideals of measure and moderation. Periodically, we have been caught up in violent artistic convulsions. But even the Greeks gave way—during the Hellenistic period—to an art of impulsive action and unstable forms. Our art, too, can be furious and explosive as well as smooth and untroubled. Often in the career of a single artist—Picasso, for instance—we see classical restraint combined with emotional violence. Nietzsche may have been right in dividing culture into two principal strains—Apollonian and Dionysiac. The Apollonian strain expresses a dream of order and serenity; the Dionysiac strain expresses frenzy, the angry discharge of energy. In the past, one strain or the other dominated art; today, both exist side by side.

Because the openness of modern culture permits artists to express their Apollonian *and* Dionysiac impulses, formal order is not our only style of artistic expression. Neither does it represent the taste of an artistic "establishment." It appears to be the natural expression of artists who are almost

instinctively drawn to stable forms and balanced composition; they seem to need a serene vision of the world. So in the West, at least, the style of formal order results from *personality* factors in the artist more than *political* factors in the culture.

Classicism, or formal order, can also be understood as a wish that the world were governed by reason and logic. From the evidence of art we can see how caution and deliberation, calculation and the weighing of alternatives, overcome the spontaneous expression of feeling. This produces Brancusi instead of Rodin, Mondrian instead of De Kooning. We see the artists planning, measuring, and refining—trying to organize their sensations and govern their emotions. For them, the greatest danger is loss of control.

## THE TRANSIENT AND THE PERMANENT

If there is a single trait that characterizes the style of formal order, it is the search for forms that are permanent. When working with a dynamic subject, the artist emphasizes its steady, unwavering qualities. This means selecting positions where the figure looks stable, avoiding the suggestion that it is about to change. Late in the nineteenth century, Rodin's *St. John the Baptist Preaching* was criticized for giving the impression of a figure walking off its pedestal. It was then believed that sculpture should seem to be immutable; it should stand still. Also, the French identify strongly with the classical tradition; a statue that "wants" to travel outside its assigned space violates that tradition. Whatever carries the viewer's eye beyond the art object negates the idea of permanence. Classical artworks try to express the durability of an individual or an idea by stressing the fixed character of their forms; viewers are supposed

Polyclitus. *Doryphorus (Spear Bearer).* **Roman copy after an original of c. 450–440 B.C. Marble, 78" high. National Museum, Naples**

Polyclitus designed his sculpture according to an ideal geometric formula, yet this figure looks completely natural. Why? Because of sensitive modeling and the rightness of the proportions underneath the surface.

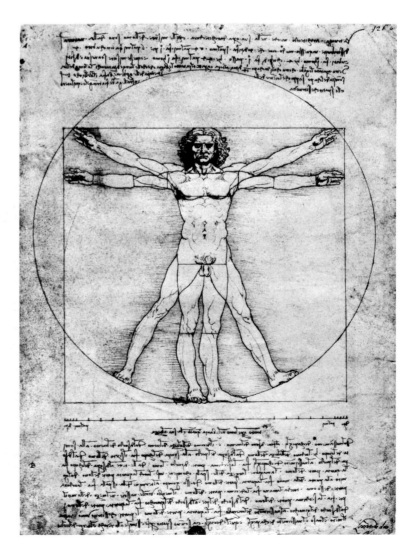

Leonardo da Vinci. *Studio del Corpo Humano.* **c. 1492. Pen and ink, 13⅛ × 9⅝". Academy, Venice**

Leonardo tried to solve an incredibly difficult problem. He wanted to show that a well-proportioned human figure—in action or at rest—fits exactly into two perfect geometric figures: the circle and the square. This would prove that man and geometry, earth and heaven, are harmoniously connected.

to feel that the monument has arrested the flow of time. Thus art represents a victory over transience or change.

Academic art instruction was usually biased in favor of formal order. Students were taught to recognize the positions that give changing shapes a permanent, classical quality. Also, the act of drawing from a static model had the effect of freezing movement; to hold a pose the model had to get into a *balanced* position. The goal of this instruction was the creation of artworks that would look resistant to the forces of change. In effect, the artist was asked to find what it is that can survive amid all the things—including ourselves—which must die.

Students of philosophy will recognize this approach to art as Platonic—the endeavor to know the permanent forms or ideas that stand behind the transient examples of the things we see. The truly beautiful is the imitation, not of surface appearances, but of ideal and unchanging essences. But essences must be known intellectually before they can be imitated visually. Accordingly, artists must study things of the mind—mathematics (geometry) first, and the ideal dimensions and proportions of things. Only then should they attempt to imitate what the eye sees. This Platonic approach is still alive in art instruction, whether we realize it or not. Artists may also be drawn to it spontaneously: formal order is an emotional and intellectual bias as well as a philosophic choice.

In *Church of the Minorites (II)* by Lyonel Feininger (1871–1956), we see the style of formal order employed by an artist under the influence of Cubism. In general, Feininger's work tries to impose the geometric order of crystals upon the visible world. Of course, architecture lends itself easily to this treatment; however, Feininger exploited a similar form language to represent organic or growing things—even people. Clearly, Cubism created the breakthrough that Feininger uses to express the clean, clear, and restful qualities of the chapel: the building and its world seem to be facets of a remarkable gem. Feininger's work implies that our universe has an underlying structure, a structure that is measured, ordered, and perhaps, divinely decreed.

In the hands of certain artists, therefore, formal order has religious implications. This is understandable, since the Greeks had an almost mystical view of mathematics; for them it possessed *divine* beauty; art was the physical manifestation of the sacredness of mathematics. Hence the implication in Feininger's work that the universe is permanent and perfect: it seems to be

Auguste Rodin. *St. John the Baptist Preaching.* 1878–80. Bronze, 6'6¾" high, at base 37 × 22½" (irregular). Collection, The Museum of Modern Art, New York. Mrs. Simon Guggenheim Fund

*far left:* Lyonel Feininger. *Church of the Minorites (II).* 1926. Oil on canvas, 47 × 43". Walker Art Center, Minneapolis

*left:* Philip Johnson. Garden Grove Community Church, Garden Grove, California. 1980

Crystalline structures have been imagined in every time and place, but in our time they have actually been built. Structural steel and plate glass produce this remarkable union of technology and spiritual striving. The Greeks would have loved it.

saying that God exists, has created the order reflected in art, and wishes it to continue. That is what a theologian might say; Feininger's painting shows how an artist would make that statement.

## KINDS OF FORMAL ORDER

Although the style of formal order is associated with stability and permanence, there are many variations within the style—different ways of playing out its possibilities. These variations—*intellectual order, biomorphic order,* and *aesthetic order*—are not absolutely separate categories, but one or the other is usually dominant in a given work or in an artist's total output.

**Intellectual Order** Perhaps Piet Mondrian is the best known modern master of *intellectual* order. His *Composition with Red, Yellow, and Blue* was created entirely with vertical and horizontal lines, with areas of unvarying color and no representational elements whatever. The elimination of curves, modeling, and subject matter forces us to examine his canvas solely in terms of its restricted formal vocabulary. Yet within this narrow pictorial language, Mondrian produces considerable variety—in the proportions of the rectangles (their ratios of height to width), in the length of the lines, in the apparent "weight" of the colored areas, and in their spatial relationships. The interactions among the forms are quite complex, yet they are largely intellectual. By reducing his vocabulary, Mondrian used the activity of the viewer's eye to create *mental* impressions of motion, balance, opposition, completeness, and rest. We interpret the elements of the design as weight, space, volume, energy, direction, and so on. But the order we experience is based on operations performed by the mind more than the imagination.

An earlier type of intellectual order appeared in Cubism, especially in the stage called Analytic Cubism (1910–12). Braque and Picasso worked together at this time, and their work is so similar that it looks as if either one could have painted any given picture. This suggests that the same *intellectual*

Piet Mondrian. *Composition with Red, Yellow, and Blue.* 1921. Oil on canvas, 15⁹/₁₆ × 13¹³/₁₆". Gemeente Museum, The Hague, The Netherlands

Georges Braque. *Man with a Guitar.* 1911. Oil on canvas, 45¾ × 31⅞". Collection, The Museum of Modern Art, New York. Acquired through the Lillie P. Bliss Bequest

*method* of analyzing form was used by both painters; artistic individuality was subordinated to the common requirements of reason or logic. In Braque's *Man with a Guitar* we see straight lines, a narrow range of color, and a figure sliced into geometric shapes. But notice that we learn nothing about the age or personality of the subject; instead we see a quiet arrangement of geometric forms that seem to be floating in shallow space. The forms are denser toward the center and more loosely distributed around the edges. Apparently, we are dealing with an approach to the nature of matter—the expression of the idea that, fundamentally, all substances have a common structure. Both Braque and Picasso seem to be saying that variations in the visible world are superficial; underneath there is an order like that of physics or mathematics. Again, the influence of Platonic thought.

Cubism offered an analysis of form that artists could use in many media for various purposes. In sculpture, *The Horse* by Raymond Duchamp-Villon (1876–1918) looks like an attempt to translate an animal into mechanical parts, using an essentially geometric vocabulary. The painterly language of Cubism was enlarged by using forms taken from machines or the drawings of mechanical engineers. But while the artist wants to visualize motion, the stability of classical order predominates. The process of analyzing an animal and reconstructing it along mechanical lines produces an essentially intellec-

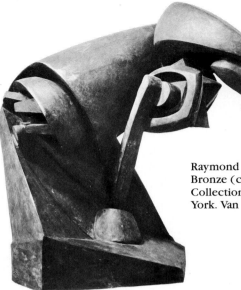

Raymond Duchamp-Villon. *The Horse.* 1914. Bronze (cast c. 1930–31), 40 × 39½ × 22⅜". Collection, The Museum of Modern Art, New York. Van Gogh Purchase Fund

*below:* Charles Demuth. *My Egypt.* 1927. Oil on composition board, 35¾ × 30". Collection of Whitney Museum of American Art, New York. Purchase, with funds from Gertrude Vanderbilt Whitney

Geometry lends itself to a style of order or of emotion. In the Demuth, the forms have been stabilized, balanced, and adjusted to each other. In the Delaunay, they express surging energy— the opposite of balance and rest.

*right:* Robert Delaunay. *Eiffel Tower.* 1911. Oil on canvas, 79½ × 54½". The Solomon R. Guggenheim Museum, New York. Gift of Solomon R. Guggenheim, 1937

tual construct; this horse cannot eat, or run, or breed: it exists for the pleasure of the mind.

Mechanization has been enormously fascinating to artists, whose reactions have ranged from approval to envy to hostility. Classical artists, in general, see their ideals of rationality and clarity realized in the machine. Perhaps that is why they borrow mechanical engineering forms so often. But when these forms are employed in art, they also function as symbols. As symbols they tend to express a classical sense of order. That is clearly the meaning of the crisp Euclidian shapes we see in *My Egypt* by Charles Demuth (1883–1935). But in the *Eiffel Tower* by Robert Delaunay (1885–1941) we see

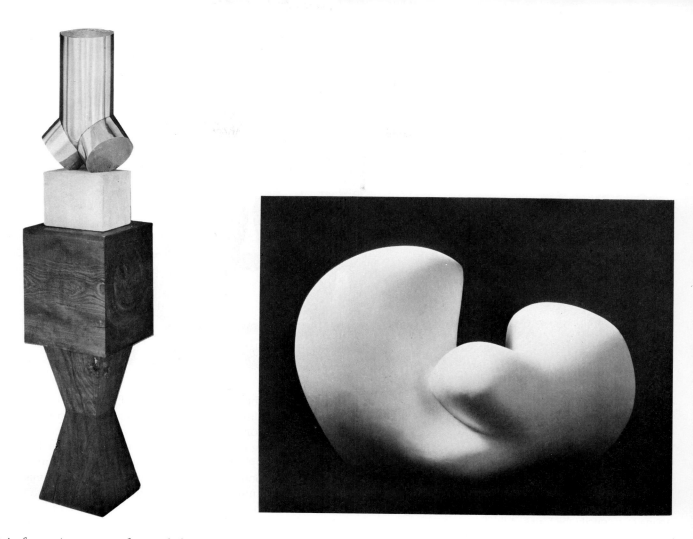

geometric forms in a state of partial disintegration: instead of resting they seem to be exploding. This shows that the choice of geometric forms offers only a clue to the artist's intentions; it is the *organization* of forms that creates the style.

In architecture, Mies van der Rohe may be our most noted apostle of formal order. As we have seen, his buildings are classically simple and severely intellectual. This may be due to the crucial importance he attached to absolute purity of surface and volume; variations have to be regular and predictable. No matter what their materials, his buildings give no visual hint of hand or craft skills. What we see is a product of pure design, that is, of thought governing the organization of standardized parts. Like Mondrian, Mies restricted himself to a narrow formal vocabulary; he gave up the emotional associations of curving lines to create an intellectual order which, strangely enough, has an almost sensuous appeal.

Mies's style has been widely imitated because it fits so logically into a world of computers and machine technology. It has been equally well used for apartment houses, libraries, and college buildings; it reflects the classicist's search for permanent and unvarying form. Indeed, Mies said he wanted to create space that could be used for any purpose. Hence his buildings rarely reflect differences in function or location. But that is a virtue from the standpoint of intellectual design: it illustrates the victory of architecture over restrictions of climate, handcraft, and tradition. It shows art transcending the personality of the artist. And the client. And the rest of us: we have to *fit into* these structures.

**Biomorphic Order** The term "biomorphic" designates forms that look as if they had developed in the same way that living organisms develop— through the subdivision of cells. An example can be seen in Jean Arp's

*left:* Constantin Brancusi. *Torso of a Young Man.* 1924. Polished brass, 18" high; with original wood base 58½" high. The Hirshhorn Museum and Sculpture Garden, Smithsonian Institution, Washington, D.C. Gift of Joseph H. Hirshhorn, 1966.

*above:* Jean Arp. *Human Concretion.* 1935. Original plaster, 19½ × 18¾". Collection, The Museum of Modern Art, New York. Gift of the Advisory Committee

Henry Moore. *Family Group.* 1948–49. Bronze (cast 1950), 59¼ × 46½", at base 45 × 29⅞". Collection, The Museum of Modern Art, New York. A. Conger Goodyear Fund

*below:* Marcel Gromaire. *Nu, bras levé, sur fond gris et or.* 1957. Galerie Leandro, Geneva

Classical artists often feel the need to reach an understanding with machines. Here we see them trying to reconcile the forms of the human body with the precise measured shapes created by engineers.

*right:* Oskar Schlemmer. *Abstract Figure, Round Sculpture.* 1962. Bronze copy after plaster original of 1921. 42⅛" high. Collection Frau Tut Schlemmer, Stuttgart. © The Oskar Schlemmer Family Estate, Badenweiler, Germany, 1988

*Human Concretion.* While some of us think of nature as chaotic, this artist finds perfection in the simplest forms of organic life. His sculpture has a soft, fleshlike quality. The connection with the human may be remote, but the identification with living form is strong. Again, in *Torso of a Young Man* by Constantin Brancusi (1876–1957), geometric and biological forms meet in the same work. Although Brancusi is devoted to a kind of mathematical perfection of form, he is determined not to break the connection with organic life. His truncated cylinders also recall ancient art—the armless or headless figures unearthed in classical Greek ruins. At the same time, the trunk and thighs of the sculpture remind us of the African carvings which so obviously influenced Cubism. So we have another classical idea: complex evocations achieved through the sensitive adjustment of simple forms.

Another classicist, Henry Moore, created sculptures which are less abstract than those of Arp or Brancusi. His family groups and reclining figures are monuments to human heroism and vital response. Moore may stress the

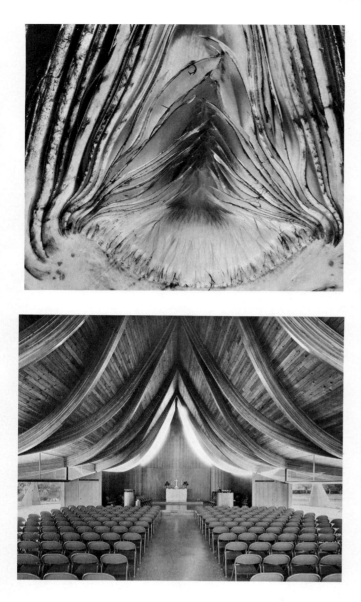

*left:* Edward Weston. Photograph of halved artichoke. 1930

The similarity between the forms here is no accident: both deal with "architecture"—the creation of protected space. The emotions generated by Lundy's church have the same source as those evoked by Weston's halved artichoke.

*below left:* Victor Lundy. St. Paul's Lutheran Church, Sarasota, Florida. 1959

Frank Lloyd Wright. Interior, The Solomon R. Guggenheim Museum, New York. 1959

roundedness of human forms, yet his people are hardly soft or weak. This is because there is a virile sense of structure underneath Moore's smooth, curving surfaces; his massive figures are supported by a dynamic system of thrusts. Moore successfully solved the problem of the tension between the human and the abstract—of monumental size and subtle surface control. As a result, his work makes one of our most powerful statements of the human capacity for growth and regeneration.

In architecture, biomorphic order has received fresh energy from a multitude of new materials and devices: collapsible domes with curved metal skins; concrete shells sprayed over inflated balloons; paraboloid roof structures combined with strong but delicate suspension systems. The dome, which has always expressed biomorphic impulses, is a device going back to the Stone Age *tumulus,* or burial mound. We associate its shape with our wish to live inside a womblike enclosure—the grave mound that unites us with Mother Earth, or the dome of the heavens symbolizing a benevolent, maternal universe. Beyond their engineering significance, these structures exhibit an order that symbolizes the ultimate biological and religious meanings of existence.

Frank Lloyd Wright practiced what he called an "organic" philosophy of architecture—one in which buildings assert their kinship with nature through cavelike spaces, rugged materials, and natural forms. His Guggenheim Museum is actually based on the structure of a living creature—an enormous

nautilus shell. The spiral form of that shell has both practical and symbolic significance: it converts the life cycle of a snail into a single, continuous chamber for the display of nonobjective art. Its curved walls and gently descending ramps may remind us of a glorious parking garage that transforms motorists into devotees of a new aesthetic religion. As a result, we might look at a real garage as an automotive Guggenheim whose outer skin has been stripped away; it turns into a concrete seashell holding gasoline engines by Ford and Chrysler instead of paintings by Mondrian and Kandinsky.

**Aesthetic Order**    Aesthetic order results from the artist's organization and adjustment of the various surface appeals of a work. It gives us pleasure mainly through the gratifying arrangement of shapes, colors, and textures. Depending very little on the optical imitation of reality, aesthetic order relies on immediate feelings of sensuous satisfaction. The simplest analogy is to our pleasure in the taste of food: the pleasure of taste does not designate something beyond itself. It appeals to a sense of rightness or goodness within us, and we respond with the emotion of delight. Perhaps aesthetic order promotes an ideal organization of bodily energies—a type of internal balance or homeostasis which makes us happy. We experience feelings of satisfaction that seem valid in themselves.

In *The Breakfast Room* by Pierre Bonnard (1867–1947), for example, we see a symphony of color not unlike the symphony of tastes in a gourmet dinner. Bonnard weaves a tapestry of textures suggested only partly by the objects before him. The table, the window, the fragmented figure, the scene through the window: these are only barely established. They really act as opportunities for the artist to play variations on yellow, yellow-green, yellow-orange, violet, blue-violet, and so on. Deep space is hardly suggested, and the drawing is very sketchy. Notice, too, that the color does not move back and forth in the picture space: it shimmers on the surface of the canvas. Painters like Bonnard do not try to remind us of the real appearance of fruit, trees, or tableware: the material we are mainly aware of is paint. Like his predecessors, Monet and Seurat, Bonnard communicates delight in paint and color apart from what they represent.

Georges Braque, Picasso's early collaborator, aimed their common intellectual style toward a sophisticated type of aesthetic order. His *Woman with a Mandolin* stresses the play of shapes, colors, and texture largely for the sake of painterly pleasure. Compared to Bonnard, however, Braque is a stronger designer: his orchestration of shapes is more varied and inventive. And he has a deeper interest in textural variation, whereas Bonnard suppresses every texture in favor of a single one—paint. Braque also uses paint additives like sand and ground eggshells to increase the tactile appeal of his surfaces. By exaggerating the wallpaper pattern, pulling it into the same plane as the figure, Braque implies that the sensuous qualities of the wall are more important than its "correct" location in space. Finally, notice that we learn very little about his subject: she functions as stuff the artist manipulates and rearranges for visual rather than cognitive effect: seeing for seeing instead of seeing for knowing.

Modernism's most elegant master of aesthetic order is Henri Matisse (1869–1954). His style was greatly enriched by the study of Persian art, which, like much Middle Eastern art, emphasizes opulent color and decorative detail. Thus we see an almost oriental emphasis on splendor in Matisse—a subordination of expressive meaning for the sake of rich aesthetic surfaces. His *Lady in Blue* shows us a work in which the Persian tradition of flat form and luxuriant color is combined with the European tradition of figurative representation in deep space. But Matisse freely chooses and discards; he finds what he needs in tradition and what is before him. Here he is attracted to the woman's rich gown, its flowing ruffles, her string of beads, her ripe features, the flowers framing her head, the furniture curves, and the drawing fragments

*opposite:* **Pierre Bonnard. *The Breakfast Room.*** c. 1930–31. Oil on canvas, 62⅞ × 44⅞". Collection, The Museum of Modern Art, New York. Given anonymously

Georges Braque. *Woman with a Mandolin.*
1937. Oil on canvas, 51¼ × 38¼".
Collection, The Museum of Modern Art,
New York. Mrs. Simon Guggenheim Fund

Henri Matisse. *Lady in Blue.* 1937. Oil on
canvas, 36½ × 29". Philadelphia Museum of Art.
Gift of Mrs. John Wintersteen

Harry Bertoia. Screen for Manufacturers Hanover
Trust Company, New York. 1954

Bradley Walker Tomlin. *No. 10.* 1952–53. Oil on
canvas, 6' × 8'6½". Munson-Williams-Proctor
Institute, Museum of Art, Utica, New York

in the background. All these elements are highly simplified; only shape is
taken from their total reality—shapes which Matisse reassembles to create a
new reality. He subordinates all forms to one pictorial effect which is meant
to be pleasurable as a whole. To enjoy this work, we have to see the entire
canvas at once. Then, if we let its shapes and colors *fill the eye*, their qualities
will be felt as a set of mutually reinforcing visual thrills. Pure aesthetic
pleasure!

An American sculptor, Harry Bertoia (1915–1978), designed a metal
screen, or wall, which richly exploits the aesthetic relationships of brass,
copper, and nickel. It acts as a partition and a plane against which we see
people going about their business in a bank. Because it functions architec-
turally, Bertoia wisely emphasized the abstract properties of the screen materials; symbolic and representational forms do not compete for the viewer's
attention. The effect is orderly and sensuous at the same time. As a result, we
are aware of a mutually enhancing relationship involving the wall, the people,
and the space they use.

The painting of Bradley Walker Tomlin (1899–1953) exhibits a type of aesthetic order that has the qualities of a Bach fugue. Like Bertoia's wall, Tomlin's *No. 10* is totally abstract. Although it is a product of measurement, calculation, and simplification, there is a sense of freedom—even joy—about it. Works of this type generate feelings much like those we get from ancient Greek art and architecture. But unlike the Greeks, modern classicists do not

## ABSTRACT MODES OF ORDER

**Alexej von Jawlensky.** *Still Life with Lamp.* 1913. Oil on cardboard, 21⅝ × 19⅝". Private collection, Hofheim/Taunus, Germany

The objects are barely identified; the intense colors try to break loose. However, a strong linear framework holds everything together; color and line live in a state of controlled tension.

**Maurice Esteve.** *Rebecca.* 1952. Oil on canvas, 36¼ × 29". Musée National d'Art Moderne, Paris

We see the typical shape and size relationships of an early Cubist still life: smaller forms tightly positioned at the core; larger forms loosely distributed around the center. The colors become lighter and brighter as we move outward. Despite the wavy, emotional quality of the shapes, we sense that they obey an overall logic.

build on our associations with the human figure. They rely, instead, on our willingness to recognize the order and rationality of machines, or electronic circuits, or crystals seen through a microscope. Aesthetic order has become a search for the order beneath surface sensation; it seems that we are looking for the key that can make the sensory excitement of modern life fit into a pattern. In addition to pleasure, we want reassurance.

Richard Diebenkorn. *Ocean Park, No. 22*. 1969. Oil on canvas, 98 × 81". Virginia Museum, Richmond. Gift of Sydney and Frances Lewis

This is the type of controlled abstraction in which the light, color, or shape of a place is lifted out of context so that its qualities are felt while its identity is obscured.

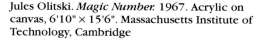

Jules Olitski. *Magic Number.* 1967. Acrylic on canvas, 6'10" × 15'6". Massachusetts Institute of Technology, Cambridge

Olitski sets up a vast yellow area whose dynamics could easily "run away" with the picture. Then he asserts his governance over the scene with some tonal modeling at the bottom of the yellow field, a hint of overlapping in the lower right corner, and a few color streaks along the edges of the canvas. Formal order is achieved with color and space and only a suggestion of shape.

Robert Delaunay. *Homage to Blériot.* 1914. Tempera on canvas, 98½ × 99". Kunstsammlung, Basel

Color theory began as a scientific idea and turned into an object—a wheel. Here the wheel becomes a bicycle, an airplane, a spinning propeller, a solar disk. Ultimately it is joined by man as bird, cosmic flyer, and, finally, Superbird.

Stanton Macdonald-Wright. *Abstraction on Spectrum (Organization, 5).* 1914. Oil on canvas, 30 × 24". Des Moines Art Center, Des Moines, Iowa. Nathan Emory Coffin Memorial Collection

The solar disk again, taken apart and reassembled to make a gorgeous color symphony—or Synchromy, as Wright called it. He was engaged in a daring attempt to put the emotional and symbolic properties of color under painterly control.

Frank Stella. *Sinjerli Variation I*. 1968. Fluorescent acrylic on canvas, diameter 10'. The Harry N. Abrams Family Collection, New York

The sun disk in a new guise—a set of intersecting protractors. Stella is playing Wright's color-wheel game but according to different rules: painterly emotion is eliminated; color symbolism is gone. We now have precise shapes, perfectly even color, and neat white lines. Design wins over gusto.

André Derain. *London Bridge.* 1906. Oil on canvas, 26 × 39". Collection, The Museum of Modern Art, New York. Gift of Mr. and Mrs. Charles Zadok

Here color sensations begin to have an independent existence. We recognize the place and the objects, but we experience the sensuous quality of the scene through color alone.

Wassily Kandinsky. *Landscape with Houses.* 1909. Oil on cardboard, 27⅜ × 37⅝". Kunstmuseum der Stadt Düsseldorf

Like Derain, Kandinsky was trying to attend to his sensations rather than to the structural qualities of buildings and trees.

Pierre Bonnard. *Nude in Bathtub*. c. 1941. Oil on canvas, 48 × 59½". Museum of Art, Carnegie Institute, Pittsburgh. Acquired through the generosity of the Sarah Mellon Scaife family

Bonnard goes further than Derain in separating color from drawing. Now space and shape are subordinated to the orchestration of surfaces with color and a rich mixture of textures.

Wassily Kandinsky. *Study for Composition No. 2*. 1910. Oil on canvas, 38⅜ × 51¾". The Solomon R. Guggenheim Museum, New York

Increasingly, Kandinsky looked inward for inspiration. This composition seems to be based on memories of Russian legends and Slavic music. The sensuous force of color and shape is blended into a medley of folklore and mysticism.

Jean-Paul Riopelle. *Vesperal No. 3.* 1958. Oil on canvas, 44¾ × 65⅝". The Art Institute of Chicago. Mary and Leigh B. Block Fund for Acquisitions

Aside from its structural qualities, this paint surface seems edible: the palette-knife technique reminds us of thick slabs of butter and globs of strawberry jam spread on bread.

Sam Francis. *Abstraction.* 1959. Oil on canvas, 72 × 50". Collection of Whitney Museum of American Art, New York. Udo M. Reinach Bequest

We see color and space, but we feel emotions largely associated with tactility. Francis is a master of the semitransparent mark, the wet stain, the moving spot, the orchestrated splash and trickle.

## CONCLUSION

Obviously, classical styles of art are closely associated with measurement and mathematics—especially geometry. But geometry is not the whole story. The essence of formal order lies in an *attitude* toward motion and rest: rest is good and motion is threatening. When dealing with moving forms, we want them to look calculated and predictable. The same assertions could be made about life as well as art. Notice that parents often judge their children by their patterns of motion: certain patterns mean trouble; others are reassuring. Somehow we have learned a visual language of motion and rest, a language that feeds us information about how to feel and think and act.

There are times in our lives when order and stability are what we want

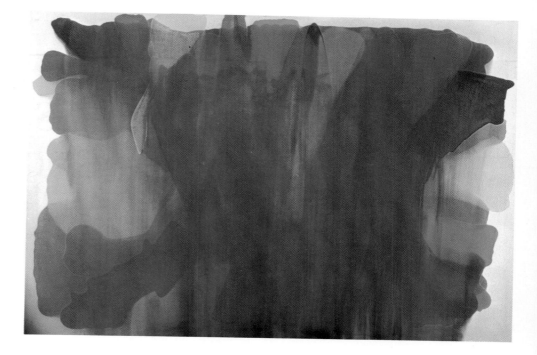

Morris Louis. *Kaf.* 1959–60. Acrylic on canvas, 8'4" × 12'. Collection Kimiko and John G. Powers, New York

Through the management of fluid, overlapping stains on unprimed canvas, the characteristic mark of the brush—hence of the hand—is bypassed. We respond to a moist, multichrome mist, seemingly created by nature, not man.

Paul Jenkins. *Phenomena in Heavenly Way.* 1967. Acrylic on canvas, 48 × 64". Collection Mr. and Mrs. Jack Stupp, Don Mills, Ontario

Wetter than the Louis work, this has more puddle and flow. As the hand and brush become more remote, we enter a world of hydrodynamic engineering made gorgeously visible.

more than anything else. At other times, stability—in art or life—strikes us as painfully dull. So, from the standpoint of society's health, the opportunity for nonformal styles to flourish alongside classical styles seems essential. Consider the hunger for American cultural products in Eastern Europe: it seems to be a sign of the anxiety and boredom that a style of forced classicism creates among people who desperately want change. When a stylistic reaction *does* emerge—sooner or later—it takes an extreme form because it has been so long repressed. The coexistence of opposite styles appears to be one of the best signs of a free society and a healthy culture; it tells us that our social and political institutions are functioning more or less well.

# CHAPTER SIX

# THE STYLE OF EMOTION

The expression of feeling occurs so often in the visual arts that we can safely refer to a "style" of emotion. For some artists it is the only possible language. Van Gogh and Soutine are examples: their pictures of people, trees, flowers—even chairs—seem to burst with passion. What matters to them is not visual accuracy or the careful construction of an ordered universe; it is the communication of pity or anxiety or rage. Strong feeling takes precedence over everything.

But if we say that emotion is important to certain artists, do we mean the emotions they feel or their stimulation of emotion in others? It can be both. As viewers, however, we are mainly concerned with the way artworks stimulate our feelings. Sometimes critics imply that artists have, in fact, experienced the emotions expressed in their work. That may or may not be true, but there is no way to find out for sure. Some people assume that aesthetic excellence depends on whether the artist truly felt the emotions we see in his or her work. However, the study of style focuses on the art object more than the artist's private life. In judging art it is better to ask: "Does this work make me believe in the world it represents?" "Are the emotions I feel based on what I see?" "Am I under the spell of the image or the artist's reputation?"

There is a vast literature about "emotion" and "expression" in art. I take the position that emotions are the names we give to neuromuscular reactions which have been triggered by the visual organization of an artwork. The *energy* for these feelings comes from the viewer, but the *kinds of feelings* we have are due to the design of the image. Accordingly, emotions in art are caused by visual forms shaped and organized so they will *work within us*. (For a discussion of "aesthetic work," see Chapter Ten.) That "work" often takes place at a subconscious or precognitive level.

Naturally, there are variations in the style of emotion. That is, images have the capacity to arouse feelings and dispositions which are strong but which differ in their content; we can be elated by one work and depressed by another. Our emotional response may be caused by the subject matter of the work, or it may be due to the kind of aesthetic "signal" the work sends out. For example, an abstract painting with no apparent subject matter can affect moods and attitudes. Something in the work's form or design must be responsible for our reactions. Consequently, we have to deal with *two* sources

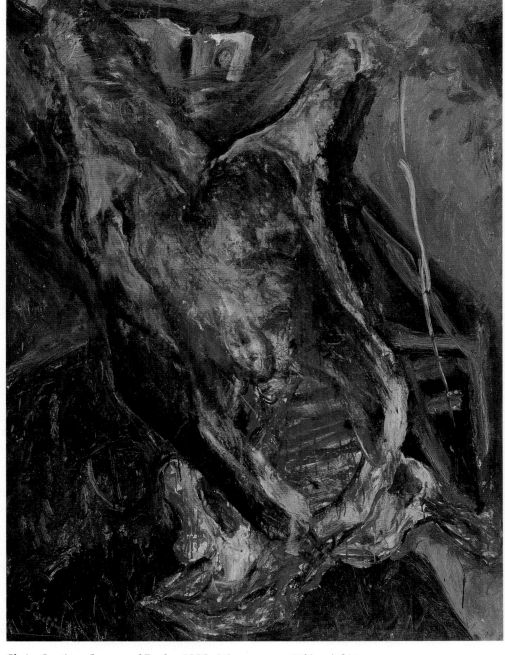

Chaim Soutine. *Carcass of Beef.* c. 1925. Oil on canvas, 55¼ × 42⅜".
Albright-Knox Art Gallery, Buffalo, New York. The Room of Contemporary Art
Fund, 1939

Germaine Richier. *The Bat.* 1952. Whereabouts unknown

Henry Moore. *Falling Warrior*. 1955-56. Bronze, 52" long. The Hirshhorn Museum and Sculpture Garden, Smithsonian Institution, Washington, D.C. Gift of Joseph H. Hirshhorn, 1966

*opposite above:* Henry E. Mattson. *Wings of the Morning*. 1936. Oil on canvas, 36 × 50". The Metropolitan Museum of Art, New York. Arthur Hoppock Hearn Fund, 1937

*opposite below:* Winslow Homer. *Northeaster*. 1895. Oil on canvas, 34⅜ × 50¼". The Metropolitan Museum of Art, New York. Gift of George A. Hearn, 1910

of aesthetic emotion: thematic or subject-matter sources, and organizational or design sources.

The style of emotion uses *any* means of arousing strong feeling, but its most stirring examples usually employ theme *and* design. We can see two examples in the *Carcass of Beef* by Chaim Soutine and *The Bat* by Germaine Richier. Both subjects are disagreeable, and the organization of forms in each case reinforces our normal feelings of revulsion—feelings clustered around ideas of pain, laceration, and death. Notice that Moore's *Falling Warrior* deals with dying, too, but its classic simplification of forms seems to sanitize the theme; we are not aware of any gory qualities. What we know about the subject does not interfere with a peculiar sense of serenity in the sculpture. On the other hand, the carcass by Soutine forces us to think about the mutilation of what was once a living creature; it records the slaughter of a beast, not the death of a hero.

Richier's bat, with webbed limbs radiating from a mammalian trunk, strikes a note of primeval terror because it stirs up a deep instinctual fear. This creature bears a resemblance to the human that arouses mixed emotions of recognition and dread. Hence we feel disturbing emotions associated with the monstrous and unnatural. Those lumpy, stringy, perforated forms, combined with the symbolic associations of bats, create a powerful sense of uneasiness.

Themes of violence and mutilation, the nonhuman and the unnatural, are frequent features of the style of emotion, especially today. But here we are not concerned with deciding whether we like or dislike this type of art; our purpose is to understand the roots of visual emotion and their connections to our world. If art reflects the times, it is worth attention whether we enjoy it or not. The style of emotion may lead us to ask what it is about modern life that produces images of cruelty and terror. Or it may raise questions about where we find joy, and why.

## ROMANTICISM AND EMOTION

As suggested above, the style of emotion can *disclose* an artist's deepest feelings. The attitude of emotional candor, of stressing highly personal reac-

Paul Gauguin. *The Spirit of the Dead Watching*. 1892.
Oil on burlap mounted on canvas, 28½ × 36⅜".
Albright-Knox Art Gallery, Buffalo, New York.
A. Conger Goodyear Collection, 1965

Theodore J. Roszak. *Spectre of Kitty Hawk*. 1946–47.
Welded and hammered steel brazed with bronze and
brass, 40¼" high, at base 18 × 15". Collection, The
Museum of Modern Art, New York. Purchase

tions to events, is also called Romanticism. For the Romantic, the important aspect of a person, place, or event is his or her feeling about it. Indeed, Romantics believe feelings *are* facts. They tend to lose themselves in "feeling-facts." They may even lose their "sense of proportion," the common-sense idea of the rightness of things. Perhaps that is why *Wings of the Morning* by Henry E. Mattson (1887–1971) can make us feel like sea dwellers. Briefly, we forget the difference between the observer and the observed, between what we see and who we are. The ocean is not only a body of water but a mysterious world in which we could somehow live. Winslow Homer, a non-Romantic artist, also painted the ocean—the same vast and powerful universe—but for him, the sea is a wholly *separate* place.

Typical of Romanticism is its interest in remote places and dangerous experiences. Romantic artists are often attracted to distant lands, as Paul Gauguin (1848–1903) was to Tahiti. Perhaps faraway places and strange customs make us forget the monotony of our lives; we can get lost in some paradise or hell of the imagination. Gauguin's *The Spirit of the Dead Watching* promotes this feeling: Tahiti is an exotic place where people live close to nature; peculiar things can happen there. Fantastic colors and flowers and a mysterious inscription appear in the picture—"Manao tupapau"—"The spirit

Darrel Austin. *The Black Beast.* 1941. Oil on canvas, 24 × 30". Smith College Museum of Art, Northampton, Massachusetts. Purchased 1941

of the dead remembers her." The girl on the bed seems to be frightened or paralyzed; an atmosphere of supernaturalism hovers over the scene. Terror and beauty, innocence and demonism, have been mixed in the same image: this is the stuff that excites the Romantic imagination.

In contrast to Gauguin's exoticism, there is the strangely ominous world of the American painter Darrel Austin (born 1907). His pictures illustrate the peculiar fascination that violence has for the Romantic imagination. In *The Black Beast* we see a tiger with a dead bird under its paws. The fierce jungle cat seems to glow because Austin has illuminated her from below, or within, creating an unreal, phosphorescent effect. The marshy landscape looks unreal, too—like a hallucination more than a real jungle scene. What accounts for the Romantic emotions in this picture? Is it the juxtaposition of a majestic killer with a frail, mangled bird? The real theme of the work becomes the duality of nature: struggle and silence, violence and peace, victory and death.

We see another Romantic work in a sculpture by Theodore Roszak (1907–1981), *Spectre of Kitty Hawk*. Here the artist has invented a frightening creature based on the pterodactyl, an extinct flying reptile. Roszak created this monster with steel, bronze, and brass to suggest the mixed results of the invention of human flight. But without the title and its reference to the Wright brothers at Kitty Hawk, would we understand this work? I think so. We would experience the same mixed emotions—feelings generated by a creature which has a predatory head and claws combined with the wings, body, and

Théodore Géricault. *The Raft of the "Medusa."* 1818-19. Oil on canvas, 16'1" × 23'6". The Louvre, Paris

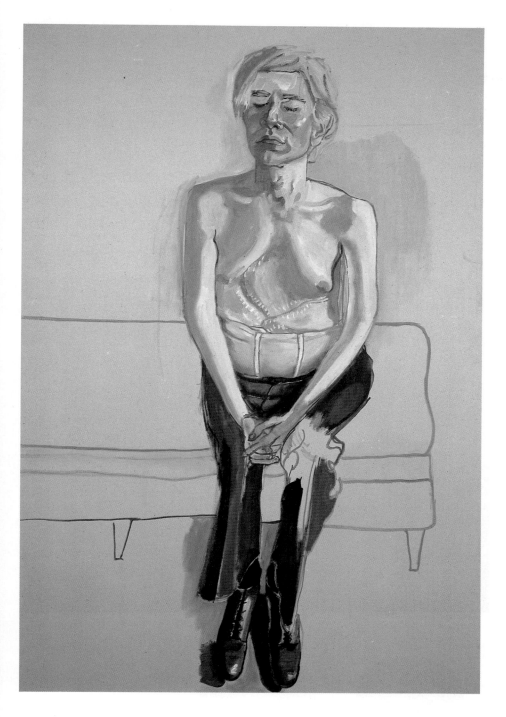

Alice Neel. *Andy Warhol.* 1970. Oil on canvas, 60 × 40". Collection of Whitney Museum of American Art, New York. Gift of Timothy Collins

Alice Neel paints Warhol's white body, sagging breasts, and red wounds—and his face seeming to savor the experience of near-death at the hands of a friend. This is the stuff of romantic emotion—the imagery of persons who are instinctively attracted to extremes, of life lived outside the bounds of respectability.

tail of an airplane. Plus the hard, hammered sculptural material suggesting the metallic glint of a crashed bird-machine.

Because Romantic artists deal with psychological associations and literary symbols as well as visual forms, they take large risks: they have to control a complex type of communication. The dangers of easy emotion or cheap sentimentality are very great. For these reasons the works of Romantic masters like Géricault and Delacroix may seem overly melodramatic. Still, *The Raft of the "Medusa"* survives as a masterpiece. Why? Because of its powerful design, its masterful execution, its magnificent display of the human figure. We may not know about the shipwreck which inspired the painting; but the forms carry conviction even though its subject has been forgotten.

# EMOTION GENERATED BY SYMBOLS

Jean Dubuffet. *Leader in a Parade Uniform*. 1945. Oil on canvas, 36⅜ × 25⅞". Collection Morton M. Neumann Family Collection, Chicago

Dubuffet's imagery derives its emotion from a source that was ignored until the twentieth century: the art of children, primitives, and the insane.

*below:* Adolph Gottlieb. *Dialogue No. I.* 1960. Oil on canvas, 5'6" × 11'. Albright-Knox Art Gallery, Buffalo, New York. Gift of Seymour H. Knox, 1961

Two immaculate disks float over a terrain filled with dirty splotches and wild writing. The painting symbolizes the world before and after it was civilized.

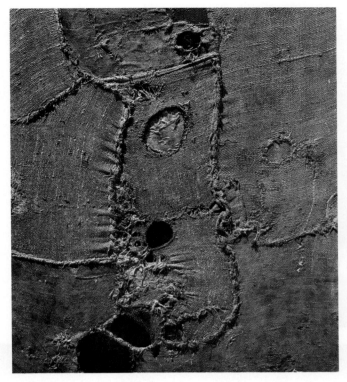

**Alberto Burri.** *Sacco B.* 1953. Burlap, sewn, patched, and glued over canvas, 39⅜ × 33½". Collection the artist

An open wound is visible through a tear in a rotting and patched sackcloth cover; other holes are burned out, dead. Does biological survival—or civilized life—depend on a fabric so worn and makeshift?

**Robert Motherwell.** *Elegy to the Spanish Republic, No. XXXIV.* 1953–54. Oil on canvas, 6'8" × 8'4". Albright-Knox Art Gallery, Buffalo, New York. Gift of Seymour H. Knox, 1957

In the background we see the bright, sunny colors of Spain. The melancholy forms in the foreground almost blot them out; they speak of death, of a maddened animal—a bull?—who will kill or be killed.

**Arshile Gorky.** *The Liver is the Cock's Comb.* 1944. Oil on canvas, 72 × 98". Albright-Knox Art Gallery, Buffalo, New York. Gift of Seymour Knox

These fowl shapes and bright colors seem to come from a cockfight—a maelstrom of claws, beaks, and feathers. We can also recognize hints of human sexual organs. Symbols of pain and pleasure, fighting and sex, living and dying, are mixed to create a beautiful/gory spectacle.

Pablo Picasso. *Night Fishing at
Antibes.* 1939. Oil on canvas, 6'9" ×
11'4". Collection, The Museum of
Modern Art, New York. Mrs. Simon
Guggenheim Fund

Two women casually watch the
spear-killing of fish attracted to a
boat by the light of the fishermen's
lantern. It is a scene of rich color
and dark irony: men are predators
at work or play. The women—one
executing a pirouette, the other
holding her bike and eating a
double ice-cream cone—enjoy the
spectacle.

Richard Diebenkorn. *Man and
Woman in a Large Room.* 1957.
Oil on canvas, 71¼ × 62½". The
Hirshhorn Museum and Sculpture
Garden, Smithsonian Institution,
Washington, D.C. The Joseph H.
Hirshhorn Foundation, 1966

Empty windows, empty walls,
empty faces, empty lives. Here
shape, color, and perspective barely
establish form and space; mainly,
they operate as symbols of a
physical and human vacuum.

# THE ROLE OF DISTORTION

Distortion generates emotion because our feelings are quickly aroused by any departure from the normal, especially in the case of the human body. But distortion of manufactured objects also disturbs us; this is due to tensions between what we know, what we expect, and what we see. Distortion means twisting, stretching, mutilating, or otherwise deforming the normal shapes and proportions of things. It refers also to exaggeration of size, color, and illumination; increased contrast between light and dark; overstated textural and surface qualities. Sometimes distortion is intentional, but usually it is a spontaneous result of the artist's attitude toward a subject.

Because of personality or training, artists may emphasize or suppress certain features of objects; or they may choose to view objects when they look deformed. Even photographs seem to be distorted when their subjects are seen at peculiar times or from odd angles of vision. Some artists use distortion for expressive purposes. Michelangelo, for example, is known for the writhing, tormented quality of his figures, especially for his famous *contrapposto*, an extreme twisting action through the shoulders, trunk, and pelvis. The apocalyptic feeling of his *Last Judgment* is due, in part, to the representation of faces, muscles, and bodies in extreme tension. Through empathy—through bodily imitation of what we see—we feel those tensions physically and emotionally.

Distortion can add emotional force to an artist's statement: sardonic detachment in Lautrec; feverish anxiety in Munch; psychological isolation in Giacometti. Van Gogh's distortion projects a kind of personal pain and mystical joy into everything he sees. Francis Bacon produces a macabre, unsettling effect by suggesting that the mentality of savages and madmen lies behind civilized faces. Some distortions, however, can be agreeable; the attenuated figures of Lehmbruck give adolescence a pleasing sort of grace. Modigliani's stretching of forms produces a heightened sensuality in the figure. Of course, these two artists are basically classicists; when they distort, it is mainly to simplify and *refine* form; they make us linger on a contour because it is lovelier than anything we are likely to encounter in real life.

Jack Levine's *Welcome Home* employs distortion to arouse indignation: the longer we look, the angrier we get. The people in this scene are held up to ridicule and contempt; their bodies become the physical containers of vices such as pride, avarice, and gluttony. Levine tends to see moral depravity in social or political power. Given this mindset, he emphasizes the elegant table service, the obsequiousness of the waiter, the fancy dress of the diners, and the sickly glamour of the scrawny woman (upper left) who is meant to represent the "filthy rich." Noteworthy, too, is Levine's use of a distorting perspective to enlarge the heads; we view these people from above and that lets us "look down" on them. This sort of satire calls for an artist with a large capacity for outrage, and Levine fits that description; he loves the signs of grossness and corruption. For him, distortion is more than an artistic device: it is a physical weapon, a way to express loathing and a means of enjoying one's disgust.

## ANXIETY AND DESPAIR

In this century we have known several terrible wars, and we live with the possibility of extermination in another. So it is not surprising that art shows symptoms of fear and anxiety. The style of emotion mirrors our periodic lapses into despair, our feelings of doubt that the world can settle its problems. Artists, like philosophers and theologians, continually try to explain what is happening to the human species. Some condemn the political or economic conditions that cause wars; others see war's roots in human nature itself. Such artists are fascinated by images of human pathology: they are peculiarly attracted to ugly behavior, the corruption of institutions, the failures of our civilization.

**Distorted photograph of a man**

The high-speed camera reveals distortions the naked eye cannot see. Or, sometimes, it *creates* distortions, as in this photo. In either case, we try to imitate internally what we see externally. That imitation produces emotion—in this case, queasiness.

**Michelangelo. Detail of *The Last Judgment*. 1534–41. Sistine Chapel, The Vatican, Rome**

In this self-portrait, Michelangelo wanted to express his personal misery and wretchedness. But notice that he used the same type of distortion we see in the high-speed photo above. Distortion can create a wide range of feelings—from physical distress to spiritual anguish.

Thus we have an eloquent tradition of artistic protest against war's inhumanity, from Goya's Disasters of War etchings to Picasso's *Guernica*. Beyond that, we have a despairing art related mainly to personal suffering—suffering without any apparent social connection. *The Scream* by Edvard Munch is an example: it shows a person on a bridge, hands held to the ears, with mouth open in what looks like a drawn-out howl. The figure's gender is uncertain, and we do not know why it is screaming. But there is something deathly about it, perhaps an anticipation of suicide. In the distance, two anonymous figures symbolize the world's indifference to private tragedy. Notice that the lines in the sky and harbor are dully repeated; they seem to force all the forms into "echoes" of the scream. Munch has used very simple artistic devices to describe what strikes him as an essential truth: all life is pain and suffering. Through one painting we encounter all the anguish of existence.

In the sculpture *Cain* by Lu Duble (1896–1970), the idea of personal torment is even more violent and explicit; this is the agony of a man who murdered his brother and fled from society. Cain's agony is expressed by powerful diagonals that produce a frantic distortion of the figure. The held-back head and bared throat tell us that Cain is asking to be killed. Perhaps a dancer would use his body this way to express guilt and absolute surrender; the figure becomes a vehicle for externalizing unbearable psychological pain. The narrative style of the Bible is rarely subtle; it speaks about our spiritual condition in black and white, but with very few grays. And that is what Lu Duble creates in her sculpture—an image that fits the moral scale of the Bible.

*Head Surrounded by Sides of Beef* by Francis Bacon (born 1909) portrays a person who has gone mad or is turning into a wild animal. The cry in Munch's painting suggested human isolation and despair; this scream declares that "civilized" men are savages. Notice that Bacon portrays a well-

Jack Levine. *Welcome Home.* 1946. Oil on canvas, 39¹⁵⁄₁₆ × 59¹⁵⁄₁₆". The Brooklyn Museum. John B. Woodward Memorial Fund

To create satire, indignation is not enough: acute observation and hostile analysis are also required.

Edvard Munch. *The Scream.* 1893. Casein on paper, 35¾ × 29". National Gallery, Oslo

Lu Duble. *Cain.* 1953. Hydrocal, 38" high. Collection
of Whitney Museum of American Art, New York. Purchase

Chris Steele-Perkins. Photograph of poster: José Napoleón Duarte, President of Salvador. 1984

Aesthetic emotion originates in real-life situations. In this defaced poster we can see several devices that are deliberately used by Abstract Expressionist painters: the splash, the smear, paint runs, and paint spatters. The paint drips on Duarte's lapel are especially ominous because they look like bloodstains.

dressed individual sitting in a chair, but instead of giving us a conventional portrait, he stresses the connection between man and beast. Naturally, the image is disturbing. Does it tell the truth about our species, about the human condition? Well, in this century we have been crueler than any animal, so it is not surprising that Bacon's style has been exceedingly influential. The American painter Hiram Williams (born 1917) may have been attracted to Bacon's imagery: the blurred features of his one-eyed *Guilty Men*, combined with their neat business suits, produce the same idea of man as a civilized beast. Both artists employ distortion and human-animal fantasy to upset any comfortable notions we may have about how much we have risen above savagery.

In *Migration to Nowhere* Rico Lebrun (1900–1964) deals with war by making a macabre dance out of the flight of its crippled victims. Using distorted perspective, he enlarges the feet of the figures to dramatize the idea of flight. The vacant horizon symbolizes hopelessness and the slim chance of escape. Notice, too, that the figures seem to lose their corporeality as they recede into the distance. Yet there is a curious grace in their movement, in their billowing garments, in their use of crutches with the skill of players in a horrible game. Ironically, Lebrun makes a desperate situation bearable by invoking the agility of the maimed. Bacon, however, finds nothing redeeming in the image of man: under a well-tailored suit he is a mad dog.

A subject similar to Lebrun's is treated by Ben Shahn in *Liberation*. Here the figures are deliberately awkward; they seem maimed but they aren't; this is an instance of Shahn's ability to find expressive distortion in the freeze-action of photographic imagery. Lebrun's figures, on the other hand, look graceful even though they are crippled. Again, irony is a major quality of the work: children, obviously undernourished, play in a bombed-out environment; they find fun in the wreckage. Just as Lebrun finds grace in deformity, Shahn finds aesthetic quality in the texture of the sky, the lean of the building, and the rendering of rubble. But if we examine the children's silhouettes, noticing especially their foreshortened, almost spastic legs, we sense the horror of broken bodies and broken cities.

The world's recurrent wars and postwar agonies have produced a type of artistic anxiety that pervades the work of Oskar Kokoschka (1886–1980). His *Self-Portrait* employs some of the typical features of Expressionist art: an oversized hand and eyes; a gaunt head illuminated by flickering light and dirty shadows; and a facial expression hovering between sadness and deep-seated guilt. The hand seems to accuse the artist while the mouth cannot speak, cannot say what it is that assails him. The restless contours of the face heighten the central idea of the work—that this is a man who can find no forgiveness.

Compared to Bacon, Kokoschka deals with the theme of modern anxiety without surrendering his essential humanity; at least his subject feels responsibility and guilt. It would be difficult to attribute these feelings to Bacon's man: an animal is *amoral*; it does not understand guilt. Kokoschka's portrait dates from before World War I, while Bacon's picture was painted in the 1950s. So, on the evidence of these two works, our time has seen considerable

*left:* Francis Bacon. *Head Surrounded by Sides of Beef.* 1954. Oil on canvas, 51⅛ × 48". The Art Institute of Chicago. Harriott A. Fox Fund

*below:* Hiram Williams. *Guilty Men.* 1958. Oil on canvas, 96 × 72". Collection Mr. and Mrs. Dalton Trumbo, Los Angeles

Rico Lebrun. *Migration to Nowhere*. 1941. Gouache, 30 × 48". Whereabouts unknown

Ben Shahn. *Liberation*. 1945. Tempera on cardboard, mounted on composition board,
29¾ × 40". Collection, The Museum of Modern Art, New York. James Thrall Soby Bequest

Oskar Kokoschka. *Self-Portrait.* 1913. Oil on canvas, 32⅛ × 19½". Collection, The Museum of Modern Art, New York. Purchase

moral deterioration. Of course, the evidence is incomplete; it may only reflect the opinions of two atypical observers. Still, our art exhibits a great deal of pain and suffering. Can we find any evidence of gladness or hope?

## JOY AND CELEBRATION

Strangely, the same style that expresses anxiety can be used to express joy. As in drama, there is a very fine line between tragedy and comedy. Indeed, the genius of a comedian like Chaplin lay in the fact that his acting approached tragedy while he was working for laughs. Perhaps celebration is related to the tragic *and* the comic spirit: we laugh *and* cry during life's exultant moments. Like drama, art can express joy because it knows about sorrow; it can affirm the goodness of living because it has seen life taken away.

Max Weber. *Hasidic Dance.* 1940. Oil on canvas, 32 × 40". The Brooklyn Museum. On loan from The Lowenthal Collection

*below:* John Marin. *Maine Islands.* 1922. Watercolor, 16¾ × 20". © The Phillips Collection, Washington, D.C.

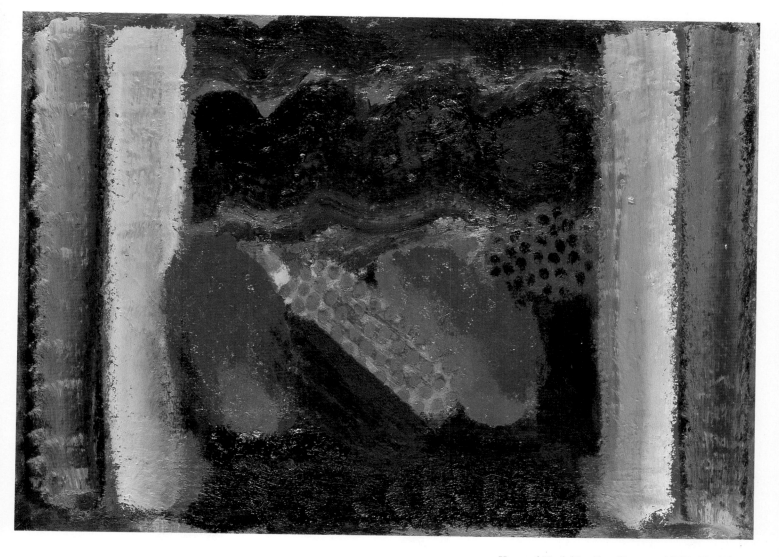

Howard Hodgkin. *Day Dreams*. 1977–80. Oil on wood, 23⅛ × 32⅛". Private collection, London. Courtesy Whitechapel Art Gallery, London

Using rhythmic abstract shapes and large, soft areas of color, Hodgkin manages to convey powerfully erotic feelings. Yet there are no figurative forms—only the chromatic richness and texture of paint, hints of pillows and bedcovers, and a window opening out to the night.

A good connection between comedy and celebration can be seen in *Hasidic Dance* by Max Weber (1881–1961). Here the members of a mystical Jewish sect dance and sing to express their feelings of exaltation in the created universe; their dance is joyous, ecstatic, and reverent at the same time. Wearing high hats and long, almost funereal garments, the men dance in a spirit of what is, for them, complete abandon. The effect is slightly comic but they don't seem to care: they are worshipping God and that makes them happy. The appeal of this work depends on a set of comic contrasts; awkward men trying to be graceful; dignified garments getting tangled up; high hats that might fall off. But the passion of these men makes them indifferent to worldly concerns; what matters is that miracles take place all the time.

From another standpoint and using a different technique, John Marin (1870–1953) expresses joy in the freshness and continuous renewal of nature. Working mainly in watercolor, Marin painted scenes that are alive with energy and movement. With a few slashing strokes he can suggest nature's whole panorama: sky, sun, air, water, and mountains. Marin's style—based on Cubism but not as heavily intellectual—was highly personal; he used an abbreviated, straight-line technique derived ultimately from Cézanne's carefully hatched planes. But Marin's approach is more vigorous and slapdash; the generous use of white paper and a fast, wet brush give his pictures genuine brilliance and sparkle. This is a happy world; Marin may even paint a few sun rays the way children do. His universe is untroubled, filled with radiant energy and growing things: the color and motion and noise are friendly to our species.

To some of us, Marc Chagall's paintings may seem naive because of their childlike belief in the power of love—its capacity to lift us above the here and the now. In *Flying over the Town* a young couple floats over a village as if in a dream; but their eyes are open and the village is real. Chagall depicts the miraculous beliefs of childhood: that gravity can be cancelled; that love transcends facts; that the world is mostly illusion and enchantment. He is a joyous artist completely devoted to the ideal of romantic love; its erotic aspects hardly exist. If he portrays a female nude, there is no suggestion of physical desire—by her or for her. Just love. Chagall's men and women appear to be conceived by the minds of children. And for that reason, perhaps, love is a weightless sort of joy—a joy so pure that it liberates us from rootedness in the earth.

Can architecture express joy? Not easily, since a building has to solve the problems of gravity and stability before anything else. Yet the Los Manantiales Restaurant by Ordoñez and Candela has a happy, festive air. Its main engineering device—thin-shell concrete in the form of hyperbolic curves resting on a circular plan—brilliantly solves the problem of structure and expression. The shell structure acts as roof, side wall, and window opening simulta-

**Marc Chagall.** *Flying over the Town.* 1914. Oil on canvas, 31⅞ × 39⅜". Collection Mrs. Mark C. Steinberg, St. Louis

Joaquín Alvares Ordoñez (architect) and Félix Candela (structural designer). Los Manantiales Restaurant, Xochimilco, Mexico. 1958

Victor Bisharat/James A. Evans and Associates. General Time Building (now occupied by States Marine Line, Inc.), Stamford, Connecticut. 1968

Using a circular plan on a masonry base and repeated inverted arches, the General Time Building is emotionally similar to Ordoñez and Candela's building. But the structural devices are entirely different. The common denominator is poured, reinforced concrete, a material that turns architects into sculptors.

neously; its visual effect suggests the delicacy of curved paper, yet the shell is very strong. As a contrast to those wavy shapes, the designers used a rugged masonry foundation and wide, gentle steps. The result is a secure horizontal base for the soaring overhead forms, producing feelings of lift and solid support at the same time.

Our pleasure in this building is something like our joy in a great cathedral: there is a thrill in structures and spaces that seems to exceed the limits of human ingenuity. Those curves send signals that can also be found in nature—in leaves, petals, seashells, and ocean waves—but rarely in man-made forms. In architecture we seldom see mathematical rhythms carried out with the feelings of a frolic. Again, an almost comic idea is connected to the sense of joy; complex calculations have been devoted to fun, serious fun. Inert materials have been organized to build a roof that sings while it keeps the rain out. So we get lightness, elegance, and gaiety—something to shout about.

# CHAPTER SEVEN

# THE STYLE OF FANTASY

As artists manipulate materials, they discover they can invent new forms—forms that were never seen before. While some will not let their work stray from what looks logical or probable, others enjoy creating strange new worlds. And most artists have the skill to make such worlds seem real. Often these imaginary creations reflect an artist's determination to change the rules of reality. Such artists create fantastic forms, or they *let fantastic forms happen*, regarding themselves as instruments that cooperate with universal processes of creation.

Everything in the man-made world almost certainly originated in someone's fantastic imagination. Architects probably imagine new shapes and spaces before they think of practical purposes for them. Even engineers must have moments when they want to build impossible structures, or possible structures that no one needs. Painters and sculptors, more liberated from practical necessity, are in a better position to pursue their visions and intuitions of form. The important point is that fantasy—the imagination of unreal objects, places, and events—is a universal human trait, and art is its principal outlet.

But if our realities were once fantasies, not all fantasies become realities. Chagall's people flying through the air are fantastic, but they do not anticipate general diffusion of the gift of levitation. (That may happen, but not because of Chagall's paintings.) However, some artistic fantasies have utopian implications: the architect who imagines an ideal city may, someday, see that dream come true. As we know, several major architects have proposed utopian structures and communities—fantastic solutions to the problems of social living. City and regional planning might be regarded as the professionalization of our tendency to imagine utopias. Certainly many of the architectural fantasies of the 1920s and 1930s have become living facts. And today, planning for communities in outer space is beginning to seem practical. So private dreams *can* become public realities.

Apart from physical communities, some utopian fantasies deal with ideal personal and social relations. A painting by Edward Hicks (1790–1849), *Peaceable Kingdom*, is based on the Biblical prophecy of a world in which natural enemies live together without conflict, and men (exemplified by William Penn and the Indians in the background) settle their affairs harmoniously. Why is this painting a fantasy? Because the world it portrays is not the

Edward Hicks. *Peaceable Kingdom*. c. 1848.
Oil on canvas, 29 × 36". Pennsylvania
Academy of the Fine Arts, Philadelphia

*below:* Master Gislebertus. Detail of *The Last
Judgment.* c. 1130. Stone relief. From the
west tympanum, Cathedral of Autun, France

Judgment—who goes to heaven and who
goes to hell. The weighing of the souls of the
saved and the damned becomes the focus of
a struggle between amazingly tall angels and
fantastically ugly devils. Notice that the naked
souls, waiting to be judged, have fairly
naturalistic proportions. It is the angels and
demons who are deformed.

one we live in. But if the world Hicks painted is unreal, the ideal it embodies *is* real. And as we have said, ideals have a way of becoming facts.

Fantastic art originates in both logical and irrational mental processes; accordingly, it has no common set of visual traits. Fantastic artworks may be objectively accurate or subjectively distorted. We can speak of a fantastic *style*, then, only because certain works exhibit a logic based on hopes, dreams, myths, and visual speculation. Of course, the visions of a trained mind can have practical potential. For that reason we discuss fantastic art in relation to science as well as myth. Science and myth are equally useful sources of imagery so far as art is concerned. Artists use all kinds of material: the shaman's magic, the scientist's conjecture, the prophecies of wise men, and the hopes of religion.

## MYTH

As children we learned stories and fables that we usually accepted without question: they seemed to explain the world in a way that satisfied our curiosity. With greater sophistication, we realized that myths were not literally true. They were entertaining as fiction but not as reliable accounts of history or as accurate explanations of the way the world works. Still, we could not entirely abandon those early fables: they were converted into folk wisdom and ultimately enshrined in our mental lives in the form of unexamined beliefs and convictions. Officially, we may think of myths and fairy tales as the fantastic entertainments of a stage we have left behind us. But have we?

When an artist like Jean Cocteau presents a fairy tale in a film, our adult sophistication receives a shock: the tale is strangely believable; the myth lives on within us. Thus folk stories have the power to stir our deepest selves long after we think we are immune to superstition. The work of the Swedish film director Ingmar Bergman is usually based on a conflict between the scientific, rational mind and the mythic, poetic, or religious mind. Often, he shows how both tendencies exist in the same person, as in *The Magician*, where a physician succumbs to fantastic fears—fears he thought were overcome by his scientific training.

Why do myths have the power to compel our belief? It is not that they are true as science defines truth, but because they establish convincing connections with the way our minds grasp reality. We are not wholly rational, not completely evolved from our primitive selves. In a sense, myths *are* truthful—truthful accounts of the way we have seen ourselves and the world for most of our life on earth. Accordingly, myths explain a great deal about the way people feel and think. For the artist this is important: even seeing has a mythic component.

In visual art, as in life, mythmaking goes on continually. The visual arts use graphic and plastic fantasy—the creation of strange forms and shapes, or strange combinations of known forms and shapes. At first these may be suggested by accidental technical effects, as in the "planned accidents" of Max Ernst. Also, many artists rely on unconscious suggestions—hidden, mysterious sources of form. Some believe that uncontrolled creation will connect their work with the mythic roots of human personality. So, surrendering to fantasy is not an abandonment of truth; it is a way of gaining access to *a special type of truth*—truth that our culture does not value highly but which nevertheless explains much of our behavior.

A well-known fantastic painting that shows the mythic imagination at work is *Hide-and-Seek* by Pavel Tchelitchew (1898–1957). It simultaneously pictures a tree, a hand, a foot, a system of nerves and blood vessels, and then, embryos, babies, and young children. Everywhere we look, passages of wet, flowing color merge with forms of biological life. The blood vessels look like illustrations for a medical anatomy; tiny lights beautifully illuminate the rendering of an ear or the place where the veins of a leaf merge with the fine capillaries feeding a human fetus.

**Film still from *The Magician*. Directed by Ingmar Bergman. 1958. Courtesy Janus Films, Inc.**

A physician, proud of his scientific knowledge, is driven close to madness by a magician using tricks and illusions. But we, as viewers, are not sure those tricks *are* tricks: the magician seems to have supernatural powers.

Pavel Tchelitchew. *Hide-and-Seek.* 1940–42.
Oil on canvas, 6'6½" × 7'3¾". Collection, The
Museum of Modern Art, New York. Mrs. Simon
Guggenheim Fund

Of course, children do not grow on trees, and the similarity between a hand and a tree is superficial. But for the mythic imagination, things that look alike are aspects of the same reality. Remember, too, that men once worshiped trees, and children are the "fruit" of our bodies; arteries and nervous systems *do* branch out like the limbs of a tree, the fingers of a hand, or the tendons of a foot. Still, the painting by Tchelitchew is not a treatise on physiology; it shows how the primitive portion of human personality confronts themes like the life of the unborn, the drama of nourishment, the connection between plants and people, the tension between dreams and reality, the teeming activity beneath the shells of living things.

## DREAMS AND HALLUCINATIONS

Dreams are further examples of the connection between fantasy and the real world. They seem to lack logical organization after we wake, but while we sleep they look very real, sometimes frighteningly real. Hence, artists often employ dream material to connect with our unconscious processes, or to shock us out of our customary ways of seeing. Often, realistic modes of representation are used; we see images that remind us of hallucinations, images like those caused by a high fever, or shock, or drunkenness. Surrealism is the major example. As an organized movement embracing art, music, and poetry, Surrealism may be dead, but as an artistic influence it is very much alive.

Obviously, an artistic approach that relies on dreams and accidents will encounter resistance from those who think of art as a planned or reasoned approach to creation. However, even rational artistic strategies employ some kind of intuition, some reliance on sources of imagery hidden mysteriously in the self. Otherwise—if art were just a matter of applying known principles to known objectives—artists could be replaced by computers. Computers are wonderful tools, but so far as I know they do not dream.

For their interest in dreams, the Surrealists were, of course, indebted to Sigmund Freud. They learned from him that dreams are only *seemingly* illogical, that they have meaning if certain principles of interpretation are known. Not that Surrealist paintings are merely collections of symbols requiring a key (a dictionary of symbols) for interpretation. They also employ the device of fantastic or shocking image juxtaposition to create new meanings. Surrealist theory maintains that shock has educative value; that is, it causes viewers to reorganize their habits of perception. But why reorganize our habits of perception? Because—according to the Surrealists—we are hopelessly enmeshed in wrong ways of thinking.

In Salvador Dali's (1904–1989) *Soft Construction with Boiled Beans: Premonition of Civil War*, we see a highly realistic technique combined with a strangely mutilated human figure. Employing strong light and shadow contrasts plus careful modeling, Dali skillfully enhances the illusion that his fantasies are real. The sky and landscape are painted in hues that could be seen in a vacation postcard or a television travelogue. This rather banal naturalism adds to the shock value of the imagery. We also have an eroded landscape with a tiny figure (lower left) which establishes the monstrous scale of the main subjects: skeletal forms, huge pieces of female anatomy, and a grimacing head attached to a breast which is being squeezed by a clawlike hand. There is also a tree trunk merging into a foot that acts as a kind of crutch. Notice the melting of objects—a typical Surrealist trait. We experience that melting in dreams, where persons and objects also exchange identities. From animal to vegetable, from natural to artificial, from mechanical to human: these changes or metamorphoses occur in mythology, too. This "logic" may or may not hold some sort of truth; it certainly asks us to change the way we think.

Meret Oppenheim. *Object.* 1936. Fur-covered cup, saucer, and spoon; cup, 4⅜" diameter; saucer, 9⅜" diameter; spoon, 8" long; overall height 2⅞". Collection, The Museum of Modern Art, New York. Purchase

The idea of a fur-covered cup, saucer, and spoon is fantastic and absurd. So we laugh. But our laughter is close to panic: this image threatens everyday logic; our world might collapse.

Salvador Dali. *Soft Construction with Boiled Beans: Premonition of Civil War.* 1936. Oil on canvas, 39⅜ × 39". Philadelphia Museum of Art. The Louise and Walter Arensberg Collection

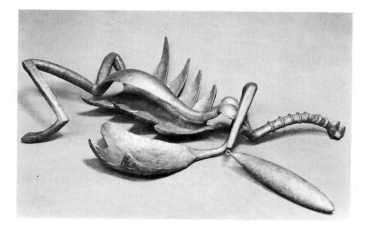

*below:* Alberto Giacometti. *Woman with Her Throat Cut.* 1932. Bronze (cast 1949), 8 × 34½ × 25". Collection, The Museum of Modern Art, New York. Purchase

A gruesome fantasy made all the more lurid because it is rendered with exquisite clarity and loving attention to form.

Art Nouveau chair. c. 1910. Wood, gesso, and silver paint, 36 × 25 × 16". Collection Leo Castelli and Jean Christophe Castelli

A chair that wants to be something else. Wavy plant stems and female heads combine to create an object that seems to be having a terrible dream.

Another example of metamorphosis can be seen in *Secretary*, a sculpture by Richard Stankiewicz (born 1922). This fantasy consists of a torso made of a boiler with a typewriter embedded in its "abdomen." Pipe-stem arms operate the typewriter which belongs to the secretary's body—an incongruous combination of the human and the mechanical. Many contemporary artworks deal with this theme: persons becoming machines, or machines becoming persons. Here, a human being assimilates a machine and then operates on its mechanical innards. Perhaps Stankiewicz is making a prediction—telling us what will happen to machines and people as they age and rust and begin to look like each other.

An interesting variation of the Stankiewicz fantasy appears in an advertisement for the Royal Typewriter Company. The idea of a typewriter emerging from a French horn is whimsical and absurd at the same time. At first it seems to be a clever way to attract attention. But why a French horn? Because it is a beautiful, carefully crafted instrument that makes a rich sound. When we see it presenting a typewriter like an artwork on a pedestal, or a mother giving birth to a "perfect child," we get a complex advertising message. In this fantasy two artificial objects are, for a moment, organically united: they exchange essential traits and they share each other's excellence.

Picasso's etching *Minotauromachy* is one of the monuments of Surrealism. This work embodies almost all the elements of fantastic art: dream, myth, hallucination, erotic reverie, incongruous juxtaposition, a man-animal monster, and more. Picasso deals with the Cretan myth of the Minotaur and with modern bullfighting; he also refers to the Greek legend in which Zeus, disguised as a bull, abducts Europa. Here, Europa is shown as a sleeping or unconscious female matador carried off by a badly wounded horse whose entrails pour out of his torn belly. But violent as the scene is, it is calmly viewed by beautiful human faces. At the left, an innocent-looking flower girl holds a light up to the Minotaur, who symbolizes chaos and violence. As with all dreams, this work is not easily interpreted, but it makes us aware of recurrent themes in ancient and modern European history. For a Spaniard like

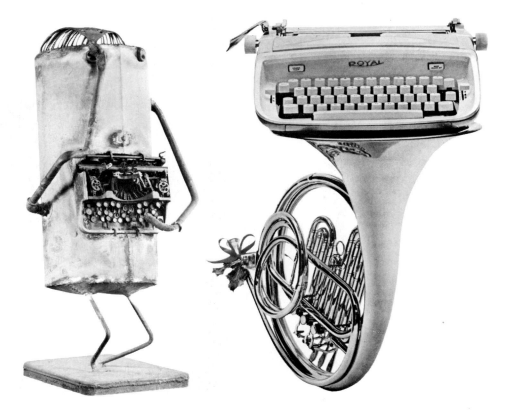

*right:* Richard Stankiewicz. *Secretary.* 1953. Mixed media, 35⅞" high. The Israel Museum, Jerusalem

*far right:* Advertisement. *A Christmas gift with keys so lively, they can go 115 words a minute.* Courtesy Royal Typewriter Company, New York

*left:* Pablo Picasso. *Minotauromachy.* 1935. Etching, printed in black; plate, 19½ × 27⁷⁄₁₆". Collection, The Museum of Modern Art, New York. Purchase Fund

*above:* Pablo Picasso. *Baboon and Young.* 1951. Bronze (cast 1955), after found objects, 21" high, base 13¼ × 6⁷⁄₈". Collection, The Museum of Modern Art, New York. Mrs. Simon Guggenheim Fund

Picasso's use of a toy automobile for the baboon's head is a good illustration of Surrealistic humor: the logic of the sculpture is stronger than the logic of the "real world."

Picasso, the tauromachy—the ritualistic killing of a bull—reenacts a pre-Christian fertility rite which is connected to ancient ideas of love and rape. Picasso explores his Spanish heritage, his erotic fantasies, and his fascination with bullfighting to serve up a large piece of history in one concentrated image. Two years later, in 1937, he painted his *Guernica,* commemorating one of the cruelest events of the Spanish Civil War. The *Minotauromachy* anticipated that work: Picasso seems to have seen—or prophesied—what would happen to Europe.

In Henri Rousseau's (1844–1910) *The Dream* we encounter a type of fantasy which is based on the imagination of a primitive artist. Here "primitive" means untrained or self-taught and perhaps childlike. Rousseau lovingly portrays his dream of a naked woman on a couch, mysteriously located in a jungle where exotic birds, animals, natives, and vegetation abound. This is not only the dream of the artist; some have suggested that it may also be the woman's dream. Naive and mildly erotic, it shows us nature's abundance conveniently arranged so that food is easily available, the animals are friendly, the natives are kind, and the environment intoxicates our senses. In this lush setting, man and woman can enjoy real love.

Rousseau produces a magnificent decorative effect by his careful rendering of flowers and foliage. And while his drawing of the nude is a bit stiff, he manages to dramatize her figure with strong illumination and careful modeling. Thus, a "primitive" artist makes a dream seem real and attainable by painting each detail with absolute conviction. Rousseau demonstrates a major principle of fantastic art: for the visionary, conviction is the key; the artist has to believe.

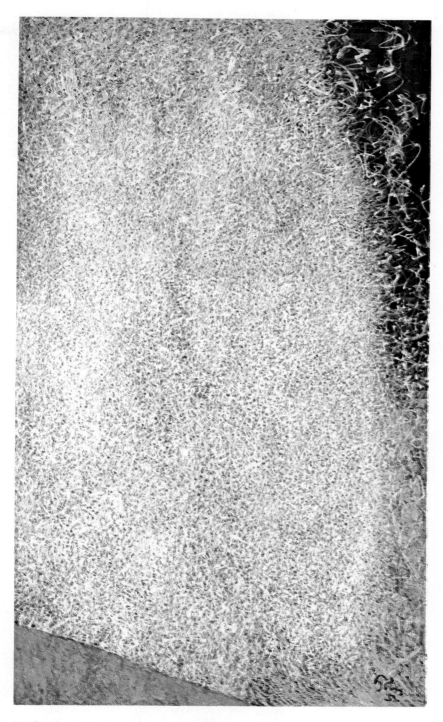

*opposite above:* Henri Rousseau. *The Dream.* 1910. Oil on canvas, 6'8½" × 9'9½". Collection, The Museum of Modern Art, New York. Gift of Nelson A. Rockefeller

For Rousseau, nature's fertility is generous and benign. For Ernst, nature is an arena of cancerous growth: plants and animals exchange identity; ceaseless reproduction spawns monsters; vegetation threatens to choke out the sky. Rousseau's dream of contentment has been replaced by an Ernstian hallucination. Which vision is right?

*opposite below:* Max Ernst. *The Joy of Living.* 1936. Oil on canvas, 28⅝ × 36". Private collection, London

Mark Tobey. *Edge of August.* 1953. Casein on composition board, 48 × 28". Collection, The Museum of Modern Art, New York. Purchase

We cannot tell where this is: Tobey uses a strange sort of writing with light to dissolve the boundaries of places and objects. Line, color, and light combine to produce a mystical sense of oneness with the world.

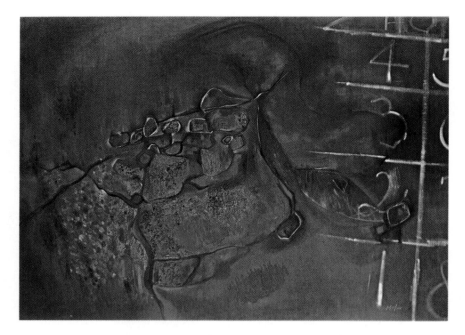

Loren MacIver. *Hopscotch.* 1940. Oil on canvas, 27 × 35⅝". Collection,
The Museum of Modern Art, New York. Purchase

These are the ordinary marks and textures we might see on a city
sidewalk—juxtaposed by accident. But MacIver does not overlook them;
she changes them into strangely beautiful emblems—signs of truth
written in a language we cannot decipher.

Matta. *Disasters of Mysticism.* 1942. Oil on canvas, 38¼ × 51⅜".
Collection James Thrall Soby, New Canaan, Connecticut

Matta depicts a gorgeous explosion of energy in outer space. We feel a
sense of release plus a certain amount of cosmic anxiety. There are great
fires in this world; if we approach them we might be incinerated.

Barnett Newman. *Adam*. 1951–52. Oil on canvas, 95⅝ ×
79⅝". The Tate Gallery, London

Newman's vertical divisions represent a parting of the
pictorial field, which then opens primordial space to the
viewer; we see the world at the beginning.

Arthur G. Dove. *That Red One*. 1944. Oil on canvas, 27 × 36".
William H. Lane Foundation, Leominster, Massachusetts

Dove tried to work his way out of nature and then back
again, cleansed by abstraction and armed with the radiant
force of a powerful symbol: a black sun.

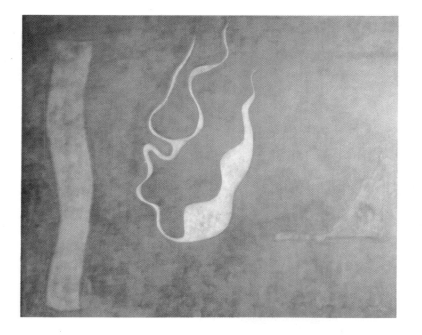

**William Baziotes. *The Sea.* 1959. Oil on canvas, 60 × 72". Collection Mr. and Mrs. Morris H. Grossmann, New York**

For a certain kind of artist, the miraculous emerges in the discovery that painting can evoke a natural world nature does not know.

**Mark Rothko. *Earth and Green.* 1955. Galerie Beyeler, Basel**

Because of its size and the floating, looming qualities of the color, Rothko's painting becomes an environment in which we feel ourselves absorbed. Our sense of self is dissolved in the act of visual contemplation.

## SCIENTIFIC FANTASY

Science and technology dominate our lives, so it is not surprising that artists have adapted their symbols. Science raises questions about outer space and submicrocosmic matter—questions that fascinate the popular imagination and stimulate endless speculation. *Artistic* speculation about technology belongs to a natural process of humanizing concepts which can radically change our notions of space, time, matter, and energy. These concepts are often threatening, so we cope with them indirectly—in dreams, jokes, and tall stories. Artists do the same thing, employing their language of images to find out whether new scientific ideas can be used expressively in their private worlds of feeling and intuition. They wonder how new discoveries about motion and energy will change the way people deal with reality. This sort of speculation may not add to our fund of scientific knowledge, but it does explain how science affects the human psyche, our collective modes of thinking and feeling.

The work of the Chilean painter Matta (Echaurren) (born 1912) offers an interesting artistic effort to deal with the world of outer space. Matta builds on a Surrealist foundation, which encourages him to examine his dreams of flying, floating, and wandering in a nonresistant environment. The result is a fantastic universe with an astrophysical look. This imagery reminds us of microphotographs of subatomic particles, showing their orbits, velocities, and collisions, their short but active life spans. As the particle paths overlap and combine, they produce forms that have both geometrical and organic qualities. In Matta's fantasies, we always detect a biological note, a hint of living form. Together with the movements of electron particles guided by the laws of physics, there is our familiar water, air, and sunlight. Outer space is not all rocks and radiation surrounded by nothingness: there are bodies out there; and some of them are burning.

Matta has not built a model of the real universe. Instead, he paints a world that might be seen by some superior eye, an eye that simultaneously understands the imagery of science and art. In other words, Matta is not producing talented technical illustration. Perhaps the best analogy to his work can be seen in the late medieval painting of Hieronymus Bosch (c. 1450–1516), where the torments of Hell are described in loving detail. Bosch painted what no one had seen but what everyone thought about—the incredible tortures of the damned according to then-current notions of cosmology and theology. Interestingly, the fifteenth-century Hell depicted by Bosch bears an uncanny resemblance to the fantastic, extraterrestrial world depicted by Matta.

## FANTASY AND ILLUSIONISM

Because they want us to believe in their fantasies, artists use a variety of representational devices. Like shamans and magicians, they work hard to create credible illusions. As we shall see, the style of fantasy calls for thorough mastery of realistic technique.

*Infinite Divisibility* by the American Surrealist Yves Tanguy (1900–1955) employs the naturalistic lighting and modeling we would expect in a conventional still-life painting. Certainly these are inanimate objects—*nature morte* or "dead nature," as the French say. Light comes from a single source, which causes these fantastic objects to cast sharp shadows that obey the laws of perspective as they move toward a horizon we cannot see. In the distance we see glowing light radiating from one, or several, suns. This light passes through an atmosphere much as sunlight sometimes reaches us on earth—through a cloud haze. The objects themselves belong to a skeletal system. But whose? They seem to have organic *and* mechanical origins: some resemble sticks or stones or geological forms. And a machine is suggested by the geometric contraption at the left.

Roger de La Fresnaye. *The Conquest of the Air.* Oil on canvas, 7'8⅞" × 6'5". Collection,
The Museum of Modern Art, New York. Mrs. Simon Guggenheim Fund

Matta. *Here, Sir Fire, Eat!* 1942. Oil on canvas, 56⅛ × 44⅛". Collection, The Museum of Modern Art, New York. James Thrall Soby Bequest

Hieronymus Bosch. *Hell* (detail of *The Garden of Delights*). c. 1500. The Prado, Madrid

Yves Tanguy. *Infinite Divisibility.* 1942. Oil on canvas, 40 × 35". Albright-Knox Art Gallery, Buffalo, New York. Room of Contemporary Art Fund, 1945

After we examine the sharp, carefully rendered forms in the foreground of Tanguy's world, everything dissolves into a luminous haze. The infinite horizon creates a dream mood, an atmosphere of silence. And since the color is mostly silvery gray, the painting has an almost photographic quality. The overall effect of the work is to induce a calm acceptance of an otherworldly environment. There is no violence in this "lunar" landscape; it seems to exist in a time *after* violence and passion have spent their force. So Tanguy's universe—so bare of the essentials needed to sustain life—is amazingly peaceful. Perhaps that is because these creatures are no longer alive. This may be the world as it would look after we (and everything else) have become extinct.

Another kind of illusionism is employed in *The Bride* by Marcel Duchamp (1887–1963). Here we have the convincing representation of geometric solids connected by some sort of mechanical-biological circulation system. The title adds a touch of Surrealistic irony by contrasting the romantic meanings of "bride" with a quasi-Cubist picture of what might be human viscera. We are shown the insides of a mysterious system that hints at human internal organs and arteries. This is the sort of imagery we might see in a catalogue for a plumbing manufacturer. Perhaps we are looking at a Surrealist "gag"—a mad, ironic image of what goes on inside the bodies we love so well.

Surrealist illusionism depends on visual discoveries made as early as the Renaissance. Today, many artists have abandoned that type of illusionism, preferring to use real objects which are glued, nailed, soldered, or welded together—for example, *Masculine Presence* by Jason Seley (1919–1983). This figure is made of welded automobile bumpers and a grill (possibly a 1955 Buick). The result looks like a man's muscle and skeletal system, with the convex machine parts producing a remarkably organic effect. Seley's figure suggests an interesting relationship between industrial design and sculpture. The original purpose of an automobile bumper was to provide a sturdy defense for a car's easily damaged metal skin. Over the years, however, designers "improved" the rugged old bumper with a variety of curvilinear shapes. That is, they treated it like sculpture, giving it quasi-figurative, usually female, qualities. Seley understands this. But in reassembling these automobile parts, he has changed their sex, returning them to the human body they were taken from. And perhaps—as sculpture—that is where they belong.

For a more whimsical fantasy we can turn to Marisol (Escobar) (born 1930), who made *The Generals* out of painted wood, plaster, and assorted odds and ends. Notice the barrel in the body of the horse and an ordinary table or bench in the legs. Marisol's sculpture plays with several levels of representation and meaning at once: overall it has a hobbyhorse quality, particularly in the horse's neck, head, and tail. The stiffness and boxlike construction of the generals suggests children's soldiers; but their painted

*above:* Jason Seley. *Masculine Presence.* 1961. Assemblage: welded chromium-plated steel automobile bumpers and grill, 7'2⅞" × 4'. Collection, The Museum of Modern Art, New York. Gift of Dr. and Mrs. Leonard Kornblee

*left:* Marcel Duchamp. *The Bride.* 1912. Oil on canvas, 35⅛ × 21¾". Philadelphia Museum of Art. The Louise and Walter Arensberg Collection

Marisol. *The Generals.* 1961–62. Wood and mixed media, 87" high. Albright-Knox Art Gallery, Buffalo, New York. Gift of Seymour H. Knox, 1962

Humorous fantasy: from silly soldiers to serious sculpture.

faces and helmets (inverted cereal bowls?) give them the rigidity of dedicated warriors. Their legs and boots are painted on the barrel like children's book illustrations; so it is hard to take their generalship seriously. For a heroic equestrian statue, the horse will not do. And why are two generals riding the same horse?

Marisol hardly tries to create fool-the-eye illusions; and only modest craftsmanship is required to mount boxes on a barrel or a barrel on a bench. Yet, with the visual hints she gives us, it is easy to imagine silly soldiers on horseback. Her art consists in planting certain satirical ideas in the viewer's consciousness: that generals look like boxes; that military posturing is a child's game; that courage means stiffness. Also, we know that generals don't go into battle on table legs (or anything else). That knowledge is also part of the work of art.

Traditional artists persuaded paint, clay, or stone to look like flesh or hair or cloth, whereas contemporary artists employ real objects along with illusionistic fragments to create several levels of reality in one work. This is what enables Seley and Marisol to "play with" the viewer's frame of reference. The result can lead to fresh insight, a vacation from reality, or a good laugh. We should remember, too, that every work of art is, in a sense, a fantasy. Artists always operate in the realm between reality and illusion, encouraging us to look a little harder at the real world. Indeed, they make us wonder what makes it real.

# PART THREE

# THE STRUCTURE OF ART

When we learned to speak, we tried almost from the beginning to express desires, feelings, and ideas. Adults helped us to pronounce words, but they did not give us definitions of nouns, verbs, and adjectives and ask us to put them together. Somehow, we learned to say words and understand them at the same time. Mostly, we learned to use language through trial and error and meaningful reactions to our talk. Much later, teachers dissected the language for us, broke it down into parts of speech and rules of usage. Before that, without consciously knowing the rules, we managed to understand what people were saying.

The same is true of art: we have been using its language, and now we are about to study its *structure*—its parts and how they are assembled to produce meaning and emotion. Studying the structure of art may not be absolutely essential for understanding its overall significance; life experiences and common sense may be as useful as formal instruction. However, there are other reasons for studying the structure of art.

First of all, the parts and organizational devices of a language have meanings which are expressive or enjoyable in themselves. What makes them "expressive or enjoyable"? Our chapter on Aesthetics tries to answer that question. Listening to the way a soprano sings certain notes yields pleasure over and above what we get from her song as a whole. There can be passages in a picture, parts of a sculpture, sections of a building, that are satisfying even though the *complete* painting, sculpture, or building does not work. This type of breakdown gives us our second purpose for studying the structure of art: to find out what is responsible for an artwork's failure or success. Finally, we want to understand the principles of artistic organization—how a work is composed or designed—because design is itself a source of information and pleasure; it tells us how artists think, how images function, and how viewers perceive what artists have created. So the discussion in the following chapters focuses on parts and wholes and the responses they evoke. We study the building blocks of art plus the tactics and strategies that make them work together effectively.

# THE VISUAL ELEMENTS: GRAMMAR

People see images, not things. Light sensations falling on the retina are carried as energy impulses to the brain, where they are almost simultaneously translated into a meaningful entity called an image. Not that there is a picture, an optical projection, in the brain. Optical processes are in the eye alone; perception is a function of the brain, body, and mind. Because of that "mind connection" we cannot experience sensations without characterizing them. An image, therefore, can be defined as *the result of endowing optical sensations with meaning*.

The images we see have labels designated by words like house, tree, sun, and sky. And just as words can be broken down into letters, images can be broken down into their visual elements: line, shape, color, and texture. Furthermore, we can learn to focus on those visual elements. In fact, when we focus on *part* of an image, that part becomes an image: our minds have a tendency to create wholes out of parts.

Here we are concerned with the visual elements as they are employed by artists. But after seeing them in art, we may recognize them in nature, too. We see the visual elements in the natural world because we *project* upon nature the habits of perception that our species has found useful or pleasurable. For that reason, studying the structure of art yields indirect dividends— added satisfaction from the perception of images regardless of their source.

Labels for the visual elements tend to vary according to the user, but what they refer to is fairly consistent. It does not matter greatly if one authority uses "shape," another "contour," and a third "form" (shape is flat and form is three-dimensional). Mainly we want to understand the visual effects that the labels designate.

## LINE

There is a difference between a *line* and *line-in-general*. A line is the path made by a pointed instrument: a pen, a pencil, a crayon, a stick. A line implies action because work was required to make it. Line-in-general suggests direction or orientation. An impression of movement can be achieved by a series of shapes; none of them needs to be thin, sharp, or linear, but collectively they can suggest sequence, direction, or thrust. In other words, a line is a mark made by a sharp, moving instrument, whereas line-in-general represents the

*opposite:* **Poncho section from Peru.**
A.D. 700–1000. **Wood, 40¾ × 19⅞".**
**The Metropolitan Museum of Art, New York.**
**The Michael C. Rockefeller Memorial Collection.**
**Bequest of Nelson A. Rockefeller, 1979**

Almost all the visual elements—line, shape, color, light, and texture—can be seen in this superb Peruvian fabric. Yet, despite its extreme geometricization, the design is representational: it depicts a feline deity holding a human-headed staff. The imagery looks highly abstract, but for the ancient Peruvians it read like a book. For us, the lesson is that abstract forms are most powerful when rooted in real objects, places, and events.

Norbert Kricke. *Raumplastik Kugel.* 1955.
Nickel, 15¾ × 17¾". Collection Hertha Kricke,
Düsseldorf

Compare Kricke's white-wire construction to the
paintings of Matta (pages 196 and 201). Both
artists use linear systems to describe subatomic-
particle trajectories, or the motion of bodies in
outer space.

Pablo Picasso. *Diaghilev and Selisburg.* 1919.
Pencil, 24⅞ × 18⅞". Collection the artist's estate

Victor Pasmore. *Linear Development No. 6:
Spiral.* 1964. Oil and gravure on board, 18 × 19".
Collection Mrs. John Weeks, London

A system of drawn lines serves as a visual
analogy for processes in nature: growth, flow,
resistance, and mutual adaptation.

viewer's conclusion that a set of forms is going somewhere. Here, we shall
be talking mainly about a *line*, a distinct series of points.

Because all of us have used lines to write, to make marks in the sand or
on walls, we know that drawing a line calls for thought: a choice must be
made about where the line will go. In learning to write we discovered that
some lines produce letters that cannot be understood. That is, there can be
right and wrong lines. In writing, a "wrong" line is one that doesn't follow
certain rules. To write legibly we have to agree about what letter forms should
look like; then we need the muscular coordination to make them right. In
drawing, too, we try to control lines so that there will be a resemblance
between the shapes we make and visual reality. The idea that there are linear
agreements about how lines communicate was established early in our lives.

When we were young, line combinations had magical properties: a circle
could be the sun, a face, a flower; lines were alive with possibilities. Sometimes, professional artists try to recapture those magical-symbolic properties
of line, using them in fresh combinations that may become new artistic
conventions. And people seem to understand them immediately. Picasso's
linear treatment of the crying woman in *Guernica* (page 51) is a good
example: we recognized what it meant the first time we saw it.

**Uses of Line in Works of Art**    For a simple demonstration of line's elo-
quence, we might examine Picasso's drawing of the ballet impresarios
Diaghilev and Selisburg. Here the artist who gave us so many distorted human
images shows his mastery of naturalistic contours. Mainly, he uses an ac-
cented line to describe the weight and volume of enclosed forms. Thus M.
Selisburg's fleshy face and hands are executed with a line of utmost precision.
The absence of shading gives an almost classical elegance to both of these
well-fed gentlemen. Notice, too, that Picasso also uses the power of geometric
forms; we sense the presence of underlying ovals, cylinders, and rectangles
in this deceptively simple drawing.

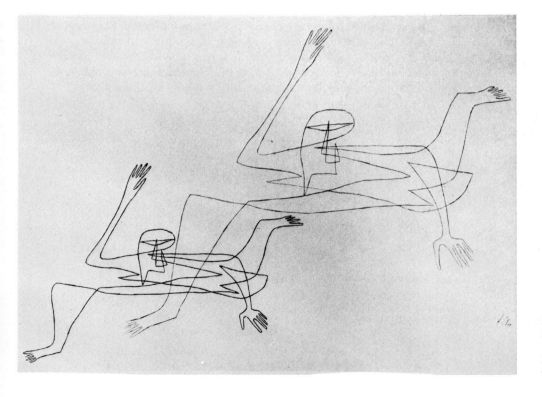

The writing on this diploma looks authentic, but it cannot be read: the artist has exploited all the linear and compositional conventions of diploma art except those concerning correct letter form.

The idea of linear energy often appears in the work of Paul Klee (1879–1940). Not only does line describe the shapes of things, it also calls attention to itself *becoming something else.* Klee enjoys a kind of metaphysical wit: he creates illusions of reality and then he tells us we have been deceived. Actually, he lets us in on a private joke: the artist is not sure whether the image he draws is "out there," inside himself, or in our agreement to share an illusion.

In Klee's *Flight from Oneself* we see a marvelous, funny-sad pattern of lines: it visualizes the ridiculous antics of a split personality. The gestures seem to be decorative echoes until we realize that they represent twin aspects of the same person. The meandering line—which looks like a disciplined scribble—is duplicated exactly in two scales. The result is two figures which are separate but joined, attached to each other by the same cord that gives them life. Thus, with one continuous piece of string, Klee portrays the shifting reality of mind, body, and personality.

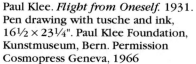

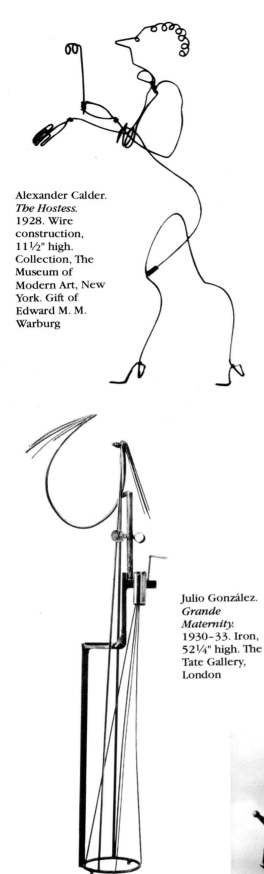

Alexander Calder.
*The Hostess.*
1928. Wire
construction,
11½" high.
Collection, The
Museum of
Modern Art, New
York. Gift of
Edward M. M.
Warburg

Julio González.
*Grande
Maternity.*
1930–33. Iron,
52¼" high. The
Tate Gallery,
London

Drawing lines occur in sculpture, too, except that they move in three dimensions. A good illustration is the humorous little wire sculpture by Alexander Calder, *The Hostess.* Here we see how much line can convey through suggestion. There is also a penetration of solid sculptural forms, a penetration which has fostered new directions in welded sculpture: Julio González (1872–1942) was one of the first modern sculptors to exploit the linear properties of metal—iron rods. Logically enough, his work grows out of the rich Spanish tradition of decorative ironwork. In *Grande Maternity*, welded rods form a stately, monumentally dignified sculpture of a woman. Notice that González composes by elimination, arriving at form by subtraction more than addition. The sweeping lines of the rods and the cagelike structure of the skirt are remarkably effective in suggesting the movement and grace of the female figure.

In *Royal Bird*, David Smith (1906–1965) plays almost musical variations on a dominant horizontal line. Here, as in Theodore Roszak's *Spectre of Kitty Hawk* (page 168), the basis of sculptural form is a bird's skeleton. The calm horizontal axis is counteracted by a fierce beak-and-jaw construction and the bird's aggressive stance. Notice that the rib-cage pattern, translated into metal, suggests the armor of a medieval knight more than Thanksgiving leftovers. But if we can suppress our associations with turkey, and see the horizontal pattern as a written script, we can almost read this sculpture as metal calligraphy.

Klee's psychological use of line appears again in his drawing *And I Shall Say.* Here, too, the figure seems to have been produced with a slightly directed scribble. The hands and feet imitate children's drawing, but the face had to be drawn by a trained artist. Klee combined several types of line to produce this psychologically convincing characterization. It is an approach that has been used by legions of modern artists, designers, and cartoonists. Klee's line can be a nervous impulse, a contour, a notion about to collapse, or a soul rebuilding itself. Notice how the inner-directed eyes express the idea of the child in the adult. We see a person pathetically wrapped in fantasy; her mouth is closed and her mind is speaking; she listens to herself answering someone in an imaginary dialogue. And most of this is accomplished with a smart scribble.

Line is perhaps the most expressive of the visual elements. Why? (1) Because the *outlines* of things are crucial keys to their identity. (2) Because of our almost universal experience with line in writing and drawing. (3) Because line is precise and unambiguous; it forces artists to "speak" clearly. (4) Because line leads the viewer's eye, implying movement and direction. (5) Because line (for some inscrutable reason) symbolizes thought.

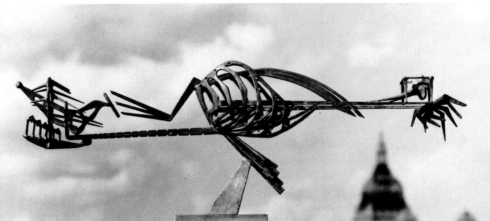

David Smith. *Royal Bird.* 1948.
Stainless steel, 21¾ × 59 × 9".
Walker Art Center, Minneapolis

Paul Klee. *And I Shall Say.* 1934. Pencil, 18⅞ × 12⅜". Paul Klee Foundation, Kunstmuseum, Bern

## SHAPE

Our discussion of line touches on shape because closed lines become the boundaries of shapes. However, shapes can be created without lines—when a painter establishes a color area, or a sculptor builds a three-dimensional form. In both cases, drawn lines are unnecessary. Shapes do have *linear* quality when our attention is drawn to their edges, or their direction, but usually we think of shapes as areas, or as silhouettes—containers of more-or-less homogeneous stuff.

The shapes that artists create have numerous sources: some are taken directly from nature; others reflect the marks of the tool used to make them. Then there are shapes which are "invented." But we cannot help seeing them—no matter how abstract—in terms of our experience with reality. That is, we cannot see a triangle without relating its corners to something sharp and pointed—something that can puncture. So triangular shapes are potentially dangerous but not necessarily. A triangle resting on its base also suggests rest or immovability, like an Egyptian pyramid. The expressive meaning of a shape depends on which of its properties the artist has emphasized. If an artist uses a triangular shape to describe something which is normally curved, that may give us a clue to its aesthetic meaning. Why, for example, does the horse's tongue in Picasso's *Guernica* (page 51) come to a sharp, daggerlike point? Because that shape, in that place, symbolizes pain—the pain of the Spanish people.

Seeing lines and shapes involves a certain amount of guessing about where they came from. When we encounter a perfect geometric shape, we doubt that it was made by hand: perfect straightness or curvature usually implies a mechanical origin; irregularity of shape usually suggests handmade forms. Because machine forms are the product of human planning and

211

Jean Arp. *Star.* 1939–60. Marble, 22½ × 20½ × 4". Collection Édouard Loeb, Paris

design, they usually have precise, essentially intellectual qualities. Of course, geometrical shapes can be found in nature—in crystals, in snowflakes, and in geological formations. But the natural objects we see with the unaided human eye usually have uneven, irregular shapes.

Our bodies and the bodies of animals are a main source of curvilinear shapes. They are modeled ultimately on the patterns of organic growth—growth through the division and integration of cells. But this principle is violated by crustaceans, living creatures that have sharp, jagged, almost geometrically shaped armor. Their armor—which has been so suggestive to sculptors—is like our fingernails; it lacks nerves and blood vessels, the capacity for sensation. So "armor" shapes look as if they feel no pain; they look as if they can *inflict* pain.

In *Star*, a sculpture by Jean Arp, we see a rounded, organic shape given to something usually conceived in geometric terms. A star is, after all, light from a distant body; we do not see its source, just its light waves—usually shown as straight, not curved, lines. But Arp has chosen a living model for the conventionally pointed star diagram; his star renounces geometry and radiating lines. Instead, it has skin and flesh, perhaps some bones, and an opening in its center. The contradiction between the standard notion of a star and Arp's organic version invites us to think of "bodies" in outer space: maybe the universe is a *biological* system.

Architecture is an unlikely source of organic shapes since its structural devices are usually geometric. However, the development of reinforced concrete has greatly enlarged the architect's vocabulary. Indeed, some contemporary buildings are faulted for being *too* sculptural; they create exciting shapes at the expense of functional efficiency. But in Le Corbusier's chapel at Ronchamp, functional requirements are satisfied while organic shapes enhance the building's symbolic expressiveness. Notice the roof shape, which might be compared to a fish; it does, in fact, resemble a sculpture by Brancusi called the *Fish*. Do we force the comparison by suggesting that the roof is deliberately shaped like a fish, an early Christian symbol? In any case, the

*left:* Theodore J. Roszak. *Sea Sentinel.* 1956. Steel brazed with bronze, 8'9" high. Collection of Whitney Museum of American Art, New York. Purchase

The weapons and armor of crustaceans offer a form language that has a curious fascination for contemporary painters and sculptors.

*below:* Spiny lobsters

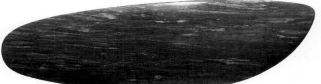

*left:* Le Corbusier. Notre-Dame-du-Haut, Ronchamp, France, 1950–55

The shapes we see in Le Corbusier's roof and in Brancusi's *Fish* are surprisingly similar. Can this be explained? Perhaps the same idea speaks to us through a similar process of abstracting from living form.

*below:* Constantin Brancusi. *Fish.* 1930. Gray marble, 21 × 71"; on three-part pedestal of one marble and two limestone cylinders, 29⅛" high. Collection, The Museum of Modern Art, New York. Acquired through the Lillie P. Bliss Bequest

biomorphic shapes in the building increase our awareness of the chapel as a living body—a religious idea that works as visual form.

Another architectural use of organic shapes can be seen in the facade of the Casa Batlló in Barcelona, designed by Antoni Gaudí (1852–1926). Clearly, he avoids geometric shapes wherever he can. In Gaudí's architecture, doors, windows, chimneys, and balconies are converted into fantastic forms, usually resembling human or animal bodily parts. His style appears to be a triumph of the biomorphic imagination over the character of materials. We see living shapes performing architectural, sculptural, and symbolic functions at the same time.

Antoni Gaudí. Detail of Casa Batlló, Barcelona. 1905–7

The fleshy facade Gaudí designed for the Casa Batlló acquires strength and firmness through the thin, bony columns that seem to support enormous Surrealistic eyelids.

213

*right:* Jean Arp. *Madame Torso with Wavy Hat.* 1916. Wood relief, 15⅞ × 10⅜". Hermann and Margrit Rupf Foundation, Kunstmuseum, Bern

*far right:* Adolph Gottlieb. *Blast II.* 1957. Oil on raw canvas, 90 × 45". Joseph E. Seagram and Sons, Inc., New York

In Arp's *Madame Torso with Wavy Hat*, shape has a comic function. We can easily identify madame's hourglass figure, but her head and hat have changed into something else. Ocean waves? An Ionic capital? An upside-down handlebar mustache? Notice, too, how the convex forms of the hips are balanced by *concave* shapes located where the thighs would fit into the torso. These shape relationships are dramatized by shadows cast by the figure's raised relief. But why do these shapes look funny? Because organic forms without structural firmness seem to wriggle like jelly. And jelly is funny because it has no bones.

*Blast II* by Adolph Gottlieb (1903–1974) is virtually a laboratory demonstration of the expressive properties of shape. The canvas is occupied by two forms of the same area and mass, but the upper one is smoothly rounded whereas the lower one is ragged and smeared at the edges. The title suggests

**below: Billowing spinnakers**

Shapes also possess volumetric meanings: we perceive them as the containers of dynamic forces. The beauty of a sailboat (and its female associations) are based on the container idea, here expressed in the spinnakers.

*right:* Paul Klee. *The Great Dome.* 1927. Pen and tusche, 10½ × 12". Paul Klee Foundation, Kunstmuseum, Bern

that we are looking at an abstract version of a nuclear explosion: the circular form must represent a mushroom cloud, while the violent shape below symbolizes destruction. The cloud has a serene, floating quality which contrasts with the angry shape underneath. Notice the blotched quality of the brushstrokes around its edge: Gottlieb emphasizes its chaotic, "dirty" character. Obviously, he is exploiting the stark contrast between a sooty, black shape and the clean, brushed-out form floating above it.

Paul Klee gives us a striking illustration of two basic types of shape—the biomorphic and the geometric. *The Great Dome* might be considered a sexual/symbolic statement in the guise of architectural description. The structure at the left represents a monument of our architectural tradition—the heavenly dome. It also describes the female breast, our prime symbol of maternal nurture. At the right Klee depicts a tower, a symbol of maleness standing erect because of a geometrical system of triangles. These shapes appear to be opposed but they are connected along the base of the composition. To engage in some amateur psychologizing, it might be said that Klee uses these shapes to say that man and woman are fundamentally different, and that they are fundamentally (at rock bottom) united. In other words, the sexes have to be joined to create a complete picture.

We see an extreme example of geometrical shapes representing human beings in *The Cardplayers* by Theo van Doesburg (1883–1931). (Cézanne's earlier *Card Players* may have anticipated the analysis of form in Van

Theo van Doesburg. *Composition: The Cardplayers.* 1917. Oil on canvas, 45⅝ × 41¾". Gemeente Museum, The Hague, The Netherlands

Paul Cézanne. *The Card Players.* c. 1890-95. Oil on canvas, 17¾ × 22½". Musée d'Orsay, Paris. Bequest of Isaac de Camondo, 1911

final Proof Hundertwasser 田 屋根の上の川

彫川嶋達夫
摺清水昭男

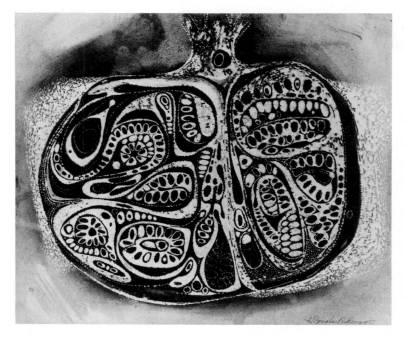

*left:* Printed circuit (used in television sets). 1958. Plastic sheet, copper foil bonded to surface, 7⅜ × 5". Collection, The Museum of Modern Art, New York. Gift of Warwick Manufacturing Company, U.S.A.

Printed circuitry and a section of fruit; their similarity shows how advanced technology approaches art and how both approach the organic.

*above:* H. Douglas Pickering. *Pomegranate.* 1955. Collection the artist

Doesburg's work.) This composition consists of a system of rectangles, loosely packed on the outside and densely packed in the center. A few large L-shapes suggest shoulders, knees, and chairs. Notice that the organization of these geometrical shapes takes precedence over visual representation. Human irregularity has been converted into strictly measured, precisely placed, units of form. It should not be surprising to learn that we have a device (a "coordinatograph") which creates electronic circuit patterns that bear a remarkable resemblance to Van Doesburg's painting. Perhaps Van Doesburg unwittingly anticipated today's computer circuits. Can we expect better coordinatographs to replace painters and sculptors? Will electronic engineers create art? They can try.

## LIGHT AND DARK

It is reported that on his deathbed Goethe uttered the words: "More light." During the eighteenth-century En*light*enment, philosophers did indeed speak about "the light of reason." For them, light dispels darkness; it symbolizes mind and reason illuminating ignorance and error. Perhaps it is unfair, but light is also a masculine symbol; all the ancient sun gods were male: Mithras, Mazda, Apollo, and Horus. The earth and the moon, which *receive* or *reflect* light, are female symbols. Yet without these female bodies, light would be invisible. It seems that reality or form requires light *and* dark—yin *and* yang.

Regardless of the bad reputation of darkness, artists use it as a positive tool: they work with shadows to imply light. Symbolically speaking, they use male *and* female elements. In Klee's *Self-Portrait,* light is the absence of shadow; the exposed paper is perceived as light because of its *contrast* with the black areas. Without contrast, we would have the sensation of light but would be unable to see line or shape. Notice how the Kasimir Malevich (1878–1935) painting *White on White* reduces the light-dark contrast and

Technician using coordinatograph to prepare pattern for microelectric circuit

*opposite:* Friedrich Hundertwasser. *End of Waters on the Roof.* 1985. Woodcut in 28 colors, 20½ × 15⅜"

Symbolic shapes. Hundertwasser's cityscapes are cryptic images of himself—the tightly wound spiral, or snake person, in the center of the composition. He looks out through mysterious window-eyes at a fence, or barricade, made of houses. They could be spear points or teeth. Will they devour Hundertwasser? Or is their main function to protect him from strangers?

*above:* Paul Klee. *Self-Portrait: Drawing for a Woodcut.* 1909. Collection Felix Klee, Bern

*right:* Kasimir Malevich. *Suprematist Composition: White on White.* c. 1918. Oil on canvas, 31¼ × 31¼". Collection, The Museum of Modern Art, New York

The eye requires contrast to see form: contrast in light and dark, contrast in color, or contrast in "temperature." Malevich gives us contrast in temperature, which is almost invisible in black and white.

almost eliminates form. Actually, Malevich played a trick: he employed two kinds of white—one warm and one cool—so that form perception is possible because of a "thermal" difference rather than a light-dark contrast.

Colors differ in degree of lightness or darkness (or value) and can be used to establish light-dark differences and thus produce form. Pure yellow is lighter than red; pure blue is darker than yellow; side by side they create contrast. Sometimes, however, colors are mixed to the same degree of light-

Henri de Toulouse-Lautrec. *Maxime Dethomas.* 1896. Gouache on cardboard, 26½ × 20¾". National Gallery of Art, Washington, D.C. Chester Dale Collection

Here the silhouette shape directs our attention outward: it creates pictorial space and alerts us to an interesting exchange of glances between the masked woman and M. Dethomas.

218

Käthe Kollwitz. *War Cycle: The Parents.* 1923. Woodcut, 20⅛ × 26¹⁵⁄₁₆". National Gallery of Art, Washington, D.C. Lessing J. Rosenwald Collection

Now the silhouette forces our eyes inward. We look for light, shape, and details to define and animate the total form.

ness or darkness, and then the eye has to discriminate between them on the basis of their chromatic quality alone.

We see the simplest type of light-dark contrast in the silhouette. Usually a solid black against a white ground, the silhouette provides a maximum of contrast and visibility. The viewer's eye is normally drawn to its shape as a source of information. Silhouettes occur in nature, as when we see an object against the light; but usually, objects receive some light, or they are illuminated by several light sources. This results in a play of light which can be

Honoré Daumier. *Two Sculptors.* Undated. Oil on wood, 11 × 14". © The Phillips Collection, Washington, D.C.

Daumier models with light almost as a sculptor models with clay.

imitated in art. The manipulation of light and dark to create illusions of form on a two-dimensional surface is called "modeling"—a term borrowed from sculpture. Objects can be modeled using only the stark contrast of two "values"—black and white. More subtle and convincing representations can be created by imitating a wider range of light intensities. This type of modeling—perfected during the Renaissance by Leonardo da Vinci—is called *chiaroscuro.*

With a great deal of effort, painters can imitate photography, as in the style called Photorealism (see page 438). However, the human eye (and the camera) can discriminate more degrees of light intensity than the artist's skill and pigments can reproduce. Consequently, most artists do not try to compete with nature *or* the camera. Usually, they look for *patterns* of light and dark which they can use to create believable and expressive effects.

As mentioned above, light symbolism is often mythic in character. In art, however, the transitions from light to dark have their own, distinctively aesthetic, meanings. For example, the gentleness or abruptness of modeling can create emotional responses. The source of illumination—from above or below—affects our feelings. The distinctness or indistinctness of shapes can be controlled by light and dark manipulation. Some shadows seem empty or opaque; others look luminous and full of life; some invite closer inspection or direct us back to the light. We have seen how architects use light: some bathe an interior in strong light while others break up the light or cast mysterious shadows. The great architects *compose* with light as much as with space.

As with line and shape, our perceptions of light and dark are guided by life experience. And in life we avoid too much of either: we can be as blinded by light as by its absence. In art, strong light-dark contrasts usually equal sharpness of focus, which usually implies closeness to the viewer. Because the eye prefers to avoid extremes of light or dark, the late afternoon seems to provide the most optically pleasing halftones and shadows. From four to seven is a good time for social life: people past the bloom of youth seem to know this. Only teenagers have the courage to have a date in the glare of fluorescent lighting, or at the sun's peak. The rest of us get together when the shadows are falling.

The use of intense color in modern painting has produced a tendency to think of light mainly in terms of color. Nevertheless, the creation of form by manipulating light and dark has been with us for a long time and it is not likely to disappear. In the following pages, therefore, we examine some dramatic examples of lighting in both traditional and modern works of art.

**Baroque Experiments with Illumination**   After the masters of the Renaissance perfected chiaroscuro, the later Mannerist and Baroque painters went on to employ unusual illumination to dramatize their subjects. For example, Caravaggio's (1571–1610) *The Calling of St. Matthew* employs a light source at the extreme right in a highly theatrical manner: about eighty percent of the figures are in shadow. We can read the forms only with the evidence provided by the light that creeps around their edges. This concentration of light or "information" in small areas has the effect of increasing our visual alertness. "Seeing" this painting involves a new kind of viewer participation. Georges de La Tour (1593–1652) went a step further, using *artificial* light to construct simple, solid forms of tremendous emotional power. In his *Saint Mary Magdalen with a Candle* we see a Baroque painter creating a dramatic stillness with a light-dark patterning which is simultaneously abstract and realistically convincing. Although most of the picture is in darkness, it is a quiet, comfortable darkness because of the careful shaping of the lights.

El Greco (1548?–1614?) carried the tradition of rich Venetian color to Spain, but he is best known as a master of flickering light—a light more animated than that of La Tour. Although both are Baroque painters, La Tour's

Caravaggio. *The Calling of St. Matthew.* c. 1597–98. Oil on canvas, 11'1" × 11'5". Contarelli Chapel, S. Luigi dei Francesi, Rome

In Baroque painting, light is an aggressive, liberating force. A small amount of it is enough to reveal the spiritual opportunities that lie hidden in the shadows.

*below:* Studio of El Greco. *The Agony in the Garden of Gethsemane.* c. 1580. Oil on canvas, 40 × 51½". The National Gallery, London

In El Greco's painting, forms are flames beckoning to each other. The spiritual life is almost always compared to fire—glowing, blazing, and consuming.

Georges de La Tour. *Saint Mary Magdalen with a Candle.* 1625–33. Oil on canvas, 50⅜ × 37". The Louvre, Paris

La Tour's light represents the cleanliness of a spirit that has been washed and scrubbed by the effects of endless moral reflection.

Rembrandt van Rijn. *Man with a Magnifying Glass.* c. 1668. Oil on canvas, 36 × 29¼".
The Metropolitan Museum of Art, New York.
Bequest of Benjamin Altman, 1913

For Rembrandt, light is the device that creates shadows, and shadows are the painter's way of listening to the soul. We see this best in his sitter's eyes—looking out but thinking in.

smoothly brushed figures seem less troubled—on the surface at least—than those of El Greco. Notice the artificial illumination in *The Agony in the Garden of Gethsemane*, especially in the Christ figure, where the contrast between light and dark conveys a powerful impression of emotional climax. El Greco seems almost modern in the inconsistency of his light sources: the angel and the swirling figures beneath her receive different kinds of illumination from that of Christ. As for the soldiers and trees in the distance, they are lit around the edges, as in Caravaggio. The result is a scene that looks real and dreamlike at the same time: the natural and the supernatural are brought together in the same space.

In Rembrandt (1606–1669) we encounter perhaps the most psychologically penetrating of Baroque experiments with illumination. The richness of forms in the light, the cultivation of mystery in the darks, and the gradual or sudden buildup of paint with brush or palette knife: these technical and aesthetic devices have never been surpassed. Rembrandt's transitional tones bear the closest study because that is where he departs from the abstract patterning of light and dark to reveal his distinctive insight into the human condition. Those halftones raise his art above merely skillful modeling. In *Man with a Magnifying Glass* the loss of light in the shadows seems to symbolize all that is vulnerable in his subject. The light areas consist of a vigorous impasto swimming in liquid glazes which manage the transition to the luminous shadows. The light areas meet our eyes first, fighting to expand

Rembrandt van Rijn. Detail of *Man with a Magnifying Glass*

From Boucher to Manet to Gauguin one travels
through distinct modes of how men have
viewed women. In one she is a delightful toy; in
the next she becomes a more complete
person—still used for pleasure, but humanized
to the point where her stare is embarrassing; in
the third, she reverts to fearful adolescence as
the child-woman imprisoned by the superstitions
of a witch.

and assert their dominance. The halftones represent modifications of light,
the feminine element that compromises by resisting in some places and
yielding in others. In the deepest shadows we see light whose fire has almost
burned out; the shadows are burial places for fires that have died. But in
Rembrandt, light never really dies; it sleeps restlessly underneath his glazes;
it can always flare up again.

**Light and Dark in Modern Art**   A spectacular break with the traditional use
of light and dark appears in the work of Édouard Manet (1832–1883), especially in his "scandalous" *Olympia.* Perhaps his merciless lighting aroused
indignation as much as his subject offended the French public. There were
moral objections to his candid presentation of a prostitute, but his flattening
of form and unsentimental paint application seriously upset conventional
visual expectations. Manet tended to eliminate subtle modeling effects: he
painted directly, without glazes, and with a preference for bluish black in the
shadows and transitions. The *Olympia* may remind us of a candid-camera
photograph in which the flash bulb has bleached out the halftones. And, since
Manet avoided linear perspective, we do not approach the subject by gradual
stages; we confront this woman suddenly and directly. Or she confronts *us,*
and that, too, is disturbing. Glaring light, flatness, and indecent subject matter:
this was enough to launch a pictorial revolution.

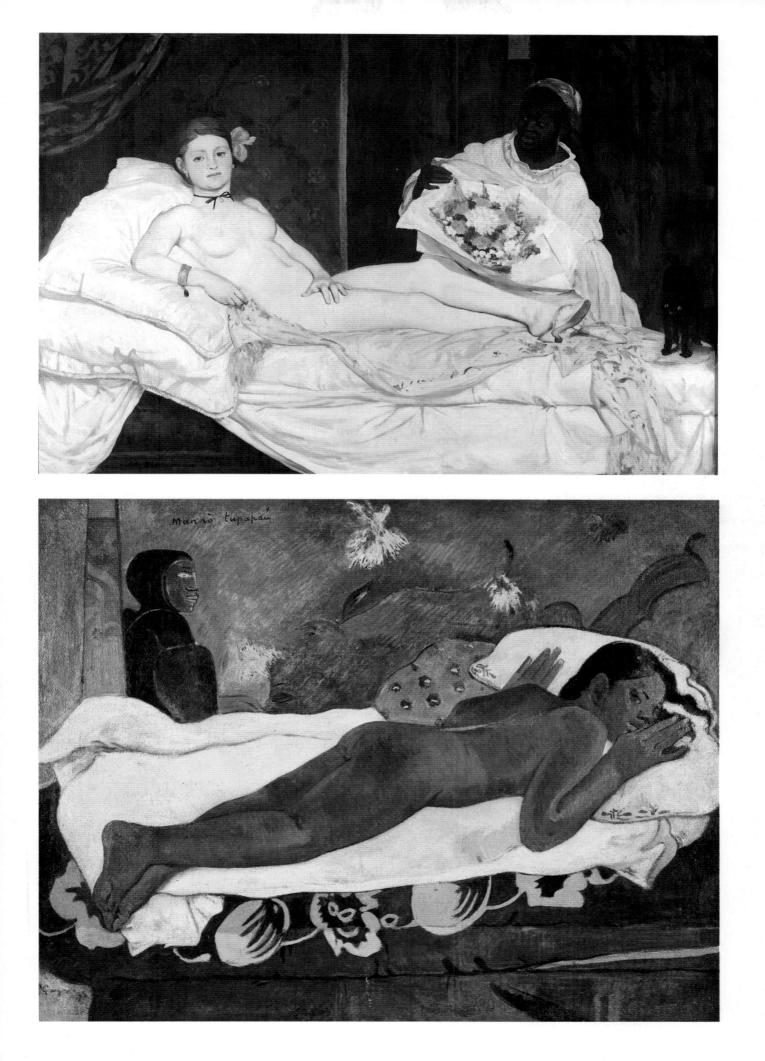

*above:* Georges Rouault. *Miserere: Dura Lex sed Lex.* 1926. Etching, 17 × 23½". Philadelphia Museum of Art. Purchase, Temple Fund

*right:* Emil Nolde. *The Prophet.* 1912. Woodcut, 15⅞ × 13½". National Gallery of Art, Washington, D.C. Lessing J. Rosenwald Collection

In Emil Nolde's (1867–1956) woodcut *Prophet,* we see again how the elimination of halftones can produce a powerfully expressive effect. Of course, the woodcut medium is highly suited to this treatment of light. But it would be difficult to accept if Manet had not blazed the path. The nose in Nolde's *Prophet* is entirely black, even though that conflicts with the logic of the head's lighting. By 1912, however, an artist could mix descriptive and abstract elements arbitrarily, in this case producing a stern effect through the dark pattern connecting the nose, brows, and mustache. The tools used to cut a wood block do not change direction easily because of the wood grain's resistance. The result is a harshness in the shapes which can be read as traits of the prophetic temperament: anger, righteousness, disappointment, sorrow.

Rouault's *Miserere: Dura Lex sed Lex* is very much in the spirit of Nolde's woodcut. Here, too, pictorial structure is based on an extreme light-dark contrast, with the addition of a few halftones to soften the glare. Using very unconventional printmaking techniques, Rouault achieves a rich texture on the plate; he produces a surface that is more like a painting than a print. The grainy, scratchy whites and the thick, pitted blacks create a painfully hard image, an image in which bitterness and resignation seem to be mixed with acid.

## COLOR

There is a vast literature on color theory—much more than most of us have the time or inclination to study. Often it provides answers to questions that artists do not necessarily ask; their knowledge about color is usually based on trial and error, the advice of teachers, or borrowings from other artists. As for color systems, they may be more concerned with the physics of light than aesthetics. Some of them have evolved from industrial needs for the classification of inks, dyes, and pigments. At any rate, artists work with color on an intuitive more than a scientific basis. The great colorists tend to make instinctive adjustments to the requirements of their vision rather than apply the findings of color physics. The French Impressionists were very interested in scientific color theory, but the paintings of other artists made the principal difference in the evolution of their style. Their opportunity to see the work of Turner and Constable in England, in 1870, was a major factor in their artistic and aesthetic development. Still, it does not hurt to know about color wheels, complementary color, analogous color, tonal color, and so on. But keep in mind that we want to understand *how color works in art*—how it affects the ideas, feelings, and information we get from artistic images.

**Color Terminology**    Whether color is intellectual or intuitive, we need to talk about it. Hence terminology: it permits orderly reference to the chromatic properties responsible for aesthetic emotion. Following are brief definitions of the terms most commonly used, chiefly to describe what is done with artists' pigments.

*Hue* refers to the names of primary colors such as red, yellow, and blue. Note that these are different from the colors of the light spectrum as taught in physics. (The "physical" spectrum, made by breaking down light into its component colors, consists of red, orange, yellow, green, blue, indigo, and violet. Plus all the colors in between, for which we may or may not have names.) The primary hues are theoretically the basis for mixtures resulting in orange, green, and violet; presumably, they are *not* the result of a mixture; that's what makes them primary. But in practice, the most intense hues are achieved by mixture. The names manufacturers use are a type of labeling meant to distinguish hues and tints from their almost identical cousins made by other manufacturers. Thus we have "Mediterranean Gold," "Colonial Yellow," "Roman Bronze," and "Canary Yellow." Artists' pigments have a label history, too: burnt Sienna, Rubens red, gamboge yellow, zinc white, and so on. But these labels mean nothing unless you have used the colors.

*Value* refers to the lightness or darkness of a color. As white is added, a color becomes "higher" in value until pure white is reached. Conversely, as black is added, or some other color which has a darkening effect, the value becomes "lower" until pure black is reached. As you approach pure white or pure black, you become less aware of chromatic or color quality and more aware of lightness or darkness, which is to say, *value*. Yellow is already high in value, so it can be used to raise the value of colors darker than itself. Blue is already low in value, so it can lower the value of lighter colors.

*Intensity* refers to the purity of a color, the absence of any visible admixture. As mentioned above, pigments seldom present a hue at its fullest intensity. For example, the pigment called alizarin crimson is quite dark; it can be made into an intense, bright red by the addition of a small amount of yellow or cadmium orange. Ultramarine blue is very dark as a pigment and becomes an intense blue hue only with the addition of white. But too much white will kill its intensity, producing a "pastel" or tint, a faded look.

*Local color* is the color we "know" an object to be as opposed to the colors we actually see. We know a fire engine is red, but depending on light conditions, its distance from the viewer, its reflective quality, and so on, it may look red, violet, orange, or even green in some places. Its highlights might be almost white. At least a painter would use these colors to represent the "redness" of a fire engine. Similarly, distant mountains appear to be blue and violet although we "know" that their local color is green and brown.

*Complementary colors* are opposites. Also, they are opposite each other on the color wheel. More fundamentally, the presence of one denotes the absence of the other: there is no yellow in blue; there is no red in green. Which means that no other color is as different from red as green. To the human eye, the *afterimage* of red is green and the afterimage of green is red. If red and green are side by side, the red looks redder and the green looks greener; the afterimage of each enhances the actual color of the other. If complementaries are mixed, they cancel each other out—that is, they pro-duce a gray or, more likely, what painters call mud; they *neutralize* each other. A small amount of red added to a large amount of green will gray the

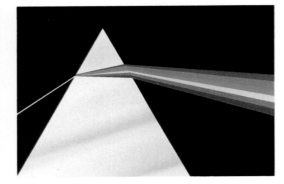

**The Color Spectrum. Illustration by Lino Semeoni**

The result of passing light through a prism.

### The Color Wheel

The results of arranging the color spectrum in a circle. The number ones are called primaries; the number twos are called secondaries; the number threes are called tertiaries or intermediates.

Color complementaries are pairs that face each other on the color wheel: red-green, violet-yellow, blue-orange, etc. With a larger wheel and more mixtures, we would have more complementary pairs.

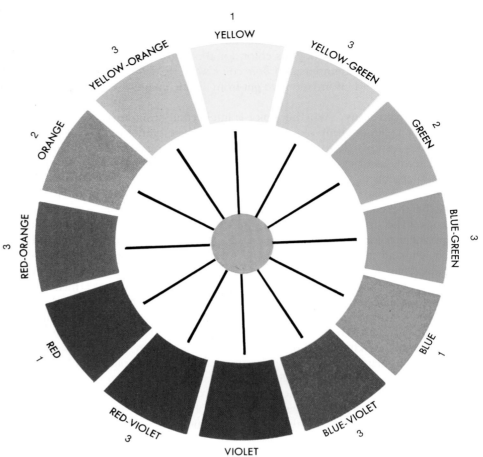

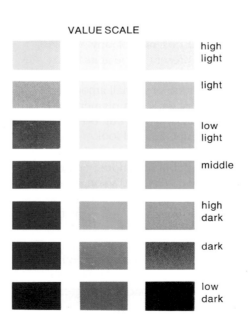

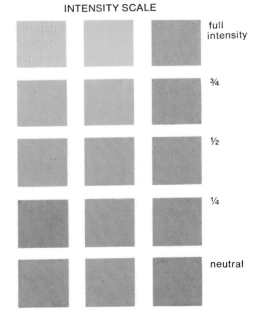

VALUE SCALE

high light
light
low light
middle
high dark
dark
low dark

INTENSITY SCALE

full intensity
¾
½
¼
neutral

**The Value Scale:**

From light to dark. High values approach white; low values approach black.

**The Intensity Scale:**

This shows the range of a color, from full saturation to low saturation or neutrality.

Victor Vasarely. *Arcturus II.* 1966. Oil on canvas, 63 × 63". The Hirshhorn Museum and Sculpture Garden, Smithsonian Institution, Washington, D.C. Gift of Joseph H. Hirshhorn, 1972

A painting that consists mainly of variations on four hues: blue, green, red, and violet. We can see it as a textbook illustration of the *values* that can be generated by adding white to strong colors. Or we can see it as a demonstration of pure chromatic power.

green; white added to the mixture will raise the value; and thus a variety of interesting grays can be mixed without using black.

*Analogous colors* are relatives or kinfolk, as opposed to strangers, like complementaries. They are related because they share the same "blood lines"—red and orange, orange and yellow, green and blue, blue and violet, violet and red. Analogous or "family" colors are next to each other on the color wheel. None of them ends distinctly at any point; they seem to "intermarry" with their close neighbors. And being relatives, they "get along," if that is true of relatives. They are compatible with each other, that is, they can mix with each other without becoming gray.

Colors are called *warm and cool* because of our associations with blood, sky, fire, or ice. Reds, yellows, and oranges are warm; blues, greens, and some violets are cool. However, these "thermal" properties are relative (all the properties of color are relative): yellow-green would be cool next to orange but warm next to blue. Painters can create form by contrasts of warm and cool rather than contrasts of light and dark. When it comes to spatial quality, the warm colors advance, and the cool colors recede. This illusion is due to the fact that the wave lengths at the warm end of the light spectrum are stronger—that is, more visible—than those at the blue-violet end. Ultraviolet, for example, is so weak that we cannot see it at all.

*Tone* refers to variations—lighter or darker—of a single hue; its meaning is similar to color value. *Tonality* refers to the overall effect of a work in which one color and its variations seem to dominate the whole. Rousseau's *The Dream* (page 194) has an essentially green tonality, for instance. We also speak of a warm or cool tonality, which is a way of referring to the "temperature" variations of the dominant color in an artwork. A painting with a blue tonality may have some reds and yellows, but bluish tones would be dominant because of their *quantity* and *distribution*. In general, tonal painting tends to produce easy color unities because it reduces the number of color variables the artist must work with.

**Color as Language**   It should be plain that little can be said about colors in isolation; they always occur in a context or relationship—in art and in life. Our ideas about advancing/receding, expanding/contracting, warm/cool relationships can be changed by color *quantity*. And, of course, the *shape* of a color area affects its meaning, as does its surface quality or texture. But in addition to the optical properties of color, there are symbolic properties to consider: we are affected by the folklore and psychology of color. Hence artists have to work simultaneously with the colors we see and how we feel *about* them.

Frank Auerbach. *Head of Catherine Lampert.* 1986. Oil on canvas, 20¼ × 18¼". Private collection

Color as a language of feeling. Of course, the thick paint and frantic brushwork express a great deal of anger, but those acidulous yellows and greens make us *feel* the anger—right in the pit of the stomach.

One of the main goals of modern painting has been the use of color as an independent language of feelings and ideas. This is especially true of abstract and nonobjective art. The intention of certain early modern painters was to imitate music, which presumably communicates through "non-objective" sounds. Wassily Kandinsky (see page 161), who thought of colors in musical terms, is credited with the first nonobjective paintings—works that try to use color as a pure language of emotion. Before him, the Fauves or "Wild Beasts" had carried the coloristic advances of Impressionist painting into the realm of arbitrary color. Several other movements—Post-Impressionism, Symbolism, and Expressionism—greatly enlarged the role of color as an autonomous language. Here, instead of discussing styles and movements we shall look at the way color speaks in specific works by some of the masters of modern art.

*London Bridge* by André Derain (1880–1954) (page 160) exhibits the crisp, bright touches of color we associate with Impressionist paint application, but the blurring of edges and the pursuit of atmospheric effects are absent. Notice, too, that the strong yellow marks on the bridge do not hold still; they jump out of their assigned places and try to act independently. Local color is also exaggerated: we see a bright orange sky without any optical "explanation." And the yellow reflections in the water look improbable. As for the drawing, it is clearly subordinate to the pattern of brushwork and the activity of paint. As we would expect at a time when Impressionism was still controversial, Derain's Fauvist color aroused exceedingly violent reactions from critics and the public.

*Still Life with Lamp* by Alexej von Jawlensky (1864–1941) (page 156) dates from the same time as Derain's *London Bridge*. However, it moves further in the direction of independent color, retaining only a nominal connection with visual reality. Although the structural organization is strong, it is really a scaffold on which to hang the intense, vigorously applied color. Jawlensky is well on the way to a type of abstraction in which pictorial structure is based on contrasting color intensities. At least four kinds of red compete for our optical attention; two or three yellows also make themselves heard; some greens try to cool things down; and a coarse black framework struggles to hold the work together. Drawing is minimal and modeling is nonexistent. It is color alone that produces this angry lamp and those frantic apples.

Like the Derain, the *Landscape with Houses* by Wassily Kandinsky (page 160) is fairly close to Impressionism in its gradations and traces of color-vibration technique. Although Kandinsky's edges are not as harsh as Derain's, his color spots do jump out. We also see an unbelievable blue house, a pair of glowing trees, and some incredibly orange rooftops. Kandinsky does not aim for the type of spatial control that Cézanne achieved in the 1890s. Instead, the color is musical: we can almost hear a flute and a mandolin. Or is it a balalaika?

Mark Rothko (1903–1970) (page 198) is famous for using color to create a mystical light that seems to surround the viewer. His pigment impregnates the canvas like a stain, so we are not aware of it as a brushed-on substance: the picture *radiates* color; it becomes a separate, light-filled world. Apparently, Rothko was trying to find a way to change the viewer's consciousness through color. Employing shape very sparingly, his paintings manage to transcend our everyday ideas and associations. We know that color is exceedingly potent in its capacity to affect the nervous system, but to experience it there must be form—shape, size, location—or design. And that is what Rothko produces with his colored rectangles floating in a colored field. Serene, deceptively simple, and pleasing to the eye, these forms find a pathway to our consciousness through our eyes alone.

As we know, Surrealism also tried to alter consciousness. Mainly, it employed outrageous juxtapositions of form and subject matter; the approach was essentially literary. As the public grew familiar with this strategy, however, its capacity for surprise diminished. Rothko found a new way to enter our consciousness, at least temporarily. With color, he could induce an agreeable, contemplative state of being. His art suggests that we may be entering an era when painting will be able to communicate directly with the neurological source of our feelings.

# TEXTURE

We speak of getting "the feel of things" as if touching is the best way to know something. In fact, feeling things is our *earliest* way of dealing with objects. But as we grow, tactile sensation gives way to visual sensation as the main mode of knowing. Still, we regard touch as more reliable than vision. If you have a bad fall, you are likely to *feel* your body—"searching" for breaks or bruises; something that "looks" all right may hide damage that has to be *felt* to be realized. As we know, babies examine objects by putting them in their mouths—*feeling* them with the lips and tongue. The time comes, however, when learning about the world through taste or touch is dangerous: seeing is safer.

Although adults look before they touch, it is possible that their looking is a kind of tactile inquiry. That is, we use vision to find out how something would feel *if* we touched it. This connection between visual and tactile sensation is so well developed that we can fall in love just by seeing: "love at first sight." However, looking contemplates tactility: we hope to hold and embrace. In other words, we return to our earliest sensory modes when seeking the complete knowledge that love implies.

Textures can be seen as well as felt. But seeing a texture really means having a good idea about its surface quality. Thus visual representation often consists of providing viewers with reliable cues about surfaces. Surfaces, in turn, are sources of very basic information. Think of modern advertising—especially photographic illustrations and their capacity to inform, to arouse desire, and to sell through texture.

*far left:* Nail fetish, from the Lower Congo. 1909. Wood and nails, 33½" high. Museum für Völkerkunde, Basel

The heavily textured surfaces of these sculptures have different functions. The nails driven into the African fetish act almost medically: they are supposed to drive out demons or activate healing energies in the body of a real person. Paolozzi's figure bears the holes left by arrows shot into the body of the martyred saint. It also looks like the torso of a man lacerated by every kind of modern illness. In both figures we see a similar symbolic drama. The nails and arrows represent powerful invasive forces that, when released, leave holes for the body's pain or energy to escape. Visually, those coarse textures are signs of a struggle to control the life force inside every person.

*left: Eduardo Paolozzi. Saint Sebastian No. 2.* 1957. Bronze, 84¾" high. The Solomon R. Guggenheim Museum, New York

What are the tactile properties of surfaces that can be rendered visually? Essentially, they are phenomena related to the light-absorbing and light-reflecting qualities of materials. These are usually represented graphically in terms of light-and-dark patterning. With pattern an artist can represent the texture of anything from burlap sacking to the surface of the moon. In the three-dimensional arts, of course, textures are created, not simulated. But painters and printmakers are not far behind: collage has taught them to attach anything to a surface—if glue can keep it there.

The early dependence on touch in human sensory development is reflected in the strength of tactile qualities in the art of tribal peoples. Their art exhibits a textural vividness which is especially popular today—particularly for artists who want their work to make direct sensory appeals. For the tribal artist, rough textural effects result mainly from using traditional tools and materials in ritualistic settings. For today's artist, coarse textures fulfill an aesthetic agenda: returning to the source; abandoning illusions in favor of composition with real objects; creating a "primitive" look to arouse the tired sensibilities of the jaded gallery-goer.

**Jean Dubuffet. *The Sea of Skin*. 1959. Botanical elements, 21⅝ × 18⅛". Collection Daniel Cordier, Paris**

This "Sea of Skin" comes from the century plant, an organism that flowers once and then dies. Dubuffet has used its textures to make a statement about all the things, including ourselves, that age and die.

Today's desire to exploit tactility in art may be due to a distrust of remote visual stimulation, as in reading, driving, and scanning—watching the world from a distance. The coarse textures of contemporary art may express an effort to reach back and down into the deepest strata of human personality. We have grown sick of smoothness and polish—in life and in art. Also, we live in a culture where our senses are regularly assaulted by loud noises and violent images; a powerful jolt of texture may be the artist's only way of being heard.

**Seymour Avigdor (designer). Interior with patterns. 1969. Material found at Vice Versa Fabrics, New York**

The appeal of overall repetitive patterns is fundamentally tactile. The patterns become textures because we cannot deal visually with so many little images—they have to be perceived in the same way that we see grains of sand, beans in a pot, or bees in a hive.

# CHAPTER NINE

# ORGANIZING THE ELEMENTS: DESIGN

No matter what its purpose, the elements of an artwork are organized to be seen. The purpose of a chair is to support someone and *to be seen*. The purpose of a poster is to persuade people and *to be seen*. Better said, a poster *must be seen* before it can persuade. Works of art have one common goal over and above their personal, social, or physical goals. That goal might be called *organization for visual effectiveness*, or *design*.

Design is a process which is common to the creation of all works of art. For that reason, we make no distinction in this book between the design of paintings or sculptures and the design of useful objects like chairs or posters or book jackets. Sometimes, the word *design* is restricted to the creation of utilitarian objects, while the creation of "nonuseful" objects like pictures and statues is called composition—a more "artistic" process. But for our purposes, design applies to any art object, regardless of its maker, its material, or its use. Why?

1. Because the useful objects of the past often become the "use*less*" objects of the present. The status of the object may change but its visual organization remains the same.

2. Because so-called useless objects (pictures, statues, decorative objects) have a purpose, although it is not necessarily a physical purpose; they function by being seen.

3. Because design, regardless of purpose, is the artist's chief way of controlling what we see.

By insisting that design is a process common to all works of art, and by refusing to set up a hierarchy of art objects—calling some *fine* art and others *applied* or *minor* art—we gain certain advantages. We avoid being embarrassed by history, as when a fertility figure becomes a "fine-art" object in a culture that employs modern medicine instead of magic. We avoid classification problems, such as how to distinguish between the physical usefulness, the psychological expressiveness, and the aesthetic value of stained glass in a Gothic cathedral. We recognize the power of all kinds of images: the Brooklyn Bridge is symbolically potent even though it was meant to carry travelers across a river. There must be a visual reason, a *design* reason, for that symbolic power.

As soon as materials are formed and assembled, they become a visual organization that succeeds or fails because of the way its elements work together. All works of art exhibit certain *patterns* of working together—patterns sometimes called "principles" of design. These principles are based mainly on the way people see effectively. In a sense, the so-called principles of design are the result of long-term trial and error. Perhaps the history of art should be considered the history of the various types of formal organization that have been effective in various times and places.

We cannot claim that any single design principle—for instance, "unity in variety"—constitutes a universal rule of artistic effectiveness. Distinguished

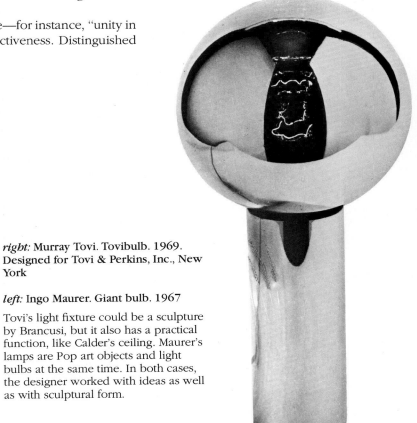

*right:* Murray Tovi. Tovibulb. 1969. Designed for Tovi & Perkins, Inc., New York

*left:* Ingo Maurer. Giant bulb. 1967

Tovi's light fixture could be a sculpture by Brancusi, but it also has a practical function, like Calder's ceiling. Maurer's lamps are Pop art objects and light bulbs at the same time. In both cases, the designer worked with ideas as well as with sculptural form.

works can be found that defy the design principles cited here or elsewhere. Remember that unity is experienced differently in different cultures: the unity of a Hindu temple is more apparent to Indian than to Western eyes; remember that twelfth-century Gothic architecture seemed ugly and *dis*unified to the peoples of the Mediterranean world. Nevertheless, the principles of design are based on fairly common habits of visual perception; they are certainly influenced by the common physiological equipment of the human race.

The habit of reading from left to right, or top to bottom, or right to left may produce differences in the way we look at images. But everyone has to measure size relationships, the distance between objects, and the speed of moving objects. Our binocular vision and perceptions of color, size, shape, brightness, texture, and depth confer more uniformity than diversity on our seeing. Because of that perceptual uniformity we can speak of design elements and principles as if they applied to everyone. In fact, as languages go, the language of vision may be the best we have for communicating the unity of the human species.

## UNITY

Perhaps unity is the *only* principle of visual organization; perhaps the others are merely different ways of achieving it. Ultimately, unity reflects the fact that we are separate individuals who see and feel and think with the equipment provided by our separate bodies and minds. We are also finite individuals; we need to close our visual experience at some point in order to move on to other things. That may be the chief reason why we need visual unity. Artists try to help us by organizing the parts of an artwork so that they will be *seen as a whole*. A failure in this effort—ineffective design—results in the premature termination of the viewer's experience: viewers stop looking. The act of "not looking" might be considered a kind of completion, but not a good one; it represents the breakdown of communication. Therefore, the artist's design objective is to create a *good* unity among the parts of an artwork *before* they are seen by a viewer. What are the principal ways of doing this?

One is *dominance and subordination.* The artist attempts to control the *sequence* in which visual events are observed and the *amount of attention* they are paid. The dominant element of a work is the one the others depend on for their visual value and their meaning. Dominance is achieved most easily by *size*, the largest form being seen first. It is also achieved by *color intensity*. Other things being equal, an intense color area will dominate a dull, pale, or grayed area of the same size. Similarly, a warm area will dominate a cool area because warm colors seem to advance toward us.

Another way of achieving dominance is through *location.* Our eyes are usually drawn toward the center of any visual field: centrally located objects are more likely to receive attention. That is why the head in most portraits is centered between left and right and slightly above the midpoint of a canvas: it corresponds to the location of the viewer's own head. The *convergence* of lines and forms on a point, or their *radiation* from a point, gives dominance to that point. *Light* is also a dominance factor: the eye—like a moth—cannot resist a place that seems to radiate light. For instance, we are tempted to look at the bright sun even though we know it will hurt our eyes. Hence, a very light area will dominate its darker surroundings, much as the sun dominates the sky.

Finally, dominance can be achieved by *difference* or *exception.* We know that nonconformity stands out: if an oval shape appears among a number of squares, it will be seen as the exception; it will stick out like the proverbial sore thumb. What is the image you associate with the novel entitled *A Tree Grows in Brooklyn*? A slender, green, plant-shaped object surrounded by massive walls of brown brick and gray stone; the tree captures our attention because it is unexpected. In our mind's eye, we see the tree before the bricks.

Paula Modersohn-Becker. *Self-Portrait*. 1906.
Oil on canvas, 24 × 19 11/16". Kunstmuseum, Basel

Notice that the face is modeled in more depth
than the body; its colors are more intense, too.
The unity of the portrait depends on the greater
dimensionality of the head. Our eyes are drawn
to the place where the plastic and psychological
values are concentrated.

*Coherence* refers to the *belonging together* of the parts of a work of art.
In life these parts may be entirely unrelated, but in art their colors, shapes,
sizes, or textures can be adjusted so that they seem almost indivisible. The
sense of coherence casts a kind of spell: once it is achieved, any change will
be noticed and it will seem to ruin the whole work. Coherence makes us
respond as if we are in the presence of a living thing; the unity of the image
is its life. The viewer comes to believe that the organization or design of an
artwork is inevitable: it could not be different and still exist.

Visual coherence is often pursued through analogous color and color
tonality—the use of one color or admixtures of it throughout a work. *Similarity* of any kind—of shape, color, size, illumination, or texture—promotes
the impression of coherence. But similarity has its perils since sameness can
lead to boredom: our tolerance for sameness is limited. We need *variety* to
satisfy our appetite for change, but not so much variety that the sense of
wholeness or coherence is sacrificed. Clearly, the artist has to walk a fine line.

Dissimilar forms can be unified by the device of clustering: closeness

*left:* Piero della Francesca. *The Resurrection of Christ.* c. 1463–65. Fresco, 88⅝ × 78¾". Palazzo Comunale, Sansepolcro, Italy

Two kinds of unity. In Piero's fresco, the placement of Christ's head at the apex of a triangle creates a powerful symbol of dominance and upward movement. In Rembrandt's etching, Christ is centrally placed but only slightly higher than the others. His figure unifies and dominates the scene through gesture, frontality, and painterly modeling of form.

*below:* Rembrandt van Rijn. *Christ Healing the Sick (The Hundred Guilder Print).* c. 1648–50. Etching, drypoint, and burin, 11 × 15⅛". Prentenkabinet, Rijksmuseum, Amsterdam

*left:* Richard Lippold. *Variation Number 7: Full Moon.* 1949–50. Brass rods, nickel-chromium and stainless steel wire, 10 × 6'. Collection, The Museum of Modern Art, New York. Mrs. Simon Guggenheim Fund

*above:* Herbert Ferber. *"and the bush was not consumed."* 1951–52. Copper, 12 × 8'. B'nai Israel Synagogue, Milburn, New Jersey

suggests coherence. When surrounded by open space, dissimilar forms which are near each other tend to be seen as a unit: the eye *prefers* likeness to unlikeness. This principle of unity is illustrated in Braque's *The Round Table* (page 38). There we see a variety of objects, shapes, and textures, almost none of which are alike. But they are held together by the encircling form of the tabletop and the open space around them. There is also an unexpected sense of "spilling up," but that is part of the fun of this work.

Unity based on converging or radiating lines is fairly common and easy to use. So the designer's problem is to avoid the obvious. An almost pure example of radiating unity can be seen in a wire construction by Richard Lippold (born 1915): *Variation Number 7: Full Moon.* But notice that Lippold creates subsidiary centers of interest; also, the color and shimmer of the fine metal lines have considerable intrinsic appeal, so they divert attention away from the radiant center. In a related type of design, *"and the bush was not consumed,"* Herbert Ferber (1906–1991) builds a composition on repeated V-forms—in the sculpture and in the wall behind it. But while the lines converge at the point of the V, Ferber introduces variations in shape and direction to escape monotony. In addition, he uses plant forms to avoid a tedious repetition of the V-shaped device.

An example of unity through central location can be seen in *Nachi Waterfall,* a silk-scroll painting from the Kamakura period of Japanese art. Such paintings had a mystical-religious function in ancient Japan, but we can see them in terms of masterful pictorial design. The dead-center placement of the waterfall would be obvious and dull except for the sensitive location of shapes and weights left and right, top and bottom. Notice the dramatic climax of the painting at the base where the falling water strikes an irregular, rocky profile. There the artist introduces rounded forms and diagonal lines to counteract the straight, dominant verticals. He also reserves the strongest light-dark contrasts for the spot where the water crashes against the rocks; after that, it trickles away to a different tune.

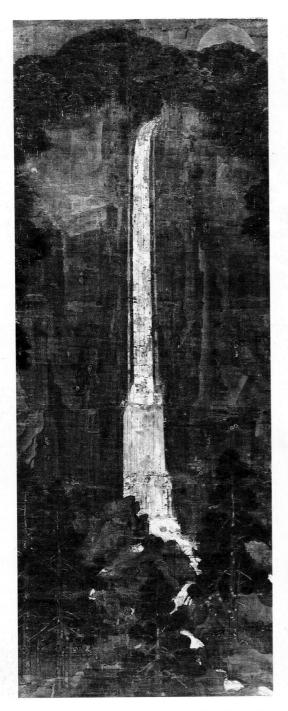

*Nachi Waterfall.* 14th century A.D. Silk, 63 × 23".
Nezu Museum, Tokyo

*right:* Henri Matisse. *Carmelina.* 1903. Oil on
canvas, 32 × 23¼". Courtesy, Museum of Fine
Arts, Boston. Tompkins Collection

Unity through frontality. Everything faces straight
ahead—the table, the mirror, the picture, the
objects on the shelf—and Carmelina. But her
hand positions are not identical, one bottle is
slightly turned, and there is some nonfrontal
imagery in the mirror. Matisse has used
psychological interest and visual variation to
enliven what could have been a dull
composition.

At first it seems that the artist has used an almost mechanical device for
achieving unity. Then we recognize his ingenious use of subordinate devices
for creating variety. A masterpiece can result from creating an impossible
problem and then solving it.

## BALANCE

The Leaning Tower of Pisa is famous because it is out of balance but still
manages to stand. What keeps it from falling? Are invisible forces holding it
up? From what we can see, the building ought to collapse; the fact that it
doesn't is funny and disturbing. Clearly, we have a deep need for balance or
equilibrium; that balance can be seen in nature, in the human figure, and in
man-made structures. We expect it in art as well as life.

In architecture, balance is largely a matter of adjusting weights and
stresses; in physics we find it in the laws of energy conservation; in the
biological world it exists in a correlation between living populations and the
food supply. In art, balance is an optical condition: weight, stress, tension,
and stability—words that are borrowed from physics or engineering—take
on perceptual meanings. Perhaps certain scientific problems are intuitively
solved by artists and viewers as they calculate whether the forms they see are
pleasing. One thing is certain: in learning to walk we went through a period
of instability; remembering that period has made us sensitive to every sign of
imbalance.

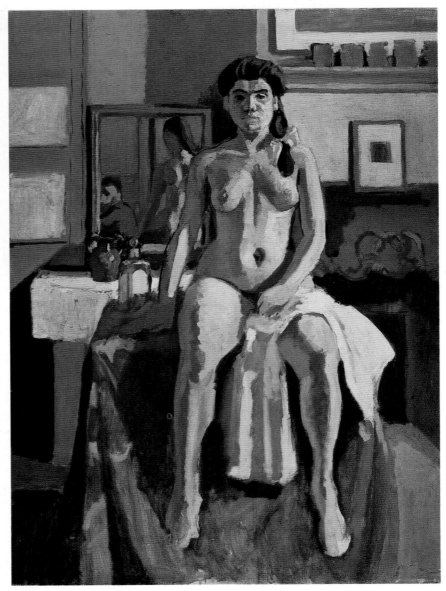

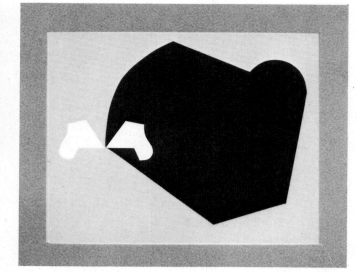

Symmetry is the simplest and least challenging type of balance. It has a spontaneous appeal which is probably due to the bilateral symmetry of the human body. Also, it requires a minimum of perceptual effort to understand. The elements in each half of an image may be very complex, but as soon as they are recognized as echoes or mirror images of each other, they acquire an interest which is curiously satisfying. Perhaps this pleasure is related to the way electrical charges are distributed over the brain hemispheres during perception. Perhaps it is just a visual reinforcement of our physical stability. *Asymmetrical balance*, which is more difficult to achieve, provides pleasure, too. But it works indirectly—through a complex system of substitutions and compensations: it "costs more" in terms of perceptual energy.

*Balance by weight* reminds us of a lever and fulcrum, or a seesaw. We unconsciously assume that the center of a picture (or of our visual field in the case of architecture and sculpture) corresponds to the fulcrum where the lever or seesaw is poised. A heavy weight on one side can be balanced by a lighter weight on the other if the lighter weight is located at a greater distance from the center. Here physics and visual perception follow the same laws. Although gravity does not actually operate on the objects in paintings, we perceive them *as if* it does.

*Balance by interest* is another asymmetrical device. It is based on stimulation of the viewer's *curiosity*, usually to counteract weight or mass. Here we deal with the fact that visual attention—its duration and intensity—adds weight. This is something artists may have known before psychologists: small forms that excite our interest can balance massive forms that leave us cold. How is psychological interest generated? By formal or symbolic complexity. Psychological interest can upset the physical forces at work in a visual image.

**SYMMETRICAL AND ASYMMETRICAL BALANCE**

*left:* Piero Dorazio. *Janus.* 1949. Marlborough Galleria d'Arte, Rome

Janus was a two-headed Roman deity, here treated as a pair of symmetrical forms. Notice how Dorazio produces variation of shape and direction within a basically symmetrical design. Arp balances his *Olympia* (remember Manet's woman of the same name?) by exploiting our interest in the pair of small forms at the left; they counteract the massive torso that occupies most of the picture space.

*above:* Jean Arp. *Olympia.* 1955. Private collection, Switzerland


**ASYMMETRICAL BALANCE USING MECHANICALLY PRECISE FORMS**

*left:* Ben Nicholson. *Painted Relief.* 1939. Synthetic board mounted on plywood, painted, 32⅞ × 45". Collection, The Museum of Modern Art, New York. Gift of H. S. Ede and the artist (by exchange)

*below:* Jean Gorin. *Composition No. 9.* 1934. Private collection

241

*above:* Edvard Munch. *The Dance of Life.*
1899–1900. Oil on canvas, 49½ × 75". National
Gallery, Oslo

This almost completely symmetrical composition
employs balancing figures at both extremes to
symbolize the opposed notions of joy and
sorrow, vitality and death.

PSYCHOLOGICAL BALANCE

*right:* Alexander Colville. *The River Thames.*
1974. Acrylic polymer emulsion on board,
30 × 30". Collection Mr. and Mrs. J. H. Clark

The thrust of the bridge and the weight of the
woman's figure are balanced psychologically by
the expanse of water. The river becomes a
symbol (of her ambition, her career, her life)
whose "weight" counteracts the forms and
forces on the left side of the composition.

We know that certain signs—a face, a cross, a flag—can arouse complex feelings and associations; they can influence perception in ways that have little to do with formal structure. Surrealist works, for example, are difficult to perceive apart from their symbolic meanings. Here we might consider Chagall's *Birthday* (page 19). The little bouquet of flowers—the special gift—carries a great deal of emotional weight; it balances the figures psychologically. Without it, the rest of the canvas makes little sense; it doesn't have to.

Balance of weight by interest is humorously illustrated in Miró's *Maternity*, a case that is virtually a laboratory experiment. Two straight lines cross in the center of the picture, forming an X. The point where they cross becomes the fulcrum for a seesaw, or a pair of scissors. At the end of one line, we see a large form shaped like a wedge of pie; this large form is balanced by a small, insectlike form at the other end of the line. A wormy shape near the insect seems aimed at a circular form on the other arm. Apparently, the wedge shape stands for the male, with the hole in the wedge acting as a kind of eye; the wormy shape is probably a sperm seeking an ovum. The other arm of the X seems to be female, and it is divided by the fulcrum point into two equal segments. One is internal, where the ovum is located; the other is external, where we see a hemispherical shape that looks like a breast. The feathered little creatures at both ends must represent the female biological symbol, ♀: both seem to be engaged in a seesaw game: the ovum swings close to, and then away from, the sperm. From the title of the picture and what we know about scissors and levers, it looks as if there is going to be a meeting; someone is going to get pregnant. So Miró has created a play out of the biology of human conception: fertilization seems to be a comic event in which physical engineering, delicate timing, and funny little bugs cooperate with chance.

# RHYTHM

The term "rhythm" applies basically to music, dance, and poetry; it relates to measures of time. Time plays a role in visual art, too, but there it is a function of space. In other words, the artist creates visual rhythms by controlling sequences and repetitions of shaped space. We might define rhythm in art as

*left:* Paul Klee. *Daringly Poised.* 1930. Watercolor on paper mounted on cardboard, 12⅛ × 9⅝". Paul Klee Foundation, Kunstmuseum, Bern

The irregular dark shape (lower right) outweighs the circular shape (upper left) until we realize that the circle may be an eye. If so, the rectangles form a head—of a man with a pipe in his mouth. Thus we get psychological interest and optical weight in the same image.

*below:* Joan Miró. *Maternity.* 1924. Oil on canvas, 35⅞ × 29⅛". Penrose Collection, London

An X, or two levers, or a pair of scissors. They have to obey the laws of physics, but psychological symbols provide their energy: symbols make the world go round, even when it comes to making babies.

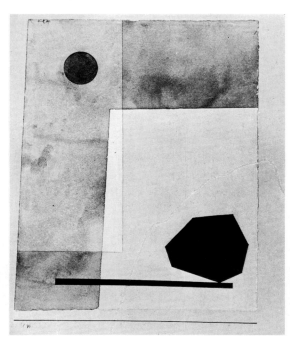

*the regular recurrence in space of one or more of the visual elements.* The main types of rhythm are called *repetitive, alternative, progressive,* and *flowing.* Usually, it is repetition of the same shape that sets up a rhythm; it makes seeing easier and more enjoyable. For some mysterious reason, our eyes will follow a repeat sequence almost against our will. Visually speaking, rhythm makes it hard to say no.

We know that people march, lift, or pull together with more effectiveness if their effort is regulated by a rhythmic stress or beat. They tire less easily, too. In performing repetitive tasks, we always try to find a comfortable rhythm or pace. Up to a certain point, *repetitive* rhythm reduces weariness and maximizes efficiency. However, industrial psychologists have shown that operators who perform repetitive tasks on dangerous machinery—stamping,

### REPETITIVE RHYTHMS

Mu Ch'i. *Six Persimmons.* c. 1270. Ink on paper, 14¼" wide. Daitoku-ji, Kyoto, Japan

The rhythm of Mu Ch'i is mainly achieved through repetition of shape, with subtle variations in spacing and tonal values. Each piece of fruit is an individual.

Wayne Thiebaud. *Seven Jellied Apples.* 1963. Oil on canvas. Formerly Allan Stone Gallery, New York

The rhythm here is deliberately monotonous, even the tilt of the sticks is boring. Thiebaud seems to be saying that all those jellied apples have the same sickly sweet taste.

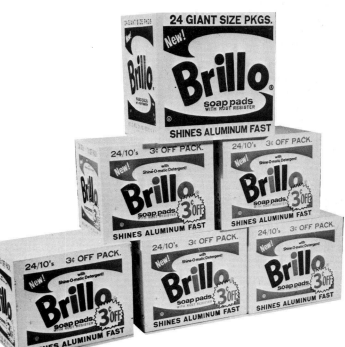

cutting, and sawing machines, for example—tend to get hurt. But injuries can be reduced by rotating operators after a certain length of time. When the human organism is bored by repetitive action, it resists by breaking the rhythm of that action.

Artists and designers try to exploit the comfortable qualities of repetitive rhythm without creating boredom or monotony. So they employ *repetition with variation*, which is like *theme and variation* in music. Thus, simple alternations between black and white, solid and void, warm and cool can be varied by introducing an unexpected element, a slight change in emphasis; the goal is to "wake up" the viewer without destroying the rhythmic pattern of his or her experience. A rhythm is like a habit: it creates unity but it can frustrate variety. So artists seek variety *within* unity by temporarily frustrating the viewer's expectations—in other words, with an occasional surprise. But ultimately, the artist has to satisfy the rhythmic expectations that were originally aroused.

A rhythmic sequence rarely occurs as the result of accident: it has to be calculated by the artist. Such calculations can easily become mechanical

*top:* Joern Utzon. Sydney Opera House. Bennelong Point, Sydney Harbor, Australia. Completed in 1973

*above left:* Andy Warhol. *Brillo Boxes.* 1964. Silkscreen on wood, 17 × 17 × 14". Leo Castelli Gallery, New York

*above:* Kasimir Malevich. *Suprematist Painting: Eight Red Rectangles.* 1915. Oil on canvas, 25⅝ × 19⅛". Stedelijk Museum, Amsterdam

patterns requiring only the capacity to follow directions. Viewers sense this and they lose interest rapidly. Some of the Pop artists—Andy Warhol in particular—have made the repetitiveness—the boring aspects of our commercial environment—the main theme of their work. We can think of other examples from architecture and product design which exhibit a deadly sort of sameness. Then what separates the artist from the patternmaker, or manufacturer of stereotypes? The ability to think of saving variations—variations that enliven a work without destroying its basic rhythm.

*Progressive* rhythm involves repetition plus a consistently repeated change. Thus the viewer's expectation is aroused in terms of a goal, a culmination. In architecture we may see it in the order of the setbacks of tall buildings. Or, when moving through a building's interior, we experience a sequence of progressively enlarged or diminished volumes. This builds suspense: we wonder what we'll see at the finish. The architect usually gives us some hints: he may then satisfy our expectations or pull a surprise out of his hat. But a surprise totally unrelated to what preceded it would sacrifice the unity of the whole. So we have a rhythmic rule: some qualities of the introductory sequence must be found in the dramatic climax. In other words, there are good surprises and bad surprises.

*Rhythm as continuous flow* is demonstrated by wave motion: the repetition of curved shapes, the buildup of emphasis at the crests, a sense of pause in the troughs, and a smooth changeover from one form to the next. The crucial feature of this type of rhythm is the transition between forms: how does the artist carry the eye from one nodal point, or crest, to the next? If the transition takes place along a curvilinear path, with no sudden changes of direction, it describes continuous flow. But there can be jagged, or staccato, rhythms, too. We see them in the paintings of Stuart Davis and John Marin. In general, flowing rhythm is more common: we see it in the sculpture of Jean Arp and Henry Moore. In architecture, we see it in the work of Félix Candela and Eero Saarinen. Alvar Aalto's bentwood experiment shows how flowing rhythm might be used in chair design. Notice, too, that this comfortable rhythm is based on the contours of the human figure: our pointy knees and elbows have been nicely rounded off.

Marcel Duchamp, in his *Nude Descending a Staircase, No. 2*, and Gino Severini (1883–1966), in his *Dynamic Hieroglyphic of the Bal Tabarin*, demonstrate the varieties of rhythm in single works of art. Thus we see repetitive,

## FLOWING RHYTHM

*below:* **Alvar Aalto. Experiment with bentwood. 1929. Courtesy Artek, Helsinki**

Aalto has created rhythm out of the flexible character of a material and the process used to shape it.

*right:* **Hans Hokanson. *Helixikos No. I.* 1968. Natural wood and elm wax, 29½ × 39 × 19". Borgenicht Gallery, New York**

Here the flowing rhythm is enhanced by a vigorous wood-carving texture that runs across the direction of the flow. We get a sense of muscular relaxation.

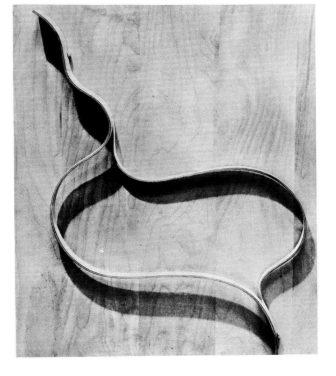

*left:* Marcel Duchamp. *Nude Descending a Staircase, No. 2.* 1912. Oil on canvas, 58 × 35". Philadelphia Museum of Art. The Louise and Walter Arensberg Collection

*below:* Gino Severini. *Dynamic Hieroglyphic of the Bal Tabarin.* 1912. Oil on canvas, with sequins, 63⅝ × 61½". Collection, The Museum of Modern Art, New York. Acquired through the Lillie P. Bliss Bequest

alternating, progressive, and flowing rhythms in combinations that can keep our eyes almost endlessly occupied. Duchamp's graceful sequence of forms was much influenced by early multiple-exposure photography; the Italian Futurist, Severini, was fascinated by the precision and energy of mechanical processes. His painting has the quality of a skillfully orchestrated, rather agreeable explosion. Both Duchamp and Severini were trying to humanize mechanical modes of seeing and making; interestingly, they relied largely on rhythm to do the job.

## PROPORTION

Proportion refers to the *size relationships* of parts to each other and to a whole. Size or scale in itself has no proportional meaning: a form must be seen in relation to other forms before we can be aware of proportion. Why do we study proportion? Is it because there are *rules* for correct or harmonious proportions? Or is this a case like color, where artists tend to follow their intuitions about what is right?

We study proportion because viewers respond to it emotionally. For more than a thousand years there have been attempts to set up rules of perfect proportion—rules that would guarantee pleasing intervals in works of art. The most enduring is the so-called Golden Section, or Golden Mean. It divides a line or a rectangle into two parts so that the smaller has the same ratio to the larger as the larger has to the whole. Expressed algebraically, the formula for the Golden Section is: $a/b = b/(a+b)$. But although the Golden Section has been used for a long time, there is nothing magic about it beyond the recognition that a line divided in half makes a dull pair of intervals. Segments of thirds are only slightly better. If we could measure the proportions of all the world's masterpieces, we would find that they come close to the Golden Section, but they vary from it, too. The variations tend to follow cultural norms differing according to time and place. For example, we would find little or no

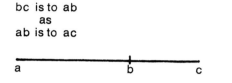

bc is to ab
as
ab is to ac

a       b     c

**Golden Section**

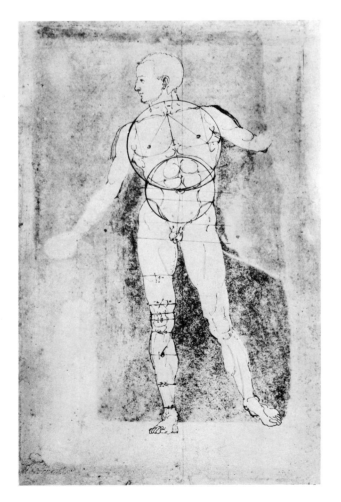

**Albrecht Dürer. *Study for Adam.* c. 1507. Pen and sepia wash. The Albertina, Vienna**

Dürer kept searching for the geometrical secret of classical figurative proportions. Compare this drawing with Leonardo's *Studio del Corpo Humano* (page 144)

similarity in the proportions of Eskimo and Polynesian figurative sculptures. Why? Different peoples, different economies, different climate, different social organization.

But even if universal rules of proportion do not exist, all of us make judgments about proportion. Certainly we have strong ideas about what constitutes *bad* proportion in art, in useful objects, and in other people. Consider this: we are larger and taller today than the knights who wore medieval armor; so when we see a suit of armor in a museum we conclude that medieval knights were generally stubby characters. Compared to us they have "bad" proportions! Apparently there has been a change in standards of proportion since the Middle Ages, but not because of a new geometrical formula. Nutrition made the big difference.

The figures in today's fashion illustrations are sometimes ten or twelve heads high. (Only basketball players can meet that standard.) Yet art students used to be taught that eight heads is right for men, and six and a half is right for women. If a model did not conform, the head could be drawn larger or smaller as needed. I suspect that average human proportions constitute our model for thinking about proportions in all things. That is, we see a ceiling or doorway in terms of the space it provides above the height of the average person. The seat of a chair is judged according to our notions about the proportions of the average person's bottom. That average changes as we grow older and more sedentary: designers have to think about these things.

People are continuously engaged in making visual calculations and comparisons. If you say about a friend: "She's my height, but a little stouter," you are making a proportional judgment. You may enter a new apartment and feel uncomfortable without knowing why. Did the builder skimp on the ceiling height, so that you feel squeezed down? You walk along a city's streets and feel depressed for no apparent reason. Are the buildings so high that you cannot see them as multiples of the human figure? Unconsciously, we make proportional judgments in deciding how an image, an object, or a space relates to our physical and, ultimately, our aesthetic, needs.

In architecture, viewers were accustomed for centuries to the proportions of classical Greek and Roman buildings. So early modern buildings— even skyscrapers—were adorned with miniature Greek temples at ground level or on their roofs. This was a recognition of the fact that the classical civilizations solved the problem of proportion and symbolism in major buildings, while we were confused about what to do. In the 1930s, when the severe flat roof of International Style architecture was introduced, it looked stark, naked, and arbitrarily cut off. Viewers wanted psychological interest at the top of a building as well as at its entrance. That is why our earliest tall buildings had to have something that looked like a "head." Good proportion meant having a *complete body.* The idea that a building needs a capital, or head, is quite literally expressed in the buttresses of the Nebraska State Capitol in Lincoln. Well, those Nebraskans could have been right in 1922, even if they used a somewhat old-fashioned idea to create "capitol" interest. Today, we have returned to the notion that a building needs a head. And we employ abstract forms to do the job; often we borrow traditional forms and give them a modern twist, or break, as in the broken pediment on top of Philip Johnson's American Telephone and Telegraph Building in New York City. Underlying the "Chippendale" look is the idea that satisfying proportions in any structure have to be modeled on something we care about. But a cabinet? A highboy? A chiffonier?

## CONCLUSION

Our discussion of unity, balance, rhythm, and proportion has shown that designers have to consider viewers' habits and needs. In other words, perception does not obey abstract, impersonal laws; it depends on perceivers— flesh and blood human beings. So, in addition to knowing the devices of the

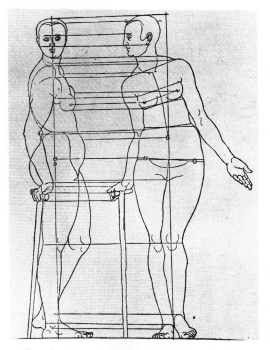

Albrecht Dürer. Study for *The Proportions of the Human Body.* 1528. Engraving. Kupferstichkabinett, Berlin

*below:* Fashion drawing

*right:* Female figure. Photograph of Debbie Drake from the jacket of her *Easy Way to a Perfect Figure and Glowing Health,* Prentice-Hall, Inc., 1961

Proportions through the ages. From Dürer's search for classical perfection, to an elongated fashion image, to an actual woman. But the proportions of "actual" women change, too. Can art be the reason?

Buttress of the State Capitol, Lincoln, Nebraska.
1922

John Burgee Architects with Philip Johnson.
Model of AT&T Corporate Headquarters, New
York. 1978–84

designer, we need to know how they affect viewers. To a considerable extent,
an artist's effectiveness depends on understanding the way people respond
to different kinds of visual organization. In addition, we should realize that
artists are guided by their personal responses to form; in the act of creation
artists become surrogates for the viewers they hope to have.

We may be tempted to use "design principles" as standards for judging
works of art; but that would be a mistake. Their use should be limited to
*explaining* the organization of the visual elements in specific cases. That may
give us some insight into the way an image works, why it is boring or exciting,
whether it has too much or not enough of something. Here we come close to
the problems of art criticism, discussed more fully in Chapters Sixteen and
Seventeen of this book. There we shall see that criticism involves philosophic
as well as design considerations. But the principles of design remain useful:
they provide many of the tools we need in undertaking art criticism.

# CHAPTER TEN

# PERCEIVING THE ELEMENTS: AESTHETICS

We have examined the visual elements and the principles of their organization or design. Now we shall examine aesthetics, which deals with the way people look at, and respond to, works of art. Although aesthetics embraces a great many things for philosophers, the subject has to be more narrowly focused for us. Our discussion will be mainly confined to what people do in the presence of art, how they interact with art, and what they get out of art.

## AESTHETIC WORK

By using words like "do," "interact," and "get," I want to stress the fact that looking at art is a type of work—physical, mental, and emotional. That work may not be as exhausting as heavy lifting, but it does involve effort that

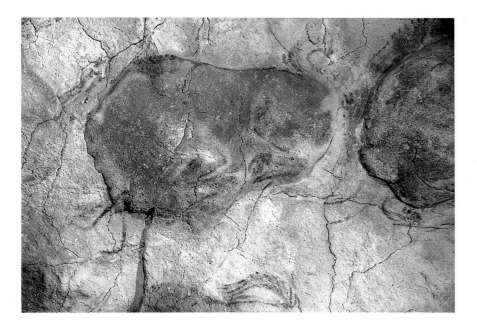

**Wounded bison. Cave painting from Altamira, Spain. c. 15,000–10,000 B.C.**

Aesthetics was there in the beginning: the first artists must have had some aesthetic impulses. We cannot escape the impression that the forms of this wounded bison were enhanced to give pleasure to the Stone Age hunter—pleasure in having killed the animal and pleasure in lingering over the "beauty" of its body.

stimulates and energizes or leaves us tired. My point is that looking at art is not a passive activity. Even bad art requires the expenditure of energy, which may explain why we don't like it: bad art makes us pay too much for what we get.

Looking at art is work if only because of the physiological processes involved. Our eyes cannot cope with sensory excitations, register colors and shapes, focus on details, and measure size relationships without expending energy. To be sure, the expenditures are small at first, but they grow larger the longer we engage in this activity. Aesthetic work also entails emotional expense. As we look at art, visual stimuli generate processes that involve virtually every part of the human organism. Those somatic or bodily processes—which we experience as emotions—have their costs: it takes fuel and a working engine to drive our muscles and organs.

As works of art run up our energy bills—and this is why art criticism is so maddening—they also make demands on our cognitive apparatus. In other words, the mind or intellect is involved. Consider the mental operations that have to be performed merely to look at a picture: we have to organize our sensations, concentrate our attention, sort out feelings, recognize forms, construct images, and compare what we see with what we have seen. Visual cognition requires that we discriminate among different *kinds* of images—those we see "out there" and those we summon up from within.

So it is no wonder that people complain about "museum fatigue." It is not only the feet that hurt; a few hours in a museum gives the entire organism a workout. Hopefully, we feel good during the workout and even better afterward. Aesthetic work is demanding; it involves all our capacities, and it requires physical fitness and mental alertness. It can also be immensely rewarding, even exhilarating. Who we are, where we have been, what we have done, and what we think we know: all these things come into play when we build an aesthetic experience.

## AESTHETIC EXPERIENCE

What *is* an aesthetic experience and how does it differ from other kinds of experience? Perhaps the best known answers to these questions were given by the philosopher and educator John Dewey in his classic *Art as Experience*, published in 1934. Here we can provide only a brief summary of Dewey's ideas on the subject.

First, we should understand that Dewey sees no fundamental difference between ordinary experience and aesthetic experience; they differ in degree but not in kind. For Dewey, the aesthetic is ordinary experience enhanced by certain "plus" factors—vividness, intensity, unity, and cohesion in recollection. Thus we can have an aesthetic experience at work, in the presence of nature, or amid the routines of everyday life. Aesthetic responses can be generated by fine art or by utilitarian art, by "high" art or by popular art. And since there is no fundamental conflict between art and life, any object, activity, or event has aesthetic potential.

What accounts for this virtually universal and continuous possibility of the aesthetic? According to Dewey, it emerges from the interactions of every human organism with its environment. Those interactions create conditions for our awareness of needs, our determination of purposes, our encounter with resistance, and our focusing of effort, followed by the disappointment or fulfillment of our expectations. Thus living itself contains the seeds of art, that is, the seeds of artistic action and aesthetic response.

It is important to realize that Dewey makes no fundamental distinction between the processes involved in making art and experiencing art. This is because "the artist embodies in himself the attitude of the perceiver while he works." As for the perceiver, "his creation must include relations comparable to those which the original producer underwent." Thus aesthetic perception entails the viewer's reenactment of the artist's creative decision-making and

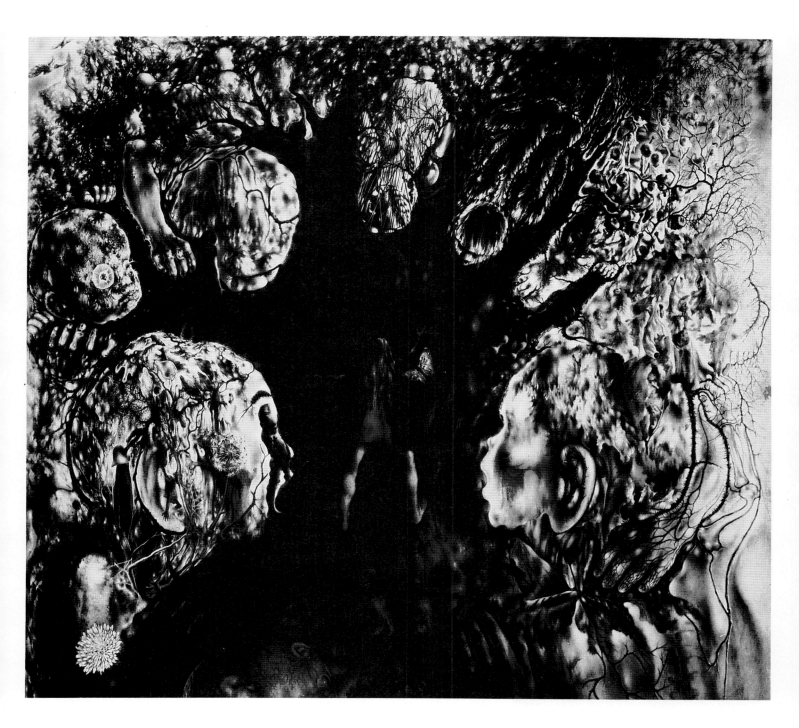

perhaps his or her personal experience. Psychologically, at least, the viewer confronts similar problems to those the artist confronted in endeavoring to create form out of the materials presented by life and the technical challenges of a particular medium or artistic tradition.

Now we come to the specific features of an aesthetic experience. According to Dewey it has all or most of the following traits: anticipation, flow, pattern and structure, vividness and intensity, economy and concentration, tension and suspense, conflict and temporary resolution, purpose and control, pauses but no holes, culmination or consummation, unity and integration. This list is long but by no means complete; furthermore, many of the listed qualities and traits are features of ordinary experience. Then what makes them distinctively aesthetic? Dewey says it is the viewer's perception of them as enjoyable "for their own sake."

Pavel Tchelitchew. *Hide-and-Seek*. 1940–42. Oil on canvas, 6'6½" × 7'3¾". Collection, The Museum of Modern Art, New York. Mrs. Simon Guggenheim Fund

Because it operates at multiple levels of meaning, *Hide-and-Seek* poses many challenges. We have to find the forms, compare the shapes, establish their identities, notice their transformations, and figure out what they signify, individually and collectively. This is hard work—*aesthetic* work—but it is enjoyable, too. And it uses all our powers of mind and imagination.

253

David Alfaro Siqueiros. *Landscape*. 1956.
Pyroxylin on Masonite, 41 × 38⅝". Instituto
Nacional de Bellas Artes, Mexico City

According to Dewey, recognizing this place and
its imagery will not produce an aesthetic
experience. The scene has to be "vividly
realized," that is, re-created in the beholder's
consciousness. To do that, Dewey says we must
engage in the same "process of organization the
creator of the work consciously experienced."

*below:* Strainer arches, crossing of the nave and
transept of Wells Cathedral. 1338

Empathy. These great arches function
structurally as reinforcements of the piers
supporting the cathedral's tower. Aesthetically,
they function as powerful arms and legs that
protect us as they hold the piers apart and
prevent the vault from collapsing. The aesthetic
effect is a product of empathy: even though the
forms are abstract, we respond to them as bodily
parts which make us feel strong and secure.

It almost seems that Dewey is a "formalist," but we cannot damn him
with that label: he does not believe artistic form exists autonomously; he
cannot conceive of art disconnected from the realities of everyday life, without linkage to meanings and events outside the art object. What ultimately
controls Dewey's thought is his doctrine of the continuity between means and
ends, between doing and undergoing, and hence between art and life.
Accordingly, one's aesthetic awareness of form is in some sense an awareness
of the experiential roots of form. We cannot enjoy a work of art without
intuiting, at least, the forces that brought it into being. Perhaps that is why art
has educational value: to experience art is to learn about the world—the
artist's world, our own world, and the connections between them.

## EMPATHY AND PSYCHIC DISTANCE

Now we can look more closely into the process of aesthetic perception. The
first one, empathy, deals with the act of "feeling into" a work of art—living
imaginatively in the world an artist has created. Psychic distance is a related
concept since it calls for deciding *how much* empathy is desirable on a given
aesthetic occasion. That is, how far should we "let ourselves go" when
looking at an artwork? How much should we identify with the persons or
things represented in it? Should we forget or try to remember that the world
of art is artificial, not real?

Before trying to answer these questions we ought to consider how empathy works. What is its mechanism? According to the psychologist Theodor Lipps, empathy is a psychological projection of the self into a work of art. This projection enables viewers to share the emotions they see expressed in or through art. Temporarily, at least, we experience a spiritual kinship with artistically created persons, places, and objects. What causes that sharing or sense of kinship? Art forms have *contagious* qualities that we catch and build on. We have little control over the process: the forms in the object beckon to the viewer's spirit, which responds by projecting its values back into the forms. Thus viewer and object feed on each other.

According to another psychologist, Karl Groos, empathy is less spiritual; it is caused by "inner mimicry," a type of neuromuscular or kinaesthetic activity that occurs as we look at art. We find ourselves tapping our feet as we

Edvard Munch. *Death in the Sickroom*. c. 1895. Oil on canvas, 59 × 66". National Gallery, Oslo

To paint this picture, Munch must have made a thousand decisions, all of which were colored by his knowledge of dying and death. Dewey maintains that viewers reenact Munch's personal and creative experience as they see and respond to his painting. That is how life's raw material is translated into aesthetic experience.

Erich Hauser. *Space Column 7/68*. 1968. Steel, 10'9½" high. Courtesy of the artist

Inner mimicry. To experience this sculpture aesthetically we must internally reenact the experience of losing balance. That enables us to "feel" the tilt, stagger, and stumble of the columns. Then we can watch the columns regain their poise and establish a new relationship with the earth.

listen to music, or gritting our teeth as we watch a horror film; both are motor reactions. These physiological responses generate emotions which the viewer "sees" in the art object. Of course, it is the artist's organization of forms that produces the physiological reactions. But it is the viewer's bodily equipment that does the aesthetic work.

Now let us consider psychic distance. According to the psychologist Edward Bullough, who originated the term, "distance" is a psychological rather than a spatial concept; it refers to the viewer's feelings of involvement in, or detachment from, a work of art. As mentioned above, psychic distance builds on empathy, on the concept of self-projection. Bullough's contribution to the subject lies in specifying the factors that increase or decrease distance. He tries to explain the aesthetic principles, or distance factors, that govern the viewer's empathic relations with an art object.

Bullough maintains that one set of distancing factors is stylistic. Thus realistic art (a typical photograph) reduces distance while highly abstract art (a Mondrian painting) increases distance. Figurative types of art (like dance and theater) decrease distance; nonfigurative types of art (like architecture and product design) increase distance. In other words, clear recognition—especially of human forms—tends to promote self-identification and emotional involvement.

Another set of distancing factors is attitudinal. Viewers with a practical interest in what is represented or expressed in art lose detachment, or distance; they become *under-distanced* (lawyers might call this "conflict of interest"). As they look at the art object, they are mainly concerned with their personal goals and needs; they lose sight of the distinctively artistic factors that give the artwork its aesthetic value. Conversely, viewers with little or no personal interest in what is represented or expressed tend to become *over-distanced*. They care too little about the form or theme or subject matter of the work; their self-involvement is not strong enough to produce an aesthetic response. Such viewers can become the cause of their own boredom.

Then what is the ideal amount of distance or self-involvement? Bullough says it is "the utmost decrease of distance without its disappearance." That seems sensible: at one extreme we experience confusion about the difference between art and life; at the other extreme we surrender to apathy and boredom. Bullough's "law" of distance is meant to give us the best of two worlds: we gain the satisfaction that comes from seeing connections between a work of art and the realities of our lives; and we have the pleasure of seeing how form, style, and technique cause those connections.

# CLOSURE AND GOOD GESTALT

Gestalt psychology, founded in 1912 by Max Wertheimer, provides us with a theory of visual perception which is shared by many artists and aestheticians. The wide influence of this theory may be due to its foundation in experimental evidence and the fact that it corresponds closely to artistic practice. That is, Gestalt "laws" seem to explain the visual thinking of artists as well as the aesthetic responses of viewers.

However, before discussing the Gestalt laws, we ought to mention some of the principles or axioms on which they are based. First, all perception is of wholes, or total *gestalten*. The human organism always seeks completion; hence incomplete forms or unstable organizations of form cause tension, suspense, and stress. Second, a whole configuration, or *gestalt,* is more than the sum of its component parts and sensory impressions. Those parts and impressions are organized by viewers using the optical information provided by the artist plus their own perceptual equipment. Thus aesthetic perception becomes a cooperative enterprise in which viewers must do a great deal of work. The *amount* of work they do and the *quality* of their work-product depend on the character of the "materials" they have to work with.

Another Gestalt principle lies in its distinction between "distant" and "proximal" stimuli. The art object is the source of (spatially) distant stimuli whose energy excites proximal (or local) stimuli when it reaches a perceiving organism. The psychologist Kurt Koffka put it as follows: "We see, not stimuli—a phrase often used—but on account of, because of, stimuli." In other words, we do not see stars, and we barely see the light from stars. We see the starlight that we generate ourselves! Now here is the crucial Gestalt proposition: viewers can register weak or distant stimuli with their eyes but they can only perceive proximal, or local, stimuli. Thus, what we "see" is to a large extent self-created. If this proposition is valid it may explain why different viewers literally see different works of art.

The "laws" of Gestalt are based on the Law of Prägnanz, a psychological application of a principle of physics called Kirchkoff's Law. That law, which originally applied to current in an electrical circuit, maintains that all the forces in a system distribute themselves according to a pattern of minimal energy production to maintain a maximum of stable, systemic function. It seems to me that this connection—between minimal energy production and maximal systemic function—explains what mathematicians, artists, and aestheticians mean by "elegance."

Now we come to the Gestalt laws of visual organization: proximity, similarity, continuity, and closure. Sometimes, these laws (generated by the Law of Prägnanz) are expressed as regularity, symmetry, and simplicity—principles that most of us recognize as rhythm, balance, and unity. For practicing artists they translate into strategies for effective composition and design, that is, effective ways of organizing visual information. For Gestalt psychologists these laws produce the so-called good gestalt.

What is a "good gestalt"? Objectively, it is a set of forms organized to produce an uninterrupted, hence coherent, hence meaningful, hence gratifying, aesthetic experience. If the organization of that set of forms is unstable, viewers will add information *through their own perceptual activity* to make up the deficit. But if the organization remains unstable, then we have to say it is incoherent, meaningless, and aesthetically disappointing: from a Gestalt standpoint the work of art fails despite the viewer's best efforts.

Finally, we come to closure, the Gestalt term for the completion of the process of aesthetic perception. If visual forms are skillfully organized to exploit the laws of proximity, similarity, and continuity, then viewers will be able to achieve closure. Which is to say, a "good gestalt" leads to fulfillment or successful closure. That closure, in turn, yields coherence, meaning, and emotional satisfaction. Why? Because it fulfills the physiological requirements

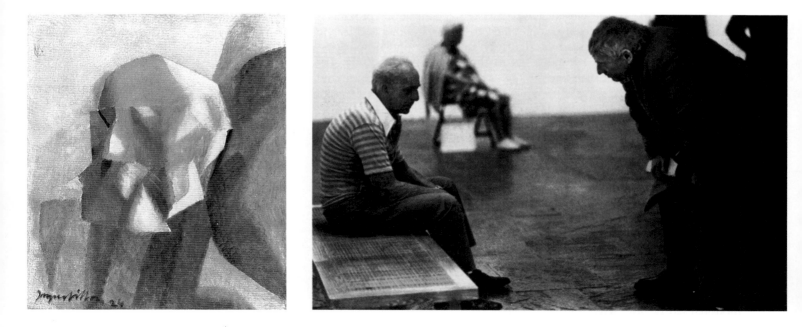

*opposite above:* David Alfaro Siqueiros. *Self-Portrait.* 1943. Pyroxylin, 39⅜ × 48". Instituto Nacional de Bellas Artes, Mexico City

Under-distancing. By violently thrusting his arm toward the viewer, Siqueiros makes it impossible to view his portrait with detachment. The first thing we see is a fist, greatly enlarged by foreshortening and perspective. With this device the artist penetrates the space between image and spectator, eliminating psychic distance at the same time. We feel threatened—not by art but by life itself.

*opposite below left:* Jacques Villon. *Portrait of the Artist's Father.* 1924. Oil on canvas, 21½ × 18¼". The Solomon R. Guggenheim Museum, New York

Over-distancing. This head can be viewed with almost complete detachment. Emphasis is mainly on the light that falls on a rhythmic succession of crisp planes. But even though this is a son's portrait of his father, there is no reference to a relationship, no identification with the subject, and no expression of feeling. As far as our aesthetic involvement is concerned, we could be looking at a Cézanne still life.

*opposite below right:* Man studying a Duane Hanson sculpture, *Man on a Bench,* at the Whitney Museum of American Art, New York. 1977

Total loss of distance. Hanson's hyper-realism confuses the viewer; he cannot respond aesthetically because he cannot tell whether he is looking at a work of art or a real person. The man's confusion shows that an art experience requires awareness of artifice: we need to see the artist's hand at work.

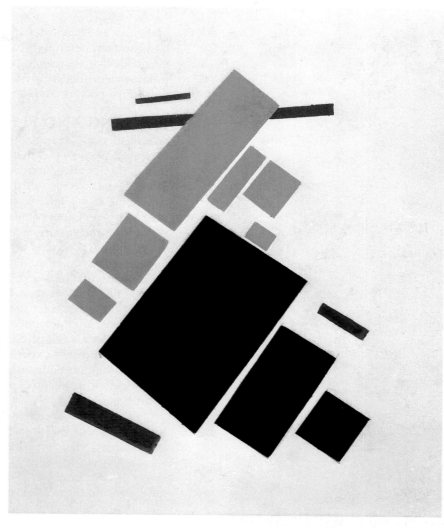

*above:* Kasimir Malevich. *Suprematist Composition: Airplane Flying.* 1915 (dated 1914). Oil on canvas, 22⅞ × 19". Collection, The Museum of Modern Art, New York. Purchase

At first we see a collection of rectangles, graded in size and floating in space. None of them touch, although there is one case of overlapping. Then we read the title, which includes the word "airplane," and suddenly we "see" wings, a fuselage, and a propeller. What creates this miracle? Closure. The aesthetic image is produced by the artist's formal suggestions, plus the title, plus the viewer's need for perceptual completion.

*left:* Nan Wood Graham and Byron McKeeby, models for Grant Wood's *American Gothic* (see page 125)

What is the basic difference between the photograph and the painting? The artist's deliberate repetition of forms, especially of ovals; that is what changes a plain couple into an aesthetic statement. By stressing the oval shapes of the faces and the pitchfork, Wood identifies these people with their work and their rural existence. The Gestalt principle of similarity produces a unified quality that the photograph does not possess.

of the Law of Prägnanz. Closure occurs because the qualities of the art object have, in fact, been perceived and understood. Indeed, Gestalt psychology maintains that completed perception *is* understanding: to see completely is to know. For that happy consummation we can thank the artist, our own perceptual powers, and, of course, Kirchkoff's Law.

## FUNDING AND FUSION

Gestalt theory is especially persuasive in its analysis of visual perception. However, we may feel that the concepts of closure and good gestalt, while useful, do not adequately account for our perception of meaning in a work of art. Gestalt seems to explain *why* we experience a work's unity without explaining its cognitive character or semantic significance. Here the philosopher Stephen Pepper comes to our rescue; Pepper offers the related concepts of *funding* and *fusion*.

Funding, according to Pepper, is based on the fact that it takes time to experience a work of art. During that time we have many separate successive perceptions of the work. Those separate successive perceptions may be similar, they may have a family resemblance, but they are not identical. However, they interact with each other: early perceptions influence later perceptions, later perceptions affect earlier perceptions, and strong perceptions dominate weak perceptions. As these perceptions accumulate in memory and in present experience, they modify and enrich each other. This modification and enrichment are what Pepper means by funding: funding gives depth to aesthetic experience. Stated otherwise, funding makes a work of art "interesting."

Our separate perceptions of an artwork and our awareness of their interactions can lead to a kind of bewilderment which is familiar even to sophisticated viewers. Funding may enrich our aesthetic perceptions, but what pulls them together? What gives our experience its unified character and sense of completeness? We know what the Gestaltists would say: it is the artist's organization of the visual field, Kirchkoff's Law, and good gestalt. What does Pepper say?

Pepper says that our separate successive perceptions of an artwork constitute a *perceptive series*. This perceptive series becomes the *aesthetic object*, the real focus of appreciation and critical judgment. But how does that aesthetic object come into being? First, through its physical constancy; second, through the viewers "perceptual grasp." What is perceptual grasp? It is the management of the process of fusion by the spectator, or "subject continuant." And what distinguishes fusion from funding? Fusion occurs *after* funding; it is the integration of our previous and partial perceptions of the art object, which Pepper calls the "physical continuant." Fusion summarizes everything we have felt, remembered, and seen *in* the physical continuant and *because of* the subject continuant.

How does fusion lead to the awareness of a pervasive or controlling quality in a work of art? Pepper speaks of a "convergence effect" produced by the culture and biological constitution of the viewer. That convergence effect cancels any tendency of the art object to disintegrate aesthetically. Thus Pepper is not far from the Gestaltists: he says funding and fusion are responsible for the "personality" of the aesthetic object, and personality is produced by forces latent in the physical continuant and active in the organism's drive toward unity, closure, and meaning.

Like Lipps and Groos, Pepper builds on the concept of empathic responses. Like Bullough he realizes that viewers exercise control over their aesthetic responses. And like the Gestaltists he distinguishes between distant stimuli (the physical continuant) and local or proximal stimuli (the subject continuant). We are especially indebted to Pepper for his analysis of aesthetic perception as a process that *takes time*. From Pepper's analysis it follows that

**Male portrait head, from Ife, Nigeria. 12th century. Bronze, 13½" high. Collection the Oni of Ife**

We like this head immediately, spontaneously, despite its non-Western origin. Why? Must we be Africans or African-Americans to appreciate the work? No. The sculpture appeals on a more generalized aesthetic level—a level that rises above race, class, or ethnicity.

Georges Seurat. *A Sunday Afternoon on the Island of La Grande Jatte.* 1884–86. Oil on canvas, 6'9½" × 10'1¼". The Art Institute of Chicago. Helen Birch Bartlett Memorial Collection

the character or flavor or meaning of a work of art is not instantly grasped: it is an "emergent," a product of the viewer's accumulated perceptions. Meaning has to be built, or as Dewey said: "A beholder must create his own experience."

## LIKING AND DISLIKING

Whether artists like it or not, we have opinions about their work, and many of us feel free to express them. Those opinions are sometimes called critical judgments, a subject treated in Chapters Sixteen and Seventeen of this book. But here we shall not discuss the reasoned judgment of critics, scholars, and connoisseurs—persons who can be expected to employ historical comparisons, appraisals of technique, and the careful marshaling of iconographic evidence. Instead, we want to look into the likes and dislikes of lay people, their more or less spontaneous responses to art.

There is a substantial literature about spontaneous liking and disliking, sometimes called *affective response* to art; much of it is based on experimental studies—usually preference tests—conducted by psychologists and aestheticians. Their findings can be instructive although they tend to tell us what we already know or might reasonably expect: that youngsters like pictures with bright colors; that most people prefer representational art to abstract art; that adults tolerate complex shapes better than children; that scenes of violence are more appealing to males than to females.

Perhaps the questions asked by the people who devise these tests do not reach the subtlety or richness of aesthetic response. Perhaps, too, their experimental data are not as objective and quantifiable as they think. Never-

Seurat's canvas presents so much to the eye: strollers, rowers, and picnickers; men relaxing, women fishing, and children playing; plus two dogs and a monkey. Plus parasols and headgear: top hats, a helmet, a cap, and women's chapeaux galore. Plus boats and water, trees and grass, sunlight and shadow. What unites all these forms, colors, creatures, and actions? Is it the picture frame? The time of day? The day of the week? The spatial envelope? Aesthetically, it is our "perceptual grasp"—our awareness of an underlying order pervading everything we see. And that awareness is produced by "fusion."

theless, there may be good reasons for conducting art preference research even if we doubt the possibility of a genuine "science" of aesthetics. Following are some questions and issues in the realm of aesthetic preference which might benefit from further investigation.

First, are aesthetic preferences purely subjective? That is, are likes and dislikes innate or learned? Obviously, this is another version of the nature versus nurture controversy. An easy answer to the question is "yes" and "no." Some likes are innate; others are learned. But regardless of whether a preference was inherited or acquired, it is felt subjectively: when I *like* a work of art, it is I—not someone else—who likes it. We need to know why that "I" likes what it likes.

Second, are the preferences of viewers related to their age, race, gender, politics, religion, social class, or educational level? Again the answer would appear to be "yes" and "no." Yes, we tend to like what people in our group or class or generation like. No, we don't *have to* like what people in our group or class or generation like. Does this mean we are free to make aesthetic choices? If so, why? If not, why not?

Third, can tastes or preferences be divided into high and low, ignorant and sophisticated, old-fashioned and modern? Well, people do make such distinctions. Sometimes "high" and "low" are references to a hierarchy of the senses, with sight and sound at the high end and touch and smell at the low end. Sometimes "ignorant" and "sophisticated" are code words for the preferences of people already classified as high or low. As for "old-fashioned" and "modern," they too are code words for good or bad, for advanced or retarded, for slow or alert. In fact, all these terms may be social, moral, or psychological judgments disguised as aesthetic preferences.

Fourth, can personal tastes be changed? And if so, should they be changed? This amounts to asking whether natural or spontaneous taste is inevitably inferior to educated or "cultivated" taste. One can think of cases

**Norman Rockwell. *Doctor and Doll*. Oil painting for *Saturday Evening Post* cover, March 9, 1929**

What is it that we like here? The cute little girl? Her doll? The kindly old doctor? The mock seriousness of the scene? All these features encourage an agreeable response to the picture. But it is not an especially *aesthetic* response. We recognize the situation, we like what it represents, and we like ourselves for liking the picture.

*above:* Juan Gris. *Fantômas (Pipe and Newspaper)*. 1915. Oil on canvas, 23½ × 28⅞". National Gallery of Art, Washington, D.C. Chester Dale Collection

*right:* Roy Lichtenstein. *Girl at Piano*. 1963. Magna on canvas, 68 × 48". The Harry N. Abrams Family Collection, New York

"Low," or popular, art often ends up as "high," or elite, art. In 1915 the Cubist collage by Juan Gris was as jarring to fine-art sensibilities as Roy Lichtenstein's 1963 "comic-strip" image was at the time of its creation. Indeed, that was a principal aim of modernism: to enlarge the language of art by breaking down false aesthetic categories.

*left:* Jeff Koons. *Ushering in Banality.* 1988. Polychromed wood, 38 × 62 × 30". Sonnabend Gallery, New York

Can taste—especially bad taste—be changed? Koons tries to do the job aesthetically—by a deliberately kitschy treatment of a kitschy idea. After this "therapy" we should be immune to pretty colors, sweet faces, and maudlin subjects forever.

*below:* Norman Rockwell. *The Connoisseur.* Oil painting for *Saturday Evening Post* cover, January 13, 1962. Printed by permission of the Norman Rockwell Family Trust © 1962

Rockwell the illustrator is commenting on an Abstract Expressionist canvas, probably a Pollock. The artist and the connoisseur must be Americans, yet we suspect a breakdown in artistic communication. Why? Whose fault is it? Apparently, aesthetic failures can occur *within* cultures as well as *between* them.

where educated taste is really a type of status striving, that is, a form of social emulation. On the other hand, we cannot deny that tastes and preferences change sincerely in the light of new experience. Not only do they change, they may actually change for the better. By "better" I mean that they represent considered choices made from a larger class of relevant alternatives. Hence our answer to the question raised above is: While we live and grow, our tastes *should* change; that is, they should be deepened, enriched, and revised. But for the right reasons.

## CROSS-CULTURAL FACTORS

Our discussion of liking and disliking leads directly to certain controversial social questions: Are aesthetic values inevitably culture-bound? Do viewers automatically prefer the art made in their own land by their own kinfolk? Can we respond authentically to works of art created outside our country by other kinds of people? For example, can Americans appreciate Chinese or Japanese or African or Indian art? Can Japanese or African or Indian viewers appreciate American art? It must be obvious that they can and do. Why, then, do we hear so much about the incompatibility, or nontransfer, of aesthetic values? Do works of art, like certain wines, turn into vinegar when they travel?

These questions arise, I believe, because of three basic misconceptions. First, we think a work of art is really a collective creation, the mystical emanation of a time, place, linguistic group, or community of believers. Second, we think an aesthetic response is really a response to the race, religion, politics, and temperament of the artist whose work we are examining. Third, we think that the differences between ourselves and other peoples are far greater than our similarities. On reflection, all these views are partially wrong or wholly mistaken: art is, in fact, created by flesh-and-blood men and women very much like ourselves.

There may be a deeper reason for the belief that aesthetic responses are culture-bound. Because we recognize differences in the art of various peoples we conclude that those differences separate us aesthetically and humanly, that is, at the very core of our being. But such a belief flies in the face of the facts. For example, I collect African and Polynesian sculpture with great pleasure. The Japanese pay huge sums for the paintings of a red-headed Dutchman, Vincent van Gogh; the English have always admired the German artist Hans Holbein and the Flemish painter Anthony van Dyck; the French are wild about an American comic, Jerry Lewis; and almost everyone loves Chinese food and ceramics. Further examples of artistic, aesthetic, and culinary transfer could be cited; my point is that culture's control over aesthetic response has been greatly exaggerated.

The lesson of art history is that some works of art easily transcend group preferences and biases, the vagaries of taste, and the boundaries of regions and states. Other works can be understood outside their original geographic and societal settings, but only with difficulty. Still others seem to be truly culture-bound: they cannot travel at all. It is possible, however, that variations in aesthetic response reflect the differences between good, mediocre, and bad art. In other words, not every failure of aesthetic communication is the fault of the viewer.

When an aesthetic experience is aborted, we have to decide whether the cause is in the work of art or in ourselves. Here the systematic study of art criticism may help in assigning responsibility. Perhaps cultural differences have clouded our vision, but before making that diagnosis we ought to consider these points: (1) the act of seeing is personal, not collective; (2) artistic images are visual organizations before they are anything else (the Gestaltists were not crazy); (3) the capacity of "strong" images to break through cultural constraints should not be underestimated; (4) good art is more about sharing than excluding; (5) great art tends to build bonds among dissimilar peoples and personalities.

*left:* Unkei (?). *Basu-Sennin.* One of 28 attendants to Kannon. 13th century. Colored wood, 63⅜" high. Myoho-in Temple, Kyoto, Japan

*above:* Donatello. *Mary Magdalen.* 1454-55. Wood, 6' high. Baptistery, Florence

Notice that both sculptors employ the same artistic devices—attenuation, realistic detail, and sharp undercutting—to express the same notion of spirituality: mortification of the body to attain the ideal of saintliness. Whether we are Japanese or Italian, our response is essentially the same: aesthetic effect transcends ethnic, geographic, and religious differences.

## CONCLUSION

The painter Barnett Newman once said: "Aesthetics is to art as ornithology is to the birds." Perhaps he was expressing an artist's contempt for theory separated from practice. Or maybe he was referring to the notoriously difficult and abstract literature of aesthetics. I hope the illustrations and captions in this chapter have helped dispel the fog by giving focus and concreteness to that literature.

Here we should bear in mind that aesthetics was not created to confuse or mystify art lovers; it constitutes a studied attempt to explain what happens when we look at works of art. We may want to understand and enjoy pictures, but we cannot deal with them intelligently if we operate on the basis of pure subjectivity or mere liking or some unexamined theory of artistic form. Without a serious explanation of the interactions between artworks and viewers we cannot really understand such "heavy" concepts as aesthetic perception, expression, communication, and cognition.

Many of us would rather look at art without the benefit (or interference) of aesthetic theory. That is, in fact, what most people (including many art scholars) do. On the other hand, ignorance of aesthetics can lead to certain grievous errors: we think aesthetic pleasure is a passive activity; we imagine that emotions are literally *in* the art object; we think art deals with feelings but not with ideas; we confuse spontaneous preference with artistic quality; and we believe works of art have meanings which are fixed and immutable. Some very intelligent people make these errors; however, the student of aesthetics knows better.

*Dignitary or priest,* from Tabasco, Mexico. 400–500 A.D. Wood and paint, 15" high. The Metropolitan Museum of Art, New York. The Michael C. Rockefeller Memorial Collection. Bequest of Nelson A. Rockefeller, 1979

We sense the nobility of this little personage regardless of its creator's origin. The sculptor was, in fact, Mexican, but he could have been Chinese or Peruvian or Egyptian. The aesthetics of the figure relies on universal human qualities, hence the carving can cross cultural barriers. In other words, "Good art is more about sharing than excluding."

# PART FOUR

# The Interaction of Medium and Meaning

How do the terms "material," "medium," and "technique" differ? We ought to understand them before studying the interactions between artistic expression and the various media. *Material* causes no difficulty: it designates the physical stuff of art, such as paint, clay, metal, and stone. These materials are available in a variety of natural or manufactured forms; artists work with them directly or supervise others who shape and assemble them according to instructions.

*Medium* is a more difficult term. In the dictionary it is defined as "the substance through which a force acts or an effect is transmitted." In other words, a medium is a vehicle for changing materials into artistic form. In painting, the word *medium* has a technical meaning: it is the *liquid* in which pigment is suspended—wet plaster, linseed oil, egg yolk, varnish, synthetic resin, and so on. But that definition would not work for architecture or sculpture. For a definition that applies to all the arts, let us say that a medium is a special use of materials for an artistic purpose. Thus architecture is not a medium, it is an art. Cast concrete, however, is a medium used in architecture. Sculpture is an art, but welded metal is a sculptural medium.

*Technique* and *medium* tend to overlap in ordinary usage, but we can define *technique* with more precision here: *a technique is a special or personal way of using a medium.* For example, many artists employ the medium of oil paint, but Jackson Pollock developed a *personal technique* of dripping paint. The sculptors John Chamberlain (page 356) and Richard Stankiewicz (page 354) use different personal techniques in the medium of welded metal. The architects Le Corbusier, Nervi, and Candela use the medium of cast concrete, but each in a different way.

In the following chapters, we attempt to show how the nature of a medium influences what is done *with* it and what is expressed *through* it. Obviously, every medium has inherent possibilities and limitations. Some

*left:* Edgar Degas. *Developpé en avant.* 1920. Bronze copy after wax original of 1880. The Metropolitan Museum of Art, New York. The H. O. Havemeyer Collection. Bequest of Mrs. H. O. Havemeyer, 1929

Two representations of woman in motion. Notice how material and technique influence form and meaning.

*right:* Robert Cremean. *Swinging Woman.* 1960. Wood mache, 58 × 35½ × 67". University of Nebraska Art Galleries, Lincoln. Gift of Mrs. A.B. Sheldon

artists submit to the limitations; they seem to know what can or cannot be accomplished within a medium. Others work on the possibilities: they try to stretch the medium's range. *Craftsmanship* might be understood as the knowledge of what can be done in a medium and the ability to do it. Still, all the possibilities cannot be known in advance: every artistic medium holds out a challenge to the judgment of the person who uses it.

Technique is important but it is not the whole story of art. Although an artist needs technical skill, it is only a means to an end. That is why, as critics, we find ourselves judging the connections between artistic means and ends; we are interested in the *quality of interaction between medium and meaning.* When examining a work of art, we want to find out how the medium has influenced the artist's overall expression. At the same time, we want to know how an expressive purpose has affected the medium's use. Needless to say, critics must know as much as possible about the technical and expressive possibilities of the various media.

Is personal artistic experience necessary to understand media/meaning relationships? It helps, but it may not be absolutely essential. Certainly, none of us has worked in every artistic medium. So the following chapters try to provide some basic information about media/meaning relationships in the major art forms. This is not easy because we are attempting to communicate through words and reproductions the sort of knowledge that is normally gained by direct observation or practical experience. Also, new technologies might make our generalizations about media obsolete. Wherever possible, then, we shall talk about specific works of art; they, at least, will stay put.

# CHAPTER ELEVEN

# PAINTING

O f all the visual arts, painting is the most widely practiced. Children and grandparents, amateurs and professionals, physicians and prizefighters—all paint, with pleasure to themselves if not always to others. Is there any reason why this art should have attracted so many devotees? There are several reasons, of course, but one of them concerns us especially: the flexibility and versatility of painting, particularly in oil, tempera, or acrylics.

The discovery of oil painting in the fifteenth century opened up immense pictorial possibilities. It was the type of technological innovation that illustrates our theme: the interaction of medium and meaning. Oil paint has blending and modeling qualities unobtainable with tempera paint. The slow-drying oil vehicle permits the artist to modify a still-wet paint film by adding paint, wiping it out, introducing darker or lighter tones, scratching in lines, and even manipulating paint with the fingers. Yet the paint will dry as a single "skin" in which all these applications and afterthoughts are physically united.

Because oil paint dries to a fairly elastic film, it does not crack if the canvas buckles slightly. Accordingly, the artist can work on a large canvas as opposed to the small wooden panels required for tempera. Before the perfection of oil painting, mural-size works had to be executed in fresco—that is, dry colors plus fresh plaster—and on the site of the wall itself. With oil on canvas, artists could execute huge works in their studios, afterward transferring them to a permanent site in a building. Using fresco, Michelangelo had to stand on a scaffold, or lie on his back, to paint the Sistine ceiling. Like a modern painter of outdoor signs, he could not stand back from his work to admire it or gauge his progress.

Painting appeals to persons varying greatly in skill and sophistication, while sculpture appears to be an art for the hardy few. Sculptors need solid technical preparation, and they have to be strong. Also, their subject matter is limited. To be sure, Bernini could carve stone to look like lace—a truly virtuoso effect. But painting has a generally larger capacity for creating illusions. Sculptors seeking naturalistic effects used to *paint* their work to produce a convincing result. In painting, however, the use of linear perspective, foreshortening, chiaroscuro, glazing, and color complementarity opened up illusionistic opportunities that nothing could match. Finally, sad

**Michelangelo.** *Isaiah* (detail from the ceiling of the Sistine Chapel). 1508-12. The Vatican, Rome

The physical condition of Michelangelo's Sistine ceiling paintings makes us wish that Leonardo had used the same fresco technique in his *Last Supper.* The color in a fresco does not *rest* on the surface; it sinks into, and becomes part of, the wall. Thus a fresco can withstand a great deal of punishment.

to say, badly executed paintings endure physically in spite of their poor craftsmanship. Painting has no "built-in" features that might discourage technical ineptness: almost everything survives.

Because the painting media are flexible and tough, because painting is attractive to many temperaments, because painting can treat almost any subject, and because works of indifferent technique can last as long as masterpieces, painting is exceedingly popular. For that reason alone, the criticism of painting is very difficult. The invention of oil painting and painting with plastic media has had amazing social as well as artistic consequences. But no matter how revolutionary the technical changes have been, we must remember that the human need to create images has been the driving force.

## THE FUGITIVE AND THE PERMANENT

In a well-designed building we can see that a truss, an arch, or a dome is *doing the work* of supporting weight and enclosing space. The forms are felt as a physical system which probably will hold together as we use it. But such factors rarely affect our perception of painted forms. Still, the art of painting has a physical basis which, as in architecture, is concerned with durability.

The stone vaults of Gothic churches were developed because fires were common and wooden-roofed churches burned down repeatedly. So the physical survival of man-made structures was very important in medieval communities. This interest in durability was reflected in all the arts. For painting, durability meant resistance to fading, peeling, cracking, warping, and splitting. Since a picture was a valuable commodity, painters had to master "correct"—that is, permanent—technique. So-called fugitive colors could fade, especially the blues and violets. Others might turn black or "bleed through." Colors applied to an absorbent ground might "sink in." The knots in a badly sealed wood panel might show through the paint film. A thousand perils hovered over every artist's brush.

During the Renaissance, painters were products of the guild system, and although masters like Leonardo, Michelangelo, and Titian had risen above the artisan class, they were deeply immersed in problems of craftsmanship; their training was based on mastery of proven techniques. Leonardo and Cennino Cennini wrote treatises on the art of painting which contain lengthy discussions of technical methods. However, Cennino's treatise is more like a cookbook, while Leonardo goes beyond cookery into questions of anatomy, physiology, optics, perspective, and even art criticism.

Thus, if painting technique begins as an interest in physical durability, it ends up in aesthetics. During the Middle Ages, artists' contracts specified the use of costly materials, much as today's architectural specifications require materials with certain performance ratings. But as the social and professional status of the painter was raised, the intangible qualities of his art were stressed. Sound technique was assumed, but patrons realized that genius consisted of more than costly materials.

Many modern painters observe ancient traditions of craft, often for stylistic reasons. A picture's technique may be its principal source of meaning; in the past it was mainly a guarantee of durability. For example, El Greco could not have employed Soutine's brilliant cadmiums and alizarins; they were not available in chemically stable, light-proof pigments. The Baroque master had to use a thin reddish glaze over a neutral tempera underpainting Soutine, on the other hand, could apply opaque crimsons and reds directly to his white-primed canvas; he could paint these twisted passages quite spontaneously. The turbulence of Soutine's imagery owes a great deal to this type of direct execution, whereas El Greco's flickering effects had to be planned in advance.

*left:* Chaim Soutine. *The Madwoman.* 1920. Oil on canvas, 37¼ × 23¼". The National Museum of Western Art, Tokyo. Presented by Mr. Tai Hayashi, 1960

*below:* El Greco. Detail of *Pentecost.* 1603–7. The Prado, Madrid. Copyright © Museo del Prado

Leonardo da Vinci. Detail of *The Last Supper.*
c. 1495–98. Sta. Maria delle Grazie, Milan

Instead of the time-honored fresco technique,
Leonardo used tempera on a masonry wall that
was badly sealed with a varnish of resin and
pitch. Moisture must have passed through the
wall into the paint film, which began to peel
soon after the work was completed. Since then,
it has suffered from poor care and numerous
restorations. We can only guess at its original
magnificence.

Inevitably, the durability of goods has a different meaning today than it
had in the scarcity economies of the past. For us, an artistic concern with
permanent technique seems old-fashioned, since we are reasonably sure of
a painting's physical survival; our concern shifts to its durability as a
significant statement. We want to know whether a painting will live as a
vehicle of *sustained aesthetic interest.* Also, we are deeply concerned with its
*originality.* As George Moore said, "It does not matter how badly you paint,
so long as you don't paint badly like other people."

The *time* required to execute a work by traditional methods worked
against a casual approach toward subject matter. But as the oil-painting
medium was perfected, technical skills could be devoted to themes of less
than high seriousness. For example, the courts of love paintings by Jean-
Honoré Fragonard (1732–1806) seem rather shallow, even by modern standards. We are more impressed by the painterly virtuosity of *The Swing:* the
drawing, brushwork, and composition rise above the picture's silly theatrics.
Today, a casual, offhand technique can be employed to treat even a major
theme. *La Mort d'Attila* by Georges Mathieu (born 1921) is such a work; it
represents the death of the "Scourge of God," as the murderous Hun was
lovingly known. But visually, it tells us more about Mathieu's wrist than about
Attila.

We do not look at a painting as Renaissance men and women did,
inquiring into its craftsmanship and its likelihood of surviving as an object that
expresses an important idea. Contemporary collectors are more inclined to

*left:* Jean-Honoré Fragonard. Detail of *The Swing.* 1766. By permission of the Trustees of the Wallace Collection, London

*below:* Georges Mathieu. *La Mort d'Attila.* 1961. Oil on canvas, 6'6¾" × 9'10⅛". Collection Jean Larcade, Paris

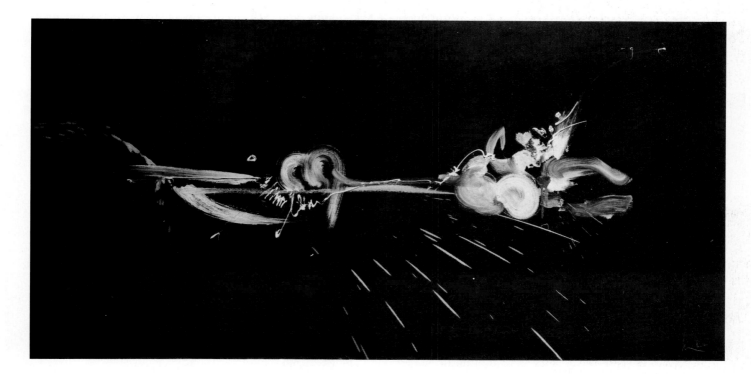

think of a painting as a possession they may sell if it ceases to be interesting or if its market value increases. We have a different sense of time and a different set of priorities. Under the impact of rapid social and technical change, our confidence in fixed values has broken down. The idea that man-made structures should last indefinitely seems old-fashioned, just as it would have seemed absurd to medieval guildsmen that anything be made *not* to last.

273

But if the decline of old notions of permanence has cost us certain artistic values, there have also been compensations. Experimentation with new materials has generated large dividends in visual variety. Painting is perhaps more entertaining—certainly more shocking—than it was. At the same time it has not abandoned serious issues. Photography, film, and television may pose a threat to the survival of handcrafted pictures, but painting appears to be responding to the challenge vigorously. Certainly it is more widely practiced and exhibited; and it has extended its range of social and personal concerns. Also, painting tries to compete with other media of information and expression: it has even acquired some of the traits of architecture, sculpture, and theater. Old as it is, painting continues to change and grow.

## DIRECT AND INDIRECT TECHNIQUES

Simply stated, direct painting seeks a final effect immediately; indirect painting calls for a stage-by-stage approach. These two approaches represent fundamental differences in technique and artistic psychology. In general, traditional methods are indirect, systematic, and planned in advance. Modern methods tend to be direct, spontaneous, and open to happy accidents.

As long as painting is an elaboration of drawing, the indirect method prevails. When painting is a process of applying color to a scheme already worked out, it makes sense to use this indirect method: it amounts to a problem in the division of labor. First comes the conception of the work, its theme, its setting, its action, illumination, and so on. Next, drawings are made to establish the spatial envelope, locate figures, and arrange landscape or architectural features. Finally, there may be an oil sketch to indicate the distribution of color, light, and shadow. Drawing, however, is the main compositional tool, the real decision-making device.

*below:* Michelangelo. Studies for *The Libyan Sibyl.* c. 1511. Red chalk on paper, 11⅜ × 8⅜". The Metropolitan Museum of Art, New York. Joseph Pulitzer Bequest, 1924

The drawing is more detailed than the final fresco painting because it truly is a "study"—a device for knowing a phenomenon visually and intellectually.

*right:* Michelangelo. *The Libyan Sibyl* (detail from the ceiling of the Sistine Chapel). 1511. The Vatican, Rome

Artists made studies of anatomy, drapery, hands, and facial expressions to assure themselves of an intellectual and visual grasp of their subject; then they felt ready to transfer their drawings to a prepared surface. After enlargement to the scale of the final work, the artist could begin painterly execution. The preliminary painting—often in tempera—was usually monochromatic; this "underpainting" fitted preparatory studies and sketches into the large compositional scheme, defined the lights and darks, and modeled the main forms. Because tempera paint dries quickly and opaquely, corrections to cover mistakes can be made easily. Oil paint, on the other hand, dries slowly and becomes somewhat transparent as it grows older; thus passages which have been painted out will eventually show through. However, tempera does not blend easily. Egg tempera, especially, is difficult to spread over large areas. So large forms have to be built up by "hatching" (creating small areas of color or tone by a series of lines painted close together); it is an essentially linear technique.

When the indirect method is used, the underpainting can be executed in cool tones because they will probably be covered with warm-tone glazes. By manipulating glazes (paint thinned with oil or varnish), painters could achieve a rich, warm-cool balance. Light areas were usually painted "higher" or "chalkier" than they would finally appear because overpainting and glazing "lowered" their value. Also, it was assumed that white pigment (usually white lead), together with final varnishing, would yellow the painting in time. That was another reason for favoring a cool tonality in the underpainting.

Before the wide use of oil painting, most pictures were completely executed in tempera (the other principal media were encaustic, which employs hot wax as a binder, and fresco, which employs lime and plaster as its binder). Tempera is usually understood as any painting medium based on a glue. Older glues came from cooked animal skins—rabbit skin, for instance. As we know from scraping breakfast frying pans, eggs are a powerful adhesive. Casein, a milk derivative, is a modern glue that makes an excellent tempera. Polymer or acrylic tempera comes close to being an ideal medium since it possesses most of the assets and none of the liabilities of the traditional tempera and oil media. Until the 1940s, however, tempera paintings were mostly executed with the traditional egg-yolk medium. Some painters, like Andrew Wyeth, continue to employ the classic egg-tempera medium.

Contemporary artists who use the traditional method of tempera painting prepare a gesso ground (thin, white, plaster-of-Paris layers applied over a coating of glue) on a wood panel (today it would be Masonite). Then they puncture an egg-yolk sac, "cook up" an egg-and-water or egg-and-oil emulsion, and mix the emulsion with powdered dry pigments. Pure egg-tempera technique is quite permanent; it does not darken with age; and it produces clean, bright color. But tempera usually calls for a rigid support and, as mentioned above, is not well suited for covering large areas. Furthermore, it dictates a slowly built-up, step-by-step mode of execution. And, like fresco, it forces the artist to think in linear terms.

*Direct painting* began when artists increased the amount of pigment in their oil glazes. The Venetians were probably the first: they employed a technique in which the brush is "loaded" with paint of a pasty, viscous consistency and then applied in short "touches" rather than spread out evenly. This technique permits freer departures from a controlling tempera underpainting. We can see a line of development in the use of direct oil painting from Titian to Rubens to Delacroix. The departure from reliance on an underpainting is very clear in Delacroix: with him, spontaneous execution asserts itself forcefully. His contemporary, Jean-Auguste-Dominique Ingres (1780–1867), painted directly but produced a surface in which brushstrokes are invisible, whereas Delacroix exploited the emotive possibilities of brushwork. His oil sketch for *The Lion Hunt* relies heavily on vigorous brushing

Jean-Auguste-Dominique Ingres. *Pauline
Eléanore de Galard de Brassac de Béarn,
Princesse de Broglie.* 1853. Oil on canvas,
47¾ × 35¾". The Metropolitan Museum of Art,
New York. Robert Lehman Collection, 1975

Ingres's technique: execution of the painting in
"one skin" and without underpainting or glazes.

gestures. The dynamism of the composition derives from an underlying
pattern of whirling forms which radiate from the center and rotate in a
counter-clockwise direction. But Delacroix is not content to rely on linear
dynamics: he supports the movement of the composition with brushwork that
has a life of its own.

In the *Lion Hunt* by Peter Paul Rubens (1577–1640) we see the technical
and thematic ancestor of the Delacroix oil sketch. Although Rubens employed
a preliminary underpainting, he relied on a direct type of overpainting executed very spontaneously. Today, we can see a similar approach in the
painting of Richard Lytle (born 1935). Clearly, direct painting technique has
an appeal—for the artist and the viewer—which ignores the passage of time.

*top:* Peter Paul Rubens. *Lion Hunt.* 1616–21.
Oil on canvas, 8'2" × 12'4". Alte Pinakothek,
Munich

*above:* Eugène Delacroix. Sketch for *The Lion
Hunt.* 1860–61. Private collection

*right:* Richard Lytle. *The Possessed.* 1959. Oil on
canvas, 8'2" × 6'7". Collection the artist

# BRUSHWORK AND EMOTION

The question arises: How does brushwork excite our emotions? Fundamentally, it is through empathy or visual imitation: we "act out" the artist's brushing behavior. Also, most of us have had experience with brushes—either in art classes or in performing personal and household tasks. So, it is easy to simulate inwardly the motions implied by the brushwork we see. This does not mean that we perform gymnastic maneuvers in front of a painting with an active surface. It does mean that brushmarks stimulate physiological reactions within the viewer, and these reactions generate feeling.

In direct technique a great many decisions are combined in the act of applying paint. The brushing gesture takes on crucial importance when color, value, shape, size, and texture are determined as the paint is laid on. Furthermore, the painter is usually trying for a spontaneous look even if he or she works slowly and deliberately. When the desired effect is not achieved immediately, the artist scrapes off the paint and tries again: oil paint is ideal for this sort of trial-and-error execution. But if the artist continues to paint over earlier efforts rather than scrape them off, the result is a rather tortured-looking paint surface. Direct technique, therefore, is not well suited to frequent "overpaints." The tones become muddy and the surface looks hesitant; clarity of color and crispness of brushwork are lost.

Because painting is in many respects a performing art, viewers are attracted by the evidence of paint mixing and brushwork. Here, Cézanne and Van Gogh are instructive performers to watch. Cézanne favors a steady buildup of planes, but his "touch," while careful, is rarely hesitant. He does not push paint around indecisively, and he seems to know the color and value of each stroke before he commits himself. Frequently, the canvas shows through, like the white paper in a watercolor painting. Consequently, Cézanne's surfaces have a freshness and sparkle that a more labored technique would destroy.

Van Gogh's *The Ravine* demonstrates the emotional power of another kind of brushstroke: he favors a pattern of short, curved, and angular thrusts. These thrusts set up staccato rhythms which reinforce the impact of the vibrating color. Thus paint application contributes to the gushing motion we "feel" in the water: blended colors and luminous glazes would surely ruin this effect. For a completely different approach to brushwork, we must go back to El Greco's *Agony in the Garden* (page 221). Here it is the *shaped areas of light* that generate a turbulent emotional effect. Using indirect painting technique, El Greco produced the agitated feeling that modern painters achieve through violent, impulsive brushwork.

If we trace the language of brushwork from its beginnings among the fifteenth-century Venetians to its full development in our own time, it seems to have paralleled the growth of individualism in society and of autonomy among artists. Direct technique played a major role because of its emphasis on the uniqueness of the painter's style; it appealed to artists who saw the expression of personality as their principal objective. Indirect technique suited more modest or secretive painters—artists who did not wish to display their "handwriting." These contrasting attitudes are visible today. The so-called hard-edge and geometric painters tend to employ a smooth, anonymous technique, relying on design and the optical effects of color to carry their message. But for "action" painters, the path of the artist's brush traveling across a canvas is often the work's principal theme.

Brushwork has become a declaration of the artist's personal freedom. For painters, what could be a more forceful assertion of individualism than the marks of the brush, left on the canvas exactly as they were applied, unretouched and undisguised? With their brushwork exposed, painters could tell all. In a post-Freudian era, artists declared that there was nothing to hide and nothing to cover up.

*opposite above left:* Frans Hals. Detail of *Governors of the Old Men's Almshouse, Haarlem.* 1664. Frans Hals Museum, Haarlem, The Netherlands

*opposite above right:* Paul Cézanne. *Houses in Provence.* c. 1880. Oil on canvas, 25⅝ × 32". National Gallery of Art, Washington, D.C. Collection Mr. and Mrs. Paul Mellon, 1973

*opposite below:* Vincent van Gogh. *The Ravine.* 1889. Oil on canvas, 23¾ × 36⅛". Courtesy, Museum of Fine Arts, Boston. Bequest of Keith McLeod

## DIRECT TECHNIQUE

The impression of swiftness and spontaneity calls for considerable assurance on the part of the artist—assurance based on solid knowledge, power of observation, and trust in the validity of one's sensations.

Leonardo da Vinci. Detail of *Portrait of a Musician*. 1490.
Biblioteca Ambrosiana, Milan

Michelangelo. Detail of *The Prophet Joel*. 1509. Ceiling of the
Sistine Chapel, The Vatican, Rome

## THE HUMAN IMAGE IN TRADITIONAL PAINTING

What generous expressions! How intelligent the eyes! The
noses and chins are constructed as nobly as Greek temples.
Even if they are idealized, such men *should* have existed.

Rembrandt van Rijn. Detail of *Head of Christ*. c. 1650.
The Metropolitan Museum of Art, New York. The Mr. and
Mrs. Isaac D. Fletcher Collection. Bequest of Isaac D.
Fletcher, 1917

For Rembrandt, the image of Jesus posed a special problem:
the Catholic Baroque tradition called for an idealized,
somewhat mannered personification, but Rembrandt's
painterly style and religious commitment had their roots in
Protestant realism. His solution: a Jewish model in whose
countenance we see a remarkably credible embodiment of
manliness and compassion.

El Greco. Detail of *Fray Felix Hortensio Paravicino*. c. 1605.
Museum of Fine Arts, Boston

Behind those penetrating eyes, which seem to take one's full
measure, the viewer senses the controlled intensity of a
totally dedicated man, a "true believer."

Peter Paul Rubens. Detail of *Self-Portrait*. 1638–40.
Kunsthistorisches Museum, Vienna

The self-assurance of an older man who has been very
successful. An intellectual as well as a highly physical
person, Rubens was never assailed by doubts about the
ultimate unity of spirit and flesh.

These are stubborn men. So were the artists who painted them—stubborn about telling the whole truth.

Albrecht Dürer. Detail of *The Painter's Father*. 1497.
The National Gallery, London

Jan van Eyck. Detail of *The Virgin and the Canon Van der Paele*.
1436. Groeningemuseum, Bruges

Jacques-Louis David. Detail of *Man with a Hat.*
After 1816. Royal Museum of Fine Arts, Antwerp

Even in the work of a classicist like David, the force
of a private personality asserts itself—especially in
this candid portrait. A new cult of individualism is
emerging in France—informal, studied, and
self-assured. The manner of aristocrats is now
enjoyed by a confident bourgeoisie.

Théodore Géricault. Detail of *The Homicidal
Maniac.* 1821–24. Musée des Beaux Arts, Ghent

Pursuing the varieties and extremes of
individualism, the Romantic painter examines one
of the most tragic forms of human suffering:
madness.

Diego Velázquez. Detail of *Pope Innocent X.* 1650.
Doria-Pamphili Gallery, Rome

A work of the seventeenth century, but thoroughly
modern in its approach to painting and personality.
Its optical realism anticipates Impressionism and
photography. The only barrier between the viewer
and a complete disclosure of Innocent's character is
the artist's aristocratic reserve.

Édouard Manet. Detail of *The Luncheon in the
Studio.* 1869. Neue Pinakothek, Munich

The self-assurance of this young man corresponds
to certain arrogant qualities in Manet's style: a
frontality based on exceedingly flat lighting, a
refusal to tamper with or idealize visual facts, a
determination to set the painterly act above
pictorial convention.

**Eugène Delacroix. Detail of *Portrait of Chopin*. 1838. The Louvre, Paris**

Here is an ideal combination: a Romantic composer portrayed by a Romantic painter. Delacroix realized that there could be a correspondence between feeling, form, and technique. We see more than the structure of Chopin's head; we see his turbulent inner life expressed through brushwork.

# THE HUMAN IMAGE
# IN MODERN PAINTING

From Cézanne to Picasso to Gris, we see the progressive analysis, breakup, and rearrangement of form. Cézanne tried to bypass subjective impressions by destroying objects and reconstructing them along rational, architectonic lines. Picasso went further by attempting to show the interpenetration of solids and voids. Even so, the human qualities of his subject show through. With Gris, we have a different objective: the creation of a geometry of form that could deal with anything—people, objects, places, or spaces. Cézanne would have approved.

Pablo Picasso. Detail of *Portrait of Ambroise Vollard*. 1909-10. Pushkin Museum, Moscow

Paul Cézanne. Detail of *Victor Chocquet Assis.* c. 1877.
Columbus Museum of Art, Ohio. Howald Fund Purchase

Juan Gris. Detail of *Portrait of Picasso.* 1912. The Art Institute
of Chicago

Georges Rouault. Detail of *The Tragedian*. 1910. Collection
Professor Hahnloser, Bern

Edvard Munch. Detail of *Puberty*. 1894. National
Gallery, Oslo

The common trait of Expressionist art is its capacity to make us spectators at the
moment when a person experiences a very personal dread. The soul, if not the
body, is invariably shown naked and shivering. We see more than a person's fear
or guilt or anxiety; we experience a feeling of awe when dreaded abstractions
become final meanings in personal existence.

Oskar Kokoschka. Detail of *Self-Portrait*. 1913. Collection, The Museum of Modern Art, New York. Purchase

Ivan Albright. Detail of *And God Created Man in His Own Image*. 1930–31. On permanent loan to The Art Institute of Chicago from the Collection of Ivan Albright

Henri Matisse. *Green Stripe (Madame Matisse)*. 1905.
Oil and tempera on canvas, 15⅞ × 12⅞". Royal Museum of
Fine Arts, Copenhagen. Rump Collection

Alexej von Jawlensky. *Self-Portrait*. 1912. Oil on cardboard,
20⅞ × 19¼". Collection Andreas Jawlensky, Locarno,
Switzerland

In a sense, Matisse, during his Fauvist period, was responsible for the development
of all these artists—even the Germans and the Slavs. While pursuing his serene
pictorial objectives through a system of arbitrary color, he opened up a new set of
emotional options for figural representation—options that were eagerly seized by
artists of restless disposition. Matisse was concerned with the human image only as
a motif in a grand scheme of light, movement, and pleasure, but these
Expressionists followed a different path—a path of agonizing self-examination and
private anguish.

Max Beckmann. Detail of *Self-Portrait in a Tuxedo*. 1927.
Busch-Reisinger Museum, Harvard University, Cambridge,
Massachusetts

Ludwig Kirchner. Detail of *Portrait of Gräf*. 1924.
Kunstmuseum der Stadt Düsseldorf

Karel Appel. Detail of *Crying Nude*. 1956. Collection Mr. and Mrs. Alan Fidler, Willowdale, Ontario

Antonio Saura. *Imaginary Portrait of Goya*. 1963. Oil on canvas, 93½ × 7⅜". Museum of Art, Carnegie Institute, Pittsburgh

Where the human image survives in painting, it is either mutilated or ridiculed. Appel and Saura convert Expressionist brushwork into a mode of abuse, trying to summon mythic power through wild painterly attacks on their subjects. Larry Rivers and Richard Hamilton are cooler: they play Pop-art games with drawn, painted, and pasted image fragments. But the game is violent; the human image is being mugged.

Larry Rivers. Detail of *Celebrating Shakespeare's 400th Birthday (Titus Andronicus)*. 1963. Collection Clarice Rivers, New York

Richard Hamilton. *Fashion-plate study (a) self-portrait*. 1969. Collage, enamel, and cosmetics on paper, 27⅝ × 19⅝". Collection Rita Donagh, London

# FROTTAGE, GRATTAGE, AND DECALCOMANIA

The spontaneous application of paint with loaded brush was one type of liberation from the traditional approach to painting. Artists exploited the fact that the marks of tools are expressive in themselves. Once this was discovered, it was a simple step to the realization that new tools produce new expressive possibilities. So artists began to devise exotic new techniques for manipulating paint; paint *itself* became the subject of their imagery. Among the most inventive was Max Ernst (1891–1976), a prolific creator of new technical procedures.

For most of his career Ernst was associated with the Dada and Surrealist movements; so, irrationality played a large role in his art. *Chance arrangement* was a principle of Dadaist composition, while fantasy and the combination of unrelated images guided Surrealism. Clearly, the movements were linked. Ernst's technical discoveries grew out of a search for imagery which could not be seriously calculated or known in advance. His was an art that originated in "accidents"—seemingly random interactions between paint and process. But while his process appears to be unplanned, Ernst worked hard to create the accidental situation.

*Frottage* is the best known of Ernst's techniques. Most of us know it as the popular art of rubbings: pencil or crayon rubbed over paper resting on a textured surface transfers a negative image of the texture underneath. Accordingly, archaeologists use frottage to make copies of stone or metal reliefs. For painters, the abstract patterns of wood grains, for example, can be transferred and worked up into recognizable images. Ernst used this method to convert nature's normal or accidental processes into artistic forms. For example, he used frottage in oil painting by placing a freshly painted canvas over a relief texture and then scraping away the paint. The unscraped paint left in the crevices of the canvas created a pattern corresponding to the textures underneath. This process did not involve rubbing, but it resulted in the transfer of a pattern by a frottage-like technique.

As with *decalcomania* (see below), the key to frottage is transfer—*informal printmaking*. Other informal printing processes involved dipping leaves, kitchen utensils, toy parts—anything that could be held in the hand—into wet paint; the object was employed like a hand stamp to transfer a pattern to canvas. Then the paintbrush was used to heighten or finish the forms suggested by the marks of real objects and surfaces.

*Grattage*, another Ernstian technique, is the grating or scratching of wet paint with a variety of tools: a comb, a fork, a razor, a needle, a piece of glass.

Max Ernst. *The Eye of Silence.* 1944. Oil on canvas, 42½ × 55½". Washington University Gallery of Art, St. Louis

The painter builds a surface through carving, scratching, and abrading; his picture is something "real" rather than a system of illusions.

Grattage exploits the plastic character of wet oil paint just as the paintbrush does. However, the brush is designed to smooth and blend paint—only secondarily to leave its mark. The tools of grattage treat paint as a kind of colored mud, or as a type of building material, like concrete. (Here it should be mentioned that Le Corbusier liked to "scratch" images into the poured-concrete surfaces of his buildings.) The conception of paint as a material that can be scratched, abraded, or otherwise tortured represents a departure from the idea of paint as a descriptive substance. In traditional painting, the pigment is not really there; it designates something else. With Ernst, paint becomes a kind of primal substance which miraculously "remembers" everything done to it.

In *decalcomania*, wet blobs of paint are squeezed between two canvas surfaces which are then separated. Variations in pressure force the paint into random patterns, forming rivulets and crevices which can be exploited for their formal and thematic suggestions: fantastic geological structures, landscapes of unknown planets, weird biological specimens, creepy projections of the fevered imagination. Still, it is the artist's ingenuity which is the creative instrument. In the end, decalcomania, frottage, and grattage are strategies for making the creative juices flow.

Another Ernstian technique, *éclaboussage*, is widely used today. It involves dropping paint or turpentine from a height to a prepared canvas. To drop the paint Ernst used a perforated tin can swung from a string suspended above the canvas. The paint splashes were then manipulated like the squeezed pigment in decalcomania. He also dropped turpentine on a freshly painted canvas in order to create splash patterns or to expose areas of bare canvas. The turpentine was blotted up, allowed to stand in a puddle, or allowed to run in random paths. From éclaboussage, or *dropping* paint, it was only a short step to *throwing* paint with a brush, or dripping it from a stick, à la Jackson Pollock.

For centuries the brush was an extension of the artist's hand, but when used to splash and spatter paint it became a different tool. One of the most bizarre methods of transferring paint was devised by Niki de Saint-Phalle (born 1930), who would fire a rifle at bags of paint suspended before a wall covered with relief sculptures. The firing of the gun and the explosion of the bag of paint created two dramatic events—the performance itself and its visual result on the wall relief. The theme of violence was captured in at least two dimensions: the gun shot became, so to speak, an act of execution, and the image became a collision report.

As the brush lost its central place in painting, and as pigment became a nonillusionistic substance, the tools and materials of image-making were

Photograph of Niki de Saint-Phalle about to paint with a rifle

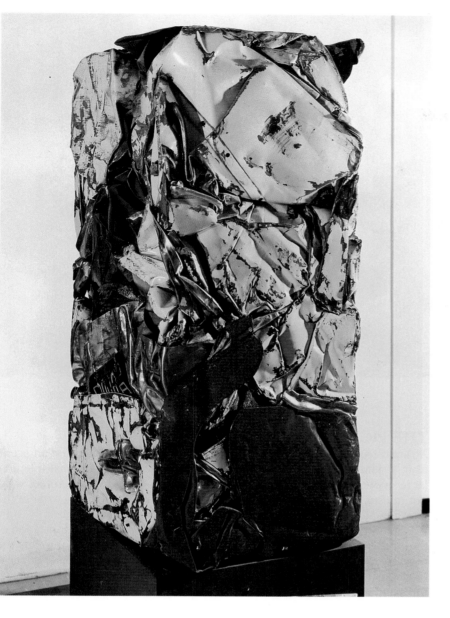

GOVERNED COMPRESSION

César. *The Yellow Buick*. 1961. Compressed automobile, 59½ × 30¾ × 24⅞". Collection, The Museum of Modern Art, New York. Gift of Mr. and Mrs. John Rewald

almost infinitely extended. For example, a bulldozer might be employed as an artistic tool, as in Robert Smithson's earthworks (see page 377). Or, images could be created with the powerful hydraulic press used to squeeze junked automobiles into compact cubes of anonymous metal. That is what César Baldaccini (born 1921) did, employing a method he called "governed compression." These dramatic gestures represented a shift of focus in visual art: from relatively small images and objects to large-scale technological effects. Increasingly, painters and sculptors wanted to be performers, or film directors, or civil engineers: they caused huge objects to be made and immense environments to be changed. But they didn't form objects and images with their hands; they used industrial technologies. Were they bored by brush, paint, and palette knife? Were they tired of drawing, mixing, and blending? Or were they trying to humanize the rifle and the hydraulic press?

The artist's desire to be a performer, an engineer, or a machine operator will be discussed below. Here we want to focus on the invention of new creative strategies. At first these strategies were tools for making art *objects*. But the next generation of artists was concerned with the strategy itself. The *process* of throwing, dripping, or exploding paint was considered aesthetically valuable apart from its results. In a subsequent section of this chapter, "Beyond Collage: Assemblage, Environments, Happenings," we shall analyze these developments in painting or drama or "performance art."

Willem de Kooning. *The Time of the Fire.*
1956. Oil and enamel on canvas, 59¼ × 79".
Collection Agnes Gund, New York

## THE PICTURE AND THE WALL

Abstract Expressionist, or "action painting," which dominated the art scene from 1946 until approximately 1960, reintroduced the huge canvas—pictures large enough for a Baroque palace. Dimensions of up to sixteen feet were not unusual. This immense new scale signaled a fundamental change in the way a picture was meant to operate in its setting and for its public.

Action painting depended for its effectiveness on the communication of the artist's brushing gestures—gestures accomplished mainly through the movements of the large muscle groups of the body. The dramatic effect is obvious in a work such as De Kooning's *The Time of the Fire.* To appreciate this painting, the viewer's reaction must be kinesthetic as well as optical. Its reproduction in a book, no matter how faithful, cannot stimulate the appropriate bodily responses: it lacks grand scale.

Large pictures were created in the past, but their size was based on the need to accommodate many figures (often lifesize or larger), plus buildings, interior details, and so on. Scale and format were keyed to the actual dimensions of real objects. However, with the growing importance of landscape painting and the mastery of atmospheric perspective, vast spaces could be portrayed on small canvases. Then, with Impressionist painting, the viewer's distance from the *picture surface* became crucial for understanding the work. At one distance, perception would be of color patches and fragments of form. At a greater distance, color areas and fragments came into *focus*, yielding an image that made sense as a whole, but not in its separate parts.

The vital—possibly accidental—discovery of the Impressionists was that unfocused color areas could sustain interest as images in themselves. Furthermore, the emotional potential of these color areas could be exploited if they were detached from objects and surfaces. This is exactly what we see in the combination of free color, active brushwork, and abstract design in a huge canvas-mural, *Water Lilies,* painted by Monet around 1920. The work is fourteen feet wide and is executed in broad, loosely brushed color areas. Because of its size we cannot see the entire canvas at once. Instead, we see a succession of fragments which are essentially abstract: areas of color take precedence over visual description; the big brushing gestures are as significant as the flowers and water they represent.

*opposite:* Claude Monet. *Water Lilies.* c. 1920.
Oil on canvas; triptych, each section 6'6" × 14'.
Collection, The Museum of Modern Art, New York. Mrs. Simon Guggenheim Fund

*above:* David Teniers. *The Picture Gallery of Archduke Leopold Wilhelm.* c. 1650. Oil on canvas, 41¾ × 50¾". The Prado, Madrid

The display of paintings in the seventeenth century emphasized their separate character: each picture represents a self-contained world independent of the architectural setting in which it was encountered.

*right:* Office of David Rockefeller, Chase Manhattan Bank, New York. 1961

Here the forms in the painting harmonize with the furniture and floor covering of the room. Painting and architecture are on speaking terms because they use the same abstract language: no figures, no illusions of deep space. Then why does the figurative sculpture from Asia look so right? Because it makes no illusionistic claims; because it occupies real space; because it functions as a real presence.

The enlarged scale of modern painting has had important implications. First, passages of color and texture are frequently larger than the viewer, making it difficult to maintain an attitude of detachment as we view them. Painted areas and shapes are not so much objects of perception as *part of our environment*: they surround the viewer. Certainly Mark Rothko has made skillful use of this effect. We are reminded of the difference between the television image and the motion-picture image. Empathy is easier with the large screen than with the home tube. Movies communicate emotion visually, whereas the television image feels more like an extension of radio: much of its information is carried through the spoken word. Thus, the small image employs a literary logic while the large image employs the logic of the body and the emotions.

A second implication of large-scale painting lies in the tendency of the picture to merge with the wall; it becomes part of a building's architecture. It ceases to be a view seen through a window, a device for *dissolving* the wall. Painting thus returns to its mosaic and stained-glass antecedents. This development began with the flattening of space by Cézanne and the Cubists, who realized that illusionistic effects violated the integrity of the wall. Today, the painted image *rests* on the wall surface; it doesn't claim to carve out deep space. Increasingly, therefore, modern painting and large-scale graphics function as architectural accents; many of our buildings would be uninteresting without them.

The return of painting to architecture is part of a drive to create environments. In this development, painters have been encouraged by modern architectural practice. Some architects design interior surfaces that function like paintings or sculptural reliefs. Buildings by Wright and Le Corbusier look very complete without pictures. Indeed, many painters feel that Wright's Guggenheim Museum dominates the pictures in it: the building's design satisfies most of our visual and plastic requirements and pictures become superfluous. Buildings by Mies van der Rohe, however, seem to need painting and sculpture.

In general, there is an abundance of anonymous space and plain wall surfaces in modern American building. Perhaps this creates a vacuum that painters instinctively want to fill. Besides, the large scale of modern painting has effectively removed it from the domestic dwelling; public buildings are its natural, perhaps its only, habitat. Increasingly, painting has become an art for the expansive walls of museums, the lobbies of public buildings, or the executive suites of banks.

Some small works are still created for private dwellings, but major works by "important" painters can rarely fit into the homes, even of the rich. Major

Selina Masombuka. Mural in living room of her house in Pieterskraal, South Africa. Courtesy of Margaret Courtney-Clarke

Painting returns to architecture. In Africa it never left. For traditional Ndebele women, wall painting was a ritual act that converted a room into an *ikumba*, a mother's personal space.

collectors have to design special facilities for their collections. Clearly, paintings have escaped the category of Victorian knickknacks: they are too large, too bright, and too disturbing to rest quietly against the wallpaper, sharing the soft light of a table lamp with family photographs, collections of china, and travel souvenirs. Painting has become an art of public statement and performance.

Today's large-scale paintings are created with the awareness that they are destined ultimately for public ownership and display. What will happen to small pictures, easel paintings? Will they be replaced by Happenings and Environments—visual extravaganzas that can fill virtually any available space? Or will they end up as handmade decorations—wall spots—for hotel rooms and doctors' offices? I think pictures regarded as ornaments, traded like furniture and other household items, will continue to be created. However, they will not occupy a position close to art's mainstream. Large or "important" paintings will be created for public places only. As for the small picture—the serious easel painting—it will be made for reproduction in print and electronic formats. But that will be the way millions of people encounter the world's best visual thinking.

## BEYOND COLLAGE: ASSEMBLAGE, ENVIRONMENTS, HAPPENINGS

In every generation, some painters feel their elders have carried the art as far as it can go, and that they must find radically new directions in materials, technique, and creative approach. One reason for their dissatisfaction is the attraction of the film—an understandable attraction since motion pictures are the most important extension of the art of image-making since the Stone Age. Spurred by the need to compete with powerful new media of communication, painters have tried to cross the lines separating their art from theater, cinema, sculpture, and architecture. Many have abandoned representation, creating works which are "real." They have fashioned works that spectators can enter physically, like actors in a play. Such innovations can be understood as an attempt by "old-fashioned" image makers to compete with materials and technologies that seem to threaten their existence.

*Assemblage* is an example. As the word implies, it is art created by putting things together—usually by combining them in new contexts. Because of

Romare Bearden. *The Prevalence of Ritual: Baptism.* 1964. Photomechanical reproductions, synthetic polymer, and pencil on cardboard, 9⅛ × 12". The Hirshhorn Museum and Sculpture Garden, Smithsonian Institution, Washington, D.C. Gift of Joseph H. Hirshhorn, 1966

The painter as collagist. Bearden used photographic fragments and assorted odds and ends, which he reorganized in a pictorial scheme that combines French Cubism with images drawn from African-American life. The combination makes sense visually and historically: Cubism had African roots.

their training, painters can think of trash and debris in terms of their line, shape, color, and textural qualities. Instead of imitating surface appearances with brush and paint, artists employ "real" materials in their work. This reduces the need for conventional skills in the *re*-presentation of reality. For many painters, then, traditional skills have grown less important as photographic, cinematic, and graphic reproduction techniques have advanced.

The technical foundation for *assemblage* was prepared by *collage*. These media are similar except that collage calls for *gluing* materials to a surface. Assemblage employs *any* method of joining things together, producing results that look much like sculpture. Many painters have practiced sculpture but as painters they usually approach three-dimensionality by manipulating textures and by creating illusions of depth. However, the differences between painting and sculpture began to break down under the assaults of Dada artists like Schwitters, Arp, Ernst, and Duchamp. As a result, today's painting studio looks very much like a sculpture studio.

Among modernist practitioners of collage and assemblage, Jean Dubuffet (1901–1985) can be compared to Max Ernst in imaginative and technical fertility. His mixtures of pigment, asphalt, cement, varnish, glue, sand, and so on convert the artist's canvas into a kind of *wall*. His "wall" becomes a new kind of fresco, this time inspired by *graffiti*, the markings

Jean Dubuffet. *My Cart, My Garden.* 1955. Oil on canvas, 35⅛ × 45¾". Collection, The Museum of Modern Art, New York. James Thrall Soby Bequest

found on sidewalks, fences, toilets, and subway cars. Like the Dadaists, Dubuffet has been powerfully attracted to the artistic possibilities of rubbish. His works have been made with driftwood, banana peels, butterfly wings, tobacco leaves, papier-mâché, metal foil, fruit rinds, coal clinkers, and dirt. Again, the downgrading of paint in favor of discarded and "worthless" materials.

An industrial civilization produces vast and varied kinds of debris—used up and rejected materials that possess a built-in visual history. For an artist like Dubuffet there is an obsessive delight in employing garbage of one sort or another *instead of* paint or in conjunction with it. He also borrows images from the art of the insane: they, too, are part of society's debris. In much of his work, Dubuffet seems to be saying that the most interesting things we produce—human, vegetable, or mineral—are the things we ignore or throw away.

Now that pigment is being displaced, industrial wastes, garbage, and earth itself—stones, gravel, minerals, and dirt—provide the materials of "painting." Inventing problems with materials becomes one of the burdens of our creative freedom: old technical constraints are gone. Also, there is no hierarchy of subject matter: one theme is as good as another. As for the public, its hostility toward the new has largely evaporated. Moving from a position of alienation, painters are often celebrated culture heroes—supported by foundations, employed as "stars" by universities, and encouraged to decorate the walls of important buildings. For some painters, the combination of social acceptance and technical freedom may seem unnatural. Artists have always thrived on resistance: the stubbornness of materials, the restrictions of traditional technique, the anger of the public. So, without this resistance, artists contrive to reintroduce it. Perhaps that explains their use of strange substances and outrageous subject matter: painters keep trying to shock the unshockable middle classes.

**Pop Art and Combine Paintings**    Almost everything in the built environment has been designed to inform, persuade, entertain, or sell. Especially to sell. In our culture an enormous amount of material is reproduced to carry out the functions of visual communication and display. Hamburgers and hot dogs, soft drinks and bathing suits, automobiles and stereo sets: their images greet us on television, jump out of road signs, crowd the pages of magazines, and fill the precious shelf space of drugstores and supermarkets. When we do not see this imagery, we hear it described in other media. To carry on our daily lives we have to *adjust* to a world saturated with images. So we become visually anesthetized, or we learn to see graphic images selectively. Pop artists chose this image-world as the source of *their* imagery; they were determined to make us see what our nervous systems had mercifully managed to suppress.

In the strategy of Pop, large scale was very important. Another major feature was repetition—mechanical repetition, as in *Twenty-five Colored Marilyns* by Andy Warhol (1928–1987). Radio and television commercials rely heavily on repetition—a device that eventually overcomes resistance. For that reason, perhaps, Warhol used visual repetition in his paintings, prints, and "sculptures"—reproductions of containers for soap, soup, breakfast foods, and so on. Obviously, he was not selling products; he was making a statement about a large part of our environment. Warhol truly understood publicity—perhaps even better than Dali.

Anonymity was another feature of Pop. Robert Indiana's (born 1928) paintings based on stenciled signs tell us little about the personality of the artist except his word choice, lettering skills, and determination to capture the viewer's attention. And Warhol's Campbell's Soup labels—hundreds of them—might have been painted by some other, equally neat, designer. Although signs of skill are visible, they do not seem to belong to any particular

Tom Wesselmann. *The Great American Nude,
#54.* 1964. Phone, radiator, table, chair, and
painting, 7' × 8'6½". Neue Gallery, Aachen,
Germany

Wesselmann's erotically displayed woman shows
that he can "do" a Matisse, a vulgar Matisse, if he
wants to. Beyond that, he throws a Pop-art
curve: the woman presented as another cheap
object in an environment of cheap objects.

Andy Warhol. *Twenty-five Colored Marilyns.*
1962. Acrylic on canvas, 89 × 57". Collection of
the Modern Art Museum of Fort Worth, Texas.
The Benjamin J. Tillar Memorial Trust, acquired
from the collection of Vernon Nikkel, Clovis,
New Mexico, 1983

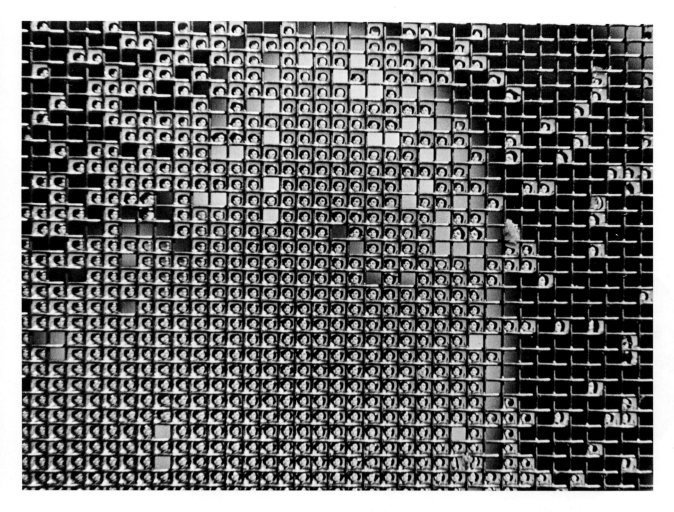

artist. Pop echoed the homogenized character of commercial graphics instead of the highly individualized creations of gallery artists.

Other Pop artists—Robert Rauschenberg, Wayne Thiebaud, and James Rosenquist—approached painting more personally, but they still exploited the stereotypes of popular culture for their imagery. Rauschenberg (born 1925) used this imagery very much like an Abstract Expressionist painter. However, he was more inclined to paste up or silk-screen a photograph than

**Charles McGowen. Photograph of raindrop reflections in a screen door. 1970**

We see a marvelous repetitive order in the chance interaction of natural and man-made structures. But nature is less resolute than man: given the slightest opportunity by the shape of the wire mesh, nature affords variety, or, at least, relief. Compare this photo with the Warhol.

**Audrey Flack. *Golden Girl*. 1979. Collection Mr. and Mrs. Walner, Illinois**

Flack uses an airbrush technique to produce a Photorealist world of female artifacts and movie-star symbols: lipsticks, makeup, a glossy black-and-white photo, a background of print, and rainbows of paint and light. Marilyn Monroe's tragic career is summed up in a pair of cupcakes with cherries on top, and, in the end, a burning candle.

301

Robert Indiana. *The Beware-Danger American Dream # 4*. 1963. Oil on canvas, 8'6" × 8'6". The Hirshhorn Museum and Sculpture Garden, Smithsonian Institution, Washington, D.C. The Joseph H. Hirshhorn Foundation, 1966

to paint an image. He used paint mainly to splash or spatter a composition made of reproductions. Thus paint became a kind of visual glue to connect, soil, or insult images manufactured by the world of commerce. Because his vision was essentially that of a collagist, the work of Rauschenberg seemed to declare the death of the "hand-painted" image.

In his "combine" paintings, Rauschenberg freely associated many of the technical and stylistic developments of twentieth-century art. In a work like *Canyon*, the principal ingredient is collage combined with attached objects— a stuffed eagle and a suspended pillow—plus brushed areas, paint drippings, and a stick nailed to the wooden picture support. The work is not easy to explain in terms of any single idea which the materials and their organization express. As in Dada, the prevailing theme is nonmeaning, the absurdity of art and everything else.

Choice of materials tells us a great deal about the world of Pop. It is a world of simultaneous fascination and disgust with the visual environment,

Robert Rauschenberg. *Canyon.* 1959. Combine on canvas, 81¾ × 70 × 24". Collection Mr. and Mrs. Sonnabend, Paris

particularly as manifested in packaging, labels, trademarks, and hard-sell advertising. The use of printed matter by early collagists like Picasso, Braque, and Gris was based on the color, texture, and real-life origin of these materials. Pop artists, however, paid more attention to the *meaning* of the printed words—words like Eat, Love, Pow, Wham, and Gosh. Also, as in action painting, paint smears and drippings were frequently used to simulate mud or other substances thrown at a wall. Splash and splatter became an important tool of painting. For artists like Sam Francis it was a decorative device, but it was also a highly expressive symbol of anger and defiance.

Generally, Pop artists seemed unable to decide what stance to take toward the advertising environment. For example, when viewing the work of Andy Warhol, it is difficult to tell whether he was repelled by our culture's commercialism or whether he wanted to merge with it. We look for signs of a point of view, but we receive only an exclamation point. As in Wow! Or Cool!

**Happenings** Architecture is the art of creating physical environments where people can live and work. In the past, painting and sculpture were *parts* of architecture—focal points in architectural space. Now painters also create environments—environments which change as they exist. Instead of being a statement *about* life, art becomes an activity which is part of life: it is lived as it is created. It is an art consisting of images made by ordinary spectators moving through a space organized by an artist. These transient images have been described by their inventor, Allan Kaprow, as "surrounding(s) to be entered into" or "Happenings" and "Environments." They look suspiciously like theater.

Happenings originated in collage and a type of environment created by the Dadaist Kurt Schwitters (1887–1948) in his famous Merzbau constructions. Built in Schwitters's home in Hanover, a Merzbau might be described as an architectural collage, a modulation of interior space using garbage and found objects as structural and decorative elements. Schwitters worked on one for several years, bringing it to completion in 1924 and giving it the title *Cathedral of Erotic Misery*. Another one, dated about 1933, was more architectonic, less reminiscent of collage techniques. Schwitters built little grottoes into his constructions, dedicated them to friends, and incorporated discarded clothing and other "nonart" items, much as Robert Rauschenberg has included old sheets and pillows in his "combine" paintings. Significantly, Schwitters was quoted as having said, "Anything the artist spits is art." Spit, splash, and splatter: these became the buzzwords of a new painterly aesthetic.

Schwitters wanted his constructions to synthesize the arts of architecture, painting, poetry, and drama. His was a revolutionary type of creativity that flourished in the generally disillusioned social environment of Central Europe after World War I—an environment that saw the rise of National Socialism (Nazism), Communism, and Fascism. Horribly depressed conditions combined to create a watershed in history for many artists and intellectuals who felt trapped by the war, oppressed by the economy, and betrayed by their civilization. The institutions, values, and forms that had existed up to and through the war were associated with disaster. Dadaism and its products have to be seen against this background of extreme demoralization.

Happenings and Environments in American art can be regarded as ritualized versions of the Dadaist antiart of the 1920s. Schwitters had made a plaster cast of a friend's discarded socks and put the casting into one of his Merzbau grottoes. That sounds familiar. Such gestures resemble our modern expressions of revolt: (1) used possessions and discarded materials are preferred to traditional art media; (2) "beauty," especially museum-type beauty, is avoided like the plague; (3) the process of creation is more important than its result; (4) wit and wisdom grow out of defiance of authority; (5) the gap between art and life is narrowed as much as possible; (6) caves and grottoes

Wayne Thiebaud. *Pie Counter.* 1963. Oil on canvas, 30 × 36". Collection of Whitney Museum of American Art, New York. Purchase, with funds from the Larry Aldrich Foundation Fund

*below:* Roy Lichtenstein. *Little Big Painting.* 1965. Oil and synthetic polymer paint on canvas, 68 × 80". Collection of Whitney Museum of American Art, New York. Purchase, with funds from the Friends of the Whitney Museum of American Art

The drips, dribbles, and broad brushing gestures of the Abstract Expressionist style are meticulously "reproduced" on Lichtenstein's canvas. What we have is a hilarious burlesque—the inspired smears of action painting reduced to commercial art.

*above:* Edward Kienholz. *The Beanery.* 1965. Mixed media, 7 × 72 × 22'. Stedelijk Museum, Amsterdam

This Environment is the replica of a real place—a bar in West Hollywood. Kienholz has carefully reproduced its cozy squalor to make a statement about the mixed assortment of people gathered there—"clock-heads" wasting their "time" and wasting each other.

*right:* Kurt Schwitters. *Merzbau,* Hanover. 1924–37. (Destroyed)

proliferate. Notice, too, that Merzbau constructions *and* Happenings favor cavernous, womblike spaces.

Even "primitives" were affected. In the 1950s, a little-known American, Clarence Schmidt, created a series of grottoes within his winding, cavelike house on a hill in Woodstock, New York. Schmidt had general carpentry and building skills, but he had no formal artistic training and was almost certainly unaware of Kurt Schwitters. Yet his fantastic house can be compared in important respects with a Merzbau construction. Like Schwitters, Schmidt recited poems of his own composition; he seemed to think of himself as a reincarnation of Walt Whitman. Schwitters's Merzbau began in the basement of his house, and it grew until an attic tenant had to be evicted. Schmidt also lived in his "house" and kept adding to it; eventually it resembled a "many chambered nautilus," with new rooms and grottoes appearing as the construction ran down the hill and burrowed into the earth.

The Happenings of Allan Kaprow were more formally organized: there was a script or scenario to control the spectators who moved through the gallery space where the first events were "staged." Kaprow says these events grew out of his work in collage and assemblage, and he lists the typical materials used: "painted paper, cloth and photos, as well as mirrors, electric lights, plastic film, aluminum foil, ropes, straw; objects that could be attached to, or hung in front of, the canvas along with various sounds and odors. These materials multiplied in number and density, extending away from the flat canvas surface, until that pictorial point of departure was eliminated entirely." As the two-dimensional canvas was left behind, real environments were simulated: "a subway station, penny-arcade, forest, kitchen, etc." Then the gallery gave way as a place for staging Happenings to "a craggy canyon, an old abandoned factory, a railroad yard, or the oceanside."

Unlike conventional theater, Happenings had no developed dramatic structure—that is, a beginning, a middle, and an end; plot and character development; conflict, climax, and resolution. The connection to assemblage was retained, plus elements of other art forms—dance, music, and poetry. As for Environments, Kaprow defined them as "slowed-down, quieter, happening(s)"—large-scale dioramas that could last for several weeks; the Happenings compressed time and lasted only a few hours. Of course, motion pictures are better at compressing or expanding time. And they have the advantage of being reproducible, whereas a Happening is so spontaneous that it is confined to a single enactment and viewing.

What is the meaning of the Happening for painting? We have mentioned its resemblance to theater and film, although it has less dramatic structure than theater and less pictorial control than film. As painting, the Happening surrenders fixity and permanence: it cannot linger before our vision. However, the collage origins of Happenings and Environments suggest different objectives. Happenings by Kaprow and Environments-plus-Sculpture, like those of George Segal, appear to be efforts to discover a hidden order beneath the surfaces of ordinary things and events. Like Schwitters and Dubuffet, these artists wanted to find meaning in what is apparently chaotic and worthless.

Still, the Happening was unable to become a vehicle of durable aesthetic value. It worked better as a creative exercise for the artist, as a means of discovering fresh sources of imagery. The painter's imagination is often stimulated by literature, music, dance, and film; thus Happenings, like collage, represented a way of generating awareness of new forms and sensations. In addition, it satisfied the artist's desire to *interfere with* reality; Happenings could dissect events and reveal their unsuspected meanings. In retrospect, it was significant mainly as a creative strategy—a strategy foreshadowed in techniques like Merzbau constructions, Surrealist automatic writing, and the nihilistic stunts of the troubled generation that lived between the two world wars.

**Op Art**   Op, or optical, art, followed the premature decline of Pop art in 1964. Painters now attempted to construct artworks that would rely solely on the physiology of vision. In a sense, Impressionist color divisionism (which depended on afterimages to create sensations of colors that were not there) paved the way for the new style. Op painters employed artificial light filtered through prisms, mechanical motion, and images that shift according to the viewer's angle of vision. Op brought the science of optics into aesthetics; the sociological comments of Pop yielded to a type of art that bypassed the viewer's mind and imagination. And in its own terms, the effectiveness of Op was undeniable: it produced feelings of excitement or physical disorientation by visual means alone.

Op had physiological effects similar to those created by modern biochemistry, but perhaps that is only coincidental. In any case, Op vividly demonstrated startling new powers in painting. And painting, as a result, found a new claim on human attention: art could compete with tranquilizers

*right:* Photograph of Clarence Schmidt in residence, 1964

*below:* Allan Kaprow. From *Orange.* Happening. 1964

A form of expression that wants to escape framing, geometric positioning, specific location in time or space. Art without limits cannot be exclusive; everyone gets into the act.

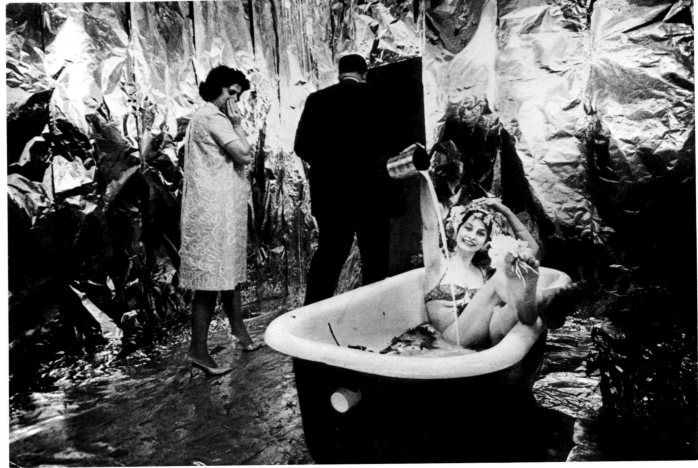

and mood-altering drugs as a stimulant or a depressant. Much earlier, Matisse had said he dreamed of an art "which might be for every mental worker . . . like an appeasing influence, like a mental soother, something like a good armchair in which to rest from physical fatigue." Op, of course, was not especially effective as a pacifier or soporific: one psychoanalyst compared it to a plunge into a cold shower. But if images could shock the nervous system, perhaps they could also induce the soothing feelings Matisse longed for.

As objects of aesthetic value, Op works are not easy to judge. They create a difficulty which the psychologist Theodor Lipps (see page 255) saw as an obstacle to aesthetic response: awareness of one's bodily sensations instead of ideas and feelings. Also, a purely optical response can be disappointing to those who expect emotional, intellectual, or formal nourishment from art. According to a West Coast painter, Jesse Reichek: "The question seems to be whether optical tricks that massage the eyeball, and result, in some cases, in physiological effects, provide a sufficient task for painting. I don't believe such tricks are sufficient."

Perhaps the desire to transform the physical basis of consciousness has always been latent in painting. We have seen it in Mark Rothko's work; in Op art we witness a systematic attempt to seize the human organism and change its psychic condition. But the movement failed to develop a rationale that would guide its further evolution. Its main influence was on psychedelic poster art. In the end, Op was arrested at a stage more related to physics than aesthetics—a stage where it was unable to join the humanistic mainstream.

**Bridget Riley. *Blaze I.* 1962.
Collection Louise Riley, London**

Kurt Schwitters. *Cherry Picture.* 1921. Collage of colored papers, fabrics, printed labels and pictures, pieces of wood, etc., and gouache on cardboard background, 36⅛ × 27¾". Collection, The Museum of Modern Art, New York. Mr. and Mrs. A. Atwater Kent, Jr., Fund

Collage and assemblage might be regarded as an unconscious return to tribal modes of artistry, particularly in their emphasis on textures. But instead of using seeds, shells, and fibers, the modern artist employs commercial garbage—the abundant rubbish of our textile, print, and home-furnishing industries.

far left: Robert Rauschenberg. *Odalisk.* 1955–58. Construction, 6'9" × 2'1" × 2'1". Museum Ludwig, Cologne

From a certain standpoint, both works can be seen as elaborate displays of the taxidermist's art: stuffed pedestals for stuffed birds. However, the purposes they serve are internal to art: to get away from calculation, deliberate design, and cerebral form—to reestablish the status of things as things.

left: Joan Miró. *Object.* 1936. Assemblage: stuffed parrot on wood perch, stuffed silk stocking with velvet garter and doll's paper shoe suspended in a hollow wood frame, derby hat, hanging cork ball, celluloid fish, and engraved map, 31⅞ × 11⅞ × 10¼". Collection, The Museum of Modern Art, New York. Gift of Mr. and Mrs. Pierre Matisse

Edward Kienholz. *The State Hospital.* 1964–66. Mixed media, 8 × 12 × 10'. Moderna Museet, Stockholm

As an impresario of mixed media, Kienholz bears a curious resemblance to the Baroque sculptor Bernini: the theatrical requirements of the spectacle take precedence over rules about the separation of painting, sculpture, and architecture. But this spectacle celebrates misery, not mystical transcendence.

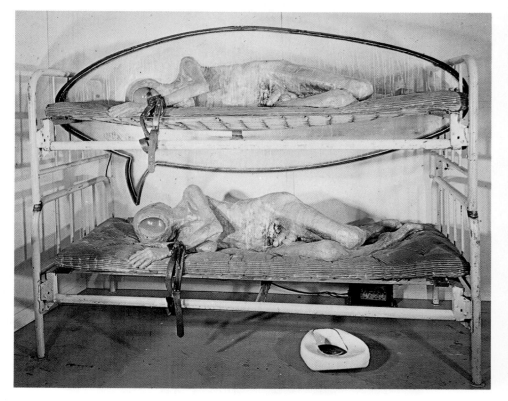

*left:* Mirror fetish, from the Lower Congo. c. late 19th–early 20th century. Wood, resin, animal teeth, bone, mirror, and other media, 18⅞" high. Ethnographical Museum, Antwerp

The fetish figure has to be a "mixed-media" construction since it functions as a container for magical substances in its abdominal cavity. In the Congolese fetish, a mirror serves to frighten off demons. In the contemporary "fetish" by Arman, tubes of paint embedded in a female torso pour ribbons of color into her polyester belly and womb.

*right:* Arman. *La Couleur de mon amour.* 1966. Polyester, 32¼" high. Collection Mr. and Mrs. Philippe Durand-Ruel, Buzenvale, France

*left:* Antoni Gaudí. Detail of spire, Church of the Sagrada Familia, Barcelona. 1883–1926

Gaudí and Rodia conceived of architecture as the creation of expressive forms that appear to have grown by natural accretion. This view demanded labyrinthine passages, surfaces like tribal sculptures, and brilliant coloristic effects. A mixed-media approach is almost inevitable when the designer feels that every part of a structure is magically alive.

*opposite:* Simon Rodia. Detail of Watts Towers, Los Angeles. 1921–54

## MINIMAL AND COLOR FIELD PAINTING

Reductionism is a persistent tendency in recent art: painting keeps trying to cast off its inherited baggage in hopes of truly being itself. Of course, artists disagree about what is essential and what is expendable. Nevertheless, they feel the need to redefine their art periodically, to breathe in an aesthetic environment unconstrained by the aims of their predecessors. For Minimal and Color Field painters, these inherited aims are storytelling, symbol making, social commentary, and artistic autobiography. Minimalists tend to react against styles that connect art to history, literature, politics, psychology, or

**Josef Albers.** *Homage to the Square: Red Series—Untitled III.* 1968. Oil on board, 32 × 32". Norton Simon Museum of Art, Pasadena, California

Albers established an important precedent for Minimalist painters by showing that pictorial values can be generated almost solely through the color interactions of simple geometric forms.

religion. What is left? Pure mathematics. Or the ineffable—imagery so pure it can only be seen, not talked about.

The seeds of this art were sown by Malevich, Kandinsky, Mondrian, and more recently, Josef Albers (1888–1976). It was called "art as art" by the painter Ad Reinhardt (1913–1967), who said: "Art-as-art is a concentration on Art's essential nature. The nature of art has not to do with the nature of perception or with the nature of light or with the nature of space or with the nature of time or with the nature of mankind or with the nature of society." Minimalists satisfy those specifications; they want to create forms that are

Ad Reinhardt. *Abstract Painting.* 1960-61. Oil on canvas, 60 × 60". Collection, The Museum of Modern Art, New York. Purchase (by exchange)

Reinhardt forces the viewer to look long and hard, to search, and, perhaps, to meditate. Sometimes, a cruciform image seems to emerge, but its meaning is unclear. All we know is that our eyes desperately search for form in the blue-blackness.

purely visual, complete in themselves, and unsoiled by contact with the world. This is to say that Minimal art aspires to the status of *ultimate* form, behind which there is nothing more, less, better, worse, or the same as.

In appearance, Minimalist canvases are large, abstract, bright, frequently hard-edged, and highly simplified in color. Figure-ground relationships created through overlapping, color-value differentials, and perspective devices are usually suppressed. Especially avoided is the painter's "handwriting," as in Abstract Expressionism. So there is a certain impersonality about Minimalist forms and painted surfaces which leads viewers to feel they are in the presence of machine-made objects. Similar results are visible in minimal sculpture, which can be manufactured industrially according to the sculptor's specifications through written or spoken instructions.

Color Field painting is more flexible; it permits considerable formal variation—from floating mists to hard-edge geometry. Its techniques are varied and ingenious: staining unprimed canvas; applying pigment with a squeegee, paint roller, or airbrush; pouring diluted paint onto a canvas, which is then turned and tipped to create shapes with controlled puddles and spills. (We are reminded of Max Ernst, but here the color is brighter and wetter.) These techniques afford great variety of edge and a wide range of depth, transparency, melting, and interpenetrating illusions. At the same time, they avoid the brushed look, the drawn line, and the painterly marks of wrist, fingers, and thumb. We have the impression that the medium itself does the job. A human being *initiates* the process, which then seems to operate according to its own laws or "intelligence." Unwittingly, perhaps, the Minimalists and Color Field painters were preparing us for computer art.

**Charles Hinman. *Red/Black.* 1964. Acrylic emulsion on canvas, 67 × 60 × 9". Krannert Art Museum, University of Illinois, Champaign**

New visual problems are created for the artist who paints on a surface of curved and bent planes. The irregular contours of the canvas no longer "frame" the image; they are part of it. As for color, it sets up a conflict between real and illusionistic space. The painter has to reconcile a variety of optical and perceptual claims.

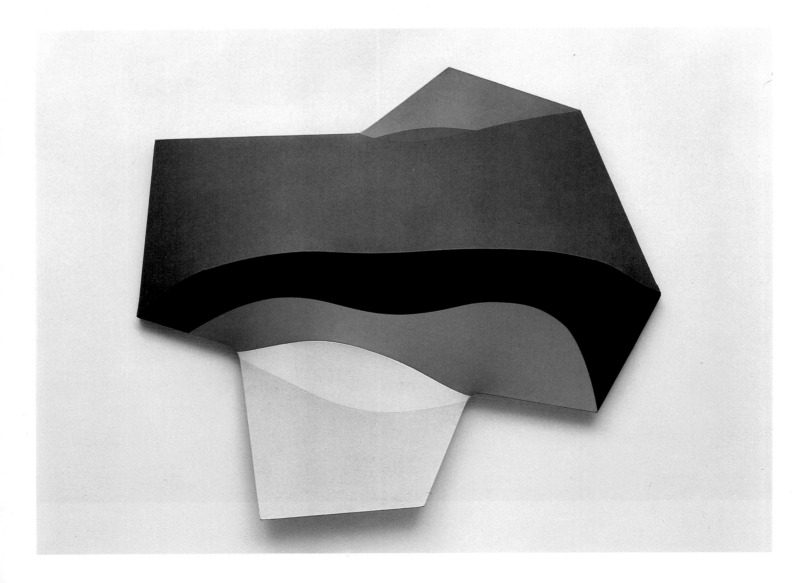

# THE SHAPED CANVAS

Theoretically, the rectangular canvas is one of many possible shapes. It dominates the other shapes mainly because of the Renaissance idea of a picture as a window opened on the world. This tradition is so strong that we are hardly aware of it; it even crops up in domestic architecture as the "picture window." In a sense, pictures have always been "windows"—images shaped by architectural design. Certainly architecture shaped mosaics, stained glass, frescoes, and mural paintings. Even cave paintings followed the shape of the rock wall. Historically, painting has obeyed externally determined formats.

But modern pictures circulate: they are not meant to hang on any particular wall. In other words, paintings are autonomous images. With the growth of abstraction the painted image ceased to symbolize something else; the shape of its frame could be determined by internal, that is, design requirements. In effect, the real locus of the image shifted from the wall to the viewer's eye. The shaped canvas became a device for organizing the forces inside the viewer's head.

It would be a mistake, however, to think of the shaped canvas as a type of painted sculpture. The strategy and tactics of this sort of painting are pictorial without being illusionistic. We cannot, as with sculpture, walk around a shaped canvas. So the painting has been liberated from architecture, yet it falls short of free-standing sculpture. The only space it can effectively occupy is within the eye—retinal space; that is where this new kind of pictorial experience is designed to begin and end.

The older painting traditions endeavored to enlist the total apparatus of vision—eye, brain, and mind. Plus the heart, liver, and spleen, if possible—not the optical organ alone. Patrons of painting—kings, princes, and popes—were concerned about the career of the image *after* it passed beyond the retina: How would it affect the viewer's thought and behavior? Today, the

Frank Stella. *Pergusa.* 1981. Mixed media on etched magnesium, 8'2" × 10'5" × 2'4". Collection Holly Hunt Thackberry, Winnetka, Illinois. Courtesy of M. Knoedler & Co., Inc., New York

Now the shaped canvas has moved into the gray area between pictorial art and sculptural relief. However, Stella's inspiration comes mainly from Abstract Expressionist painting. His old-time geometry and flatness (see page 159) have been replaced by wormy curves and fishlike squiggles. The snaky shape at bottom casts two shadows: one is real and one is painted. We get a rollicking sense of fun and media play—from painting and sculpture to architecture, mosaics, and fabric design.

image is increasingly controlled by artists themselves, and their expertise lies in the optical arena—a place where complex visual forces interact. Thus many painters want to create an art which is exclusively retinal—an art that defies interpretation along symbolic or intellectual lines. Frank Stella (born 1936) put their case well in commenting on his shaped canvases: "I always get into arguments with people who want to retain the old values in painting, the humanistic values that they always find on the canvas. My painting is based on the fact that only what can be seen there is there. It really is an object."

## EROTIC ART

One of the earliest functions of visual art was the stimulation of sexual feeling, if only to encourage human reproduction. Yet today, when human over-population is an urgent concern, we continue to witness the creation of artworks devoted to erotic themes. Some of us react with a sense of being liberated from what seems to be the repression of healthy sexual feeling. Others are offended: they see erotic art as obscene or pornographic and leading to the breakdown of civilized restraints on the expression of our sexuality.

The public celebration of the human body, especially the female nude, is a well-established tradition in Western art. This public art has usually been accompanied by a more or less underground art in which human figures are shown engaging in explicit sexual practices. But in today's permissive climate, that underground art is openly exhibited. The change is not so much in the fact that erotic art exists but that it is abundantly visible.

Much erotic art is created as a mode of protest. Perhaps that is due to the intergenerational conflicts and class antagonisms that have grown so intense in the industrial nations of the world. Thus the unlovely or obscene content

Joan Miró. *Persons Haunted by a Bird*. 1938. Black chalk, touch of brown chalk, and watercolor, 16⅛ × 13". The Art Institute of Chicago. Gift of Peter B. Bensinger Charitable Trust

In 1938, Miró's phallic fantasies could be assimilated by the Surrealist format of dream symbolism and sexual horseplay. But before he was a Surrealist, Miró was a humorist.

Jean-Léon Gérôme. *Roman Slave Market.*
c. 1884. Oil on canvas, 25¼ × 22½".
The Walters Art Gallery, Baltimore

The official art of the nineteenth century was often an exercise in disguised voyeurism. Under the pretext of teaching history, some painters catered to the prurient interest of the public.

*below:* Balthus. *The Golden Days (Les Beaux Jours).* 1944–45. Oil on canvas, 58¼ × 78⅜".
The Hirshhorn Museum and Sculpture Garden, Smithsonian Institution, Washington, D.C.
Gift of Joseph H. Hirshhorn Foundation, 1966

The awakening sexuality of the girl adolescent has absorbed much of the career of Balthus. His art thrives on the conflict between bourgeois respectability, as represented by comfortable, well-appointed interiors, and the less-than-innocent reveries of "good" little girls.

*above:* Jean-Auguste-Dominique Ingres. *Odalisque with a Slave.* 1840. Oil on canvas mounted on panel, 29⅜ × 39⅜". Fogg Art Museum, Harvard University, Cambridge, Massachusetts. Bequest of Grenville L. Winthrop

The reclining nude has a venerable tradition in Western painting. By the nineteenth century, however, that tradition had been carried to an incredible stage of too-muchness. Still, Ingres was serious about his erotic objectives; Wesselmann satirizes that eroticism, as well as our own commercialization of female bodies.

*right:* Tom Wesselmann. *Great American Nude No. 51.* 1963. Oil and collage on canvas, 10 × 12'. Courtesy Sidney Janis Gallery, New York

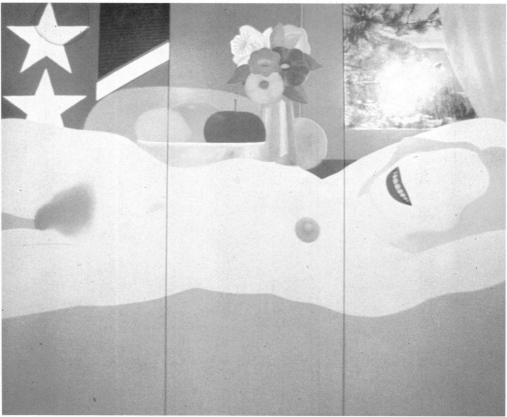

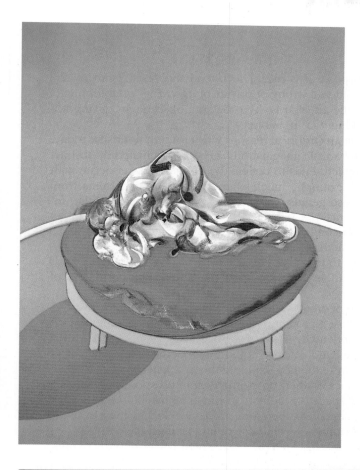

Francis Bacon. *Triptych—Studies from the Human Body.* 1970. Oil on canvas, each panel 78 × 58". Private collection

Today, artists feel free to deal with the theme of homosexuality. In Bacon's work, this motif is overshadowed by a consistently animalistic view of man—even in his efforts at love—which resemble the copulation of beasts.

*below:* Larry Rivers. *Celebrating Shakespeare's 400th Birthday (Titus Andronicus).* 1963. Oil on canvas, 58 × 77¾". Collection Clarice Rivers, New York

A mutilated female nude, symbol of Venus and maternity; a "cool" diagram of dismembered human parts; the portrait of a solemn black man; and a reference to one of Shakespeare's plays. Here we see the main areas of contemporary social concern: art, race, sex, and violence.

of erotic art has a purpose: it is meant to offend the "establishment" by celebrating what is considered wrong or private or ugly. The "establishment" reacts by co-opting erotic art, that is, by collecting obscene art, giving it a stylistic name, and making it fashionable.

There are important art-historical reasons why erotic art flourishes today. For almost a century the artistic imagination has been dominated by abstract and nonobjective art which tends to deflect the impulses we associate with sexual expression. For example, much of modernist painting stems from Cézanne, a painter whose genius was inhibited in the presence of the unclothed human figure—male or female. An erotic vision of man or woman appears to have been uncongenial to his tastes as a painter. What he left us was a structural or geometric legacy; understandably, Cézanne's artistic descendants built on the foundation he established. Thus his work stands in relation to modern art as the Epistles of Paul to the development of Christianity.

So the prominence of erotic art today may be due to the difficulty artists have experienced for close to a century in perceiving the human figure with affection. Painters shied away from the voyeurism of a Gérôme or a Bouguereau, on the one hand, and the hothouse eroticism of a Modigliani or a Pascin, on the other. Instead, they explored the problems of space organization and color dynamics opened up by the Post-Impressionists in the late nineteenth century. But space is a medium in which human beings move and encounter *each other*. Ultimately, therefore, artists decide they must examine all forms of human encounter—even those of utmost intimacy.

Perhaps, too, we are faced with an exaggerated reaction to the expression of anonymity on a large scale—as in Minimal and serial art, not to mention much of our public architecture. Thus gallery art and our popular culture exhibit a great deal of brutal imagery substituting for genuine erotic feeling. Often, this art associates sexuality with pathological behavior, as in Larry Rivers' *Titus Andronicus*. But these are the excesses that accompany the easing of a long repression; sooner or later it will play itself out.

## CONCLUSION

Schwitters's use of trash-can contents in collage; Dubuffet's use of dead leaves, flower petals, fruit rinds, and butterfly wings; the Cubist and Dadaist incorporation of "real" objects in pictures; the Pop use of package labels and advertising slogans; Happenings that look suspiciously like theater improvisations: these and other developments suggest new connections between painting and gardening, spectator sports, psychodrama, refuse collection, and media hype. Everything is fair game. Some artworks echo the processes of food preparation, eating, and collecting leftovers. Others echo the processes of emptying the garbage, recycling the garbage, and making something new and necessary.

Years ago, Jimmy Durante had a nightclub act in which he tore a piano apart in a kind of comic tantrum. The public loved it. Clearly, the processes of disintegration have their own aesthetic fascination, as can be confirmed by watching the demolition of an old building, a staged auto crash, or a child knocking down a house of blocks. In César's "controlled-compression" sculpture, the crushing of an automobile is converted into an artistic act (see page 293). These activities might be regarded as efforts to find an affirmative meaning in all the acts of needless destruction and senseless consumption that mark our culture.

Artists are not always aware of the ultimate meanings of their work, but civilization operates through them nevertheless. Hopefully, their experimentation with new materials, processes, and themes will turn out to have humanizing results. One thing is certain: history will look back and make a surer judgment than we can. In the meantime, we can watch what's Happening with fascination.

# CHAPTER TWELVE

# SCULPTURE

Like painting, sculpture began with the making of figures for primitive sorcery and, later, for religious ritual. For that reason, it has always seemed to have a magical quality. The Greek myth of Pygmalion and Galatea gives us an idea of the almost supernatural power ancient peoples attributed to this art. Pygmalion, a sculptor, falls in love with Aphrodite and, because she will not have him, he makes an ivory figure of the goddess and prays to her. Eventually she takes pity on him and enters into his carving, making it live as a real woman, Galatea. Galatea then marries Pygmalion and bears him two sons.

The myth expresses the essential ingredients of sculptural creation. The artist's motive arises from an emotional crisis—personal distress caused by yearning for the impossible. He tries to control reality by fashioning an object that portrays what he wants. The goddess cannot withhold her pity, so she gives life to the artist's image. Then he falls in love with that image—an image *he* has created. Art thus acquires a life of its own, and the union of creature and creator results in a continuation of life. A man's longing for love is converted into living reality by the artist's anguish and compelling skill.

Painting has magical associations, too, but its reality is largely illusionistic, whereas sculpture gives real substance to the artist's hopes and fantasies. For that reason, sculptures were more commonly employed to represent the gods, to serve as vessels for the souls of the departed, or to function as totems and idols for primitive peoples.

Regardless of material, the capacity of sculpture to occupy real space and to compel belief distinguishes it from painting and graphic art. Throughout its history of changing form, sculpture has remained the same art that Pygmalion practiced—the art of making three-dimensional materials come alive. It makes fantasies real, it remembers the dead, and it satisfies human longings for perfection.

## MODELING, CARVING, CASTING, AND CONSTRUCTING

The sculptural processes are simply the most effective ways of working available materials. Stone can be chipped, scraped, carved, drilled, and polished, so it appeals to artists who are comfortable with highly resistant

Tlingit Indian shaman's mask in the form of a
bear, from Alaska. c. 1840–60. Wood, opercula,
rawhide, and pigment, 10⅝ × 7⅞ × 2¾".
Peabody Museum, Harvard University,
Cambridge, Massachusetts

Sculpture has roots in masks like this one, which
enabled a tribal shaman to transform himself
psychologically into a bear. The spirit of the bear
enters the body of the shaman and makes him
potent as a healer. What we regard as art—the
superbly carved and painted sculpture—is really
magic, the enhancement of the shaman's
therapeutic powers. The marvelously active
baby otters are his spirit helpers.

materials. Wood can be worked by the same processes, but modern technology permits it to be permanently bent and molded, as in Thonet and Eames chairs (see page 114). Metals can be cast, cut, drilled, bent, filed, forged, stamped, and extruded. Today, *powdered* metals combined with plastic binders can be modeled almost like clay. Metals can also be *assembled* by welding, soldering, and riveting; and they can be joined together with adhesives. As for plastics, we are beginning to overcome their associations with cheap imitations of costly materials. Now with our new plastics, metal alloys, and high-fired ceramics, there is no telling what sculpture will become.

In traditional sculpture, mastery of the basic processes—modeling, carving, and casting—constituted the principal artistic challenges. These processes are still important but not indispensable because, as in painting, technology permits materials to be formed and assembled by other means. However, modern sculptors confront new problems of aesthetic choice due to the variety of materials and processes available to them.

Monumental statuary is an example: in the past it was cast in bronze or carved in marble. Today, welded and riveted metal is more common, espe-

Henry Moore. *Two Forms.* 1934. Pynkado wood, 11 × 17¾" on irregular oak base, 21 × 12½". Collection, The Museum of Modern Art, New York. Sir Michael Sadler Fund

Only eleven inches high, this sculpture has the monumental force of a much larger work. Why? Because Moore knows how to establish a real dialogue between abstract forms: they speak about relationships that matter—between mother and child, between lover and beloved.

cially as figurative art declines and sculptures virtually become environments. Naturalistic statuary, of course, has to be modeled and then cast in bronze; or it is carved in stone or marble. It can still be seen in public buildings and parks, and it continues to be commissioned by conservative groups. But sculptors who can create such works are a diminishing minority. Contemporary buildings seem to be more friendly to sculpture which is, in general, more geometric, more open, less monolithic in form.

Consider Rodin's *Burghers of Calais.* It would be difficult to conceive of such a group being created through any process other than bronze casting. The naturalistic treatment of bone and flesh; the psychological characterization of the figures; the sensitive control of light; the subtle manipulation of

Auguste Rodin. *Burghers of Calais.* 1886. Bronze, 82½ × 95 × 78". Rodin Museum, Paris

surfaces: these could not be achieved by welding or assemblage. Yet contemporary sculptors carry out monumental commissions. The nuances of modeling with clay or marble may be sacrificed, but grand scale and a marvelous freedom of extension into space have been gained. In addition, modern sculptors can employ the techniques of industrial production and fabrication. Thus the mallet and chisel have been joined by the acetylene torch, the electronic welder, and the hydraulic press.

The Greeks knew the art of bronze casting, and they also had an abundance of good white marble. But they must have prized marble for its durability more than its look, since their statuary was usually painted. It was not the stone's whiteness or texture they admired so much as its capacity to reveal form with exceptional clarity. Their purpose was to capture the body in action or repose and to preserve their notion of perfect human proportions. Through marble and bronze they expressed a typically Greek ideal—the merger of reality and mathematical perfection in the human body.

For Michelangelo, sculpture was the art of releasing the forms hidden, or imprisoned, in marble. This, too, is a classical Greek idea; it typifies the attitude of the carver—one who begins with the wood log or stone block and cuts away until the form in his mind's eye is revealed. Carving is a *subtractive* process, and it has always been considered the most difficult of sculptural processes because it requires a conception of the result before the work begins. The carver subtracts nonessential material to liberate an image which "already exists." However, the grain of wood or stone significantly influences the forms that emerge. For example, diorite and basalt—the hard granitic stones used in ancient Egypt—resist detailed carving. Consequently, Egyptian

*below:* Michelangelo. *Crepuscolo (Evening)* (detail from the Tomb of Lorenzo de' Medici, Florence). 1520–34

Stone carving: the forms seem to emerge from the marble. But notice that Michelangelo employed an almost Cubist technique to find out where they were.

*right:* Luca della Robbia. Detail of *Madonna and Angels.* c. 1460. National Museum, Florence

Polychromed terra-cotta: clay, fired and glazed white in imitation of marble, but capable of being mass produced. For the della Robbias it was an art and a family business.

sculpture is characterized by large, simplified forms which closely follow the shape of the stone block as it was quarried.

Casting, on the other hand, reproduces the complex forms and tool marks of an original clay or wax model. Its main advantage lies in the translation of clay or wax into a material which is more durable than the original. Furthermore, it can be duplicated and transported without breaking. Today, durability and surface quality rather than duplication are the chief motives for using casting techniques. Bronze, the most common casting material, has beautiful color characteristics: its surface develops a rich patina with age, and it can be burnished or treated with chemicals to produce a wide range of color from bright gold to a deep, lustrous brown to greenish black.

It should be remembered that the earliest sculptures were painted, glazed, or inlaid with gems and other materials; their main purpose was to create convincing and vivid effigies. Today, similar effects can be achieved with plastics. Frank Gallo's (born 1933) *Swimmer*, made of polyester resin, gives us an idea of the realism pursued by the ancients, even in its Pop art prettification. Perhaps store-window mannequins are the closest modern counterparts to ancient polychrome sculptures. Made of painted papier-mâché or plastic, adorned with synthetic hair and eyelashes, and dressed in real clothes, these figures might be considered up-to-date "temple sculptures." No one worships them openly, but they seem to have genuine cultic significance.

*far left: The Lady Nofret.* c. 2570 B.C. Limestone, 44" high. Egyptian Museum, Cairo

*left:* Jōkei. *Shō-Kannon*. Kamakura period (1185–1333). Painted wood, 5'10" high. The Kurama Temple, Kyoto, Japan

*above:* Frank Gallo. *Swimmer.* 1964. Polyester resin, 65 × 16 × 41¼". Collection of Whitney Museum of American Art, New York. Gift of the artist and purchase, with funds from the Friends of the Whitney Museum of American Art

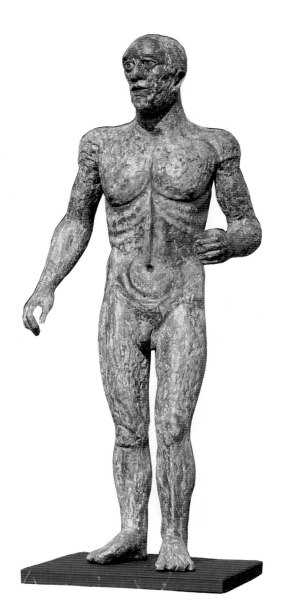

**Elizabeth Frink.** *Riace II.* 1986. Bronze, 86" high. Collection the artist

Frink sees the male nude as simultaneously sensuous and violent, powerful and vulnerable, decisive and tentative. She achieves these soft/tough effects with a technique used by Moore, Giacometti, and Richier (see page 14)—modeling in clay followed by direct carving in the hard plaster before final casting in bronze.

Unlike Michelangelo, Rodin defined sculpture as "the art of the hole and the lump." Although he (or his assistants) produced many carved marble works, Rodin's statement is typical of the sculptor as modeler—one who builds form *additively.* Also, clay is more responsive than wood or stone; the marks of the sculptor's hands are visible in the material. But while clay is very personal and direct, it has distinct limitations compared to wood or stone: it possesses little strength in tension or compression; it requires an armature for support; and it is not a permanent material. If work in clay is fired, it is limited by kiln size and a variety of engineering considerations. Therefore, clay is mainly used to make preparatory "sketches" for sculpture to be executed in other materials. As ceramic sculpture, however, clay is durable and reproducible, and it can be given a wide range of color and texture. Most important, clay is cheap: it encourages formal experimentation; it allows sculptors to take chances.

One pleasure of bronze sculpture arises from our knowledge that a soft, plastic material has been "frozen" into a hard, durable material. Bronze castings are actually hollow but they *look* heavy and solid; they retain the earthy quality of clay or rock. Hence, clay seems to call for bronze casting. In the work of a master like Rodin, clay's tactile variety—its capacity to imitate textures and modulate light while describing shape—is a principal attraction. Even though bronze casting is difficult and expensive, clay's versatility—its feel and look—makes it one of the most satisfying ways of "thinking" in three dimensions.

Wood is appealing for its grain, its color, and its sense of originating in a living tree. Also, it has greater tensile strength than stone, so it can be given projecting forms with less fear of breaking. Unlike metal, which is cold, or stone, which is abrasive, wood is warm and pleasant, even sensuous to the touch. The disadvantages of wood lie in its dimensional instability—its tendency to warp or crack. Wood can be worked more easily than stone, yet it offers enough resistance to cutting to require carving tools that leave their characteristic marks. An important advantage of wood—often exploited in contemporary work—is its adaptability to constructed sculpture. There is a special expressiveness in wooden joints, whether those of the skilled cabinetmaker or of the sculptor using improvised methods of joinery. Finally, there is the long tradition of painted wood sculpture, covered with metal or fabric, or with foreign materials embedded in it. Old though it is, wood fits easily into modern strategies of collage and assemblage.

We see a particularly modern use of wood in John Anderson's (born 1928) *Wall Piece.* Here carving and construction are combined in a sculpture that has mechanical pretenses. Forms projecting from a slot look like levers, doorknobs, or faucet handles, suggesting that we should pull, lift, or twist them. The fact that these operations cannot be performed does not prevent the sculpture from arousing our expectations: it looks *as if* it could work mechanically. It looks *as if* it could turn on a light, throw a switch, put an engine into neutral. These connections between form and meaning are logical enough, since knobs and levers are meant to be grasped, and wood is inviting to the touch. So we have a curiously magical-mechanical device; through carved forms and limb fragments it makes connections with tribal animistic sculpture; through its knobs and levers it connects with modern mechanization.

The sensuous potential of plywood, a construction material which is usually concealed, is beautifully revealed in the laminated wood sculptures of H. C. Westermann (1922–1981). In *The Big Change,* he carves a huge wooden knot, creating a Surrealistic contradiction between form and function, material and shape. Despite its absurdity and its use of a material without ancient credentials, this work manages to exhibit the unity of form, finished craftsmanship, and monolithic stability of classic sculpture.

H. C. Westermann. *The Big Change.*
1963. Laminated pine plywood, 56 ×
12 × 12". Collection William N.
Copley, New York

John Anderson. *Wall Piece.* 1963.
Wood. Allan Stone Gallery, New York

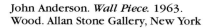

**Portrait jar, from the Chicana Valley,
Peru.** A.D. 400–600. **Painted
sun-baked clay, 4¾" high. The Art
Institute of Chicago**

Painted clay. Utilitarian function
united with realistic portraiture
seemed entirely plausible to ancient
sculptors. Commemorative or effigy
vessels evolved from an early belief
in the soul as a liquid substance,
hence the combined pottery-portrait
form.

Few final sculptures are done in wax because it is not very permanent. Also, it can easily be damaged in handling. But wax was a congenial material for the nineteenth-century sculptor Medardo Rosso (1858–1928). In *The Book-maker*—modeled wax over plaster—we see a painterly interest in light similar to that of Rodin and Degas, both of whom made sculptures in wax. Rosso's figure is unusual for its delicate treatment of a heavy body; it reminds us of Rodin's monumental *Balzac*. The transitions from form to form are so gentle that they seem to be blended with a soft brush. The work may be small, but it suggests large-scale statuary because wax has no grain, no texture visible to the eye. We can see that wax has an almost infinite capacity for detailed modeling.

Great changes in sculptural attitude have taken place since Rosso modeled his delicate figures in the 1890s. The critic Clement Greenberg summarizes some of them: "Space is there to be shaped, divided, enclosed, but not to be filled. The new sculpture tends to abandon stone, bronze, and clay for industrial materials like iron, steel, alloys, glass, plastics, celluloid, etc., etc., which are worked with the blacksmith's, the welder's, and even the carpenter's tools. Unity of material and color is no longer required, and applied color is irrelevant: a work or its parts can be cast, wrought, cut, or

Medardo Rosso. *The Bookmaker.* 1894. Wax over plaster, 17½ × 13 × 14" (irregular). Collection, The Museum of Modern Art, New York. Acquired through the Lillie P. Bliss Bequest

*right:* Auguste Rodin. *Balzac.* 1892–97. Plaster, 78¾" high. Musée Rodin, Paris

*far right:* Leonard Baskin. *St. Thomas Aquinas.* 1962. Walnut, 42 × 24 × 2". St. John's Abbey Church, Collegeville, Minnesota

330

simply put together; it is not so much sculptured as constructed, built, assembled, arranged."

Clearly, we live in the midst of a revolution in sculptural materials and technique, a revolution that reflects the unprecedented technical, social, and spiritual changes of modern life. Naturally, new materials and methods generate new aesthetic effects, which we shall examine in the following sections.

## THE ANCESTRAL COUPLE

**Ancestor figures of the Dogon tribe, Mali. Wood, 24⅝" high. Reitberg Museum, Zurich. Von der Heydt Collection**

As long as the original parents are perceived as the source of an awesome generative power—a power still active in tribal life—their effigies must be rigidly frontal, solemn, unmoved. Any deviation from verticality is felt as the weakening of a force that must endure through eternity. But notice the variety of forms and spaces that can be achieved within this vertical format.

Heavenly couple from Khajuraho, India. c. 11th century A.D. Over-lifesize. Archaeological Museum, Khajuraho, India

In India the affection of the ancestral pair assumes an explicitly sexual character. Innocent of Western prudery, medieval Hindu temples were densely populated with "loving couples" in exuberant settings much like their teeming earthly communities.

King Mycerinus and his queen, Kha-merer-nebty II, from Giza, Valley Temple of Mycerinus. 2628–2530 B.C. Graywacke, 54½" high. Courtesy, Museum of Fine Arts, Boston

Unswervingly pointed toward eternity, the royal pair also evidences an interest in the pleasures of marital intimacy. This interest is based on the discovery of the body as aesthetically pleasing and erotically exciting—ideas visible in the figures' contrasted forms: his—athletic and virile; hers—soft, rounded, and sensuous.

**Detail of sarcophagus, from Cerveteri. c. 520 B.C. Museo Nazionale di Villa Giulia, Rome**

To preserve the alive quality of this couple, the Etruscan sculptor shows them with their hands arrested, as if caught in a moment of animated conversation. The vividly painted eyes, hair, and skin must have compensated for the archaic stiffness of the heads.

*Ekkehard and Uta.* 1250–60. Stone, over-lifesize. Naumburg
Cathedral, Germany

Conjectural portraits of the founders of the cathedral. One
hardly doubts they are a contemporary, that is, a Gothic, couple.
Their relationship—more realistic than romantic—
seems based on a "sensible" arrangement: the alliance of an
influential, somewhat cynical German margrave with a stylish
and elegant Polish princess.

Ludwig Munstermann. *Adam and Eve.* c. 1620. Wood, 10¼"
high. Landesmuseum, Oldenburg, Germany

Equally guilty, Adam and Eve cannot face each other. The
sculptor—a German Mannerist—has composed their restless
forms in parallel to express the idea that they are partners in
sin.

# FROM MONOLITH TO OPEN FORM

The sculpture of antiquity reflected the tree log, the stone block, or the marble slab from which it was carved. Projecting forms in stone or wood could be broken by the sculptor's hammer and chisel; hence tribal sculptures closely resemble tree trunks, and Egyptian figures follow the form of the granite block. Only the casting process could produce long extensions and complex open shapes; but it was mainly used to fashion weapons, jewelry, and harness decorations. Sculpture in general, and carved sculpture in particular, tended to be monolithic (similar in form to a single stone). A notable exception, the Hellenistic figure group *Laocoön*, was carved from several blocks of marble, and although it represents a remarkable technical achievement, it is not considered aesthetically successful because its parts seem disunited. The feeling of a single, embracing shape—the *monolithic feeling*—has been lost.

In addition to considerations of material and process, monolithic form dominated traditional sculpture for religious and psychological reasons. We associate permanence and resistance to change with uncomplicated shapes. Open and complex forms suggest motion, the enemy of stability and time-lessness. That is why the pyramids of Egypt and the temples of Greece favor a triangle resting on its base, or a triangle supported by repeated verticals. In

Seymour Lipton. *Storm Bird.* 1953. Nickel silver on steel, 20 × 37 × 9⅝" . **Private collection**

Working directly with modern metallic materials, Lipton creates forms that combine the effects of the acetylene torch's cutting action with the surface qualities of modeled clay.

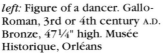

*left:* Figure of a dancer. Gallo-Roman, 3rd or 4th century A.D. Bronze, 47¼" high. Musée Historique, Orléans

*right:* Henri Matisse. *Serpentine.* 1909. Bronze, 22¼" high. The Hirshhorn Museum and Sculpture Garden, Smithsonian Institution, Washington, D.C.

Extended and penetrated forms in marble and in bronze. The *Laocoön* is anything but monolithic; those holes and projections are more typical of bronze casting. So we get mixed signals: the Gallo-Roman figure and the Matisse look like what they are—bronze castings of clay models. But the *Laocoön* marble also looks like a casting, which is aesthetically disturbing.

Agesander, Athenodorus, and Polydorus of Rhodes. *Laocoön.* Late 2nd century B.C. Marble, 7' high. Vatican Museum, Rome

religious sculpture, too, permanence is expressed through forms that look as if they can resist the ravages of time. The sacred sculpture of all ancient peoples tends to be solid, frontal, and monolithic.

Open-form sculpture comes to us mainly from the barbarian peoples whose invasions of Europe from the steppes of Asia eventually destroyed Greco-Roman civilization. Their metalworking skill and nomadic existence encouraged an art of restless linearity. Also, heated metal lends itself to curved, serpentine, and spiral shapes—ideal for peoples who are fascinated by ceaseless travel. Accustomed to wandering, hunting, and fighting, the barbarian nomads felt free to move in any direction along the seemingly endless Eurasian plains. Not surprisingly, they were late to discover the concepts of enclosed space and monolithic form. These wanderers, who eventually settled Europe from Russia to Ireland, produced an art of continuous twists and turns on a flat plane. Their small three-dimensional sculpture was created mainly by assembling two-dimensional, linear forms.

Much of Western art can be seen as a struggle between Mediterranean closed-form, or monolithic, ideas and nomadic open-form ideas. On one hand, sculptors from Michelangelo to Maillol preserved the classical ideal of monolithic form; on the other, Romanesque and Gothic sculptors held fast to the barbarian ideal of convoluted form. If the Gothic cathedral is the culmination of Christian art, then nomadic conceptions of form and space prevailed. The Renaissance attempted to revive classical notions of form, but it could not entirely displace the taste for twisting motion inherited from barbarian art. With this background, modern sculpture in the West would be expected to reveal anticlassic tendencies: it should resist clear forms and balanced relationships; it should prefer shapes that look like knots and coils; it should favor linear detail instead of plain surfaces.

*left:* Maori prow ornament, from Polynesia. 60⅝" high. Museum für Völkerkunde, Munich

Vikings and Polynesians—both warlike, seafaring peoples—created a complex linear art in which spirals, interlaces, and elaborate perforations almost obliterate their much-loved animal motifs.

*right:* Animal head, from the Oseberg ship-burial. c. A.D. 825. Carved and drilled maple, 20⅞" high. University Museum of Antiquities, Oslo

These expectations are, in fact, borne out in recent sculpture: anticlassic tendencies predominate. The sense of the monolith, based mainly on the carving tradition, has been largely abandoned. Still, the monolith survives conspicuously in the work of a master like Henry Moore, although his holes and serpentine shapes show traces of the old barbarian consciousness.

A good example of modern monolithic sculpture can be seen in Leonard Baskin's (born 1922) *Seated Man with Owl.* Yet this work seems to be a version of a theme we have encountered in Egyptian art, as in the *Pharaoh Khafre.* There, the hawk-god, Horus, stands behind the king's head, whereas the bird in the modern work—a rather inflated owl—stands on the man's arm, almost obscuring him from view. Baskin's sculpture shares the frontality and immobile expression of the pharaoh, but otherwise we see a modern personality. Where Khafre is slim, athletic, and youthful, the modern man is middle-aged, overweight, and clumsy looking. The Egyptian sculpture conveys a sense of enduring mass because it shows no trace of motion; Baskin's figure, on the other hand, exhibits the ponderous bulk of a flabby man whose sitting down is an act of collapse. The pharaoh looks confidently toward the future while Baskin's man looks bored. Apparently, a monolith can express opposite qualities: power and optimism, or resignation in the face of life's everlasting sameness.

Other examples—from the work of Maillol, Brancusi, and Arp—would show that monolithic form lives on. However, these sculptors are among the "old masters" of modernism. As we approach the present, artists seem to prefer media that yield twisted, perforated, and abstract forms. All of which suggests that the classical, monolithic tradition is dead. However, the taste for dynamic, broken forms can be oversatisfied; a desire for its opposite may emerge. In time, the stylistic pendulum may swing back to the monolith.

**Henry Moore.** *Reclining Mother and Child.* **1937. Cast bronze, 86½ × 33½ × 54". Walker Art Center, Minneapolis**

In Moore's penetrated forms we see the culmination of a long process of accommodation between the nomadic obsession with open, serpentine shapes and the classical Mediterranean concern for balance and stability.

Leonard Baskin. *Seated Man with Owl.* 1959.
Cherry wood, 30 × 16¹⁵⁄₁₆ × 17¾". Smith
College Museum of Art, Northampton,
Massachusetts

*Pharaoh Khafre.* c. 2600 B.C. Green diorite,
66" high. Cairo Museum

339

## CONSTRUCTIVISM

Constructivism was an early-twentieth-century movement which tried to abandon the monolith and the central axis as the basis of sculpture. It introduced new materials like Plexiglas, celluloid, and metal wire; and it treated the human figure like an engineering project. Its leading personalities were two Russian brothers with different names: Naum Gabo (1890–1977) and Antoine Pevsner (1886–1962). They advocated an approach which could bring sculpture into harmony with physics and mathematics—mainly through the use of engineering principles.

After the Russian revolution of 1917, the Constructivists were supported by the Communist government, but by 1921 the Soviets became unsympathetic to abstract art. Although Gabo and Pevsner wanted to revolutionize architecture and industrial design as well as painting and sculpture, theirs was a revolution the Party didn't like. So, leaving Russia in 1922, the Constructivists carried their ideas to the Bauhaus in Germany. In 1946 Gabo settled in the United States, making his home in Connecticut. By 1960 the Constructivist ideas of Gabo and Pevsner were firmly established throughout the West.

How did the Constructivists influence modern sculpture? Mainly by stressing the value of transparency, interpenetrating forms, overlapping planes, and the use of lines in tension to represent energy and space. Their sculpture often reminds us of mechanical drawings executed in three dimensions, as in Gabo's *Linear Construction #1*. Its curves are perfectly regular because they do not record organic shapes. Pevsner's *Torso* has all the geometric precision of a Cubist figure painting. And, as in the sculpture of another Russian, Archipenko, it uses negative, or concave, volumes to represent forms that are actually convex. Employing translucent plastic sheets and copper, the Constructivists were determined to avoid thick, dense materials. The thinness of wire and the transparency of plastic enabled Pevsner to stress the negation of mass. Thus, two traits of the monolith were undermined: (1) the solidity of form; and (2) the mass or weight of form.

Gabo's *Monument for an Institute of Physics* tries to eliminate the dis-

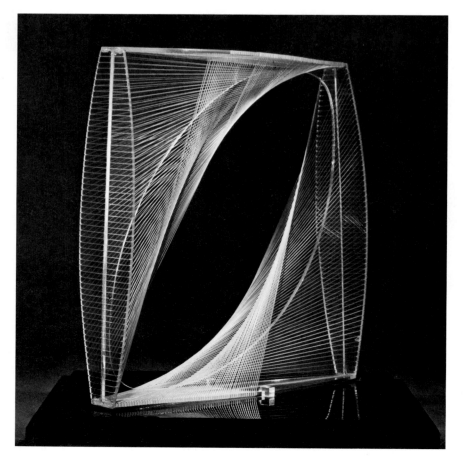

Naum Gabo. *Linear Construction #1.* 1942–43. Plastic, 12¼ × 12¼ × 2½". The Hirshhorn Museum and Sculpture Garden, Smithsonian Institution, Washington, D.C. Gift of Joseph H. Hirshhorn, 1966

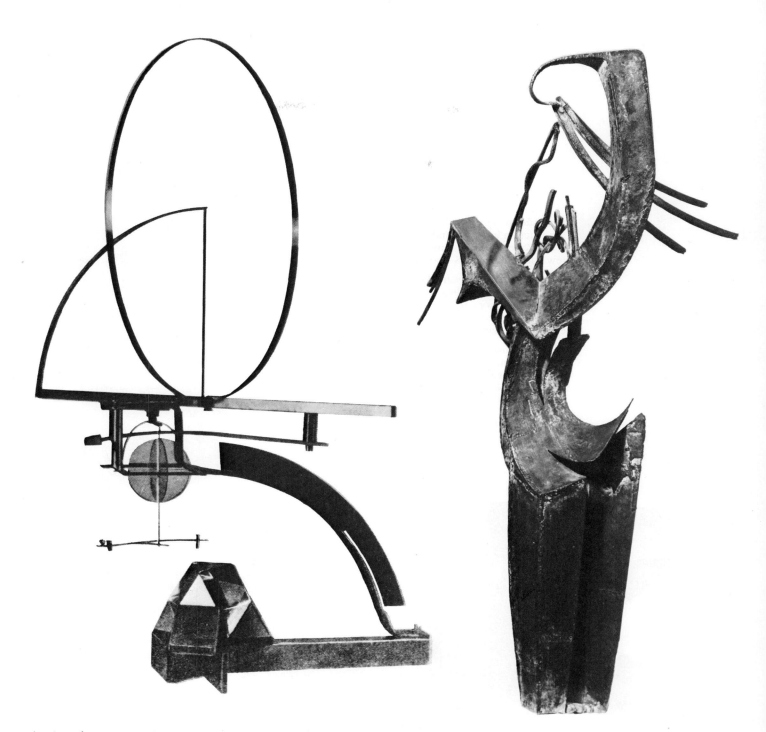

tinctions between sculpture and architecture. The model is made of plastic, glass, and bronze, but it bears an interesting resemblance to a wrought-iron sculpture by Julio González, *Woman Combing Her Hair*. Both artists demonstrated the new openness of sculptural space. Liberated from its agelong rootedness in the earth and seemingly independent of the laws of gravity, sculpture began its move into a kind of interstellar space.

Although modern physics has altered our ideas about the concreteness of matter and the uniformity of space, the Constructivists were unable to abandon opaque and volumetric materials entirely. Even plastics, wire, and glass have shape, color, weight, and substance. Increasingly, Pevsner began to use solid metals, particularly bronze rods bonded into curved planes, as in *Developable Column*: apparently, sculptural openness and the nullification of matter had limits. In the end, the sensuous appeal of metal, or even plastic, counteracted the artist's urge to dematerialize form.

*left:* Naum Gabo. *Monument for an Institute of Physics and Mathematics.* 1923–25. Glass, bronze, and plastic, 17⅜" high. Private collection, London

*above:* Julio González. *Woman Combing Her Hair.* 1936. Wrought iron, 52 × 23½ × 24⅝". Collection, The Museum of Modern Art, New York. Mrs. Simon Guggenheim Fund

*right:* Antoine Pevsner. *Torso.* 1924–26. Construction in plastic and copper, 29½ × 11⅝". Collection, The Museum of Modern Art, New York. Katherine S. Dreier Bequest

In the nearly twenty years that separate these two sculptures, Pevsner's forms grew progressively more abstract. At the same time, his surfaces became sensuously richer. There seems to be a law of compensation at work.

*below:* Antoine Pevsner. *Developable Column.* 1942. Brass and oxidized bronze, 20¾" high, base 19⅜" diameter. Collection, The Museum of Modern Art, New York. Purchase

*left:* Constantin Brancusi. *Adam and Eve.* 1921. Oak, chestnut, and limestone, 99¼" high. The Solomon R. Guggenheim Museum, New York

In the Brancusi, a scarred Adam supports a smoother and rounder Eve. By presenting the figures in a vertical plane, Brancusi creates a type of hierarchy. Giacometti places man and woman on the same horizontal plane; there the man becomes a sexual aggressor.

*below:* Alberto Giacometti. *Man and Woman.* 1928–29. Bronze, 17¾" high. Collection Henriette Gomès, Paris

**Max Ernst.** *Le Capricorne.* 1964. Bronze, 94½ × 80¾ × 51⅛".
Musée National d'Art Moderne, Centre Georges Pompidou, Paris

Ernst compromises the dignity of royalty by presenting this couple as a
pair of hybrid creatures compounded of geometric elements and pieces
of man, fish, goat, steer, and giraffe anatomy.

**Etienne-Martin.** *Le Grand Couple.* 1946. Bronze, 78¾"
high. Collection Michel Couturier & Cie., Paris

The united couple is compared to a powerful, earthy
generative force by heightening their resemblance to a
huge convoluted tree root.

Barbara Hepworth. *Two Figures.* 1954–55. Teak, 54"
high. Collection Mr. and Mrs. Solomon Byron Smith,
Lake Forest, Illinois

Which is the man and which is the woman? (I think
"he" is on the left.) These figures are so abstract that
we can differentiate them sexually only by their height.
Perhaps there are some gender clues in the ovals. Or
perhaps they are both women.

Henry Moore. *King and Queen.* 1952–53. Bronze, 65" high. The Hirshhorn Museum and Sculpture Garden, Smithsonian Institution, Washington, D.C. Gift of Joseph H. Hirshhorn, 1966

In this royal couple, Moore tries to gain access to those mythic feelings that connect the destiny of a land and its people with the strength and harmony of its rulers.

Joan Miró. *Man and Woman.* 1962. Wrought
iron, ceramic, and wood, 98½ × 23¼ × 13¾".
Pierre Matisse Gallery, New York

Beyond the cartoony sort of humor, Miró shows
how the *range* of sculpture can be extended.
This is funny in a *sculptural* way, and it doesn't
degenerate into kitsch.

Kenneth Armitage. *Diarchy.* 1957. Private collection, Chicago

The slablike device makes a literal unit of the couple, forcing us
to view the unit frontally and magnifying the impression of
obstinate regal power.

Marisol. *The Bicycle Race.* 1962–63. Wood and mixed media, 68 × 66".
The Harry N. Abrams Family Collection, New York

An almost Egyptian solemnity pervades this work. However, it also
contains a satirical comment about a couple of earnest bicycle riders: he
is No. 1, and she is No. 2—and they hate each other.

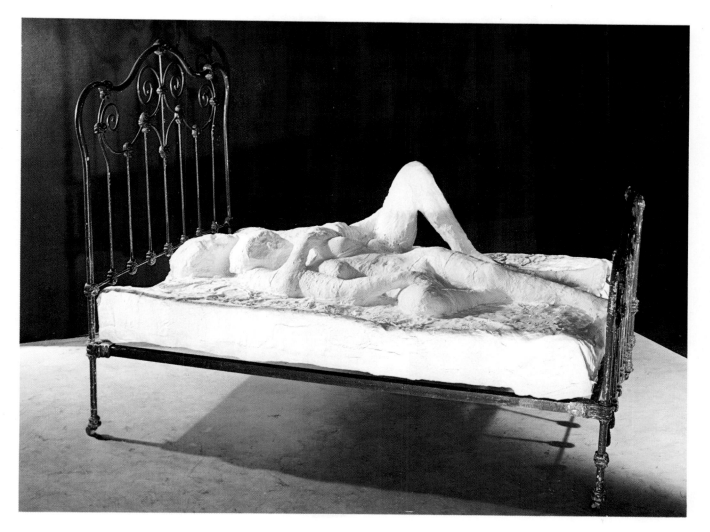

George Segal. *Lovers on a Bed II.* 1970. Plaster and metal, 62 × 56 × 84".
Sidney Janis Gallery, New York

A couple who *succumb* to love; the emptiness of the setting and the
plainness of the lovers make their embrace a compromise between Eros
and fatigue.

Eve Renée Nele. *The Couple.* 1961. Bronze, 21½ × 13⅜". Bayerische Staatsgemäldesammlungen, Munich

This is the fetish pair of a civilization consecrated to engineering: in their abdominal cavities nuts and bolts are renewed and armatures are magically rewound.

## SCULPTURAL ASSEMBLAGE

Assemblage is revolutionary in the history of sculpture because it abandons carving, modeling, and casting. It begins with materials which already have a rich body of meaning and association. It parallels the flight of painting from the creation of illusions—pretending that stone is flesh or that metal is hair. Seley's automobile bumpers (see page 203) are sculptural because they occupy real space, but they do not cease to be bumpers. In other words, assemblage does not involve the *total* transmutation of materials; it is composition with the substance and meaning of materials *as they are found*.

The sculptor's reluctance to transform materials completely constitutes a profound change in art. During the Middle Ages, alchemists tried to transmute ordinary materials into gold because they believed in *a hierarchy* of substances. Modern artists do not accept that hierarchy; science and technology have encouraged this attitude, since many of the things we value are derived from cheap, abundant substances like coal, petroleum, nitrogen, and soybeans. Moreover, the processes of creating illusions have acquired some of the associations of deceit. The Bauhaus slogan "honesty of materials" has spread from craftsmen and designers to painters and sculptors: they work in an aesthetic climate in which changing the inherent properties of a material seems unethical or foolish.

Assemblage is also related to the inadequacy a sculptor may feel when confronting industrial feats of forming and fabrication. When Cellini made his famous saltcellar, he could rightly feel that it represented the highest degree of technical mastery of his age. But the modern artist is exposed to miracles of miniaturization that make hand carving and casting look like minor achievements. In the light of computerized technologies, carved stone and ivory seem to be quaint medieval survivals. So it makes practical sense for sculptors to use industrial products in their art. As a result, creative strategies have shifted from an emphasis on forming skills to an emphasis on ideas—composition with meanings already given.

The range of sculptural effects made possible by assemblage with manufactured materials is enormous; it almost seems we are dealing with a new art form. In the following examples, however, the viewer with a good memory may recognize some familiar melodies: the old themes persist.

Benvenuto Cellini. *Saltcellar of Francis I.* 1539–43. Gold and enamel, 10¼ × 13⅛". Kunsthistorisches Museum, Vienna

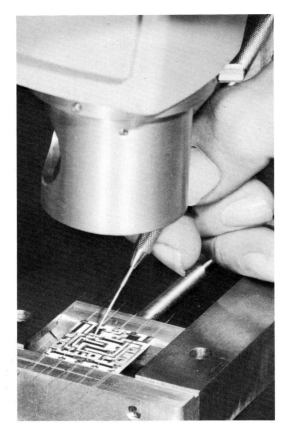

Ultrasmall electronic circuit, a high-speed binary electronic counter for use in a spacecraft

*above right*: Claes Oldenburg. *Soft Pay-Telephone*. 1963. Vinyl, kapok, and wood, 46½ × 19 × 12". Collection William Zierler, New York

A fire-damaged telephone echoes Oldenburg's soft telephone. Using nonrigid materials like canvas, vinyl, and kapok, Oldenburg has elevated limpness to high status among the expressive qualities of sculpture.

Burned phone, from advertisement for Western Electric Phone Company. 1968. Courtesy Cunningham & Walsh, Inc., New York

Life imitates art. There may have been a tragic fire, but somehow this phone looks ludicrous. Oldenburg bears some responsibility for this.

**An Assemblage Anthology**    In a relief made of canvas stretched over bent steel wire mounted on a metal frame, Lee Bontecou (born 1931) uses old *and* new "assemblage" techniques. The forms of her sculpture may remind us of the tribal costume of the Northwest American Indians. At the same time, her technique recalls early aircraft manufacture—stretching and gluing fabric over a wire-frame skeleton. Visually, the most prominent elements in her work are ovoid apertures; we cannot help seeing them as eyes, or as openings in a strangely hypnotic mask.

The fundamental metaphors here are the mask and the membrane. The sculpture's light, sturdy construction is reminiscent of the Indian practice of building a canoe by stretching hides over a wooden frame. That membrane arouses primitive, animistic feelings: air trapped inside the construction seems to exert an outward force—an invisible force of the type that holds up airplane wings. Yet all these ideas depend on a simple type of assemblage—canvas stretched over a wire frame.

In *Europa on a Cycle*, Richard Stankiewicz draws and constructs with old rods and chains; he uses mechanical parts as they are found, or cuts metal shapes with a torch. The various kinds of metal—wire, pipe, sheet, rod, spring, tube, bar, and plate—are united by a single method of attachment—welding—and a single color or texture—rust. This unity of material and surface enables the sculptor to concentrate on the problems of volume and contour, movement and balance, illusion and reality. The notion of a beautiful woman carried off by a rusty bike is the kind of Surrealist idea that would have appealed to Picasso; he also composed with handlebars.

*The Juggler* by Robert Mallary (born 1917) is made of an especially exotic material—plastic-impregnated fabric. Using a man's shirt and trousers soaked in plastic and attached to a burnt-wood support, Mallary creates a figure with the clothes meant to cover it. The hollow arms and legs are almost rigid; they function as real limbs and heavy rags at the same time. The plastic freezes the action of the fabric, which is stretched by its own weight and suspended from a wooden frame like a crucifix. Remember, too, that burnt wood is a primal material of religious sacrifice. Clearly, Mallary has assembled some of the basic symbols of suffering and transfiguration. The juggler,

Painted leather shirt. Tlingit Indians of Alaska. Collected in 1918. Painted leather, 38½ × 24½". University Museum, Philadelphia

The magical motifs of tribal artists are often taken up unconsciously or intentionally by the creators of "museum" art. But little has changed except the labels assigned by critics and historians.

*below:* Lee Bontecou. *Untitled.* 1962. Welded steel and canvas, 5'5" × 9'3" × 1'8". Collection Mr. and Mrs. Seymour Schweber, Kings Point, New York

Richard Stankiewicz. *Europa on a Cycle.* 1953. Rods and chains. Whereabouts unknown

*below: Eau de Vroom.* Advertisement for Crêpe de Chine perfume. 1967. Courtesy Berta, Grant & Winkler, Inc., New York

The sculptural strategy of assemblage is brilliantly illustrated in a perfume advertisement that combines masculine machinery (the Honda), a soft saddlebag (can it symbolize Europa?), and a precious fragrance.

Gabor Peterdi. *The Black Horne.* 1952. Etching, 24 × 20". Collection Yale Art School

*below:* Pablo Picasso. *Bull's Head.* 1943. Assemblage of bicycle saddle and handlebars, 13¼ × 17⅛ × 7½". Musée Picasso, Paris

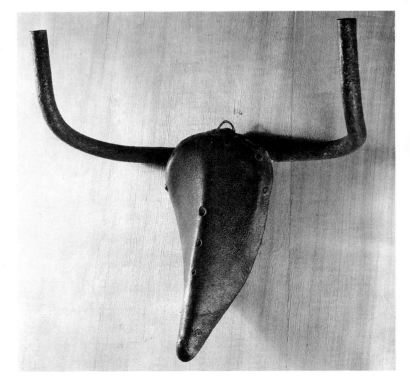

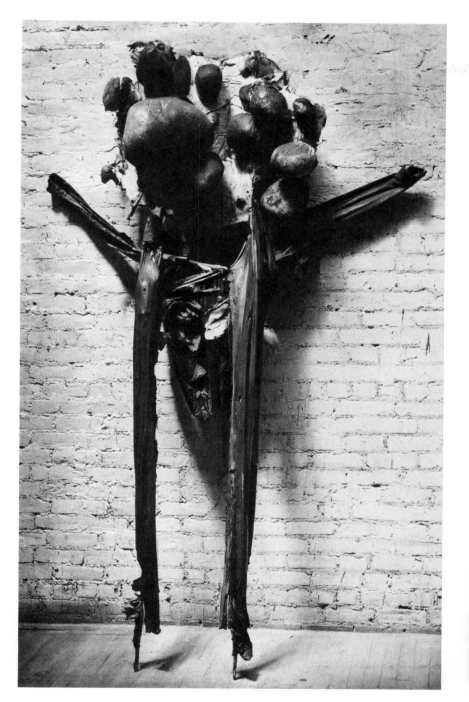

Robert Mallary. *The Juggler.* 1962. Polyester, resin, fiberglass, tuxedo, steel, and crushed stone, 9' × 5' × 1'6". Allan Stone Gallery, New York

Claes Oldenburg. *The Stove.* 1962. Metal, porcelain, paint, and plaster, 58 × 28 × 27½". Private collection

"putting on his act," falls into the position of Christ on the cross; we get a sense of dying-in-living and failure-in-success—the tragic ideas at the heart of existence.

A Pop type of sculptural assemblage can be seen in *The Stove* by Claes Oldenburg. It consists of painted plaster "food" displayed on a real but antiquated cooking range. The luridly colored food is enough to give us anorexia. Obviously, art as the pleasing organization of forms is irrelevant here; the design principles of unity, balance, and rhythm have been ignored. Instead, we are asked to regard food and food preparation as disgusting. The artist has directed a program of sabotage against what the housekeeping magazines, with their luscious colorplates, want to sell. We see the nakedness of groceries and cooking; a familiar event becomes truly ugly.

*above:* Nancy Graves. *Zaga.* 1983. Cast bronze with polychrome chemical patination, 72 × 49 × 32". The Nelson-Atkins Museum of Art, Kansas City, Missouri. Gift of the Friends of Art. Courtesy M. Knoedler & Co., Inc., New York

Animal and vegetable parts cast in bronze and assembled to make a creature that might have lived in the imagination of a prehistoric shaman or a medieval wizard. Seeds and roots, ferns and bones, wheels and rods: we seem to be watching an experiment in the laboratory of nature and technology. Graves can produce this strange, floating amalgam of mechanical and growing things because of the openness of modern sculpture.

*right:* John Chamberlain. *Essex.* 1960. Automobile body parts and other metal, relief, 9' × 6'8" × 3'7". Collection, The Museum of Modern Art, New York. Gift of Mr. and Mrs. Robert C. Scull and Purchase

John Chamberlain's (born 1927) assemblage of crumpled automobile parts looks like an earlier stage in the process of machine destruction seen in César's "compression" sculptures. These parts are found in junkyards, but Chamberlain bends, welds, and paints them himself; the total work reflects its automotive origins only partially. In other words, a dead automobile has been used as a source of cheap raw material. The title *Essex* acknowledges a venerable vehicle as its ancestor, but we see the work as a large, colored metal "painting." And that is its objective—the creation of an Abstract Expressionist "canvas" in metal. Yet despite the painterly format and screaming color, this sculpture cannot forget its roots in a machine that regularly commits vehicular homicide. The power of the work depends on aging metal clashing with the shiny new paint film provided by the artist. Chamberlain forces us to witness a new kind of conflict between old and new, tranquility and violence, death and life.

The employment of *wrappings* in assemblage enlarges the artistic vocabulary of terror. Using methods we associate with mortuaries or shipping rooms, two sculptors, Bruce Conner (born 1933) and Christo (born 1935), have independently developed a gruesome and mysterious sculptural rhetoric. Both create images in which shrouded objects or figures seem to be struggling to escape their bonds. The situation has psychopathic as well as sculptural overtones, since it exploits the viewer's fear of confinement. The chained or bound figure has a history as old as Prometheus; in Michelangelo's *Rebellious Slave*, for example, we witness a drama of imprisoned form which, in various disguises, appears in almost all his works. Conner's drama of imprisonment—*Child*—shows a mutilated wax figure on a highchair enmeshed in a gauzelike material made of torn nylon stockings; but they also look like cobwebs. The nylons function like Francis Bacon's blurred contours, creating an illusion of strangled movement—the quality of a silent, agonized scream.

*Package on Wheelbarrow* by Christo describes the struggle of an unknown thing against a random system of knots and bindings. A sheet wrapping maintains the anonymity of the creature, or object, and the wheelbarrow keeps its secret, adding only the possibility that its writhing form will be carried away. As a result the viewer experiences strange, more or less abstract tensions. But an imagination nourished on horror films may discover more ghoulishness than abstract art at the core of this work.

*Little Hands* by Arman (born 1928) continues the macabre note struck by Conner and Christo. Consisting of dolls' hands (many of them broken) glued into a wooden drawer, this construction yields a series of grisly perceptions. We start with a collection of mutilated toys and end with the uncovered mass graves that turn up so tragically in wartime. The drawer functions first as a frame, then as a container, and finally as a tomb (see section below, "Niches, Boxes, and Grottoes"). To equal its horror, we would have to go back to Hieronymus Bosch. Even then, painted images cannot muster the clinical detachment of the artist who assembles limbs originally meant to function as parts of a normal body.

In *Chopin's Waterloo* Arman shows his humorous side. Many citizens, it seems, harbor a secret desire to tear apart a piano. Arman has done it for them and has given permanent form to the ritual of piano sacrifice. The visual effect is one of splendid destruction—ivories, splinters, and piano wire in gorgeous disarray. To some of us, a piano may be more interesting when dismembered than when healthy and whole. Also, by tearing it open, the sculptor reveals it as a type of machine. Then, gratifying our desire to annihilate machines, he

*left:* Bruce Conner. *Child.* 1959-60. Assemblage: wax figure with nylon, cloth, metal, and twine in a high chair, 34⅝ × 17 × 16½". Collection, The Museum of Modern Art, New York. Gift of Philip Johnson

*right:* Michelangelo. *The Rebellious Slave.* 1513-16. Marble, 7'⅝" high. The Louvre, Paris

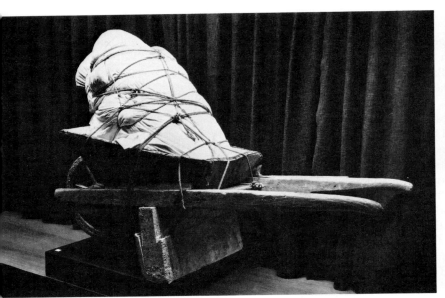

Christo. *Package on Wheelbarrow.* 1963. Cloth, metal, wood, rope, and twine, 35⅛ × 59½ × 20¼". Collection, The Museum of Modern Art, New York. Blanchette Rockefeller Fund

Jean Tinguely. Piano before its incorporation into *Homage to New York.* Self-destroyed March 17, 1960, in the garden of The Museum of Modern Art, New York

Rico Lebrun. *Bound Figure.* 1963. Bronze, 7½ × 11". Collection Constance Lebrun Crown, Malibu, California

kills it. For these or other reasons, Jean Tinguely (1925–1991), a Swiss sculptor celebrated for self-destroying machines, included a peeled and plucked piano in his kinetic sculpture performance at New York's Museum of Modern Art, *Homage to New York.* Both pianos may represent the aesthetic vindication of small boys who take clocks apart but cannot put them together again.

Violent or gruesome phenomena can be seen in all forms of art and popular culture. There is, for example, a vigorous market for the horror films of Vincent Price; all of us like to watch the Marx brothers break up a set; and Rock stars have been known to smash their guitars during a performance. Assemblage can be employed to fit the pattern: the sculptor dissects a complex object and explores the forces that hold it together. This exploration takes the form of tearing up the object and reassembling it to memorialize the process of destruction. In other words: reverse assemblage.

Arman. *Little Hands.* 1960. Dolls' hands glued in wooden drawer, 14⅝ × 17⅞ × 2⅞". Collection the artist

*below:* Arman. *Chopin's Waterloo.* 1962. Broken piano on wood panel, 6'1½" × 9'10" × 1'7" . Musée National d'Art Moderne, Centre Georges Pompidou, Paris

## NICHES, BOXES, AND GROTTOES

The niche is a recessed place in a wall where a sculptured figure or bust can be located. This encourages us to think of niche sculptures as *born from* walls, conceived as centers of dramatic interest on a plane surface. The niche encloses the sculpture physically and governs the angle of vision from which we see it. Psychologically, the niche defends a sculpture, sheltering it from full exposure to the elements. Apparently, the niche sculpture needs protection, perhaps because it holds a precious secret.

Our psychological associations with niche sculpture also adhere to the box sculptures and constructions which figure so prominently in twentieth-century art. Box sculptures can be regarded as detached niches, secular shrines taken from architectural settings that never existed. Looking at the boxes produced by our industrial civilization, it is not difficult to summon up many of our associations with cathedral niches or the recesses in a temple wall—the mysterious little places we see in private and address in reverence and awe.

**MEDIEVAL AND RENAISSANCE NICHE SCULPTURES**

*below: Apostle.* c. 1090. St. Sernin, Toulouse

From the medieval carving, which is part of the wall, to the Renaissance work, which stands free, we can see sculpture moving progressively away from architecture. But not too far: the niche is psychologically necessary; it creates a sense of the sacred, of a person who is divinely protected.

*right:* Donatello. *St. Mark.* 1411–13. Marble, 92⅞" high. Orsanmichele, Florence

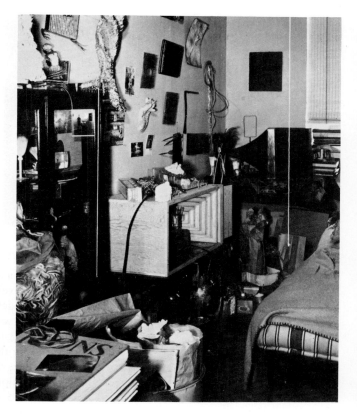

*above left:* Frederick Kiesler. Interior, Living Room, *Endless House.* 1949–60. Photograph courtesy, The Museum of Modern Art, New York

*above:* Lucas Samaras. Detail of *Room.* 1964. Pace Gallery, New York

*left:* Antoni Gaudí. Original attic (garret), Casa Milá Apartment House, Barcelona. 1905–10

The grotto, like the niche, is a man-made recess or excavation, but it has no connection to the wall: it belongs instead to the convoluted inner spaces of the natural cavern. This brings us to Frederick Kiesler's (1896–1965) shaped interior spaces—a type of hybrid sculpture/architecture. As an art form, however, the man-made grotto has little relation to shelter; it is better understood as interior sculpture. That would explain Schwitters's Merzbau, or quasi-Cubist grotto. And in the grotesque—that is, grotto-like—passageways of Antoni Gaudí, we see truly sculptural concavities. All of these interior sculptures remind us that we have never really forgotten our prehistoric existence in caves.

The *Room* by Lucas Samaras (born 1936) is a twentieth-century grotto, a three-dimensional interior assemblage consisting of possessions randomly attached to the walls of a teenage cave. Its claim to style lies in its lack of style, and its realism is reinforced by our knowledge that the room is very typical. The visual disorganization here may comment on the lifestyle of American adolescents but we should remember that it accurately mirrors the large-scale environment we have created for generations. Perhaps *Room* is a form of rebellion against the austerities created by Mondrian and Mies; perhaps it

*above:* André Bloc. *Sculpture Habitacle No. 2.* 1965

A sculpture in which one could live, or a dwelling that invites the plastic responses appropriate to sculpture.

*right:* André Bloc. Detail of *Sculpture Habitacle No. 2*

exhibits a logic that architects and designers do not yet understand—the logic of the niche, the grotto, and the box.

Boxes differ from niches and grottoes because they can close and become packages—packages that can be carried. The niche belongs to a stationary wall, whereas the box is a portable container for something worth keeping. It has many of the sanctified associations of a reliquary—a container holding the bones of a saint, a sacred text, or a precious remnant. These religious uses of boxlike containers hint at the magical ancestry of modern box sculpture; we see much more than their physical materials.

The authority of the niche is eloquently demonstrated in the sculptures of Louise Nevelson (1904–1988)—sculptures that seem to be collections of boxes or cells—little rooms. Usually painted black, they convey an impression of compulsive neatness, of well-arranged, frequently cleaned drawers. Without knowing what the contents are, we sense they have been carefully ordered, put there for a purpose. They consist, in fact, of pieces of wood molding, bowling pins, newel posts, chair legs, and so on. The secret of *Totality Dark* is not in the origin of its lumberyard odds and ends; it is in the control of their placement. These wooden objects have a power that defies logic. Why?

Just as monolithic sculptural form expresses authority and order, the box form commands belief: it convinces on sight. Nevelson's boxes constitute a type of latter-day magical-religious art; she uses this form because she thinks like a sorcerer or shaman. Her box sculptures became containers for the fetish objects that a shaman typically owns. It is not necessary to know the symbolism of the wooden shapes so long as we believe they ward off evil—the pains and anxieties normally treated with pills. In fact, the namelessness of the box contents enhances our faith in their magical power: the *form of presentation* dominates the material presented.

Marcel Duchamp's *Boîte-en-valise* (*The Box in a Valise*) consists of a craftily compartmented little museum-in-a-box that resembles an attaché case. Its carefully dimensioned spaces make room for small reproductions of each of the sixty-eight principal works Duchamp created before abandoning art for chess. Altogether, he built three hundred editions of this little "museum." But the box is more than a handy container for copies of Duchamp's artistic output: it is an ironic device. By miniaturizing artworks originally meant for a museum, and storing them according to the impartial logic of the valise, the objects become a type of business inventory—merchandise in a salesman's sample case. Is that what gallery art is?

Joseph Cornell's (1903–1972) boxes are surreal containers, too—collections of objects that seem related until we realize that they frustrate common-

Louise Nevelson. *Totality Dark.* 1962. Wood painted black, 8'2" × 10'7" × 7½". Pace Gallery, New York

*Crafts for Tour* advertisement. 1963. Courtesy The 7 Santini Brothers Fine Arts Division, New York

Compare this box to Duchamp's valise—or to Nevelson's sculpture. What principle do they illustrate? Answer: boxes make powerful magic; the container takes over its contents.

Marcel Duchamp. *Boîte-en-valise (The Box in a Valise).* 1938–42. Sixty-eight reproductions of works in green clothbound board box, 16 × 14¾ × 3⅛". The Solomon R. Guggenheim Museum, New York

sense logic. *Soap Bubble Set*, for example, has the simplicity and serenity of a Chardin still life. But its objects are not anonymous, like Louise Nevelson's wooden fragments; they have identities that induce dreams of old places and possessions, recollections of lost things like childhood toys, tastes, and smells. Somehow, Cornell manages to scramble our time sense; he plays with the cues that tell us where our minds have wandered. The experience is slightly

Joseph Cornell. *Soap Bubble Set.* 1950. Mixed media, 9½ × 14½ × 3¾". Collection Mr. and Mrs. Daniel Varenne, Paris

Joseph Cornell. *Blériot.* 1956. Collection Mr. and Mrs. E.A. Bergman, Chicago

H. C. Westermann. *Memorial to the Idea of Man, If He Was an Idea.* 1958. Mixed media. Collection Lewis Manilow, Chicago

disorienting but it leaves no scars. These collections carry us back to a distant dream time; then the frame takes us home.

Cornell began creating his enigmatic little constructions in the 1930s, apparently uninfluenced by other developments in art. The connection with sculpture is slight; he is more nearly a poet who uses small objects and spaces to create opportunities for reverie and irony. His *Blériot* has some of the spare, open structure of Constructivist sculpture, but it is much more witty: the rusted spring mounted on a parrot's perch symbolizes the first Frenchman to fly across the English Channel. Cornell's range of expression is unusually wide: he plays with a metaphor that compares man to a bird, a spiral, a trapeze artist, and a creature in planetary orbit. Then back to a bird in its cage.

H. C. Westermann's boxes are distinguished by careful craftsmanship and grotesque references to the human body. In *Memorial to the Idea of Man, If He Was an Idea* we see a large, well-made cabinet-and-Cyclops wearing crenellations for a crown, like the battlements on a castle tower. But this is a man: the door of his torso, when opened, reveals an interior lined with bottle caps. The insides also contain a headless baseball player and an armless acrobat, plus a black ship sinking in a sea of bottle caps. Bottle caps, baseball, and incomplete bodies form the idea of man! Not much of an idea, according to Westermann.

It is not unusual for the abdominal cavity of a fetish figure to hold magical substances. Writing about African art Werner Schmalenbach said: "A [fetish] figure can be used as one only when it is charged with some magic content. . . . Every conceivable thing is used as a magic content: bits of bone, teeth, animal claws. . . . They are often placed in a cavity hollowed out in the head or belly, or, too, in a little horn on top of the head." Clearly, Westermann follows the African formula: the interior of his box is important even if we don't see it. This approach to sculpture is unlike anything we have seen in museums: the outer form is only part of the statement; the artist fabricates the visceral contents too. The craftsmanship and durability of Westermann's box tell us that he wants to make "real" beings who exist by virtue of their built-in equipment. The fact that their insides are filled with the debris of an afternoon at a baseball stadium is no more remarkable than the fact that our insides contain partly digested hotdogs, onions, and Coke.

**Kenny Scharf.** *Extravaganza Televisione.* **1984. Courtesy Tony Shafrazi Gallery, New York**

The ultimate box—a television set—adorned with Day-Glo stripes and plastic, kitschy add-ons. This could be a way of acknowledging the magic of our principal household shrine. Also, the frame can now compete with its contents.

# BEYOND CONSTRUCTIVISM: PRIMARY STRUCTURES

Under the influence of Constructivism, sculptors tend to discard figurative, gestural, and symbolic meanings. Instead, they employ materials and movement as if art were an extension of physics or engineering. At the same time, the penetration of solid forms goes forward, producing a breakdown of classical notions of form. Thus sculpture seems to be redefining itself; it is becoming a new type of visual inquiry—an exploration of mechanical and architectural space through primary structures.

Primary structures are not precious objects designed to be worshiped, admired in private, or employed as architectural adornments. Instead, they are the by-products of spatial investigations undertaken to discover the impact of large-scale forms on human awareness. Often they have an architectural look except that we live *with*, not *in*, them. They may appear to be abstract and impersonal but they have a strong physical presence: seeing these structures makes us feel the need to arrange ourselves around them.

Images of persons are rarely found in primary structures, but bodily responses to their openings and enclosures are intended. These kineasthetic responses are what abstract artists invoke when they insist that a humanistic art does not require figurative *representation*: they still compose with the perceptual and physiological behavior of human beings in mind.

Primary structuralists differ in the way they employ intuition or calculation in design. Often, they surrender the control of form to prepared number systems, equations, and formulas. For them, the computer looks especially attractive as a sculptural tool. Here we should remember that artists have sought a mathematical science of proportion since the ancient Greeks. Presumably, it saves work and is free of human idiosyncrasies. Of course, human idiosyncrasies can be aesthetically interesting, but that kind of aesthetics may be dead. Thus primary structuralists exhibit our perennial hope of finding *laws* of art—laws that can transcend the chaos of human thought and desire.

Today, labels like "serial sculpture," "systems sculpture," and "ABC art" are used to describe works that rely on simple arrangements of basic volumes and voids, mechanically produced surfaces, and algebraic permutations of form. The impact on the viewer, however, is anything but simple: architectural emotions are often involved because of the implied invitation to move under, around, and through a work. Still, the forms seem engineered rather than crafted, and tactile qualities are conspicuously absent. Of course, textures can be programmed by computer, but who knows whether that can produce the surfaces of a Rodin bronze or a Henry Moore carving? It all remains to be seen.

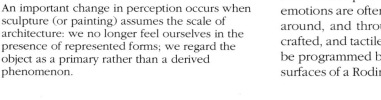

Ronald Bladen. *Cathedral Evening.* 1969. Wood, 10 × 29 × 24'. Albany Mall Project, Albany, New York

An important change in perception occurs when sculpture (or painting) assumes the scale of architecture: we no longer feel ourselves in the presence of represented forms; we regard the object as a primary rather than a derived phenomenon.

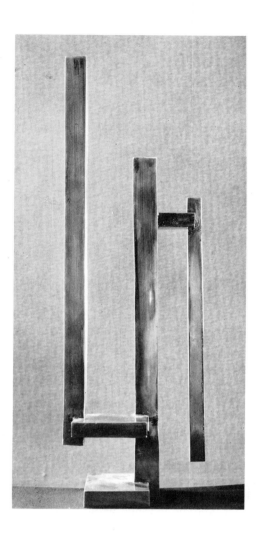

*left:* Georges Vantongerloo. *Construction y= 2x³– 13.5x²+ 21x.* 1935. Silver, 15⅛" high. Kunstmuseum, Basel

An early and austere example of sculpture created according to a mathematical equation. But notice the uncontrolled reflections, shimmers, and diffractions in the nickel-silver surfaces. Were they also planned?

*below:* Donald Judd. *Untitled.* 1968. Painted steel in eight sections, each 12 × 48 × 2". Collection Mr. and Mrs. Frederick B. Mayer, Denver

Through the absolute predictability of serial imagery, the sculptor tries to empty his forms of emotional and historical "debris." But then a conflict arises: these constructions occupy real space on a real planet whose gravity, atmosphere, and motion (night and day, dark and light) inevitably affect our perceptions of them.

Isamu Noguchi. *Floor Frame.* 1962. Bronze, 9½ × 34 × 26". Collection Mr. and Mrs. Robert A. Bernhard, Portchester, New York

Sculpture becomes the art of engineering a stately geometric twist, or of subjecting post-and-beam forms to diagonal stresses, seeming to bury and then resurrect them. Despite their monumental scale, these are humorous works.

Tony Smith. *Cigarette.* Conceived 1961, executed 1967. Cor-Ten steel, 15 × 18 × 26'. Albright-Knox Art Gallery, Buffalo, New York. Gift of the Seymour H. Knox Foundation, Inc., 1968

# KINETIC SCULPTURE

Sculpture-in-motion has a history as old as the Trojan horse and as recent as the figures that strike the hour in front of Macy's department store. We see it in the widely owned but aesthetically unmentionable Swiss clock, and in millions of spring-driven toys, quartz-driven watches, and transistorized household appliances. The combination of sculpture with mechanical motion occupied the best minds of the Renaissance, notably that of Leonardo da Vinci, who earned good fees by designing sculptural-mechanical toys for his princely patrons.

Leonardo also designed an early flying machine, repeating the mythic feat of the Greek sculptor Daedalus, who achieved successful flight but with disastrous results for his son Icarus. Icarus flew too close to the sun, which melted his wax wings; so the boy fell into the sea and drowned. This was how the ancients described the fate of men and women who try to usurp the prerogatives of gods. Daedalus may have been the mythical ancestor of all kinetic sculptors, since he also devised dolls with movable limbs for the daughters of the king of Sicily. (A great sculptor never gives up.) At any rate, the desire to make objects that move by themselves seems to live permanently in the sculptural imagination.

The mystery surrounding motion fascinates artists. Do we see form or do we see movement? Can we see energy? In kinetic sculpture, motion becomes a visual element like shape or color. As we know, the Futurists dedicated their art to the glorification of movement—especially mechanical movement—which they considered more beautiful than Greek sculpture. However, the Futurists were confined to the static conventions of painting and sculpture; motion was *represented* in their art but it did not become part of the art object itself.

In 1920 Naum Gabo created the first modern kinetic sculpture and exhibited it in Berlin. Then his brother, Antoine Pevsner, wrote their *Realist Manifesto*, which became the foundation statement for kinetic sculpture and Constructivist aesthetics: "We free ourselves from the thousand-year-old error of art, originating in Egypt, that only static rhythms can be its elements. We proclaim that for present-day perceptions the most important elements of art are the kinetic rhythms."

Richard Hunt. *Icarus.* 1956. Steel, 78 × 38". Albright-Knox Art Gallery, Buffalo, New York. Gift of Seymour H. Knox, 1959

In Hunt's sculpture, Icarus is supported from below. The original Icarus was not so lucky

*left:* Bruno Lucchesi. *Seated Woman # 2.* 1963. Bronze, 14½" high. Whereabouts unknown

*right:* Luciano Minguzzi. *Woman Jumping Rope.* 1954. Bronze, 70⅞" high. Collection Alfons Bach, Palm Beach

**MOTION SIMULATED IN STATIC SCULPTURE**

REAL MOTION BECOMES
PART OF SCULPTURE

Alexander Calder. *Red Gongs.* 1955. Sheet
aluminum, sheet brass, steel and wire, red paint,
12' long. The Metropolitan Museum of Art,
New York. Fletcher Fund, 1955

Gabo's work concentrated on constructions which penetrate volume and minimize mass, but he created few works that actually employ movement. It was an American sculptor, Alexander Calder, who created an art form in the 1930s—mobiles—in which motion is an integral part of the sculpture. Calder's mobiles are sensitively balanced, three-dimensional systems which move in response to the gentlest of air currents. While receiving their motive force from the invisible environment, the mobile's parts and subsystems travel in orbits that the sculptor has designed. The energy which actuates the system may be random, but the mobile's movement is anticipated, that is, shaped and controlled.

Calder's sculpture can be discussed as if it were static sculpture, but his original contribution was to make it possible to control the *quality* of movement. Seen in static terms, Calder's forms resemble those of Arp and Miró. Mostly, they are playful, biomorphic shapes reminiscent of fish, animals, and leaves. But his sculptural *movement* is unique. Some works suggest the stately sway of tree branches; others are as comic as Charlie Chaplin hopping and skipping his way down a street. Mobiles have enormous appeal—they have almost become an American folk art—because their control of motion seems to unlock one of life's great secrets. Perhaps the mobile and the animated film are America's greatest twentieth-century artistic achievements.

Rube Goldberg. Cartoon of an absurd machine.
Reprinted with special permission of King
Features Syndicate, Inc.

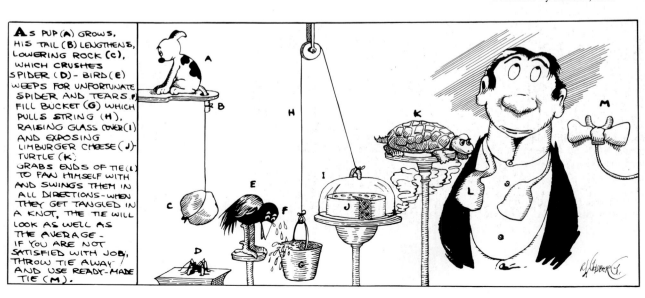

AS PUP (A) GROWS,
HIS TAIL (B) LENGTHENS,
LOWERING ROCK (C),
WHICH CRUSHES
SPIDER (D)- BIRD (E)
WEEPS FOR UNFORTUNATE
SPIDER AND TEARS F
FILL BUCKET (G) WHICH
PULLS STRING (H),
RAISING GLASS COVER (I)
AND EXPOSING
LIMBURGER CHEESE (J)-
TURTLE (K)
GRABS ENDS OF TIE (L)
TO FAN HIMSELF WITH
AND SWINGS THEM IN
ALL DIRECTIONS—WHEN
THEY GET TANGLED IN
A KNOT, THE TIE WILL
LOOK AS WELL AS
THE AVERAGE -
IF YOU ARE NOT
SATISFIED WITH JOB,
THROW TIE AWAY
AND USE READY-MADE
TIE (M).

*above:* Isamu Noguchi. *Big Boy.* 1952. Karatsu ware, 7⅞ × 6⅞". Collection, The Museum of Modern Art, New York. A. Conger Goodyear Fund

Noguchi's little person, though static, aims at the same dynamism as the swinging-girl whistle.

*above right:* **Effigy whistle: Girl on swing.** Remojadas region, Veracruz, Mexico. 7th–9th century. Ceramic, 9¾ × 10". The Metropolitan Museum of Art, New York. The Michael C. Rockefeller Memorial Collection. Bequest of Nelson A. Rockefeller, 1979.

**Examples of Kinetic Sculpture**   The machine as an idea and a permanent presence inevitably attracts artists. For kinetic sculptors mechanical motion is especially interesting; the problem is how to use it artistically. Some kinetic sculptures are themselves machines, intended only to exhibit their operation. They are different from real machines in that they perform no "serious" work. The cartoonist Rube Goldberg (1883–1970) humorously exploited this idea: he would "invent" an incredibly complex apparatus to do a minor job like swatting flies or sprinkling salt on French fries. His cartoons had a serious side: they showed how our love affair with machines had reached the stage

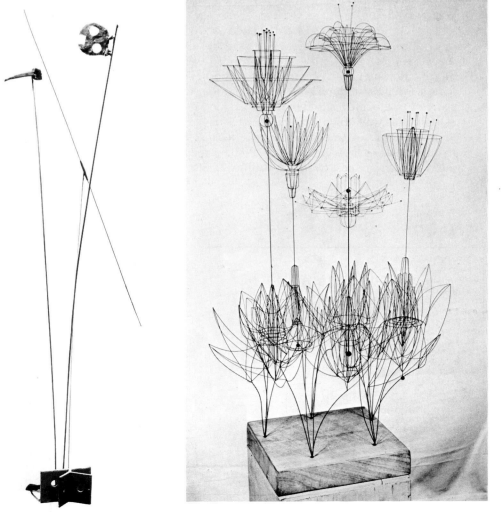

*right:* Takis. *Signal Rocket.* 1955. Painted steel and iron, 48" high, at base 5¼ × 5". Collection, The Museum of Modern Art, New York. Mrs. Charles V. Hickox Fund

*far right:* Konstantin Milonadis. *Flower Garden.* 1961. Collection Dr. and Mrs. Malcolm A. McCannel, Minneapolis

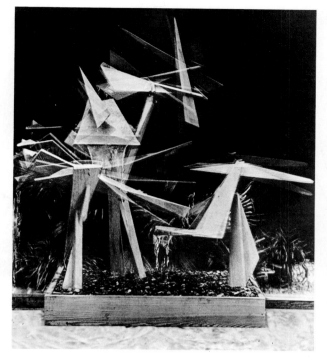

Arthur Secunda. *Music Machine.* 1964–65. Mixed media. Whereabouts unknown

*below:* Lin Emery. *Homage to Amercreo (Aquamobile).* 1964. Pine, 6' high. American Creosote Works, Inc., New Orleans

of disenchantment: mechanization can be perfect and absurd at the same time.

Arthur Secunda's *Music Machine* achieves a kind of Goldbergian absurdity. We see an operational sculpture consisting of gilded wood, metal, and machine parts built around a music box. Associations with the mechanics of sound are abetted by radio antennae, a built-in xylophone, a guitar handle, and a variety of electronic odds and ends. Gears, springs, wires, and so on are exposed in an effort to produce visual poetry with mechanized innards. There is also a hint of human irony in the suggestion that a musician is a machine wired to make noise.

We see a more practical kinetic sculpture in Lin Emery's *Homage to Amercreo,* a mobile fountain whose forms fill with water until they tilt over, empty themselves, and return to be filled again. The work functions as a machine, but its mechanical action shows the visual delight we can get from abstract forms doing a job clearly and efficiently. The same virtue can be seen in many of our mechanical contrivances. Of course, the purpose of a fountain is to create visual entertainment with moving water, and that can lead to some strange spectacles. Perhaps we should be grateful that Emery's fountain is not populated with sea nymphs and dolphins acting out an ancient Greek soap opera.

*Study: Falling Man (Figure on Bed)* by Ernst Trova consists of an aluminum figure strapped to a circular apparatus with mechanical-experimental overtones. The work is frightening because the apparatus is so obviously calculated to carry out some sort of dehumanizing operation. Trova's man is usually urban and middle-aged—swaybacked, faceless, slightly paunchy, and curiously without arms. He could be the mannequin used in an autocrash experiment. Trova's image of man would be an ideal subject for clinical experimentation, but we do not know *the purpose* of the experiment. Will he be rocked and rotated like an astronaut undergoing an exercise in weightlessness? Will his manhood survive? In another work, *Study: Falling Man (Landscape #1),* Trova offers three versions of the same person, once again involved with mechanical equipment. His nakedness, high-tech accessories, and shiny aluminum skin eerily evoke that depersonalized humanity de-

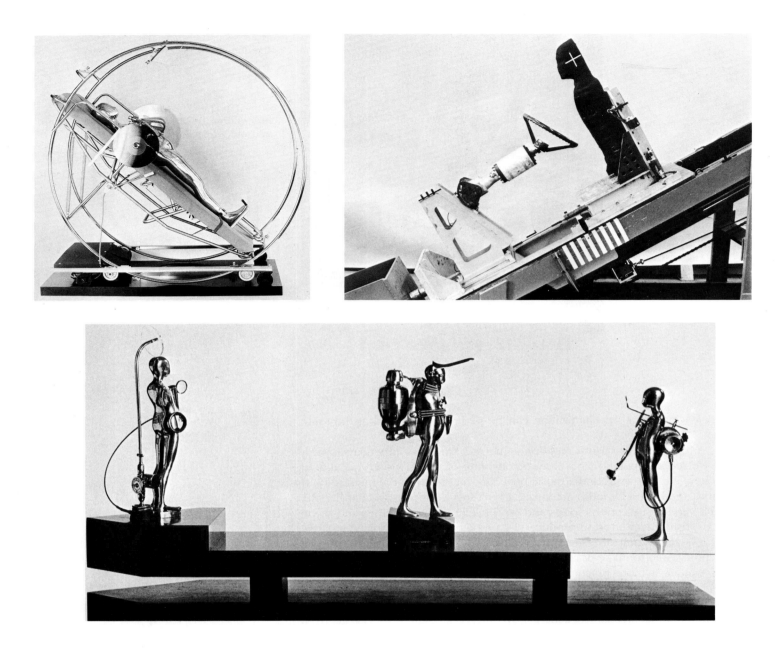

scribed by George Orwell in his not-so-fantastic novel, *1984.* This harmless creature is about to participate in some remarkable maneuvers. Will he fly? Or will the equipment fly him?

Jean Tinguely's kinetic sculptures are mechanical poems about the absurdity of machines and of a civilization governed by machines. His *Homage to New York* was a type of mechanized Happening. In addition to the battered piano mentioned earlier, it contained drums, bicycle wheels, Coke bottles, a typewriter, a drawing machine, and a weather balloon. Fifteen rickety motors powered the shabbily constructed affair, which was designed to make music, create drawings, write reports, give birth to machine babies, and finally to set itself on fire and "die." The noise, the drawings, the typed reports, and the frenzied activity were aimless, in true Dada fashion. But *Homage* had an aim: suicide. This machine was really a junkyard parody of contemporary culture.

The short career of *Homage* was witnessed by a distinguished audience in the garden of the Museum of Modern Art on March 17, 1960. Contrary to

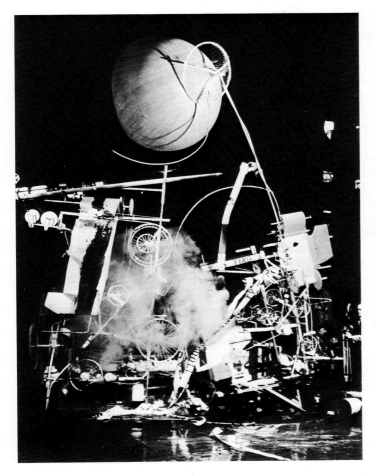

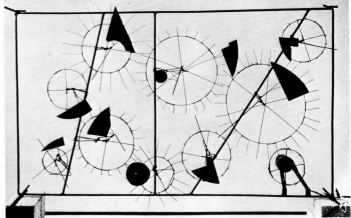

Jean Tinguely. *Méta-Mécanique*. 1954. Museum of Fine Arts, Houston. Purchased with funds donated by Dominique and John de Menil

*left:* Jean Tinguely. *Homage to New York*. 1960. Self-destroyed March 17, 1960, in the garden of The Museum of Modern Art, New York

expectations, the machine did not destroy itself as planned, so Tinguely and the fire department intervened to set it on the path to self-immolation. With their aid, the whole whirring, flapping thing began to smoke; at last it exploded into flame. The "useful" life of *Homage* was ended with a fire extinguisher.

Because of its brief existence, *Homage to New York*, like Kaprow's Happenings, may belong to theater more than sculpture. However, Tinguely has also created works which do not self-destruct. *Méta-Mécanique* exhibits his fascination with bicycle wheels, discarded metal parts, and belt-driven systems for transmitting energy. In general, Tinguely's kinetic sculptures move and sound like a one-man band, with motors substituting for the frantic musician. They thump and pound, oscillate and vibrate, producing to-and-fro alternations or ongoing cycles. In *Homage*, soft-drink bottles were endlessly sent down an inclined plane—but not to be packed, delivered, and sold; they were meant to self-destruct in a single crashing finale. Tinguely was making a statement.

From Greek water clocks to Leonardo's mechanized entertainments for the Duke of Milan, to Calder's mobiles, to Rube Goldberg's crazy inventions, to Tinguely's automated disasters: it has been a long kinetic voyage. Tinguely's machines never caught up with modern, electronically guided tools; they look more like the stuff that filled the bicycle shop of Orville and Wilbur Wright. Today, the old mechanical noise and clutter have been replaced by quieter and more efficient tools of automation. Perhaps that is why *Méta-Mécanique* is not frightening but quaint, like antique spinning wheels and sculpture that stands still.

# SCULPTURE AND THE CRAFTS

For two generations, at least, the crafts have been seeking a divorce from useful manufacture, trying to strengthen their claims to fine-art status. They may have begun as useful art forms, but they are increasingly prized for their nonutilitarian values. Handmade ceramic pots, for example, cannot compete economically with mass-produced containers made of metal, glass, or plastics. Yet, they continue to be made by potters, exhibited in museums, sold in department stores, and purchased by collectors. Clearly, they satisfy aesthetic as well as utilitarian needs. Pots are frequently made with no intention of functioning as containers. The potter's wheel has become a tool of sculpture.

Peter Voulkos (born 1924) has been a leader in exploring the expressive possibilities of forms developed by potters. His *Gallas Rock*, which was created by combining hand-built pottery forms, has the quality of a sculptural assemblage. The act of putting these forms together—or crushing them against each other—produces the kind of violent excitement we associate with action painting. Indeed, Voulkos might be regarded as an "action potter." He has made the crucial move away from the pot as container: the footing is lost, the handles and spouts are gone, the holes and hollows survive as sculptural space.

Similarly, jewelry and metalwork, silversmithing and enameling, look like small-scale sculpture practiced with special materials. Woodworking in combination with metal, fabric, or leather falls into the same sculptural category. The same is true of glassmaking and textile fiber construction. Clearly, the crafts have emerged from their "previous condition of servitude." This liberating development is welcome if craftsmen can get better prices for

Peter Voulkos. *Gallas Rock*. 1959–60. Fired clay, 9" high. Dr. and Mrs. Digby Gallas, Los Angeles

**Bruce Kokko. *Paint Can with Brush*. 1965. Whereabouts unknown**

A ceramic "craft" object that violates all the craft ideals: it can't be used; the paint spills are very uncraftsman-like; and the "truth to materials" principle is ignored.

**Roger Lucas. *Three-finger ring*. 1969**

Without a visual cue to its scale, this ring might easily be mistaken for a monumental sculpture.

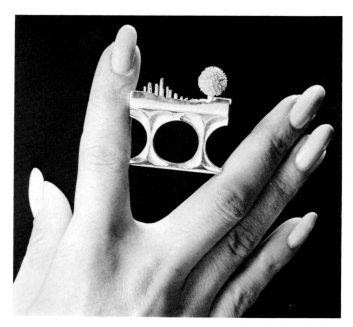

their work. And if sculptors are encouraged to pay more attention to craft, that, too, is welcome. But if our objects of daily use are left to the tender mercies of engineers, we may have cause for regret.

**Beyond the Museum: Earth Sculpture**   We know that almost everything *in* the environment has been designed by men and women. Now, many artists want to work *on* the environment. Directly. Their "environment" is more than the local space of human communities; it is the land, water, and air that make up our planet. Like civil engineers they try to shape the earth. Natural land and space become materials for a new kind of sculpture: earthworks, sky-works, and waterworks.

Today, a sculpture can be a cliff wrapped in canvas, a hole in a park, a trench in the desert, some stones piled on a gallery floor, shafts of light in the sky, or floating, luminescent gas bags made of plastic. Like Happenings, these objects, places, and events are usually too large, fragile, or temporary to be experienced directly. But we can see pictures of them or read about them. Earthworks can be commissioned, but they are difficult to buy, hard to see, and meaningless to own. Most of them can't be exhibited in museums. And that is the point: earthworks express disdain for museums and galleries; they satirize commodity ownership. The artist issues certificates testifying to the ownership of a piece of an earthwork, just as a broker sells certificates for shares in cotton, grain futures, or pork bellies. We never see the pork bellies we have bought, but we know they exist.

The growth of ecological concern in our time has stimulated artistic thinking in terms of planet-wide ecosystems; we wonder what we can do for, or to, the biosphere, the noosphere, and the atmosphere. Thus, immense creative vistas open up for the artist: perhaps earth sculpture represents the beginning of a marvelous new synthesis between human forming capacities and the earth sciences. Thus far, however, earth sculpture appears to be a type of antiart—a gesture of disillusionment with art institutions and boredom with the artistic traditions of usefulness, object-ness, and visual meaning on a comprehensible scale. From an airplane, farmland looks better.

Otto Piene. Stage of *Manned Helium Sculpture,* one of three days of "Citything Sky Ballet," Pittsburgh. 1970

*left:* Michael Heizer. *Isolated Mass/Circumflex.* 1968. Massacre Dry Lake, Nevada

These earthworks have little to do with the ecological ethic emerging today. They are meaningful mainly with reference to what they reject: the traditional scale, materials, and purposes of art.

*below:* Dennis Oppenheim. *Annual Rings.* Aerial photograph of the frozen St. John River at Fort Kent, Maine, the time-zone and international boundary between the U.S. and Canada. 1968. Courtesy Mr. and Mrs. Kelly Anderson

*below:* Mary Miss. *Field Rotation.* 1981. Wood, steel, gravel, and earth on 5-acre site. Governors' University, Park Forest South, Illinois

Here is a carefully designed, more-or-less permanent structure, which is not meant to function as shelter or as any other kind of architecture. Its main purpose is to make us think about the shape, direction, and fullness of a large piece of earth space. Perhaps it should be called "outside sculpture from the inside."

Alan Saret. *Untitled.* 1969–70. Galvanized chicken wire, 6' high. Art Gallery of Ontario, Toronto

Dirt, assorted trash, and industrial waste have been dumped where they are not supposed to be. We are invited to examine them sympathetically—not as something to get rid of.

Robert Morris. *Earthwork.* Installed in the Dwan Gallery, 1968. Courtesy Leo Castelli Gallery, New York

Robert Smithson. *Nonsite.* 1968. Painted wood bins filled with rocks, 16½ × 82". Collection Virginia Dwan, New York

Through the progressive design of the containers for these rocks, Smithson expresses a forming and not merely a collecting intention. Perhaps the rocks were too anonymous without their shaped enclosures.

## CONCLUSION

It can truly be said of sculpture that in the midst of change there is abiding sameness. Magic and sorcery survive even though materials and techniques have undergone radical transformations. Through all its innovations in form and concept, sculpture has retained its identity as an art of physical materials occupying real space, operating in real time, persuading us to believe in the aliveness of its forms. In the history of sculpture, the pursuit of vitality remains constant.

Sculpture may have lost volume and mass—from the monolith to the metal filament; but it has gained in motion—from the static statuary of ancient Egypt to the kinetic sculpture of the twentieth century. Today we find sculpture knocking at the door of physics: think of what lasers and holography may do. But it is interesting that Gabo, Pevsner, and Moholy-Nagy—artists with strong scientific interests—were increasingly attracted to the sensuous qualities of materials as their careers unfolded. It seems that three-dimensional media make powerful tactile claims—claims that cannot be denied. In other words, sculpture is an art that involves us in physical reality; it forces us to celebrate the world in concrete form. The substance must precede the idea.

Pratt & Whitney RL10 rocket engine, from advertisement for United Aircraft Corporation. 1969. Courtesy Cunningham & Walsh, Inc., New York

The resemblance is accidental, of course. Still, those exhausts look like snakes, and the whole engine has a humanoid look. Why? Because this is the sculpture of the twentieth century. Our technology inspires faith: we want to believe in it.

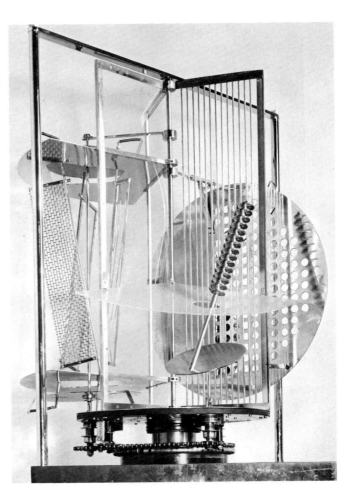

László Moholy-Nagy. *Light-Space Modulator.* 1923–30. Busch-Reisinger Museum, Harvard University, Cambridge, Massachusetts

Seventy years ago, Moholy-Nagy anticipated many of today's experiments with light-and-motion sculpture. His machine is not only a working device but also a kinetic sculpture.

*Snake Goddess.* c. 1600 B.C. Faience, 13½" high. Heraklion Museum, Crete

*opposite above:* Magdalena Abakanowicz with her sculpture, *Women.* 1985. Burlap and resin, 67 × 19¾ × 4". Courtesy Xavier Fourcade, Inc., New York

Headless, armless figures seen only from the back. They look like mummies, unwrapped after waiting thousands of years to be brought back to life. By using organic materials that have the capacity to age, wrinkle, and decay, and by placing the figures on the same floor we stand on, Abakanowicz draws us into their company—the company of the dead. Seeing sculpture becomes a funereal rite.

*opposite left:* Arnaldo Pomodoro. *Large Sphere.* 1966–67. Cast bronze, 12' diameter. Mt. Sinai Hospital, New York

Further evidence of the powerful attraction that contemporary sculpture has, not only for craftsmen but also for industrial designers.

*opposite right:* Francesco Bocola. Quasar lamp. 1970

# CHAPTER THIRTEEN

# ARCHITECTURE

Buildings result from the interaction of many factors: site, climate, function, client, building codes, workmanship. For any given structure, one or more of these factors can assume crucial importance. But all of them must be considered in the solution of an architectural problem. We see the physical result but rarely know the priorities which affected the architectural solution. Indeed, it would be impossible to know all the facts about a building's design and construction. However, it *is* possible to know the materials and devices available to architects and to understand how they work.

Architecture relies on structural devices like arches, domes, and trusses, which can be made of materials like wood, stone, or steel. These devices are basic because they shape the space a building encloses. Materials are important, too, because they determine how structural devices operate. For example, a truss can be made of wood or metal; a post can be made of stone or steel. Different materials require different dimensions to do the same job; hence, the visual results depend on the materials and devices the architect chooses.

The art of architecture emerges in the quality of these choices. There are usually several ways to support weight, enclose space, admit light, or finish a surface. So architects have to make their choices in the light of *an idea*—usually an idea about the way shaped spaces affect people. (Churchill once said, "We shape our houses and then they shape us.") If architects did not have to make human choices, their services could be performed by computers, and architecture would not be an art. Alas, some buildings look as if they were designed by computers: impersonal solutions have been used again and again; everyone's convenience (except the building's users) has been served. Perhaps the standardization of materials and construction processes is responsible for our architectural monotony. Certainly, the *great* modern buildings show that every architectural problem is unique and that design alternatives always exist.

## THE CLASSIC MATERIALS

The earliest builders used materials that were close at hand and in good supply. Then, as now, building devices and techniques resulted from a combination of ingenuity and the inherent possibilities of available material.

Detail of Stonehenge, Salisbury Plain, Wiltshire, England. c. 2000 B.C. Approx. 13' high

Today, the African villager builds with sticks, mud, and grass because these are the most profuse materials in the environment. For the same reason, Eskimos build an ice igloo when they settle down for the winter. On the move, they construct with reindeer skins and bone, much as American Indians built tepees with wooden poles and animal hides. The igloo is a domical structure resting over an excavation in the ice; in a way it solves the same problem as Michelangelo's dome of St. Peter's. The Indian's tepee is a type of portable housing which, as architectural form, is surely superior to a modern auto trailer. As for the African grass hut—a cone-shaped roof resting on a cylindrical base—it would be hard to surpass aesthetically.

During the great periods of Egyptian and Greek architecture, stone was the favored material. But the Mesopotamians had little stone, so they used brick and glazed tile. In most places, wood preceded stone as a building material; it served as a supporting framework for "curtain-walls" of fiber and mud. The earliest peoples reserved stone for religious and commemorative purposes, as in their mighty *menhir* statues (upright stones in which departed spirits lived) and *dolmens* ("table" slabs resting on upright stones and used as altars or open tombs). Stone construction grew more complex in the *cromlech*—a circular arrangement of menhirs around a dolmen; it probably served religious and astrological purposes. Oriented toward the sun (as at Stonehenge), the cromlech may have been the architectural ancestor of all our temples, churches, and mosques.

It is important to recognize ecological influences on the beginnings of architecture. Egypt had an abundance of granite plus a great river, the Nile, along which heavy stone could be transported to construction sites. The wood of native palm trees was weak and the importation of stronger woods

Moroccan picnic hut. Courtesy Hispanic Society of America, New York. Anderson Spalding Collection

Even basketry has been used in architecture. Notice the progressive rhythm of the geometric forms and the textural interest produced by the woven fibers. The combination is aesthetically pleasing, and it lets in light and air, too.

Detail of court, Temple of Amon-Mut-Khonsu, Luxor, Egypt. c. 1390 B.C.

was too expensive; so the Egyptians used stone roof lintels instead of timbered ceilings. But stone cannot span very wide spaces, so their interiors look like forests of columns.

Working with little more than the lever, the pulley, and the inclined plane, the Egyptian builders had thousands of efficient human engines in their slaves. For the pharaohs, it was economical to raise grain in the fertile Nile valley, feed it to peasants, and exploit their labor for a lifetime longer than that of a modern machine. Our civilization would rather convert grain into alcohol and use it as fuel to operate machines. Of course, power machinery had not been invented in 3000 B.C. But remember, too, that slavery discourages invention.

The classic materials—wood, stone, and brick—tell us a great deal about the civilizations that use them. In examining their availability and working properties we discover a number of interesting connections between architecture, economics, and politics.

**Wood**  Wood appears in nature as a structural material rather than an inert mass like stone. Its distribution in all but the most arid regions and its strength and adaptability to tooling enable it to compete with many specialized materials. It can be a covering surface or a structural member, but its grain—the principal source of wood's beauty—also accounts for its structural unreliability. In the natural state, wood varies in strength; consequently, wood construction requires wide safety factors: large dimensions and frequent reinforcement to prevent failure due to hidden defects.

American building has always been lavish in its use of wood, but the disappearance of the frontier and the development of competing materials will probably reduce the excessive use of wood. Still, wood has distinct disadvantages. (1) It is highly combustible; consider the magnificent Scandinavian and Russian churches that have been lost because of fire. (2) Wood is highly responsive to temperature and moisture changes; its dimensions are not stable. Joints loosen and nails shift as wood dries out and shrinks. (3) Wood is an organic material, so it is subject to attack by rot, fungus, and insects.

Some of these liabilities have been overcome by technology. For example, plywood made of wood veneers glued together at right angles cancels out the tendency to warp. Wood veneers, made by a rotary shaving of the log, constitute a very economical use of the raw material. Also, plywood is more consistently uniform in strength than natural wood; it can be used in skeletal structures or in stressed skin and shell structures. In general, plywood is remarkably light for its strength—especially useful in the construction of small and medium-size buildings. A recent invention—laminated wooden beams—opens up a wide array of architectural possibilities. Indeed, plywood, molded wood, pressed wood, and fiberboard constitute wholly new building materials—a far cry from the tree.

*left:* **Smith & Williams. Detail of plywood supports, Congregational Church, California City. 1964**

Smooth, slender, and graceful, these curved plywood supports are amazingly strong for their weight. They create an upward-striving effect in contrast to the coarse, earthbound masonry wall on the inside.

*below:* **Church of Lazarus, Kizhi Island, U.S.S.R. 14th century**

Wood is warm in color, flexible in form, but, alas, combustible.

*above:* Stone wall built by the Incas in Cuzco, Peru

*right:* Masayuki Nagare. Wall of the Japan Pavilion, New York World's Fair. 1964

Traditional stone masonry technique employed in a contemporary setting.

*below:* Harbeson, Hough, Livingston & Larson. The Sam Rayburn House Office Building, Washington, D.C. 1965

**Stone** Our ancestors originally found shelter in the mouths of caves and under stone ledges. They used stone for their tools and weapons and kindled their first fires within stone enclosures. The stone fireplace is still a symbol of safety and warmth in dwellings that otherwise bear no resemblance to a cave. Heavy and virtually indestructible, stone was probably the first material used to commemorate the dead. But piling up stones was not, strictly speaking, building. *Construction* with stone began with the building of so-called Cyclopean walls—made by placing rough stones on top of each other, a type of masonry in which sheer weight and bulk produce a crude form of stability. When satisfactory cutting tools were developed, it became possible to shape and fit stones to create true masonry. It was then feasible to build stone shelters—not only for the dead but for the living.

The earliest construction employed no mortar; instead, stone blocks were carefully fitted together. A knife blade could not be inserted into the joints of the masonry used to face the pyramids. The same is true of the stone walls built by the Incas of Peru. The Greeks did not develop mortar until the Hellenistic period, so they used metal dowels and clamps to prevent their marble blocks from shifting. The use of stone masonry with mortar was a great advance: the precision of dry masonry was no longer needed, and greater resistance to shifting became possible. The weight and bulk of stones joined by mortar created a structural fabric of tremendous durability.

But stone is heavy, costly to transport, and expensive to erect. Like brick, it is rarely used in modern building as a structural material. Mostly, stone and marble veneers are laid over steel, concrete, or cinder-block structures. For us, stone masonry is a cosmetic operation—a long way from the pure stone engineering of the pyramids, the Parthenon, or the Romanesque and Gothic cathedrals. The Romans may have been the first large-scale builders to use stone or marble slabs as a veneer over brick or rubble masonry. The Babylonians used what little stone they had for statuary but followed a practice similar to veneering by facing brick walls with glazed tiles at key locations.

Today, stone has enormous prestige; great cities and important buildings must exhibit large expanses of it. The Sam Rayburn House Office Building for the House of Representatives is an example; it cost between eighty and one hundred million dollars, mostly because of the simulated classical masonry that covers it. Almost universally regarded as an architectural disaster, one critic said that it is "not only the most expensive building of its kind in the world but probably also its ugliest." The lesson here is that poor design cannot be rescued by mountains of marble and limestone.

**Brick** Lacking fuel to fire brick, and living in an arid land where wood was scarce, the Sumerians made sun-dried bricks much like the adobe bricks of the Southwestern American Indians. Even in a dry climate, however, the "mud-brick" wall erodes easily and needs to be repaired regularly. Fired brick, however, is durable and maintenance-free. Brick is really a type of artificial stone with several advantages over natural stone: cheapness, standardized dimensions, uniform strength and lightness, a wide range of color and texture, and adaptability to mass-production.

Since brick is a ceramic material, it looks like a mosaic when laid up in a wall. Although it is a structural material, brick is most commonly used as a veneer. So it really *is* a mosaic—a type of wall "painting." Today, brickwork is valued for its color and texture as well as its association with skilled hand fabrication. Because it is such an ancient material, and because of its warm

*left:* The Mission of St. Francis of Assisi, Taos, New Mexico. 1772–1816

*below:* Spiral minaret of Samarra, Iraq. 9th century

SUN-DRIED BRICK

colors and weather-resistant qualities, brick inspires confidence: viewers know that a brick wall has been laboriously built by tried and true methods.

But brick walls are expensive, and their mortar joints are a problem. A large proportion of a brick wall consists of joints which require careful hand labor and are subject to more shrinkage than brick itself. Also brick walls are fabricated slowly, and for large buildings an elaborate scaffolding is required. That is why metal panels are increasingly used for the exterior walls of tall structures. Finally, brick provides good sound insulation, but like stone it transmits dampness unless combined with additional insulating material.

In the stone and brick architecture of Egypt and Mesopotamia the amount of interior space compared to the amount of overall volume was very low. To us, this type of construction is inefficient and appalling in its social implications: it shows how slave labor inhibits architectural imagination. Perhaps the ratio of interior space to overall volume in the architecture of any civilization is an index of its people's freedom. Today's light, thin-walled buildings create interior space almost equal to a building's overall volume. So, aside from aesthetic considerations, architecture tells us something about the valuation placed on human labor, since space is a good reflection of the wages paid to artisans.

To say that wood, stone, and brick are classic materials does not mean they have disappeared from contemporary architecture. They continue to be used, but less frequently for structural reasons: their contribution is largely symbolic, since they have lost most of their weight-bearing functions. The classic materials may linger awhile in small-scale domestic dwellings, but even there, glass, steel, aluminum, and plastics are supplanting them. Yesterday's structural material becomes today's aesthetic adornment.

## DESIGN IN THE URBAN ENVIRONMENT

**Piazza San Marco, Venice. Begun 1063**

Underlying the visual pleasure of the piazza is a governing proportion that can be felt only by people on foot—citizens standing, walking, and talking to each other. A marvelously exhilarating arrangement of buildings and open space, it depends on a scale that encourages human modes of watching, moving, and meeting.

**Rockefeller Center, New York. 1931–37**

Compared with the Venetians, who built horizontally, the Americans
build vertically. They have to; horizontal space is very, very expensive.
So they invented the skyscraper. The only way urban spaces can be
created is by enclosing shopping areas with monumental steel and
concrete slabs. The result is a new kind of grandeur—clean and rational
but somewhat bland.

**John Portman and Associates. Interior, Plaza Hotel, Renaissance Center, Detroit. 1977**

An interior space that has many of the qualities of an outdoor park: shrubs, pools, and hanging vegetation, plus cantilevered trees and natural light filtering down between concrete columns and curving ramps. The main excitement comes from the spectacular overhead spaces and the sight of people moving up, down, and around at different levels in an enormous light well.

**Bertrand Goldberg Associates. Marina City, Chicago. 1964**

Here is Chicago's pragmatic solution to the storage of automobiles (in the first eighteen stories of each Marina City tower), the storage of people (in the rest of the tower), the control of traffic, and even the flow of the Chicago River. These towers generate the feeling of masculine vigor celebrated in Carl Sandburg's poetry about the city with "broad shoulders."

*opposite:* **John Jerde & Associates. Horton Plaza, San Diego, California. 1985**

How to keep shoppers downtown. Instead of an enclosed shopping mall, the Horton Plaza architects redesigned a substantial portion of the inner city, retaining its crooked streets, sharply angled spaces, and jazzy imagery. The colors are deliberately dirty pastels or ochers; the shapes are large, bold geometrics; the styles, a blend of everything imaginable. Typically American.

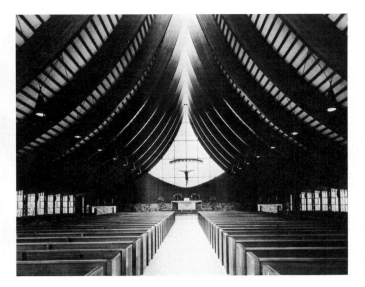

*above:* Prefabricated stack houses in housing project in Israel. 1965

Reinforced-concrete rooms, cast on the site, are lifted into place.

*right:* Interior, the shrine chapel of Our Lady of Orchard Lake, Michigan. 1963

Laminated wood beams.

## MODERN MATERIALS

Steel, concrete, and glass are old materials, but their structural use is comparatively new. The Romans mixed stone rubble with mortar to construct walls, a practice which was really an extension of masonry. But the use of *poured* or *cast* concrete reinforced with steel rods is entirely different. Similarly, the tempered-steel weapons of medieval warriors have little in common with the rolled-steel I-beams of today's steel-frame construction. As for the opalescent glass bottles of ancient Egypt, they are only distantly related to the sheets of plate glass used in modern steel and concrete structures.

Architecture has been transformed by these "new" materials because specialized techniques of mass manufacture can produce a superior product at reasonable cost. Today, factory manufacture can reduce costs and improve quality; ironically, the handcraft operations that survive in building are associated with waste, uneven quality, and frequent delays. Now structures of reinforced-concrete are formed at the building site, although many concrete beams and slabs are factory-produced like steel beams. Even so, ferroconcrete construction is not a handcraft process in the classical sense; it is better described as manufacturing at the site.

Laminated wooden beams have to be manufactured in a factory and carried to the site. Here again, the techniques of bending and gluing wood were known in antiquity, but the old animal-skin glues cannot compare with today's powerful adhesives. As a result, we have the technology to exploit the lightness, strength, and resilience of wood in continuously curved, load-bearing members which are exceptionally graceful. They permit the spanning of large spaces without interior supports, creating some of the structural excitement we see in Gothic stone arches. Laminated beams and arches are monolithic, too, so they can be erected by cranes, thus avoiding the complex scaffolding of stone masonry. The warmth of wood, the pattern of its grain, and the rhythmic effect created by repeated laminations make these beams very attractive. And they are practical for homes as well as churches and auditoriums.

**Cast Iron**  Cast iron was the first metal substitute for wooden posts and stone columns. It has characteristics similar to stone: great strength and weight; but it is brittle and it develops internal strains as the iron cools in its mold. However, cast iron made it possible to erect tall buildings without prohibitively thick walls. During the second half of the nineteenth century, huge yet delicate structures were built with prefabricated cast-iron columns and beams. Often, they imitated the stone masonry of Italian Renaissance buildings, which accounts for the magnificent factory and warehouse facades built during the 1850s. Today, we are desperately trying to preserve these buildings (they make good artists' lofts) to show the delicacy of a material that used to be considered ugly.

**George Herbert Wyman. Interior, Bradbury Building, Los Angeles. 1893**

Here we see cast iron employed structurally and decoratively at the same time. The effect may seem Victorian, but it is really an elegant demonstration of the delicacy and strength that could be achieved by a sensitive designer using a new building material.

*below:* **Louis Sullivan. Main Entrance, Carson Pirie Scott Department Store, Chicago. 1899–1904**

Sullivan said that form follows function, but he interpreted "function" very liberally. The cast-iron foliage that decorates this building functions visually and psychologically but not structurally.

SUSPENSION-BRIDGE ENGINEERING APPLIED
TO ARCHITECTURAL DESIGN

*above:* Eero Saarinen. Dulles Airport, Chantilly,
Virginia. 1962

*right:* Pier Luigi Nervi. Detail of Burgo Paper
Mill, Mantua, Italy. 1964

SUSPENSION STRUCTURES IN ARCHITECTURE

Cast iron set the stage for steel-skeleton construction in the railroad sheds, exhibition halls, and libraries of the nineteenth century. Bridge engineers appreciated iron and steel better than architects, who had used iron structurally (as in the dome of the United States Capitol) but made sure to conceal it. Even today, few architects are willing to expose structural steel. When cast iron was brought out of hiding, it was often given a form based on stone or wood. Since cast iron is a plastic material like concrete, it lends itself to a variety of derivative shapes. So it has been fair game for some questionable sculptural impulses. The ornamental cast-iron columns of the Art Nouveau designers, for example, use the material to imitate terra-cotta panels or High Gothic stone filigree. The engineers Paxton, Roebling, and Eiffel used metal more authentically. Their aesthetic contribution to building was to design metal structures that could excite the emotions while performing a practical function.

Suspension bridges made of rope and wood have been used since prehistoric times, but it was nineteenth-century suspension engineering that revealed the structural and aesthetic possibilities of metal under tension. Thus modern designers like Pier Luigi Nervi (1891–1979) and Eero Saarinen employed suspension engineering to create superb interior spaces. Joseph Paxton's (1801–1865) Crystal Palace, built for the London Exposition of 1851, was made of prefabricated wrought- and cast-iron units and glass panes. They were manufactured throughout England and bolted together on the site, one story at a time. The result was the largest structure in the world, enclosing seventeen acres under one roof; yet its construction time was six months. The building was easily dismantled when the Exposition was over and erected again at another site, where it stood until 1935.

Paxton's use of an iron skeleton anticipated today's riveting and welding of prefabricated steel components into a cagelike structure. He showed that the manufacture of standardized parts for on-site assembly was practical and economical. Masonry domes and vaults, whose strength depended on mass (plus iron chains embedded in their mortar), could now be replaced by thin membranes of concrete or glass. Structural strength could be achieved by substituting lightness and precision for heaviness and bulk.

**AESTHETIC PROBLEMS IN IRON-AND-STEEL CONSTRUCTION**

Gustave Eiffel. A joint of the Eiffel Tower, Paris, 1889

Eduardo Torroja. A joint of the Tordera Bridge

Sir Joseph Paxton. The Crystal Palace, London.
1851

**Structural Steel**   The principles of skeleton construction, known as "Chicago construction," were developed with iron. This work, which led to the development of the skyscraper, was carried out with a wrought-iron or rolled-iron framework. Iron I-beams were a great improvement over cast-iron columns, but iron is not as strong as steel (particularly under tension). Accordingly, high-rise iron structures (above twelve or fifteen stories) were impractical; so steel completely replaced iron in modern construction.

The cost of steel per pound is higher than that of any other structural material. Therefore, steel beams are designed in shapes that exploit the material's strength while keeping down its weight. The I-shaped beam is most common because its sections can be quite thin while resisting forces that try to break it. But large structural members like trusses and built-up girders cannot be manufactured in the form of a single rolled-steel beam; they have to be assembled—usually in the form of latticework—to reduce weight and take advantage of steel's tensile strength. This produces visually complex geometric openings and weblike patterns of metal. From a distance, such openings and patterns seem quite poetic, but when seen close up they look harsh. Indeed, when we think of engineering as the enemy of art, we are probably remembering some defiantly ugly piece of steel construction.

But the technology of steel manufacture and fabrication has advanced in response to the competition of other structural materials. Today, welded steel connections yield cleaner joints and better continuity within a structural system. Also, tubular, extruded, and corrugated steel products have opened up new visual possibilities. A few architects have used exposed steel construction with considerable sensitivity, but covering steel with other materials is more common: skins of brick, marble, stone, and glass are used because their colors, textures, and historical associations seem more acceptable.

Oddly enough, the versatility of steel-cage construction creates problems for designers, especially in skyscrapers: they do not know what to emphasize. Should the building look like a box, a canister, a honeycomb, or a crystal? Is it a tower or a layer cake? In 1921 Mies van der Rohe proposed a circular steel-and-glass skyscraper; in 1963 Gropius helped design a huge slab with tapered ends—the Pan Am Building—but not many people like it. Van der Rohe's glass skyscraper was not accepted, but many circular towers have since been built. One of the most successful is Lake Point Tower in Chicago, a modern version of Mies's earlier proposal. Today, steel construction still dominates high-rise architecture; its flexibility has inspired a great deal of experimentation with rooftop forms. But when exciting horizontal space is called for, when we want an arena, a chapel, or an air terminal, the best buildings seem to be made of concrete.

*left:* **Ludwig Mies van der Rohe. Model for Project: Glass Skyscraper. 1922. Photograph courtesy, Mies van der Rohe Archive, The Museum of Modern Art, New York**

Circular glass towers—alone, clustered, or melting into each other—have fascinated architects for decades. They reveal the amazing lightness of steel-cage construction, and they avoid the boxy look of the typical skyscraper.

*below:* **Schipporeit-Heinrich, Inc. Lake Point Tower, Chicago. 1968**

**Reinforced Concrete**    The ancient Romans developed a mortar based on volcanic ash, but it was not until 1824 that the first Portland cement was produced by an Englishman, Joseph Aspdin. In 1868 a French gardener, Jacques Monier, hit on the idea of reinforcing concrete flower pots with a wire web, thus creating a small-scale reinforced structure. But reinforced concrete, or *ferroconcrete*, was not widely employed as a building material until the 1890s.

Today's continuously curved and warped ferroconcrete slab is wholly new—a structural member that does not imitate masonry, wood, or metal. Since complex stress patterns are distributed throughout the slab, there is no distinct break between the functions of supporting and being supported. Thus the curved ferroconcrete slab is the logical and organic fulfillment of the older structural systems. It is also more permanent, more efficient, and potentially as beautiful.

But if stone slabs and shells are visually appealing, their curves have to be correct from an engineering standpoint. Interestingly, as engineering

THE SCULPTURAL QUALITY OF REINFORCED CONCRETE

Elevated highway, Berlin. 1963

*opposite above:* Louis I. Kahn. Interior, Kimbell Art Museum, Fort Worth, Texas. 1972

*opposite below:* Fritz Wotruba. Church of the Holy Trinity, Vienna. 1965-76

criteria are perfected, their visual results tend to look like natural forms. Some of the most dramatic ferroconcrete structures exhibit curves that resemble the organic forms we see in seashells, honeycombs, mushrooms, and soap bubbles. Like the egg, the strongest and most pleasing containers exhibit a harmonious relationship between external forces and material structure; this is the relationship that ferroconcrete seems ideally suited to create.

It is generally agreed that joints are the weakest points in classical structures: that is where loads change direction and complex stresses occur. But curved ferroconcrete members virtually eliminate joints; as with the eggshell, loads are distributed over the entire surface. This is accomplished by placing steel rods at the points of greatest tensile stress—the points where concrete particles would tear or pull apart. At points of greatest compression, the concrete is thickest: that is where the particles might be crushed. The steel rods are covered with enough concrete to prevent rusting, and they are given slight surface irregularities to prevent slippage after the concrete hardens. As a result, ferroconcrete has the virtues of steel and stone without their disadvantages.

Aside from its practical value, ferroconcrete appeals to designers because it offers so many structural possibilities: they can express their forming and shaping impulses in a variety of ways. Of course, these "sculptural" impulses are limited by the wooden forms which have to be built to hold concrete during pouring and curing. But as ferroconcrete technology advances, wooden framework may become a thing of the past. As more is known about types of aggregates and the usefulness of additives to lower weight, speed up drying, add color, and transmit light, the range of aesthetic effects possible in ferroconcrete will greatly increase.

One of the supposed disadvantages of concrete is its unsuitability as a surface material. As with steel, many architects use it for structural purposes only, covering it with veneers of brick, stone, marble, metal, and so on. Others cover concrete with stucco and paint. But these cosmetics should be unnecessary; Le Corbusier has shown what rich textures can be obtained by exposing concrete and letting the marks of the formwork show. Furthermore, rough concrete surfaces enhance the quality of smooth materials like metal and glass.

Together with the steel-frame skeleton, ferroconcrete has transformed architecture by eliminating the weight-bearing masonry wall. Combined with recessed columns, steel or concrete skeletons permit a skin to be composed almost totally of glass. That is what we see in Dallas: one crystal palace after another. The structural revolution produced by steel and ferroconcrete has changed the appearance of all our cities. Furthermore, it has changed many of our deep-rooted attitudes about space and shelter, privacy and strength. We are a much more open society than we used to be, largely because we can move freely in and out of public spaces. Steel and concrete have done a great deal to make that possible.

## THE STRUCTURAL DEVICES

To enclose space, materials must be systematically organized; that means structure. Architectural structure is the art and science of shaping, organizing, and fastening materials to resist the opposition of gravity, the attacks of weather, the wear caused by human use, and the processes of fatigue within materials themselves.

To experience architectural forms intelligently, we have to understand structure: it adds to our enjoyment of architecture, it enables us to visualize the forces that work to make a building safe and durable. And beautiful. Architecture is more than the interplay of pleasing shapes and surfaces, important though they are. We must be able to see architectural surfaces and shapes in terms of their strength and thickness; in terms of the weight they support; in terms of the space they enclose; in terms of the forces they resist.

This type of seeing and sensing has to be informed by awareness of the way materials are organized to stretch or squeeze, brace or bend, span or cover, lift or hold. Notice that these processes suggest the activities of our bodies: buildings are bodies, too. We enjoy them in the same way—by feeling the exertion, relaxation, and coordination of our bones, muscles, sinews, and skin as we go about the business of living.

**The Post-and-Lintel**    The post-and-lintel is the most ancient construction device and it is still widely used. It consists of two vertical supports bridged over by a horizontal beam. The prehistoric dolmen was an approximation of the post-and-lintel, with upright stones serving as posts and a horizontal table rock acting as a lintel. The Egyptians used the post-and-lintel exclusively, because of its stability and capacity to support great weights. Visually, the system offers a distinct separation between supporting and supported members, a feature that was especially appealing to the Greeks, admirers of clarity and precision in all things.

   Stone was the principal material used in ancient post-and-lintel construction. But steel and ferroconcrete are preferred in today's post-and-lintel construction, especially in large buildings. It is a system that resolves all forces into vertical and horizontal components, permitting an exceptionally rational organization of space and considerable efficiency in the use of materials. Since each structural member is very specialized, a high degree of standardization becomes possible. And that leads to prefabrication, mass production, and lowered costs.

   Post-and-lintel construction is also responsible for our strong emphasis on window walls in modern building. A steel cage affords large openings, which permit wide windows, which facilitate wide vision, which create

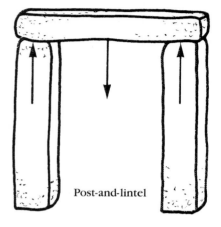

Post-and-lintel

Walter Gropius. Laboratory Workshop, The Bauhaus, Dessau, Germany. 1925–26. Photograph courtesy, The Museum of Modern Art, New York

generous display possibilities. With supporting posts set back from exterior walls, these windows need not be interrupted: window design is limited only by the size of glass panes and the framework needed to hold them in place. In the Bauhaus building designed by Walter Gropius, we see an early use of continuous bands of glass uninterrupted by walls or posts. This type of design became common for buildings—such as factories—requiring a great deal of daylight. Today, designers rely mainly on artificial illumination for factories, department stores, office buildings, and so on. But the glass wall is still popular—especially one-way and tinted glass—because its reflections help to harmonize a building with its environment.

In addition to its role in glass-wall design, the post-and-lintel system provides regular spacing of posts and partitions, creating interchangeable cubical spaces. Such spaces have advantages in modern business: efficient sale and rental; standardized design of fixtures and furnishings; orderly circulation of people. From a commercial and technocratic standpoint, the space created by arches, vaults, and domes is wasteful; the lofty spaces in a church, a library, or a museum represent uneconomic expenditures of funds. So the post-and-lintel system makes sense to engineers, and it suits capitalism. Socialists like it, too.

**The Cantilever**   A cantilever is basically a beam or slab extended horizontally into space. Its free end is unsupported, and the point where it rests on its post acts like the fulcrum of a lever. If the inside end of the beam were not bolted down, the cantilever would rotate around that fulcrum. But since that end is fixed, the free end is rigid. So the cantilever is secure if its material does not break and its internal end is firmly tied down.

The cantilever principle might have been seen in the first overhanging stone ledge. A tree branch also resembles a cantilever; but the earliest human societies saw no reason to build cantilevers. That may explain why we are slightly fearful of them: we think they might break. Today, however, cantilevers are very popular because strong materials are available at reasonable cost. We see wooden cantilever beams in many domestic dwellings, even though they cannot be extended as far as steel. Multiple dwellings use them, too, as narrow balconies and sunbreaks. But the *dramatic* impact of a cantilever is not felt unless an extension approaching the limits of the material is created. As with the suspension bridge and the lightweight truss, beauty and excitement seem to depend on defying gravity.

In buildings with a continuous window band, the portion of the floor projecting beyond the columns is usually cantilevered. The supporting columns are concealed inside the wall partitions so that no posts are visible. Thus, instead of being extended freely in space, the edge of the cantilevered floor becomes an attachment for a curtain wall of glass or metal panels. Although the cantilever is invisible, its operation is essential for producing the curtain-wall effect.

The most exciting uses of the cantilever, however, are seen in canopies, grandstands, aircraft hangars, and theater balconies: usually, they are made of ferroconcrete. Here the imagination of the architect and the ingenuity of the engineer combine to create some of the most striking forms in contemporary art. Nothing excites the imagination like a massive concrete form hovering in space.

**The Truss**   The truss is an application of the geometric fact that no angle of a triangle can be changed without altering the dimensions of its sides. A truss is a system of triangles arranged to work like a beam or lintel. Because truss systems can be made very rigid, and thus capable of bridging very wide spans, they are used where great spaces must be spanned with few or no interior supports. Wood and metal are the principal materials used because these materials possess high tensile strength for their weight; most of the members

*opposite above:* Frank Lloyd Wright. Dallas Theater Center, Kalita Humphreys Theater, Dallas, Texas. 1959. Photograph courtesy, The Museum of Modern Art, New York

Cantilevers in reinforced concrete. During the 1960s and early 1970s architects were seized by a fortress mentality. Whether designing a theater or a museum, they made the same statement: art needs to be defended.

*opposite below:* Mario Ciampi & Associates. University Arts Center, University of California, Berkeley. 1965–70

Roof truss, Old Ship Meetinghouse, Hingham, Massachusetts. 1681

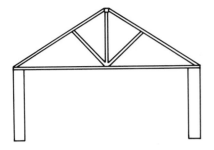

Wooden roof truss

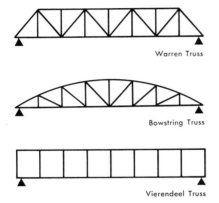

Warren Truss

Bowstring Truss

Vierendeel Truss

Types of trusses

of a truss are in tension. In bridges, theaters, convention halls, gymnasiums, and assembly plants, the truss is indispensable.

The Greek temple pediment may be the most beautiful application of the truss in the shape of a triangle. It is so firmly established in our consciousness that it is hard to imagine a traditional house, barn, or church without a triangular gable. Even though the short distances between the walls of houses can be spanned in other ways, the triangular gable roof "feels" safe. We accept a flat roof very reluctantly, if at all, in low structures. In addition, the space *inside* the gable is useful—in the form of a loft, an attic, or merely as insulation. In the sturdy Cape Cod cottage, Yankee ingenuity used gable space for extra bedrooms, which accounts for the popularity of the New England saltbox today. In more modern houses, flat ceilings can be eliminated and gable space can be converted into the prestigious "cathedral ceiling." More practically, the gable roof sheds rain and snow efficiently and offers a profile of low resistance to wind.

Although trusses are systems of triangles, their overall shape need not be triangular: most trusses are long rectangles shaped like a beam. This beam-truss has stiffening struts, braces, or bars where the solid material in a wood, metal, or stone beam would be. Another truss—the so-called bowstring truss—is straight along the lower edge and arched along the top. Structurally, the upper edge of a truss is in compression while the lower edge and the diagonals are in tension.

If we travel over a bridge supported by trusses, or if we stand under a roof made of trusses, we may wonder how so much space can be spanned by such thin members. We feel slightly insecure because we underestimate the strength of materials—especially of steel—in tension. But the parts of a truss have been designed so that loads work to *pull apart* rather than *bend* it. In the case of steel, its crystalline structure makes it almost impossible to pull apart; and its braces are usually given a cross-sectional shape that stubbornly resists bending. So, the fears based on our prehistoric memories can be set aside. Of course, a little fear produces architectural excitement; we need that, too.

**The Arch**     A post-and-lintel represents the simplest way of using gravity to enclose space; an arch is much more sophisticated. In both cases, vertical posts or columns are used, but the means of bridging over space—always the central problem of architecture—is very different. The arch relies on the compressive strength of bricks or cut stone. The separate units, or *voussoirs*, of an arch are squeezed together by the weight above them; in effect, they

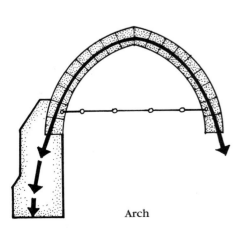

Arch

402

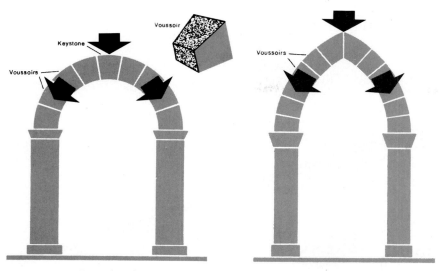

Round arch              Pointed arch

are "welded" into a single curved member. The arch does not begin to function, however, until the voussoir in its center—the *keystone*—is set in place. But since the keystone is the last stone to be placed, the arch has to be supported during construction by a structure of wooden forms called *centering*. Centering may be expensive, but it results in a uniquely beautiful curve.

The arch that the Mesopotamians developed—about four thousand years ago—is semicircular. The load it carries to its supporting posts develops almost horizontal reactions, called *thrusts*, which tend to force the posts outward, leading to collapse. These outward thrusts have to be resisted by buttressing or by a heavy masonry wall called a *spandrel*. The spandrel, which prevents bulging of the arch under pressure, was the principal mode of reinforcement used by ancient builders. A *free* arch, on the other hand, relies on the correctness of its design and the strength of its materials. In medieval architecture, buttresses began to be used in place of spandrels to counteract the outward thrusts of the free arch. Necessary from an engineering standpoint, these buttresses also produced some of the aesthetic effect so much admired in Gothic architecture.

In Renaissance construction the arch is employed in combination with the post-and-lintel, but usually as part of a wall and without external buttresses. The triangular pediment shape, based on the roof truss, was commonly alternated with the arch over windows and doors, often as a decorative rather than a structural element. Builders of this period had the engineering capacity of their Gothic predecessors, but their architectural tastes differed: they concealed structural functions while using arches, pilasters, pediments, and blind arcades—the full range of classical devices—for largely aesthetic purposes.

The arch tempts builders to become great engineers. It permits large, high openings, and the successive placement of its frames can establish a pleasing rhythmic pattern. The arch is also versatile, lending itself to the rugged honesty of early church architecture in which coarse masonry walls were used for abutment; or to the delicate, soaring effects of Gothic structures in which weight-bearing walls were virtually eliminated. In both cases, tall, vertically shaped space was the objective. The early churches had darkly mysterious interiors, lit mainly from within. Like early Christians themselves, they were indifferent to their outer garments. By contrast, Gothic interiors were richly illuminated by the outside light that passed through their stained-glass windows.

Because the pointed Gothic arch sent its thrusts more directly downward, its buttresses could be quite slender, and its stained-glass windows could be relatively free of thick masonry abutments. In addition, the pointed arch raised the height of ceilings, increasing overhead space. Eventually, Gothic ribs, or half-arches, created vaults that were in effect segmented domes. The

*opposite:* Point du Gard, Nîmes, France. 1st century A.D.

**Crypt, Speyer Cathedral, Germany. 1040**

The round Romanesque arch, resting on columns that look like massive tree trunks, generates a powerful sense of stability.

area between the ribs was filled with a masonry fabric that functioned almost like the membrane materials we use in today's thin-shell structures.

The modern, free arch is used mainly to support bridges or large domed and vaulted structures. Made of laminated wood, reinforced concrete, or steel, today's arch is monolithic and much stronger than its brick and stone ancestors. In wide-spanning arches, as in Eero Saarinen's Kresge Auditorium at M.I.T., supporting posts are entirely omitted. The arch springs (begins its curve) at ground level; thus it resembles the action of a huge bowstring truss. But true arch action is involved: the entire curve is in compression while the ground itself acts as a kind of tie-rod.

Today, the arch combined with stressed-skin shells produces enormous curved openings (see Saarinen's TWA Terminal, page 416) and floating ceiling effects that would have amazed the ancients. Indeed, architects have achieved a mastery of structure that permits an almost organic unity of form; there is hardly any separation between skin and bone. Increasingly, we build the way nature builds.

*left:* **Eugène Freyssinet. Airport hangar, Orly, France. 1921**

A modern arch structure so beautiful that it has been converted into a museum.

*below:* **Eero Saarinen. Kresge Auditorium, Massachusetts Institute of Technology, Cambridge. 1954**

This is not a true arch; it is an archlike opening in a spherical, thin-shell structure. Like the Gateway Arch in St. Louis, this "arch" functions aesthetically and symbolically; the shell does the work.

**The Vault**  The classical vault was a series of identical arches in file order—one behind the other. A bridge or an aqueduct was an arcade, a series of arches in rank order—side by side. Interior space of any size was spanned by arches in the form of a semicylinder—the so-called barrel vault. Even the dome was based on the arch; we can think of it as an arch rotating around its vertical axis. The groined vault used in Romanesque and Gothic building was a great advance; it was originally produced by the intersection of two barrel vaults, creating four ribs or half-arches.

The disadvantage of the old barrel vault was that it could not be pierced by windows without being greatly weakened. That is why early Romanesque churches were so dark. By replacing barrel vaults with groined vaults, however, church naves could go higher: their vaults were lighter in weight and they did not require such heavy walls for support. By the twelfth century, the round Romanesque arches and heavy groins began to be replaced by Gothic pointed arches and rib vaulting. These Gothic ribs were lighter than the groins they replaced, so they could be placed wherever they were needed—not just at the points where the old barrels would have intersected. Then, by adding ribs, the stone panels between them could be narrowed and constructed with lighter-weight stone. The ribs then multiplied—for decorative and structural reasons—and their weight-bearing function was spread over the whole vault surface.

Again, we witness a dynamic pattern of distributing loads, as in modern stressed-skin and shell construction. What are the architectural principles here? Arch structures disperse their stresses and tend to seek organic form; post-and-lintel structures concentrate their stresses and tend to seek geometric form. We get the classic confrontation of styles—between natural and abstract, between biological and mechanical, between measured and free.

**The Dome**  The vault evolved as a solution to the problem of bridging great spaces without interior supports while avoiding wooden trusses, which might burn, or stone lintels, which could break. As we have seen, this solution was based on arch combinations. The dome represents another solution. Essentially a hemisphere, the dome can bulge into the bulbous shape of an onion, as in the multiple domes of St. Basil's Cathedral in Moscow. Often a circular

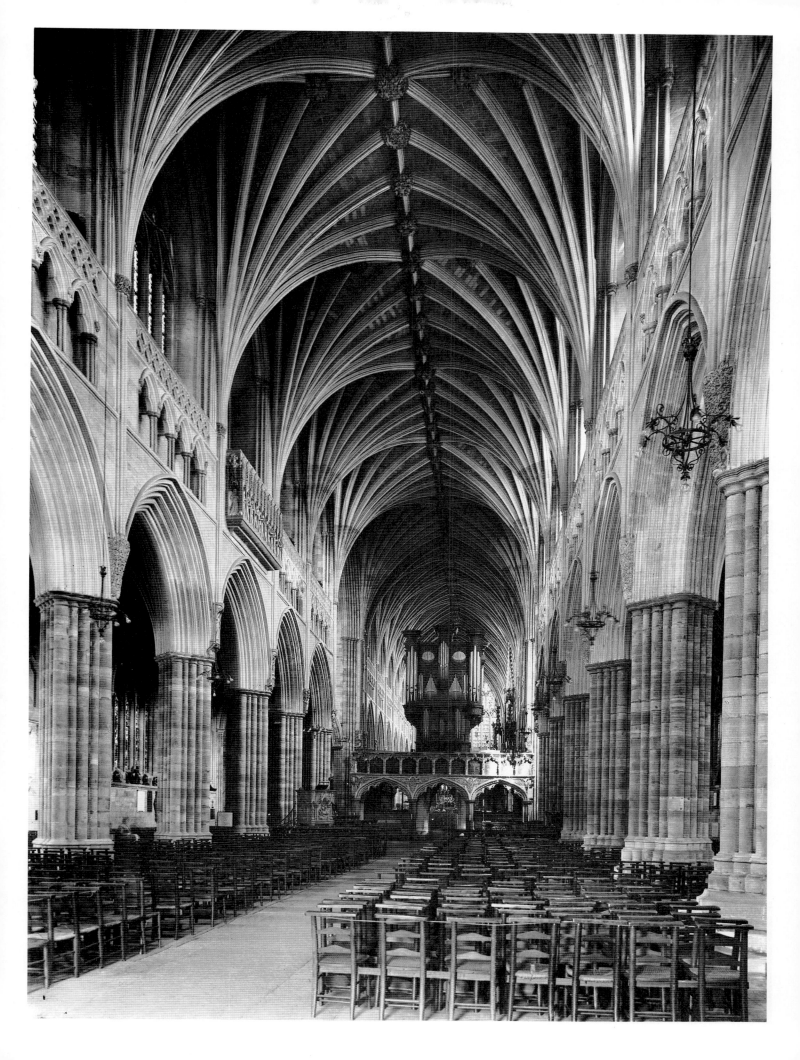

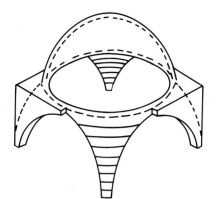

A dome on pendentives

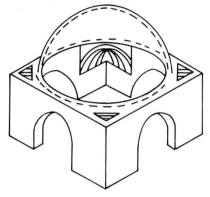

A dome with squinches

opening or skylight—called an *oculus* (or a *lantern* if it has a tower)—is placed at the top. Of course, the tower's weight increases the tendency of a dome to bulge. Hence chains or metal rings were often embedded in the masonry of classical domes. Or a high, thick mass of masonry surrounded the dome up to its haunch (a point about halfway up to the dome's top). From the outside, the dramatic exterior form of the dome is destroyed, as in Rome's Pantheon. Compared to St. Peter's, it looks like a shallow mound.

Placing a dome on a cylindrical drum over a circular foundation is logical from the standpoint of geometry. Yet most domed structures—in the West, at least—rest on rectangular foundations. Why? Because the Western church liturgy required a rectangular plan. Eastern churches favored a central plan, a plan that focuses attention on a point directly under the dome. In the Middle East, where the dome probably originated, the ceiling was regarded as an image of the cosmos; so it was frequently covered with stars. (Is that why today's planetarium is dome-shaped? Is outer space shaped like a dome?) Clearly, the dome has had religious and cosmological meaning from the beginning.

A number of devices have been used to transfer the load from the circular edge of a dome to the rectangular foundation on which it usually rests. The most common devices are called *pendentives* and *squinches*. The pendentive system places the dome on a drum which rests on four arches springing from four powerful piers located at each corner of a square plan. The arches touch the drum's rim at only four points. Between these points are four curved triangular sections, called pendentives; they connect the curves of the arch to the rim of the drum and carry its weight down to the piers.

The Pantheon, Rome, A.D. **118–125**

Michelangelo. St. Peter's, Rome. 1546-64 (dome completed by Giacomo della Porta, 1590)

Hagia Sophia in Istanbul, built in A.D. 532–37, offers the oldest and perhaps best example of a dome on pendentives. The great outward thrusts produced by its arches and pendentives are carried to the ground by a beautiful system of half domes and exterior abutments. The dome itself has no oculus; it is pierced instead by windows running continuously around its lower edge. This device creates the impression that the dome is floating—a miracle in itself, considering the dome's immense weight. In addition, the effect of the cathedral being in another world is enhanced.

DOMES: TRIUMPHANT, JOYOUS, PLAYFUL . . .

*left:* Cathedral of St. Basil, Moscow. 1555-60

*below:* John Nash. The Royal Pavilion, Brighton, England. 1815-18

*right:* Corn Palace, Mitchell, South Dakota. 1921

Domes, turrets, cones, and annually rotated mosaics made of corn. This is folk architecture: all building traditions are fair game; anything goes.

*below:* Philip Johnson. Roofless Church, New Harmony, Indiana. 1960

A wood-shingle dome that looks like a magician's trick handkerchief. This dome, without a building underneath, sits in a walled garden; it has overtones of a mosque, a Hindu temple, and a revivalist tent. But where do the people sit?

The squinch system, used mainly by Islamic builders, is not as rationally articulated as the pendentive solution. It, too, rests the dome on four arches sprung from four corner piers, creating a square support for a circular edge. But instead of pendentives in the corners, smaller arches called *squinches* are substituted, forming an octagonal support at eight different points. The octagon approximates a circle better than a square; and so, with some adjustments in the masonry, the dome rests on what is, in effect, a polygonal drum.

Squinches have this advantage: they create opportunities for numerous niches in the corners between the main arches. These form semidome shapes

... AND EXUBERANT

*left:* Detail of Mosque of Ahmed I (Blue Mosque), Istanbul. 1609–16

*below:* View into outer portal, Masjid-i-Shah, Isfahan, Iran. 1616

E.H. Brenner. Women's Clinic, Lafayette, Indiana.
1965

A complex of seven interlocking domes built by
spraying concrete over a wire-mesh framework
resting on a structure of curved polystyrene
planks.

R. Buckminster Fuller. American Pavilion, EXPO
67, Montreal. 1967

Buckminster Fuller's geodesic dome was ideal
for a World's Fair exposition building. It could
also be used by the military for radar stations in
the Arctic. But despite high expectations, it
never caught on as "architecture." Most people
associate civilized living with square-shaped
spaces.

that rhythmically repeat the shape of the major dome. But, as can be seen in the interior of the mosque at Isfahan, squinches are very prolific; they seem to give birth to more squinches, and we get an effect like a honeycomb. The surfaces between the arches are so richly decorated that the sense of architectural structure is lost. The effect may be gorgeous but we cannot see how the space is created.

**Shell Structures**    Modern shell structures enjoy the advantages of reinforced concrete and superior mathematical tools for calculating the strength and stress of materials. Compared to classical domes, our shell structures are flatter and wider; yet they don't need deep masonry drums. Concrete shells are so thin that their dead weight is negligible; the engineering problem lies in maintaining their stability and resistance to buckling because of stresses caused by rain, snow, or uneven heating by the sun. But shells are worth the trouble: they enclose a great deal of space with very little material. And they are economical to build and easy to maintain.

We seek the tent experience—for religious or secular purposes—because of the sense of protection it fosters while we feel bathed in a wonderful overhead light.

*left:* Umbrellas over trade section, Swiss National Exposition, Lausanne. 1964

*below left:* Frank Lloyd Wright. Interior, Wayfarer's Chapel, Palos Verdes Estates, California. 1951

*below right:* Wallace K. Harrison. Interior, First Presbyterian Church, Stamford, Connecticut. 1958

Shells can be made of metal as well as concrete. Buckminster Fuller's (1895–1983) geodesic domes have been made of aluminum, steel, wood, concrete, plastics, even paper. Eventually, plastic and fiberglass sheets stretched over cable systems or metal-mesh supports will compete with concrete in shell construction. These materials produce forms similar to those we see in tents, kites, and umbrellas. Shell structures can also be constructed by spraying cement over inflated rubber balloons. Sprayed plastics and weatherproof textiles are also being seriously investigated.

Because fair and exposition architecture is temporary, it is often used for experiments with new materials and structural systems. The Berlin Pavilion at the New York World's Fair of 1964–65 consisted of a tent structure made of vinyl-coated canvas stretched and supported by steel masts and tension cables. The result was visually pleasing as well as inexpensive. In the future, such buildings may be permanent if problems of long-term durability and weather resistance can be overcome. Our social, industrial, and domestic needs continually change; hence innovative structures of this type might come into widespread use.

The ability to enclose enormous spaces safely and efficiently may lead to the design of total communities in single structures—in so-called *mega-structures*. We already house small cities in our great hotels, ocean-going superliners, shopping centers, industrial parks, and universities. By locating all building units on a single raised platform, architects have suggested the direction of the future: comprehensive design of communities through integration of their major forms, with utilities and systems in a single structure to which additional units can be added—"clipped on"—as needed. This idea is not as radical as it seems; it confirms in architectural terms what is already a fact—namely, that communities are multicelled organisms increasingly connected by common systems of power, transportation, communication, and administration.

## THE ARCHITECTURE OF INTERIOR SPACE

**Frank Lloyd Wright. Interior, The Solomon R. Guggenheim Museum, New York. 1959**

Wright's museum is like a cathedral—much in the tradition of early Christian domed churches. But unlike the mosaics of St. Mark's or Hagia Sophia, the pictures in this "church" keep changing. The building and its art do not explain, they only tolerate, each other.

*opposite:* Interior, Hagia Sophia, Istanbul. A.D. 532–37

414

*opposite above:* Le Corbusier. Interior, Notre-Dame-du- Haut, Ronchamp, France. 1950–55

Rectangular openings in a thick concrete wall dramatize the process of light entering an interior at many eye levels. It is as if a sculptor had reinvented the window.

*opposite below:* Eero Saarinen. Interior, TWA Terminal, Kennedy International Airport, New York. 1962

The sweeping structural shapes and curved edges are clearly meant to suggest the trajectories of flight. The interior expression is of a great womblike cave, with light from a multitude of organic openings penetrating its earthly recesses.

*left:* Safdie, David, Barott, and Boulva. Detail of Habitat, EXPO 67, Montreal. 1967

Superb opportunities for light modulation and a truly sculptural environment present themselves in the sheltered transitional spaces formed by interlocking units.

*below:* Schoeler Heaton Harvor Menendez. Interior, Charlebois High School, Ottawa, Canada. 1971–72

A Post-Modernist conception of space in which ducts, plumbing, and trusses are brought out of concealment and used as "sculpture" or as symbols of change and growth. This, after all, is what a high school should be about.

*above:* I.M. Pei. Interior, Everson Museum of Art, Syracuse, New York. 1965–68

A monumental room achieved in a small museum by attention to fundamentals: honest and uncomplicated enclosure of space, a practical device for bathing the walls with light, and wall punctuation that allows the art objects to breathe.

*opposite:* James Stirling and James Gowan. Interior, History Building, Cambridge University, England. 1964–67

An inspiring space for university students. Stirling shows how standard industrial parts can be organized to express the idea of collective movement through time. The horizontal, no-nonsense working levels have been framed by angular glass-and-steel planes to produce an exciting sense of upward striving.

Paul Rudolph. Project for Graphic Arts
Center, New York. 1967

A megastructure planned for the center
of Manhattan. Paul Rudolph proposed
one immense, articulated building
complex that would carry out the
unwitting logic of the island's
architecture since the skyscraper mania
began in the early twentieth century.

## CONSTRUCTORS AND SCULPTORS

Can we see any pattern in contemporary architecture as a whole? Is there a
common idea about building shapes or structural systems that pervades
architectural practice today? The answer has to be "No." Almost everywhere,
buildings are being erected which express divergent philosophies while using
similar materials and structural devices. Yet, in all this diversity it may be
possible to discern two main tendencies expressed through two types of
architect: constructors and sculptors. What are their typical attitudes toward
engineering, architectural emotion, and the purposes of design?

Constructors are designers who favor the dramatization of engineering
devices to create exciting architecture. The word "constructor" is used in
Europe to designate a person who practices what Americans call structural
engineering. In both Europe and America, architecture and structural engineering are independent though cooperating professions. The professions
may be formally distinct, but each shares many of the competencies of the
other. That is why we can think of some architects as constructors. For them,
the engineering solution is fundamental; architecture is, as Nervi has called
it, "structural truth."

The label "sculptor" can be applied to designers who are mainly interested in plastic and symbolic form as sources of architectural emotion. Natu-

rally, they use structural devices to build, but these are regarded as means rather than ends. Sculptural architects are interested in the play of light over forms for the sake of visual excitement; they try to invent space-enclosing shapes that will symbolize the purpose of a building or the attributes of its users. Such designers believe that architecture should express ideas and feelings more than building systems.

In today's Post-Modernist architecture, the form of many buildings goes beyond the strict requirements of structure and utility. Philip Johnson's orchestration of domes for the Dumbarton Oaks Museum shows the "sculptor" at work; it involves the decorative rather than structural employment of a building device. Here the symbolic—not the engineering—function of the dome is exploited. Johnson used the idea of the dome as a complete and separate world to create a contemplative and mystical atmosphere for the examination of small, exquisitely displayed art objects.

From the standpoint of the constructor, architectural "sculptors" have turned away from the basic principles of modernism; their work revives the old building traditions, using modern materials and devices in place of the

*left:* Reed, Torres, Beauchamp, Marvel. Chase Manhattan Bank, San Juan, Puerto Rico. 1969

Two branch banks, both in warm climates. One expresses the engineer's mind and method; it works but it lacks the power to stir the imagination. The other strains for the picturesque. (Are the arches supposed to echo palm trees?) The result is kitschy.

*above:* Wimberly, Whisenand, Allison & Tong. Model of Waikiki branch, Bank of Hawaii. 1965

*left:* Philip Johnson. Museum of Pre-Columbian Art, Dumbarton Oaks, Washington, D.C. 1963

*below:* Philip Johnson. Plan of Museum of Pre-Columbian Art

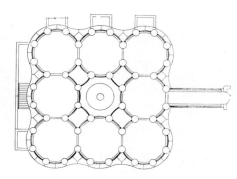

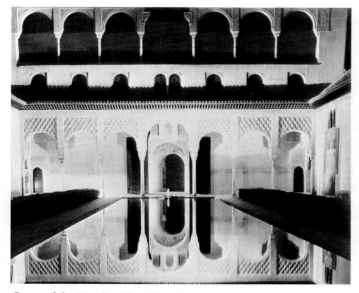

Court of the Myrtles. The Alhambra, Granada, Spain. 1368

*above:* Naramore, Bain, Brady & Johanson and Minoru Yamasaki & Associates. IBM Building, Seattle. 1961

Steel arches at ground level covered with marble: they may be strong and secure, but they look funny at the corners. A cantilever made of half arches is not very reassuring.

*left:* Edward Durell Stone. Beckman Auditorium, California Institute of Technology, Pasadena. 1960

classical orders and decorative systems. For example, Minoru Yamasaki uses Gothic arches made of metal and pagoda-like roof canopies made of ferro-concrete. The symbolic associations of old construction systems have been "borrowed" and adapted. Edward Stone (1902–1978) also used modern materials and devices to resurrect architectural memories—particularly of Persian and Moorish structures built during the late Middle Ages. His arcades, columns, and perforated walls remind us of Islamic palaces. Perhaps they represent a search for symbols by a designer who is not too proud to learn from the past. In theory, materials and technology change, but symbols never lose their power. So Stone's Beckman Auditorium at Cal Tech goes back seven centuries to a Moorish-Spanish palace, the Alhambra. Does that make sense for nuclear physicists and genetic engineers?

Constructors take pride in an unsentimental approach to design. As a result, the harsh label "new brutalism" was applied to the work of a British group of architects in the 1950s. We see an example of their tough-minded approach in the Hayward Art Gallery in London—a combination of the ideas of sculptors *and* constructors. The rugged strength of the building is not

*opposite:* **Michael Graves. Portland Public Services Building, Oregon. 1980–82**

Post-Modern architecture (see the examples by Philip Johnson, page 250, and Charles Moore, page 101) is both a reaction against Bauhaus design and a reassertion of the importance of color, ornament, and symbolism in building. Graves creates a medley of arbitrary shapes, mechanical proportions, and geometric patterns. Form and function seem almost completely divorced; instead we get playful allusions to ancient Egypt, Art Deco, and downtown signage, with Greek temples set on top of everything, like icing on a birthday cake.

*above:* **Pier Luigi Nervi. Palazzo del Lavoro Exhibition Hall, Turin, Italy. 1959**

*right:* **Pier Luigi Nervi. Little Sports Palace, Rome. 1957**

merely the result of coarse, poured-concrete construction; it also grows out of a no-nonsense solution to the light and space requirements of an art museum and the job of managing circulation through its galleries. There are no signs of axial design, traditional ornament, or obvious symbolism. Instead, we get a harsh, aggressive statement of what the building does. It looks like sculpture but its forms are justified as engineering.

## CONSTRUCTORS

**Skidmore, Owings and Merrill. Alcoa Building, San Francisco. 1968**

The crisscross beams designed to brace the structure against earthquakes convert the facade of this building into a single, huge truss.

*opposite:* **John Warnecke & Associates and Peterson, Clark & Associates. Hennepin County Government Center, Minneapolis. 1968–76**

Here the crisscross braces add visual excitement as well as strength. Notice how light and buoyant they look against the windows.

The "sculptors" do not invent forms arbitrarily; they just pay close attention to the visual associations of materials under stress.

Riccardo Morandi. Parco del Valentino
Exhibition Hall, Turin, Italy. 1958–60

Eugène Freyssinet. Basilica of Pius X, Lourdes, France. 1958

*right:* Eric Mendelsohn. Einstein Tower, Potsdam, Germany. 1920–21. (Destroyed)

*below:* Eric Mendelsohn. Drawing for Einstein Tower. 1919

Mendelsohn's powerful ink drawing reveals the approach of a sculptural designer—one who initially *feels* a form and then creates a structure to match his emotion.

left: Minoru Yamasaki & Associates. North Shore Congregation Israel Synagogue, Glencoe, Illinois. 1964

Reinforced concrete is versatile enough to convey the slender grace of Yamasaki's synagogue or the formidable power of Bennett's art gallery.

below: Hubert Bennett & Associates. Hayward Art Gallery, London. 1968

Pier Luigi Nervi was one of the great modern constructors, but he probably used more columns than were structurally needed in his Palazzo del Lavoro in Turin, Italy. The same is true of Wright's Administration Building for the Johnson Wax Company (see page 82). Nervi designed a modern equivalent of Gothic fan vaulting; like all man-made "trees," these columns provide a sense of scale, a structural reference to which people can relate and thus "feel" the dimensions of a great interior space. Bodily references are often present in the work of the constructors: Morandi's Parco del Valentino Exhibition Hall in Turin and Freyssinet's Pius X Basilica in Lourdes express a sense of powerful supporting legs, arms, and ribs. Both structures are earth-covered and both employ prestressed concrete arches and braces. But these enormous "caverns" are humanized by concrete forms that function structurally and symbolically at the same time.

Architectural emotion, therefore, arises from multiple sources: it may result from the careful adjustment of spaces and solids—from the magic of geometry; or it may rely on deep memories of life under ledges, in front of caves, or beneath woven boughs and bundles of straw. It may depend on the tent experience—a thin membrane barely separating a private world from the vastness of space. Or it may recall great stones modeled to resemble human bodily parts, the places where procreative power lives. At different stages of our development we have tried to live in the bowels of the earth or on the tops of mountains. Depending on mood or luck, we return to one or the other.

RHETORIC AND RESTRAINT IN REINFORCED
CONCRETE

Paul Rudolph. Interior, Southeastern
Massachusetts Technological Institute, North
Dartmouth. 1966

Louis I. Kahn. Stairwell in residence hall,
Bryn Mawr College, Bryn Mawr, Pennsylvania.
1964–65

Some of us are still nomads, psychologically, and that is why architecture is
so changeable.

The superiority that constructors feel toward "sculptors" reflects an agelong conflict between abstraction and empathy, between geometric designers
and pictorial designers. One camp believes architecture is structure, and
structure is measure, and measure is geometry, and geometry is reality. The
other camp believes architecture is sculpture, and sculpture is magic, and
magic is illusion made real. Of course, both of them are right.

# CHAPTER FOURTEEN

# PHOTOGRAPHY

A great friend of photography, James Agee, once said: "It is doubtful whether most people realize how extraordinarily slippery a liar the camera is." The camera is also sensitive, seductive, and instructive, but photographs have to be closely analyzed if we want to enjoy them without being deceived. And that is what we shall do in this chapter: examine photography as a remarkable way of seeing, knowing, and remembering. Photographs have tremendous power to please our eyes and persuade our minds; if we could understand that power—the product of an intimate man-machine collaboration—we might gain access to some of the deepest secrets of visual art and human communication.

Today we are surrounded by photographs and photographic reproductions. Children encounter photographic (or televised) representations of reality before they can speak. For the rest of us, pictures made with light have almost become substitutes—*preferred* substitutes—for the real world. It is important to emphasize that at the earliest stage of consciousness, the stage where the attitudes and habits of a lifetime are established, we experience photographs as real in the same sense that people, places, and things are real.

It should be remembered, too, that photography is closely connected to graphic reproduction. This book would be impossible without both. Today, art could not be taught or studied without photography and its supporting technologies of reproduction and printing. Photographs of artworks and photographs *as* artworks give us access to more places and objects than we could possibly visit in a lifetime. In this sense, photographs are like books that introduce the words and ideas of persons we cannot meet personally because they live too far away, or because they are no longer alive. The photographic reproduction of a building or a sculpture is not identical to the original. Still, it resembles the original more closely than an ancient text translated into a modern language.

Faults can be found with the photograph as a copy. And certainly it is better to visit a museum than to see its holdings in a catalogue of reproductions. Yet, we should not forget the profound changes that photographic copies have wrought in our lives. They have given us the capacity to see the faces of humanity throughout the world, the places where people live, the work they do, the things they make. If these gains have been won at the expense of demystifying original artworks, divesting them of their remote-

*above:* Diane Arbus. *Mexican Dwarf in His Hotel Room in New York City.* 1970. © 1971 The Estate of Diane Arbus

The secret of a photograph by Diane Arbus lives in her matter-of-fact approach to individuals who are condemned to be outsiders. Because she refuses to be shocked by their abnormality, Arbus forces us to look at them as persons when our instinctive reaction is to look away.

*right:* Diego Velázquez. *Sebastian de Morra.* 1643–44. Oil on canvas, 41¾ × 31⅛". The Prado, Madrid

*opposite above:* Sandy Skoglund. *Radioactive Cats.* 1980. Cibachrome color photograph, 30 × 40". Courtesy Castelli Graphics, New York

Skoglund changes the relation of photography to reality: her photos are staged. The tenement room, people, furnishings, and cats were arranged, or installed, and then photographed. Of course, this is what cinematographers do—and some photojournalists, too. But in straight photography the effect is surreal.

*opposite below:* Cindy Sherman. *Untitled.* 1982. Color photograph, 45¼ × 30". Courtesy Metro Pictures, New York

Cindy Sherman lighted, directed, and filmed by Cindy Sherman. As with Skoglund, cinematography and photography merge. But Sherman has added "performance" art: her figure, wig, props, and acting become the subject of her "movie," which is the subject of her photograph.

ness, uniqueness, and preciousness, so be it. The fact is, photographs are one of our most enjoyable ways of transcending time and space.

In this chapter photographs are juxtaposed with paintings and sculptures to bring out their similarities and differences. The similarities lie in their fundamentally visual character, no matter how the image was made. The differences are mainly due to the superior accuracy of the photograph. This superiority creates an illusion of objectivity and authenticity that has established photography—plus film and television—as exceedingly powerful instruments of information and education. Also, by comparing photographs with other visual media we become more aware of their distinctive aesthetic effects. Finally, in examining photographs seriously we should gain insight into *all* visual sources of knowing, feeling, and valuing.

## PHOTOGRAPHY AND REALITY

A close connection between the photographic print and objective reality was assumed almost from the nineteenth-century beginnings of the art. As lens, camera, and plate were perfected, the painter's hand and eye came under suspicion as truthful recorders of reality. But if the photograph seemed more reliable from an optical standpoint, it was painting that gained ground as a vehicle of psychological expression. The split between photography and painting—or between science and art—is still with us. Ironically, it is founded on the fact that the camera resembles the human eye: it captures light rays and records them by a process that excludes the human hand. The painter's hand—more than his or her eye—raised doubts about the artist's ability to represent reality in complete detail. And the brain—the neural tissue behind the eye—raised doubts about the artist's ability to tell the truth objectively.

The camera seemed to circumvent human imperfection. At least that is the impression created by its capacity to receive and record visual facts automatically. As a result, viewers attributed a special kind of credibility to the photograph, a credibility they would not grant to any painterly style, no matter how realistic. The photograph was seen as truthful in a scientific and historical sense; from that combination of virtues we got the idea of a photographic "document," the man-made image that is more reliable than words, less time-consuming than reading, and free of human bias.

Because it records only what is seen by a neutral "eye," the photograph offers viewers a fundamentally new way of knowing; the photographic print assures us that its imagery is more honest and complete than the data

delivered by human sensory equipment. No matter that the photographer chooses a subject, selects "the decisive moment," and manipulates a print in a thousand ways. The photographic record of reality still seems completely true. This has led us to believe that in seeing a photograph we come into actual contact with the world. Today, that conviction is part of a general consensus. Like perspective in the fifteenth century, photography entered human consciousness as an art that controls a superior cognitive technology.

## PHOTOGRAPHY AND PAINTING

Historically, photography emerged from painting. Its earliest practitioners were portrait painters. When the daguerreotype was perfected—about 1839—lifesize painted portraits went into decline and hand-painted miniatures died out; it was a simple case of technological obsolescence. The same process took place as history painting was replaced by still photography and then newsreel photography which, in turn, gave way to television "documentaries." As always, technological change produced unanticipated social and cultural side effects.

Today, almost everyone owns dozens, even hundreds of photographs. And almost everyone owns one or more cameras—often miniature cameras that can be carried anywhere. So photography is a folk art as well as a fine art. It is practiced by far more people than ever practiced the arts of drawing and painting. In this connection we should remember that a few centuries ago most people saw themselves only in a mirror (which gives a limited view

Evelyn Hofer. *Brownstones on the West Side.*
1974. New York Times Pictures

*below:* Edward Hopper. *Sunlight on
Brownstones.* 1956. Oil on canvas, 30 × 40".
Wichita Art Museum, Kansas. Roland P. Murdock
Collection

Both Hopper and Hofer are poets of urbanism. But Hopper is more strictly wedded to the city's rectangular relationships; notice how his couple look at nature wistfully through a square opening in the canvas. Hofer, on the other hand, finds delight in a format of converging diagonals; she sees a speedier, more dynamic harmony in the repeated masonry forms. The result is a brownstone counterpoint that skips and sings. Hofer discovers melody where Hopper felt a pervasive silence.

as well as a reversed image). Wealthy persons might see themselves in painted portraits, but the working classes and the poor had no idea—no *visual* idea—of themselves. Now that has changed: rich and poor see themselves in dozens of images—large and small, old and young, formally posed or caught off guard. In other words, all of us have seen our friends, our relatives, and our ancestors photographically; and these images confirm the fact that we exist. Thus photography has had immense importance for the development of a modern sense of self.

Photography has also taught us how much artists change what they see. Oddly enough, we are less conscious of the fact that the camera also changes reality: we do not realize that the photographer manipulates what the camera sees. Most of us believe that the photograph cannot be false no matter who operates the camera. (We are much more suspicious of statisticians.) So photography has taken over the "truth" franchise in our culture. Only photography represents reality in a way that commands universal acceptance; today even painters use photographs.

In the past, painters used photographs in secret. Most of them regarded photographs as a crutch, a device employed by artists who were weak in drawing—too lazy to analyze and reconstruct what they saw. The history of the relationship between painting and photography has been brilliantly written by Van Deren Coke (see Bibliography, page 526), who provides an abundance of evidence about the painter's use of photographic "aids." It runs from pure and simple copying to highly sophisticated references to photographic ways of seeing. Indeed, the camera's one-eyed optic is widely celebrated: photorealism is now a major style of art.

But photography creates problems for painters who prefer the record of the camera's glass eye to their own, human mode of perception. In copying photographic imagery, painters also reproduce its frozen, or "stop-action," quality. Or they reproduce the camera's typical distortions of form and space. The camera distorts inevitably because of its monocular way of seeing; as a result, the painter's copy may have an inauthentic or "dead" look. Some artists conceal their photographic sources: they can use the camera without being

Both Dong Kingman and Berenice Abbott see the "El" as a kind of carnival or bazaar. However, Mrs. Abbott stresses the grittiness of the city scene whereas Kingman is impressed with its gaiety. The watercolor medium seems ideally suited to Kingman's lyrical vision of steel girders and cast-iron lightposts because it subtracts from their mass and presents them as a collection of light, dancing surfaces. The photograph, on the other hand, retains the weight of the steel: no danger of turning the city's shadow patterns into tissue paper and lace.

used. Others deliberately simulate the photograph's frozen action; they use it to make a statement about the sameness, or the reproducibility, of everything we see and do. In any case, photographic imagery can be dangerous because it is so seductive. The painter who sets out to use it can become its captive. Instead of an image that has passed through a human consciousness, we may see no more than a painted snapshot.

# THE AMATEUR WITH A CAMERA

The rudiments of taking a photograph are quickly and easily learned, and cameras are inexpensively available to almost everyone. This combination of

*above:* Arman. *Little Hands.* 1960. Dolls' hands glued in wooden drawer, 14⅝ × 17⅞ × 2⅞". Collection the artist

Arman and Hartmann converge, not only in their choice of doll or mannequin parts to express the obscenity of Buchenwald, but also in their use of "real" objects to suggest the horror of a real event. Notice that Arman's hands do not touch; they are clearly dismembered and mutilated. Hartmann's hands and arms are intertwined and they reach toward the viewer rather gracefully. We have a more complex idea expressed in the photograph: it is a peculiar grace of writhing bodily parts. As viewers we are caught in a tension that is both moral and aesthetic—the contradictions between what we know and feel. Hartmann forces us to view the concentration-camp murders as a kind of high-fashion ballet. It is a deeply disturbing experience.

*right:* Erich Hartmann. *Mannequins.* © 1969 Magnum Photos

*left:* Ivan Albright. *Self-Portrait.* 1935. Oil on canvas, 30⅜ × 19⅞". The Art Institute of Chicago. Mary and Earle Ludgin Collection

Ivan Albright's *Self-Portrait* and Douglas Jeffery's photograph of John Gielgud portraying the aged Shakespeare offer an unusual opportunity to compare a painting and a photograph dealing with the same theme—the irony and disillusionment of old age. An interesting difference emerges: Albright's painting is hyper-realistic, more than photographic in its accumulation of detail. The photograph of Gielgud, on the other hand, is realistic by definition. Albright builds a case against himself; the symbols of life's futility are patiently and lovingly assembled. Jeffery focuses our attention on a different sort of drama—the spectacle of a great Shakespearean actor, late in his career, playing the role of his aged master. The photograph functions simultaneously as a theatrical document and a work of visual art.

*below:* Douglas H. Jeffery. *John Gielgud as Shakespeare in Edward Bond's* Bingo. August 25, 1974. Royal Court Theatre, London. © Douglas H. Jeffery, 1974

*above:* George Tooker. *Government Bureau.* 1956. Tempera on gesso panel, 19⅝ × 29⅝". The Metropolitan Museum of Art, New York. George A. Hearn Fund, 1956

The contrast between the photograph and the painting enhances our understanding of the distinctive excellence of each; their common theme is the impersonality of bureaucratic existence. How does each picture make its point? In Tooker's case it is through repetition of human and architectural forms within a fast-receding space. Michals uses the same device: the central figure is much reduced in size compared to the foreground figure. His people are also destined to be swallowed up in a prisonlike office-tomb. But Tooker dwells on the paranoid atmosphere of the bureau, the sense of being spied upon; Michals emphasizes the alienation of man from man. His theme is Giacometti's theme—isolation. Here a photographic liability becomes an asset: the monocular lens of the camera produces an optical shrinking of the older, bald-headed man in the corridor. Thus we witness his tragic reduction in spiritual size.

*right:* Duane Michals. *Intersecting Corridors.* 1974. Courtesy Duane Michals

factors has spawned a multitude of amateurs—persons who make photographs well or badly for their own enjoyment. So photography can be called a folk art without detracting from its status as one of the so-called fine arts. Actually, a good photograph is good regardless of the training or status of the person who made it. A more important question has to do with the consequences of the fact that millions of people now have the means of making pictures.

One result of photography's popularity is the discovery that everything that can be seen can be photographed. The idea that anything can be recorded by a camera is similar to the child's discovery that anything in the world can be named: it is a linguistic and cognitive revelation. As millions made this discovery, the philosophic outlook of our time was fundamentally changed. People realized that the scientific developments beginning in the eighteenth century had yielded immense technological benefits for the twentieth century—benefits going beyond the substitution of machines for human or animal effort. Machines seemed to be adequate, or more than adequate, substitutes for human mental and perceptual work. Who can doubt this today, in an age of electronic computers?

The mechanization of seeing began with the perfection of the camera. And from this initial success a marvelous feeling of cultural confidence emerged: not only seeing but perceiving and thinking could be mechanized. That is, we began to believe that machines would enable us to think faster and better. Because millions of people could record the environment almost as spontaneously as they could see it, they developed a new sense of mastery over that environment; to "capture" something on film was the psychological equivalent of controlling it. In a very real sense, the invention of photography in the nineteenth century was as revolutionary as the invention of printing in the fifteenth century.

Because the masses could take pictures of themselves and pieces of their world, photography raised the possibility that most people could understand what they were looking at. In addition, the amateur photographer became something of a critic—not only of photographic prints but also of photographic reality. This does not mean that amateur photographers became sophisticated connoisseurs of art. Usually, the amateur is more interested in the realism of a snapshot than its aesthetics. But the fact that cameras are used by millions has produced a fundamental change in the history of art and society.

First, the privilege of owning images has been extended to the masses. Second, the ownership of images has produced a quantum leap in the capacity of ordinary people to see themselves and their environment objectively. Third, the ability to take photographs, and to judge them, seems to confer more capacity to participate in cultural affairs generally. Fourth, greater participation in cultural affairs increases participation in politics. Fifth, collecting paintings is relegated to old elites whose status is secure, or to a new class that aspires to elite status.

Not surprisingly, the invention of photography and the steady improvement of photographic reproduction have led to a general democratization of life in technologically advanced countries. A "revolution of rising expectations" began when large numbers of people could see pictures of places, products, and lifestyles that were normally beyond their experience. Then motion pictures, followed by television, created a second "revolution of rising expectations." But there can be little doubt that photography started the process: this new art/technology changed the modern world.

## INSTANTANEOUS SEEING

Because of the realism of the photographic image we may not realize that its "stop-action" image is unnatural: we do not see the way the camera sees. A still frame taken from a roll of 35 millimeter motion-picture film gives us a better idea of what the human eye sees: it catches a generalized glimpse of things, a glimpse that becomes an image which is somewhat blurred and indistinct. In other words, film reality depends on the illusion of *motion* more than sharpness and clarity of *contour*: motion pictures prove that "there are no outlines in nature." The still photograph is different; it produces a "high resolution" image—an image so sharp, clear, and instantaneous that it seems to stop time.

John Pregulman. *The Rebecca Kelly Dance Company.* 1985

Stop action: the flow of time and motion condensed into a single, instant image.

*opposite above:* Film still from *The Grapes of Wrath:* the Joad Family. Directed by John Ford. 1940. © 1949. Twentieth Century-Fox Film Corp.

There is a continuous exchange of influence between photojournalists, documentary filmmakers, and film and television directors. The Arthur Grace photograph here is very reminiscent of John Ford's film which, in turn, descended from the motion-picture documentaries of Pare Lorentz and the photographs of Walker Evans, Dorothea Lange, and Margaret Bourke-White. Their common theme is the timelessness of rural poverty.

*opposite below:* Arthur Grace. *Nellie Hart and Sons.* 1974. New York Times Pictures

When we say the photograph "stops" time, we mean that it compresses the flow of time into a single instant. That instant, which is a moment in real time, isolates a split second in the life of the object. This visual isolation of a moment can be understood in terms of the physics of the camera. However, it also has a psychological and aesthetic dimension: because we simulate what we see internally, we try unconsciously to "stop" our personal or biological time as we view a photograph. As a result, photographic forms acquire a quality that we rarely experience when looking at painted forms. That quality might be called immediacy: the camera reveals what the naked eye cannot catch. Or, we realize that the camera has caught what the eye sees but the brain does not register.

So photography gives us access to a dimension of reality that normally eludes us. That seems to be the reason why photographs cast a spell over the spectator. Clearly, the modern, high-speed camera is a magical instrument even before we consider the artistry and outlook of the person who uses it. Like the microscope or the telescope, the camera "invades" an invisible realm and makes it visible.

## PHOTOJOURNALISM

"Art" photography, scientific photography, and portrait photography are older than photojournalism. But it is mainly the association with print journalism and inexpensive print reproduction that accounts for the success of photography. By "success" I mean more than popular acceptance or high commercial value; I mean that many of the world's best photographs have been made by newspaper and magazine photographers. The photojournalistic tradition of *Life* and *Look* continues to operate vigorously in today's newspapers and newsmagazines; it is also a strong influence on television news coverage and motion-picture photography.

As the documentary photograph became our most trusted medium of

Barbara Gluck Treaster. *Huyn Thanh and Descendants*. 1972. New York Times Pictures

Paul Strand. *The Family.* 1953. © 1971 The Estate of Paul Strand

Paul Strand gives us a family of distinct individuals, mutually supportive but absolutely independent. Barbara Treaster's people are entirely dependent on each other. Where Strand emphasizes the spatial separation and parallelism of his figures, Treaster gives hers a common root in the old man's feet. All the forms in the photograph seem to converge on a little area where man and earth meet. Form and idea coincide in each of these photographs.

information, its cheap reproduction by the printing press made it a prime contender with the printed word in a continuing struggle for control of the public mind. If we reckon the progress of that struggle by the changed ratio of words to pictures in printed or electronic form, it is clear that photographs have won. When advertisers decided to shift most of their expenditures from magazines to television, they shifted to a medium that was almost wholly visual, with words heard mainly in "voice-over" commentary. Unfortunately, the consequences for verbal literacy have been disastrous. Still, the public is not ignorant of national and international events; it might even be argued that functional illiterates know more about world affairs than literate persons knew two or three generations ago. From the standpoint of disseminating general information, the technology of the cheaply reproduced image may be superior to printed words.

Photography, then, provides the masses with an eyewitness account of contemporary history. To them it seems more truthful than written history or print journalism: becoming informed becomes fun. Now what accounts for the immense appeal of photojournalism? Aside from low cost and ease of access, we can cite the following factors: (1) photogravure and photo-offset printing yield very good reproductions of photographic originals; (2) the frozen action qualities of the photograph—its candid quality—make viewers believe they are looking at authentic, unposed events; (3) the realism of the photographic image gives it an inherent advantage over the abstract language of print when it comes to reconstructing "the sense" of what actually happened; (4) photojournalism satisfies our voyeuristic impulses better than any other medium of visual or literary art.

Photojournalism became the parent of today's flood of books, magazines, and posters devoted to visual gossip, erotic imagery, and hard- or soft-core pornography. This potential was always latent in photography as a medium, and now it has become an actuality. The camera functioning as a detachable eye—an instrument capable of seeing quickly, secretly, and from odd angles—made photography the ideal medium of voyeurism. Here again, literature could not compete. The candid camera made it possible to see without being seen, to investigate reality without interfering in reality—a kind of triumph over Heisenberg's law.

In the photojournalism of Mathew Brady, people could see the gory side of the Civil War—a dead Confederate sniper—up close. Erich Salomon let us into meetings of international statesmen; we could watch Mussolini's facial acting—up close. That may be why the great war photographer Robert Capa said: "If your pictures aren't good, you're not close enough." Eventually he was killed. So were Werner Bischof and David Seymour ("Chim"): they changed the imagery of war as presented by painting and prints; in their photographs war became a painful, almost tactile, experience. The ugly facts of battle had always been softened by verbal accounts. Literary journalism and historical painting had built-in conventions for creating psychological distance. But photojournalism changed all that: the viewer was transformed from a spectator into a participant. The hand-held camera (still or video) placed viewers' eyes so close to the action that they felt totally involved: this was the "pornography" of war. In peacetime it became the pornography of civil violence. From there it was a short step to pornography in the erotic sense of the word.

## PRINCIPLE OF THE FRAME

The painter's picture frame has architectural roots. This is clear when we realize that mosaics and frescoes were a kind of "fill-in" art: their shapes were defined by a building's structure. It was not until the late Middle Ages that the pictorial image became a window image—the result of seeing *out* of an enclosed space, a room. At this point painting and photography merged in their fundamental outlook: the first *camera obscura* was in fact a darkened room that admitted light through a small opening in one wall, forming an inverted image on the opposite wall.

Photography might not have been invented if Renaissance painters had not begun to think about art in optical and scientific terms. The development of perspective was a reaction against the flat, conceptual approach to imagery that we see in Byzantine art. The Renaissance artist, inspired by classical models of realism and encouraged by a new spirit of openness to sense experience, substituted his eye for the *framed* opening—the window—of a room. And that is essentially what a photographer does.

If we look at a landscape through a window or look at an object through a rectangular opening in a piece of paper, we get the idea of framing as it was understood by the Renaissance painter and the modern photographer. Moving the "window" closer or farther away from the eye enlarges or reduces the size of the visual field. Moving the "window" around in the same plane

Michael Dressler. *Man on a Bicycle*. 1980. New York Times Pictures

A bicyclist speeding past a Los Angeles mural depicting crushed automobiles in a sardine can. The picture's symbolic force depends on a very unusual juxtaposition of images. Obviously, it could not have been posed: this is the poetry that only photojournalists can create.

*left:* Erich Salomon. *Visit of German Statesmen to Rome.* 1931. International Museum of Photography, Eastman House, Rochester, New York

Erich Salomon pioneered the use of photography to show how statesmen actually operate. Visually, at least, his candid camera broke the barrier between the small circles of powerful men who negotiate the fate of mankind and the large body of humanity that looks on. His pictures are historical documents as much as they are works of art. In Teresa Zabala's picture the political photograph is carried beyond journalism: she gives us a psychological reading of these men that transcends the event itself. Whereas Salomon used the grouping of furniture and figures to generate an ominous conspiratorial quality among his politicians, Zabala probes people's faces, appraising them with a thoroughness we have not seen since the doctors in Rembrandt's *Anatomy Lesson* (page 130).

*below:* Teresa Zabala. *Carter with Congressional Leaders.* 1977. New York Times Pictures

has the effect of composing reality as if it were made of flat shapes collected within the frame. This concept of composition relies on the idea of a portable window that can be moved with as much freedom as the human eye itself. The camera, of course, is the photographer's movable window frame.

A further refinement of framing is the device of cropping, a way of *re*framing the image captured in the photographer's print. Cropping represents the photographer's "second chance" to arrange life. The "first chance" was the selection of a piece of reality to be photographed and to live again. That is a seemingly godlike act: not only do photographers choose what viewers see; they also control what is there to be seen. This is creation in an almost primal sense.

The ability to frame and crop reality lies at the heart of the photographer's art. These operations go by names borrowed from painting—"composition" or "design"—but in photography they have different meanings. Photographers isolate and juxtapose objects already created; painters *make* the forms they arrange, and the process takes time. When viewers see a photograph, they think the photographer has seen the image, recorded it, and framed it all at once. That is why they believe the recorded image does not lie. But it does. The photographer's manipulation of edges and tones, negatives and prints, changes the *gestalt*, or configuration, of the image. And if the gestalt is changed, the whole image is changed.

## PHOTOGRAPHY AND ABSTRACTION

Every photograph (like every artificial image) is an abstraction. Its small size, frozen action, flatness, and color (or lack of color) produce simplifications and generalizations of reality. For a variety of reasons we accept these simplifications and generalizations: we agree to see the part for the whole, black-and-white for color, flatness for depth, and stillness for continuous action. *Deliberate* photographic abstraction goes even further: it tries to investigate visual form by surrendering the representational function of photography.

There are essentially two kinds of photographic abstraction. The first might be called "straight abstraction" because it involves no alteration of the camera's optics and very little manipulation of the print during development. Instead, the photographer uses close-ups, unusual angles of vision, or unfamiliar fragments of familiar wholes. Our attention is drawn to patterns and structures which, although they are real, cannot be easily recognized. The purpose of this type of abstraction is to persuade viewers that the real world holds infinite resources of undiscovered beauty. Underlying the work of the straight abstractionist is the well-known formalist aesthetic—the conviction that every part of the universe has been harmoniously designed and assembled.

We have to admit, however, that modern photography finds it ridiculously easy to produce thousands of these formal revelations. They may be aesthetically interesting at first, but the public finds them increasingly boring. Why? Because discovering the world's microscopic realities needs to be done only once. After that viewers lose interest: formal patterns and textures hold our attention only to the extent that we can see their connections to larger patterns of human concern.

A second type of photographic abstraction might be called "synthetic" abstraction. Here the image is more artificially created and is virtually independent of objective or "seen" reality. The connection with the camera itself is somewhat thin: synthetic abstraction relies on the fact that visual forms can be recorded directly on a light-sensitive surface. Man Ray's *rayographs* and Moholy-Nagy's *photograms* tell us through their terminology that they are an essentially new art form—image construction without an eye or a lens.

For the art historian a new classification must reflect a fundamental artistic change, and in synthetic abstraction a new conception of artistic

Paul Caponigro. *Rock Wall No. 2, W. Hartford, Connecticut.* 1959

Photographic abstraction. The rocks are real; this is a "straight," not a manipulated, photograph. But we are forced to concentrate on form and texture rather than on symbol and context. Indeed, light, shape, and texture have been lifted *out of context* and presented purely as aesthetic phenomena.

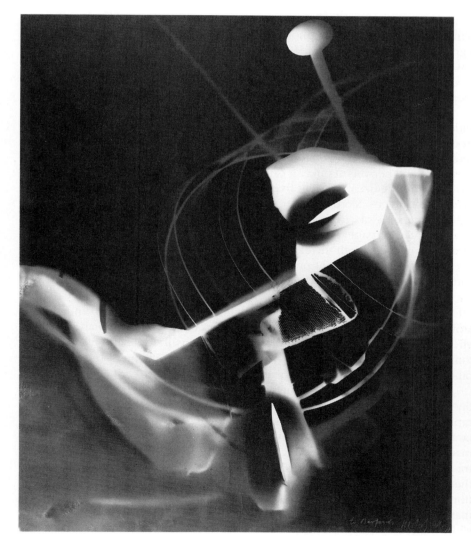

*left:* László Moholy-Nagy. *Untitled (Abstraction) Photogram.* 1924. Courtesy The Art Institute of Chicago. Gift of George Banford, 1968

Synthetic abstraction. Real objects are recorded on photographic paper without the intervention of a camera lens. Through multiple exposures, reversals of light and dark, and manipulation of tones we get an essentially nonobjective, photographic image.

*below:* Willie Vicov. *Heavy Turnout for Philippine Elections.* 1984. UPI/Bettmann Newsphotos

Photographic abstraction. Again, this is "straight" photography; but here we have to concentrate on *patterns* of repetition and variation. The overall image is abstract because it is not about nuns or voting. Not really. The real subject is the variation of similar shapes in similar enclosures. Our pleasure is mainly aesthetic: the contrasts between dark and light, the tilting and turning of forms, and slight changes in size relationships.

imagery is clearly at work. The idea of the lens as a surrogate eye, or witness, or advocate, is substantially abandoned. The synthetic abstractionist works more like a nonobjective painter or printmaker. So, from the standpoint of art history, this type of imagery represents an antiphotographic step—the continuation of a painterly idea with new materials. Photography is redefined as painting with light.

## THE PHOTOGRAPHIC SLIDE

Today, many photographers make slides instead of prints. In fact, more film is sold for slide transparencies than for any other purpose. Unlike the film negative, which has to be printed to make a positive, the slide carries a positive image as soon as it is processed. To see that image, the photographer merely projects it on a screen. So making slides rather than prints has grown in popularity among serious photographers. The advantage of slides lies in their low cost and ease of storage for easy retrieval. Also, color slides kept in a dark box are less subject to fading than color prints. For this reason alone, slides are very useful in scientific and educational work. We may be reluctant to think of the slide as an art object because we do not usually see it, only its projected image. But neither do we see the film in a movie, or the tape in a video-cassette.

One of the truisms of our time is that weddings and birthday parties are staged for the benefit of the photographer. As for the old-fashioned touristic pilgrimage, many of us do not really see the monuments because we are too busy taking pictures. Mostly, these pictures are processed as slides that will be shown at home. So the ridiculous spectacle of a photographer thrusting himself into the most solemn moment of a wedding, for example, has serious significance: the authentic witnessing of the event does not take place until a few close friends and relatives meet in a dark room to see the slides. The wedding or Bar Mitzvah was not a charade, not exactly. It was a piece of folk theater meant to be solemnized under the auspices of the slide projector.

Aesthetics comes into play as we consider the image created when the slide is projected on a screen. What the viewer sees is light reflected back from a screen, or, in the case of rear projection, light transmitted through a screen. The image can be quite large—cinema size, if desired—and it can be seen by many persons at once. It can even be projected into the night sky; at Las Vegas any citizen can pay five dollars and have his image spread out across the heavens. More importantly, when the image consists of transmitted light, it is capable of carrying a wider range of color and tonal values than an image printed on paper. Thus the slide projection has all the blown-up realism of cinema imagery, with the exception of motion.

The photographic print produces an image by a process of darkening a surface—usually paper—covered with a photographic emulsion. The forms we see are created by *subtracting* light from a surface that is white, or off-white, but not as bright as a source that seems to generate its own light. However, the slide projection glows (special screen coatings enhance that effect) and thus it has more vividness. Perhaps this is why students accustomed to slide lectures are disappointed when they encounter originals: an oil-on-canvas image cannot compete with the silver screen.

The slide image represents only one line of photographic evolution—the line that connects it to film and television. The other line connects photography to graphic art. Here the frame format inherited from painting is important. It would be difficult to conceive of "art" photography apart from pictures matted and framed like drawings, etchings, or easel paintings. However, traditional paintings and prints are limited in size; only a few persons can see them at once; they become mass media only through cheap print reproduction. The slide projection, on the other hand, is ideal for low cost, high quality mass viewing. The slide image (or the image created by projecting several slides simultaneously) is unaffected by graphic constraints; its edges are not governed by carved moldings or printed pages. Also, slide projections are not graspable objects; they enter experience in a dematerialized fashion, like light or air. So the future of the projected image may be limited only by the physiological and cognitive capabilities of the human organism.

It seems likely that slide images will evolve into something beyond photography as we know it. At the same time, photographic *prints* will probably consolidate and perfect themselves along traditional, pictorial lines. Thus photography will behave like the older art forms; it will spawn new offspring while itself remaining the same.

## THE PHOTOGRAPHER AS ARTIST

Oddly enough, amateurism strongly affects the practice of photography as a "fine art." The factors that account for the spread of amateurism among painters also influence serious photography. An inexpensive and easily used technology enables photographers to function more independently than painters and sculptors. Photographs can be cheaply reproduced and they are not hard to display; indeed they can be passed from hand to hand. Unlike writers, photographers do not depend on the costly technology of the printing industry; they need not contend with editors and publishers; they can function without a literate reading public. Photographers are more like independent craftsmen; they can reach the public without too much trouble, and most people can afford to buy photographs.

Because the same equipment is available to almost everyone, the professional photographer's *attitude* becomes the distinctive instrument of his or her art. A painter's eyes, fingers, and wrist are unique; they are integral parts of the act of painting. But we cannot make the same claim for the photographer's finger on the shutter-release: the photographer's visual and intellectual equipment is crucial. A camera has no built-in mechanism of selection, so the photographer's decision-making turns out to be the most creatively significant aspect of the art. But choices made instantaneously

*left:* Claes Oldenburg. *The Stove.* 1962. Metal, porcelain, paint, and plaster, 58 × 28 × 27½". Private collection

The derisory statement made by Oldenburg's stove relies, in a sense, on the homely old image of a stove in the Evans photograph. Before he could make it ridiculous, Oldenburg had to festoon the stove with large portions of specially constructed, inedible food. Evans, on the other hand, celebrates the beloved cast-iron monster as the only solid, durable object in a seedy environment. The photographer's manipulation of context—the frontal "pose" of the stove, the decision to "place" the pots and pans at eye-level—is less obvious than Oldenburg's manufacture of a sleazy meal. But it is no less an act of artistic selection and organization.

*below:* Walker Evans. *Frank's Stove, Cape Breton Island.* Yale University Art Gallery, New Haven. Director's Purchase Fund

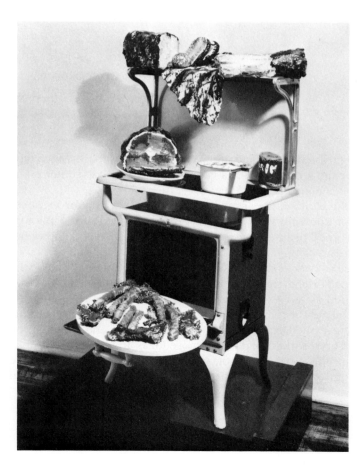

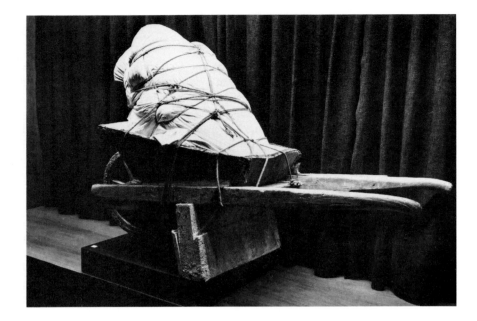

Christo. *Package on Wheelbarrow.* 1963. Cloth, metal, wood, rope, and twine, 35⅛ × 59½ × 20¼". Collection, The Museum of Modern Art, New York. Blanchette Rockefeller Fund

The bound or wrapped figure has been used as a symbol of confined power from Michelangelo to Rodin to Christo. Carolyn Watson's photograph retains the form but changes its meaning: her figures are more nearly related to Henry Moore's sleepers in the London underground during World War II. Why is this a great photograph? Because Watson saw a universal image in these two sleepers. Her print transcends the fact that two Americans had to bed down on a bench in London because of a shortage of hotel rooms. The capacity to leap from the recording of a local event to the representation of a general idea accounts for the extraordinary power and poetry of *Crash Pad.*

Carolyn Watson. *Crash Pad.* June 1971. Courtesy Monkmeyer Press Photo Service

depend on a lengthy period of incubation. Photography is more than a type of mechanical seeing; it presupposes a capacity to sense what is interesting, to recognize what is humanly *worth* seeing.

In stressing the photographer's mental and cultural preparation we stress the importance of knowing what makes a picture good to see. A photographer who takes good pictures consistently has more than luck on his or her side: he is obviously *looking for something*; good pictures are proof of *focused knowledge* as well as darkroom skill. Viewers expect a photograph to be the product of informed seeing: they want to believe their perceptions have been shaped and guided by an exceptional human intelligence; otherwise the values of a photograph become a matter of good or bad optical recording. Ultimately, the great photographers give us the sense of encountering the world through an artist's mind—an artist whose ideas and biases are visible. Whether we share those biases or not, we need to be convinced they are there. In photography, point-of-view has optical *and* philosophical significance.

# PHOTOGRAPHIC CRITICISM

The criticism of photography is largely undeveloped for three reasons. First, in its perfected form the medium is less than a century old—not long enough for a solid body of aesthetic theory to develop. Second, most scholarly writing about photography deals either with technical questions or the history of photography, that is, the history of camera equipment, developing processes, and the biographies of famous photographers. Third, in the struggle to free itself from the parent art of painting, photographic criticism often neglects the theory developed by the older visual arts.

It is unfortunate, too, that conventionally trained art historians have paid little attention to the evolution of photography as an art. They may mention the influence of photography on Courbet or on Degas and the French Impressionists, but they rarely discuss the role of photography in our visual culture as a whole; they ignore the changes photography has wrought on contemporary modes of seeing and thinking. Without addressing these questions, however, photographic criticism cannot rise above shop talk; the central problems of aesthetic value are encountered only when critics deal with photography as it confronts the major questions of society and mankind.

The battle to recognize photography as a full-fledged art form has been fought and largely won—by Alfred Stieglitz, Edward Steichen, Beaumont Newhall, Minor White, Helmut Gernsheim, John Szarkowski, Aaron Scharf, Peter Pollack, Van Deren Coke, and many others. For criticism, winning this battle has important consequences: membership in the fine arts "club" means that photographs can be judged like other works of visual art. The early status of photography as a bastard art form excluded it from serious consideration. That has now changed. But does the emergence of photography as a new art form create a new set of aesthetic expectations? No. The sources of artistic form may vary, but human needs with respect to any visual presentation are remarkably consistent. So the factors that make a good photograph are similar to those that operate in the case of drawings, paintings, and prints.

But if the criteria of greatness in visual art are similar, there are nevertheless "local" factors that operate uniquely in each art, including photography. These grow out of the technical features of the camera, the physical character of photographic prints, and the economic factors that govern their reproduction and distribution. The small size of the photograph should be mentioned—its portability and accessibility as a hand-held object. The photograph is a possession that can be carried everywhere because it fits into a wallet or a purse. Like books, photographs can be privately studied and savored. Yet they can also be vastly enlarged. As large-scale images for advertising, information, and display, photographs are perhaps the most public of visual art forms. That public character connects photography to society and history in a manner that gives the aesthetics of photography its own unique flavor.

We come, then, to photographic criteria of excellence. What separates a great photograph from a good one? Naturally, we must judge a photograph according to the way it uses the opportunities and overcomes the limitations presented by the medium. At the same time, we cannot forget that photography is an art of ideas as well as images. Therefore, our critical method should enable us to see connections between quality of technique and quality of thought or feeling; it should enable us to recognize and evaluate the interactions between medium and meaning.

The qualities that photographs must possess in order to be judged excellent can be identified. They can be designated as positions on six scales or *continua*; one end of each scale stands for a minimum of quality, while the other end represents a maximum. Since any given photograph is unlikely to fulfill every ideal expectation, we have to estimate its cumulative achievement on all six scales to form an overall judgment of its merit.

## A PAINTING THAT LOOKS LIKE A PHOTOGRAPH

Chuck Close. *Susan.* 1971. Acrylic on canvas, 8'4" × 7'6". Courtesy Pace Gallery, New York

A painting that looks like a photograph; a photograph that looks like a painting. Are we witnessing an identity crisis? Certainly we are faced with serious problems of photographic criticism. Siskind didn't *make* this photograph, he *took* it—and created an image with all the Abstract Expressionist power one could want. Now, what does that say to a "real" painter?

Aaron Siskind. *Lima 89 (Homage to Franz Kline).* 1975. Courtesy Light Gallery, New York

## A PHOTOGRAPH THAT LOOKS LIKE A PAINTING

Following are the scales, each of which goes from low to high: (1) from surface to depth, (2) from optical to tactile, (3) from pattern to idea, (4) from part to whole, (5) from singular to typical, and (6) from record to original. The first three scales emphasize technical qualities. The last three scales stress the conceptual factors affecting the evaluation of a photograph, assuming it has met our technical requirements. A photograph that scores "high" on any one of these six scales would be interesting; a high evaluation on several scales suggests the possibility of greatness. In Chapter Sixteen of this book, the discussion dealing with "Kinds of Critical Judgment" presents the general criteria on which these photographic scales are based.

***From Surface to Depth.*** Obviously, we are not referring to depth-of-field—the right aperture and focal length of the camera lens. Photographic depth refers to the volumetric quality of form; its lack is felt as thinness, lightness, or flatness. Lightness or thinness designates an unconvincing representation of the mass or weight of forms; it may be due to improper exposure and/or poor lighting. More fundamentally, it results from the photographer's failure to represent the invisible tensions and strains that contribute to the weight and shape of an object. Flatness is the failure of the image to account photographically for the distribution of objects in space.

The formal values of a good print depend very much on the photographer's ability to represent three-dimensional volumes with a mo-

Walker Evans. *Graveyard in Easton, Pennsylvania.* 1936. Library of Congress. Farm Security Administration Collection, Washington, D.C.

Andreas Feininger. *Cemetery in New York City.* 1948. *Life* magazine. © 1948, Time, Inc.

## FROM SURFACE TO DEPTH

The convincing distribution of objects in deep space calls for skillful technical control of the photographic medium. But technical control, while indispensable, cannot of itself produce depth as we intend it here. The ability to capture surface changes has to be the servant of a poetic sensibility. That is, textural change and spatial differentiation must be subordinate to the cognitive and emotive requirements of the image. Evans does only an adequate job of rendering the texture of the limestone cross, the scrubby grass, the brick-front houses, and the smokestacks. Edward Weston or Ansel Adams could have produced a better print. But Evans's point of view and his choice of a flat light over his shoulder have yielded a type of depth that no amount of textural detail could equal. It is his angle of vision—just next to the large cross— that gives the spacing to the other grave markers. This is what causes the rapid reduction in size relationships, especially between the cross and the brick dwellings. It even helps to compress the layers of rooftops, chimneys, and buildings near the horizon. Thus a squeezing down in the distance produces a pressure that seems to spread out the foreground objects, thrusting the graves toward us. This manipulation of depth, as much as the symbolism of the cross, creates photographic quality. The principal objects receive precisely the amount of space and light needed to define their forms and, more importantly, to reach a significant level of human meaning.

Feininger is a more "scientific" photographer; hence his approach to three-dimensional depth is a model of technical control. Yet it is a poetic device that creates the aesthetic depth of the work. Feininger has to contend with the fact that his telephoto lens foreshortens space, pressing distant forms into the frontal plane. He copes with this flattening effect by relying on an Eastern pictorial device: movement upward means movement inward. But how can Western viewers be persuaded to accept this way of seeing? Feininger eliminates the horizon as well as enclosing or framing lines. As a result we are forced to see the photograph as if it were a tapestry of gravestones. Our perceptual energies are concentrated on the texture of the fabric, so to speak. Now we can see subtle changes of light and dark seeming to form an S-curve that leads the eye gradually into the upper fifth of the picture. There the gravestones lose their detail; they retain only their rectangular shapes, like the crisp gray notes around the edges of a Cubist composition. This Cubist dissolution of mass, accomplished in a gently ascending movement, suggest a lovely analogy. In the bottom of the photograph the dead have begun to exchange their identities; by the time we reach the top their souls are dancing.

## FROM OPTICAL TO TACTILE

Here are three strong photographs that rely heavily on the sense of touch. Which is not to say they are merely textural studies. However, they do demonstrate the power of the medium to create monumental effects without pictorial trickery. What we see is optical rendering carried to a peak of tactile expressiveness. Notice that the subjects are all presented frontally; the problems of composition are uncomplicated; and there is little or no appeal to narrative values. To be sure, Strand's *Ranchos de Taos* touches on regional and historical ideas, but it is mainly the weight and volumetric quality of the architectural forms that account for the impact of his image. The Weston *Cabbage Leaf* is an even purer demonstration of the power of photography to generate plastic, i.e., sculptural, values with very commonplace materials. It is significant that Weston achieves a lyricism here that one cannot imagine in any other medium. Raymond's photograph is a tactile triumph of another sort. To be sure, the soft chenille fabric receives much of its sculptural quality from the bed and pillow underneath. But Raymond has also been attentive to the active notes struck by the folds at the head and foot of the bed. Finally and most photographically, these are contrasted to the flat, quiet texture barely visible in the wallpaper pattern. We know that black-and-white photography operates within a narrow visual range. Hence our criterion—from optical to tactile—emphasizes the control of volumes through the visual orchestration of textures. It shows that while still photography can suggest the qualities of the nonvisual senses—sound, taste, kinesthesia, and even smell—it is through rendering tactility that photography's claim to represent reality is most powerfully achieved.

Edward Weston. *Cabbage Leaf.* 1931. Courtesy Cole Weston

Paul Strand. *Ranchos de Taos, New Mexico.* 1931. © 1977
The Estate of Paul Strand

Lilo Raymond. *Bed in Attic.* 1972. Courtesy the photographer

nocular instrument. Because we are binocular creatures, we expect to see depth. In the pictures of Edward Weston or Ansel Adams, we think we see depth—beautifully. The effect is caused by a masterful control of light gradations. That control communicates the physical substance and spatial location of forms through purely photographic means. Something of this quality must be present in every good print.

*From Optical to Tactile.*    Photography approaches reality from a distance and from a wholly visual standpoint. Yet the reality of matter is best recognized through the feel, or tactility, of forms. Now, photography employs a developing process that subtracts light, and the loss of light can produce a loss of textural detail. Painting has the advantage of being able to construct form by adding light, or adding shadow, or both—achieving texture either way. Thus the photographer is caught between the proverbial rock and a hard place: he or she needs optical detail to suggest the weight and texture of reality; at the same time the chemistry of photography tends to darken prints and to eliminate detail. So the photographer is always engaged in seeking an optimal balance between light and dark to preserve visual facts and textural quality.

Connoisseurs know that the grain of photographic emulsions and papers can supplement or "improve" upon the visual facts. Beyond a certain point, however, such work becomes manipulative or nonphotographic—the simulation of painting or printmaking. Our rule here is: the tactility of a good photograph must be perceived as the product of an ocular process. In other words, the tactile values of a print must be photographic in origin; that excludes effects achieved through darkroom maneuvers.

*From Pattern to Idea.*    The photograph devoted to pure pattern is a commonplace achievement for the camera; often it represents good technique combined with a modest level of insight. But the camera is better employed

**George Gerster. *Sahara Pollution.* © 1976 Foto George Gerster. Courtesy Photo Researchers, Inc., New York**

An eloquent example of pattern employed in a cognitive, as opposed to a formal, context. It is the juxtaposition of beautifully patterned sand and seemingly casual deposits of trash that makes the forms work expressively. By themselves, the wavelike sand forms would look like a thousand other photographs of desert rhythms. As for the trash piles, they are curiously, almost perversely, satisfying. Perhaps that is because the endless regularity of the sand patterns makes us hunger for signs of visual randomness. Notice, too, how the human figures on the upper left horizon provide a sense of scale for the picture as a whole. At the same time they hint at the essential idea of the picture—the painful connection between human settlement and pollution.

as a machine that sees in order to know, to admire, to express, and to explain. The mere recording of patterns becomes photographic kitsch—a pretense to aesthetic profundity. Of course, patterns can be truthful as visual reports, but to sustain our interest they have to *signify* something beyond their own existence.

Patterns that require labels to be understood must be judged unsuccessful as photographic art. For a pattern to succeed aesthetically we have to *see* its meaning or significance, not read it. In other words, the formal values of a photograph require a larger context—the context of mind—as an essential support. Discovering patterns in nature or the manufactured environment becomes aesthetically potent when the photographer *shows us* their connections to the unfolding processes of nature, or reveals them as products of human powers of invention and transformation. Otherwise we feel we are looking at a kind of empty ornament—easily seen and easily forgotten.

*From Part to Whole.* The camera can only record fragments but art has to reveal universals. This is not a question of picturing large subjects or panoramic scenes. It is rather a problem in selecting and organizing what is partial or incomplete so that viewers believe they see something finished and whole. Bad photographers seek the effect of wholeness by manipulation—usually by simulating the painter's tonalities and subordination of detail. This might be called "forced" unity. Good photographers rely on (a) selecting the significant feature of a subject; and (b) framing and composing a subject so that we sense its belonging to a complete universe. Obviously, choosing the significant detail is crucial; that choice may be visual, intellectual, or intuitive.

**Werner Bischof.** *Boy Leaving His Sick Grandfather, Korea.* Undated. Courtesy Magnum Photos, New York

The purpose of photographic composition is to make fragments of reality enter into complete relationships. Here portions of two figures have been organized into a whole that augments the expressive power of each part. The square window does more than frame the boy and concentrate our attention on his anguish: its placement initiates all the visual events within the image; it explains the darkness of the room; it dramatizes the somber texture of the wall; it contrasts the glaring outdoor illumination with the soft light barely crossing the grandfather's body. Most important, the diagonal formed by the boy's arm movement connects the pieces of the image with its narrative: it gives the angle and destination of his gaze; it makes us attend to the direction of the old man's stare—over the viewer's right shoulder and into the distance. Finally, it opposes the weight of the boy's arm and shoulder to the weightlessness of the sick man's hands. In purely design terms it relates the window to the room; in symbolic terms it compares the vertical situation with the horizontal situation. Bischof believed, and here demonstrates, that the pictorial dynamics of a photographic statement are inseparable from its human meaning.

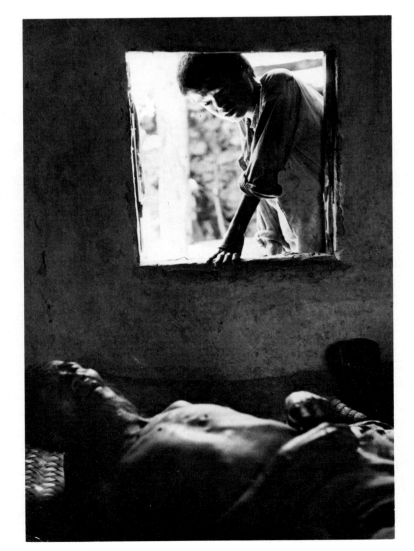

The important point is that viewers should be able to sense the totality of a situation through seeing a part of it.

*From Singular to Typical.*    Compared to the other visual arts, photography can easily capture the exotic, the peculiar, and the freakish. It can readily gratify the human interest in weird people and strange actions. That is what photojournalism often does in carrying out the responsibilities of reportage. But photography as art must go beyond the recording of shocking events or grotesque phenomena. Otherwise it degenerates into a search for perversity, abnormality, and violence.

Henri Cartier-Bresson. *Children Playing in the Ruins, Spain.* 1933. Courtesy Magnum Photos, New York

In the introduction to his book *The Decisive Moment,* Cartier-Bresson says: "Above all, I craved to seize the whole essence, in the confines of one single photograph, of some situation that was in the process of unrolling itself before my eyes." Our criterion—from singular to typical—stresses this same objective. Cartier-Bresson's famous photograph illustrates the concept perfectly; both incident and idea are captured in a single image. Notice how Ben Shahn's *Liberation* (page 180) employs the same notion of a picture; it is essentially a photographic approach: the grotesque incident frozen and transmuted into an idea. To some extent we can explain the expressive force of Cartier-Bresson's photograph in compositional terms: the children in the rubble-strewn street distributed along an S-curve that comes to an abrupt halt with the boy on crutches; the jerky rhythm created by the repeated angles of the children's bodies. But there are psychological factors at work here, too: in the tension caused by our fear that the boy's crutches will be caught in the stones and he will fall down hard; in the cruelty of boys at play; and in the contrast between the laughing faces and the rough frame created by a shell hole. Most important is the rapid divergence of the lines forming the wall against which this drama unfolds; it propels the crippled youngster forward like a shot. These devices, and more, lie beneath the photographic surface of the work. It has taken me some time to see them and a paragraph to describe them even briefly; Cartier-Bresson caught them in an instant. Such mastery must be the product of a long apprenticeship, a quick mind, an intelligent eye. By "intelligent eye" I mean the photographer's ability to make an immediate, almost instinctive connection between what he sees in a scene, what it signifies at the moment, and what it means in depth—what it means as an idea that can occupy the mind permanently.

Robert Walker. *Find Coffee House.* 1971.
New York Times Pictures

Here is a work that epitomizes the distinction between a photograph that copies or records an
event and a photograph that makes a discovery
which is aesthetically and humanly significant.
Walker's photograph, in my judgment, bears comparison with the works of Pieter Brueghel, Adriaen Brouwer, and even of Rembrandt. Consider
the Caravaggesque lighting that bathes the figure
in the upper left: it is a little masterpiece in itself.
The hand and head of the woman in the lower
right could have been taken from an interior by
Vermeer. Now these comparisons are not made to
establish the greatness of a photograph by dem-
onstrating its genealogy in the history of painting.
It is rather to say that the same factors which
make a masterwork of a Brouwer or a Vermeer
operate in the present instance. Notice how the
size and focal properties of the man advancing
with his crutches create a tension-filled space between him and the figures in the background. It is
a space modeled in the tradition of the great Baroque canvases. At the same time, the scale relationships and perspectival effects are purely photographic. The ground plane moves up and away
from us about as fast as the central figure moves
toward us. The result is a powerful and dramatic
pair of opposed movements, each culminating in
an episode that demands our compassion in a different way. An isolated figure, almost lost in
shadow (right middle-ground), provides precisely
the right amount of interest and space modulation
needed in that quadrant of the composition. The
photograph satisfies our surface-to-depth requirements; it nourishes our tactile feelings through optical representation; it transcends the unusual or
special character of the place and its people. And
it takes up several great themes: helplessness,
courage, loneliness, and love.

Some photographers confuse visual or moral shock with aesthetic
surprise. Here Velázquez is our best model: he could portray human deformity without losing sight of what is noble in human beings. Diane Arbus skates
on thinner ice: she brings us face-to-face with physical and psychological
abnormalities, but it is uncertain whether she is exploiting freaks or asking us
to realize that her people are fellow sufferers. Discovering universal human
qualities in people who are outcast, ugly, or afflicted is morally and aesthetically admirable. So the photographer's rule should be: Show us the truth
about the human condition but do not use human misery as a source of thrills.

*From Record to Original.*    The photograph as record tells us what we
would have seen or known if we were "there." This kind of image is a
convenient mechanical substitute for personal witness: it enables us to travel
without leaving home, to remember without summoning up mental images.
Such pictures are valuable to the extent that they are reliable, that is, accurate.
An "original" photograph, on the other hand, represents a fresh discovery.
That "discovery" is partially related to the character of the photographic act:
"taking" a picture means searching, getting warm, getting hot, and finally
finding something new.

So it is not enough for the photographer to be "there" with his or her
camera; it is necessary to be humanly "there." Otherwise the photograph will
merely record what a mindless machine would record. Great originals result
from alertness to the unusual—an instinctive recognition of images that say
something new. Good photographers are allergic to visual clichés and
stereotypes. So again, the mental preparation of the photographic artist must
be emphasized: When the preparation is right and when the execution is
timely, the photograph represents a live birth—in the creator and the spectator. We may have seen an object or a place a thousand times before, but it
has to strike us as a revelation. Great photographs should enable us to see
innocently—like children.

# CHAPTER FIFTEEN

# IMAGES IN MOTION: FILM AND TELEVISION

*"Until there is a chapter on film in every textbook of art . . . we shall not have firmly established in the consciousness of our generation this most important artistic development of our century." Bela Balazs,* Theory of the Film, *1952.*

A complex technology stands behind motion pictures and television, yet it is correct to think of both media as extensions of painting and picture-making. The pioneers of still photography operated on the basis of a painterly sensibility, and, even today, a long pictorial tradition supports the work of photographers and cinematographers. This will remain true as long as film and television are seen in a two-dimensional, rectangular format. The great change, of course, was the creation of a credible illusion of motion on a flat surface: it opened up the ancient art of painting and transformed it into a revolutionary force in modern life.

The illusions created by film and TV are so convincing that we are hardly aware of their pictorial connections. We are like Renaissance viewers discovering the optical miracles created by the newly discovered science of perspective. In the fifteenth century, the convincing representation of objects in depth liberated the imagination of artist and viewer alike. A long-standing goal of the pictorial tradition had been the creation of lifelike illusions; each new triumph in pictorial representation encouraged viewers to believe they were watching man's conquest of reality. Now, motion pictures and TV seem to have accomplished the ultimate—the complete simulation of reality. But

**Film still from *Modern Times*. Directed by Charles Chaplin. 1936**

Chaplin's tramp, a born loser, gets caught up in the wheels and gears of industry. Here we see how the main idea of the film—the crazy conflict between man and mechanization—is captured in a single image.

*above:* Käthe Kollwitz. *Peasant War Cycle: Sharpening of the Scythe.* 1905. Etching, 11½ × 11½". Courtesy, Museum of Fine Arts, Boston. Gift of L. Aaron Lebowich

After World War I, a Central European film style emerged based on German Expressionist graphic art, which had generated a powerful message by demoniacal lighting of subjects from below. Notice how the shadows work: they create a mood of terror by using pictorial devices taken from the design of woodcuts and etchings.

*right:* Film still from *The Cabinet of Dr. Caligari: Dr. Caligari.* Directed by Robert Wiene. 1919

technology does not stand still: lasers and holography promise to make the three-dimensional simulation of reality even more convincing.

Motion pictures and television depend on two separate but interdependent factors. First is the long artistic tradition that tries to re-present our world and our experience. Second is the continuous stream of new technologies that record reality: the camera, flexible film, film projection, synchronous sound and imagery, color photography, the iconoscope or videocamera, videotape, holography, and so on. With these technologies we have created aesthetic devices like montage, close-up, slow motion, split screen, wide screen, freeze-frame, and instant replay. It can be argued that artistic necessity motivated these technical developments. Or, perhaps technology changed according to its own internal laws. In either case, we have to consider the interaction of technical and aesthetic factors in order to understand film as an art form.

## THE MANIPULATION OF SPACE-TIME

Artists have always tried to represent movement; they blurred the edges of forms, added "speed" lines to contours, and visualized the imagined positions of bodies in motion. Without the capacity to use real motion they relied on suggestion—something close to magic. Well, some forms of magic are more convincing than others: motion pictures rely on magic, too. If you look at film footage you can see that it consists of thousands of fixed images.

Why are we willing to believe in the filmmaker's magic—the illusion of reality created by little pictures on film passing across a beam of light at the rate of twenty-four frames per second? Apparently, more than magic is involved; there are physiological effects, too. Each picture lingers as an after-image; that image is not instantly extinguished in the viewer's eye; our eyes fail to see the empty intervals (lasting 1/48 of a second) between the separate still images. Neither can we see the swift motion of the electronic beam that scans the TV tube to create pictures with little points of light. The optical persistence of the still image (or the "running together" of points of light on the TV tube) combined with our delayed perception of the changes from image to image make us believe we are witnessing real movement. Movement, in turn, is one of the most reliable indicators of life. So a chain of physical, physiological, and psychological events identifies the viewing of motion pictures with the viewing of reality.

As technology succeeded in representing motion credibly, a new artistic exploitation of space and time became possible. Filmmakers could manipulate space and time for the following reasons: (1) they controlled a technology that converts time into lengths of film; and (2) viewers identify cinematic space-time with real space-time. The cinematographer was no different from the Renaissance draftsman who could draw lines converging on a horizon line and thus convince viewers that they were seeing reality in depth. The

Marcel Duchamp. *Nude Descending a Staircase, No. 2.*
1912. Oil on canvas, 57½ × 35". Philadelphia Museum
of Art. The Louise and Walter Arensberg Collection

When exhibited at the Armory Show in 1913, this
picture was called, by some smart critic, "an explosion
in a shingle factory." The germ of truth here is more
important than its attempt at humor: Duchamp did in
fact paint movement as an explosion; his painting also
resembles a strip of motion-picture film seen very
quickly. It looks like an explosion until the projector
runs it past our eyes at a speed of twenty-four frames
per second.

Renaissance perspectivist could speed up or slow down a viewer's optical
journey by shortening or lengthening the lines moving toward the horizon
(which was an illusion). Similarly, cinematographers can represent the crossing of great distances or the passage of long time periods by controlling
lengths of film. Short distances can be extended and brief events made to last
seemingly forever. Using slow motion, reverse motion, or speeded-up motion, cinematographers have a "time machine" that lets them control pieces
of reality captured on film. Through editing, or montage, they compose with
film footage and, in effect, play with the viewer's perception of the "real"
world; actually, the viewer lives in *his* or *her* (the cinematographer's) world.
Oddly enough, the technology that makes these things possible is primitive
compared to much of modern applied science—the computer, for example.
Still, it is revolutionary as far as human imaginative life is concerned. But the
wheel was a simple machine, too.

**Film Devices**    The artistic devices available to the filmmaker can be divided
into two categories: (1) those that simulate the natural activity of the eye as it
examines objects in space; and (2) those that simulate our mental activity as
we experience the duration and quality of time.

The basic tool of cinematic space and object scanning is the *visual
continuity sequence*. This consists, very simply, of the long shot, the medium
or transitional shot, and the close-up. The camera imitates the eye as it scans
a scene: it establishes the overall situation, selects a subject within the situation, moves closer to it, and concentrates on significant details of the subject
by inspecting its details and enlarging their size on the screen—the close-up.

David W. Griffith is generally credited with the earliest use of the close-
up, a device he employed sparingly but eloquently. As an aesthetic device,
the close-up is tremendously powerful; it exaggerates the most subtle and
transient visual effects, and it generates a unique sense of intimacy. The

Film still from *The Sea*. Directed by Patroni Griffi. 1962

Even though cinema is a public medium, it gives us access, through the motion-picture camera, to scenes of the utmost intimacy and tenderness. The film close-up breaks the conventional distance between ourselves and other people. This nearness, plus over-lifesize imagery, creates over-lifesize emotions.

Film still from *The Loves of a Blonde*. Directed by Miloš Forman. 1967. Courtesy CCM Films, Inc.

close-up, in turn, created a distinctive type of screen style—facial acting. On the cinema screen, limited facial movements acquire immense expressive meaning. Also, the enormous enlargement of persons and objects emphasizes the tactile qualities of the film image. Thus a director can draw attention to significant details while generating an intense awareness of their slightest movement and texture. In addition, film close-ups destroy cultural conventions about the "right" distance between a viewer and another person. As these conventions of distance are broken down, visual images generate tactile feelings which produce strong emotional reactions.

As visual continuity is established, persons and objects are located in space. However, the visual continuity sequence is only a primitive unit of the motion-picture art; it corresponds to words, phrases, and sentences in writing. By themselves, their meaning is limited; they have to be assembled and orchestrated in paragraphs and chapters to support the sort of meaning encountered in a story or a novel. We need visual narrative or plot—the combination of images in sequences that express developments *in time.*

Assembling and orchestrating images would be merely decorative if it did not attempt to shape the viewer's experience of time. In film art, time is *abstracted from* things and felt increasingly for its own qualities. The other visual arts—painting, sculpture, and architecture—also try to manipulate time, but they do not enjoy the technical advantages of the motion-picture or TV camera, which converts time into linear-feet of film or tape. By cutting, inserting, and splicing film, the filmmaker can manipulate time more directly than the painter or sculptor. The filmmaker can govern the amount of time you and I spend on objects and events. The result is an extraordinary degree of control over the viewer's imaginative life for a real-time period that can last for hours.

Following are some of the main technical and artistic terms used in making motion pictures.

| | |
|---|---|
| Frame Shot | A single picture on a strip of film. |
| Shot | The fundamental compositional unit in a film sequence; a visual unit consisting of many frames. One element in a film scene; sometimes called a "take." |
| Sequence | A single filmic idea consisting of one or more shots or takes. It corresponds to a paragraph in prose. |
| Montage | The editing of film through various kinds of cutting and dissolves. |
| Cut-in | Insertion of a detail, usually a close-up, taken from the main action of a film sequence. |
| Cut-away | Insertion of a detail outside of, but metaphorically related to, the main action of a film sequence. |
| Overlap | Repetition of action from an immediately preceding sequence at the beginning of a new sequence. |
| Fade-in | The gradual emergence of the film image from darkness. |
| Fade-out | The gradual disappearance of the film image into darkness. |
| Dissolve | The fade-out of one image as another, over which it has been superimposed, takes its place. |
| Wipe | The displacement of a film image by another image or shape; it takes any direction across the screen as it erases its predecessor. |
| Dollying | Continuous motion of a platform-mounted camera toward or away from a subject, causing its image to grow larger or smaller on the screen. |
| Panning | Following the action of a subject with the camera, or moving the camera across relatively stationary objects. |
| Zooming | Rapid movement toward the subject by dollying, or by using a zoom lens, which achieves the same effect with a stationary camera. |

# FILM AND TV TYPES

Like all new media, movies and television began as new ways of presenting established art, information, and entertainment forms. Film and television continue to use the older forms: the novel, the stage play, the lecture, the sermon, the magazine, the short story, the outdoor poster, the carnival sideshow, party games, and combinations of all of them. Because of this mixed and varied ancestry, Pauline Kael may have been right when she described film as "a bastard, cross-fertilized super-art."

Translated into new media, the older art forms become documentaries, commercials, daytime serials, sitcoms, sermonettes, celebrity interviews, and game shows. To the extent that they adapt to the new media, the traditional art forms acquire new aesthetic identities. This is especially true of the film documentary, the soap opera, and the TV commercial. But when the older art forms are reproduced unchanged, their aesthetic power is usually weakened. A televised lecture—the well-known talking head—can be very dull. But sometimes, skillful camera work manages to create new and exciting visual content, as in the thirty-second TV "spots" for boring politicians. Thus film and TV do more than enlarge the audience for traditional forms of information and entertainment; they fundamentally change what is said and how it is seen and understood. Thus today's media managers also manage content.

"I didn't read the book but I saw the movie." Does that mean I "know" the novel? Of course not; even the plot was probably changed in the movie. But a more fundamental change occurs when a novel becomes a film, or a magazine ad becomes a TV commercial. The basic difference lies in the organization of space—unilinear and unidirectional in the case of print; multilinear and multidirectional in the case of film. The rules for reading print are quite strict, whereas the rules for reading film are more lenient, if only because there is so much more to see. So we get more information with less effort in the film or TV presentation. Because the visual media tell several stories at once, they accomplish more than print in a given amount of space.

No wonder, then, that advertisers favor visual images over words; they get "more bang for the buck." It is a matter of selecting a superior technology for the delivery of their message. Does this mean that aesthetic values are sacrificed in the transition from old to new media? Not at all. The new media simply exercise a different set of aesthetic capacities. The film and TV viewing public seems to know this very well: people watch TV commercials for detergents, deodorants, and "lite" beer with a great deal of pleasure. Why? Because of the simultaneous imagery; the multidirectional organization of space on TV is very good. As for the words, few of us give them serious attention.

**Scene from the television show *All in the Family.* Courtesy Columbia Broadcasting System**

The Archie Bunker family eating, talking, and complaining all at once. Small as it is, the TV tube manages to carry a great deal of simultaneous action, dialogue, and detail. How? By using old-fashioned pictorial composition; the same grouping of figures can be found in nineteenth-century genre painting. Of course, Archie had a great nineteenth-century mind.

# FILMED VERSUS TELEVISED IMAGERY

The technical differences between filmed and televised imagery can be exaggerated. Both media use basically similar tools: the creation of images with light, and the convincing reproduction of motion. Of course there are differences in accuracy of color, the size of their pictures, and the quality or resolution of their images. Also, we view each medium under different circumstances. Still, these differences will probably be minimized by technical improvements in television, which, in any case, relies heavily on the broadcasting of film. In all likelihood, the media will converge because both are responsive to one central drive: the persuasive representation of reality on a flat surface.

A fundamental difference between filmed and televised imagery lies in their social effects, which, in turn, grow out of differences in their modes of production, distribution, and presentation. These differences account for the special qualities of television: representation and transmission are simultaneous; TV alone permits us to witness events immediately, as they occur. When viewing a "live" telecast, we know we are "there," and this knowledge becomes a factor in our aesthetic experience. However, motion-picture film must be processed; there is a time lapse between an event and its presentation to the public. This lapse provides opportunities to heighten or isolate events through editing. Accordingly, cinema is the more "artistic" of the two media,

*left:* Film still from *Potemkin:* woman holding wounded child. Directed by Sergei Eisenstein. 1926. Courtesy Rosa Madell Film Library. Artkino Pictures, Inc.

Eisenstein's films are designed visually. Their emotional and ideological impacts rely on more than the accumulation of realistic detail. They are composed like the pictorial masterpieces of Goya. Picasso was aware of both of these masters.

*above:* Pablo Picasso. Detail of *Guernica.* 1937. The Prado, Madrid

Photograph from a *Dick Cavett Show.* From left: Noel Coward, Cavett, Lynn Fontanne, and Alfred Lunt. 1970. Courtesy Daphne Productions, Inc., New York

The collective TV interview has become an electronic version of an old, perhaps obsolete social form—conversation. Emphasis is on the glamour, opinions, and wit of famous guests. The popularity of the genre demonstrates the effectiveness of the medium in exploiting spontaneous human interactions.

Film still from *The Accused*. Directed by Jonathan Kaplan. 1988. Paramount Pictures

Movies have been less than honest in handling the ugly subject of rape. Usually they treat it as the result of the victim's provocative behavior. However, in *The Accused,* Jodie Foster plays a victim who fights that charge in court and wins.

Film still from *Steel Magnolias*. Directed by Pamela Berlin. 1989. Tri-Star Pictures

A film that celebrates the strong bonds that have always existed among working-class Southern women. The beauty shop is their "club." This is the place where distinctions of status disappear and women can rejoice or grieve openly, together.

whereas television seems to be more "historical." Of course, TV news can be edited to shape the record, but there is less time for subtle manipulation of events and contexts.

Motion pictures are normally seen by a large audience, although it is possible to attend private screenings. Accordingly, films are planned with the expectation of group responses. Television shows are also intended for groups—millions of viewers—but they are usually seen by individuals alone, or by the family alone. So television cannot depend on a large audience to influence viewer response. Unfortunately, television often tries to *simulate* large audience response with recorded noise and laughter, or by televising performances before live audiences recruited to be heard and seen. Here, TV tries to reproduce the experience of theater, but the result feels false.

The closeness of television to living events is best exploited in sports coverage and news reporting in general. Here TV demonstrates its superiority over the old filmed newsreel, which reached an audience after it had learned about the same events through radio and the newspapers. However, our awareness of the immediacy of TV coverage and transmission can give us a false idea about the medium's accuracy. (The same is true of photography.) We tend to believe in the truth of what we see—compared to spoken or written accounts—and do not realize that events can be staged, abbreviated, or isolated from context while appearing photographically accurate.

The public has not yet built adequate defenses against partial and biased TV presentations. Ironically, our political life is endangered by the same source that deepens and extends our historical experience. Although we know more about what is happening, too much of what we know is wrong, slanted, or out of context. Perhaps it is only in televised sports events that we can suspend historical judgment and surrender to the purely aesthetic pleasures of a magnificent visual medium. As for the news—especially political reporting on TV—it needs to be supplemented by outside reading.

## FILMS AND DREAMS

The darkened theater, a soft, comfortable seat, controlled temperature and humidity, and thousands of shadowy images moving across the screen: these strongly suggest the dream world. Cinema can be thought of as the manufacture of synthetic dreams. Psychological experiments reveal that individuals deprived of dreams—allowed to sleep but awakened when they begin to dream—move into a psychotic state. Clearly, dreaming is a biological and cultural necessity; in some mysterious way our human psychobiological equipment is purged and regenerated while we sleep. It seems that our sanity is maintained by a curious, illogical flow of images called dreams. But why do we need dreams during the waking state?

It might be argued that art has always served mankind as an alternative source of dreams. That is, we have always manufactured visions to supplement our real dreams. Now science has not demonstrated that dream-deprived individuals are satisfied by artificial dreams like pictures and films. Or perhaps such experiments have not been attempted. But speculation does not have to be carried that far. From the evidence of daydreaming, art history, and our obsession with film and television viewing, it is plain that we have a strong need for a waking fantasy life.

Here, it is the technical resemblance of films to dreams that arouses our interest. One of the first uses of motion-picture photography was in the study of animal movement; and today films have great value as tools of scientific investigation. But that is not the use which has stimulated their highest development. Films have moved steadily in the direction of imitating the type of perception associated with our imaginative life. Indeed, it is possible that film and TV images are technically superior to the images, or dreams, that we build inside our heads.

Apparently, our civilization, which has created the most complex tech-

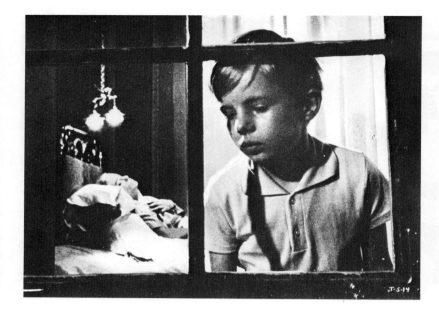

nology in history, needs to create dream-generating devices for the people who use that technology. In other words, the need for synthetic dreams grows in direct proportion to the growth of complex technical systems in our work, play, and interpersonal relations. The dreams we create biologically have to be supplemented by dream machines so we can maintain some sort of balance, or sanity, in our lives and our culture. Perhaps this explains the invention in the twentieth century of two major art forms—cinema and television—both of which simulate human dream-life. The timing of these inventions does not seem to be an accident.

## THE DEMOCRACY OF FILM

Film and television work to eliminate distinctions based on money or class because access to them is relatively cheap. But they are democratic in a more fundamental sense; every seat in a motion-picture theater is equal. That is, each viewer sees the same imagery; film actors cannot play to the boxes; seats in the balcony are as good as seats in the orchestra; sound is audible throughout the house. As for TV, despite a certain amount of family scrambling, each viewer has a prime location. Film and TV imagery tends to devour the space between the screen or tube and the viewer; each member of the audience feels that the performance is being played for him or her alone. Furthermore, the moving camera has a compelling power to lead the viewer's eye into its represented spaces and places. We forget our own physical location as we enter cinema space. Happily, there is room in it for everyone.

Close-ups, especially, eliminate the distance between actors and audience—a distance that is social as well as spatial. Early in the film industry, this produced the star system and the phonemenon of the fan who takes a deep personal interest in the actors' lives. More important, cinema encourages active processes of psychological identification; thus film and television audiences experience lifestyles that are not necessarily available to them in reality. Film fantasies also become economic and cultural facts: as people "enjoy" products and services normally reserved for the rich and successful, they acquire tastes for products and services that they want to satisfy in their real lives.

Obviously, the democracy of film can lead to commercial exploitation, but it can also play more constructive roles. The first lies in its educational influence on the lives of illiterate or impoverished people. Cinema gives them access to types of personal and social behavior normally associated with educated persons. Film and TV viewing may not solve basic problems of

*left:* Film still from *The Silence:* boy in room of dying aunt. Directed by Ingmar Bergman. 1962. Courtesy Janus Films, Inc.

Two Scandinavian masters who use the same device to express the pain of dying and living. The tension between old and young is rendered in the stark contrast between horizontality and verticality.

*above:* Edvard Munch. *The Dead Mother.* 1899–1900. Oil on canvas, 39⅜ × 35⅜". Kunsthalle, Bremen

Film still from *The Grapes of Wrath:* the Joad Family. Directed by John Ford. 1940. © 1949. Twentieth Century-Fox Film Corp.

Every generation and every group need their own image—the mythic or historical account of their founding. For the displaced Southern and Midwestern farmers of the 1930s, that account was provided by John Ford's version of Steinbeck's novel. Using a realistic style based on the documentaries of Pare Lorentz, Ford fashioned a classic epic of migration and resettlement on a continental scale.

*above:* Film still from *The African Queen:* Katharine Hepburn and Humphrey Bogart. Directed by John Huston. 1951. Horizon, United Artists

The test of a very good film image: it tells us a great deal about her, about him, and about them—without words.

*right:* Film still from *Kramer vs. Kramer:* Dustin Hoffman and Justin Henry. Directed by Robert Benton. 1979. Stanley Jaffe Productions. © 1979 Columbia Pictures Industries, Inc.

Again, the silent image speaks volumes: mother isn't there; daddy is new to shopping; the little boy's thoughts are far away. Notice how ironically this plays against the screaming soapbox graphics: BOLD (Hoffman is cautious); DASH (both of them seem to be dream walking); JOY (no one is happy).

ignorance and poverty, but it is probably the chief contributor to a desire for change—personal as well as social, political, and economic.

A second democratizing result of films and television applies mainly to advanced industrial societies—the capacity to generate a large-scale sense of community and social cohesion. Television, especially, unites the alienated citizens of a depersonalized mass society. As spectators of the same media events, millions share a common set of actual and imagined experiences. It is especially through televised events that the masses have an opportunity to recognize and validate powerful symbols of communal anxiety, achievement, and hope. Without these events it would be difficult to satisfy our need for identification with a community larger than the family or the neighborhood—social units that appear to be increasingly fragmented and temporary. So, apart from their merits as art, the moving picture media perform a vital civic function: they help create a national community out of millions of separate, more or less isolated, viewers.

## THE CRITICAL APPRECIATION OF CINEMA

Despite a vast literature devoted to the film—historical, technical, and sociological—very little material tells viewers how to look at films for increased pleasure and understanding. Critics give us plot summaries; they praise or condemn actors and directors; and they publish anthologies of their own writing. Most of all, they discourse learnedly on the theory of filmmaking. But interesting though it is, this literature does not tell viewers how to look at films, how to enjoy them as art.

Our approach here is based on one theoretical assumption: whatever else it is, film is fundamentally a visual medium. Such great film directors as Eisenstein, Bergman, and Fellini are supreme visual artists. This means that our critical approach to the other visual arts applies to film as well. After all, movies are like other pictures in many ways; they are still seen on flat surfaces within a rectangular frame.

But what about the elements of time and motion? Are they not genuinely new factors that have led to the creation of a genuinely new art form? Yes, provided we recognize that time and motion in the film are illusions created by still images. Again, look at a strip of motion-picture film. From our standpoint, a film is as good (or bad) as the sum of impressions made on us by those thousands of little images that constitute the shots and sequences of a motion-picture presentation.

We may remember a film's dialogue and sound effects, its actors' voices and diction, the physical interaction of the characters, the development of its

Film still from *La Dolce Vita:* party scene. Directed by Federico Fellini. 1960

The combined man-and-woman forms are skillfully used here to suggest animality—the loss of human dignity in Fellini's image and a crude parody of physical love in the Antonioni image.

Film still from *Blow-Up:* photographer and model. Directed by Michelangelo Antonioni. 1966. © Metro-Goldwyn-Mayer, Inc., 1966

*below:* Nam June Paik. Charlotte Moorman wearing *TV Bra for Living Sculpture.* 1969. Photo © 1969 by Peter Moore, New York

The bra consists of two small television sets fastened to Ms. Moorman's body. As she plays the cello, the TV images change in response to the musical vibrations. This is video art—high-tech and old-tech joined to create a new kind of visual imagery. The arrangement is ingenious, to be sure, but as for the pictures themselves . . .

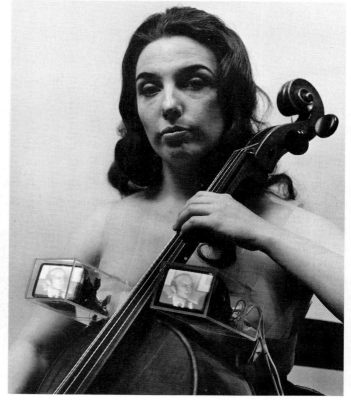

plot. Obviously, these are major aesthetic components of the film experience—auditory, literary, and dramatic. Still, it is visual imagery that converts sounds, words, and movements into the phenomenon we call *a film.* We may not remember what Bogey said to Lauren Bacall (people often get it wrong) but we cannot forget how they looked at each other.

One final point: study of films, talk about films, and writing about films takes place *after we have seen* a film. This means that film criticism is something we do with *remembered* images. Here a book may be useful: it can reproduce certain images—still images, of course—to help us recollect and concentrate on our film experience. That is what we have tried to do, modestly, in a context provided by the other arts. I hope the lesson is not lost: the criticism of film art, like the criticism of painting or photography, begins with the examination of visual images.

## CONCLUSION

Writing in *The New Yorker* about film, television, and literature, the critic Michael Arlen said: "The audience for the serious music of language seems to be drifting away, as if mesmerized by paintings, photographs, moving pictures, videotape—by the new power of visual imagery." He speaks also of a "childish battle . . . between the print and visual interests . . . in which the visual team now appears to have the upper hand." Then he concludes that "the real issue remains in doubt: respect for man and his art." Arlen sounds unhappy about the closing of a cultural gap, the equalization of the visual and verbal arts in our media of communication and expression. He fears that fine literature is taking a beating from the visual media, and as a result the prospects for art and humanity don't look very good.

A major premise of this book is that the visual arts—including the newer media of photography, film, and television—have been engaged in restoring balance to a cultural situation that has grown badly out of kilter. Over the centuries, the dominance of printed words in the arts of communication and expression has produced an *under*development of our visual sense and, perhaps, a distortion of consciousness itself. However, the rise of the visual media today does not mean that civilization will revert to barbarism. It is just that new and almost forgotten forms of power are being developed. After these forms are fully developed and understood, it is unlikely that our visual sense will be so powerfully repressed again.

**Film still from *La Dolce Vita:* Christ figure suspended from a helicopter. Directed by Federico Fellini. 1960**

In one of the great symbolic sequences of film art, Fellini defines modern decadence. Cynical promoters exploit popular religious feeling by staging a fake miracle. Fellini includes himself among the promoters: he, too, creates spectacles and encourages people to believe in them. That is what filmmakers do.

# PART FIVE

# THE PROBLEMS OF ART CRITICISM

Most of us think we are art critics. At least, we deliver critical opinions regardless of what we know about art or art theory. Perhaps this is because a democracy encourages its citizens to believe their views on any subject have equal weight, just as their votes count equally in politics. As a result, there is a great deal of heat generated in critical discussions of art—especially contemporary art. Here we would like to add some light to that heat. Unfortunately, our educational system devotes very little time to developing a foundation for practicing criticism. Well-informed persons—even artists—find themselves delivering opinions that have been foisted on them, or offering their own views without knowing where they came from. When it comes to art criticism, most people seem to rely on instinct.

In an effort to approach the subject rationally, we devote the next two chapters to critical theory and method. My main goal is to give viewers a commonsense approach to the business of forming interpretations and making judgments about works of art. Although there are no permanently correct interpretations and evaluations of particular artworks, there are systematic procedures for going about the work of criticism. We should know what those procedures are and be able to use them. At least we should be able to defend the way we arrive at our opinions.

Whatever else it is, criticism is something we *do*. It is a practical activity (with theoretical underpinnings) in which it is possible to gain proficiency. But first we need to know what criticism is for, what different kinds of critics do, and how critics justify their judgments. Finally, we need critical procedures that work—procedures that advance our understanding of art without spoiling the fun of looking at it.

**Vernon L. Smith.** *Looking at John Chamberlain's* **Essex** *(1960) at the Guggenheim Museum.* **1972. New York Times Pictures**

Everyone does criticism but not everyone does it well. Is this because some of us have a "good ear" for art while the rest of us are tone deaf? No. Can we get better with study and practice? Yes. Do artists make the best critics? Not necessarily. What about art historians? Same answer. Then who can be trusted? You must judge that for yourself.

# CHAPTER SIXTEEN

# THE THEORY OF ART CRITICISM

T he chief goal of art criticism is understanding. We need a way of
looking at art objects that will yield a maximum of insight into their
meanings and merits. Although a work of art yields information to
the trained viewer, we are also interested in how that information is
related to its excellence. For this reason, archaeological, historical, and bio-
graphical data *about* art and artists may be interesting but not necessarily
useful in art criticism. Our main goal is to understand the causes *in* the work
of the effect it has upon us.

A second goal of art criticism—perhaps as important as the first—is
pleasure or delight. To be sure, we get pleasure from understanding, from
knowing what it is in art that causes our gratification. The trained viewer
should also be able to experience more of the satisfactions a work is capable
of yielding; criticism enables us to carry on the search systematically. The
satisfactions we get from art depend on two things: the quality of the object
itself, and our capacity to use our own experience in seeing it. So art criticism
increases pleasure while teaching us to focus our knowledge and experience
in an aesthetic situation.

Some people think that serious study of art kills the pleasures it can yield.
They probably think that too much knowledge about art is deadening. And
some kinds of art scholarship seem to confirm those fears. But the information
sought by critics is mainly about the sources of their satisfaction, about the
bearing of a work on their experience, and the meaning of their existence in
the world. As we look at art we may discover that we are stimulated or
depressed, frightened or excited, angered or soothed. Then, being human
and curious, we want to know why.

But the search for meaning and pleasure is not the only function of art
criticism: we have a real desire to share what we have found. It is very difficult
to know or enjoy something without thinking about the reactions of someone
else. That is probably why we talk about art, music, films, and books: we want
to know whether others have had the same responses. Or we want to
persuade them to accept our interpretations and opinions. So there is always
a social motive in criticism—assuming that, whatever else it may be, *art
criticism is talk about art.*

Why do we enjoy talking about art? Because it is one of the best ways to
communicate our feelings without embarrassment. That may be why few

Jack Levine. *The Art Lover.* 1962. Oil on canvas, 56⅛ × 49". National Museum of American Art, Smithsonian Institution, Washington, D.C. Gift of S.C. Johnson & Son, Inc.

A caricature of the aesthete: his standards are so high that he doesn't like anything. Actually, liking and disliking are only minor features of criticism; the important task is to *understand* a work, and that requires interest, sympathy, and imagination. If we can't understand the work, we can't judge it.

people can resist the impulse to deliver critical judgments: we want others to *know* us in a special way. But the great critics have more than a desire to talk; they have an unusually rich and varied capacity for aesthetic pleasure. By disclosing their discoveries, they enlarge our capacities for understanding and delight. In this sense, art criticism is like teaching; it is the communication of ideas about art and often about life, the soil in which art is nourished.

One commonly accepted purpose of criticism is to make a statement about the worth or rank of an art object. Indeed, the purposes mentioned above may be considered preliminary to judging "how good" a work is. Here we face a persistent human tendency—the need to say that something is "better than" or "worth more than" something else. This probably derives from our wish to possess what is valuable, a very human motive that may account for the development of art criticism as a serious discipline.

So we need a sound foundation for judging what is good, better, and best. Why? Because we want to feel secure about what we like. Furthermore, artistic fame and prestige depend on our critical judgments. To some extent, art history began as an effort to sort out artists and artworks. Then, as the "greatness" of artists was established, the discipline developed ingenious ways of determining the authenticity of artworks, especially when dealers wanted to sell them. If a work could be attributed to an important master, it would be *worth* a great deal in money. (Money values and aesthetic values are not total strangers.) But scholars found that in answering questions of origin and authenticity, they learned much that is *humanistically* valuable. The history and criticism of art became disciplines that enable us to see connections between art and the major patterns of human thought and behavior.

Collectors are involved in criticism, too, since their purchases confirm their own or someone else's critical judgment; all the activities that surround the buying, selling, and display of art have critical significance. Criticism carried on by reviewers and journalists in newspapers and·magazines, and by implication in galleries and museums, influences what artists create. This leads to an interesting result: criticism affects the production of what it criticizes. Artists need the support of the public, whose expectations have been shaped and defined by critics. In their pursuit of recognition, artists try to discover the critical standards by which they will be judged in the places where they wish to be admired.

So criticism may begin with the need to understand and enjoy art, but it ends with the formulation of ideas and opinions that act as standards for artistic creation. We may not have set out to influence what artists create, but in teaching art, talking about art, and buying art, we bring critical standards into being. These standards shift, of course, and they are difficult to formulate with precision. Nevertheless, a process of critical communication seems to be constantly at work. In one way or another, all of us participate in a process that affects the politics, economics, and aesthetics of art. So, we need to do the job of criticism with as much integrity as we can muster.

## THE TOOLS OF ART CRITICISM

What kind of equipment does a critic need in order to function adequately? What must we know, what skills must we have, what experience is needed to be a critic?

Obviously, wide acquaintance with art—especially the kind we expect to judge—is fundamental. Usually, this is acquired through study, especially of art history. It is important that this knowledge be gained through seeing original works of art as well as reproductions. Also, it helps to see student work, unfinished work, even "bad" work. Artists have a considerable advantage here: they can recognize errors of technique that theoreticians often miss. Acquaintance with masterpieces seen in color slides is fine, but not enough by itself. We have to go to galleries and museums and studios. All over the world, if possible. Seeing the world's art is the best excuse for leaving home.

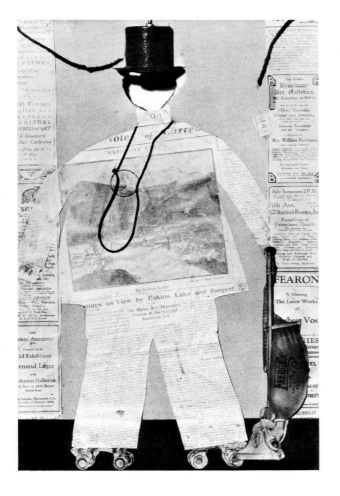

**Arthur G. Dove. *The Critic.* 1925. Collage, 12½ × 9". Terry Dintenfass Gallery, New York. Arthur G. Dove Estate**

The artist's mischievous image of the critic—a ridiculous, top-hatted figure who rides around the galleries on roller skates, carrying a magnifying glass and wielding a vacuum cleaner.

Knowing about art implies more than visual recognition of the monuments of art history. It also calls for understanding the styles and functions of art, the social and cultural contexts in which artists have worked, the technical factors that affect artistic execution in various media. The chief benefit of a broad acquaintance with art is breadth of taste. A critic should appreciate a wide range of artistic creativity as a defense against critical narrowness—the tendency to employ standards based on a meager knowledge of styles and limited experience with technical methods. Fortunately, we have access—through reproductions and travel—to art created throughout the world. This was not possible for most people only a few generations ago. As a result, our standards of art criticism are richer and more complex (or they *should* be) than those of our grandparents.

Artists would probably have more respect for critics if their judgments were based on artistic experience. Of course, some critics have had this experience, and some are artists themselves. But most criticism is done by persons with mainly literary and theoretical preparation. Still, scholars have an advantage: they are presumably free of the rivalry, partisanship, and jealousy that can color artists' opinions of other artists' work. Some have argued that artists are constitutionally incapable of judging their peers objectively—a harsh judgment in itself. The question will probably be argued as long as there are artists and critics. For a long time, colleges and universities employed only theoreticians to teach art. Today, happily, we employ theoreticians *and* practitioners—persons who often have both kinds of training.

Critics with only theoretical preparation are poorly equipped to assess quality of execution in works of art. Some have a tendency to denigrate technical facility: they think it is superficial and often they do not recognize faulty craftsmanship. The art world is regularly embarrassed when the work of amateurs, practical jokers, and animals is given serious attention (or prizes!) in art exhibitions. These stunts—probably intended to ridicule modern art—have little to do with the achievement of serious artists. Nevertheless, they constitute a scandal in the practice of art criticism; certainly they raise questions about the competence of some critics. In an effort to be fair and open to all forms of artistic expression, some critics simply abdicate their responsibility to the public. To be more than art publicists or promoters, critics must be reasonably good judges of artistic technique: technique plays a major role in determining form, and form is inseparable from content. Without *some* technical expertise, our critical judgments may be entertaining but hardly defensible except as literature.

Another requirement of the critic might be called "breadth of sensibility." This designates the capacity to respond to a wide range of artistic expression. We know that individuals vary in the kind and quality of emotion they feel in connection with real-life events. Likewise, they vary in capacity for feelings encountered in art. Critics, however, must have access to a generous range of aesthetic emotion; they must be flexible in the realm of feelings and ideas; otherwise, their usefulness is limited. It is possible that many of our differences of opinion about art are due to restricted sensibility or limited capacity for aesthetic perception. Enlarging and deepening our responses to art—extending our aesthetic range—is a humanly enriching enterprise. That is why the development of critical capacity should be one of the main goals of a liberal education.

Of course, a critic is more than an empty slate. He or she carries a host of biases and unconscious preferences. So another item of critical equipment might be called *judicious temperament.* This means the ability to withhold judgment until all the aesthetic evidence is in. Many of us make judgments too quickly: we state conclusions and then look for reasons to justify them. A judicious temperament, however, allows time for sensations, impressions, associations, and half-formed valuations to interact; it permits our intelligence to carry out the work of sifting, sorting, and organizing. When we examine a work of art, our feelings are being skillfully assaulted; so we need time to exercise logic and rationality. In art, or in a court of law, there should be no "rush to judgment."

# TYPES OF ART CRITICISM

Although we speak of a person called an art critic, there are in fact several kinds of critic, differing according to the social or professional roles they perform. The most familiar type is probably the *journalistic* critic—someone who writes reviews of exhibitions, plays, books, and concerts. There are several varieties within this category. Sometimes a newspaper employs only one reporter to "do" art, music, and drama criticism; these are journalists who might better be called "art writers." On the other hand, an art magazine may employ a number of critics with specialized art backgrounds. Another kind of criticism takes place in schools, colleges, and universities—wherever art is taught. This criticism, conducted by teachers, might be called *pedagogical* criticism; spoken rather than written, it has tremendous influence. In addition, there is *scholarly* criticism, which appears mainly in learned journals; it can affect artistic production and art collecting, though somewhat indirectly. There is also the *popular* criticism conducted by lay people. They clearly constitute the majority of critics, and while they vary in expertise, their opinions cannot be ignored.

Finally, the artist, too, is a critic; every decision he or she makes has a critical dimension; the creative act is one of continuous re-examination and revision, that is, acceptance or rejection of forms and meanings in the light of the artist's expressive goals and critical standards. This subject—the artist's use of mental images and ideals during the process of creation—would be worth a book by itself.

Following is a more detailed examination of the critical types outlined above.

**Journalistic Criticism**    The main point about journalistic criticism is that it is a category of news. It is meant to inform readers about events in the art world and to retain their loyalty to a particular newspaper or magazine. Usually, we read a "review"—a brief summary of an exhibition; it is rarely long enough to constitute a systematic analysis of the main works in a show. Indeed, there is a style of review writing which endeavors to create verbal equivalents of the work in an exhibition. Obviously, criticism which reports the news and tries to substitute words for visual and aesthetic experience, while also giving critical judgments, labors under an impossible burden. Usually, the brevity of journalistic criticism forces the writer to bypass analysis and to rely on critical conclusions to create exciting copy. Unfortunately, this kind of writing also appears in longer magazine articles where there is less excuse for pages and pages of long-winded opinion and speculation passing as critical analysis.

Still, considering that journalists have to satisfy the curiosity of many readers and describe works their readers have not seen, some fine critical writing can be found in newspapers and newsmagazines. Specialized monthly journals have the space to do more: they engage in aesthetic debates, promulgate a "party line," or scold museums and foundations for failing to support their favorites. However, they serve a good purpose; they stoke the fires of critical controversy; and by expressing biases forcefully they help create the atmosphere of striving and rivalry that artists, collectors, and the general public seem to require.

Journalistic critics write under pressure of deadlines, so their output can suffer from the perils of much newswriting: inaccuracy, hasty conclusions, the substitution of opinion for analysis, and a tendency to be witty at the artist's expense. But discriminating readers can discount for errors and biases in advance. Or they compensate by reading several critics, comparing them for

Honoré Daumier. *The Influential Critic.* Published in *Le Charivari*, June 24, 1865. Lithograph, 9⅜ × 8½". The Metropolitan Museum of Art, New York

Artists tend to dislike critics, but they save good reviews. Here they surround and fawn over a top-hatted old scribbler, hoping for favorable mention. In private, of course, they hate him.

accuracy and insight. Best of all, they try to see art shows personally. Without these safeguards, our critical understanding would consist of trendy opinions about the principal current reputations. Coteries and intrigues are not unknown in the art world; art journalism is certainly part of the endless jockeying for position that characterizes a realm where talented people struggle for recognition. So we can use journalism for news while reserving critical judgment for ourselves.

**Pedagogical Criticism**   The purpose of pedagogical criticism is to advance the artistic and aesthetic maturity of students. Beyond rendering judgments of student work it should enable them to make judgments themselves. To do this well, the teacher of art must be familiar with the art of beginners and amateurs as well as "museum art." The art of young and old, of the naive and sophisticated, of the technically adept and the technically inept, of trailblazers and plodders, innovators and imitators: teachers of art must know them all. Pedagogical criticism calls for tremendous range.

An important task of the teacher of art—one that demands great sensitivity and critical skill—is the analysis and interpretation of a student's work *to the student*. This is how students learn to analyze and interpret their own work; this is how advanced students learn to see the directions their work is taking. For beginning students, an instructor functions as a critic *during* the process of execution. Student work represents a delicate kind of critical collaboration—a collaboration that should not become a form of artistic dependency.

In the past, students sought out teachers whose art they admired and wished to imitate. Most of them wanted criticism to inculcate the standards visible in an artist-teacher's work. As a result, a teacher often reproduced his artistic personality endlessly among his students. Robert Henri was an exception; he had strong artistic views but his instruction did not constrict the growth of students. Thomas Benton, on the other hand, produced "little Bentons" as if on an assembly line. Either from the force of his personality or the narrowness of his vision, he dominated students technically and aesthetically. Jackson Pollock was one of them; his early work was touchingly Bentonesque. But as history shows, he changed. The lesson here is that strong teachers can nurture a student, strangle a student, or create the foundation for a lifelong rebellion.

Today's philosophy of pedagogical criticism seems to call for a certain amount of restraint on the part of the artist-teacher. Its main goal is to assist in the development of critical standards *within* the student—standards which are compatible with a student's emerging artistic personality. Yet the art teacher worth his or her salt should have strong convictions. So achieving the right blend of qualities in a teacher is not easy; we need a combined father, mother, and midwife who possesses well-developed artistic skills, great powers of aesthetic discrimination, plus the ability to recognize genius in others.

**Scholarly Criticism**   Scholarly art criticism is the fully developed product of long study, specialization, and refined critical sensibility. Its function is to provide the kind of analysis, interpretation, and evaluation that academic independence makes possible. In other words, it takes time. For the living artist, scholarly criticism represents an approximation of "the judgment of history." Settled in the safety of academic tenure and undergirded by traditions of scrupulous research and disinterested truth-seeking, scholarly critics are in a position to render the informed and sensitive judgment that serious art deserves. Unfortunately, not all artists live to see that judgment, but it is reassuring to know that it will eventually come to light.

Academic critics often reexamine styles and reputations which have been categorized and set aside. Since each era has its characteristic way of seeing, artists who were scorned in their own day may be shown to have fresh

*above:* Thomas Hart Benton. *Arts of the West.* 1932. Tempera on composition board, 7'10" × 13'3". The New Britain Museum of American Art, New Britain, Connecticut. Harriet Russell Stanley Fund

Early in his career Pollock fell under the Benton spell. We can see what he got from his teacher: extreme contrasts of light and dark; torn, jagged contours; explosive composition; a taste for violent action.

*right:* Jackson Pollock. *Untitled.* c. 1936. Oil on board, 10⅞ × 16⅜". Courtesy of Jason McCoy, New York

meaning now. Museums perform this function when they resurrect the reputation of an artist, a school, or a style which has fallen into disesteem. Think of the current vogue for Art Deco—a style that was considered of only minor decorative value; today it is having a lively revival. We should remember, however, that the history of art does not repeat itself identically. Originally (during the 1930s), Art Deco was part of a progressive thrust in the arts of design; today it is bathed in nostalgia, a nostalgia colored mauve, dusty rose, off-white, and teal blue. Why have we rediscovered these colors? Because a few scholars and critics decided they had meaning for our time.

**Popular Criticism**   Any discussion of art takes place against a background of criticism by the public at large. The average citizen continues to judge art whether we think he is qualified or not. Therefore, the existence of a large body of popular critical opinion has to be considered in its effect on the total art situation. We should also remember that the general public does not consist entirely of fools. As Mark Twain said: "The public is the only critic whose opinion is worth anything at all."

If critical opinion influences what artists create, we have to consider popular as well as elite criticism. The concept of an avant-garde, of a body of artists working in advance of popular taste, assumes the existence of masses of people who are too sluggish and dull to keep up with the latest thing. But if it were not for these dull people and their backward tastes, there would be nothing for the avant-garde to rebel against! Actually, the idea of progress in art—of advanced and retarded taste—is a myth: it confuses progress in history with progress in aesthetics. Nevertheless, that myth has considerable influence, especially among those who think of art as a branch of the fashion industry.

Popular criticism changes very little; it judges art in terms of its representational power. Most people believe normal vision is adequate equipment for the conduct of art criticism. The critical consensus of these people is consistent through history, so their standards cannot be easily ignored: they want art to be faithful to the visual facts. We have discussed this type of art in connection with the style of objective accuracy. Today, photography and film satisfy the popular desire for visual truth; indirectly, this gives artists a good reason for departing from purely optical realism. But abandoning reality entirely seems to be something that popular criticism will never forgive.

Perhaps aesthetic education will enable people to discriminate among the various types of realism. It should not be impossible to see the difference between styles of unselective realism and styles that portray the character and inner existence of persons and places, objects and events, while remaining faithful to their appearance. Within its own standards of fidelity to human vision, popular criticism can become wise and discriminating; it is a matter of having access to a full range of stylistic options and aesthetic intentions.

## KINDS OF CRITICAL JUDGMENT

How do critics justify their evaluations? Or do they judge art intuitively? Do they measure each work against a master they happen to admire? Or do they have general standards, formulated in advance, for judging each new work of art?

From our standpoint it would be well if critics withheld judgment until they had carried out the preliminary tasks of description, analysis, and interpretation. After that, judging would be more responsive to the character of the art object. But when critics "rush to judgment," certain ideas of excellence seem to underlie what they say is good. Following are the main ones.

**Formalism**   Once we have abandoned the notion that great art is the skillful imitation of surfaces, we can turn to what is called formalist criticism. Here excellence is located in visual organization—in successful relationships among the visual elements of an artwork regardless of labels, associations, or symbolic meanings.

For a formalist, successful relationships are *designed;* they result from an artist's calculation and planning rather than a viewer's subjective reactions. Artists like Poussin, Cézanne, or Mondrian appeal to the formalist because they minimize accidental effects; they aim deliberately at a harmony of forms. We have no uncertainty about the artist's purpose or method: it is to create a work that does not depend on "extraneous," that is, nonartistic, considerations to be effective.

Formalist excellence does not require a geometric, a hard-edge, or an abstract style. For example, Poussin gives us softly rounded representational forms moving in naturalistic space. But his compositions, considered in their totality, are organized so that the main shapes, directions, and masses are related to each other with remarkable precision: every tree, hill, and figure has been measured, weighed, and balanced. So we witness a perfect reconciliation of visual forms; we experience a pleasure that must be like that of an accountant auditing a perfect set of books.

Formalist critics are capable of finding interest in subject matter; they can learn about religion, history, or politics from the persons and objects represented in artworks. However, they consider an artwork excellent only insofar as its *form*, its underlying organization, is responsible for their enjoyment. For example, they must admire the bronze-metal skin of Mies van der Rohe's

Seagram Building, not just because bronze is inherently beautiful, but because its bronze parts have the right dimensions and are located at the right intervals in relation to the window size, the color of the tinted glass, the overall shape of the building, and the size of the space around it.

Formalist criticism takes an interest in craftsmanship, since putting things together carefully and working them to the "right" degree of finish suggests a search for pleasing relationships. But craftsmanship is based on the logical and economic use of tools and materials—essentially utilitarian concerns. The formalist responds to this logic only if it produces results that seem to harmonize great forces in the universe. In other words, the formalist wants works of art to depend solely on the principle of *unity in variety*. The unity or harmony or *beauty* of the artwork should be a kind of grand reconciliation—like the unified field theory that Einstein never quite discovered.

Formalism has had a healthy influence on art mainly in its negative teaching, that is, when it has insisted on the unimportance of literary or historical associations as vehicles of aesthetic meaning. But on the positive side, formalism has trouble in establishing what its idea of excellence is. That is, how do we know which formal relationships are pleasing or significant? The formalist critics Roger Fry and Clive Bell never really specified the criteria of formal excellence. Mainly they told us what it is not. Their expression, "significant form," sounds good but it doesn't help much in doing criticism.

If pressed, the formalist might say that an organization is good when it embodies the ideal structural possibilities of the forms we see in it. ("Structural" is an okay word for formalists to use since it has no literary or historical associations.) But how do we *know* when a visual organization embodies the *ideal* possibilities of its components? Here, formalists must fall back on the quality of their perceptions—that is, they must feel that their perceptions in the presence of the work are inherently satisfying. Bernard Berenson relied on formalist ideas of aesthetic value when he employed the term "life-enhancing" to describe the most important characteristic of art. This term (which is really an elegant way of saying "good") represents a viewer's conviction that great art makes us feel stronger, more confident, or more vigorous: this happens *regardless* of subject matter.

The qualities we call "beautiful" or "life-enhancing" are presumably the qualities any intelligent and sensitive person would consider pleasing. In other words, there are *norms* or *ideal standards* in art which connect with something in us that seeks such norms. Thus we come to a theory of communication that underlies the formalist's idea of excellence. He believes there is an ideal or perfect embodiment of all things and that excellent art reveals or *communicates* that ideal to certain people. Who are they? They are persons who, because of their biological makeup and cultural background, can recognize and enjoy ideal form. This sounds like a circular argument, and it is. Formalism is ultimately a philosophy of art that enables certain people to realize that they like the same things, or the same combinations of qualities.

Many artists and critics are formalists without knowing it. Their ideas of excellence are based on intuitive feelings of sympathy with the organization of an art object. Perhaps those feelings come from affirmative signals received from their glandular, nervous, and muscular systems. But we shall never know. Formalism is most useful in providing us with a guide to the values it rejects as aesthetically irrelevant: historical information, social connotation, literary reference, religious association, and mechanical imitation. Beyond that it offers us the form preferences of the normal person—the sensitive and cultured normal person. We have to hope that we fall into that category.

**Expressivism**  Expressivist criticism sees excellence as the capacity of art to communicate ideas and feelings vividly, intensely, and truly. It is not especially interested in formal organization for its own sake. Children's art offers a good example of what expressivist critics admire. Children usually

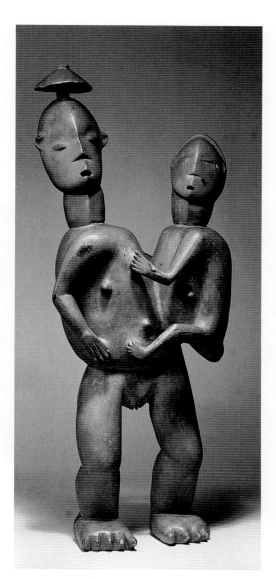

*Mother and Child,* by a Mangbetu sculptor, northeastern Zaire, Central Africa. c. 1910. Wood, 23½" high. Courtesy Department of Library Services, American Museum of Natural History, New York

For a formalist critic this sculpture supports aesthetic values that transcend its anthropological context. The twist of the mother's torso, the tilt of her head, her subtly suggested features, the formal echoes in the child's figure all add up to a type of self-contained elegance that formalists prize above social, religious, or historical meaning.

*above:* Nicolas Poussin. *Landscape with the Burial of Phocion.* 1648.
Oil on canvas, 47 × 70½". Hôtel Matignon, Paris

*opposite above:* Paul Cézanne. *Lac d'Annecy.* 1896. Oil on canvas,
25⅝ × 31⅞". Courtauld Institute Galleries, London

*opposite below:* Fernand Léger. *Nudes in the Forest.* 1909–10. Oil on canvas,
47¼ × 67". Kröller-Müller Museum, Otterlo, The Netherlands.

## THE FORMALIST AS PAINTER

First, the formalist tries to capture nature within a measured, orderly
framework (Poussin); next he tries to represent nature's vitality without
losing control of its underlying structure (Cézanne); finally, he fits nature
into his vision of the universe as a perfect machine (Léger).

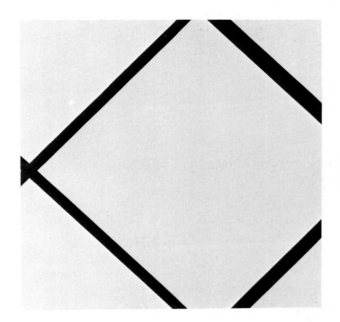

The formalist sensibility. To understand this work, we measure and compare forms: lengths, thicknesses, angles, convergences, and divergences. We do this with the negative spaces, too. When all the measuring and comparing are done, we can examine our feelings of balance and imbalance, tension and harmony, action and repose. Some bodily responses are involved, but they are based almost wholly on our optical activity. The experience has nothing to do with history, religion, philosophy, sociology, or politics.

**Drawing by a four-year-old child**

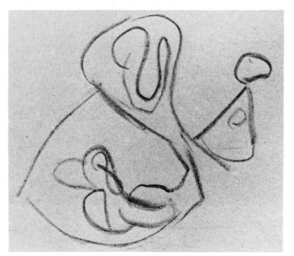

Paul Klee. *Shame.* 1933. Brush drawing, 18½ × 24¼". Paul Klee Foundation, Kunstmuseum, Bern

The expressivist sensibility. Klee uses a childlike way of seeing to represent an adult way of feeling. The goal here is emotional resonance, psychological reality, primal truth.

lack the patience or skill to produce art that exhibits a finished and calculated organization of form. For them, the impulse to communicate, to describe an event, or express an emotion is stronger than the desire to adjust forms so they will be "perfect" or "beautiful" as adults understand these words. The art of children pleases us because of its uninhibited color, design, and imagery—its naiveté. In describing their world, children "tell it like it is."

All art, regardless of style, communicates ideas or feelings. Consequently, expressivist criticism must help us decide whether a work goes beyond "mere" communication. To deal with this problem, we have the idea of intensity of experience. Art is best when it arouses powerful feelings—feelings stronger than those we experience in everyday life. We must be simultaneously aware of the real-life origin and the artistic sources of our feelings. Consider the photograph of an air attack. We know what it represents, but the image looks mechanical and ordinary: it fails to communicate the violence of the event *even though* it is obviously accurate. But when Grosz or Dix deal with the same theme, we realize that our emotional responses have been heightened by the artist without destroying the underlying truth of the event.

Clearly, expressivist critics believe art should "have something to say," which implies that *artists* should have something to say. Expressivists, like many lay people, want art to be a source of insight about life: the great artist should be wise in a way that others are not. That is, the artist discovers certain truths about life, and, through skill and imagination, finds a way to express them forcefully. Therefore, *originality, relevance*, and *cognitive validity* become expressivist criteria of aesthetic excellence. Technique and formal organization are important only insofar as they help communicate significant ideas.

The expressivist standard of relevance amounts to a demand that art contribute to the meaning of existence *now*. The emphasis on "now" suggests that a work of art succeeds when it conveys feelings and ideas that have immediate meaning in our lives. "Immediate meaning" for the expressivist is tied to originality and truth—ideas that have scientific force. The reasonably perceptive individual knows when these standards have been met. Again, we have the concept of the normal person, but now that mythical individual has been recruited for a new task—the establishment of a standard of relevance that includes all of us.

**Instrumentalism**   Instrumentalism conceives of art as a tool for advancing some moral, religious, political, or economic purpose. Therefore, excellence does not depend exclusively on the artist's ability to solve problems inherent in the use of materials or the creation of form—problems *internal* to the artistic enterprise. Neither is excellence based on expressivist criteria like vividness, credibility, and relevance. Instrumentalists are concerned with the *consequences* of the ideas and feelings expressed in art; they want art to serve ends more important than itself.

The instrumentalist idea of art might be illustrated by the background music for a film. The music should support the dramatic action, heightening its meaning and anticipating climactic moments but never calling attention to itself. That should be the relation of art to social, political, or moral goals.

Pablo Picasso. *Woman Weeping.* 1937. Penrose Collection, London

This is not a pretty picture: expressivist art is not meant to please. Picasso's achievement is to employ form in a fresh way (originality), to make an honest statement (truth) about the human condition as it really affects us (relevance).

*above:* Otto Dix. *Lens Bombed.* 1924.
Watercolor, 27½ × 20½". Philadelphia Museum
of Art. Gift of anonymous donor

*above right:* George Grosz. *Punishment.* 1934.
Watercolor, 27½ × 20½". Collection, The
Museum of Modern Art, New York. Gift of Mr.
and Mrs. Erich Cohn

*right:* Photograph of an air attack on a tank
during World War I

Another example of this idea of art might be seen in the illustration for an ad:
it should visualize the words or the message as a whole. In presenting that
message it can be witty or beautiful, but not so witty or beautiful that we forget
the name of the product.

In a sense, the history of art is the history of its service to society's
principal institutions, ideals, and social agendas. It is only in the modern era
that art has functioned as a free-floating activity, unattached to a church, state,
or ruling elite. Today, museums, universities, and foundations have emerged
as the chief sponsors of art and artists, but they rarely try to change the
unattached character of artistic creativity. Their support does not usually
require aesthetic loyalty. However, when it comes to art that is not made for
museums, galleries, and foundations—commercial art, graphic communication, product design—then it is clear that instrumentalism is very much alive.
The people who sponsor this kind of art have very clear ideas about what it

is for, and they employ artists and designers who can do the job they want done. The results—like the instrumentalist art of the past—are often very impressive.

Instrumentalist criticism encounters trouble when we consider art that is admired for reasons other than those it was created to serve. Medieval art was meant to communicate the doctrines of the Church to people who could not read. But *we* can read—most of us; our religious indoctrination comes from other sources. Still, we admire Romanesque sculpture for its vigor, emotional honesty, and unity of form and expression. Does this mean that with the passage of time instrumentalism loses its validity as an explanation of artistic greatness?

Not exactly. Instrumentalist theory is really based on a shrewd analysis of artistic creativity. Instrumentalists realize that art which once served purposes outside itself may eventually be prized for formal or expressive qualities. Those qualities were originally "built into" the art object so that it would function effectively: the service of chief or church or monarch requires excellence in *all* respects. For the instrumentalist, the highest motivation is indispensable for the creation of great art.

Is the instrumentalist critic really a formalist or expressivist who requires that art have extra-artistic motivation? No, because the instrumentalist maintains that motivation and purpose cannot be separated. For instrumentalist critics, aesthetic values do not exist independently; the meanings and pleasures of art are fully experienced only when we recognize their involvement in life's larger goals. Michelangelo's *Pietà* is a masterpiece not only because it illustrates a central religious event but also because it supports crucial ideas about maternal love and grief. Form, purpose, and idea are identical. Thus, instrumentalists experience the visual organization of forms and their expressive function at the same time. They need not speculate about whether an organization has realized its ideal possibilities; they know the purpose of the work when they see its form. If they cannot "see" or feel or understand the purpose of the work, they *know* it has failed. Criticism is much easier that way.

Michelangelo. *Pietà.* 1498–99. Marble, 68½" high. St. Peter's, Rome

Instrumentalism: its masterpieces are formalist masterpieces, too. But the forms are organized to serve purposes above and beyond form.

Diego Rivera. *Night of the Rich.* 1923–28.
Fresco. Ministry of Education, Mexico City.

Diego Rivera. *Two Women.* 1941. Oil on canvas,
77 × 64". The Arkansas Arts Center, Little Rock.
Gift of Abby Rockefeller Mauzé, 1955

These works employ approximately the same
form-language, using it to express bourgeois
complacency or revolutionary disgust. Which
shows that Cubism supports formalism or
instrumentalism, depending on how the artist
feels at the time.

Jean Metzinger. *Tea Time.* 1911. Oil on canvas, 29⅞ × 27⅝". Philadelphia Museum of Art. The Louise and Walter Arensberg Collection

**David Alfaro Siqueiros. Detail of *New Democracy.* 1945. Whereabouts unknown**

The female nude in the service of politics. The fusion of voluptuous form with the idea of revolutionary violence.

There is a vulgar kind of instrumentalism which expects art to deal with stereotyped political ideas. Thus Marxist critics want artists to illustrate certain ideological themes: the class struggle, capitalist oppression of the masses, imperialist exploitation, the heroism of workers, and so on. At its best, this criticism offers an interesting explanation of the economic relations between creators and users of art, but it tends to be unsatisfactory in dealing with

Pieter Brueghel the Elder. *The Painter and the Connoisseur.* c. 1565. Pen drawing, 10 × 8½". The Albertina, Vienna

In the sixteenth century the critic might be literally *there,* observing the birth of a masterpiece and probably offering advice. Today's critic is rarely present in the flesh, but the artist is well aware of his or her spirit: it hovers over everything, occasionally holding back the brush or making the paint hard to spread.

questions of artistic form and quality. In the mural art of Diego Rivera, for example, we see numerous scenes depicting the oppression of the Mexican masses. Their purpose was to create the motivation for revolutionary change. But the form-language of these murals is indistinguishable from non-revolutionary works painted by Rivera and other Cubists early in this century. In other words, Rivera's enduring reputation rests substantially on formalist grounds; his Communist content was superimposed on a style of bourgeois formalism.

The Soviets were notorious for their sponsorship of art which advocates the standard Party line; most of it was consistently mediocre. But this mediocrity may not have been due to instrumentalism; more likely the culprit was bureaucratic clumsiness and rigidity. In the Western democracies, too, citizens and politicians often adhere to theories of vulgar instrumentalism: art is good when it celebrates officially proclaimed goals; art is bad when it makes us uncomfortable. Art is especially bad when it is ugly; the problem here may be that vulgar instrumentalists are really closet formalists.

Despite its abuses—especially in bureaucratic censorship—instrumentalism provides useful grounds for criticizing art. First, it encourages critics to investigate the social, moral, and economic purposes that art serves. Second, it emphasizes the worthiness of art which is related to society's dominant concerns. Third, it acts as a corrective to the tendency of artists to become excessively involved with narrowly technical problems. In other words, instrumentalism is not a bad critical philosophy; certainly it is a durable philosophy, but it can become a crude weapon when politicians get hold of it.

## CONCLUSION

There are so many kinds of art that no single critical theory is adequate for evaluating all of them. When criticizing architecture, the crafts, and industrial art, for example, we must find ways to consider the aesthetic value of utility, workmanship, and the expressiveness of forming and fabrication processes. What we must *not* do is decide that certain classes of objects are aesthetically irrelevant; we must also guard against the tendency to consider only the kinds of art that fit our favorite critical principles. When we say that something is *not* art, we are probably avoiding the task of criticizing what we dislike. But if we want to understand art, theories that exclude objects before we have examined them are not very useful. We ought to employ a definition of art that includes potentially everything that human beings make. Then, equipped with suitable critical procedures, we can examine the merits of any work that "asks" to be judged.

David Seymour. Photograph of Bernard Berenson at the Borghese Gallery in Rome, 1955

The critic as connoisseur. Is it an original? By whom? When did he make it? Who has owned it since then? Has it been altered or retouched? How much was done by the master and how much by assistants? How much was "created" by restorers? What do the other experts think? Why are they wrong? Why am I right? Incidentally, is it any good?

# CHAPTER SEVENTEEN

# THE CRITICAL PERFORMANCE

Having discussed the qualifications of critics, the purposes of their work, and the arguments they use to support their judgments, we can turn to the critical performance itself. Much of the commentary in this book consists of criticism. That would be true of most statements about art, since it is difficult to discuss the subject without carrying out some critical operations. But now it is time to describe the critical performance in detail; we want to stress that it is an orderly and sequential process.

Our guiding assumption is that there is a systematic way of acting like a critic, just as there is a systematic way of behaving like a lawyer. For lawyers there is a form for presenting evidence, refuting adversaries, citing precedents, appealing to reason, and so on. And while art criticism does not have the form of legal debate, it *does* have form. To do criticism well, therefore, we need a form or system that makes the best possible use of our knowledge and experience and powers of observation.

Art critical *performance* can be divided into four stages: Description, Formal Analysis, Interpretation, and Evaluation or Judgment. To some extent these stages overlap, but they are fundamentally different operations; their sequence proceeds from the specific to the general and from easy to difficult. That is, we focus on particular visual facts before making inferences about their overall meaning and value.

## DESCRIPTION

Description is a process of taking inventory, of noting what is immediately visible in an artwork. At this stage we try to *avoid* inferences, judgments, and personal responses. We want to arrive at a simple account of "what is there." In description, the language of the critic should be as "unloaded" as possible; that is, it should not contain hints about the meaning or value of what is being described.

The reason for deferring inferences and value judgments is to make certain that our description is as complete as possible. Making value statements at this stage might tempt us to justify them, and that would prevent us from completing the description, finding what is "there" to be discovered. Interpreting or judging a work on the basis of partial evidence can be very embarrassing.

Gerald Gooch. *Hmmm.* 1968. Pencil drawing, 3 panels, each 40 × 16". Hansen-Fuller Gallery, San Francisco

What do we try to describe in a work of art? First, the most obvious things. In dealing with a realistic work, we mention the *names* of the things we can see, and we try to use terms that will minimize disagreement. For example, we might say that Picasso's *Les Demoiselles d'Avignon* shows the figures of five women. But, despite the title, it may seem that one of the figures is not a woman. Then we should say the painting has five *figures*, four of which appear to be women. It would be better for the critic to *prove* that the fifth figure is a woman. Perhaps the uncertainty about that figure will be useful in forming an interpretation.

When artistic imagery is abstract, it becomes difficult to name persons, objects, places, and so on. The things we normally recognize disappear, or become something else. Hence we describe the main shapes, colors, and directions we see. A shape may be large or small, ovoid or rectangular, hard-edged or soft-edged; but we should not say it is beautiful or ugly, vigorous or sluggish. The same applies to the other visual elements: they can be described without being judged. The point of this operation is to give us *time*—time to see, time to build up a body of perceptions, time to let the visual facts "soak in."

We can also call attention to characteristics of execution—preferably the *visible* characteristics. We can see whether paint has been brushed out or mixed on the canvas. We can tell if a surface consists of several transparent layers or has been applied in one coat. In architecture, we can recognize cast iron or steel or concrete or brick. Often, but not always, we can see how these materials have been shaped and assembled. In the case of handcraft or manufactured objects, we should describe processes of fabrication: Is a container turned, stamped, built up by hammering, cast, welded, or soldered? Can we see the marks of the tools that formed and finished it? Answers to these questions affect our perceptions of an object, our understanding of its form, and our notions about its use.

Discussions of technique usually depend on our practical knowledge. Again, the critic should deal with technique in terms of its visible effects. In other words, we do not want a lecture on lost-wax casting while we are looking at a Rodin bronze. Professor Vincent Scully gives us just enough technical information in architectural criticism: "Moreover, the Beinecke Library wall is actually a Vierendeel truss; it thus need be supported only at the four corners of the building. But the truss does not look structural to the eye, which therefore sees the building as small, since the span looks to be a little one. Yet the building is huge and therefore disorienting to the viewer." Scully seems to be saying that the engineering qualities of the span have been visually violated. The little squares that make up the wall deceive us about the way the building is actually constructed. According to Scully, structure and appearance should correspond. And since they don't, the building is "disorienting to the viewer." This brief excerpt tells us how technical analysis can lead to an aesthetic judgment—visual disorientation—hardly a virtue in a great library. Scully concludes: "It all ends, I think, by creating an atmosphere of no place, nowhere, nobody, matched only by some of De Chirico's images of human estrangement and by a few similarly motivated Italian buildings of the Thirties and early Forties."

Devastating as it is, Scully's critique is based on more than subjective opinion; he lays a technical foundation for his view. Then he tries to *persuade*

**Skidmore, Owings and Merrill. Beinecke Rare Book and Manuscript Library, Yale University, New Haven, Connecticut. 1963**

Scully's comparison of the Beinecke Library to one of De Chirico's "images of human estrangement" shows how the aesthetic sense operates in the work of criticism. The library and the painting do not look alike, but they convey a similar feeling.

**Giorgio de Chirico. *Delights of the Poet.* c. 1913. Oil on canvas, 27⅜ × 34". Collection Helen and Leonard Yaseen, New York**

489

us by offering an aesthetic impression of the library—using an analogy to the forlorn imagery of Giorgio de Chirico, and comparing the building to the architecture of Italy during the Fascist era. Whether we agree with Professor Scully or not, it is clear that he has earned the right to pronounce judgment.

## FORMAL ANALYSIS

In formal analysis, we try to go beyond a descriptive inventory to discover *the relations among* the things we have named. We may have identified five female figures in *Les Demoiselles*, but now we want to examine their organization as shapes, colors, and textures, and as forms with particular locations in space.

Some of the figures in *Les Demoiselles* (see page 499) are made of flat, angular planes of color, whereas the two central figures are quite curvaceous; they have gentler transitions of color and they seem less distorted. Also, white lines are employed in one of them to show its main shapes. Strangely, the outer figures have heads which are radically different from their bodies. And the central figures, while frontally posed, present the nose in profile. Finally, one figure looks very insecure, like a statue that might fall off its pedestal. The woman's torso is erect, but her feet are too far to the left to support her body.

This observation about the figure that seems to be falling illustrates an important source of inference in art criticism: the erectness of human posture and the influence of gravity on form. No matter what style of art we examine, certain physical and biological assumptions about people are shared by artist *and* viewer. We cannot look at a tilted representation of the human figure without feeling that it may fall. Thus the expectation of collapse creeps into our perception of the work.

Continuing our formal analysis: the color in *Les Demoiselles* seems to model the forms, but we have very little impression of depth. The figures exist in a shallow space implied by their overlapping shapes. But there are no perspective devices, no changes in size, focus, color intensity, or sharpness of edge to suggest a representation of space much deeper than the picture plane. Does this mean that Renaissance picture-making is finally dead? Is single-point perspective finished, along with the unity of pictorial space?

Notice that the drawing of the hand in the central figure involves some skill in foreshortening; so it is more or less believable. But the other two hands in the picture are crudely drawn; one is childlike, while the other is stiff and schematic—part of an arm that looks like wood or stone more than flesh. Yet that arm—on the left side of the canvas—is painted in the typical pink tones of European figurative art. There seems to be a conflict between the drawing of the arm and its color and paint quality. Is this the type of unintentional conflict that Scully noted in his architectural critique? Or is it an *intended* conflict—part of the meaning of the work?

We also recognize three kinds of distortion in the heads of the three outer figures. In the head at the left, color shifts from pink to brown, the eye is much enlarged, and the planes of the nose are simplified as in African wood sculpture. However, the *shape* of the head remains naturalistic, and it is naturally illuminated. Moving to the upper-right head, we depart completely from logical representation. Harsh green lines are used to indicate the nose plane in shadow, and a rough, unfinished kind of execution is employed in the head and the area around it. Finally, the breast has a squarish or diamond shape. Strange.

Still, the upper-right head has a normal connection to the body, whereas the head on the seated figure (lower right) is very uncertain in its attachment. Its nose has been flattened out and the convention of a shadow plane has been used as if it were a decorative element in a "synthetic" composition based on a head. Also, the alignment of the eyes is illogical and the mouth is too small. It seems that a collection of shapes taken from a head has been arbitrarily assembled and placed on the figure's shoulders. From this "head"

alone we cannot deduce the age, sex, race, or any other distinguishing characteristic of a person. Only the hips and thighs—plus the title—confirm that it is a woman.

Finally, at the extreme left of the canvas, we see a brown area which looks like a close-up of a female figure, employing forms typical of African art. Is it one of the *demoiselles?* It seems to be an echo of a woman's back, painted brown to look like carved wood sculpture. Perhaps it announces the *leitmotif,* the subtopic, of the painting. Perhaps it is an enlarged rear view of the figure at the left.

Pablo Picasso. *Les Demoiselles d'Avignon.* 1907. Oil on canvas, 8' × 7'8". Collection, The Museum of Modern Art, New York. Acquired through the Lillie P. Bliss Bequest

Details of *Les Demoiselles d'Avignon*

The viewer's expectations are very important in formal analysis: on the basis of what we see, what do we *expect* to see? Remember that artists are usually aware of our visual and cultural conditioning. Certainly Picasso knows how to use fixed-point perspective, and he knows that viewers in the Western world expect illusions of depth to create the space for figures to move around. Nevertheless, he breaks up any possibility of deep space. The still life at the bottom of the painting provides the merest hint of a plane leading *into* the picture space. But Picasso does not follow through: he locates the foot of the figure on the left in the same plane and at the same height as the still life. This foot *has to be* on the floor, yet the floor cannot be on the same level as the tabletop and the still life. Obviously, our expected logic of spatial representation has been deliberately destroyed.

It is plain that in making a formal analysis we have been accumulating evidence for interpreting and judging the work. At first, Picasso's breakdown of Western spatial logic suggests that something is seriously wrong. But perhaps a different logic has been created. Or would *any* logic of space be irrelevant here? It seems reasonable to say that the activity of each figure takes place in its own space in a shallow area parallel to the picture plane.

Notice that the linear and coloristic clues in *Les Demoiselles* keep us close to the surface. When our eyes try to travel inward, they are turned to one side. Picasso makes us feel we must move to make sense of the profile view of the nose. From a fixed position we cannot deal with a front view of the face and a profile of the nose in the same head. So we must move imaginatively from left to right as we view the two central figures: we move in the *same direction* as the "falling" central figure. That movement reinforces our tendency as Westerners to "read" everything in a clockwise direction. Yet there are numerous violations of our *other* expectations; Western ideas of form and proportion are repeatedly disobeyed. By the time we reach the seated figure at the right, we are ready for anything; we may even be willing to accept the joining of the shoulder, arm, forearm, and hip in a single continuous form. Indeed, emphasis has shifted away from the shape of the limbs to the *shape of the openings* they form.

Our analysis now moves from an objective description of forms to a statement about the way we perceive them. We seem to be groping for a principle of organization, an idea that can account for the way the total work is structured. As our observations grow, as information accumulates, it becomes increasingly difficult to postpone the work of interpretation. But now we can undertake that job with modest feelings of security: we have identified the things we see; we have *tried* to be objective in our description; we have examined the main form relationships; we have tried to build a consensus about the visual facts and their "behavior." Now how do they add up?

# INTERPRETATION

Interpretation in art criticism is a process of finding the overall meaning of a work that the critic has described and analyzed. This does not mean that critics give verbal equivalents for art forms. Neither does it mean judging the work. Obviously, we are not in a position to judge a work until we have decided what problems it tries to solve, what it seems to say, what it means now.

Interpretation or explanation is the most important part of the critical enterprise, and it is tremendously challenging. Indeed, if we have thoroughly interpreted a work, the business of evaluation may seem superfluous: we feel satisfied with what we have found out. Perhaps that is because good interpretation involves discovering the meaning of a work of art and stating its relevance to our lives and the human situation in general.

Certain assumptions underlie critical interpretation. We assume that an art object, being a human product, cannot escape the value system of the artist. Values and ideas are almost like germs; we pick them up everywhere. Just as human beings "pick up" values, art objects pick up ideas. As critics we are not primarily interested in whether these ideas are faithful to the artist's beliefs. That is, we do not use art to find out what an artist thinks. But we *are* interested in the fact that art objects become charged with ideas—ideas that may enter a work without the artist's conscious knowledge. It is our function as critics to discover those ideas and communicate them to others.

An important principle of criticism is that the artist is not necessarily the best authority on the meaning of his or her work. As critics we are interested in what artists think about their work; indeed, we are interested in *anything* they can tell us. But their views cannot be swallowed whole: whatever artists say needs to be confirmed by our own methods of analysis and interpretation.

Does interpretation violate or distort the qualities of art that are not readily verbalized? Is it possible to talk about shapes, colors, and textures except in highly imprecise terms? My reply is that art criticism is not a substitute for aesthetic experience. If visual content could be verbally ex-

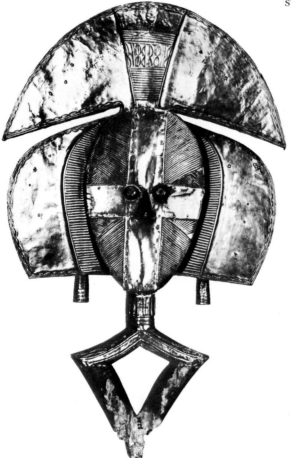

*below:* Guardian figure, from the Bokota area, Gabon. 19th–20th century. Ethnographic Collection of the University, Zurich.

Picasso's *Dancer,* painted about the same time as *Les Demoiselles,* gives us a good idea of the way he used African art, and how his powers of visual transformation work. The Gabon figure is a grave marker: symmetrical, armless, and austere. Picasso converts it into a female dancer displaying her charms.

*right:* Pablo Picasso. *Dancer.* 1907. Oil on canvas, 59 × 39¼". Collection Walter P. Chrysler, Jr., New York

pressed, it would be unnecessary to make the artwork in the first place. The function of language in critical interpretation is to deal with the formal and sensuous qualities of the art object in terms of their impact upon our feelings and intelligence. When we examine an artwork, its qualities seem to organize themselves into a perceptual unity, and it is this unity that we try, however badly, to verbalize.

During description and analysis we used words to *direct the viewer's attention* to actual colors and shapes in the art object, not to our language about them. Our verbal formulations may vary somewhat, and that suggests perceptual variation or different emphases in what we see. But now we need a device that can organize our various perceptions into a single statement. In the discussion that follows we try to reconcile these variations in the form of a *hypothesis*—a tentative interpretation of the perceptual facts. We want to arrive at an explanation that will make sense to many viewers of the same work.

**Forming a Hypothesis**    How do we begin the work of interpretation? Well, during description and analysis, several possible explanations presented themselves almost spontaneously. Now we have to formulate an explanation deliberately; we want it to summarize the evidence we have been accumulating. The explanations which came up as we analyzed the art object were based on incomplete evidence; technically, they were *explications*—partial explanations of the work as it unfolds. However, partial explanations contain useful hints: perhaps we can use one or more of them as *hypotheses* to see if they will work as explanations of the whole.

In science, more than one hypothesis can account for a given phenomenon. And the same is true of art: more than one hypothesis can explain an artwork. Since changing social, personal, and cultural conditions affect our perceptions, it is not surprising that the same work can be interpreted differently at different times or by different persons. What is important is that the interpretation be responsive to a particular set of visual facts. In practical criticism, we find that the various interpretations tend to have a "family resemblance." But if more than one hypothesis can explain a work, should the critic abandon the effort to develop a single explanation? To some extent the answer depends on the public a critic serves. For example, a teacher of children might explain Seurat's *A Sunday Afternoon on the Island of La Grande Jatte* as a picture of people enjoying a day off: they stroll, rest in the shade, watch fishermen, and meet friends. In other words, an adequate interpretation might consist of little more than an account of the picture's subject matter. For others, the picture might be explained in terms of the representation of light, the flattening of forms, the control of contours, and the pointillist application of paint. The critic might also contrast the dignity, order, and *silence* of the painting with the sounds (boat whistles, dogs barking, kids shouting) which we hear. Or do we hear them? Is this a picture of silent sound?

Finally, we might offer the hypothesis that this is "really" an abstract painting which uses familiar objects to sustain our attention until we become aware of its complex formal relationships of light and dark, flat and deep space, and chromatic imitations of sunlight. Another hypothesis, not incompatible with the others, is that the picture is a *game* the artist plays with viewers—a game employing the pictorial conventions of linear perspective, dark silhouettes, cast shadows, and a new way of coloring flat surfaces. Seurat persuades us to recognize familiar things in forms which are mainly his own inventions. The viewer is taken in by a few contours and perspective devices; we have been "fooled" into believing these patterns are people.

**The Mimetic Theory**    How are hypotheses formed? We get a hint from the remarks people make about "modernistic" art—works that seem "wild,"

"A picture is not thought and settled beforehand. While it is being done it changes as one's thoughts change. And when it is finished, it still goes on changing, according to the state of mind of whoever is looking at it."

Picasso

495

"crazy," or "childish," as in Seymour Lipton's *Cerberus*. We know what people do when they are frustrated: they become angry or they try to be funny. Here is a free-form sculpture that might remind us of a "dog waiting to take a bite out of a mailman's leg." The remark is questionable as humor, but that's what we often hear; it expresses annoyance and embarrassment as much as anything else. It also reveals the normal impulse to use what might be called the "looks-like," "feels-like," and "reminds-me-of" reaction. The mind, confronted with material it cannot organize, struggles to find some correspondence between present, confusing perceptions and past perceptions that have been organized and understood. The "humor" is only a symptom of the struggle.

At a certain level, Lipton's sculpture *does* look like a watchdog waiting to bite someone. But the comic-strip saga of dog biting mailman explains few of the visual facts. So we must employ the "looks-like" reaction at a more sophisticated level. What is there about a dog-bites-man episode that corresponds with the art object? This fierce little beast, with his sharply pointed equipment, has only one aim in life: to bite strangers. Which makes him a marvelous guardian. Yet somehow, man—a noble creature—becomes entangled in the low concerns of this single-minded creature. So the Cerberus episode may be an "excuse" for the artist to deal with the themes of animality and dignity. No humans are present but we respond to those forms like humans: we're ashamed to be afraid of *Cerberus*.

A simple "looks-like" or "reminds-me-of" reaction can lead to a fairly complex hypothesis *if* the visual evidence will support us. If not, we must modify our statement until it fits the facts.

**Interpreting *Les Demoiselles*** To illustrate interpretation, let us return to Picasso's *Les Demoiselles*. We can discard some hypotheses first: the work is not a celebration of female beauty (although it does evoke works of that type: Rubens's *Judgment of Paris* or Raphael's *Three Graces*). But notice that it displays very little artistic virtuosity—skill in drawing and brushwork, painterly modeling of forms, sensitive representation of light; color and shape are not employed as sources of sensuous delight. In other words, the value of the painting lies in something other than optical enjoyment of its surface. The forms we have analyzed serve mainly to designate or symbolize ideas. Indeed, it is possible that *Les Demoiselles* expresses ideas which are original in a historical or philosophical sense.

Perhaps we can build our interpretation on the basis of the clue offered by Picasso's left-central figure; it *looks like* a statue that has lost its base. The

Otto Piene. *Carousel.* 1980. Helium-filled balloon, 150' long. On roof of Passenger Ship Terminal, New York City

The title of a work may give us a clue to its interpretation, but critics should also trust their "looks-like," "feels-like," and "reminds-me-of" reactions. Here the impression of a spider combines with the floating effect of helium and the circular motion of a carousel to produce the image of a walking, whirling, striving creature we have never seen. Or have we? Could it be us?

496

figure seems to be falling, but, being a statue, it maintains a serene expression: the statue *does not know* it is collapsing. Picasso's painting tells us that someone or something is in a state of collapse without being aware of it.

We noticed earlier that Picasso used white lines to delineate forms in the central figure. It is a use of line we may have seen in ancient Greek vase painting. The faces of the two central figures also have the expressionless stare which is characteristic of archaic Greek female images. A more recent ancestor of the central figure might be found in a highly sentimental work by Ingres: *Venus Anadyomene.* But even without this information we can sense the origins of the central figures: they embody the classical ideal of female beauty developed in the cultures of the ancient Mediterranean world; they belong to Picasso's own tradition (indeed, they look like Picasso!). By contrast, the other standing figures are derived from non-Western sources—African or Pre-Columbian. And, as observed earlier, they employ angular as opposed to curvilinear shapes. These figures disappoint the expectations of Mediterranean pulchritude aroused by the central figures: the upper-right figure is aggressively ugly; and the left figure has the sort of leg we do not see in the cities of the West.

So we witness a change of race along with a change in artistic treatment. Picasso has intentionally juxtaposed Western and non-Western racial types to express the *fall* of Western ethnocentrism. First, the classical beauty symbolized by the central figures is contrasted with the angular forms of the other standing figures; then they are synthesized in the hybrid figure at the lower right. Its head is based on non-Western plastic forms subjected to a kind of Western cerebral play. In the "fall" of the classical figures we see the decline of a culture in which beauty is the object of serene contemplation. The ideal of female passivity is displaced by ideals of female activity and magical aliveness.

Jim Dine. *Five Feet of Colorful Tools.* 1962. Oil on canvas surmounted by a board on which thirty-two tools hang from hooks; overall, 55⅝ × 60¼ × 4⅜". The Sidney and Harriet Janis Collection. Gift to The Museum of Modern Art, New York

After attending to the objects, their colors, their negative shadows, their placement, the space below them, the paint spatters, the board on top, the hooks, the frame, and their relationships—we are about ready to interpret. Some suggestive hypotheses might help, and we get them by raising the following questions: Is this work about carpentry? About neatness? About craft in relation to painting? About dancing tools? About the souls of useful objects? About what happens between the real objects and their airbrushed echoes? Has the glossy paint changed the identity of the tools? What caused the vertically shaped paint spatters? Are the hammers and saws bleeding? Are they perspiring in color? Are they happy to be what they are, where they are? Are we looking at musical notes? Should we sing?

Seymour Lipton. *Cerberus.* 1948. Collection Mr. and Mrs. Alvin S. Lane, New York

Pablo Picasso. *Les Demoiselles d'Avignon.* 1907. Oil on canvas, 8' × 7'8".
Collection, The Museum of Modern Art, New York. Acquired through the Lillie P.
Bliss Bequest

Can this work be explained wholly on the basis of what we see? Or must it be
approached via the history of art? Must we know the Western conventions for
dealing with the pose and composition of female nudes before we can adequately
appreciate Picasso's departure from those conventions? The answer depends on
whether we regard the work as one document in a continuing story or whether we
see it as an independent, organic thing. It is possible, however, with agility in
shifting one's perceptual gears, to understand the work through visual sensibility
*and* scholarly intelligence. Of course, that obliges us to discipline our seeing and
knowing.

Raphael. *The Three Graces.* 1500. Oil on panel, 6¾ × 6¾". Musée Condé, Chantilly, France

Raphael uses these women for a superb demonstration of classical equipoise: they are balanced on their feet, within the pictorial space and on the picture plane. Is it essential to remember this painting as we look at Picasso's?

Peter Paul Rubens. *The Judgment of Paris.* 1638–39. Oil on panel, 57 × 75".
The National Gallery, London

In Rubens's picture, as in Picasso's, the display of female flesh is an important part
of the story. The women compete with one another—one even addresses herself
to the viewer. Again, must we keep her in mind as we look at the central figures in
*Les Demoiselles?*

**Jean-Auguste-Dominique Ingres.** *Venus Anadyomene.* 1848.
Oil on canvas, 64⅛ × 36¼". Musée Condé, Chantilly, France

This insipid painting embodies many of the ideals of
nineteenth-century French academic art. Surely Picasso reacted
against everything it represents: *Les Demoiselles* is, among other
things, a picture of that reaction.

Pablo Picasso. *Head of a Woman*. c. 1909.
Gouache and black crayon, 24⁵⁄₁₆ × 18¾".
The Art Institute of Chicago. The Charles L.
Hutchinson Memorial Collection

Further support for our interpretation of *Les Demoiselles*. In 1909—two years after *Les Demoiselles*—Picasso was still trying to fit African sculptural forms into a European pictorial format.

Art historians know that Picasso originally intended to paint a brothel scene showing a sailor surrounded by nude women, fruit, flowers, and a symbolic intimation of death. However, the final version of the canvas does not embody this plan. Here it should be stressed that a defensible interpretation of the work need not follow Picasso's intent; indeed, we can be misled by the artist's plan (assuming it is possible to know what it was). Our critical procedure is designed to get at the meanings which can be *visually* confirmed in the work—meanings the artist may not have consciously intended.

In 1907, well before the two world wars and the dissolution of European colonialism in Africa and Asia, Picasso's painting represented a remarkable anticipation of the political and cultural changes that would take place some forty years later. So, if my explanation is right, Picasso's painting has meaning for general history as well as the development of a major artistic style. Generally regarded as the first Cubist, or proto-Cubist, picture, this work also represents a great advance in the capacity of painting to deal with world-historical ideas.

Our interpretation of *Les Demoiselles* has led to an appraisal, or judgment, of its importance: clearly it has enormous artistic and intellectual significance. Now, we should look more closely into the business of making value judgments about works of art.

## JUDGMENT

Judging a work of art means giving it a rank in relation to other works of its type. This aspect of art criticism is much abused and may be unnecessary if a satisfying interpretation has been carried out. Nevertheless, for a variety of motives, human beings often want to rank art objects. Also, there are practical situations where ranking and appraisal are unavoidable. Museums are anxious to acquire works which are "important": there are "good" collections of French Impressionists and there are "great" collections of French Impressionists. As for individuals, they may buy what pleases them but they like to feel that what pleases them is good, that is, *comparatively* good—better than something else.

Certain kinds of critics are called connoisseurs—persons who "know" a great deal about matters of taste and technical excellence and are hence considered good judges. When dealing with older artworks, connoisseurs are usually concerned with authenticity. For example, the importance of Giorgione has long been established; hence connoisseurship may involve deciding whether he did, in fact, paint a certain picture (if the "Giorgione" is really a Titian, then it is probably worth less; paintings by Giorgione are rare, but Titian lived a long time and painted many pictures—not all of the same high quality); when in his career the work was executed; whether other versions exist; and whether it is a *good* example of his style. In general, connoisseurs seem to be best at judging artworks in comparison to other works by the same artist or the same school of artists.

In the case of contemporary art, different problems arise. Authenticity is not often a problem; most of the facts about the work are known. But many collectors and gallery owners want to acquire works of art *before* their creators have become famous and expensive. They have to exercise critical judgment almost like an investor in low-priced mining stock; such persons want to identify artistic excellence before it is widely recognized. Hence, the criticism of contemporary art is closely related to the *prediction* of aesthetic values. Somehow, the critic must anticipate what discriminating persons are going to like. Hopefully, they will like good art. Well, what makes it good? The judgment of history, but who can wait?

**Comparisons with Historical Models**   In making a critical judgment, we try to relate a work of art to the broadest possible range of comparable works. A common error of young artists and critics is to form judgments with reference to a very recent or narrow context of artistic creativity. But to take

John Sloan. *Connoisseurs of Prints.* 1905. International Business Machines Corporation, New York

Connoisseurs are critics of a special type; they usually specialize in a particular kind of art or in the style of a particular artist. Their expertise is gained by close scrutiny of the minutest details of material and technique. That is what Sloan satirizes here—connoisseurs concentrating on every stain, blemish, or scratch in a print. Does this mean they miss the big picture?

a critical judgment seriously we must feel assured that it is based on the consideration of a wide range of comparable objects in time and space. Since we know examples of artistic creativity beginning over twenty thousand years ago and continuing to the present day, the range of relevant objects is enormous. Knowing the history of art (as much of it as possible) is the best defense we have against pure subjectivity in critical judgment. Fortunately, modern education, the wide dissemination of reproductions, and the frequent display of original works greatly extends the known history of art. So there is little excuse for the critic who judges according to standards based only on the work of a certain school, region, style, period, or cultural setting.

Perhaps it seems paradoxical to say that judging art calls for relating it to historical examples while expecting it to express current needs and values. But a comparison with the best work of the past does not imply *imitation* of the past. Historical examples are not supposed to be copy models; we employ them intelligently when using them as benchmarks or touchstones of excellence. When judging excellence in sculpture, for example, the masters from Michelangelo to Henry Moore should shape our ideas about the capacity of genius to operate within specific historical and cultural contexts.

Accordingly, we can admire Max Beckmann's *Self-Portrait* as much as the *Portrait of a Young Man* by Bronzino. Both works make eloquent use of form to describe the outer man and his inner ideals. Bronzino, in addition to establishing the self-confidence of a handsome young man, concentrates on creating a credible illusion of skin, clothing, and architectural surroundings. The magnificently drawn and modeled hands testify to the values of the age and the quality of the painting *at the same time*. Beckmann, facing himself, portrays an older person—a man with an experienced and cynical expression. The pose has a certain elegance but the portrait is hardly a celebration of manly beauty. Despite the formal clothes and the nonchalance of the hands, we get an ominous and troubled impression. In the Bronzino portrait,

*left:* Agnolo Bronzino. *Portrait of a Young Man.* c. 1535–40. Oil on panel, 37⅝ × 29½". The Metropolitan Museum of Art, New York. The H. O. Havemeyer Collection. Bequest of Mrs. H. O. Havemeyer, 1929

*above:* Max Beckmann. *Self-Portrait in a Tuxedo.* 1927. Oil on canvas, 54½ × 37¾". Busch-Reisinger Museum, Harvard University, Cambridge, Massachusetts

Lucian Freud. *Reflection (Self-Portrait)*.
1985. Oil on canvas, 22⅛ × 20⅛".
Private collection

The relevance of technique. We cannot focus on this image without being aware of the way it was made. That colors our perception of the man. Compare Freud's gritty paint application to Auerbach's furious brushwork (page 229). Clearly, all impastos are not the same: some are angrier than others.

psychological analysis is minimal; in the Beckmann portrait, psychological analysis predominates, especially in the grim set of the mouth, the lighting of the face from two sides, and the exaggerated sharpness of the facial planes. Bronzino's young man symbolizes an age of reverence for learning: he holds a book to suggest the intellectual interests of the Renaissance. Beckmann's man holds a cigarette, also symbolizing an age—an age of neurosis. Both men desire poise and serenity, but they go about it differently.

The more we examine Beckmann's portrait, the more we are convinced that it makes a significant artistic and psychological statement. Obviously its values are different from those of the Bronzino, yet both pictures belong to the same type or genre. It is this similarity which enables us to compare them, to seek a range of meaning and a power of expression in the modern work which is comparable to the range we find in the sixteenth-century work. We do not seek the same values, but the same *capacity to support values*. Thus the harshly manipulated planes in the Beckmann become a vehicle of aesthetic expressiveness as much as the flawless surface of the Bronzino. Which means that the Beckmann is *as good as* the Bronzino.

**The Relevance of Technique**    For the purposes of art criticism, what is the role of craftsmanship, mastery of technique, skill and facility in the use of materials? To answer, we can begin with the proposition that *art is making*; it is what the Greeks called *techné*. Art is not an idea *followed by* technical expression; art is idea *and* materials united by technique. The notion of technique as subordinate to idea is a philosophic error that has bedeviled aesthetics and art criticism for a long time. We cannot afford to ignore craft or technique in criticism because making and forming processes are themselves expressive and satisfying.

Technical analysis has already been mentioned in connection with critical description. Now we want to examine craftsmanship as a vehicle of aesthetic value. In art, technique is not only a means toward an end, it is an end in itself. There is a special sort of aesthetic pleasure we derive from technique; it probably comes from our strong identification with our hands and hand tools. The logical and effective use of tools is one of the most fundamental demonstrations of human mastery over the environment: we are, after all, tool-using animals.

How, then, do we decide whether a work is technically good? Is it good if it works, or is it good because it looks good? In the past, good technique was chiefly concerned with the durability and magical effectiveness of an object. Craftsmanship was also a visible sign of labor and materials expended; it signified the power to command skilled labor. Durability remains important but it is less prominent in today's art because modern materials permit even badly crafted works to survive. As for the evidence of human labor, it is less significant as a mark of status since our most costly possessions are often made by machines. For us, then, craftsmanship or technical excellence means (1) logic in the use of tools and materials; and (2) close correspondence between appearance and function. Although technical excellence is difficult to judge, we can be alert to these qualities at least: utility (in practical objects), logic and economy (in the use of materials), and a sense of connectedness between form, purpose, and meaning.

Since the physical properties of materials govern what can be done with them, craftsmanship consists of extracting the maximum of performance from materials without violating their nature. Perhaps craftsmanship can be defined as the *morality* of materials and technique: certain things that can be done with materials *should not be done*. Plastics can be treated to look like anything from marble to wood, but we feel cheated when we discover the deception. Of course, our notions about the appropriate use of tools and materials cannot be fixed forever; a new "logic" of materials can be invented. Engineers continually extend our ideas about the use of old materials; artists,

Aristocles. *Stele of Aristion,* from Attica. 510–500 B.C. Carved and chiseled Pentilic marble. National Archaeological Museum, Athens

Pablo Picasso. Detail of *Les Demoiselles d'Avignon.* 1907. Collection, The Museum of Modern Art, New York. Acquired through the Lillie P. Bliss Bequest

The resemblance between these two figures may be entirely accidental. Or perhaps Picasso was using the archaic Greek figure in the same way he used African wood sculpture: to contrast the early, vigorous stage of culture with the late, overripe stage of civilization.

Claes Oldenburg. *Two Cheeseburgers, with Everything (Dual Hamburgers)*. 1962. Burlap soaked in plaster, painted with enamel, 7 × 14¾ × 8⅝". Collection, The Museum of Modern Art, New York. Philip Johnson Fund

designers, and craftsmen do this, too. Sometimes they employ a *perverse* logic of materials: they deliberately violate our sense of rightness in craft or technique; *anticraftsmanship* becomes one of the expressive meanings of a work.

This is often the case with Pop art. In *Two Cheeseburgers, with Everything (Dual Hamburgers)* by Claes Oldenburg we have an intentionally "ugly" sculpture of an everyday object. These oversized hamburgers are made of plaster painted in vivid, garish colors. With this crudely painted plaster, distorted scale, and general lack of "finish," the artist achieves a strong sense of cheapness and vulgarity. Technique is used to violate our feelings about size, color, texture, and logic in the use of materials. Oldenburg tells us that we are looking at something meant to be eaten, but his craft makes it look exceedingly unappetizing. Imagine sinking your teeth into painted plaster: the "aesthetic" reaction becomes physical revulsion. Has this ruined us for fast-food burgers forever?

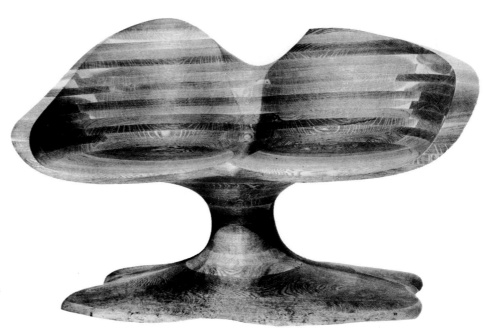

**Wendell Castle. Double chair. 1968**

The criticism of craft objects raises special problems: the work asks to be judged as sculpture and as seating equipment simultaneously. Thus Wendell Castle puts himself in double (or triple) jeopardy—and wins his case! The chair succeeds as utilitarian form, expressive image, and skilled performance.

508

*Correspondence between appearance and function* requires technique to express the meaning or use of an object. Our rule is that objects should *look like* what they do. From this rule we get what amounts to a moral position in the crafts and industrial art: inferior materials and poor craftsmanship should not be "covered up" with skins that deceive us about what is going on inside. Honesty in materials also implies honesty in appearance. Here ethics and aesthetics meet; they require that surfaces satisfy our visual needs for reliable information about weight, dimension, textural quality, and structural purpose. But in speaking of "inferior materials" we do not mean that some materials are intrinsically superior to others. Materials become "inferior" only when they are used inappropriately from the standpoint of durability, honesty, and logic of forming and fabrication.

Craftsmanship becomes especially elusive in the criticism of painting, drawing, and graphic arts. This is because technique in the pictorial arts is closely associated with the capacity to create illusions, whereas the crafts stress utilitarian results. In today's painting and design, however, technique is almost independent of illusionism (although Photorealism is an important

**Isabel Bishop. *Nude*. 1934. Oil on composition board, 33 × 40". Collection of Whitney Museum of American Art, New York. Purchase**

Technique. The mood of this work is inseparable from the paint application. Through half-covering glazes alone, Bishop carries us a long way—from the surface of a woman's skin to the center of her dreams.

Stuart Davis. *Visa*. 1951. Oil on canvas, 40 × 52".
Collection, The Museum of Modern Art,
New York. Gift of Mrs. Gertrud A. Mellon

Words constitute an integral part of the imagery
of this work; the critic has to consider them from
the standpoint of color, shape, size,
meaning—and even of sound.

exception). Accordingly, the critic has to examine technique in terms of
artistic *performance*. We study execution—the application of paint, the manipulation of tones, the handling of color—to see whether the artist controls
his or her performance. Does the performance exhibit inventiveness, dexter-
ity, and expressive use of the medium? Is the technique consistent with the
design of the work as a whole? Does it heighten our awareness of material,
form, and idea *at the same time*? This is the great challenge of technique: to
display skill or virtuosity without losing touch with the idea or purpose of the
work.

## CONCLUSION

This discussion of technique and its connection to the main idea of an artwork
has broad implications. For one thing, it suggests that there is such a thing as
*too much* craft—overdoing or over-finishing a work. That would apply to a
book as well as a painting. The process of creation is alternately frustrating
and satisfying. I think the pleasures outweigh the frustrations, and for that
reason we are reluctant to stop working. But the author of a book dealing
with criticism should recognize the perils of over-finishing or over-writing. If
nothing else, that author should know when the danger point has been
reached. I think the time has come: this book is done.

# GLOSSARY

*Cross references are indicated by words in* SMALL CAPITALS.

ABSTRACT EXPRESSIONISM. A style of painting (mainly American, 1950s and 1960s) emphasizing spontaneous execution, large brushing gestures, bursts of muscular energy, and non-representational imagery. See "ACTION" PAINTING.

ABSTRACTION. The essential form after superficial or changeable features have been taken away; sometimes used (incorrectly) to mean any image that does not resemble its model in reality.

ACADEMIC. The artistic approach taught in the eighteenth- and nineteenth-century art academies of Europe; a philosophy of art based on bland imitations of ancient CLASSICAL art; by extension, any systematic, traditional, anti-experimental type of art.

"ACTION" PAINTING. A style in which the meaning or content of a picture relies strongly on the implied activity of the painted surface, especially the signs of brushing, spattering, and dripping paint; related to ABSTRACT EXPRESSIONISM.

AERIAL PERSPECTIVE. Creation of depth illusions in painting through the use of diminishing intensity of colors, the use of cooler colors for distant objects, softening of edges, and blurring of focus.

AESTHETIC. Pertaining to art theory or matters of taste and appreciation in art; the beautiful as opposed to the good, true, or useful; any vivid or intense experience. Also *an* aesthetic: an artistic or stylistic point of view; a philosophy of art.

AFFECTIVE. Pertaining to emotion, especially the emotions that accompany or result from seeing works of art.

ALLA PRIMA. Italian for "all at once"; DIRECT PAINTING; immediate achievement of final effects; the painting has one "skin" rather than many layers; the opposite of indirect painting.

ARABESQUE. Imagery that resembles the flowing interlaces of Islamic art; stylized ornamental motifs based on plants and flowers; intricate and fantastic decorative pattern of ORGANIC or geometric origin.

ARCHAIC. Primitive, antiquated, or obsolete; Greek art before the seventh century B.C. Also, archaic smile: the expression, almost a smile, of Greek sculptured heads before the seventh century.

ARCHITECTONIC. Architectural. Paintings, sculptures, or craft objects that exhibit the structural or textural traits of buildings.

ARMATURE. The skeleton or framework inside a wax or clay (usually) sculpture; it supports the work while it is being modeled.

ART NOUVEAU. French for "new art" (JUGENDSTIL in German); highly decorative style of the 1890s; emphasis on the whip-lash curve, rich color, flat patterns, floral ornamentation, vertical attenuation.

ASSEMBLAGE. Creation of imagery by the aggregation of different materials, often fragments of recognizable images and objects.

AUTEUR THEORY. The view that the artistic quality of a motion picture is mainly the responsibility of the film director, who is the real cinema "artist."

AVANT-GARDE. French word for those who are advanced, "ahead of the times"; artists who point out the direction others will follow.

AXIS. The center line, real or imaginary, around which the parts of a work of art are composed and balanced.

BAROQUE. Art of the seventeenth century in Europe; characterized by irregularity of form, illusions of infinite space, theatricality of color and lighting, grandiose gestures, over-lifesize figuration.

BASILICA. Originally a Roman building used as a court of law or for public meetings; evolved under Christianity into the church, a building with a long, narrow NAVE, side aisles, and an apse at the end, formerly occupied by the judge or emperor's representative.

BAUHAUS. The school of art and industrial design founded in 1919 by Walter Gropius to promote the unity of all the arts; closed by the Hitler regime in 1933.

BIOMORPHIC. Having the qualities of living form. See ORGANIC.

BROKEN COLOR. Painting technique typical of IMPRESSIONISM; short touches of bright color, often complementaries, placed side-by-side to create a vibrating effect.

BRUTALISM. An architectural style of the 1950s featuring exposed steel and large areas of coarse, undecorated concrete; the building treated almost like an Expressionistic sculpture.

BYZANTINE/BYZANTINE ICONS. The art and architecture, mainly religious, of the Byzantine Empire; icon paintings of sacred persons venerated in the Eastern Orthodox Church; style of strict frontality, little or no naturalistic modeling, rich decoration, otherworldly outlook. See MOSAICS.

CALLIGRAPHIC. Pertaining to the art of beautiful writing as in the scripts of Persia, China, and Japan; an artistic style characterized by graceful flowing curves.

CANTILEVER. The free part of a horizontal member that projects into space, seemingly without support, while its internal end is anchored in the main structure.

CAPITAL. The head or topmost part of a column or pier; depending on its characteristic shape and decoration, it may be called Doric, Ionic, Etruscan, or Corinthian.

CARTOON. A full-scale preparatory drawing for a painting, MURAL, or tapestry; a humorous sketch or caricature; a series (as in a comic strip), usually made for a newspaper or magazine.

CHIAROSCURO. In painting, the MODELING of form with light and dark; any artistic treatment that stresses the contrast between light areas and shadows.

CHROMATIC. Pertaining to color, especially HUE. See also POLY-CHROMATIC, MONOCHROMATIC.

CLASSICAL. The art of ancient Greece and Rome; any work exhibiting the traits of ancient Greek art; an art of formal order stressing simplicity, dignity, clearly defined intervals, mathematical proportion. A "classic" is, by extension, a work generally accepted as a masterpiece.

CLOSED FORM. The sense of unbroken space characteristic of CLASSICAL composition in painting, sculpture, and architecture.

COGNITION. The act of knowing; in art, the knowledge that results from aesthetic perception.

COLLAGE. From the French coller, to paste; any artistic composition made by gluing assorted materials (cloth, newsprint, wallpaper, wood veneers) to a flat surface, usually a canvas or a panel.

CONCEPTUALISM. An art movement (after 1960) emphasizing the transient character of the creative act rather than its outcome; art objects become the report, written or spoken, of an event; deemphasis of visual imagery. Related to Process Art.

CONNOISSEUR. Literally, one "who knows" and is therefore competent to offer critical judgments of art; an expert in a particular branch of art who can recognize certain techniques, establish dates, verify authenticity, estimate prices; a person of discriminating taste in art, cooking, etc.

CONSTRUCTIVISM. Twentieth-century nonrepresentational sculpture style, associated with the Russians Naum Gabo and Antoine Pevsner; theoretical foundations in modern physics, engineering, and technology; an endeavor to treat volume with a minimum of mass.

CONTRAPPOSTO. A twisting of the human figure in such a manner that the head, chest, abdomen, hips, and thighs may face in different directions. The various directions create an opposition of forces within the figure, which is felt as emotional tension by the viewer.

CRITICISM. The act of describing, analyzing, interpreting, and judging works of art; informed talk about art; incorrectly used to mean censure or fault-finding.

CROSS-CULTURAL. Pertaining to artistic and aesthetic phenomena that transcend local traditions, habits, and preferences.

CUBISM. A style of art originated by Picasso and Braque in Paris about 1907; emphasis on the geometrical foundations of form, the two-dimensionality of the picture surface, multiple views of the same objects, superimposition and interpenetration of forms. Intellectual phase is *Analytic Cubism* (1909–12); decorative, playful phase is *Synthetic Cubism* (1912–14).

DADAISM. Post-World War I style stressing accidental images and events, the "logic" of absurdity, irrationality in art, literature, and morality. Related to SURREALISM.

DAGUERREOTYPE. An early photographic process (1839) named after L. Daguerre, employing silver salts, iodine, and mercury vapor in developing a picture.

DIRECT PAINTING. See ALLA PRIMA. A technique that stresses spontaneity or the appearance of spontaneity in execution; a minimum of reworking; avoids transparent effects and "building up" a surface with several layers of paint.

DOCUMENTARY. A photographic, motion-picture, or television presentation of unposed or uncontrived events; a style of art that *seems* to report actual events.

EARTH SCULPTURE. A form of art in which the sculptor excavates earth, relocates boulders, digs water channels, etc., to create pleasing or expressive aesthetic effects. Also Earthworks and ENVIRONMENTAL ART.

ECLECTICISM. A style based on many borrowings; the combination of recognizable elements from several styles to fashion something new.

EMPATHY. The imaginative projection of feelings or thoughts into another person, creature, or thing.

ENCAUSTIC. A painting medium using hot wax to bind colors to a wood panel or a wall.

ENTABLATURE. The portion of a CLASSICAL building facade between its column capitals and its roof; it contains the architrave, frieze, and cornice.

ENTASIS. A slight convexity or swelling in the shaft of a CLASSICAL column; it counteracts the optical effect whereby perfectly straight columns seem to be narrower in the center.

ENVIRONMENTAL ART. Any ordered arrangement or reconstruction of the natural or built environment; a garden, for example. See EARTH SCULPTURE and HAPPENINGS.

EXPRESSIONISM. A style of modern painting, originally Central European, emphasizing intense color, agitated brushwork, and violent imagery to express painful emotions, anxiety, and hallucinatory states.

EXPRESSIVISM. A term used here to describe the critical position that greatness in art results from the vivid, intense, and convincing expression of emotion.

FAUVISM. From the French *fauve* (wild beast). An early-twentieth-century painting style emphasizing the juxtaposition of extremely bright areas of color, arbitrary drawing unrelated to the color, and distorted linear perspective. Main aim is breakdown and reform of traditional pictorial structure; not as anguished as German EXPRESSIONISM, which it resembles.

FETISH. A charmed or magical object; often a sculpture regarded as the home or embodiment of a spiritual substance, much as the *ka*, or other self, of an Egyptian pharaoh is believed to reside in the many statues of him; a psychological obsession with an object or part of the body which results in an erotic response.

FORESHORTENING. The representation through drawing of three-dimensional forms on a flat surface to create the illusion of their depth, as of an arm and hand extended toward the viewer. See Mantegna, *The Lamentation* (page 138).

FORMALISM. The doctrine that the meaning, emotion, and value of an artwork depend wholly on the organization of its lines, shapes, colors, and textures.

FRESCO. A type of MURAL, or wall painting, in which dry colors are mixed with water and applied to a wet plaster surface; *fresco* means "fresh" in Italian.

FRONTALITY. The full-face or head-on presentation of the human figure; planarity in the organization of forms, that is, emphasis on forms parallel to the frontal plane.

FUNCTIONALISM. The doctrine prominent in the early twentieth century that architecture, furniture, and other useful objects should be designed to reveal their materials and process of making, to work well and to endure, and to express their practical purpose; the view that aesthetic excellence results from successful utilitarian design and performance.

FUTURISM. An Italian painting style (about 1910) derived from CUBISM; devoted to the celebration of speed, the representation of motion, and the dynamization of civilized life.

GEODESIC. Word invented by R. Buckminster Fuller to describe his basically hemispherical domes, which rely for strength on a geometric grid of thin, straight members in tension and compression.

512

GESSO. The mixture of chalk or plaster and glue applied to wooden panels and (rarely) to canvas to serve as a ground for tempera painting.

GESTALT. A pattern or configuration. In psychology, the theory that wholes are greater than (not identical to) the sum of their separate parts.

GLAZE. A semitransparent film of pigment and oil or varnish used to color or model an underlying painting that is usually MONOCHROMATIC or limited in color range; imparts a lustrous effect.

GOTHIC. Originally applied to the art and architecture of France, then Europe, from the twelfth to the mid-sixteenth century; emphasis on vertical space, basilican plan, long, narrow NAVE, slender masonry construction, progressive enlargement of window area, ribbed groin VAULTS, flying buttresses, stained glass.

GRAPHICS. Also the graphic arts; from the Greek word for drawing or writing. Applied to engraving, etching, woodcut, lithography; any method of printmaking or communication through line, especially when reproduced in books, magazines, posters, and by electronic transmission.

GUILDS. Free professional and social associations of medieval artisans, merchants, and tradesmen, organized to protect their interests, to maintain standards of craft, to govern the training of apprentices and journeymen, the admission of members, the preservation of trade secrets, and the control of business and work.

HAPPENING. A quasi-theatrical event staged or contrived in non-repeatable form, employing people, places, and objects to make a visual-sculptural-satirical statement. See ENVIRONMENTAL ART.

HATCHING. A drawing and printmaking technique; a kind of shading in which fine lines placed close together create a tone that models form; in painting, a series of parallel strokes (as in Cézanne) that create the appearance of planes or facets of form.

HEDONIC. Pertaining to pleasure; art created to generate agreeable sensations.

HUE. The name of a color, such as red, blue, or yellow; the quality of light (wavelength) that separates one color from another.

ICONOGRAPHY. The conventional meanings of the images used to convey or symbolize ideas in works of art; an artist's distinctive use of visual SYMBOLS.

ICONOLOGY. The historical study and interpretation of visual SYMBOLS in art, with particular attention to their literary origins; the study of religious symbolism.

IDEALIZATION. Visual representations that omit defects or imperfect variations in a form; a type of ABSTRACTION; a type of STYLIZATION; representations that follow perfect models.

IMPASTO. From the Italian word for paste; paint applied in thick slathers or lumps.

IMPRESSIONISM. A late nineteenth-century (mainly French) style of painting; the extension of REALISM to the scientific analysis of color and light; stress on capture of transient atmospheric effects; use of BROKEN COLOR and color complementaries to render form; outdoor painting and direct observation of subjects emphasized.

INSTRUMENTALISM. A term used here to describe the critical position that greatness in art results from effectiveness in advancing the objectives of humanity, usually as defined by one of a number of major social or economic institutions: family, church, state, GUILD, firm, political party, corporation.

INTENSITY. In color, a high degree of brightness; the fullest manifestation of a color's chroma, its freedom from black, white, or gray. In AESTHETICS, high emotional excitation.

INTERNATIONAL STYLE. First applied to Gothic art; the style of architecture and utilitarian design developed in the 1920s by Walter Gropius, Mies van der Rohe, and Le Corbusier; an outgrowth of the Bauhaus philosophy.

JUGENDSTIL. See ART NOUVEAU.

JUNK ART. The use of rubbish and trivial objects (by Schwitters, Duchamp, Dubuffet, and others) to create images and objects; an extension of the COLLAGE idea.

KEYSTONE. The wedge-shaped stone in the center of a masonry arch.

KINAESTHETIC. Muscle sense. Pertaining to the feelings that works of art generate by stimulating the activity of the muscles, joints, tendons, and organs.

KINETIC ART. Mainly three-dimensional or sculptural art that seems to move spontaneously in space (as in a Calder mobile) by the aid of a mechanism or through some naturally recurring force, such as tide, wind, or water.

KITSCH. Mediocrity in the highest degree. In aesthetics, pretentiously bad art; bad taste in art; cheap, mass-produced objects and images designed to arouse easy emotions.

LANTERN. An open cylindrical construction that lets light in through the top of a dome. See OCULUS.

LINEAR. Pertaining to line. One of Wölfflin's categories stressing the creation of form by outlines or contour lines. Also a main trait of the graphic arts.

LINTEL. The horizontal member of the POST-AND-LINTEL structural device that supports the weight above an opening in a wall.

LOCAL COLOR. The natural or daylight color of an object, seen closely, as opposed to its OPTICAL COLOR, as seen from a distance or as influenced by reflections, weather, or surrounding objects.

MANNERISM. A post-Renaissance, mainly sixteenth-century aristocratic style, characterized by elongation of the figure, artificial poses and gestures, strange distortions of the figure, forced perspective, and strident color; affectedness in art as well as behavior.

MATTE. Having a dull, almost nonreflective surface; the opposite of glossy. Matte varnishes protect a painting without adding gloss.

MEGALITHS. Immense stones such as were used in the construction of Stonehenge. Menhir: a single, uncut, prehistoric megalith.

MIMESIS. The Greek word for imitation or reproduction; the theory, generally attributed to Aristotle, that art is the imitation of human beings in action.

MINARET. The tall, slender tower attached to a mosque; it has one or more balconies from which the muezzin calls Muslims to prayer.

MINIMALISM. A style of nonrepresentational art restricted to very few visual elements, organized as simply as possible.

MODELING. In sculpture, the direct forming of materials such as wax, clay, wood, stone. In painting, the creation of more-or-less sculptural illusions.

MODULE. A standard or unit for measuring and designing; in architecture a device for standardizing the sizes and proportions of building parts and furnishings.

MONOCHROMATIC. Pertaining to a single color or HUE; a composition organized around tonal variations of one color.

MONTAGE. A method of composition in photography, cinema, and television; the technique of combining imagery from various sources to create a unified visual presentation; film editing: superimposition, intercutting, overlapping, etc.

MONUMENTALITY. The combined quality of dignity, grandeur, and impressiveness, especially in architecture and sculpture, regardless of actual size.

MOSAICS. A surface decoration or picture made with pieces of colored glass, stone, or ceramic (called TESSERAE) set into cement or mastic; typical of wall, apse, and dome decoration of BYZANTINE churches.

MURAL. Any large wall painting. See FRESCO.

NAIVE ART. The art of untrained or self-taught artists; the art of preliterate peoples. See PRIMITIVE ART.

NATURALISM. The doctrine that art should consist of the exact transcription of visual appearances. See Chapter Four, "The Style of Objective Accuracy."

NAVE. The central part of a church, used by the congregants, running from the main entrance to the altar; usually flanked by side aisles and bordered by piers and columns.

NEOLITHIC. Also New Stone Age; starting about 10,000 or 8,000 B.C.; beginnings of settled living: farming, animal husbandry, spinning and weaving, fired pottery.

NEO-PLASTICISM. A twentieth-century style of painting, mainly associated with Piet Mondrian and the De Stijl group in Holland; characterized by limited palette (black, white, and the primaries) and restriction to absolutely vertical and horizontal forms.

NONOBJECTIVE ART. Literally, art without objects, wholly nonrepresentational art; an art whose images have no obvious models in physical reality. Should not be confused with abstract art.

OCULUS. The "eye," or circular opening, at the top of a dome. See LANTERN.

OP ART. A style of painting in which disorienting effects are created by juxtaposing vibrating colors, after-images, perspectival illusions, and subtle, progressive changes of repeated shapes.

OPTICAL COLOR. The perceived color of an object; color modified by intervening conditions. See LOCAL COLOR.

ORGANIC. Pertaining to forms that resemble the structure of living things; shaped like the parts of plants and animals rather than machines; natural.

ORPHISTS. A school of abstract painters in Paris about 1912—grouped around Robert and Sonia Delaunay—who combined Cubist form with bright, vivid color.

PALEOLITHIC. Also Old Stone Age; from 32,000 B.C. to about 8,000 B.C.; the period of the cave dwellers who employed tools of stone and bone and lived mainly by hunting and gathering.

PALETTE. The thin panel (often with a thumb hole) on which a painter mixes pigments; also the colors usually employed by an artist.

PAPIER-MÂCHÉ. A sculptural material made of pulped paper or strips of paper mixed with paste; can be pressed, molded, or modeled when moist; dries hard.

PATINA. The mellow, greenish-brown film created on a copper or bronze sculpture either through natural oxidation or by applying chemicals and heat.

PEDIMENT. The triangular space formed by the gable end of a CLASSICAL building; the shape created by the sloping roof and the horizontal cornice; usually holds sculptured figures.

PENDENTIVES. The curved, triangular areas of masonry that support a dome resting on a square base.

PERCEPTION. Mental activity stimulated by seeing, hearing, touching, etc.; the process of knowing through the senses.

PERSPECTIVE. A system for creating illusions of depth on a flat surface; usually a linear system is meant. See also AERIAL, or atmospheric, PERSPECTIVE.

POLYCHROMATIC. Made of many colors, as in painted statuary or the multicolored ceramic sculpture of the Della Robbia family. See MONOCHROMATIC.

POP ART. A style of painting (and sculpture) originating in the 1960s, employing enlarged images and motifs from commercial art, road signs, comic strips, and outdoor advertising.

POST-AND-LINTEL. The principal structural device of CLASSICAL Greek architecture employing two vertical members, or posts, and a horizontal beam, or lintel.

PRIMITIVE ART. The art of preliterate peoples; a slightly opprobrious term for untrained or unsophisticated art; mistakenly applied to European paintings before the Italian Renaissance. See NAIVE ART.

PROVENANCE. Also prevenience; origin or source, especially of a work of art.

REALISM. A nineteenth-century style of painting associated with Gustave Courbet and related to the novels of Zola; emphasis on a truthful account of human existence; opposed to idealized and academic art. See SOCIAL REALISM.

RENAISSANCE. Also Renascence. The fifteenth-century "rebirth" of art and letters, that is, the revival of CLASSICAL art in Italy and afterward throughout Europe. The Renaissance style displaced medieval GOTHIC and BYZANTINE art.

ROCOCO. A late form of BAROQUE architecture and decoration, but more intimate and secular; playful, witty, and often erotic; ornate decor; light colors; irregular form; reflects the effeteness of the French court in the late eighteenth century.

ROMANESQUE. The art and architecture of Europe from the ninth to the twelfth century; characterized by heavy masonry construction, dark church interiors, and mystical, restless sculptural forms.

ROMANTICISM. In art, an eighteenth- and nineteenth-century style emphasizing subjective feeling and the emotions associated with exotic life-styles, escape from the present, extreme danger, suffering, nostalgia, myth, and historical evocation.

SEMANTIC. Pertaining to meanings, especially of words but also of visual signs and symbols.

SERIAL ART. Also series painting, systems sculpture, and "ABC art." A style of the 1960s and 1970s in which simple geometric configurations are repeated with little or no variation; sequence becomes important as in mathematics and linguistic theory.

SFUMATO. The soft, "smoky" treatment of contours, notably by Leonardo, to avoid edginess and to create an impression of rounded volume.

SHAMAN. Sorcerer, magician, medicine man, priest of the Old Stone Age hunting cultures; he was probably responsible for the pictures of animals painted on the cave walls and ceilings.

SOCIAL REALISM. The style of art, allegedly Marxist, which is based on the doctrine that painting and sculpture should accurately represent the workers' experiences, especially their oppression by class enemies and their triumphs of production.

STYLING. As used in industrial or product design: superficial change. The stylist alters the appearance of the product for marketing, rather than functional, reasons.

STYLIZATION. The process of making visual representations conform to a conventional model. See IDEALIZATION.

SURREALISM. A literary and artistic style stressing the subconscious and nonrational sources of imagery; influenced by Freudian psychology. See also DADAISM and Chapter Seven, "The Style of Fantasy."

SYMBOL. In art, an image employed to designate something else. Symbolism: the systematic use of visual symbols according to mythical, religious, literary, etc., traditions; see ICONOGRAPHY. Symbolists: a late nineteenth-century school of painters (including Gauguin) who used color especially to suggest ideas and emotions; also Synthetists.

TACTILE. Pertaining to the sense of touch; in painting, the use of textured materials or the treatment of surfaces to induce sensations of touch. "Tactile values": an expression of the connoisseur Berenson to designate the convincing or authentic qualities of a painting.

TECTONIC. Pertaining to architecture and construction; one of Wölfflin's categories meaning "closed-form," where it applies to painting and sculpture, too. Also, ARCHITECTONIC.

TEMPERA. A type of paint whose medium or binder is egg yolk, glue, or casein; water soluble until it dries.

TERRA-COTTA. A reddish-brown baked clay used for earthenware, sculpture, and building construction, as in terra-cotta tiles, pipes, and fire insulation.

TESSERAE. Pieces of colored glass, stone, or ceramic used in making MOSAICS.

TONAL BLENDING. In painting, modeling a form by changes in tones of a single color instead of changes in HUE.

TOTEM. The protecting creature, usually an animal or bird, to which a clan believes itself related; the emblem that represents a clan or family. Totem pole: a carved and painted wooden post showing figures of totemic protectors or ancestors.

TRANSEPT. The crossarm in a basilican church; it meets the NAVE at right angles, separating the NAVE from the apse; the main altar is usually under the crossing of NAVE and transept.

TROMPE-L'OEIL. "Fool the eye" in French; a highly illusionistic method of painting, as in the works of Harnett and Peto; see also NATURALISM.

UNDERPAINTING. The first stage of the indirect painting method; the establishment of the chief shapes, lights, darks, and masses, usually with a limited palette or in monochrome.

UNITY. A coherent relationship among the parts or elements of a work of art.

VALUE. The lightness or darkness of a color. In aesthetics: any perceived quality; any source of appeal in a work of art; the artistic satisfaction of a human interest.

VAULT. A masonry, brick, or concrete arched structure forming a ceiling or roof over a hall; *barrel* vault, *groin* vault, *ribbed* vault.

VEHICLE. The binder or glue that holds the coloring matter in pigment and makes it adhere to a surface.

VOUSSOIR. A wedge-shaped block used in the construction of a masonry arch. See KEYSTONE.

WASH. A thin, semitransparent film of paint, highly diluted with turpentine or water (as in watercolor painting), and applied with a broad, continuous sweep of the brush.

ZIGGURAT. The almost pyramid-shaped monument of the ancient Babylonians and Assyrians, consisting of four or five stages or stories stepped back to form terraces; outside stairways lead to temples and a shrine at the top.

ZONING. Partitioning a city or town by ordinance into specific areas or zones for manufacturing, recreation, and residence.

ZOOMORPHIC. Pertaining to animal art; ascribing animal forms or attributes to humans, especially to gods and goddesses.

| TIME | TYPICAL OBJECT, IMAGE, MONUMENT | MAKER, ARTIST | MATERIAL, MEDIUM, PROCESS | PLACE | PERIOD OF CULTURE | USER, SPONSOR, PATRON |
|---|---|---|---|---|---|---|
| No Date | Child's Drawing (page 480) | Four-year-old child | Crayon and paper (any pointed instrument; any surface), 4" high | Universal | All cultures | Autonomous creation; art sponsored by the artist |
| c.. 30,000–25,000 B.C. | *Venus of Willendorf* (page 15) | Unknown shaman-artist | Limestone carving, 4⅜" high | Austria | Upper Paleolithic (Old Stone Age, Aurignacian culture) | Child-bearing woman; mother cult (?); fecundity rites |
| No Date (probably 19th century) | Ancestor figures of the Dogon tribe (page 331) | Tribal carver; village smith/medicine man (?) | Wood carved with iron adze and knife; rubbed, charred, and oiled, 26⅝" high | Mali (Sudan), West Africa | Neolithic Metal Age (Dogon culture) | Probably commissioned by secret society of male elders and priests |
| A.D. 400–600 | Portrait jar (of ruler?) with stirrup-spout handle (page 329) | Unknown potter-portraitist | Painted sun-baked clay, 4¾" high | Chicama Valley, Peru | Late Neolithic (Mochica; pre-Inca); (comparable to pre-Dynastic Egypt) | All classes used effigy jars decorated according to social status |
| c. 2600 B.C. | *Pharaoh Khafre* (Chephren) with hawk-god, Horus (page 339) | Unknown temple sculptors | Green diorite; carved, abraded, and polished, 66" high | Giza, Egypt | Old Kingdom, Fourth Dynasty | The pharaoh is sponsor and only beneficiary |
| c. 2000 B.C. | Stonehenge (page 381) | Bands of farmers and herdsmen supervised by priests and skilled stoneworkers | Upright stones with lintels (about 13' high, up to 50 tons) arranged in ritual circle, or *cromlech* | Salisbury Plain, England (Also Carnac, Brittany; Maltese Islands) | Late Neolithic (Bronze Age), megalithic, pre-Celtic | Bronze Age farming, herding-hunting community |
| c. 1600 B.C. | *Snake Goddess* (or priestess) (page 378) | Unknown sculptor/priestess (?) | Faience (glazed, multicolored pottery), 13½" high | Knossos, Crete | Aegean (Late Minoan Bronze Age) | Cult of mother goddess (?) |
| c. 1350 B.C. | Tutankhamen's throne (page 117) | Unknown palace craftsmen under direction of priests of Amon | Gold-sheathed wood, carved and inlaid with precious stones | Thebes, Egypt | New Kingdom, Eighteenth Dynasty | Commissioned by king for his tomb |

| FUNCTION, PURPOSE | SOCIAL ORGANIZATION AND CHARACTERISTICS | KEY EVENTS: POLITICAL, ECONOMIC, RELIGIOUS, TECHNOLOGICAL |
|---|---|---|
| To overcome fear of outside world; to control environment through magic; to "name" things; to assert own existence | Any kind of human family | Discovery of fingers and thumbs as tools of expression; discovery of relationship between visual form and real world; ability to control reality through representation; beginning of separation of world from the self: people, places, and things organized *around* the self. This art, or something very much like it, preceded the specimens of prehistoric art known to us |
| To promote fertility, induce pregnancy; good-luck charm, amulet; sympathetic magic | Nomadic hunting band, about 60 people; some division of labor between sexes; everyone forages; males hunt | Homo sapiens emerges; Cro-Magnon man supersedes Neanderthal man; incest taboo defines family relationships; improved tools for hunting and fishing; better spears, harpoons; bow and arrow invented; animal trapping; burial of dead; red ocher a symbol of blood and life |
| To preserve the spirits of ancestors; to guard and advise the family; to accompany genealogical accounts of clan's founding at annual feast; to express dualism of male and female principles | Tribal, extended family; polygamous, exogamous (girls marry outside the group); men hunt, women cultivate small plots; men's and women's societies act as check on power of chief, govern initiation of boys and girls | Settled agriculture, hoe cultivation, some hunting; ruling class descended from stock raisers, mounted warriors; local wars produced captives who become slaves; monopolies of metalwork (especially in gold) exercised by king's family and courtiers |
| Placed in boxlike grave; held liquid believed to sustain life of deceased | Warrior-hunter caste enslaved farmers; served by priests, artisans, dancers; close village life, some leisure; human sacrifice practiced | Copper, silver, and gold work; textile manufacture; frequent wars; irrigation systems; maize farming, ocean fishing; pyramids of adobe brick; worship of sun, moon, jaguars, serpents; no potter's wheel, no wheeled vehicles, no draft animals; no written language |
| To provide a permanent home for the *ka*, or soul, of the king in case his mummy is damaged or stolen; hawk symbolizes the sun-god, Re, and the royal descent of Khafre | Matriarchal; brother and sister marriages in royal house; pharaoh (who could be a woman) is god-king and absolute ruler | Unification of Upper and Lower Egypt, c. 3100 B.C.; royal household governs through small group of priests and officials; hieroglyphic writing, 3000 B.C.; great pyramid construction (2680–2500 B.C.); Hyksos invasions (1730–1580 B.C.) end isolation of Egypt |
| Shrine for worship of Great Mother deity; possible observatory to sight solstices, plot solar and lunar movements, predict eclipses; mother goddess causes sunrise, return of spring, renewal of earth's fertility; for rites connecting earth and sky gods | Egalitarian farming communes; tribal chieftains; some matriarchal survivals; fear of witches among herdsmen | Gold trade with Ireland; amber trade with Baltic countries; copper trade with Near East; flint mining; stone imitations of bronze weapons; wood, mud, reed houses; underground burial in gallery graves; cattle, sheep, and swine raised to supplement low-yield agriculture |
| To worship woman as embodiment of fertility principle; snakes symbolize earthly insemination (the male principle), controlled by the goddess | Mercantile aristocracy; luxury-loving leisure class; matriarchal customs survive in freedom; flirtatiousness of upper-class women | Palace civilization based on Mediterranean sea trade; Linear A writing; Hyksos invasions, earthquakes destroy palaces, 1720 and 1450 B.C; high style of fresco painting, no monumental art; elaborate dresses for women: full skirts, bared breasts |
| To show King "Tut" as upholder of *maat* (truth/justice) as evidenced by sun's rays bathing him and his queen | Powerful priesthood and priestly bureaucracy control throne; drive out "subversives," including rebellious army officers | Ikhnaton's monotheism challenges priesthood (1372–1358 B.C.); his successor, 18-year-old Tutankhamen, restores priests and ancient cult; stonecutters obliterate sun-disk, the name of the one god, Aton; priests interpret Amon's oracle, thus control politics; restoration of gigantic architecture and statuary |

# CLASSICAL AND MEDIEVAL ART

| TIME | TYPICAL OBJECT, IMAGE, MONUMENT | MAKER, ARTIST | MATERIAL, MEDIUM, PROCESS | PLACE | PERIOD OF CULTURE | USER, SPONSOR, PATRON |
|---|---|---|---|---|---|---|
| 510–500 B.C. | *Stele of Aristion* (page 507) | Aristocles | Carved and chiseled Pentelic marble; color added | Attica, Greece | Archaic Greek (transitional) | Family of Aristion or his fellow hoplites |
| c. 450–440 B.C. | *Doryphorus (Spear Bearer)* (page 144) | Polyclitus | Carved marble (Roman copy of bronze original, which was decorated with colored stones, pastes, gold, and silver), 78" high | Argos, Greece | Classical Greek | Citizens of Athens |
| c. 225 B.C. | *Dying Gaul* (page 35) | Epigonus | Carved marble (Roman copy of bronze original) | Pergamum, Asia Minor | Early Hellenistic (Greek) | General Attalus I |
| A.D. 118–125 | The Pantheon (page 408) | Unknown architects | Coffered dome on cylindrical base; brick, stone rubble, marble, granite, concrete, and gilded bronze | Rome | Late Hellenistic (Roman) | Emperor Hadrian |
| A.D. 532–37 | Cathedral of Hagia Sophia (page 415) | Anthemius of Tralles and Isidorus of Miletus, architects | Dome-on-pendentive construction; brick, stone rubble, marble, mosaics, and fresco | Constantinople (Istanbul) | Byzantine (First "Golden Age") | Emperor Justinian |
| C. A.D. 825 | Animal head, from the Oseberg ship-burial (page 337) | Unknown carver/shipwright | Carved and drilled wood, 20⅞" high | Oslo, Norway | Early Medieval (Northern Carolingian) | Crew of Viking longship |
| c. 1095–1115 | Nave, St.-Savin-sur-Gartempe (page 406) | Unknown masons, craftsmen, and painters | Hall church; barrel- or tunnel-vault construction; painted ceiling of nave, cut-stone arcade; pillars painted to imitate marble | Poitou, France | Western Romanesque | Religious community and people |
| c. 1130 | *The Last Judgment* (page 187) | Master Gislebertus | Stone relief carving | Cathedral of Autun, France | Romanesque | The Cluniac Order |

| FUNCTION, PURPOSE | SOCIAL ORGANIZATION AND CHARACTERISTICS | KEY EVENTS: POLITICAL, ECONOMIC, RELIGIOUS, TECHNOLOGICAL |
|---|---|---|
| Gravestone marker; memorial to aristocratic "warrior-gentleman" | Tribal, aristocratic: gods, heroes, heroic dead, kings, noble families, free workers, peasant farmers, slaves; "barbarians" the lowest caste | Rule of *polis* (Greek city and surrounding pasture) by old Dorian clans; armored infantrymen (*hoplites*) replace horsemen; the phalanx (*hoplites* fighting in unison); military comradeship weakens tribal ties; egalitarianism of warriors extended to civic life; poor farmers enfranchised; more money spent on public building |
| To symbolize the union of reason, action, and correct proportion in the ideal Greek man or god; to establish a perfect, i.e., geometrical, standard of physical beauty | Old aristocracy weakened by insurgence of mercantile class and prosperous laborers; *polis* becomes democratic city-state | Greek cities defeat Persians, 448 B.C.; Athenian fleet and merchants dominate Eastern Mediterranean and Black Sea; spread of Hellenism—Greek art, language, and literature; emergence of Athens as model of an open society: free speculation unfettered by priests and tyrants, but for citizens only; Athens defeated by Sparta in Peloponnesian War (431–404 B.C.) |
| To celebrate victory over Celtic or Galatian invaders; to memorialize bravery of barbarians, their worthiness as men and foes | Oligarchic control of Hellenistic cities; large estates; independent farmers disappear; emergence of small, rich leisure class living off land rents and slave labor | Alexandrian conquests (336–323 B.C.); Oriental colonization; spread of Greek culture (330 B.C.–A.D. 100) to Rome, Egypt, Syria, Asia Minor, Persia, India; imperial bureaucracy; standardized city planning; great library in Alexandria; much prestige in philosophy; Roman conquest of Corinth (146 B.C.), Greece controlled by Rome |
| Officially dedicated to the gods of the seven planets; to create a vast interior space symbolizing the cosmos; to glorify Hadrian | Imperial state; cosmopolitan capital city; large-scale importation of European slaves; laborers and artisans live in tenements | Growth of mystery religions, Zoroastrianism, Manichaeism, astrological cults; Roman economic exploitation of the provinces; death of Jesus (c. A.D. 30); Jewish rebellion (A.D. 60); death of Paul (c. A.D. 65); Christian underground; slave revolts; growth of large proletariat in Rome; free "bread and circuses" for urban masses |
| To express the Eastern Christian idea of the unity of God and light in a great vertical space; announces emperor is God's deputy on earth, empress is God's wife | Absolute monarchy supported by urban aristocracy of merchants, monopolists, priesthood, civil service, and army of spies; the commercial model for Venice | Roman legalization of Christianity in A.D. 313; Constantine establishes new imperial capital at Byzantium, 330; Rome sacked by Goths, 410; Justinian and Theodora rule in Constantinople, 527–65; Gregory the Great becomes Roman pope, 590; birth of Muhammad, c. 570; Muslim conquests begin, 632; Jerusalem taken, 638; Arabs defeated at Poitiers by Charles Martel, 732; Charlemagne becomes Holy Roman Emperor of the West, 800 |
| Figurehead (dragon?) for sailing vessel/war galley protects raiders, terrifies farmers and villagers; ship buried with chieftain | Tiny kingdoms subsisting on farming, fishing, trapping, and piracy; polygamy and primogeniture produce younger sons without property, looking for loot | Viking sea raiders invade Ireland, England, France, Italy, and Sicily, penetrating inland on shallow-draft ships (830–900); Central Asian nomads invade Europe, 890; feudal system in Europe; monastery at Cluny, France, founded, 910 |
| To express the Latin Christian idea of salvation in a long, horizontal space culminating in the chancel, altar, reliquary, and choir | Manorial feudalism and monasticism well established; conversion of Roman estate slaves into serfs by victorious raiders who set themselves up as new nobility; employment of foreign artisans as builders | Norsemen and Huns become Christians, c. 1000; England conquered by William of Normandy, 1066; international pilgrimages to holy sites, veneration of saints' relics; schism between Roman Catholic and Eastern Orthodox Churches, 1054; Capetian dynasty in France under Louis VI guided by Abbot Suger (1081–1151); reconquest of Spain from Arabs begins, 1085 |
| To remind the faithful, as they enter the church, that they must answer for everything they do in life | Restless and pugnacious nobility addicted to feuds, killings, destruction; higher clergy (abbots, bishops) chosen from their peaceful sons | St. Bernard preaches Second Crusade, 1146; sends knights to fight Islam for possession of Jerusalem; European barbarians exposed to Middle Eastern wealth, learning, and civilization; deep-cutting plow opens northern European plains to agriculture, rotation of crops; more protein in diet; peasants more vigorous |

# RENAISSANCE AND BAROQUE

| TIME | TYPICAL OBJECT, IMAGE, MONUMENT | MAKER, ARTIST | MATERIAL, MEDIUM, PROCESS | PLACE | PERIOD OF CULTURE | USER, SPONSOR, PATRON |
|------|----------------------------------|---------------|----------------------------|-------|--------------------|------------------------|
| c. 1495–98 | *The Last Supper* (page 272) | Leonardo da Vinci | Egg tempera plus oil glaze on stone wall covered with plaster and sealed with varnish | Refectory of Sta. Maria delle Grazie, Milan | Italian Renaissance (Florentine School) | Commissioned by Duke Ludovico Sforza for the monastery of Sta. Maria delle Grazie |
| 1500 | *The Three Graces* (page 500) | Raphael | Oil on wood panel, 6¾ × 6¾" | Perugia (?), Italy | Italian Renaissance (Roman School) | Made for the artist himself (?) |
| c. 1507 | *Study for Adam* (page 248) | Albrecht Dürer | Pen and sepia wash on paper | Nuremberg, Germany | Northern Renaissance | Study for the artist |
| 1546–64 | St. Peter's (page 409) | Michelangelo (dome completed by Giacomo della Porta, 1590) | Stone, marble, mosaics; metal chains in dome fabric; fusion of central plan and basilican plan; 452' high | Rome | Early Baroque | Pope Paul III |
| c. 1580 | *The Agony in the Garden of Gethsemane* (page 221) | El Greco | Oil on canvas, 40 × 51½" | Toledo, Spain | Mannerism | Church in Toledo (?) |
| 1638–39 | *The Judgment of Paris* (page 501) | Peter Paul Rubens, his pupils and assistants | Oil on panel, 57 × 75" | Antwerp, Flanders (Belgium) | Northern (Flemish) Baroque | Private patron |
| 1650 | *Pope Innocent X* (page 282) | Velázquez | Oil on canvas | Rome | Spanish Baroque | Painted for the pope during Velázquez's trip to Italy (1649–51) |
| c. 1648–50 | *Christ Healing the Sick* (page 238) | Rembrandt | Etching, 11 × 15⅛" | Amsterdam | Northern (Dutch) Baroque | For sale by the artist through his dealer, Pieter de la Tombe; price: one hundred guilders |

| FUNCTION, PURPOSE | SOCIAL ORGANIZATION AND CHARACTERISTICS | KEY EVENTS: POLITICAL, ECONOMIC, RELIGIOUS, TECHNOLOGICAL |
|---|---|---|
| To enable the prior and monks, while eating, to contemplate Jesus' last meal with his disciples; to create psychological studies of Jesus and each of his disciples | Italy's city-states ruled by feudal princes (dukes), bankers, landed aristocrats, and mercenaries (condottieri); brief republic in Florence (1494–1512) | World exploration: Columbus (1492), Vasco da Gama (1497–99), Balboa (1513), Magellan (1519–22); Byzantine and Gothic styles repudiated; classical Greek and Latin texts published in Italy; intellectual life flourishes in ducal courts; artists emerge from artisan class |
| To express ideas drawn from ancient humanistic texts; to revive the classical ideal of beauty in the nude; to visualize perfection embodied in human form | Roman popes and curia dominate regional dukedoms (except Venice) | Alexander VI (Borgia) and Julius II consolidate power of papacy; best artists go to Rome, now the world's financial center; Michelangelo paints Sistine Chapel ceiling (1508–12) while Raphael works on frescoes for papal apartments in the Vatican; nominally religious art with strong pagan-classical flavor |
| To master "the science of proportion" in preparation for his figure paintings and engravings; to represent nature truly, i.e., in the "new" Italian manner | Mercantile aristocrats in Nuremberg and Augsburg (the Fuggers) imitate Italian princes, patronize artists and scholars, resent flow of funds to Rome | Martin Luther posts his theses, 1517; Luther excommunicated, 1521; Luther publishes German Bible in 1522 with woodcuts by Lucas Cranach the Elder; Peasant Revolt in Germany (1524–25); iconoclasm, confiscation of ecclesiastical art and property (1520–40) |
| Rebuilding initiated by Julius II in 1505 to contain his tomb; to restore prestige of city of Rome after sack in 1527; to combine dome-of-heaven symbolism of the early Church with the longitudinal orientation of Latin Christianity | Papal household dominates Rome; cardinals and bankers compete in self-glorification | German army sacks Rome, 1527, artists scatter; Henry VIII breaks with Rome, 1534; Council of Trent (1545–63) fails to reconcile Protestants; Spain rules much of Italy through local surrogates; Michelangelo paints Last Judgment (1534–41) |
| To combine the qualities of Spanish religiosity with the aims of the Counter-Reformation; to render the Passion of Christ in terms of noble suffering and mystical transcendence | Feudal Spain is bankrupt; imperial Spain milks American colonies; nobility impoverished; intense otherworldly religious feeling | Reconquest of Spain completed; Jews expelled by Ferdinand and Isabella, 1492; Ignatius Loyola founds Jesuit Order, 1540; large infusions of American gold and silver destabilize Spanish economy; Spanish naval power destroyed by English pirates; Armada defeated (1588) by Drake |
| To express the compatibility of Catholic courtly culture, Renaissance humanism, and the grandiose lifestyle of the aristocratic merchants of Flanders | Jesuits control art, education, and architecture; sponsor devotional art for the masses, classical studies for sons of the rich | The Netherlands gains freedom from Spain, 1609; Antwerp, Amsterdam, Augsburg, and Ulm become major banking centers; French, English, and Dutch settlements established in North America; Hudson's Bay Company organized, 1670; Spanish Hapsburg influence lingers in Flemish art, education, and upper-class behavior |
| To emphasize the power and sagacity reposed in the head of the Roman Catholic faith | Spaniards dominate Italian politics and religion; Roman Baroque dominates art of Europe | Galileo tried for heresy by the Inquisition, 1633; end of Thirty Years' War, 1648; Catholicism triumphs except in northern Europe; skepticism of Descartes (d. 1650) undermines intellectual authority of Rome; France becomes most poweful nation in Europe; French Academy established, 1635 |
| To render the miracles of Jesus according to the egalitarian ideals of Protestant Christianity and the realistic outlook of the prosperous Dutch burgher class | Dutch towns ruled by wealthy, conservative bourgeoisie supported by Calvinist clergy | Dutch East India Company (chartered 1602) monopolizes Southeast Asian trade; Harvey discovers circulation of blood, 1628; Rembrandt paints Anatomy Lesson, 1632; Dutch ruling class sponsors secular art, realistic style, everyday subject matter |

# FROM ROCOCO TO MODERN

| TIME | TYPICAL OBJECT, IMAGE, MONUMENT | MAKER, ARTIST | MATERIAL, MEDIUM, PROCESS | PLACE | PERIOD OF CULTURE | USER, SPONSOR, PATRON |
|---|---|---|---|---|---|---|
| 1752 | *Miss O'Murphy (Nude on a Sofa)* (page 224) | François Boucher | Oil on canvas, 23¼ × 28⅞" | Versailles (?) (now in Alte Pinakothek, Munich) | Rococo | Louis XV |
| c. 1816 | *Man with a Hat* (page 282) | Jacques-Louis David | Oil on canvas | Brussels | Neoclassicism | Portrait commission |
| 1830 | *Liberty Leading the People* (page 44) | Eugène Delacroix | Oil on canvas, 8'6⅜" × 10'1" | Paris | Romanticism | Painted for first Salon, sponsored by Louis Philippe |
| 1886 | *The Burghers of Calais* (page 325) | Auguste Rodin | Bronze, 82½ × 95 × 78" | Calais, France | Romanticism-Impressionism-Symbolism | The people and town fathers of Calais |
| 1890–95 | *The Card Players* (page 215) | Paul Cézanne | Oil on canvas, 17¾ × 22½" | Aix-en-Provence | Post-Imressionism | Painted for himself; later (1895) exhibited by the dealer Ambroise Vollard |
| 1909 | Robie House (page 77) | Frank Lloyd Wright | Steel beams, wood, brick, glass, stucco; cantilever and masonry pier construction | Chicago | International Modern Prairie style | Frederick D. Robie |
| 1937 | *Guernica* (page 51) | Pablo Picasso | Black, white, and gray oil paint on canvas, 11'5½" × 25'5¾" | Paris (now in The Prado, Madrid) | Late Cubist-Expressionist | For Spanish Pavilion, Paris World's Fair |
| 1960 | *Homage to New York* (page 373) | Jean Tinguely | Piano, drums, wheels, gears, typewriter, electric motor, Coke bottles | Museum of Modern Art, New York (self-destroyed) | Abstract Expressionism, kinetic "metamatic" art | For audience in the garden of the Museum of Modern Art, New York |
| 1975 | Old Folks Home, from *Ruckus Manhattan* (page 97) | Red Grooms and Mimi Gross | Wire, cloth, wood, plastic, metal, paint | New York City | Installation art; Pop diorama | Walk-in public |
| 1983 | *To the Unknown Painter* (page 29) | Anselm Kiefer | Oil, emulsion, shellac, latex, woodcut, straw, 9'2" square | Germany | Neo-Expressionism | The artist, the German people, all Europeans |

| FUNCTION, PURPOSE | SOCIAL ORGANIZATION AND CHARACTERISTICS | KEY EVENTS: POLITICAL, ECONOMIC, RELIGIOUS, TECHNOLOGICAL |
|---|---|---|
| To portray the king's mistress as his plaything; to express a lighthearted, spontaneous approach to love; to join the idea of childlike innocence with eroticism | French aristocracy concentrated in royal court, loses governing function; people impoverished by royal wars and extravagance | Louis XIV rules France as absolute king (1643–1715); "Glorious Revolution" and English Bill of Rights, 1689; Hobbes (d.1679) questions absolute monarchy; Locke (d. 1704) urges representative government; J. J. Rousseau (d. 1778) justifies revolution; Watt perfects steam engine, 1765; Adam Smith writes *Wealth of Nations*, 1776; American Revolution, 1775–83; French Revolution, 1789–94 |
| A tribute to the elegance and fastidiousness of Euope's newly rich class of businessmen and industrialists; David integrates the noble form language of Neoclassicism with the naturalistic detail desired by his wealthy clientele | Powerful entrepreneurial class struggles to control European society after revolutionary radicals are overthrown in France | Napoleon dominates French and European history (1799–1814); David is artistic dictator during French Revolution *and* under Napoleon; Goya portrays Spanish resistance to Napoleonic invasions, 1814; Napoleon defeated at Waterloo, 1815; David exiled; French Academy reinstated, 1816 |
| To idealize fighting on the barricades; satisfies bourgeois appetite for a life of action and danger; substitutes exciting color and brushwork for controlled feeling of classical drawing and modeling | Bitter alienation of artists from society; bohemianism; growing split between art and science; doctrine of art for art's sake | Revolution of 1830 in France and throughout Europe in 1848; Daguerre perfects photography, 1839; Marx's *Communist Manifesto*, 1848; Courbet paints *The Stone Breakers*, 1849; Baudelaire publishes *Fleurs du Mal*, 1857; Darwin publishes *Origin of Species*, 1859; serfs nominally freed in Russia, 1861; American Civil War, 1861–65 |
| To dramatize the heroism of a group of ordinary citizens; to demonstrate the possibility of a democratic public monument; to analyze the emotions of men facing death by execution | Factory system establishes new managerial class; terrible exploitation of industrial workers; middle class firmly controls art, politics, and education | Tolstoy writes *War and Peace* (1863–69); Marx writes *Das Kapital* (1867–94) in England; Edison invents light bulb, 1879; germ theory of disease demonstrated by Pasteur, 1881; Roebling builds Brooklyn Bridge (1869–83); Manet paints Emile Zola (1868) |
| To create a harmony of colors, shapes, and their interrelations; to demonstrate the geometrical roots of form; to fix and record the artist's perception of objects in space | Industrial societies dominate the world; Western imperialism; strong belief in progress through education, science, technology; business enterprise | Monet paints haystack series, 1891; Spanish-American War (1898); U.S. emerges as world power; skyscraper invented in Chicago (1885–1900); revolutions in China and Mexico begin, 1911; World War I (1914–18); Russian Revolution, 1917; League of Nations, 1919 |
| To express the unity of the house with the land by emphasizing horizontality; to make the dwelling seem to belong "organically" to its site; to create decorative and textural effects by exposing natural building materials | Boom atmosphere in U.S.; massive immigration, powerful corporations; blacks and women still disenfranchised; culture essentially WASP | Freud publishes *Interpretation of Dreams*, 1900; Planck's quantum theory, 1900; Wright brothers' flight, 1903; Einstein's relativity theory, 1905; Ford assembly line, 1909; Futurist Manifesto, 1909; U.S. opens Panama Canal, 1914; Griffith directs *Birth of a Nation,* 1915; Americans in World War I, 1917 |
| To protest Franco's bombing of civilians and to denounce Fascism; to create a form language that can simultaneously describe the bombing and its emotional impact; to relate modern war to ancient, subconscious memories of violence | Worldwide depression, unemployment, wild speculation destabilize capitalist societies; mass communication plus charismatic leaders result in mass-movement dictatorships | Mussolini's Fascists take over Italy, 1922; Surrealist Manifesto, 1924; Wall Street "Crash" and Great Depression, 1929; Hitler's Nazis take over Germany, 1933; Gropius and the Bauhaus (1919–33); F. Roosevelt and the New Deal, 1933; Spanish Civil War, won by Franco's Nationalists (1936–39); Hitler-Stalin nonaggression pact, 1939; World War II (1939–45) |
| To entertain; to ridicule mechanization; to dramatize the "suicide" of a machine; to condemn industrial cilization and the "machine aesthetic" | Growing independence of "Third World" peoples; "loss of nerve" in Europe and America; "backward" Russia emerges as "superpower" | Atomic bombs dropped on Hiroshima and Nagasaki, 1945; United Nations formed, 1945; British leave India, 1947; State of Israel founded, 1948; Marshall Plan for Europe, 1947; Soviets explode atomic bomb, 1949; U.S. explodes hydrogen bomb, 1954; Soviets launch Sputnik, 1957; Cuban missile crisis, 1962; John F. Kennedy assassinated, 1963; Solzhenitsyn describes Gulag (1962), wins Nobel Prize (1970), moves to U.S. |
| To enable public to participate in lives of street people, service workers, welfare clients; to break the barriers between viewers and artwork | Women's Movement; Environmentalism; Gay-Liberation; abortion legalized; test-tube babies; new health diets; personal computers; spread of Eastern mysticism | Watergate burglary, 1972; Picasso dies, 1973; Vitenam War ends, Nixon resigns, 1974; Civil War in Nicaragua, 1978; Iranian revolution, U.S. hostages, Margaret Thatcher, 1979 |
| To expiate guilt for Holocaust; to memorialize artist victims of Nazism | Post-modern architecture; declining SAT scores; Japan and Germany dominate world markets; AIDS epidemic; crack cocaine; junk bonds; affirmative action; multiculturism | Reagan elected, 1980; antinuclear demonstrations, 1982; Wall Street sponsors leveraged buyouts; Chernobyl disaster, 1986; fall of Berlin Wall, liberation of Eastern Europe, 1989; Russian/U.S. disarmament treaty, Soviet Union collapses, 1991 |

# SELECTED BIBLIOGRAPHY

Following is a list of books related to the major subjects discussed in this volume. Its purpose is to cite principal sources and suggest the range of published material that can be consulted in connection with questions raised in the text. Specialized monographs and publications about individual artists have been omitted, and the listing of periodicals has been kept to a minimum. World histories of art are not included on the assumption that the reader is already familiar with them or has access to a bibliography of the outstanding works of comprehensive art history.

## THE FUNCTIONS OF ART

Antal, Frederick. *Florentine Painting and Its Social Background*. London: Routledge and Kegan Paul, 1948.

Attenborough, David. *The Tribal Eye*. New York: W. W. Norton, 1976.

Baxandall, Michael. *Painting and Experience in Fifteenth Century Italy*. New York: Oxford University Press, 1983.

Boime, Albert. *A Social History of Modern Art*. Chicago: University of Chicago Press, 1987.

Cole, Bruce. *The Renaissance Artist at Work: From Pisano to Titian*. New York: Harper & Row, 1983.

Dorner, Alexander. *The Way Beyond "Art."* New York: New York University Press, 1958.

Feldman, Edmund B. *The Artist*. Englewood Cliffs, N.J.: Prentice-Hall, 1982.

Gedo, Mary Mathews. *Picasso: Art as Autobiography*. Chicago: University of Chicago Press, 1980.

Hauser, Arnold. *The Social History of Art*. 2 vols. New York: Knopf, 1951.

Huyghe, René. *Art and the Spirit of Man*. New York: Abrams, 1962.

Lommel, Andreas. *Shamanism, The Beginnings of Art*. New York: McGraw-Hill, 1967.

Marshack, Alexander. *The Roots of Civilization: The Cognitive Beginnings of Man's First Art, Symbol, and Notation*. New York: McGraw-Hill, 1971.

Mayor, A. Hyatt. *Prints and People: A Social History of Printed Pictures*. New York: The Metropolitan Museum of Art, 1971.

Pollitt, Jerome J. *Art and Experience in Classical Greece*. Cambridge, Eng.: Cambridge University Press, 1972.

Read, Herbert. *The Grass Roots of Art*. New York: Wittenborn, Schultz, 1947.

Selz, Peter. *Art in Our Times: A Pictorial History*. New York: Harcourt Brace Jovanovich and Abrams, 1981.

## THE STYLES OF ART

Ackerman, James. "Style," in Ackerman and Rhys Carpenter, *Art and Archaeology*. Englewood Cliffs, N.J.: Prentice-Hall, 1963.

Brion, Marcel. *Art of the Romantic Era: Romanticism, Classicism, Realism*. New York: Praeger, 1966.

Gablik, Suzi. *Has Modernism Failed?* New York: Thames and Hudson, 1984.

Hauser, Arnold. *Mannerism: The Crisis of the Renaissance and the Origin of Modern Art*. 2 vols. New York: Knopf, 1965.

Hunter, Sam, and John Jacobus. *Modern Art: Painting, Sculpture, Architecture*. New York: Abrams, 1985.

Lucie-Smith, Edward. *Movements in Art Since 1945*. New York: Thames and Hudson, 1984.

Meisel, Louis. *Photo-Realism*. New York: Abrams, 1980.

Nochlin, Linda. *Realism*. New York and Baltimore: Penguin Books, 1971.

Rosenblum, Robert. *Cubism and Twentieth-Century Art*. New York: Abrams, 1966.

Rubin, William S. *Dada, Surrealism and Their Heritage*. New York: The Museum of Modern Art, 1968.

Schapiro, Meyer. "Style," in *Anthropology Today*. Edited by A.L. Kroeber. Chicago: University of Chicago Press, 1953.

Tomkins, Calvin. *Post- to Neo-: The Art World of the 1980s*. New York: Holt, 1988.

Wölfflin, Heinrich. *Principles of Art History*. Translated by Mary D. Hottinger. New York: Dover, 1950.

Worringer, Wilhelm. *Abstraction and Empathy: A Contribution to the Psychology of Style*. Translated by Michael Bullock. New York: International Universities Press, 1953.

## THE STRUCTURE OF ART

Anderson, Donald M. *Elements of Design*. New York: Holt, Rinehart and Winston, 1961.

Arnheim, Rudolph. *Art and Visual Perception*. Berkeley and Los Angeles: University of California Press, 1954.

Chermayeff, Ivan, et al. *The Design Necessity*. Cambridge, Mass.: MIT Press, 1973.

Gombrich, E. H. *The Sense of Order*. Ithaca, N.Y.: Cornell University Press, 1979.

Hill, Edward. *The Language of Drawing*. Englewood Cliffs, N.J.: Prentice-Hall, 1966.

Itten, Johannes. *Design and Form: The Basic Course at the Bauhaus*. New York: Reinhold, 1964.

Klee, Paul. *Pedagogical Sketchbook*. New York: Praeger, 1953.

Moholy-Nagy, Lázló. *The New Vision*. 4th rev. ed. New York: Wittenborn, Schultz, 1949.

Munsell, Albert H. *A Grammar of Color*. New York: Van Nostrand, 1969.

Richardson, John Adkins; Floyd W. Coleman; and Michael J. Smith. *Basic Design: Systems, Elements, Applications*. Englewood Cliffs, N.J.: Prentice-Hall, 1984.

Sommer, Robert. *The Behavioral Basis of Design*. Englewood Cliffs, N.J.: Prentice-Hall, 1969.

Wölfflin, Heinrich. *The Sense of Form in Art. A Comparative Psychological Study*. New York: Chelsea, 1958.

## PAINTING

Arnason, Harvard H. *History of Modern Art*. 3rd ed. Revised by Daniel Wheeler. New York: Abrams, 1986.

Baigell, Matthew. *A Concise History of American Painting and Sculpture*. New York: Harper & Row, 1984.

Daix, Pierre. *Cubists and Cubism*. New York: Rizzoli, 1982.

Doerner, Max. *The Materials of the Artist*. Translated by Eugen Neuhaus. New York: Harcourt, Brace, 1949.

Goldstein, Nathan. *Painting: Visual and Technical Fundamentals*. Englewood Cliffs, N.J.: Prentice-Hall, 1979.

Haftmann, Werner. *Painting in the Twentieth Century*. 2 vols. New York: Praeger, 1960.

Henri, Robert. *The Art Spirit*. Philadelphia: Lippincott, 1923.

Read, Herbert. *A Concise History of Modern Painting*. New York: Praeger, 1959.

Seitz, William C. *The Art of Assemblage*. New York: The Museum of Modern Art, 1961.

——. *Abstract Expressionist Painting in America*. Cambridge, Mass.: Harvard University Press, 1983.

Selz, Peter. *New Images of Man*. Prefatory note by Paul Tillich. New York: The Museum of Modern Art, 1959.

Vogt, Paul. *Expressionism: German Painting, 1905–1920*. New York: Abrams, 1980.

Williams, Hiram. *Notes for a Young Painter*. Englewood Cliffs, N.J.: Prentice-Hall, 1963.

## SCULPTURE

Brasser, Ted, et al. *Stones, Bones and Skin: Ritual and Shamanic Art*. Toronto: The Society for Art Publications, 1977.

Burnham, Jack. *Beyond Modern Sculpture*. New York: Braziller, 1968.

Elisofon, Eliot, and William Fagg. *The Sculpture of Africa*. New York: Hacker, 1978.

Elsen, Albert E. *Origins of Modern Sculpture: Pioneers and Premises*. New York: Braziller, 1974.

Giedion-Welcker, Carola. *Contemporary Sculpture: An Evolution in Volume and Space*. New York: Wittenborn, Schultz, 1955.

Hammacher, A. M. *The Evolution of Modern Sculpture*. New York: Abrams, 1969.

Krauss, Rosalind E. *Passages in Modern Sculpture*. Cambridge, Mass.: MIT Press, 1981.

Leuzinger, Elsy. *The Art of Black Africa*. New York: Rizzoli, 1977.

Moore, Henry. *Henry Moore at the British Museum*. New York: Abrams, 1981.

Read, Herbert. *A Concise History of Modern Sculpture*. New York: Praeger, 1964.

Rickey, George. *Constructivism: Origins and Evolution*. New York: Braziller, 1967.

Schmalenbach, Werner. *African Art*. New York: Macmillan, 1954.

Tucker, William. *The Language of Sculpture*. London: Thames and Hudson, 1974.

Wittkower, Rudolf. *Sculpture: Processes and Principles*. London: Allen Lane/Penguin Books, 1977.

## ARCHITECTURE

Arnheim, Rudolf. *The Dynamics of Architectural Form*. Berkeley and Los Angeles: University of California Press, 1977.

Burchard, John, and Albert Bush-Brown. *The Architecture of America*. Boston: Little, Brown, 1961.

Conrads, Ulrich, and Hans Sperlich. *The Architecture of Fantasy: Utopian Building and Planning in Modern Times*. New York: Praeger, 1962.

Drexler, Arthur. *Transformations in Modern Architecture*. Boston: New York Graphic Society, 1980.

Duby, Georges. *The Age of the Cathedrals: Art and Society 980–1420*. Chicago: University of Chicago Press, 1981.

Giedion, Sigfried. *Space, Time and Architecture: The Growth of a New Tradition*. Cambridge, Mass.: Harvard University Press, 1954.

Goldberger, Paul. *On the Rise: Architecture and Design in a Postmodern Age*. New York: Times Books, 1983.

Jencks, Charles A. *The Language of Post-Modern Architecture*. New York: Rizzoli, 1977.

Kostof, Spiro. *A History of Architecture: Settings and Rituals*. New York: Oxford University Press, 1985.

Macaulay, David. *Cathedral: The Story of Its Construction*. Boston: Houghton Mifflin, 1973.

Norberg-Schulz, Christian. *Meaning in Western Architecture*. New York: Praeger, 1975.

Rasmussen, Steen Eiler. *Experiencing Architecture*. Cambridge, Mass.: MIT Press, 1959.

Rudofsky, Bernard. *Architecture Without Architects: An Introduction to Non-Pedigreed Architecture*. New York: The Museum of Modern Art, 1964.

Scully, Vincent J. *American Architecture and Urbanism*. New York: Praeger, 1969.

Torroja, Eduardo. *Philosophy of Structures*. Translated by Milos and J. J. Polivka. Berkeley and Los Angeles: University of California Press, 1958.

Trachtenberg, Marvin, and Isabelle Hyman. *Architecture from Prehistory to Post-Modernism*. New York: Abrams, 1986.

Venturi, Robert. *Complexity and Contradiction in Architecture*. New York: The Museum of Modern Art, 1977.

Wittkower, Rudolf. *Architectural Principles in the Age of Humanism*. London: Academy, 1973.

Wolfe, Tom. *From Bauhaus to Our House*. New York: Farrar, Straus and Giroux, 1981.

Zevi, Bruno. *The Modern Language of Architecture*. Seattle: University of Washington Press, 1977.

## CITY PLANNING

Bacon, Edmund N. *Design of Cities*. New York: The Viking Press, 1967.

Blake, Peter. *God's Own Junkyard: The Planned Deterioration of America's Landscape*. New York: Holt, Rinehart and Winston, 1964.

Goodman, Paul, and Percival Goodman. *Communitas: Means of Livelihood and Ways of Life*. New York: Vintage Books, 1960.

Halprin, Lawrence. *Cities*. Cambridge, Mass.: MIT Press, 1972.

Jacobs, Jane. *The Death and Life of Great American Cities*. New York: Random House, 1961.

Lynch, Kevin. *The Image of the City*. Cambridge, Mass.: Technology Press and Harvard University Press, 1960.

Mumford, Lewis. *The City in History*. New York: Harcourt Brace Jovanovich, 1961.

Rosenau, Helen. *The Ideal City: Its Architectural Evolution*. New York: Harper & Row, 1972.

Rudofsky, Bernard. *Streets for People: A Primer for Americans*. New York: Doubleday, 1969.

Sitte, Camillo. *The Art of Building Cities*. New York: Reinhold, 1945.

Zucker, Paul. *Town and Square*. New York: Columbia University Press, 1959.

## THE CRAFTS AND INDUSTRIAL DESIGN

Banham, Reyner. *Theory and Design in the First Machine Age.* New York: Praeger, 1960.

Feldman, Edmund B. *Thinking About Art.* Englewood Cliffs, N.J.: Prentice-Hall, 1985.

Giedion, Sigfried. *Mechanization Takes Command.* New York: Oxford University Press, 1948.

Gropius, Walter, and Ise Gropius. *Bauhaus, 1919–1928.* Edited by Herbert Bayer. New York: The Museum of Modern Art, 1938.

Harvey, John H. *Medieval Craftsmen.* London: Batsford, 1978.

Klingender, Francis D. *Art and the Industrial Revolution.* London: Royle Publications, 1947.

Lucie-Smith, Edward. *The Story of Craft: The Craftsman's Role in Society.* Ithaca, N.Y.: Cornell University Press, 1981.

Mumford, Lewis. *Technics and Civilization.* New York: Harcourt, Brace, 1934.

Papanek, Victor. *Design for Human Scale.* New York: Van Nostrand Reinhold, 1983.

Paz, Octavio. *In Praise of Hands.* Greenwich, Conn.: New York Graphic Society, 1973.

Pevsner, Nikolaus. *Pioneers of Modern Design from William Morris to Walter Gropius.* New York: The Museum of Modern Art, 1949.

Pye, David. *The Nature and Aesthetics of Design.* London: Barrie and Jenkins, 1978.

Read, Herbert. *Art and Industry.* London: Faber & Faber, 1934.

## PHOTOGRAPHY

Barthes, Roland. *Camera Lucida: Reflections on Photography.* New York: Hill & Wang, 1981.

Coke, Van Deren. *The Painter and the Photograph.* Albuquerque: The University of New Mexico Press, 1972.

Coleman, A. D. *The Grotesque in Photography.* New York: Summit Books, 1977.

Gernsheim, Helmut, and Alison Gernsheim. *The History of Photography from the Camera Obscura to the Beginning of the Modern Era.* London: Thames and Hudson, 1969.

Grundberg, Andy, and K. M. Gauss. *Photography and Art.* Los Angeles: Los Angeles County Museum of Art, 1987.

Kahmen, Volker. *Art History of Photography.* New York: The Viking Press, 1973.

Lucie-Smith, Edward. *The Invented Eye.* New York: Paddington Press, Ltd., 1975.

Newhall, Beaumont. *The History of Photography.* New York: The Museum of Modern Art, 1964.

Pollack, Peter. *The Picture History of Photography.* New York: Abrams, 1969.

Scharf, Aaron. *Art and Photography.* London: Allen Lane/Penguin Press, 1968.

Schuneman, R. Smith, ed. *Photographic Communication.* New York: Hastings House Publishers, 1972.

Sontag, Susan. *On Photography.* New York: Farrar, Straus and Giroux, 1977.

Szarkowski, John. *Looking at Photographs.* New York: The Museum of Modern Art, 1973.

## FILM AND TELEVISION

Eisenstein, Sergei M. *The Film Sense.* Translated and edited by Jay Leyda. New York: Harcourt, Brace, 1942.

Kael, Pauline. *Deeper into Movies.* New York: Bantam Books, 1971.

Kracauer, Siegfried. *Theory of Film: The Redemption of Physical Reality.* New York: Oxford University Press, 1960.

MacGowen, Kenneth. *Behind the Screen: The History and Techniques of the Motion Picture.* New York: Delacorte Press, 1965.

Monaco, James. *How to Read a Film.* New York: Oxford University Press, 1977.

Newcombe, Horace, ed. *The Critical View: Television.* New York: Oxford University Press, 1976.

Nilsen, Vladimir. *The Cinema as a Graphic Art.* New York: Hill and Wang, 1959.

Sarris, Andrew. *The Primal Screen.* New York: Simon & Schuster, 1973.

Spottiswoode, Raymond. *Film and Its Techniques.* Berkeley and Los Angeles: University of California Press, 1966.

Tyler, Parker. *The Three Faces of the Film.* Cranbury, N.J.: Barnes, 1967.

Whitaker, Rod. *The Language of Film.* Englewood Cliffs, N.J.: Prentice-Hall, 1970.

Williams, Raymond. *Television: Technology and Cultural Form.* New York: Schocken Books, 1975.

## AESTHETICS

Arnheim, Rudolph. *Visual Thinking.* Berkeley: University of California Press, 1980.

Beardsley, Monroe. *Aesthetics: Problems in the Philosophy of Criticism.* New York: Harcourt Brace and World, 1981.

Bell, Clive. *Art.* New York: Frederick A. Stokes, 1914.

Bernheimer, Richard. *The Nature of Representation.* New York: New York University Press, 1961.

Bullough, Edward. *Aesthetics.* Stanford: Stanford University Press, 1957.

Clark, Kenneth M. *The Gothic Revival: An Essay in the History of Taste.* New York: Humanities Press, 1970.

Dewey, John. *Art as Experience.* New York: Minton, 1934.

Dorfles, Gillo. *Kitsch: The World of Bad Taste.* New York: Universe Books, 1970.

Goldstein, Kurt. *The Organism.* New York: American Book, 1939.

Gombrich, Ernst. *Art and Illusion.* 5th ed. London: Phaidon, 1977.

Köhler, Wolfgang. *Gestalt Psychology.* New York: Liveright, 1947.

Lipman, Matthew. *What Happens in Art.* New York: Appleton-Century-Crofts, 1967.

Morgan, Douglas. "Creativity Today," *Journal of Aesthetics and Art Criticism* 12 (1953).

Munro, Thomas. *Toward Science in Aesthetics.* New York: Liberal Arts Press, 1956.

Osborne, Harold, ed. *Aesthetics in the Modern World.* London: Thames and Hudson, 1968.

Rader, Melvin, ed. *A Modern Book of Esthetics.* New York: Holt, Rinehart and Winston, 1960.

Vivas, Eliseo, and Murray Krieger, eds. *The Problems of Aesthetics.* New York: Holt, Rinehart and Winston, 1953.

Wertheimer, Max. *Productive Thinking.* Chicago: University of Chicago Press, 1982.

## ART CRITICISM

Armstrong, Robert P. *The Affecting Presence: An Essay in Humanistic Anthropology.* Urbana: University of Illinois Press, 1971.

Berger, John. *Ways of Seeing.* New York: Penguin Books, 1977.

Boas, George. *A Primer for Critics.* Baltimore: Johns Hopkins University Press, 1937.

Cahn, Walter. *Masterpieces: Chapters on the History of an Idea.* Princeton, N.J.: Princeton University Press, 1979.

Clark, Kenneth. *What Is a Masterpiece?* London: Thames and Hudson, 1979.

Crews, Frederick C. *The Pooh Perplex: A Freshman Casebook.* New York: E. P. Dutton, 1963.

Danto, Arthur. "Narratives of the End of Art," in *Encounters and Reflections: Art in the Historical Present.* New York: Farrar Straus and Giroux, 1990.

Diamonstein, Barbaralee. *Inside New York's Art World.* New York: Rizzoli, 1979.

Foster, Stephen C. *The Critics of Abstract Expressionism.* Ann Arbor, Mich.: University Microfilms, 1980.

Gottlieb, Carla. *Beyond Modern Art.* New York: Dutton, 1976.

Greene, Theodore M. *The Arts and the Art of Criticism.* Princeton, N.J.: Princeton University Press, 1947.

Guilbaut, Serge. *How New York Stole the Idea of Modern Art.* Chicago: University of Chicago Press, 1983.

Hughes, Robert. *The Shock of the New.* New York: Knopf, 1981.

Krauss, Rosalind E. *The Originality of the Avant-Garde and Other Modernist Myths.* Cambridge, Mass.: MIT Press, 1985.

Margolis, Joseph. *The Language of Art and Art Criticism.* Detroit: Wayne State University Press, 1965.

Panofsky, Erwin. *Studies in Iconology.* New York: Harper & Row, 1972.

Pepper, Stephen C. *The Basis of Criticism in the Arts.* Cambridge, Mass.: Harvard University Press, 1949.

Podro, Michael. *The Critical Historians of Art.* New Haven: Yale University Press, 1982.

Russell, John. *The Meanings of Modern Art.* New York: The Museum of Modern Art, 1981.

Venturi, Lionello. *History of Art Criticism.* New York: E. P. Dutton, 1936.

# INDEX

Page numbers are in roman type. Page numbers on which illustrations appear are in *italic* type.

## A

Aalto, Alvar: experiment with bentwood, 246; *246*
Aarnie, Eero: Gyro Chair, 112; *112*
Abakanowicz, Magdalena: photograph of, *379;* *Women,* 378; *379*
Abbott, Berenice: *"El" at Battery,* 433; *433*
abstract art: color and, 230; emotional response to, 164, 166; formal order and, 156–59; graphic design and, 62; nature and, 197, 198; psychic distance and, 256; realism and, 131, 132, 207; satire and, 61
Abstract Expressionism, 178, 263, 294, 301–2, 305, 316, 317, 341. *See also* action painting
acrylic painting, 269, 275
action painting, 294, 304. *See also* Abstract Expressionism
Adams, Ansel, 449, 451
adolescence, in art, 12, 24, 25, 27, 132, 134, 319, 361
Adrian, Barbara: *Bed of Stones,* 20; *20*
advertising art, 107, 363, 372, 378; assemblage used in, 354, 363; fantasy in, 192; for film, 63; Op art in, 71; photography and, 231, 447; Pop art and, 299, 301, 304, 352; purpose of, 43; in radio and television commercials, 299; texture used in, 231. *See also* commercial art; graphic design
aesthetic experience, 252–54, 255, 259, 264
Aesthetic Movement, 37
aesthetic object, 260

aesthetics, 36–42, 251–66; aesthetic experience, 252–54, 255, 259, 264; aesthetic work, 251–52, 253, 256; architecture and, 76, 85; beauty and, 42; closure, 257, 259, 260; cognition involved in, 252; of craftsmen, 107; cross-cultural factors and, 264–66; drawing "errors" and, 137; emotion and, 164, 166, 252, 255, 256; empathy, 254, 255–56; film and, 460; of formal order, 146, 153–57, 254; function of, 36–42; funding, 260–61; fusion, 260–61; Gestalt theory, 257, 259–60, 264; of materials, 509; photography and, 442, 444; physiological processes in, 252, 254–55; preferences (liking and disliking), 261–64; psychic distance, 254, 256, 258–59; psychology and, 36, 253, 254, 255–56, 257, 259–60, 264; recognition and, 37; significance of, 265–66; technology, effect on, 76
aesthetic work, 251–52, 253, 256
African art: fetish figures, 312, 365; form and function and, 116, 117; influence: on Cubism, 150, 298, 503; on Modigliani, 66; on Picasso, 490, 491, 494, 497; sculpture, 22, 43, 67, 231, 260, 312, 477; village architecture, 381, 382
Agee, James, 429
Agesander: *Laocoön* (with Athenodorus and Polydorus), 335, 336; *336*
Albers, Josef, 315; *Homage to the Square: Red Series—Untitled III,* 314; *314*
Albright, Ivan, 28, 131; *And God Created Man in His Own Image,* 286; *287; Into the World There Came a Soul Called Ida,* 131–32, 134; *133; Picture of Dorian Gray, The,* 131; *131; Self-Portrait,* 28, 435; *30, 435*
Alhambra, Granada, Spain, 423; Court of the Myrtles, *423*
*All in the Family,* scene from television show, 460; *460*
Allner, Walter: cover for *Fortune* magazine, 69; *69*
Analytic Cubism, 146–47
Ancestor figures of the Dogon tribe, Mali, 331; *331*
Andersen, Gunnar Aagaard: armchair, 115; *115*
Anderson, John, 328; *Wall Piece,* 328; *329*
Andrews, John: Scarborough College, University of Toronto, 105; *105*
animal head, from the Oseberg ship-burial, 337; *337*
Antonioni, Michelangelo: *Blow-Up,* film still from, 465; *465*
anxiety and despair, in art, 175–81
apartment houses, 84–85, 94, 105. *See also* domestic architecture
Apollonian culture, 143
*Apostle,* St. Sernin, Toulouse, 360; *360*
Appel, Karel, 290; *Crying Nude,* 290; *290*
Aptecker, George: photograph of a wall at Coney Island, 63; *63*
Arbus, Diane, 454; *Mexican Dwarf in His Hotel Room in New York City,* 430, 454; *430*
arch construction, 254, 380, 400, 402–5
Archipenko, Alexander, 340
architects: as constructors, 420, 421–22, 427–28; as sculptors, 393, 398, 417, 420–21, 423–24, 426, 428
architecture, 380–428; air conditioning and, 75, 99; aluminum and, 386, 414; apartment houses, 84–85, 94, 105; aqueducts, 388; arches in, 254, 380, 400, 402–5; Art Nouveau style and, 78; balance and, 240; brick, 381, 383, 385–86, 402; bridge engineering and, 392, 393, 402, 405, 406; buttressing in, 403; cantilevers in, 400, 423; cast iron, 78, 390–93; Chicago construction and, 394; classic materials of, 380–86; decorative devices of, 385, 391; domes in, 380, 381, 393, 400, 403, 406–13, 421; domestic, 74–86; dwellings, 74–86; eco-

nomics and, 382, 383, 385, 386, 400; emotion expressed through, 178, 184–85, 427–28; engineering and, 72, 73, 76, 105; environmental concerns and, 105; experimental, 414; expression of joy and, 184–85; external veneers used in, 385, 394–95, 398; fantasy and, 186; formal order and, 145, 149, 151, 153; furniture and, 86; geodesic domes, 412, 414; glass, 75, 145, 386, 390, 393, 398, 400; Happenings as, 304, 306–7; Industrial Revolution and, 72; interior design and, 86; interior space and, 386, 388, 393, 403, 406, 413, 414–19, 427, 428; International Style, 76, 78–79, 249; light and, 220, 413, 417, 419; materials of, 74–75, 81–83, 86, 151, 380–86, 390–98; media/meaning relationships and, 267–68; megastructures and, 105, 414, 420; mixed media and, 312–13; modern materials of, 74–75, 83, 151, 390–98; new brutalism and, 423–24; organic shapes and, 184–85, 212–13, 396, 398, 405; painting and, 296, 297; pendentives and, 408, 409; physical function of, 72–105; plastics and, 386, 414; politics and, 383, 386; post-and-lintel, 399–400, 402, 403, 406; Post-Modern, 417, 421, 423; poured concrete, 81–83, 184–85; prefabrication and, 390, 399; prehistoric, 381; proportion and, 249; psychic distance and, 256; reinforced concrete (ferroconcrete), 81–83, 91, 184–85, 212, 390, 393, 395, 396–98, 399, 400, 405, 413, 414, 427, 428; rhythm and, 246; sculptural impulses of, 212, 297, 393, 398, 417, 420–21, 423–24, 426, 428; sculpture and, 361, 362, 366; shell structures, 413–14; skyscrapers, 387, 394, 395, 420; as social art, 74, 85, 87, 91, 105; spandrels in, 403; spiritualism and, 145; squinches in, 408, 411, 413; standardization of parts and materials and, 380, 393, 399, 400; steel, 145, 380, 386, 390, 393, 394–95, 398, 399, 400, 402, 405, 414; stone, 380, 381–82, 383, 384–85, 386, 390, 399, 402; structural devices of, 380, 398–414; structural engineering (constructors) and, 420, 421–22, 427–28; Surrealist forms in, 213; suspension-bridge engineering applied to, 392, 393, 400; symbolic aspect of, 420–21, 423; technology and, 74–75, 76, 85, 145, 390, 394, 398; tents as, 413, 427; trusses in, 380, 400, 402, 403, 424; in the urban environment, 85, 89, 90–91, 386–89; utopian, 87, 186; vaults in, 393, 400, 406; window walls and, 399–400; wood, 380, 381, 383, 386, 390, 400, 405, 414; wrought-iron, 394. *See also* city planning; domestic architecture

Aristocles: *Stele of Aristion,* 507; *507*
Arlen, Michael, 466
Arman, 357; *Chopin's Waterloo,* 357–58; *359; Couleur de mon amour, La,* 312; *312; Little Hands,* 357, 434; *359, 434*
Armitage, Kenneth: *Diarchy,* 347; *347*

Armory Show, New York City, 457
Arp, Jean, 18, 115, 246, 298, 338, 369; *Human Concretion,* 149–50; *149; Madame Torso with Wavy Hat,* 214; *214; Olympia,* 241; *241; Star,* 212; *212; Torso Gerbe,* 18; *18*
art: aesthetic purpose and, 38, 494–95; aesthetics of, 36–42, 251–66; affective responses to, 261–64; Apollonian, 143; changing relationship to architecture and sculpture, 304; communication and, 11, 12–13, 43, 477, 480–83; Dionysiac, 143; as dream source for mankind, 462; emotion and, 13, 45, 140; as experience, 252–54, 255; functions of, 11–71; high, 252, 262; humanitarian concerns in, 49–51; as language, 12–13, 43, 121, 205, 236; low, 252, 262; making and experiencing, 252–53; mathematics and, 143, 144, 145, 147, 148–49, 162; Nature in, 15; photography and, 123; Platonic approach to, 145, 147; representation of movement and, 456–57; responsibility and purpose of, 45; ritual and, 43; role of, as propaganda, 43, 47; role of, in transmitting information, 126; social function of graphic art and, 62–71; social responses to, 43; structure of, 205–50; style and, 121; utilitarian aspect of, 106–8. *See also* architecture; painting; sculpture
art collectors: art criticism and, 470, 473, 504; contemporary, 272–73, 296–97, 437, 504
art criticism, 467–510; aesthetic experience failure and, 264; art collectors and, 470, 473, 504; art history and, 471, 504–5; authenticity and, 504; comparison with historical models, 504–6; connoisseurs and, 261, 263, 486, 504; craftsmanship and, 506, 508–9; description and, 487–90, 495; difficulty of, 270; effect on artists, 471, 473, 486; energy needed for, 252; evaluation (judgment) and, 487, 494, 503–10; expressivism and, 477, 480–81, 483; of films, 464, 466; formal analysis and, 487, 490–93, 495; formalism and, 476–77, 478, 480, 481, 483, 484, 486; forming a hypothesis and, 495, 496; goals and purposes of, 469–71, 494–95; information sought by, 469, 470; instrumentalism and, 481–86; interpretation and, 487, 493, 494–503; journalistic, 473–74; judgment of excellence (evaluation) and, 470, 471, 476–86, 487, 494, 503–10; Marxism and, 485–86; media/meaning relationships and, 268; mimetic theory and, 495–96; pedagogical, 473, 474; performance of, 487–509; persuasion and, 489–90; of photography, 447–54; popular, 473, 475–76; prediction of aesthetic value and, 504; problems of, 467; process of, 487–510; requirements for, 471–73; scholarly, 473, 474–75; social motive of, 469–70; systematic procedures for, 467, 487–510; technique and, 488, 506,

508–9; theory of, 469–86; tools of, 471–73; types of, 473–76; understanding design principles and, 241, 250
Art Deco style, 475
art education, 109–10, 145, 474. *See also* art history
art history, 122, 447, 470; as tool for art criticism, 471, 504–5
artists: aims of, in social functions, 43; aims of, through realistic techniques, 127; avant-garde, 475–76; choice of style and, 144, 145, 186, 188, 278, 301–2; as colorists, 226–27; as craftsmen, 106; as critics, 473; as culture heroes, 299; as detached observers, 127–29; education of, 109–10; effect of art criticism on, 471, 473, 486; individualism and, 262; as industrial designers, 72, 73, 108, 109–10, 112; private vision of, 12; responsibility of, 45; selective eyes of, 129, 131–34. *See also* art; painting; sculpture
Art Nouveau style, 61, 78, 106, 114, 191, 393
Aspdin, Joseph, 396
assemblage, 297–99, 302, 306, 310–11; sculpture and, 298, 328, 351–59, 361–62. *See also* collage
Athenodorus: *Laocoön* (with Agesander and Polydorus), 335, 336; *336*
Auerbach, Frank: *Head of Catherine Lampert,* 229; *229*
Austin, Darrel, 170; *Black Beast, The,* 170; *169*
automobiles, 93, 202–3; assembly lines for, 108–9; *108;* grilles, 111; *111*
Avigdor, Seymour: interior with patterns, 233; *233*
Azaceta, Luis Cruz: *Apocalypse: Now or Later,* 47; *47*

# B

Babylonian architecture, 385
Bacon, Francis, 42, 175, 176, 357; *Head Surrounded by Sides of Beef,* 176, 178, 179; *179; Triptych—Studies from the Human Body,* 321; *321*
Bacon, Peggy, 61; *Patroness, The,* 61; *60*
balance, as design principle, 240–43, 249; architecture and, 240; asymmetrical, 241, 242, 243; Gestalt laws and, 257; by interest, 241, 243; psychological, 241, 242, 243; by weight, 241, 243
Balazs, Bela, 455
Baldaccini, César. *See* César
Balthus, 319; *Golden Days, The,* 319; *319*
Baroque art, 220–24, 280
Baskin, Leonard, 338; *St. Thomas Aquinas,* 330; *Seated Man with Owl,* 338; *339*
Bass, Saul, 66, 70; advertisement for film *The Two of Us* (with Goodman), 63; *63;* poster for Pabco Paint Company, 66; *70*
Bauhaus, 82, 109–10, 340, 351, 423; ar-

chitecture of, Dessau (Gropius), 400; *399*

Baziotes, William: *Sea, The,* 198; *198*

Beals, Jesse Tarbox: Photograph of Italian children, *55*

Bearden, Romare: *Prevalence of Ritual: Baptism, The,* 298; *298*

Beckmann, Max: *Columbine,* 142; *142; Self-Portrait in a Tuxedo,* 289, 505–6; *289, 505*

Bell, Clive, 477

Benday screening, 64

Bennett, Hubert, & Associates: Hayward Art Gallery, London, 423–24, 427; *427*

Benton, Robert: *Kramer vs. Kramer,* film still from, 464; *464*

Benton, Thomas Hart, 474; *Arts of the West,* 475; *475*

Berenson, Bernard, 477; photograph of (Seymour), *486*

Bergman, Ingmar, 188, 464; *Magician, The,* film still from, 188; *188; Silence, The,* film still from, 463; *463*

Berlin, Pamela: *Steel Magnolias,* film still from, *462*

Berlin Pavilion, New York World's Fair, 414

Bernini, Gianlorenzo, 269, 311

Bertoia, Harry, 155; screen for Manufacturers Hanover Trust Company, New York City, 155; *155*

billboards, 94

biomorphic shape. *See* organic shape

Bischof, Werner, 441; *Boy Leaving His Sick Grandfather, Korea,* 452; *452*

Bisharat, Victor/James A. Evans and Associates: General Time Building, Stamford, Connecticut, 185; *185*

Bishop, Isabel: *Nude,* 509; *509*

Bladen, Ronald: *Cathedral Evening,* 366; *366*

Bloc, André: *Sculpture Habitacle No. 2,* 362; *362*

Bloom, Hyman, 29; *Corpse of an Elderly Female,* 29; *31*

Boccioni, Umberto: *Development of a Bottle in Space,* 120; *120*

Bocola, Francesco: Quasar lamp, 378; *379*

Bohrod, Aaron, 54; *Landscape near Chicago,* 54, 56; *56*

Bonnard, Pierre, 153; *Breakfast Room, The,* 153; *152; Nude in Bathtub,* 161; *161*

Bontecou, Lee, 353; *Untitled,* 353; *353*

Bosa, Louis, 54; *My Family Reunion,* 54; *54*

Bosch, Hieronymus, 199, 357; *Hell* (detail of *The Garden of Delights*), 199; *201*

Bouché, René, 132; *Elsa Maxwell,* 132; *133*

Boucher, François: *Miss O'Murphy,* 224; *224*

Bouguereau, Adolphe William, 322

Bourke-White, Margaret, 438

boxes, as sculpture, 360, 362–65

Brady, Mathew, 441

Brancusi, Constantin, 144, 150, 235, 338;

*Adam and Eve,* 343; *343; Fish,* 212, 213; *213; Sculpture for the Blind,* 112; *112; Torso of a Young Man,* 150; *149*

Brandt, Marianne: Teapot, 110; *110*

Braque, Georges, 37, 42, 66, 139, 146, 304; *Man with a Guitar,* 147; *147; Round Table, The,* 37–38, 239; *38; Woman with a Mandolin,* 153; *154*

Brenner, E. H.: Women's Clinic, Lafayette, Indiana, 412; *412*

Breuer, Marcel, 76

brick, in architecture, 381, 383, 385–86, 402

Brockhurst, Gerald Leslie: *Adolescence (Portrait of Kathleen Nancy Woodward),* 25, 27; *25*

Broderson, Morris: *Earth Says Hello, The,* 140; *140*

Bronzino, Agnolo: *Portrait of a Young Man,* 505–6; *505*

Brooklyn Bridge, New York City, 234

Brouwer, Adriaen, 454

Brueghel, Pieter, the Elder, 454; *Painter and the Connoisseur, The,* 486; *486*

brushwork, emotion and, 275–76, 278, 283, 294

Buchanan, Beverly: *Shack South: Inside and Out,* 74; *74*

Bullough, Edward, 256, 260

Burchfield, Charles, 15; *April Mood, An,* 15, 16; *16*

Burgee, John, Architects: American Telephone & Telegraph Company Building, New York City (with Johnson), 249; model, *250*

burned phone, from advertisement for Western Electric Phone Company, 352; *352*

Burri, Alberto, 28; *Sacco B,* 28, 32, 173; *32, 173*

buttressing, in architecture, 403

Byzantine art, 441

# C

Calder, Alexander, 40, 369, 373; *Acoustical Ceiling,* 235; *235; Hostess, The,* 210; *210; International Mobile,* 40, 42; *40; Red Gongs,* 369; *369*

*camera obscura,* 441

Candela, Félix, 185, 246, 267; Manantiales Restaurant, Xochimilco, Mexico (with Ordoñez), 184–85; *185*

cantilever construction, 400, 423

Capa, Robert, 441

Caponigro, Paul: *Rock Wall No. 2, W. Hartford, Connecticut,* 443; *443*

Capp, Al, 58; *Li'l Abner* Ugly Woman Contest, panels from, 58; *58*

Caravaggio, 220, 454; *Calling of St. Matthew, The,* 220, 221; *221*

caricature, 59, 470

Carter, Donald Ray: photograph of Galleria Vittorio Emanuele, Milan, 98; *98*

Cartier-Bresson, Henri, 453; *Children Playing in the Ruins, Spain,* 453; *453*

cartoon art, 58, 59, 317, 370–71

carving, in sculpture, 323, 324, 326, 328, 335

Cassatt, Mary, 15; *Toilette, La,* 15, 17; *17*

casting, in sculpture, 108, 323, 324, 325, 326, 327, 328, 335, 336

cast iron, in architecture, 78, 390–93

Castle, Wendell, 114; double chair, 508; *508;* oak-and-leather chair, 114; *114*

Cathedral of St. Basil, Moscow, 406; *409*

cave paintings, 22, 124, 251, 317

Cavett, Dick, photograph of, *461*

Cellini, Benvenuto: *Saltcellar of Francis I,* 117, 351; *117, 351*

Cennini, Cennino, 271

César (Baldaccini), 293; *Yellow Buick, The,* 293, 322; *293*

Cézanne, Paul, 45, 183, 230, 259, 278, 284, 296, 322, 476; *Card Players, The,* 215; *215; Chocquet Assis,* 284; *285; Houses in Provence,* 279; *279; Lac d'Annecy,* 478; *479*

Chagall, Marc, 18–19, 184, 186; *Birthday,* 18–19, 243; *19; Flying over the Town,* 184; *184*

chair design, 82; Art Nouveau, 191; *191;* industrial design and, 112–15; *112–15;* as sculpture, 112, 508; *508*

Chamberlain, John, 267, 356; *Essex,* 356; *356, 468*

Chaplin, Charles, 181, 369, 455; *Modern Times,* film still from, 455; *455*

Chardin, Jean-Baptiste, 363

*chiaroscuro,* 220, 269

Chicago construction, 394

children's art, 97, 124, 477, 480

Chirico, Giorgio de, 489, 490; *Delights of the Poet,* 489; *489*

Christo (Javacheff), 357; *Package on Wheelbarrow,* 357, 446; *358, 446*

Chryssa: *Fragments for the Gates to Times Square,* 57; *57*

Churchill, Winston, 59, 380

Church of Lazarus, Kizhi Island, U.S.S.R., 383; *383*

Ciampi, Mario, & Associates: University Arts Center, University of California, Berkeley, 400; *401*

cinema. *See* film

city planning, 86–105; Broadacre City (Wright), 89–90; plan of, *89;* Cumbernauld, Scotland, 92; *92;* Daly City, California, 88; *88;* decentralization and, 89; elements of, 91–105; Garden City (Howard), 87, 88; greenbelts, 87; highways, 90, 93–94, 95, 96, 396; industrial and commercial structures and, 100–105; plazas, malls, civic centers, 94, 96, 98–100; residential grouping, 91–93; shopping malls, 75, 94, 96, 98, 99–100; single-family dwellings, 91–93; social problems and, 105; suburbs, 85, 87, 90; transportation and, 90–96, 105; utopian, 86, 89–90, 186; Vällingby, Sweden (Markelius), 93; *93;* Ville Radieuse, La (Le Corbusier), 90–91; plan for, *91*

civil engineering, 72

classicism, 144, 148, 150, 156–57, 162; in Greek art, 143, 144, 150, 156. *See also*

formal order, style of
Close, Chuck: *Susan,* 139, 448; *139, 448*
closure, 257, 259, 260
Cocteau, Jean, 188
Coke, Van Deren, 432, 447
collage, 66, 322; assemblage and, 298, 310; Cubist, 262; Dada and, 304; fantasy art and, 202–4; Pop art and, 302, 304; sculpture and, 202–4, 328; texture and, 232, 310. *See also* assemblage
color, as visual element in art, 207, 226–31; afterimage and, 227; analogous, 229, 237; arbitrary use of, 138; complementary, 227–29, 269; contrast and, 218; drawing and, 160, 161; emotional and intuitive response to, 226–27; formal order and, 160–63; hue, 227; Impressionist theories of, 127–28, 129, 226–27, 307; intensity and, 227, 228, 236; *228;* as language, 229–31; local, 227; in modern art, 230–31; mystical aspect of, 195; objective accuracy and, 138; sensuous surface and, 160–63; spectrum of, 228; *228;* symbolic properties of, 174, 229; Synchromy and, 158; terminology of, 227–29; theories of, 158, 226; tonality and, 229, 237; tone and, 229; value and, 227, 228, 229; *228;* warm and cool, 218, 229, 236, 275; wheel, 228, 229; *228*
Color Field painting, 314–15, 316
Colville, Alexander: *River Thames, The,* 242; *242*
"combine" paintings, 302, 304
commercial art, 137, 299, 301, 482–83. *See also* advertising art; graphic design
community planning, 86–87. *See also* city planning
computer-aided design (CAD), 108
computer-aided manufacture (CAM), 108
computer art, 64, 217, 316, 366
concrete, in architecture: poured, 81–83, 184–85; reinforced (ferroconcrete), 81–83, 91, 184–85, 212, 390, 393, 395, 396–98, 399, 400, 405, 413, 414, 427, 428
Conklin and Wittlesey: town center, Reston, Virginia, 88; *88*
Conner, Bruce, 356; *Child,* 356–57; *357*
connoisseurs, 263, 268, 486, 504
Constable, John, 227
constructing, in sculpture, 323, 328
Constructivism, 340–42, 366, 369
*contrapposto,* 175
coordinatographs, 217
Cornell, Joseph, 362–64; *Blériot,* 364; *364; Soap Bubble Set,* 363–64; *364*
Corn Palace, Mitchell, South Dakota, 394; *394*
Courbet, Gustave, 447
crafts (craftsmanship), 72, 106–8; art criticism and, 477, 506, 508, 509; defined, 506; industrial design and, 109, 113–14, 120; materials and, 506, 509; range of medium and, 268; revivals, 109; as sculpture, 374–75
*Crafts for Tour* advertisement, 363; *363*
Cremean, Robert: *Swinging Woman,* 268; *268*

criticism. *See* art criticism
cromlechs, 381
cross-cultural factors, aesthetics and, 264–66
Cubism, 21, 37, 42; African sculpture and, 150, 298, 490, 491, 494, 497, 503; Analytic, 146–47; collage and, 66, 298, 322; flattening of space and, 296; formal order and, 145, 146–47, 156, 484; influence of, 62, 66, 68, 81, 145, 183; instrumentalist traits of, 484; perspective and, 139; photography and, 449; sculpture and, 147–48

# D

Dada, 291, 298, 299, 302, 304, 322, 372
daguerreotype, 431
Dali, Salvador, 190, 299; *Soft Construction with Boiled Beans: Premonition of Civil War,* 190; *191*
Darius, king of Persia, 108
Daumier, Honoré: *Two Sculptors,* 219; *219*
David, Jacques-Louis: *Man with a Hat,* 282; *282*
Davidson, Bruce: photograph of people on East 100th Street, 74; *74*
Davis, Stuart, 42, 246; *Report from Rockport,* 41, 42, 94; *41; Visa,* 510; *510*
death and morbidity, in art, 12, 22–25, 27–29, 255
Debschitz, Wilhelm von: inkstand, 111; *111*
decalcomania, 291, 292
*Decisive Moment, The* (Cartier-Bresson), 453
Degas, Edgar, 128, 129, 330, 447; *Developpé en avant,* 252; *252; Glass of Absinthe, The,* 128, 129; *129*
Deitrick, William H., 102, 105; J. S. Dorton State Fair Arena, Raleigh, North Carolina (with Nowicki), 102, 105; *104*
de Kooning, Willem, 42, 61, 144; *Time of the Fire, The,* 294; *294; Two Women,* 140; *141; Woman, I,* 61; *60*
Delacroix, Eugène, 45, 171, 275, 283; *Liberty Leading the People,* 44, 45; *44; Lion Hunt, The,* sketch for, 275–76; *277; Portrait of Chopin,* 283; *283*
Delaunay, Robert, 148; *Eiffel Tower,* 148–49; *148; Homage to Blériot,* 158; *158*
Demuth, Charles, 148; *My Egypt,* 148; *148*
*Denver Church Opens Doors to Homeless: Eddy Wade at the Holy Ghost Roman Catholic Church,* 49; *49*
Derain, André, 161, 230; *London Bridge,* 160, 230; *160*
description, social function of, 51–55
design, principles of, 115–20, 234–50; artistic organization and, 205; balance and, 240–43, 249; coherence in, 237, 239; composition in, 234; dominance in, 236, 238; proportion in, 248–49; rhythm in, 244–48, 249; symbolism and, 234, 241, 243; unity in, 236–40,

249; in useful and fine art, 234, 235. *See also* industrial design
Dewey, John, 261; *Art as Experience,* 252–54, 255
*Dick Cavett Show,* photograph from, 461; *461*
Diebenkorn, Richard: *Man and Woman in a Large Room,* 174; *174; Ocean Park, No. 22,* 157; *157*
dignitary or priest, from Tabasco, Mexico, 266; *266*
Dine, Jim: *Five Feet of Colorful Tools,* 38, 498; *498*
Dionysiac culture, 143
distortion, in art, 175, 178, 179
Dix, Otto, 126, 480; *Lens Bombed,* 480; *482; My Parents,* 126–27; *125*
Doesburg, Theo van, 215; *Composition: The Cardplayers,* 215, 217; *215*
dolmens, 381, 399
domes, 380, 381, 403, 405, 406–13; economics and, 400; geodesic, 412, 414; iron used for, 393; oculus in, 408; pendentive system and, 408–9; space created by, 400, 406, 408; squinch system and, 408, 411, 413; symbolism of, 408, 421
domestic architecture, 74–86; air conditioning and, 75; apartment houses, 84–85, 94, 105; development of, 74; dwellings, 74–83; environment and, 75–76, 85; family life and, 74; interior design and, 86; of Le Corbusier, 81–83, 85; of Mies van der Rohe, 78–81; modern materials and, 74–75; Prairie Houses (Wright), 76–78; principles of, 75, 85–86; as social art, 74, 75, 85, 91; structural devices of, 400, 402; technology and, 74–75, 76, 85; of Wright, 76–78
Donatello: *Mary Magdalen,* 265; *265; St. Mark,* Orsanmichele, Florence, 360; *360*
Dorazio, Piero: *Janus,* 241; *241*
Douglas, Melvyn, photograph of, *30*
Dove, Arthur G.: *Critic, The,* 471; *471; That Red One,* 197; *197*
Drake, Debbie; photograph of, *249*
dreams and hallucinations: in art, 188, 189–94; in film, 462–63
Dressler, Michael: *Man on a Bicycle,* 441
Dreyfuss, Henry, 113
Duble, Lu, 176; *Cain,* 176; *177*
Dubuffet, Jean, 42, 298–99, 307, 322; *Devidoir enregistreur,* 97; *97; Leader in a Parade Uniform,* 172; *172; My Cart, My Garden,* 298; *Sea of Skin, The,* 232; *232*
Duchamp, Marcel, 202, 298; *Boîte-en-valise (The Box in a Valise),* 362, 363; *363; Bride, The,* 202; *203; Nude Descending a Staircase, No. 2,* 246, 248, 457; *247, 457*
Duchamp-Villon, Raymond, 147; *Horse, The,* 147; *148*
Durante, Jimmy, 322
Dürer, Albrecht, 248; *Four Horsemen of the Apocalypse, The,* 47; *Painter's Father, The,* 281; *281; Proportions of the*

*Human Body, The,* study from, 249; *249; Study for Adam,* 248; *248*

dwellings, 74–83. *See also* domestic architecture

Dyck, Anthony van, 264

# E

Eakins, Thomas, 129; *Agnew Clinic, The,* 28, 32, 129; *32, 130; Gross Clinic, The,* 129; *131*

Eames, Charles, 113; chaise longue, 115; *115;* lounge chair, *114*

Early Christian art, 47

earth sculpture, 375–77

*Eau de Vroom,* advertisement for Crêpe de Chine perfume, 354; *354*

éclaboussage, 292

effigy figures, 329, 331

effigy whistle: girl on swing, Romojadas region, Veracruz, Mexico, 350; *350*

egg-tempera painting, 275. *See also* tempera painting

Egyptian art: architecture, 335, 381–82, 385, 386, 399; monuments, 22; sculpture, 326–27, 332, 335, 338; symbolism and, 117

Eiffel, Gustav, 393; Eiffel Tower, Paris, joint of, *393*

Einstein, Albert, 477

Eisenstein, Sergei, 464; *Potemkin,* film still from, 461; *461*

*Ekkehard and Uta,* from Naumburg Cathedral, Germany, 334; *334*

"elegance," Kirchkoff's Law and, 257

Emery, Lin: *Homage to Amercreo,* 371; *371*

emotion, style of, 164–85; anger and, 61; anxiety and despair and, 175–81; architecture and, 184–85, 427–28; brushwork and, 275–76, 278, 283, 294; Expressionism and, 286, 288, 290; joy and celebration and, 181–85; role of distortion in, 175, 178, 179; Romanticism and, 166–71; sculpture and, 166, 170–71, 176; as source of artistic response, 164, 166; symbolism and, 172–74, 176; violence and, 166, 170

empathy, 254, 255–56

encaustic painting, 275

engineering, 148; architecture and, 72, 73, 76, 105. *See also* mechanical engineering

Enlightenment, 217

environmental design, 73

Environments, 304, 306, 307

Epigonus: *Dying Gaul,* 35; *35*

Epstein, Jacob, 15; *Head of Joseph Conrad,* 138; *137; Madonna and Child,* 15, 17; *17*

Epstein & Sons: Kitchens of Sara Lee Administration Building, Deerfield, Illinois, 103; *103*

Erni, Hans: *Atomkrieg Nein (Atom War No),* 45

Ernst, Max, 188, 291, 292, 298, 316;

*Capricorne, Le,* 344; *344; Eye of Silence, The,* 291; *291; Joy of Living, The,* 195; *194*

erotic and obscene art, 15–16, 18, 183, 192–93, 318–22, 332, 349

Esteve, Maurice: *Rebecca,* 156; *156*

Etienne-Martin: *Grand Couple, Le,* 345; *345*

Etruscan art, 333

Evans, Walker, 438; *Frank's Stove, Cape Breton Island,* 445; *445; Graveyard in Easton, Pennsylvania,* 449; *449*

Exeter Cathedral, England, nave of, 406

Expressionism, 27–28; Abstract, 178, 294, 301, 305, 316, 317, 356; color and, 230; distortion and, 179; emotion and, 286, 288, 290; German, 456; objective accuracy and, 126–27

Eyck, Jan van: *Virgin and the Canon Van der Paele, The,* 281; *281*

# F

fantasy, style of, 186–204; architecture and, 186; dreams and hallucinations and, 188, 189–94; emotion and, 178; in films, 188; human-animal, 178; humor and, 190, 193, 203–4; idealism and, 186, 188; illusionism and, 190, 199, 202–4; irrational origins of, 188; logical origins of, 188; metamorphoses and, 190, 192; mystical transcendence and, 195–98; myths and, 188–89, 190, 192; primitive art and, 193; science and technology and, 188, 199; sculpture and, 187, 192, 202–4; Surrealism and, 190, 193, 199, 202; utopian vision and, 186, 188

fashion illustration, 249; *249*

Fauvism, 230, 288

Feininger, Andreas: *Cemetery in New York City,* 449; *449*

Feininger, Lyonel, 145; *Church of the Minorities (II),* 145–46; *145*

Fellini, Federico, 464; *Dolce Vita, La,* film stills from, 465, 466; *465, 466*

Ferber, Herbert, 239; *"and the bush was not consumed,"* 239; *239*

ferroconcrete. *See* reinforced concrete

fertility objects, 15, 234

fetish figures, 231, 312, 354, 362, 365

figure of a dancer, Gallo-Roman, 336; *336*

film, 437, 455–66; aesthetic devices of, 456, 457–59; aesthetics of, 460; animated, 369; close-up, as device of, 457–58, 463; critical appreciation of, 464, 466; democracy of, 463–64; documentary, 460; dreams and, 462–63; effect of, on content, 460; fantasy in, 188; German Expressionism and, 456; image of, vs. television, 296, 461–62; importance of, to image-making, 297; objectivity of, 430; photography and, 437, 440, 444, 447; reality and, 438, 456–57, 476; relationship to painting

and picture-making, 274, 298, 455; social effects of, 461, 463–64; space-time manipulation and, 456–59, 460; technology and, 455, 456–57; types of, 460; visual continuity sequence and, 457–59; visual imagery of, 464, 466

Flack, Audrey: *Golden Girl,* 301; *301*

folk art, 63, 122, 431, 436

Ford, Henry, 108, 109

Ford, John: *Grapes of Wrath, The,* film still from, 438, 463; *439, 463*

Ford Motor Company assembly line, 108; *108*

foreshortening, 138, 269. *See also* perspective

form, 284; Dewey on, 254; psychic distance and, 256; as visual element in art, 207–8. *See also* shape

formal order, style of, 143–63; abstract modes of, 156–59; aesthetics and, 146, 153–57, 254; architecture and, 149, 151, 153; art education and, 145; biomorphic shapes and, 146, 149–51, 153; classicism and, 143, 144; Cubism and, 145, 146–47, 156, 484; intellectual, 146–49; permanency of forms and, 144–46; religious implications of, 145–46; sculpture and, 149–51, 155; sensuous surfaces and, 160–63; social control and, 163

Forman, Miloš: *Loves of a Blonde, The,* film still from, 458; *458*

Foster, Jodie, 462

Fragonard, Jean-Honoré, 272; *Swing, The,* 272; *273*

Francis, Sam: *Abstraction,* 162; *162*

Frankenthaler, Helen: *Rapunzel,* 38; *39*

Freire, Segundo, 62; Carnival poster, 62; *64*

fresco painting, 269, 270, 274, 275, 299

Freud, Sigmund, 190

Freyssinet, Eugène: airport hangar, Orly Airport, France, 405; *405;* Basilica of Pius X, Lourdes, France, 426, 427; *426*

Frink, Elizabeth: *Riace II,* 328; *328*

frottage, 291, 292

Fry, Roger, 477

Fujiwara, Tsuneji, 66; cosmetics poster by, 66, 67; *67*

Fuller, R. Buckminster, 414; American Pavilion, EXPO 67, Montreal, 412; *412*

functions of art, 11, 12–120; personal, 11, 12–42; physical, 11, 72–120; social, 11, 43–71

funding, 260–61

furniture, 86. *See also* chair design

fusion, 260–61

Futurism, 248, 368

# G

Gabo, Naum, 340, 368, 377; *Linear Construction #1,* 340; *340; Monument for an Institute of Physics and Mathematics,* 340–41; *341*

Gallo, Frank, 327; *Swimmer,* 327; *327*

Gallo-Roman art, 336
Gateway Arch, St. Louis, 405
Gaudí, Antoni, 213; Casa Batlló, Barcelona, 213; facade, *213;* Casa Milá Apartment House, Barcelona, 361; original attic, *361;* Church of the Sagrada Familia, Barcelona, 312; *312*
Gauguin, Paul, 169; *Spirit of the Dead Watching, The,* 169–70, 224; *168, 225*
geodesic domes, 412, 414
geometric forms (geometry), 135, 148–49, 162, 284; Greek art and, 143, 144, 145; human figures and, 147, 215, 217; Minimal painting and, 314; power of, in art, 207, 208
Géricault, Theodore, 27, 29; *Homicidal Maniac, The,* 282; *282; Madwoman,* 27; *26; Raft of the "Medusa," The,* 171; *170*
German Expressionism, 456
German Rose Engine, London, 110; *110*
Gernsheim, Helmut, 431
Gérôme, Jean-Léon, 322; *Roman Slave Market,* 319; *319*
Gerster, George: *Sahara Pollution,* 451; *451*
gesso, 275
Gestalt theory, 257, 259–60, 264; good Gestalt, 257, 260
Ghirlandaio, Domenico, 28; *Old Man and His Grandson, An,* 28, 30; *30*
Giacometti, Alberto, 13, 175, 436; *Man and Woman,* 343; *343; Man Pointing,* 13, 14; *14; Woman with Her Throat Cut,* 191; *191*
Gielgud, John, 435; photograph of (Jeffery), *435*
Giorgione da Castelfranco, 504
glass, in architecture, 75, 145, 386, 390, 393, 398, 400
Goethe, Johann Wolfgang von, 217
Gogh, Vincent van, 31, 164, 175, 264, 278; *Landscape with Olive Trees,* 16; *16; Ravine, The,* 278, 279; *279; Starry Night, The,* 29, 31, 34; *34*
Goldberg, Bertrand, Associates: Marina City, Chicago, 388; *388*
Goldberg, Rube, 370–71, 373; cartoon of an absurd machine, 370–71; *369*
Golden Section (Golden Mean), 248; *248*
González, Julio, 210; *Grande Maternity,* 210; *210; Woman Combing Her Hair,* 341; *341*
Gooch, Gerald: *Hmmm,* 488
Goodman, Art: advertisement for film *The Two of Us* (with Bass), 63; *63*
Gorin, Jean: *Composition No. 9,* 241
Gorky, Arshile: *Liver Is the Cock's Comb, The,* 173; *173*
Gothic art: architecture, 270, 337, 385, 390, 403, 406; sculpture, 334, 337
Gottlieb, Adolph, 214; *Blast II,* 51, 214–15; *214; Dialogue No. I,* 172; *172*
Gowan, James: Engineering Building, Leicester University, England (with Stirling), 419; interior, *418*
Goya y Lucientes, Francisco José de, 461; Disasters of War series, 51, 52, 176; "Nothing more to do" from, 52; *52*

Grace, Arthur: *Nellie Hart and Sons,* 438; *439*
Graham, Nan Wood, *259*
graphic design, 62–71, 299, 429, 482–83. *See also* advertising art; commercial art
grattage, 291–92
Graves, Michael: Portland Public Services Building, Oregon, 423; *422*
Graves, Nancy: *Zaga,* 356; *356*
Greco, El (Domenikos Theotokopoulos), 220, 222, 271; *Agony in the Garden of Gethsemane, The,* 221, 222, 278; *221; Fray Felix Hortensio Paravicion,* 281; *281; Pentecost,* 271; *271*
Greek art, 506; architecture, 249, 335, 337, 381, 385, 399, 402; classicism and, 143, 144, 150, 156–57; Hellenistic period, 143; ideals of beauty and, 143; mathematics of proportion (geometry) and, 143, 144, 145; sculpture, 144, 326, 497, 507; vase painting, 497
Greenberg, Clement, 330
Griffi, Patroni: *Sea, The,* film still from, 458; *458*
Griffith, David W., 457
Gris, Juan, 14, 139, 284, 304; *Fantômas (Pipe and Newspaper),* 262; *262; Portrait of Max Jacob,* 14–15; *14; Portrait of Picasso,* 284; *285*
Gromaire, Marcel: *Nu, bras levé, sur fond gris et or,* 150; *150*
Grooms, Red: *Ruckus Manhattan* (with Gross), 97; *97*
Groos, Karl, 255–56, 260
Gropius, Walter, 76, 109–10; Bauhaus, Dessau, Germany, 400; Laboratory Workshop, *399;* Pan Am Building, New York City, 395
Gross, Mimi: *Ruckus Manhattan* (with Grooms), 97; *97*
Grosz, George, 13–14, 480; *Couple,* 21; *21; Poet Max Hermann-Neisse, The,* 13–14; *14; Punishment,* 480; *482*
grottoes, 361–62
guardian figure, Bokota area, Gabon, Africa, 494; *494*
Guglielmi, Louis: *Terror in Brooklyn,* 54; *54*
guild system, 271
Guimard, Hector, 78; Métropolitain station, Place de l'Etoile, Paris, 78; *79*
Gutenberg, Johannes, 108

# H

Hagia Sophia, Istanbul, 409, 414; interior, *414*
Hals, Frans, 12; *Governors of the Old Men's Almshouse, Haarlem,* 279; *279*
Hamilton, Richard, 290; *Fashion-plate study (a) self-portrait,* 290; *290*
handcrafts. See crafts
Hanson, Duane: *Man on a Bench,* man studying, 259; *258; Shoppers, The,* 124; *124*
Happenings, 304, 306–7, 322, 372, 373

Harbeson, Hough, Livingston & Larson: Sam Rayburn House Office Building, Washington, D.C., 385; *384*
Hare, David, 40; *Juggler,* 40, 42; *40*
Harnett, William M.: *Old Models,* 137; *136*
Harrison, Wallace K.: First Presbyterian Church, Stamford, Connecticut, 413; interior, *413*
Hartley, Marsden: *Indian Composition,* 37; *37*
Hartmann, Erich: *Mannequins,* 434; *434*
Hauser, Erich: *Space Column,* 256; *256*
heavenly couple from Khajuraho, India, 332; *332*
Hecker, Zvi: apartment house, Ramat Gan, Israel (with Neumann), 94; *94*
Heizer, Michael: *Isolated Mass/Circumflex,* 376; *376*
Henri, Robert, 474
Hepworth, Barbara: *Two Figures,* 345; *345*
Hersey, William: Piazza d'Italia, New Orleans (with Moore), 100; *101*
Hicks, Edward, 186; *Peaceable Kingdom,* 186, 188; *187*
highways, 90, 93–94, 95, 96, 396; *95, 96, 396*
Hinman, Charles: *Red/Black,* 316; *316*
Hockney, David: *First Marriage, The,* 20; *20*
Hodgkin, Howard: *Day Dreams,* 183; *183*
Hofer, Carl, 21; *Early Hour,* 20, 21; *20*
Hofer, Evelyn: *Brownstones on the West Side,* 432; *432*
Hokanson, Hans: *Helixikos No. I,* 246; *246*
Holbein, Hans, 264
Holocaust, 29
holography, 456
Homer, Winslow, 169; *Northeaster,* 167
Hopper, Edward, 55, 131; *Gas,* 94; *97; House by the Railroad,* 55, 56; *56; Nighthawks,* 131; *132; Sunlight on Brownstones,* 432; *432*
Horyu-ji, Nara, Japan, caricature from ceiling of, 58; *58*
Howard, Ebenezer, 87; Garden City, 87, 88
human figures, 42, 246; ancestral couples in sculpture, 331–34; in architecture, 213; couples in modern sculpture, 343–50; distortion and, 175; in erotic and obscene art, 318–22; in fashion illustrations, 249; geometric shapes used to depict, 147, 215, 217; from machine parts, 150, 192, 199, 202; in modern painting, 284–90; nudes, 13, 143, 144, 318–22; in traditional painting, 280–83
humanitarianism in art, 49–51
humor, in art, 58–59, 214, 243, 318; fantasy and, 190, 193, 203–4; in sculpture, 347, 367. See also satirical art
Hundertwasser, Friedrich: *End of Waters on the Roof,* 217; *216*
Hunt, Richard: *Icarus,* 368; *368*
Huston, John: *African Queen, The,* film still from, 464; *464*

# I

Ibsen, Henrik, 25
igloos, 381
Illinois Institute of Technology, Chicago, 110. *See also* Mies van der Rohe, Ludwig
illumination in Baroque art, 220–24. *See also* light and dark
illusionism, in art: fantasy and, 190, 199, 202–4; Surrealism and, 202. *See also* objective accuracy, style of
illustration. *See* commercial art
image, visual elements of, 207
Impressionism (Impressionists), 127–29, 230; color theories of, 127–28, 129, 226–27, 302; forerunner of, 282; Japanese influence on, 129; objective accuracy and, 127–29; perception and, 294; photography and, 447
Incan stone wall, Cuzco, Peru, 385; *384*
Indiana, Robert, 299; *Beware-Danger American Dream #4, The, 302*
Indian village, Taos Pueblo, New Mexico, 94; *94*
industrial and commercial structures, 100–105
industrial design: art and, 72, 73, 106, 109–10; Bauhaus and, 109–10; chairs and, 112–13, 114–15; craft and, 114, 120; emergence of, 109–10; form, function, and 110–12, 117; mass production and, 108–9; modern materials and, 115; physical function of, 72, 73, 106, 108–14; planned obsolescence and, 111–12; psychic distance and, 256; sculpture and, 202–3, 378; styling (redesign) and, 72, 109, 111
industrial engineering, 72
Industrial Revolution, 72, 108, 109
information design, and graphic arts, 66–71
Ingres, Jean-Auguste-Dominique, 275; *Odalisque with a Slave,* 320; *320; Pauline Eléonore de Galard de Brassac de Béarn, Princesse de Broglie,* 276; *276; Venus Anadyomene,* 497, 502; *502*
inner mimicry, 255–56
interior design, 86
International Style, 76, 78–79, 249
Isaacs, Kenneth: Ultimate Living Structure, 75; *75*
Islamic architecture, 409, 411

# J

Jahn, Helmut: model for Donald Trump's "Television City" in Manhattan, 87; *87*
Japanese art, 58, 239–40; influence on Impressionism, 129
Jawlensky, Alexej von, 230; *Self-Portrait,* 288; *288; Still Life with Lamp,* 156, 230; *156*
Jeanneret, Pierre: chaise longue (with Le Corbusier and Perriand), 115; *115*
Jefferson, Thomas, 89
Jeffery, Douglas H.: *John Gielgud as Shakespeare in Edward Bond's Bingo,* 435; *435*
Jenkins, Paul: *Phenomena in Heavenly Way,* 163; *163*
Jerde, John, & Associates: Horton Plaza, San Diego, 388; *389*
Johnson, Philip, 81; American Telephone & Telegraph Company Building, New York City (with Burgee), 249, 423; model, *250;* Garden Grove Community Church, Garden Grove, California, 145; *145;* Glass House, New Canaan, Connecticut, 81; *81;* Museum of Pre-Columbian Art, Dumbarton Oaks, Washington, D.C., 421; *421;* plan of, *421;* Roofless Church, New Harmony, Indiana, 410; *410*
Jōkei: *Shō-Kannon,* 327
joy and celebration: in architecture, 184–85; in art, 12, 181–84
Judd, Donald: *Untitled,* 367; *367*
jug, Kültepe, Anatolia, 119; *119*

# K

Kael, Pauline, 460
Kahlo, Frida: *Two Fridas, The,* 27; *27*
Kahn, Eli J., 102; Municipal Asphalt Plant, New York City, 102, 104; *104*
Kahn, Louis I.: Bryn Mawr College, Bryn Mawr, Pennsylvania, stairwell in residence hall, *428;* Kimbell Art Museum, Fort Worth, *396*
Kandinsky, Wassily, 230, 315; *Landscape with Houses,* 160, 230; *160; Study for Composition No. 2,* 161; *161*
Kane, John, 135; *Self-Portrait,* 135; *135*
Kaplan, Jonathan: *Accused, The,* film still from, 462; *462*
Kaprow, Allan, 304, 306–7, 373; *Orange Happening,* 308; *308*
Kiefer, Anselm, 29; *To the Unknown Painter,* 29; *29*
Kienholz, Edward: *Beanery, The,* 306; *306; State Hospital, The,* 311; *311*
Kiesler, Frederick, 361; *Endless House,* living room interior, 361; *361*
kinetic sculpture, 358, 368–73, 377
Kingman, Dong: *"El" and Snow, The,* 433; *433*
King Mycerinus and his queen, Kha-merer-nebty, from Giza, Egypt, 332; *332*
Kirchkoff's Law, 257, 260
Kirchner, Ludwig: *Portrait of Gräf,* 288; *289*
Klee, Paul, 209, 210; *And I Shall Say,* 210; *211; Daringly Poised,* 243; *243; Flight from Oneself,* 209; *209; Great Dome, The,* 215; *214; Self-Portrait,* 217; *218; Shame,* 480; *480*
Koffka, Kurt, 257
Kohlmeyer, Ida: *Mythic Chair,* 113; *113*
Kokko, Bruce: *Paint Can with Brush,* 374; *374*
Kokoschka, Oskar, 18, 179; *Self-Portrait,* 179, 181, 286; *181, 287; Tempest, The (The Wind's Bride),* 19, 21; *19*
Kollwitz, Käthe, 22, 23; *Death and the Mother,* 22; *22; Nude,* 31; *31; Peasant War Cycle: Sharpening of the Scythe,* 456; *456; Self-Portrait,* 42; *42; War Cycle: The Parents,* 219; *219*
Koons, Jeff: *Ushering in Banality,* 263; *263*
Kricke, Norbert: *Raumplastik Kugel,* 208; *208*

# L

Lachaise, Gaston, 15, 18; *Standing Woman* (1912–27), 15; *18; Standing Woman* (1932), 15–16; *18*
*Lady Nofret, The,* 327
La Fresnaye, Roger de, 21; *Conjugal Life,* 21; *21; Conquest of the Air, The,* 200
Lanceley, Colin: *Inverted Personage,* 40; *40*
landscape painting, 15, 16, 294
Lange, Dorothea, 438
Laroye, Samuel: bicycle mask of the Gelede Secret Society, Yoruba tribe, 43; *43*
lasers, 456
Latin American art, 45–48
La Tour, Georges de, 220; *Saint Mary Magdalen with a Candle,* 220, 221; *221*
Laury, Jean Ray: *Pieced Crazy Quilt,* 37; *37*
Lautrec. *See* Toulouse-Lautrec, Henri de
Law of Prägnanz, 257, 260
Lawrence, Jacob, 54; *Pool Parlor,* 54; *53*
Leaning Tower, Pisa, 240
Lebrun, Rico, 178; *Bound Figure,* 358; *Migration to Nowhere,* 178–79; *180*
Le Corbusier (Charles Edouard Jeanneret-Gris), 81–83, 85, 267, 292, 296, 398; architectural philosophy of, 74, 91; chaise longue (with Jeanneret and Perriand), 115; *115;* Chandigarh, India, city built at, 83; city planning and, 90–91, 93; domestic architecture of, 81–83, 85; High Court Building from, *83;* influence of, 85; Notre-Dame-du-Haut, Ronchamp, France, 83, 212, 213, 417; *213;* interior, *416;* Unité d'Habitation, Marseille, 85; *84;* Villa Savoye, Poissy-sur-Seine, 81–82; *82;* Villa Shodan, Ahmedabad, India, 82–83; interior, *83;* Ville Radieuse, La, 90–91; Voisin Plan for Paris, *91*
Léger, Fernand, 62; *Nudes in the Forest,* 478; *479; Three Women,* 62; *65*
Lehmbruck, Wilhelm, 12, 134, 175; *Seated Youth (the Friend),* 134; *133*
Le Nain, Louis: *Peasants at Supper,* 15; *15*
Leonardo da Vinci, 59, 73, 220, 271; *Caricature of an Ugly Old Woman,* 59; *58; Drawing for an automated spool-winding machine,* 73; *73; Last Supper, The,* 270, 272; *272; Portrait of a Musi-*

*cian*, 280; *280;* sculptural-mechanical devices of, 368, 373; *Studio del Corpo Humano*, 144, 248; *144*

Levine, Jack, 61, 175; *Art Lover, The*, 470; *470; Feast of Pure Reason, The*, 61; *59; Welcome Home*, 175, 176; *176*

Lewis, Jerry, 264

Lichtenstein, Roy, 64; *Ceramic Sculpture I*, 107; *107; Girl at Piano*, 262; *262; Little Big Painting*, 305; *305*

*Life* magazine, 438

light and dark, as visual elements in art, 217–26; in architecture, 220; *chiaroscuro* and, 220; contrast and, 217–20; creation of form through, 218–20; emotional response to, 220; illumination in Baroque art and, 220–24; modeling with, 220, 224; in modern art, 224–26; mystical aspect of, 195; objective accuracy and, 137; symbolic aspects of, 217, 220

Lincoln Center for the Performing Arts, New York City, 100; *100*

Lindner, Richard: *Hello*, 142; *142*

line, as visual element in art, 207–10; contour drawings and, 208; energy of, 209; expressive quality of, 210; magical-symbolic properties of, 208; mystical aspect of, 195; psychological use of, 209, 210; relationship to shape, 211; in sculpture, 210

Lippold, Richard, 239; *Variation Number 7: Full Moon*, 239; *239*

Lipps, Theodor, 255, 260, 309

Lipton, Seymour, 496; *Cerberus*, 496; *498; Storm Bird*, 335; *335*

Loewy, Raymond, 113

*Look* magazine, 438

Lordi, Tony: *Lucky Star/The Empire State Building*, 100; *100*

Lorentz, Pare, 438, 463

Los Angeles Fine Arts Squad: *Isle of California*, 56; *56*

Louis, Morris: *Kaf*, 163; *163*

love, in art, 15, 17, 18–21, 27, 28, 184, 193

Low, David, 45, 59; *Rendezvous*, 59; *59; Very Well, Alone*, 45

Lucas, Roger: three-finger ring, 374; *374*

Lucchesi, Bruno: *Seated Woman #2*, 368

Lundy, Victor: St. Paul's Lutheran Church, Sarasota, Florida, 151; *151*

Lustig, Alvin, 62; cover design for *Fortune* magazine, 66; *66*

Lytle, Richard, 276; *Possessed, The*, 277

# M

Macdonald-Wright, Stanton, 159; *Abstraction on Spectrum (Organization, 5)*, 158; *158*

McGowen, Charles: photograph of raindrop reflections in a screen door, 301; *301*

machinery: in film, 455; in painting, 135, 136, 137, 150, 369–71; in sculpture, 147, 150, 192, 202–3, 369–71

MacIver, Loren: *Hopscotch*, 196; *196*

McKeeby, Byron, *259*

magic realism, 137

Maillol, Aristide, 337

male portrait head, from Ife, Nigeria, 260; *260*

Malevich, Kasimir, 217, 315; *Suprematist Composition: Airplane Flying*, 259; *259; Suprematist Composition: White on White*, 217–18; *218; Suprematist Painting: Eight Red Rectangles*, 245

Mallary, Robert, 353; *Juggler, The*, 353, 355; *355*

Manet, Édouard, 224, 226, 282; *Dead Christ with Angels, The*, 138; *138; Luncheon in the Studio, The*, 282; *282; Olympia*, 224, 241; *225*

Mannerism, 220, 334

man-size mannequin, from advertisement for Ford Motor Company, *372*

Mantegna, Andrea: *Lamentation, The*, 138; *138*

Manzù, Giacomo, 132; *Girl in Chair*, 132, 134, 138; *133*

Maoist poster, 45; *45*

Maori prow ornament, New Zealand, 337; *337*

Margoulies, Berta, 49; *Mine Disaster*, 49; *49*

Marin, John, 183, 246; *Maine Islands*, 183–84; *182*

Marisol (Escobar), 204; *Bicycle Race, The*, 348; *348; Family, The*, 52; *52; Generals, The*, 203–4; *204*

Markelius, Sven: *Vällingby, Sweden*, 93; *93*

marriage, in art, 15, 18, 20, 21

Marx brothers, 358

Masjid-i-Shah, Isfahan, Iran, 413; view into outer portal, *411*

mask, from Ivory Coast, Africa, 66; *67*

Masombuka, Selina: mural in her house in Pieterskraal, South Africa, 297; *297*

mass production, 107, 108–10. *See also* industrial design

Master Gislebertus: *Last Judgment, The*, 187; *187*

materials: of architecture, 380–86, 390–98, 414; craftsmanship and, 506, 508–10; debris as artistic, 299; meaning created by different, 13, 15, 267–68; of painting, 267, 292–93; in Pop art, 304; in sculpture, 323–31, 340. *See also* techniques

mathematics, 143, 144, 145, 147, 148–49, 162

Mathieu, Georges, 272; *Mort d'Attila, La*, 272; *273*

Matisse, Henri, 153, 300, 309; *Carmelina*, 240; *240; Green Stripe (Madame Matisse)*, 288; *288; Lady in Blue*, 153, 155; *154; Serpentine*, 336; *336*

Matta (Echaurren), 199; *Disasters of Mysticism*, 196, 208; *196; Here, Sir Fire, Eat!*, 208; *201*

Mattson, Henry E., 169; *Wings of the Morning*, 169; *167*

Maurer, Ingo: Giant bulb, 235; *235*

mechanical engineering, 72; forms of, in art, 147–49

mechanization, 148

medium, in art, 267–68

megastructures, 105, 414, 420

Mendelsohn, Eric: Einstein Tower, Potsdam, Germany, 426; *426;* drawing for, *426*

menhir statues, 381

Mesopotamian architecture, 381, 386, 403

Metzinger, Jean: *Tea Time, 485*

Michals, Duane: *Intersecting Corridors*, 436; *436*

Michelangelo Buonarroti, 73, 137, 271, 446, 505; architecture of, 381, 408; *Crepuscolo (Evening)*, 326; *326; Drawing for the Fortification of Florence*, 73; *73;* drawings of, 73, 137, 274; *Isaiah*, 270; *270; Last Judgment, The*, 175; *175; Libyan Sibyl, The*, 274; *274;* studies for, *274; Pietà*, 483; *483; Prophet Joel, The*, 280; *280; Rebellious Slave, The*, 356; *357;* St. Peter's, Rome, dome of (completed by della Porta), 381, 408; *409;* sculpture of, 326, 328, 337; Sistine Chapel frescoes, 175, 269, 270, 274, 280

Micronesian stool for grating coconuts, Mariana Islands, 119; *119*

Mies van der Rohe, Ludwig, 76, 78–81, 85, 149, 296, 361; "Barcelona" Chair, 112–13; *114;* Crown Hall, Illinois Institute of Technology, Chicago, 79, 103; *80;* Farnsworth House, Plano, Illinois, 79; *80;* floor plan of, *80;* Model for Project: Glass Skyscraper, 395; *395;* Seagram Building, New York City, 476–77; Tugendhat House, Brno, Czechoslovakia, 79; living room, *80*

Milonadis, Konstantin: *Flower Garden*, *370*

Minguzzi, Luciano: *Woman Jumping Rope*, 368

Minimal art, 314–16, 322

Miró, Joan, 66, 115, 318, 369; *Man and Woman*, 347; *347; Maternity*, 243; *243; Nursery Painting*, 66; *70; Object*, 311; *311; Persons Haunted by a Bird*, 318; *318*

mirror fetish, Lower Congo, Africa, 312; *312*

Miss, Mary: *Field Rotation*, 376; *376*

Mission of St. Francis of Assisi, Taos, New Mexico, *385*

mobiles, 40, 42, 235, 369

modeling: in painting, 219–20, 224; in sculpture, 323, 324, 326, 328, 330

modernism, 262

Modersohn-Becker, Paula: *Self-Portrait*, 237; *237*

Modigliani, Amedeo, 18, 66, 175, 322; *Anna de Zborowska*, 66, 67; *67; Reclining Nude*, 18; *18*

Moeschal, Jacques: sculpture for Mexico City's Route of Friendship, *96*

Moholy-Nagy, László, 110, 378; *Light-Space Modulator*, 378; *378;* photograms, 442; *Untitled (Abstraction) Photogram*, 443; *443*

Mondrian, Piet, 55, 144, 149, 256, 315, 476; *Broadway Boogie Woogie,* 55, 57, 361; *57; Composition with Red, Yellow, and Blue,* 146; *146; Painting, I,* 480; *480*

Monet, Claude, 127, 153; *Cathedral in Fog,* 127–28; *128; Cathedral in Sunshine,* 127–28; *128; Water Lilies,* 294; *295*

Monier, Jacques, 396

Moore, Charles: Piazza d'Italia, New Orleans (with Hersey), 100, 423; *101*

Moore, George, 272

Moore, Henry, 35, 246, 338, 366, 446, 505; *Falling Warrior,* 166; *166; Family Group,* 150–51; *150; King and Queen,* 346; *346; Reclining Figure,* 35; *35; Reclining Mother and Child,* 338; *338; Two Forms,* 325; *325*

Moorman, Charlotte, photograph of, *465*

Morandi, Riccardo: Parco del Valentino Exhibition Hall, Turin, 426, 427; *426*

Moroccan picnic hut, Africa, 382; *382*

Morris, Robert: *Earthwork,* 377; *377*

Morris, William, 72, 109

Mosque of Ahmed I (Blue Mosque), Istanbul, detail of, *411*

*Mother and Child,* by Mangbetu sculptor, northeastern Zaire, *477*

Motherwell, Robert: *Elegy to the Spanish Republic, No. XXXIV,* 173; *173*

motion pictures, 456, 458. *See also* film; television

Mourgue, Olivier: chairs, 115; *115*

movable type, invention of, 108

Mu Ch'i: *Six Persimmons,* 244; *244*

multiple dwellings, 85. *See also* apartment houses

Munari, Bruno: *Campari, 63*

Munch, Edvard, 12, 23, 25, 28, 175; *Dance of Life, The,* 242; *242; Dead Mother, The,* 23, 25, 463; *23, 463; Death in the Sickroom,* 255; *255; Puberty,* 25, 27, 286; *25, 286; Scream, The,* 45, 176; *177*

Münstermann, Ludwig: *Adam and Eve,* 334; *334*

*Murder on a Bad Trip* (Drummond), advertisement for, 71; *71*

"museum fatigue," 252

music and art, 42, 55, 230, 371

mystical transcendence through painting, 195–98

myths: fantasy in art and, 188–89, 190, 192; folktales and, 188; Greek, 307; metamorphoses and, 190, 192; symbolism of light and, 217, 220

## N

*Nachi Waterfall,* 239–40; *240*

Nagare, Masayuki: Japan Pavilion, New York World's Fair (1964), wall of, *384*

nail fetish, Lower Congo, Africa, 231; *231*

Naramore, Bain, Brady & Johanson: IBM Building, Seattle (with Yamasaki & Associates), 423; *423*

Nash, John: Royal Pavilion, Brighton, England, *409*

Neel, Alice: *Andy Warhol,* 171; *171*

Nele, Eve Renée: *Couple, The,* 350; *350*

Nelson, George, 113

Neolithic era, 108

Nervi, Pier Luigi, 267, 393, 420; Burgo Paper Mill, Mantua, Italy, *392;* Little Sports Palace, Rome, *424;* Palazzo del Lavoro Exhibition Hall, Turin, Italy, 427; *424*

Nessim, Barbara: Computer art for *Ms.* magazine, 64; *64*

Neumann, Alfred: apartment house, Ramat Gan, Israel (with Hecker), 94; *94*

Nevelson, Louise, 362, 363; *Totality Dark,* 362, 363; *363*

new brutalism, 423–24

Newhall, Beaumont, 447

Newman, Barnett, 265; *Adam,* 197; *197*

*New Yorker* magazine, 466

niches, 360, 361–62

Nicholson, Ben: *Painted Relief, 241*

Nietzsche, Friedrich, 143

Noguchi, Isamu: *Big Boy,* 370; *370; Floor Frame,* 367; *367*

Nolde, Emil, 226; *Prophet, The,* 226; *226*

Nowicki, Matthew, 105; J.S. Dorton State Fair Arena, Raleigh, North Carolina (with Deitrick), 102; *104*

nudes, in art, 13, 143, 144, 318–22, 328

## O

objective accuracy, style of, 123–42, 476; color and, 138, 140; concealment of technique and, 127; detached observation and, 127–29; devices of, 137–39; Expressionist aspect of, 126–27; imitation of appearances and, 123–27; Impressionism and, 127–29; magic realism and, 137; narrative aspect of, 124, 126–27; perspective and, 138–39, 140; popularity of, 123, 124; psychological aspect of, 124; selective eye of artists and, 129, 131–34; variations of the style of, 134–37

oil painting, 269, 270, 272, 275, 278

Oldenburg, Claes: *Lipstick Ascending on Caterpillar Tracks,* 120; *120; Soft Pay-Telephone,* 352; *352; Stove, The,* 355, 445; *355, 445; Two Cheeseburgers, with Everything (Dual Hamburgers),* 508; *508*

Old Ship Meetinghouse, Hingham, Massachusetts, roof truss of, *402*

Olitski, Jules: *Magic Number,* 157; *157*

Op art, 71, 307, 309

Oppenheim, Dennis: *Annual Rings,* 376; *376*

Oppenheim, Meret: *Object,* 107, 190; *107, 190*

optics, 137, 139, 207, 307

Ordoñez, Joaquin Alvares, 185; Manan-tiales Restaurant, Xochimilco, Mexico (with Candela), 184–85; *185*

organic shapes, 110, 113, 149–51, 153, 217; in architecture, 184–85, 212–13, 396, 398, 405

Orozco, José Clemente, 45; *Gods of the Modern World,* 45–47; *46*

Orwell, George, 372

Oseberg ship-burial, animal head from, 337; *337*

Our Lady of Orchard Lake, Oakland, Michigan, interior, 390; *390*

over-distancing, 256, 258, 259

## P

Paik, Nam June: *TV Bra for Living Sculpture,* 465; *465*

painting, 269–322; acrylic, 269; action painting, 294, 304; as architectural accent, 296, 297; assemblage and, 297–99, 302, 307, 310–11; collage and, 298, 302, 304, 307, 310–11, 322; Color Field, 314–15, 316; "combine," 302, 304; decalcomania and, 291, 292; direct technique and, 274, 275–76, 278, 279; durability of, 270–74; éclaboussage, 292; as elaboration of drawing, 274–75; emotive brushwork and, 275–76, 278, 283, 294; encaustic, 275; Environments and, 304, 306, 307; erotic and obscene, 15, 18, 183, 192–93, 318–22; flexibility of, 269; formalism and, 476–77, 478; fresco, 269, 270, 274, 275, 299; frottage and, 291, 292; gesso and, 275; glazing technique and, 269, 271, 275; grattage and, 291–92; guild system and, 271; Happenings and, 304, 306–7, 322; hard-edge/geometric, 278; human image in modern, 284–90; human image in traditional, 280–83; indirect technique and, 274–75, 278; large-scale, 269, 294, 296, 299, 316; materials and tools of, 267, 292–93; media/meaning relationships and, 267–68; Minimal, 314–16, 322; mystical transcendence through, 195–98; objectivity and, 430; oil, 269, 270, 272, 275, 278; originality of style and, 272, 274, 278, 297; photography and, 259, 274, 298, 430–33, 441–42, 454; popularity of, 269–70, 274; psychological expressions through, 430; as public statement, 297; relationship to film and television, 455; shaped canvases and, 316, 317–18; technology and, 293; tempera, 126, 269, 272, 275; texture and, 232, 310; underpainting, 271, 275, 276; Venetian, 275, 278; as walls, 294–97; as windows, 317. *See also* techniques

Paleolithic cave painting, 22, 124, 317

Pantheon, Rome, 408; *408*

Paolozzi, Eduardo: *Medea,* 41; *41; Saint Sebastian No. 2,* 231; *231*

Parthenon, Athens, 385

Paschke, Ed: *Caliente,* 53; *53*

Pascin, Jules, 322
Pasmore, Victor: *Linear Development No. 6: Spiral*, 208; *208*
Paulin, Pierre: undulating furniture, 86; *86*
Paxton, Joseph, 393; Crystal Palace, London, 393; *394*
Pearlstein, Philip: *Two Seated Models*, 140; *141*
Pedersen, B. Martin: dust jacket for *Typography 5*, 68; *68*
Pedersen, G.: ice bucket with lid (designed by Stephensen), 118; *118*
Pei, I.M.: Everson Museum of Art, Syracuse, 419; interior, *419*
pendentives, 408–9
Pepper, Stephen, 260–61
perception. *See* visual perception
perceptive series, 260
perceptual grasp, 260
Perriand, Charlotte: chaise longue (with Le Corbusier and Jeanneret), 115; *115*
Persian art, 153
personal functions of art, 11, 12–42; aesthetic expression and, 36–42; death and morbidity as, 12, 22–29; illness as, 27–29; love, sex, marriage and, 15–21, 27, 28, 193; psychological expression and, 12–15; spiritual concern and, 29, 31–36
perspective, 174, 253; objective accuracy and, 138–39; Renaissance, 441, 455–56, 457
Peruvian art, 207, 329, 368, 385
Peterdi, Gabor: *Black Horne, The, 354*
Pevsner, Antoine, 340, 341, 368, 377; *Developable Column*, 341, 342; *342; Torso*, 340, 342; *342*
*Pharaoh Khafre*, 338; *339*
photography, 429–54; abstraction and, 442–44; accuracy of, 430, 462; aesthetics of, 442, 444; amateur, 433, 436–37; the camera and, 430, 433, 437, 438; credibility of, 430–31, 432, 438, 440, 442; criticism of, 447–54; cropping and, 442; distortion and, 175, 432; *175;* economic factors of, 447; as educational tool, 429, 430, 447; film and, 437, 440, 444, 447; as fine art, 429, 431, 435, 436, 440, 442, 444–45, 447–54; as folk art, 431–32, 437; formalist aesthetics and, 442; graphic reproduction and, 429, 440; humanitarian concern and, 49, 51; influence of, 128, 129, 135, 139, 248, 447; invention of, and art, 123, 431–33; light and dark and, 220, 451; objectivity of, 430; optical to tactile, 259, 447, 450, 451; painting and, 274, 298, 430–33, 441–42, 454; part to whole, 448, 452–53; pattern to idea, 448, 451–52; as photojournalism, 126, 431, 438–41, 453; pornography and, 440; principle of the frame and, 441–42; prints and, 444–45; psychic distance and, 256; qualities of excellence in, 447–54; reality and, 123, 429, 430–31, 435, 437–38, 440, 476; record to original, 448, 454; relationship to film and television, 430, 438, 440, 444, 447;

significance of, 429–30, 431–32, 433, 436–37; singular to typical, 432, 453–54; slides and, 444–45; social and cultural side effects of, 431, 433, 436–37, 438, 440; stop-action image and, 437–38; "straight," 49; surface to depth, 448–49, 451
photojournalism, 124, 431, 438–41, 453
Photorealism, 220, 301, 432, 438, 509–10
physical functions of art, 11, 72–120; city planning, 86–105; crafts and industrial design, 106–14; domestic architecture, 74–86
Piazza San Marco, Venice, 100, 386; *100, 386*
Picasso, Pablo, 25, 27, 37, 42, 153, 284, 495; African sculpture and, 490, 491, 494, 497; artistic style of, 143; *Baboon and Young*, 193; *193; Bull's Head, 354;* collages of, 66, 304; Cubism and, 139, 146–47; *Dancer*, 494; *494; Demoiselles d'Avignon, Les*, 488, 490–93, 494, 496–97, 499–503, 507; *475, 492–93, 499, 507; Diaghilev and Selisburg,* 208; *208;* drawings of, 137, 208; *Frugal Repast, The*, 28; *28; Girl Before a Mirror*, 24, 25, 27; *24; Guernica*, 51, 176, 193, 208, 211, 461; *51, 461; Head of a Woman*, 503; *503;* influence of, 62, 66; *Minotauromachy*, 192–93; *193; Night Fishing at Antibes*, 174; *174; Ornamental Design: Pierrot and Harlequin*, 64; *64;* portrait of (Gris), 284; *285; Portrait of Ambroise Vollard*, 284; *284;* sculpture of, 193, 353, 354; *Suze, La*, 66; *66; Woman Weeping*, 481; *481*
Pickering, H. Douglas: *Pomegranate*, 217; *217*
picnic hut, Morocco, 382; *382*
Piene, Otto: *Carousel*, 496; *Manned Helium Sculpture*, stage of, *375*
Piero della Francesca: *Resurrection of Christ, The*, 238; *238*
Pintori, Giovanni: poster for Olivetti 82 Diaspron, 69; *69*
planned obsolescence, 111–12. *See also* styling
plastics, in architecture, 386, 414
Platonic approach to art, 145, 147
plazas, malls, civic centers, 94, 96, 98–100
political and ideological expressions, in art, 45–51
Pollack, Peter, 447
Pollock, Jackson, 35–36, 263, 267, 292; *Number I, 1948*, 36; *36; Untitled*, 475; *475*
Polyclitus: *Doryphorus (Spear Bearer)*, 144; *144*
Polydorus of Rhodes: *Laocoön* (with Agesander and Athenodorus), 335, 336; *336*
Pomodoro, Arnaldo: *Large Sphere*, 378; *379*
Pont du Gard, Nîmes, France, 404
Pop art, 61, 62, 235, 290, 299–304, 305, 307, 322, 508; sculpture and, 327, 355
Porta, Giacomo della, 409
Portman, John, and Associates: Plaza

Hotel, Renaissance Center, Detroit, 388; interior, *388*
portrait jar, Chicana Valley, Peru, 329; *329*
portraits, 13–15, 236, 431; modern, 284–85, 288–90; traditional, 280–83
post-and-lintel construction, 399–400, 402, 403, 406
poster art, 45, 62, 63, 66, 67, 69, 70, 234, 309
Post-Impressionism, 230, 322
Post-Modern architecture, 417, 421, 423
poured concrete, 81–83, 184–85
Poussin, Nicolas, 476; *Landscape with the Burial of Phocion*, 478; *478*
Prägnanz, Law of, 257, 260
Pratt & Whitney RL10 rocket engine, from advertisement for United Aircraft Corporation, 378; *378*
prefabricated stack houses, Israel, 390; *390*
Pregulman, John: *Rebecca Kelly Dance Company, The*, 438; *438*
Price, Vincent, 358
priest or dignitary, from Tabasco, Mexico, 266; *266*
primitive (naïve) art, 135, 193, 306
Prip, John: silver teapot, 110; *110*
proportion, as design principle, 143, 144, 248–49, 366
psychic distance, 254, 256, 258–59
psychological expressions, in art, 12–15, 45, 49, 58–59, 124, 430
Puccini, Giacomo, 28
pyramids, Egypt, 385

**R**

Ramos, Mel: *Chiquita Banana*, 62; *62*
Rand, Paul: poster for Advertising Typographers' Association of America, 69; *69*
Raphael: *Three Graces, The*, 496, 500; *500*
Rauschenberg, Robert, 301–2, 304; *Canyon*, 302; *303; Odalisk*, 311; *311*
Ray, Man, 442
Raymond, Lilo: *Bed in Attic*, 450; *450*
realism, 123, 126. *See also* illusionism; objective accuracy, style of
*Realist Manifesto*, 368
Reed, Torres, Beauchamp, Marvel: Chase Manhattan Bank, San Juan, Puerto Rico, 421; *421*
Reichek, Jesse, 309
reinforced concrete (ferroconcrete), 390, 393, 395, 396–98, 399, 400, 405, 413, 414, 427, 428
Reinhardt, Ad, 315; *Abstract Painting*, 315; *315*
religious art, 29, 31, 145–46, 151, 323, 324, 329, 331–32
Rembrandt van Rijn, 222, 454; *Anatomy Lesson of Dr. Tulp*, 129, 441; *130; Christ Healing the Sick (The Hundred Guilder Print)*, 238; *238; Head of Christ,*

280; *280; Man with a Magnifying Glass*, 222, 224; *222, 223*

Renaissance art, 73, 317, 441; architecture, 72, 73, 390, 403; *chiaroscuro* and, 220; guild system and, 271; perspective and, 441, 455–56, 457; sculpture, 337, 360

revolutionary art, 45–48, 484, 485–86

rhythm, as design principle, 244–48, 249; alternating, 244, 248; flowing, 244, 246, 248; Gestalt laws and, 257; progressive, 244, 245, 246, 248; repetitive, 244–46, 248

Richier, Germaine, 13; *Bat, The*, 166; *165; Feuille, La (The Leaf)*, 13, 14; *14*

Riemerschmid, Richard, 106; table flatware, 106; *106*

Riley, Bridget: *Blaze I, 309*

Riopelle, Jean-Paul: *Vesperal No. 3*, 162; *162*

Rivera, Diego, 45, 47, 486; *Billionaires, The*, 47, 48; *48; Night of the Poor*, 47, 48; *48; Night of the Rich*, 484; *484; Two Women*, 484; *484*

Rivera, José de, 38; *Construction "Blue and Black,"* 38, 40; *40*

Rivers, Larry, 290; *Celebrating Shakespeare's 400th Birthday (Titus Andronicus)*, 290, 321, 322; *290, 321*

Robbia, Luca della: *Madonna and Angels*, 326; *326*

Rockefeller, David: office of, Chase Manhattan Bank, New York City, 296; *296*

Rockefeller Center, New York City, 99–100, 387; *99, 387*

Rockwell, Norman: *Connoisseur, The*, 263; *263; Doctor and Doll*, 262; *262*

Rodia, Simon: Watts Towers, Los Angeles, 312; *313*

Rodin, Auguste, 15, 137, 144, 328, 330, 366; *Balzac*, 330, 446; *330; Burghers of Calais, The*, 44, 137, 325; *44, 137, 325; Kiss, The*, 15, 17; *17; St. John the Baptist Preaching*, 144; *145*

Roebling, John A., 393

Roman art, 94; architecture, 249, 385, 390, 396

Romanesque art: architecture, 385, 405, 406; sculpture, 337, 360, 483

Romanticism, 27, 282, 283; style of emotion and, 166–71

Rosenquist, James, 301

Rosso, Medardo, 330; *Bookmaker, The*, 330; *330*

Roszak, Theodore J., 170; *Sea Sentinel*, 212; *212; Spectre of Kitty Hawk*, 170–71, 210; *168*

Rothko, Mark, 230–31, 296, 309; *Earth and Green*, 198, 230; *198*

Rouault, Georges, 29; *Miserere: Dura Lex sed Lex*, 226; *226; Three Clowns*, 29, 34–35; *33; Tragedian, The*, 286; *286*

Rousseau, Henri, 193; *Dream, The*, 193, 195, 229; *194*

Royal Typewriter Company, advertisement for, 192; *192*

Rubens, Peter Paul, 275, 276; *Judgment of Paris, The*, 496, 501; *501; Lion Hunt*, 276; *277; Self-Portrait*, 281; *281*

Rudolph, Paul, 83; Art and Architecture Building, Yale University, New Haven, 83; *84;* Project for Graphic Arts Center, New York City, 420; *420;* Southeastern Massachusetts Technological Institute, North Dartmouth, interior, *428*

Ruskin, John, 109

Ryder, Albert Pinkham, 22, 23; *Death on a Pale Horse (The Race Track)*, 22–23; *22*

# S

Saarinen, Eero, 105, 246, 393; Dulles Airport, Chantilly, Virginia, 392; Kresge Auditorium, Massachusetts Institute of Technology, Cambridge, 405; *405;* TWA Terminal, Kennedy International Airport, New York, 105, 405, 417; *104, 418*

Safdie, David, Barott, and Boulva: Habitat, EXPO 67, Montreal, 105, 417; *105, 417*

St.-Etienne, Caen, France, nave of, *406*

St. Mark's, Venice, 414

Saint-Phalle, Niki de, 292; photograph of, *292*

St.-Savin-sur-Gartempe, Poitou, France, nave of, *406*

Salomon, Erich, 441; *Visit of German Statesmen to Rome*, 441; *441*

Samaras, Lucas, 361; *Room*, 361–62; *361*

sarcophagus, Cerveteri, Italy, 333; *333*

Saret, Alan: *Untitled*, 377; *377*

satirical art, 47, 58–61, 175, 176, 320, 348, 504

Saura, Antonio, 290; *Imaginary Portrait of Goya*, 290; *290*

Scharf, Aaron, 447

Scharf, Kenny: *Extravaganza Televisione*, 365; *365*

Schipporeit-Heinrich, Inc.: Lake Point Tower, Chicago, 395; *395*

Schlemmer, Oskar: *Abstract Figure*, 150; *150*

Schmalenbach, Werner, 365

Schmidt, Clarence, 306; photograph of, *308*

Schoeler Heaton Harvor Menendez: Charlebois High School, Ottawa, Canada, 417; interior, *417*

Schwitters, Kurt, 298, 304, 306, 307; *Cathedral of Erotic Misery*, 304; *Cherry Picture*, 310; *310; Merzbau, 306;* Merzbau constructions, 304, 306, 307, 361

science and technology, in fantasy art, 188, 199

Scully, Vincent, 488–90

sculpture, 323–79; ABC art and, 366; African, 22, 43, 67, 231, 260, 312, 444; ancestral couples in, 331–34; appeal of, 260; architecture and, 361, 362, 366; architecture as, 212, 297, 393, 398, 417, 420–21, 423–24, 426, 428; assemblage as, 298, 328, 351–57, 361; barbarian, 337; boxes, 360, 361–65; bronze, 324, 325, 326, 327, 328, 336, 341; carving and, 323, 324, 326, 328, 335; casting and, 108, 323, 324, 325, 326, 327, 328, 335, 336; ceramic (clay), 324, 326, 328, 335, 374; collage as, 328; constructed, 323, 328; Constructivism and, 340–42, 366, 368; couples in modern, 343–50; and crafts, 374–75; cross-cultural factors and, 265, 266; durability and, 327, 335, 337; earthworks, 375–77; emotion and, 166, 170–71, 176; Environments as, 307; erotic, 332, 349; fantasy and, 187, 192, 202–4; formal order and, 147, 149–51, 155; grottoes, 361–62; Happenings as, 372, 373; humor in, 347; industrial design and, 203, 378; kinetic, 358, 368–73, 377; limitations of, 269; line and, 210; magical associations of, 323, 324, 353, 365, 377; marble, 324, 325, 326, 336; media/meaning relationships and, 267–68; metal, 324, 328, 340, 341; Minimal, 316; mixed media and, 312; mobiles, 40, 42, 235, 369; modeling and, 323, 324, 326, 328, 330; monolithic, 335, 337–39, 340, 362; monumental, 326, 366–67; motion simulated in static, 368; naturalistic, 325; niches, 360, 361–62; nomadic, 337; objective accuracy and, 137, 138; open-form, 335, 337; plastics, 324, 327, 340, 341; as primary structure, 366–67; religious ritual and, 323, 324, 329, 331–32; rhythm and, 246; satire in, 348; serial, 366, 367; shape and, 212; social functions of, 49; stone, 323–24, 326–27, 328; store-window mannequins as, 327; systems, 366, 367; techniques of, 323–31; technology and, 324, 326, 330–31, 335, 340, 351, 378; terra-cotta, 326; texture and, 231, 232, 366; unity in design and, 239; wax, 328, 330; welded and riveted, 210, 324–25, 335; wood, 324, 326, 328

Secunda, Arthur: *Music Machine*, 371; *371*

Segal, George, 15, 307; *Dinner Table, The*, 15; *15; Execution, The*, 52; *52; Lovers on a Bed II*, 349; *349*

Seley, Jason, 202–3, 204; *Masculine Presence*, 202–3, 351; *203*

self-portraits, 135, 179, 258, 259, 281, 287–90

Seurat, Georges, 153; *Sunday Afternoon on the Island of La Grande Jatte, A*, 261, 495; *261, 497*

Severini, Gino, 246; *Dynamic Hieroglyphic of the Bal Tabarin*, 246, 248; *247*

sexual art, 15–16, 18, 21, 215, 224. *See also* erotic and obscene art

Seymour, David, 441; Photograph of Bernard Berenson at the Borghese Gallery in Rome, *486*

Shahn, Ben: *Handball*, 134–35; *134; Liberation*, 179, 453; *180; Passion of Sacco and Vanzetti, The*, 25, 28; *23*

shape, as visual element in art, 207, 211–17; biomorphic, 215; comic purpose of, 214; expressive meaning of, 211–12; functions of, 213; geometric, 135, 148–49, 162, 215, 217, 284; linear quality of, 211; organic, 110, 113, 149–51, 153, 212–13, 217; sculpture and, 212; symbolic aspect of, 174, 211, 214–15, 217; volumetric quality of, 214

shaped canvases, 316, 317–18

Sheeler, Charles, 127, 135; *City Interior,* 127; *127; Upper Deck,* 135, 136, 137; *136*

shell structures, 413–14

Sherman, Cindy: *Untitled,* 430; *431*

shopping malls, 75, 94, 96, 98, 99–100

silhouettes, 219

single-family dwellings, 91–93. *See also* city planning; domestic architecture

Siqueiros, David Alfaro, 45; *Echo of a Scream,* 45; *46; Landscape,* 254; *254; New Democracy,* 485; *485; Self-Portrait,* 259; *258*

Siskind, Aaron: *Lima 89 (Homage to Franz Kline),* 448; *448*

Skidmore, Owings and Merrill: Alcoa Building, San Francisco, 424; *424; Beinecke Rare Book and Manuscript Library, Yale University, New Haven, 488–90; *489; Lever House, New York City, 102; *103*

Skoglund, Sandy, 430; *Radioactive Cats,* 430; *431*

skyscrapers, 387, 394, 395, 420

Sloan, John: *Connoisseurs of Prints,* 504; *504*

Smith, David, 210; *Royal Bird,* 210; *210*

Smith, Tony: *Cigarette,* 367; *367*

Smith, Vernon L.: *Looking at John Chamberlain's Essex (1960) at the Guggenheim Museum,* 468

Smith & Williams: Congregational Church, California City, 383; plywood supports, *383*

Smithson, Robert, 293; *Nonsite,* 377; *377 Snake Goddess,* 378; *378*

social functions of art, 11, 43–71; description of life as, 51–55; graphic communication as, 62–66; humanitarian, 49–51; information design and, 66–71; photography and, 431, 437, 438, 440; political and ideological, 45–51; public monuments as, 44; satire as, 58–61; social protest as, 49, 51

Soutine, Chaim, 27, 28, 164; *Carcass of Beef,* 166; *165; Madwoman, The,* 27, 127, 140, 271; *26, 141, 271*

Soyer, Isaac, 49; *Employment Agency,* 49; *49*

spandrels, 403

Spanish Civil War, 51, 193

Spencer, Stanley, 29; *Christ Preaching at Cookham Regatta: Series No. VI: Four Girls Listening,* 29; *33; Self-Portrait,* 135; *135*

Speyer Cathedral, Germany, 405; crypt, *405*

spiral minaret, Samarra, Iraq, *385*

spiritual art, 29, 31, 34–36, 145, 195–98, 221, 265, 266

spontaneous liking and disliking, 261–64

squinches, 408, 411, 413

Stamford Town Center Mall, Connecticut, 98; *98*

Stankiewicz, Richard, 192, 267; *Europa on a Cycle,* 353; *354; Secretary,* 192; *192*

State Capitol, Lincoln, Nebraska, 249; buttress of, *250*

steel, in architecture, 145, 380, 386, 390, 393, 394–95, 398, 399, 400, 402, 405, 414

Steele-Perkins, Chris: photograph of poster of José Napoleón Duarte, President of Salvador, 178; *178*

Steichen, Edward, 447

Steinbeck, John, 463

Steinberg, Saul: *Diploma,* 209; *209*

Stella, Frank, 318; *Pergusa,* 317; *317; Sinjerli Variation I,* 159; *159*

Stephensen, Magnus: ice bucket with lid (executed by Pedersen), 118; *118*

Stieglitz, Alfred, 49; 447; *Steerage, The,* 49, 51; *50*

Stirling, James: Engineering Building, Leicester University, England (with Gowan), 419; interior, *418*

stone, in architecture, 380, 381–82, 383, 384–85, 386, 390, 402

Stone, Edward Durell, 423; Beckman Auditorium, California Institute of Technology, Pasadena, 423; *423*

Stonehenge, Salisbury Plain, Wiltshire, England, detail of, *381*

Stradivari, Antonio: violin, 106; *106*

Strand, Paul: *Family, The,* 440; *440; Ranchos de Taos, New Mexico,* 450; *450*

structure of art, 205–50; design principles and, 234–50; visual elements and, 207–33

style: artists' choice of, 144, 145, 186, 188, 262, 317–18; artistic meaning of, 121; changes of, 122; defined, 121; of emotion, 164–85; fantasy and, 186–204; of formal order, 143–63; of objective accuracy, 123–42, 476; psychic distance and, 256; social change and, 122

styling (redesign), and industrial design, 72, 109, 111

suburbs, 85, 87, 90

Sullivan, Louis, 110; Carson Pirie Scott Department Store, Chicago, 391; *391*

Sumerian architecture, 385

Surrealism, 48, 49, 55, 107, 230–31, 307; in architecture, 213; Dada and, 291; dreams and hallucinations and, 190, 318; fantasy and, 190, 193, 199, 202, 291; forerunners of, 137; humor and, 193; illusionism and, 202–3; influence on graphic design, 66; perspective and, 139; sculpture and, 328, 353; symbolism and, 243, 318; theory of, 190

Swiss National Exposition, Lausanne, umbrellas over trade section at, 413; *413*

Symbolism, 230

symbolism (symbols), 72, 148, 192, 217, 234, 241, 243, 318; in architecture, 420–21, 423; color and, 174, 229–30; Egyptian art and, 117; emotion generated by, 172–74, 176; of light and dark, 217, 220; of line, 208

Synchromy, 158

Szarkowski, John, 447

# T

Takis: *Signal Rocket, 370*

Tanguy, Yves, 199; *Infinite Divisibility,* 199; *202*

taste, aesthetic preferences and, 261–64

Tchelitchew, Pavel, 188; *Hide-and-Seek,* 188–89, 253; *253*

techniques: airbrush, 301; art criticism and, 488, 506, 509; carving, 323, 324, 326, 328, 335; casting, 108, 323, 324, 325, 326, 327, 328, 335, 336; Color Field painting and, 316; constructing, 323, 328; decalcomania, 291–93; defined, 267, 268; direct (modern), 274, 275–76, 278, 279; durability and, 271; frottage, 291–93; glazing, 269, 271, 275; of governed compression, 293; grattage, 291–92; hatching, 275; improved materials and, 271–72; indirect (traditional), 274–75, 278; "loaded" brush, 275, 291; meaning created by different, 13, 15, 267–68; modeling, 220, 224, 323, 324, 326, 328, 330; paint manipulation and, 291–93; permanence and, 270; in printmaking and graphic art, 226; psychic distance and, 256; sculptural, 323–31; technology and, 324, 326, 330–31, 335, 340, 351; underpainting, 271, 275, 276. *See also* painting; sculpture

television, 94, 96, 437, 455–66; accuracy of, 462; aesthetic devices of, 456, 457–59, 460; commercials on, 460; democracy of, 463–64; effect of, on content, 460; graphic design for, 62; image of, vs. film, 296, 461–62; interview shows on, 460, 461; news reporting on, 461–62; objectivity of, 430; perception and, 456; photography and, 438, 440, 444, 447; reality and, 455–56, 457, 462; relationship to painting and picture-making, 274, 298, 455; soap operas, 460; social effects of, 461, 462, 463–64; space-time manipulation and, 456–59, 460; sports coverage on, 462; technology and, 455, 456; types of, 460

tempera painting, 126, 269, 272, 275

Temple of Amon-Mut-Khonsu, Luxor, Egypt, detail of court, *382*

Teniers, David: *Picture Gallery of Archduke Leopold Wilhelm, The,* 296; *296*

tepees, 381

texture, as visual element in art, 207, 231–33, 310, 366

Thiebaud, Wayne, 301; *Pie Counter, 305; Seven Jellied Apples,* 244; *244*

Thonet, Gebrüder: rocking chair, 114, 324; *114*

Tinguely, Jean, 358; *Homage to New York,* 358, 372–73; *373;* piano from,

358; *Méta-Mécanique,* 108, 373; *373*
Titian, 271, 275, 504
Tlingit Indian painted leather shirt, Alaska, 353; *353*
Tlingit Indian shaman's mask in the form of a bear, Alaska, 324; *324*
Tobey, Mark, 55; *Broadway,* 55, 57; *57; Edge of August,* 195; *195*
Tomlin, Bradley Walker: *No. 10,* 156; *155*
Tooker, George, 49; *Government Bureau,* 48, 49, 420; *48, 420; Subway, The,* 55; *55*
Torroja, Eduardo, Tordera Bridge, joint of, *393*
Toulouse-Lautrec, Henri de, 128, 175; *Maxime Dethomas,* 218; *218; M. Boileau at the Café,* 128–29; *129*
Tovaglia, Pino, 62; railway poster, 62; *65*
Tovi, Murray: *Tovibulb,* 235; *235*
transportation, 90–96, 105. *See also* highways
Treaster, Barbara Gluck: *Huyn Thanh and Descendants,* 440; *440*
Trova, Ernest, 371; *Study: Falling Man (Figure on a Bed),* 371; *372; Study: Falling Man (Landscape #1),* 371–72; *372*
truss construction, 380, 400, 402, 403, 424
Turner, Joseph Mallord William, 227
Tutankhamen's throne, 117; *117*

## U

under-distancing, 256, 258, 259
United States Capitol, Washington, D.C., 393
unity, as design principle, 236–40, 249; central location and, 239–40; coherence and, 237, 239; converging or radiating lines and, 239; dominance and subordination and, 236–37, 238; frontality and, 240; funding and fusion and, 260; Gestalt laws and, 257, 260
Unkei: *Basu-Sennin,* 265; *265*
urban living, 85, 89, 90–91, 386–89. *See also* city planning; domestic architecture
utopian art: architecture, 87, 186; city planning and, 86, 89–90, 186; fantasy and, 186, 188
Utzon, Joern: Sydney Opera House, Australia, *245*

## V

Vail, Lawrence: *Bottle with Stopper,* 120; *120*
Valadon, Suzanne: *Reclining Nude,* 13; *13*
Vandermolen, Mimi: dashboard of the 1985 Ford Taurus, 109
Vantongerloo, Georges: *Construction y=2x³-13.5²+21x,* 367; *367*

Vasarely, Victor: *Arcturus II,* 229; *229; Vega,* 71; *71*
vault construction, 393, 400, 406
Velázquez, Diego, 454; *Pope Innocent X,* 282; *282; Sebastian de Morra,* 135; *135, 430*
Venetian painting, 275, 278
*Venus of Willendorf,* 15; *15*
Vermeer, Jan, 454
Vicov, Willie: *Heavy Turnout for Philippine Elections,* 443; *443*
video art, 465
Viking art, 337
Villon, Jacques: *Portrait of the Artist's Father,* 258; *258*
visual elements of art, 207–33; color, 207, 226–31; form, 207; light and dark, 217–26; line, 207–10; organization of (design), 234–50; shape, 207, 211–17; texture, 207, 231–33
visual perception: design and, 234–36; Impressionism and, 137, 139, 294; optics and, 137, 139, 207, 307; physical function of, 207; physics and, 240–41
Voulkos, Peter, 374; *Firestone,* 41; *41; Gallas Rock,* 374; *378*

## W

Walker, Robert: *Find Coffee House,* 454; *454*
war, reaction to, in art, 28, 43, 51, 59, 176, 179, 193, 304, 402
Warhol, Andy, 299, 304; *Brillo Boxes,* 245; portrait of (Neel), 171; *171; Twenty-five Colored Marilyns,* 299; *300*
Warnecke, John & Associates: Hennepin County Government Center, Minneapolis (with Peterson, Clark & Associates), 424; *425*
Watson, Carolyn: *Crash Pad,* 446; *446*
Weber, Max, 183; *Hassidic Dance,* 183; *182*
Wells Cathedral, strainer arches in, 254; *254*
Wertheimer, Max, 257
Wesselmann, Tom: *Great American Nude No. 51,* 320; *320; Great American Nude #54, The,* 300; *300*
Westermann, H.C., 328, 364; *Big Change, The,* 328; *329; Memorial to the Idea of Man, If He Was an Idea,* 364, 365; *364; Nouveau Rat Trap,* 61; *61*
Weston, Edward, 449, 451; *Cabbage Leaf,* 450; *450;* photograph of halved artichoke, 151; *151*
White, Minor, 447
Whitehead, Alfred North, 69
Whitney, Eli, 108
Wiene, Robert: *Cabinet of Dr. Caligari, The,* film still from, 456; *456*
"Wild Beasts." *See* Fauvism
Wilde, Oscar, 131
Williams, Hiram, 178; *Guilty Men,* 178; *179*
Wimberly, Whisenand, Allison & Tong:

Bank of Hawaii, Waikiki, model of, 421; *421*
women, in art, 24, 140, 142, 174, 192; anger and, 61; antifeminine imagery, 142; graphic design and, 70; ideal visions of, 66; love, sex, marriage and, 15–21, 27, 28, 184, 193, 224; machine image of, 192; nude, 318–22. *See also* human figures
Wood, Grant, 126; *American Gothic,* 126; *125;* models for, 259; *259*
wood, in architecture, 380, 381, 383, 386, 390, 400, 405, 414
wooden door with carving in relief, Baule, Ivory Coast, Africa, 116; *116*
World War I, 304; photograph from, *482*
World War II, 28, 29, 59
Wotruba, Fritz: Church of the Holy Trinity, Vienna, 397
Wright, Frank Lloyd, 75, 76–78, 82, 85, 93, 110, 296; architectural philosophy of, 76, 78, 151; Broadacre City, 89–90; plan, *89;* city planning and, 76, 89–90; Dallas Theater Center, Kalita Humphreys Theater, Dallas, 400; *401;* Fallingwater, Bear Run, Pennsylvania, 76; *77;* Guggenheim Museum, New York City, 151, 153, 296, 414; interior, *151, 414;* influence of, 76, 85; Johnson Wax Administration Building, Racine, Wisconsin, 82, 102, 411; *102;* interior, *82;* Johnson Wax Research Tower, Racine, Wisconsin, 102; *102;* Prairie Houses, 76–78; Robie House, Chicago, 76; *77;* Taliesin East, Spring Green, Wisconsin, 78; interior, *78;* Wayfarer's Chapel, Palos Verdes Estates, California, 413; interior, *413*
Wright, Russel, 113
Wyeth, Andrew, 126, 131, 275; *Christina's World,* 126, 134–35; *126*
Wyman, George Herbert: Bradbury Building, Los Angeles, 391; interior, *391*

## Y

Yamasaki, Minoru, 102, 423; St. Louis Airport Terminal, 102; *104*
Yamasaki, Minoru, & Associates: IBM Building, Seattle (with Naramore, Bain, Brady & Johanson), 423; *423;* North Shore Congregation Israel Synagogue, Glencoe, Illinois, 427; *427*

## Z

Zabala, Teresa: *Carter with Congressional Leaders,* 441; *441*
Zaragoza, José: cover for Brazilian edition of *Vogue* magazine, 68; *68*
Zerbe, Karl, 29; *Aging Harlequin,* 29; *30*

# Photo Credits

*The author and publisher wish to thank the libraries, museums, galleries, and private collectors named in the picture captions for permitting the reproduction of works of art in their collections. The following picture sources are gratefully acknowledged below:*

Copyright A.C.L., Brussels: 282 above right; Courtesy Air India, New York: 332 above right; Alinari (including Anderson and Brogi), Florence: 73, 238 above, 270, 272, 274 left, 280 above left, 280 above right, 360 right, 408; American Crafts Council, New York: 111 above; Courtesy Department of Library Services, American Museum of Natural History, photo by Lynton Gardiner: 477; AP/ Wide World Photos: 49 below, 87; Architect of the Capitol: 384 below; © The Art Institute of Chicago. All Rights Reserved: 17 right, 30 above right, 53 above right, 125 top, 131 below, 132, 133 above left, 141 above, 162 below, 179 left, 261, 285 right, 318, 329 below, 497, 503; Courtesy of ARTnews, New York: 259 below left; Art Resource, New York: 470; Asuka-en, Kyoto: 265 left; © Craig Aurness, West Light, Los Angeles: 313; Australian News and Information Bureau: 245 above; Courtesy Austrian Press and Information Service, New York: 397 below; © Morley Baer, Carmel, CA: 401 below, 424 below; Ronald Baldwin, New York: 461 below; Bank of Hawaii, Honolulu: 421 above right; H. Baranger, Paris: 426 above right; Ken Bell Photography Ltd., courtesy University of Toronto Public Relations Department: 105 above; Oscar Bladh, Stockholm: 93; Hans-Ludwig Blohm/Public Archives Canada/PA–145886: 417 below; Blue Ridge Aerial Surveys, Leesburg, VA, courtesy of Gulf Reston, Inc.: 88 below; Lee Boltin, Croton-on-Hudson, NY: 117 above; Office of E. H. Brenner, Lafayette, IN: 412 above; The Bridgeman Art Library, London: 194 below; Photographie Bulloz, Paris: 187 below; Rudolph Burckhardt, New York: 107 above, courtesy of Leo Castelli Gallery, 120 below left, 320 below, courtesy of Sidney Janis Gallery; Hillel Burger, Cambridge, MA, 69–30–10/1609, T700–B1, © President and Fellows of Harvard College 1981: 324; R. D. Burmeister, Clovis, NM: 300 below; Robert Burroughs/NYT Pictures: 389; California Division of Highways, Sacramento: 95 below; California Institute of Technology, Pasadena: 423 below; Canadian Consulate General, New York: 412 below; Ludovico Canali, Rome: 100 below, 386; CBS Television Network, New York: 30 below right; Ron Chamberlain, Warwick, NY: 358 below; Victor Chambi, Cuzco, Peru: 384 above left; Chase Manhattan Bank, New York: 296 above right, 421 above left; Chicago Architectural Photo Company: 391 below; Geoffrey Clements, New York: 69 below, 130 above, 131 above, 321 below; Lee Clockman: 300 below; Colorado Highway Commission: 96 above; Commonwealth United Entertainment, Inc., Beverly Hills, CA: 465 above, 466; Community Service Society, New York: 55 below right; © Margaret Courtney-Clarke: 297, back cover; Craft Horizons, New York: 114 above left, 371 right; Craftsmen Photo Company, New York: 463 above left; Thomas Y. Crowell, Inc., New York: 119 above, from *Primitive Art* by Erwin O. Christensen; George Cserna, New York: 151 below left, 413 below right, courtesy of Harrison & Abramovitz; © 1985, Mark C. Darley, New York: 104 top; Design M—Ingo Maurer, Munich: 235 below left; The Drabinsky Gallery, Toronto: 242 below; Dwan Gallery, New York: 376 above left, 376 above right; John Ebstel, New York: 428 below; Edholm & Blomgren Photographers, Lincoln, NE: 250 left; Susan Einstein, Santa Monica, CA: 56 above; Richard Einzig © Arcaid, England: 418; Michael Fedison, courtesy of Western Pennsylvania Conservancy: 77 below; Fischbach Gallery, New York: 366, 367 below right; Ford Motor Company, Dearborn, MI: 108, 372 top right; Copyright David Gahr, New York: 373 above left; Roger Gain, Paris: 115 below; Lynton Gardiner, New York: 155 above; General Instrument Corporation, Microelectronic Division, New York: 217 be-